Service Operations Management

Robert G. Murdick
Florida Atlantic University

Barry Render
Rollins College

Roberta S. Russell
Virginia Polytechnic Institute and State University

ALLYN AND BACON
Boston   London   Sydney   Toronto

To Emily—RGM
Bill and Jeanne—BR
Fred, Travis, and Amy—RSR

Editorial-production service: Technical Texts, Inc.
Cover administrator: Linda Dickinson
Production administrator: Lorraine Perrotta
Manufacturing buyer: Tamara Johnson
Series editor: Rich Wohl
Senior editorial assistant: Kelley Saunders-Butcher

Library of Congress Cataloging-in-Publication Data

Murdick, Robert G.
    Service operations management / Robert Murdick, Barry Render,
  Roberta Russell.
      p. cm.
    ISBN 0–205–12250–7
    1. Service industries—United States—Management. 2. Industrial
management—United States.   I. Render, Barry.   II. Russell,
Roberta.   III. Title.
HD9981.5.M87   1990
658—dc20   89–18422
                                                           CIP

ISBN 0–205–12250–7
ISBN 0–205–12510–7 (International)

Printed in the United States of America.
10 9 8 7 6 5 4 3   94 93 92

CONTENTS

PREFACE

About five years ago, based on the textbook used, a student could complete a degree in business administration and hardly be aware that service firms existed. Marketing was concerned with the marketing of *products* in manufacturing and retailing firms. Finance and accounting focused on manufacturing firms. Production management and quantitative methods focused on the production of goods. Currently, more and more texts are giving a nod to services by including brief sections and problems that deal with service situations. Traditional operations management instructors stand firmly behind the credo that manufacturing principles cover service firms almost completely.

A new view of operations management is rapidly emerging. Students see service activities all about them in everyday life but rarely see manufacturing plants. Is it any wonder that with 7 out of 10 American workers employed in service organizations, most students envision careers in services? Is it any wonder they do so when 95 percent of the 25-million jobs created in the United States since 1969 have been in the services, while employment in manufacturing has changed relatively little?

Rather than teach common production principles in a manufacturing setting, it appears more logical today to teach them in a service organization setting. Despite commonalities, we believe that there are enough differences between service operations management and manufacturing management to justify distinctly different courses. For example, could a machine shop manager successfully operate a ski resort, or vice versa? Could an automobile production line manager successfully run an advertising agency, or vice versa?

The characteristics of most service firms differ widely from those of manufacturing firms. Further, a greater variety of organization, operations, and functions exists within the service industry than within the manufacturing industry. Manufacturing can be more nearly rationalized so that, with technological advances, productivity has increased far more in manufacturing than in service firms. A coherent theory for services and greater productivity increases in services are needed. The challenges and the opportunities for schools of business and for their graduates will extend into the future for service organizations.

Since the Harvard group of W. Earl Sasser, R. Paul Olson, and D. Daryl Wyckoff coauthored their ground-breaking book of text, cases, and readings on management of service operations in 1978, the literature on services operations management (SOM) has grown in both the management and functional fields. Several SOM journals have been born, and a small number of other texts have appeared with specialized perspectives of SOM.

Our book is based on a framework of service activities that allows common principles of both manufacturing and service organizations to be observed. Similarities, contrasts, and unique topics in each industry are pointed out so that the widest variety of instructors may feel comfortable with new material. In addition, the text is designed to accommodate most teaching styles and to support either a qualitative or quantitative approach to the topic. The combination of text, many short cases, and readings make this book suitable for an introductory course. Lengthy cases and a detailed term service project in Chapter 18 provide an opportunity for in-depth analysis for those who desire this approach. For quantitative courses, the language of mathematics is placed in stand alone parts or in supplements to each chapter, with enough depth to make this book good for a rigorous treatment of the subject. The book was developed to meet AACSB requirements for an operations management course.

Although this book has been widely reviewed by eminent authorities in the field, the final selection of material has been ours. Through wide use of such a text, feedback from users of this text, and increased research in service operations management, a sound general theory of service operations management can evolve.

ACKNOWLEDGMENTS

The authors wish to thank the following individuals for their support on this very exciting, but demanding, writing project: James L. Heskett, Harvard University; David A. Collier, Ohio State University; Vincent A. Mabert, Indiana University; Aleda V. Roth, Duke University; Tim Davis, Cleveland State University; Ted Helmer, Northern Arizona University; Scott Shafer, University of Miami; John Larsen, Indiana University; Asoo Vahkaria, University of Arizona; Peter Mills, University of Santa Clara; Pradeep Korgaonkar, Florida Atlantic University; Sid Das, George Mason University; and Joanna Baker, Virginia Polytechnic Institute and State University.

We also appreciate the fine work of our support staffs, editors, and graduate assistants, including Anne Strauss, Sue Crabill, Sylvia Seavey, Jay Teets, John Geissler, and Keith Becker.

PART I

Introduction

CHAPTER

1

Services in Our Society

INTRODUCTION

For some, it is a hard realization that services are the predominant force in our society, that McDonald's has more employees than U.S. Steel, and that perhaps golden arches, not blast furnaces, symbolize the American economy.[1] For others, services represent the essence of American culture—closeness to the consumer, responsiveness, innovation, dependency on labor, management of small groups of employees, and entrepreneurial opportunities. Whatever your orientation, services are an integral part of our society and deserve careful study.

Good service doesn't just happen by chance; it is not the result of an extraordinary employee who goes out of his or her way to please a particular customer. Good service must be planned and managed, from the design of the service to the delivery of the service, from maintaining efficient operations to ensuring that the quality of the service is both high and consistent.

There must be a strategy for providing service that matches the target market with the strengths of the service company. Decisions in support of the service strategy,

---

[1] This oft-quoted statement comparing McDonald's to U.S. Steel is attributed to George F. Will, a well-known syndicated columnist.

3

such as location, layout, capacity, inventory, distribution, and quality assurance, must be in place. The management of technologies and human resources must be effectively addressed. Some of these issues can be resolved by borrowing techniques from the manufacturing sector; others are uniquely service-oriented and require special consideration.

This text covers a wide range of issues in managing service operations. It is designed to provide a more comprehensive, systematic coverage of service operations than ''service examples'' found in production/operations management texts or narrative expositions on service quality found in management books.

We begin here in Chapter 1 by defining services and exploring the role of services in our society.

WHAT ARE SERVICES?

The material gains of a society are achieved by adding value to natural resources. In advanced societies, there are many institutions which extract raw materials, add value through processing them, and transform intermediate materials and components into finished end products. There are, however, many other institutions which *facilitate* the production and distribution of goods and add value to our personal lives. The outputs of this latter group are called **services.**

Services can be defined as economic activities that produce time, place, form, or psychological utilities. A maid service saves the consumer's *time* from doing household chores himself or herself. Department stores and grocery stores provide many commodities for sale in one convenient *place.* A database service puts together information in a *form* more usable for the manager. A ''night out'' at a restaurant provides *psychological* refreshment in the middle of a busy workweek.

Services also can be defined in contrast to goods. A **good** is a tangible object that can be created and sold or used later. A **service** is intangible and perishable. It is created and consumed simultaneously (or nearly simultaneously).[2] Although these definitions may seem straightforward, the distinction between goods and services is not always clearcut. For example, when we purchase a car, are we purchasing a good or the service of transportation? A television set is a manufactured good, but what use is it without the service of television broadcasting? When we go to a fast-food restaurant, are we buying the service of having our food prepared for us or are we buying goods that happen to be ready-to-eat food items?

In reality, almost all purchases of goods are accompanied by *facilitating services,* and almost every service purchase is accompanied by a *facilitating good.*[3] Thus the key to understanding the difference between goods and services lies in the realization

---

[2] Chapter 2 describes the special characteristics of services in more detail.

[3] The term *facilitating good* was suggested by John Rathmell in *Marketing in the Service Sector* (Cambridge, Mass.: Winthrop Publishers, 1974). For more discussion of facilitating goods and services, see W. E. Sasser et al., *Management of Service Operations* (Boston: Allyn and Bacon, 1978), Chap. 2.

that these items are not completely distinct, but rather are two poles on a continuum. Exhibit 1–1 shows such a continuum.

Referring to Exhibit 1–1, we would probably classify the first three items as "goods" because of their high material content. There is little service to self-service grocery stores; an automobile is mostly a physical item; and while its installation does require some service, carpet is predominantly a good. The remaining items we would probably classify as "services" because of their high service content, although some physical materials may be received. For instance, restaurants not only give the customer a meal of physical food and drink, but also a place to eat it, chefs to prepare it, waiters to serve it, and an atmosphere in which to dine. Motels are almost pure service, with very little material goods (perhaps matches or a postcard) received by the consumer. Can you identify the goods and services content of the other examples in Exhibit 1–1?

A Service Taxonomy

If it is difficult to distinguish between goods and services, it is equally as difficult to define what constitutes a service firm or a service industry. Even government agencies disagree. An example will illustrate the problem. The *Statistical Abstract of the United*

_____ EXHIBIT 1–1 _____

- *A Comparison of Various Goods and Services*

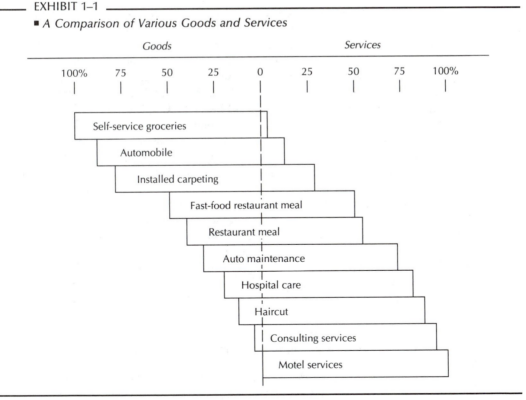

Source: From Earl W. Sasser, R. P. Olsen, and D. Daryl Wyckoff, *Management of Service Operations,* p. 11. Copyright © 1978 by Allyn and Bacon. Reprinted with permission.

—— EXHIBIT 1–2 ——————————————————————————————————————

■ *A Taxonomy of Services*

Distributive Services: Physical and Informational

Retail and Wholesale Trade

Nonprofit Services

Producer Services
Finance
Insurance
Real estate
Business services
Legal services
Membership organizations
Miscellaneous professional services

Consumer Services
Health care
Education
Personal services
Auto repair, garages, miscellaneous maintenance
Hotel/motel services
Restaurant/food services
Leisure services
Private households

States classifies the economy into such industries as mining; construction; manufacturing; transportation and public utilities; wholesale and retail trade; finance, insurance, and real estate; and government. The last four industries are considered services. Under construction are "special trade contractors." Many of these contractors are involved only in repair work, never in original construction, and yet they are not classified as services. However, national studies on services submitted to the General Agreement on Tariffs and Trade (GATT) nations *do* include construction in the service sector. These same studies include utilities in the manufacturing sector!

Within the service sector, different classifications, or **taxonomies,** also have emerged.[4] The U.S. Census Bureau classifies services by function. The Bureau of Labor Statistics uses production as a basis for classification. Still another government classification scheme is provided in the Standard Industrial Classification (SIC) code. While researchers may disagree on how services should be classified, it is still useful to select some classification scheme when studying services in order to identify similarities and differences in managing certain service operations. As an example, Exhibit 1–2 shows a service taxonomy based on service function.

In Exhibit 1–2, distributive services include the physical distribution of goods or people by the transportation industry, as well as the distribution of information by the telecommunications or information-processing industries. Retail and wholesale trade represent all commerce of physical goods. Nonprofit services consist of various government agencies, and public- and private-sector organizations that serve the public without personal gain. Producer services are basically intermediate services provided to the corporate sector, whether manufacturing- or service-oriented. They consist of a diverse group of services usually classified as "overhead" when provided within a

---

[4] For example, see N. N. Foote and P. K. Hatt, "Social Mobility and Economic Advancement," *American Economic Review,* Vol. 43 (1953), pp. 364–378; M. A. Katouzian, "The Development of the Service Sector," *Oxford Economic Papers,* Vol. 22 (November 1970), pp. 362–382; and H. C. Browning and J. Singleman, *The Emergence of a Service Society: Demographic and Sociological Aspects of the Sectoral Transformation of the Labor Force in the U.S.A.* (Springfield, Va.: National Technical Information Service, 1975).

—— EXHIBIT 1–3 ————————————————————————————————————

■ *Employment Prospects for the Year 2000 (in millions)*

Industry	1965		1986		2000	
Goods						
Mining	.6 ⎫		.8 ⎫		.7 ⎫	
Manufacturing	18.0 ⎬	36%	19.0 ⎬	25%	18.2 ⎬	21%
Construction	3.2 ⎭		4.9 ⎭		5.8 ⎭	
Services						
Transportation and utilities	4.0 ⎫		5.2 ⎫		5.7 ⎫	
Wholesale and retail trade	12.6 ⎪		23.6 ⎪		30.0 ⎪	
Finance, insurance, and real estate	3.0 ⎬	64%	6.3 ⎬	75%	7.9 ⎬	79%
Miscellaneous services	8.9 ⎪		22.5 ⎪		32.5 ⎪	
Government	10.1 ⎭		16.7 ⎭		18.3 ⎭	
Total	60.4	100%	99.0	100%	119.1	100%

Source: *Statistical Abstract of the United States* (U.S. Government Printing Office, 1988), p. 380.

company. Consumer services consist of a wide range of social and personal services provided to the individual, in most cases to enhance the quality of life.

From the taxonomy in Exhibit 1–2 it can be discerned that the markets for producer services and consumer services are very different, requiring different approaches to service design and marketing. These issues are discussed in Chapters 4 and 17. Similarly, retail and wholesale trade requires extensive knowledge of forecasting and inventory techniques (presented in Chapters 3 and 12). Nonprofit and public service organizations also require special study. Their sources of authority, funding, and organizational characteristics differentiate them from profit-making organizations. Chapters 4, 9, and 14 discuss the differences in public or nonprofit versus profit-making organizations in terms of service design, human resources, and quality assessment. Finally, technological advances have affected distributive services more dramatically than any other service class. Chapter 10 discusses technology and information services, and Chapter 13 presents some techniques for efficient service distribution.

THE SERVICE SECTOR OF OUR ECONOMY

From a macro viewpoint, our economy may be divided into three different sectors for study: the extractive sector (which includes mining and agriculture), the manufacturing sector, and the service sector. The service sector has had a tremendous impact on the U.S. economy, as indicated by the following statistics:

■ Seven out of every 10 American workers are employed in the service sector.[5] By the year 2000, it is expected that almost 8 out of every 10 American workers will have service jobs. Exhibit 1–3 demonstrates these trends in employment.

---

[5] Another way to look at this statistic is that 7 out of every 10 students in this class will work in the service sector!

- Services account for 95 percent of the 25 million net new jobs created since 1969. Of the additional 21 million new jobs predicted by 2000, practically all will be in service-producing industries. Exhibit 1–4 illustrates how jobs in the service sector have soared.
- Of the more than 22 million women entering the work force over the past 20 years, 33 out of 34 have found employment in service-sector jobs.
- Service-sector industries purchased in one year more than 80 percent of $25 billion of computers, office equipment, and communication equipment shipped.
- By 1987, manufacturing contributed less than 20 percent to the gross national product (GNP), whereas services contributed over 70 percent to GNP in the United States. Exhibit 1–5 projects manufacturing and service contributions to GNP from the 1980s to the year 2000.

These statistics lend credence to the labeling of the U.S. economy as a ''service economy.''

───── EXHIBIT 1–4 ──

- *How Jobs in the Service Industry Have Soared*

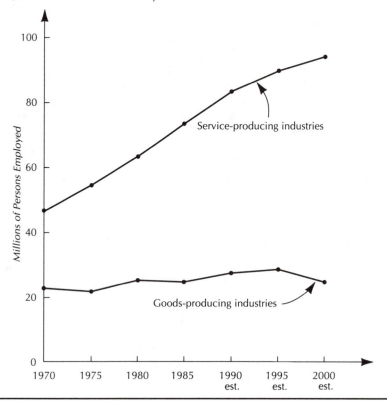

Source: *Statistical Abstract of the United States* (U.S. Government Printing Office), 1987, p. 389, and 1988, p. 380.

—— EXHIBIT 1–5 ————————————————————————————

■ *Manufacturing and Services as Percentages of Gross National Product*

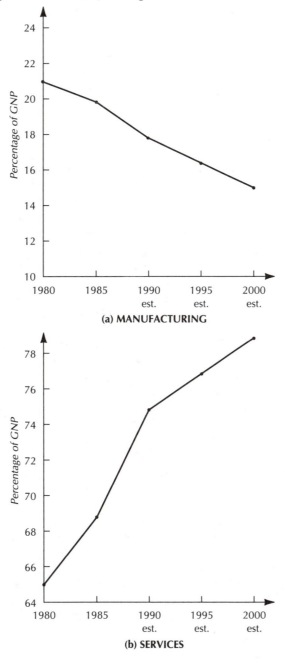

(a) **MANUFACTURING**

(b) **SERVICES**

Estimates for years 1990 to 2000 by the authors
Figures exclude agriculture, forestry and fisheries,
mining, and construction

Source: *Statistical Abstract of the United States* (U.S. Government Printing Office, 1989), p. 422.

Defining the Service Sector

The range of services provided in a society may be quite broad. Producers of a service may provide the service with no interaction with the consumer beyond the formal sale (vending machine, for example). At the other extreme, the producer of the service may be the consumer, as in the case of the homemaker or the do-it-yourself person who fixes his or her own car or mows his or her own lawn. In the latter case, there is no economic transaction, so the value of these services does not appear in national product data, yet the value must be huge.

Most services included in the service sector of our economy fall between these extremes. The producer and user of the service are distinct, but both participate in providing the service. For example, the lawyer and client work together, the restaurant and customer both contribute to the design of a specific meal and the timing of service, and the school and the student design the student's program and constrain the content and timing of topics in a single course.

Service organizations also exist within manufacturing firms. Internal service organizations in manufacturing firms consist of all personnel, departments, and staff groups not directly participating in changing the form of physical materials. Accounting, research and development (R&D), sales distribution, corporate staff, and human resource groups are examples. In automated factories, such groups may far outnumber the number of workers in the actual production process. Thus traditional manufacturing firms increasingly need to manage services supplied to both external customers and internal management.

Many companies that have always viewed themselves as manufacturing companies may soon learn to see themselves as primarily service companies. General Electric, for example, can attribute only one-fifth of its profits to manufacturing, while RCA's revenues from broadcasting and car rentals are now greater than its revenues from manufacturing. *Fortune* magazine annually publishes a list of the top 500 (i.e., largest) firms in manufacturing and the top 500 firms in services. *Fortune*'s definition of a service firm is one that derives more than 50 percent of its sales revenue from the services it provides. Examples of companies originally listed in the Industrial 500 but now appearing in the Service 500 include RCA, Bally Manufacturing, Turner Construction, and Exxon Pipeline. These companies have truly been caught up in the "service sector revolution."

Of particular interest to us today are the growing roles of service workers in information-processing and in high-tech industries. These are areas in rapid growth today. It is estimated that information workers currently account for over 50 percent of the American work force.[6] Exhibit 1–6 shows the interrelationships among services, nonservices, high-tech industries, and the information economy. Note the size of the service sector in relation to the nonservice sector and the types and amount of services required to support the information and high-tech industries.

---

[6] Paul A. Strassman, *Information Payoff* (New York: The Free Press, 1985), p. 5.

—— EXHIBIT 1–6 ——————————————————————————————————————

- *The Interrelationships of the Services, High-Technology, and Information Sectors in the Private-Sector Economy of the United States*

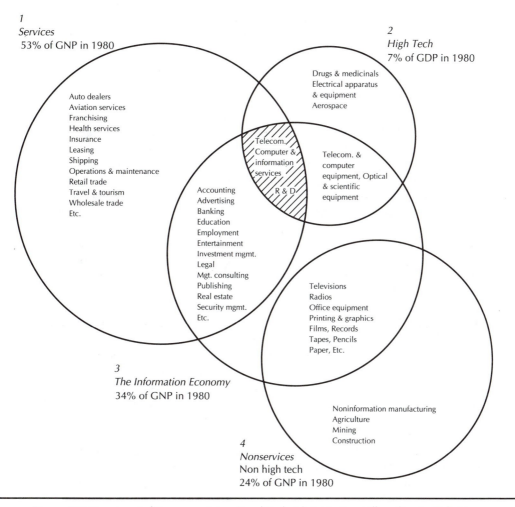

1
Services
53% of GNP in 1980

2
High Tech
7% of GDP in 1980

Drugs & medicinals
Electrical apparatus
& equipment
Aerospace

Auto dealers
Aviation services
Franchising
Health services
Insurance
Leasing
Shipping
Operations & maintenance
Retail trade
Travel & tourism
Wholesale trade
Etc.

Telecom.
Computer &
information
services

R & D

Telecom. &
computer
equipment, Optical
& scientific
equipment

Accounting
Advertising
Banking
Education
Employment
Entertainment
Investment mgmt.
Legal
Mgt. consulting
Publishing
Real estate
Security mgmt.
Etc.

Televisions
Radios
Office equipment
Printing & graphics
Films, Records
Tapes, Pencils
Paper, Etc.

3
The Information Economy
34% of GNP in 1980

4
Nonservices
Non high tech
24% of GNP in 1980

Noninformation manufacturing
Agriculture
Mining
Construction

Source: U.S. Department of Commerce, International Trade Administration, Office of Service Industries.

Theories Explaining the Growth of Services

The growth of services in an economy has been attributed by various theories to

— The increase in efficiency of agriculture and manufacturing that releases labor to services
— The linear flow of workers from agriculture and other extraction to manufacturing and then to services

— The application of comparative advantage in international trade
— A decrease in investment as a percentage of gross domestic product (GDP) in high-income industrialized countries or an increase in the percentage of the GDP in low-income countries
— A rise in per capita income
— An increase in urbanization
— An increase in international trade
— Joint symbiotic growth of services with manufacturing

The first four theories are based on the production factors of labor and capital. The first theory is based on data indicating that services grow because of a simultaneous flow of labor from agriculture and manufacturing as each of these sectors becomes more efficient. The second theory describes a more sequential progression of labor from agriculture to manufacturing and then to services.

Comparative advantage traditionally has been studied from the view of manufactured products and industrialized countries. However, services also can provide a comparative advantage. Early in England's history, its wealth came from shipping and finance because of its location. Switzerland gained its financial position because of its physical location and its neutralist policies. Many other countries have large tourist industries. These examples cast doubt on the theories that services increase solely to absorb excess labor from production.

Theories that assume a growth in services independent of manufacturing have not been extensively explored because of the assumption that only industrialized countries have a substantial service sector. However, even in the most backward countries (characterized by mainly extractive production, low per capita GNP, and low quality of life), services exist. Exhibit 1–7 shows how the traditional focus on labor inputs has obscured the importance of the service sector. At the lower levels of per capita GNP, extractive employment is clearly dominant, even though services provide the greatest percentage of GNP. At slightly higher values of per capita GNP, the service sector dominates both in employment and GNP percentages.

In an affluent society, as people continue to acquire goods, their desires for services increase as their needs for goods become more nearly satisfied. Thus manufacturing output tends to stabilize relative to the population. With automation, robotics, and other manufacturing efficiencies, it is only natural that fewer people are employed in manufacturing.

OPPOSING VIEWS OF A SERVICE ECONOMY

The term **postindustrial economy** is widely used to denote a service economy that succeeds a manufacturing economy. Most U.S. business and popular writers, focusing on the decline of manufacturing and the increase of the service sector, have predicted as inevitable the shift of America to a service economy. This shift, sometimes called the "McDonaldization of America," is not always viewed as desirable.

—— EXHIBIT 1–7 ——————————————————————————

▪ *Sectoral Percentages for Employment and GDP*

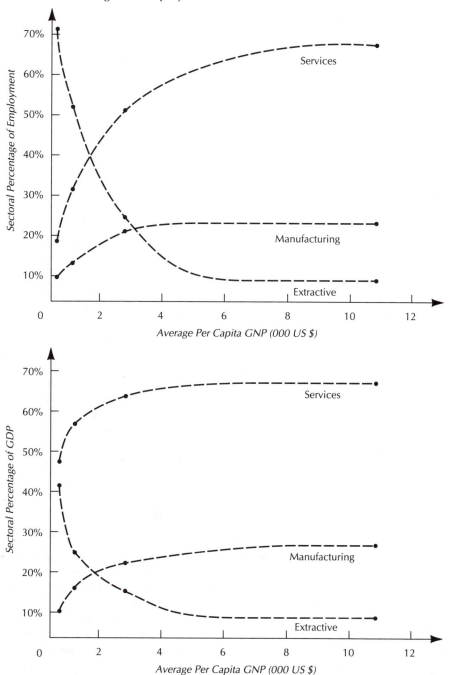

__ EXHIBIT 1–8 _____

■ *Service Wages Lag Behind Manufacturing Wages*

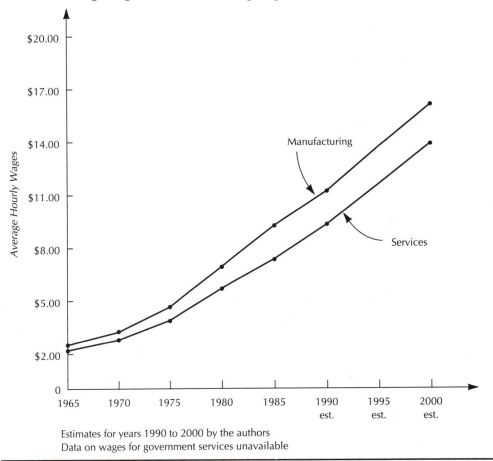

Estimates for years 1990 to 2000 by the authors
Data on wages for government services unavailable

Source: *Statistical Abstract of the United States,* (U.S. Government Printing Office, 1989), p. 397.

The Pessimistic View

The pessimistic view of a service economy is derived from the belief that manufacturing is the "engine of growth." Service jobs do not generate as much economic growth as manufacturing jobs because they are lower paying and less productive. Private-sector service jobs pay only about 90 percent of the average wages of manufacturing jobs (see Exhibit 1–8). Moreover, there are hidden costs in the shift from a manufacturing to a service economy. A key source of economic growth is improved productivity resulting from research and development. The manufacturing sector, while accounting for only a fifth of the gross domestic product, is responsible for more than 96 percent of all research and development expenditures.

In addition, purchases by manufacturing firms represent more than a third of the gross domestic product, and manufacturing shipments account for nearly 60 percent of the gross domestic product. Unlike service-sector jobs, every manufacturing job creates three other jobs in the economy.[7] These observations tend to support economists' views that reliance on a service economy will lower our standard of living.

Many economists also predict that the current growth in services will be short-lived. This is based on the belief that services are linked to manufacturing, so that as manufacturing declines, services also will decline at a lagging rate.

Regardless of the relationship between manufacturing- and service-sector growth, assumptions that Americans somehow are more skilled at providing services than manufacturing goods are dangerous at best. The same lack of attention to quality and the customer that has caused the decline in American manufacturing competitiveness is evident in American services too. We saw London decline from being the center of international finance and banking as New York took over. Now financial services are growing and shifting to Japan. Reading 1.1 at the end of this chapter demonstrates a level of quality in service by the Japanese that will be difficult to match. Thus, unless services are managed more efficiently, they may be the next victims of international competition.[8]

The Optimistic View

While no one advocates the total replacement of the manufacturing sector with the service sector in our economy, there are certain benefits that a strong service economy can provide. It should be noted that growth in the service sector has not caused the decline of manufacturing, but rather, its relative strength has helped the American economy and the American people withstand bad times in the manufacturing sector.

One advantage of a service economy is that it resists cyclical changes better than manufacturing. The reason is that services do not engage in large inventory buildups that depress prices and produce losses during economic downswings. It must be admitted, however, that interest-sensitive financial services are affected adversely by swings in interest rates and market conditions (as we saw, for example, in the fallout from "Black Monday").

Among the fastest growing services are those provided to manufacturers. Manufacturers, in fact, may look for opportunities to expand in-house services into new external opportunities, as Borg-Warner did when it moved into dealer inventory financing. Other examples include the expansion of the General Electric Credit Corporation and the development of aircraft overhaul and maintenance services by Kimberly-Clark. Another approach is for large manufacturing companies simply to purchase service companies. Such diversification often improves the cash flow of the manufacturing company and provides more profit during recessions.

But are service-sector jobs good jobs? Certainly, the growth in the number of teachers, computer programmers, consultants, and technicians represents a growth of good jobs. In fact, one of the fastest growing job categories, information-centered

---

[7] These statistics are from William Raspberry, "Perhaps Shift to Service Economy is Neither Inevitable nor Desirable," *Roanoke Times & World News,* April 29, 1988.

[8] This point is made very clearly in J. B. Quinn and C. E. Gagnon, "Will Services Follow Manufacturing into Decline?" *Harvard Business Review,* Vol. 64, No. 6 (November–December 1986), pp. 95–103.

services, is demanding high skills and high wages, which are rising at a faster rate than those in the manufacturing sector.

Finally, the service industry can serve as a role model for manufacturing. Oftentimes, the policies and techniques that have been successful in manufacturing are advocated as routes to increase the productivity of services. Sometimes, however, the learning process can occur in reverse. Witness the current manufacturing emphasis on serving the customer and the fact that the most effective production system in the world, Toyota, was designed in large part after the policies and procedures used to service customers in American supermarkets![9] How about the planning, design, and monitoring of an operation such as Walt Disney World[10] or the efficiencies and sophistication of Federal Express? The success and advances of these ''services'' are hard to beat in manufacturing.

Probably the biggest service success story in recent years is the Scandinavian Airline System (SAS), which turned an $8 million loss into a $71 million profit in a little over a year. Reading 1.2 details ''the SAS story.'' Basically, the company was able to make such dramatic gains by refocusing its attention on the *service management concept,* i.e., serving the customer and managing the service. While the concept may seem obvious and simplistic, it should be noted that many companies do *not* focus their attention on the customer, nor do they attempt to manage the service process. Reading 1.1 illustrates this point. SAS, however, represents a different case. From design to development to delivery of its service, SAS painstakingly reflects, documents, and manages the customer's experience. The results provide valuable lessons for services and manufacturing alike.

SUMMARY

This chapter developed the concept of services from a macro viewpoint. Definitions of service and service economy were presented, as well as the importance of services in our society. Theories concerning the transition from a manufacturing to a service economy, including the pros and cons of such a move, also were discussed. The chapter ends with a reference to the service management concept, which involves serving the customer and managing the service.

The remainder of this book examines specific issues in managing service operations. However, throughout the book, regardless of the emphasis of a particular chapter, a common theme that will emerge is the service management concept. With that in mind, Chapter 2 delineates the characteristics of services that set them apart from other types of industries. Chapter 3 provides some techniques for forecasting the demand for services, an important first step in ensuring that proper service can be provided. Part II contains seven chapters that discuss different components of the service system, including design of the service and the service process, service location and facility layout, aggregate planning for services, human resource management, and the use of technology. Part III presents a more detailed analysis of the tools and

---

[9] See M. A. Cusumano, *The Japanese Automobile Industry* (Cambridge, Mass.: Harvard University Press, 1985), p. 277.

[10] Manufacturing companies from General Electric to General Motors routinely send their executives to Walt Disney World to discover how Disney motivates its employees to maintain such high service standards.

techniques involved in service operations. It consists of chapters on scheduling capacity, developing inventory systems, routing service vehicles, and managing quality. In addition, the techniques of project management and linear and goal programming are presented. Finally, the marketing of services is discussed as a facilitating system for the operations function. The book concludes with a comprehensive project and several case studies to integrate the concepts involved in managing service operations.

____ DISCUSSION QUESTIONS

1. Why is it difficult to define a service? What is meant by the term *facilitating good?*

2. What is the difference between producer services and consumer services?

3. Why do service economies necessarily follow industrial economies?

4. What indications are there that the United States is becoming a service economy?

5. What are the dangers of the United States becoming a service economy?

6. What advantages does a service economy provide?

7. Why do you think service-sector jobs pay less than jobs in manufacturing? Is there a difference in skill levels or educational requirements? Why have most women found jobs in service industries?

8. Look at the trend toward services in other countries. Is Japan, for example, also becoming a service economy?

9. "There are no such things as service industries . . . only industries whose service components are greater or less than those of other industries" (Levitt, 1972). Explain this statement. Do you agree or disagree?

10. Examine the data in Exhibit 1–9 on the top firms in *Fortune*'s 500 and *Fortune*'s Service 500. Compare the performance of the service firms with the manufacturing firms on the basis of size and profitability.

____ EXHIBIT 1–9 _____

■ *Performance Measures of Service and Manufacturing Industries*

Service Industry	Value	Manufacturing Industry	Value
Assets			
Citicorp	$203,607 million	General Motors	$87,422 million
American Express	$116,434 million	Exxon	$74,042 million
Federal Nat'l Mortgage Ass'n	$103,459 million	IBM	$63,688 million
Sales			
Sears, Roebuck	$48,440 million	General Motors	$101,782 million
K-Mart	$25,627 million	Exxon	$76,416 million
Safeway Stores	$18,301 million	Ford Motor Co.	$71,643 million
Sales per Employee			
Fed. Nat'l Mortgage Ass'n	$4,031 thousand	Tosco	$1,381 thousand
Gelco	$3,715 thousand	AG Processing	$1,150 thousand
Bindley West Ind.	$2,814 thousand	Pacific Resources	$1,053 thousand
Profits			
American Int'l Group	$1,042 million	IBM	$5,258 million
Aetna Life & Casualty	$921 million	Exxon	$4,840 million
Cigna	$728.3 million	Ford Motor Co.	$4,625 million
Return on Stockholder's Equity			
Tiger International	287.7%	Affiliated Publications	62.1%
Missouri-Kansas-Texas R.R.	155.7%	Georgia Gulf	57.4%
ServiceMaster	142.2%	Ralston Purina	54.4%

——— READING 1.1 ————————————————————————————

Japan's Got Us Beat in the Service Department, Too

My husband and I bought one souvenir the last time we were in Tokyo—a Sony compact disk player. The transaction took seven minutes at the Odakyu Department Store, including time to find the right department and to wait while the salesman filled out a second charge slip after misspelling my husband's name on the first.

My in-laws, who were our hosts in the outlying city of Sagamihara, were eager to see their son's purchase, so he opened the box for them the next morning. But when he tried to demonstrate the player, it wouldn't work. We peered inside. It had no innards! My husband used the time until the Odakyu would open at 10 A.M. to practice for the rare opportunity in that country to wax indignant. But at a minute to 10 he was preempted by the store ringing me.

My mother-in-law took the call, and had to hold the receiver away from her ear against the barrage of Japanese honorifics. Odakyu's vice president was on his way over with a new disk player.

A taxi pulled up 50 minutes later and spilled out the vice president and a junior employee who was laden with packages and a clipboard. In the entrance hall the two men bowed vigorously. The younger man was still bobbing as he read from a log that recorded the progress of their efforts to rectify their mistake, beginning at 4:32 P.M. the day before when the salesclerk alerted the store's security guards to stop my husband at the door. When that didn't work, the clerk turned to his supervisor, until a SWAT team leading all the way to the vice president was in place to work on the only clues, a name and an American Express card number. Remembering that the customer had asked him about using the disk player in the U.S., the clerk called 32 hotels in and around Tokyo to ask if a Mr. Kitasel was registered. When that turned up nothing, the Odakyu commandeered a staff member to stay until 9 P.M. to call American Express headquarters in New York. American Express gave

him our New York telephone number. It was after 11 P.M. when he reached my parents, who were staying at my apartment. My mother gave him my in-laws' telephone number.

The younger man looked up from his clipboard and gave us in addition to the new $280 disk player a set of towels, a box of cakes, and a Chopin disk. Three minutes after this exhausted pair had arrived they were climbing back into the waiting cab. The vice president suddenly dashed back. He had forgotten to apologize for my husband having to wait while the salesman had rewritten the charge slip, but he hoped we understood that it had been the young man's first day.

My Tokyo experience contrasts sharply with treatment I've received at home. In late July, without explanation or apology from Bloomingdale's, a credit of $546.66 appeared on my American Express statement for china ordered Jan. 12, paid for April 17, and never received.

Back in mid-February, the Bloomingdale's saleswoman who had promised delivery in three weeks knew nothing; it was up to Customer Service to resolve the problem. In Customer Service a Ms. X could tell me nothing either, but took all of the relevant information and said someone would get back to me. "When?" I asked. "In three weeks," she said.

Three weeks and no word from Bloomingdale's. Later, I called Customer Service and asked for Ms. X. I was told that customers cannot request to speak to a particular person in Customer Service, but have to speak to whoever happens to answer their call. How many people were employed in Customer Service? "I can't tell you that," she said. So I recounted my American Express card number, sales slip reference code, date, amount, name and address and agreed to mail new copies of the paper work to this new person. How long would it take to put this "retracer" on the first "tracer?" "Three weeks."

This time I had the nerve to ask just what could take so much time. "We have to put it through a process," she said. What process? The only description I could elicit was of a labyrinthine, slow internal communications system linking, through shuffling couriers, every video terminal and desk to the Bloomingdale's mailroom. Hoping to be helpful, I offered to deliver the paper work in person. "You can't do that!" she barked. "Customers cannot see anybody in Customer Service."

On May 10, I received a letter from Ms. Y in Merchandise Adjustments, who informed me that I had taken the purchase with me on Jan. 12, and that she hoped this clarified the matter. I looked at the copy of the sales slip she had attached as proof. It was mine, but it wasn't for the china to be delivered. The amounts, reference codes, and sales slip number for the taken merchandise didn't jibe with those of the china in question. The only similarities, in fact, were my name, the date and the department. I pointed this out to Ms. Y on the phone. She told me to resubmit all of the documentation so she could put it through the "process" once again. Could I deliver it to her in person? "No." But if I insisted, I could leave it at the regular credit window, where it would be routed to her via the mailroom.

Every employee I dealt with implied that it was my fault the store had both my money and the china. I shouldn't have paid my American Express bill, said one. I must have given Customer Service the wrong information, said another.

I'm sure this isn't a problem unique to Bloomingdale's. As I sit here, listening to my compact disk player and eating off my old china a half-year after the ordeal began, I'm struck that buyers in the U.S. cannot afford to assume a common interest with the seller, but must be ready to take up an adversarial position.

In all the current hysteria over our $37 billion trade deficit with Japan, it is often overlooked that the U.S. still enjoys a considerable surplus in trade in services with that country. It would be naive to assume this comparative advantage is permanent, however. U.S. and European pressure on Japan to liberalize its economy is drawing it into direct competition with us over this last piece of turf as well. American consumers will eventually turn to the best product (or service). Walter Mondale once warned Americans that the only jobs left for us will be "working at McDonald's and sweeping up around Japanese computers." But no nation can guarantee its people any job, even those.

———— QUESTIONS FOR READING 1.1

1. Reexamine the article and list the points of service contact for the "good" service example and the points of service contact for the "bad" service example. What accounted for the quality of the service at each point of contact with the customer?

2. Describe an instance when you received particularly good service. Now give an example of particularly poor service that you personally received. What made the service good or bad? Can the quality of the service experience be attributed to the service provider or the service system? Discuss.

3. Is there a danger of services becoming internationalized? Don't services by their nature have to be locally provided? Do we need to worry about foreign competition in services?

———— READING 1.2 ————————

The SAS Story

In 1981, Scandinavian Airlines System—SAS as it is known in the industry—was struggling with a severe downturn in business; this was true of virtually all other airlines as well. The worldwide recession had cut deeply into the airline industry, and companies were bleeding from every pore. During the year, SAS posted an $8 million loss.

The multinational board of directors of SAS

Source: Adapted from K. Albrecht and R. Zemke, *Service America! Doing Business in the New Economy* (Homewood, Ill.: Dow Jones–Irwin, 1985), pp. 20–26. © Richard D. Irwin, Inc. 1985.

was understandably concerned. The company president resigned and the board promoted to that position a young superstar, Jan Carlzon. An energetic, flamboyant man of 39, Carlzon had been managing one of the company's subsidiaries.

While most other airline companies were whittling back their expenditures with an energy bordering on desperation, Carlzon decided to go in exactly the opposite direction. He embarked on a virtual death-or-glory expedition to turn SAS around, and his strategy revolutionized the company's attitude toward its customers.

What followed was a spectacularly successful turnaround maneuver in which SAS went from the $8 million loss figure to a gross profit of $71 million on sales of $2 billion in a little over a year. SAS was voted "airline of the year" and laid claim to being the most punctual airline in Europe. The company strove for, and largely achieved, recognition as "the businessman's airline."

All of this happened in a remarkably short span of time while the rest of the airline industry was losing an aggregate of $1.7 billion per year.

Naturally, more than a few people were curious to know just how Carlzon had managed to pull that particular rabbit out of his hat. Carlzon did not attribute his success to such conventional tactics as advertising, rate cutting, and cost reduction—or even to his own leadership. He credited most of the improvement to the effects of a deceptively simple philosophy: *make sure you're really selling what the customer wants to buy.*

"Look," Carlzon began to say to everyone in the company who would listen, "for too many years we've been putting almost all our attention on the mundane aspects of flying airplanes, and not enough on the quality of the customer's experience. It's time we as a company shifted the focus of our attention. Our business is not flying airplanes, it's serving the travel needs of our public. If we can do that better than the other companies, we'll get the business. If we can't, we won't get the business and we don't deserve to."

Carlzon believed that if he could teach most SAS managers and employees to keep tabs on the kind of treatment the customer received at each of the critical stages of his or her dealings with the company, they could create a conscious impression of service quality for the customer to carry away. Said Carlzon, "We have 50,000 moments of truth out there every day." A moment of truth, by Carlzon's definition, is an episode in which a customer comes into contact with any aspect of the company, however remote, and thereby has an opportunity to form an impression.

In Carlzon's view, SAS had become an "introverted" organization which had lost its conceptual focus on the customer's needs as critically important to success. Front-line people tended to be preoccupied with their individual tasks. Managers were concerned about routine managerial duties and administrative people about forms and reports. In such an organization, the prevailing attitude seemed to be, "if only the customers would go away and leave me alone, I could get my job done."

Carlzon contended that a constant preoccupation with the customer's motivational structure—the needs of the market—would force attitudinal and structural changes in the SAS organization. This would mean a shift in the deployment of the delivery system so that it could be more in harmony with the customer's human priorities. If that happened, Carlzon reasoned, the company's image would improve. As its image improved, its performance in the market would improve, and the process would become self-reinforcing.

With the help of his key executives, Carlzon began to preach and teach this gospel of customer orientation energetically and persistently throughout the organization, taking it right down to the front-line employees. Since Carlzon was convinced that the game would be over if he had to wait for the new gospel to "take" at its own speed, he decided to jump over the management levels and take his message directly to the working people. He formed an implementation team consisting of consultants and hand-picked executives at the highest levels. He and his team embarked on an aggressive campaign to change the thinking of some 20,000 people.

Certainly, SAS did much more than merely train its employees. Out of the management meetings came a number of projects and programs for putting the SAS organization back into shape. One of the projects became known in-house as the BMA project—the businessman's airline. Carlzon decided that, rather than try to be all things to all people when, in fact, the company hadn't been much of anything to anybody, SAS should have a "best-known-for" feature. Its best bet was to become famous for catering to the needs of daytime business travelers moving regularly about Europe and Scandinavia.

SAS had for some time been operating a singularly illogical seat-pricing system on its regular flights. Of course, the airline industry is well known for its peculiar, often baffling price structures, but SAS's scheme outdid those of most companies. A business executive who had paid the full fare for a seat might often find himself or herself sitting beside a college student with a backpack who had paid a substantially lower fare. Should this point arise in the course of their conversation, the executive might well wonder, "Why am I paying more for my ticket, but not getting anything more for my money?" SAS marketing people soon realized that the company's image with business travelers, who contributed the lion's share of SAS receipts, had deteriorated badly.

This led to the creation of the highly successful Euroclass service. Even for relatively short flights, a business traveler could partake of a somewhat higher level of comfort and service, and could sit in a separate curtained-off section of the cabin. This normalization of fare structures and service levels did a great deal for SAS's image in the minds of business travelers.

A second important change masterminded by Jan Carlzon was the take-off-on-time program. Seeking to score points with business travelers, he decided to make SAS the most punctual airline in Europe. "Can we come up with a new plan in six months?" he asked his operating executives. "If so, how much do you think it will cost?" This challenge captured the imagination of a number of key players, and it became a sort of rallying idea.

The original estimate for the venture was a six-months' undertaking at a cost of about 8 million Swedish kronor, which is equal to about $1 million.

The project won so much support at so many levels that it took only three months for SAS to become the most puncutal European airline at a cost of only about 1 million kronor, which amounts to about $125,000.

Again, Carlzon's constant influence lent impetus to the effort. According to legend, he went so far as to install in his office a video showing the status of every flight in the SAS system. It was not unusual for an SAS pilot to land at his destination city and have someone hand him this message: "Mr. Carlzon would like you to call him." When the pilot dialed through, Carlzon would say, "I just wondered why your plane took off late." Perhaps there was an acceptable reason beyond normal human control, but the effect was to keep the pressure on at all levels. Few SAS pilots looked forward to the prospect of explaining to the president of the company why they didn't get their customers in the air at the advertised time.

Though Carlzon's high-profile turnaround strategy attracted considerable attention, few people understood immediately the real implications of what SAS had achieved under his guidance. What was not readily visible to the casual observer was that Carlzon had evolved, largely in an intuitive way, a unique approach to the company's management. This approach was characterized by an almost obsessive commitment to managing the customer's experience at all points in the cycle of service.

QUESTIONS FOR READING 1.2

1. How is the service management concept illustrated by the SAS story?

2. List four things that SAS did to achieve its remarkable turnaround.

3. Is the SAS approach applicable to all services?

4. Why do you think the management of services has become increasingly important in recent years?

REFERENCES

"A Strategy for Rebuilding the Economy" (editorial), *Business Week,* June 30, 1980, p. 146.

Ackoff, R., P. Brohom, and R. Snow. *Revitalizing Western Economies.* San Francisco: Jossey-Bass, 1984.

Albrecht, K., and R. Zemke. *Service America! Doing*

Business in the New Economy. Homewood, Ill.: Dow Jones–Irwin, 1985.

Berger, Joan. "The False Paradise of a Service Economy," *Business Week,* March 3, 1986, pp. 71–74.

Browning, H. C., and J. Singelmann. *The Emergence*

of a Service Society: Demographic and Sociological Aspects of the Sectoral Transformation of the Labor Force in the U.S.A. Springfield, Va.: National Technical Information Service, 1975.

Canton, Irving D. "Learning to Love the Service Economy," *Harvard Business Review.* Vol. 62, No. 3 (May–June 1984), pp. 89–97.

Chase, R. B., and D. A. Garvin. "The Service Factory," *Harvard Business Review,* Vol. 67, No. 4 (July–August 1989), pp. 61–69.

Cusumano, M. A. *The Japanese Automobile Industry.* Cambridge, Mass.: Harvard University Press, 1985.

Davidow, W. H., and Bro Uttal. "Service Companies: Focus or Falter," *Harvard Business Review,* Vol. 67, No. 4 (July–August 1989), pp. 77–85.

Foote, N. N., and P. K. Hatt. "Social Mobility and Economic Advancement," *American Economic Review,* Vol. 43 (1953), pp. 364–378.

Ginsberg, Eli. *Understanding Human Resources.* Lanham, Md.: University Press of America, 1985.

Goodman, Ann. "Are Service Jobs Good Jobs?" *Fortune,* June 10, 1985, pp. 38–43.

Guide to Service Industry Statistics and Related Data. Washington, D.C.: Bureau of the Census, September 1984.

Jonas, Norman. "The Hollow Corporation," *Business Week,* March 3, 1986, pp. 56–58.

Heskett, J. L. "Thank Heaven for the Service Sector," *Business Week,* January 26, 1987, p. 27.

Heskett, James L. *Managing in the Service Economy.* Cambridge, Mass.: Harvard Business School Press, 1986.

Katouzian, M. A. "The Development of the Service Sector: A New Approach," *Oxford Economic Papers,* Vol. 22 (November 1970), pp. 362–382.

Lewis, Russell. *The New Service Economy.* New York: Longman Group, 1973.

Mills, Peter. *Managing Service Industries.* Cambridge, Mass.: Ballinger, 1986.

Norman, Richard. *Service Management: Strategy and Leadership in Service Businesses.* New York: Wiley, 1984.

Pennar, Karen, and Edward Mervosh. "Why Service Jobs Can't Keep Stoking the Economy," *Business Week,* July 8, 1985, pp. 62, 66.

Petit, Pascal. *Slow Growth and the Service Economy.* New York: St. Martin's Press, 1986.

Quinn, J. B., and C. E. Gagnon. "Will Services Follow Manufacturing into Decline?" *Harvard Business Review,* Vol. 64, No. 6 (November–December 1986), pp. 95–103.

Raspberry, William. "Perhaps Shift to Service Economy Is Neither Inevitable nor Desirable," *Roanoke Times & World News,* April 29, 1988.

Riddle, Dorothy I. *Service-Led Growth.* New York: Praeger, 1986.

Shelp, R. K., J. C. Stephenson, N. S. Truitt, and B. Wasow. *Service Industries and Economic Development,* New York: Praeger, 1985.

Stanback, Thomas M., Jr., P. J. Bearse, T. J. Noyelle, and R. A. Karasek. *Services: The New Economy.* Totowa, N.J.: Allenheld, Osmun, 1981.

Urguhart, M. "The Services Industry: Is it Recession-Proof?" *Monthly Labor Review,* Vol. 104, No. 10 (October 1981), pp. 12–18.

Wilson, John W., and Judith H. Dobrzymski. "And Now the Post-Industrial Corporation," *Business Week,* March 3, 1986, pp. 63–66.

2

Characteristics of Services

INTRODUCTION

As noted in Chapter 1, the definition of a service business or service organization has been a continuing problem for students of productive systems. Manufacturing is often taken as the point of departure, and service firms are distinguished in terms of differences from manufacturing organizations. This approach tries to identify services by some criteria for the output, the process, or the consumption of the output that contrasts with manufacturing organizations.

Other approaches for identifying services are (1) listing service organizations or (2) specifying classes of characteristics that a service must possess and those that a service does not possess. In this chapter we present a general concept that will be of practical value in identifying service systems.

GENERAL CONCEPT OF A PRODUCTIVE SYSTEM

A **system** is, simply, a set of elements that works toward a common goal by acting on inputs to produce outputs. A productive system is one that adds value, economic or otherwise, in the conversion of inputs to outputs. A general representation of a productive system is shown in Exhibit 2–1.

A productive system consists of physical elements related to each other. There are five types of productive systems:

— Extraction of materials or energy from the environment
— Biological growth and change
— Tangible output conversion systems
— Intangible output conversion systems
— Hybrid conversion systems

Examples of each of these are shown in Exhibit 2–2. We may note that **services,** as usually defined, fall into either of the last two groups. For example, a retail store is generally considered to be a service, but its output consists of tangible items sold and the intangible utility of offering an assortment of items in one location. Manu-

EXHIBIT 2–1

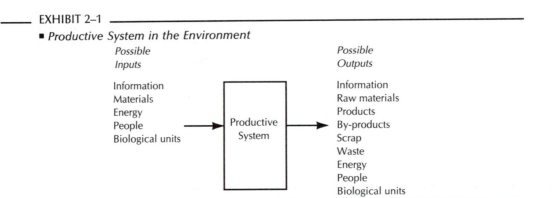

■ *Productive System in the Environment*

——— EXHIBIT 2–2 ———

- *Types of Productive Systems*

Extraction	*Intangible-Output Conversion System*
Mining the earth (or moon) surface	Consulting
Mining under the ocean	Movies
Processing ocean or other bodies of	Radio broadcasting
water (such as salt lakes)	Physical examinations
Extracting gasses from the atmosphere	Day-care centers
Biological	Public administration
Agriculture	*Hybrid Conversion Systems*
Animal and fish husbandry	Restaurants
Biological growth and genetic changing of	Book publishing
micro-organisms	Barber shop
Tangible-Output Conversion Systems	Automobile repair
Unit, or custom	Surgery
Batch	
Continuous (long runs of identifiable units)	
Process (identity of individual units is lost	
as in chemical, textile, rubber, and electrical	
power production)	

facturing organizations also fall within two groups, the third and the fifth. There is no way that the sole output of a manufacturing organization can be intangible (the fourth group). However most "manufacturing" firms provide a *combination* of tangible and intangible outputs. Consider a custom automobile "manufacturer" who works in contact with a customer throughout the process. Is this firm really a manufacturer or is it primarily a "service" firm?

From the preceding, we see that the dichotomy of "service" versus "manufacturing" is not easily maintained. Rather, there is a continuous spectrum of firms with varying amounts of tangible and intangible outputs (see Exhibit 2–3). Thus, we may prefer to simply classify firms as to whether their outputs are tangible, intangible, or both. This provides a more clearcut distinction than service versus manufacturing.

Another definition of a service based on the output of the productive system is as follows. A service is a productive system that falls into one of three classes:

1. *Class 1*. The output of the system is consumed simultaneously with its production. Examples are haircutting, medical treatment, electrical power, retailing, and movies.

2. *Class 2*. The output of the system is information or energy that has been packaged in a storage device to be used later. For example, a firm performs economic research, "stores" the output in a computer database, a brochure, or letter, and sells the output over a period of time. Another example is a company that recharges batteries for customers for use over an extended time period.

3. *Class 3*. The output of the system is that of supplying supporting activities that are not directly a part of new construction of facilities or of a client's primary manufacturing or construction activity. Examples include landscaping, janitorial services, interior decorating, consulting, communications, financial activities, transpor-

EXHIBIT 2–3

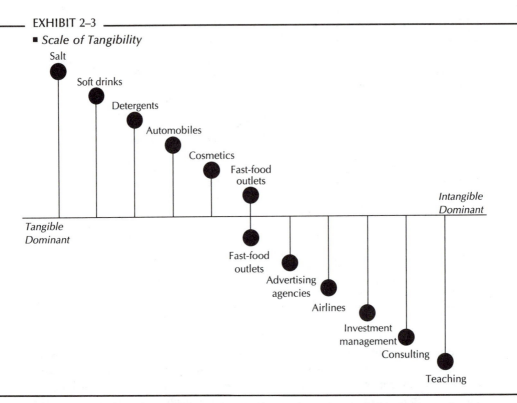

■ *Scale of Tangibility*

Source: G. Lynn Shostack, "Breaking Free from Product Marketing," *Journal of Marketing,* April 1987. Reprinted from *Journal of Marketing,* published by the American Marketing Association.

tation, legal assistance, trade assistance, and information processing. Businesses that perform construction or physical repair of equipment, etc. for other businesses are manufacturing subcontractors rather than services under this definition.

In practice, the definition of services depends on the fact that it is easy to define manufacturing, extraction, agricultural, and mining activities. If an organization does not fit into one of these groups, usually it is classified as a service. For this reason, Clark referred to service industries as the "residual."[1]

CRITERIA FREQUENTLY USED TO IDENTIFY SERVICES

Through the years, researchers and analysts have used one or more criteria to characterize services. Snyder, Cox, and Jesse, Jr.,[2] and Zeithaml, Parasuraman, and Berry[3] have identified a number of such criteria. The following list is based on their studies.

[1] C. Clark, *The Conditions of Economic Progress* (London: Macmillan, 1940).

[2] Charles A. Snyder, James F. Cox, and Richard R. Jesse, Jr., "A Dependent Demand Approach to Service Organization Planning and Control," *Academy of Management Review,* Vol. 7, No. 3 (July 1982), pp. 455–466.

[3] Valerie Zeithaml, A. Parasuraman, and Leonard L. Berry, "Problems and Strategies in Service Marketing," *Journal of Marketing,* Vol. 49, No. 2 (Spring 1985), pp. 33–46.

1. Services produce intangible output.
2. Services produce variable, nonstandard output.
3. A service is perishable; i.e., it cannot be carried in inventory, but is consumed in production.
4. There is high customer contact throughout the service process.
5. The customer participates in the process of providing a service.
6. Skills are sold directly to the customer.
7. Services cannot be mass-produced.
8. High personal judgment is employed by individuals performing the service.
9. Service firms are labor-intensive.
10. Decentralized facilities are located near the customers.
11. Measures of effectiveness are subjective.
12. Quality control is primarily limited to process control.
13. Pricing options are more elaborate.

While not all services possess each of these characteristics, they do exhibit at least *some* of these characteristics to some degree. The 13 criteria just listed emphasize the scope of unique problems that managers of service operations encounter. We will now discuss these criteria in more detail.

Intangible Output

A service such as legal advising may have no tangible output. Other services combine an intangible output with a physical output, as in the case of restaurants, gasoline stations, or interior decorating. While it is true that manufacturing output also can include intangibles (such as warranties, technical information, and prestige of ownership), manufacturing's primary output is always a physical product.

Intangibility describes the uniqueness of services more succinctly than any other characteristic. One prominent author in services management, Lynn Shostack, discusses the impact of the intangibility of services as follows:[4]

> It is wrong to imply that services are just like products "except" for their intangibility. That's like saying apples are just like oranges except for their "appleness." Intangibility is not a modifier; it is a state. Intangibles may come with tangible trappings, but no amount of money can buy physical ownership of such intangibles as experience (movies), time (consulting), or process (dry cleaning). A service is rendered. A service is experienced. A service cannot be stored on a shelf, touched, tasted, or tried on for size.

Variable, Nonstandard Output

The beauty shop, the custom dress design firm, and the executive recruiting firm provide services that vary with the individual client. It is difficult, if not impossible, to standardize the output because each client varies in terms of desires before and during the performance of the service. In addition, many services are labor-intensive, and it is often difficult to standardize the output generated by a variety of service providers. Chapter 5 discusses designing the service process to attain some uniformity in service delivery.

[4] G. L. Shostack, "Breaking Free from Product Marketing," *The Journal of Marketing,* April 1977.

Perishability

Most services, because they are simultaneously produced and consumed, are considered perishable, noninventoriable commodities. The person who phones in to a time service to find the correct time uses up the service at the time it is provided. Hotel rooms, seats on an airplane or in a theater, and an hour of a lawyer's day cannot be stored and retrieved for later use.

However, perishability may be different from a consumer's point of view. While a customer cannot carry home a service after it is produced, the customer *can* enjoy the "effects" of the service long after it has been purchased. For example, the surgeon who gives a heart transplant is providing not just a single operation, but rather a benefit that is enjoyed over the patient's life. Even a movie may be enjoyed in retrospect or provide educational benefits that extend beyond the time that the movie is presented.

The perishability of services, coupled with the highly varying demand patterns that most services experience, requires that managers allocate service capacity carefully and attempt to actively manage service demand. Chapter 8 on aggregate planning and Chapter 11 on scheduling capacity discuss these issues.

High Customer Contact Throughout the Service Process

Services are generally characterized by high customer contact throughout the service process. However, the range of customer contact may be quite broad depending on the type of service provided. As such, the following classification of customer contact is useful.

1. Constant physical contact is required throughout the service operation.
2. Constant communication contact is required throughout the service, but the customer may be remote.
3. Contact with the customer is required physically at sporadic intervals.
4. Communication (remote) with the customer is required sporadically throughout the service.
5. Contact with the customer is required physically and/or by remote communication only before and at the beginning and end of the service.

Exhibit 2–4 provides some examples of the degree of customer contact for service firms as compared to manufacturing firms.

Because of the lack of a buffer between the customer and the service provider, service employees must be carefully selected and trained to interact effectively with customers. Chapter 9 on human resource management discusses employee recruitment, selection, and training.

Customer Participation

Customer participation in services, such as restaurants, aerobics, investments, and real estate selection, is extensive and can take on different forms. For example, service customers may participate as members or subscribers of a service, such as the person

_____ EXHIBIT 2–4 _____

■ *Contact of Processor with Customer*

Contact During the Production Process	Service	Manufacturing
Constant physical contact	Barber, masseuse, cruise ship	None
Constant communication	Hot line	Large complex weapons system
Sporadic physical contact	Management consulting, plastic surgeon, restaurant	Toupee manufacturer, custom clothier
Sporadic communication	Management consulting, legal service, utility	Custom printing, tool and die manufacturer
Physical contact before, at beginning and at end of the process	Tailor, dry cleaner, mover of household goods	Kitchen cabinet manufacturer for custom homes
Communication only before, at beginning and at end of process	Stock broker conducting stock transaction, fertilizer company that sprays farms, car rental	Custom suit manufacturer located abroad, manufacturer using mail distribution

who has a telephone in the home using the service whenever it is needed. On the other hand, a service may be continuously available to a customer even though he or she is not a formal subscriber of the service. This is true of most public services, such as police protection. Or services may be available to the general public only at discrete times, such as mass transit. Exhibit 2–5 shows additional examples of continuous delivery versus discrete service transactions and formal versus informal relationships between the customers and the service organization. The degree and form of customer participation should be an important consideration in the design of a service. Chapter 4 discusses service design.

_____ EXHIBIT 2–5 _____

■ *Relationships with Customers*

Nature of Service Delivery	Type of Relationship between the Service Organization and its Customers	
	"Membership" Relationship	No Formal Relationship
Continuous delivery of service	Insurance Telephone subscription College enrollment Banking American Automobile Association	Ratio station Police protection Lighthouse Public highway
Discrete transactions	Long-distance calls from subscriber phone Theater-series subscription Travel on commuter ticket	Car rental Mail service Toll highway Pay phone Movie theater Public transportation Restaurant

Source: Christopher B. Lovelock, *Services Marketing,* © 1984, p. 54. Reprinted by permisssion of Prentice Hall, Inc., Englewood Cliffs, New Jersey.

Skills Sold Directly to the Customer

In many services, the customer buys a *skill* such as home painting, plumbing repair, landscaping, beauty treatment, or psychiatric care. In many other services, the technical skill is a core separated from the customer. Most of the membership relationships of Exhibit 2–5 are of this nature. The design of the service (presented in Chapter 4) and service process (presented in Chapter 5), as well as the marketing of a service (presented in Chapter 17), are all affected by the manner in which skills are provided.

Mass Production

One view that has distinguished services in the past is that they cannot be mass produced. For the most part, this is true. Each customer brings different requirements for service. However, some services can actually go beyond mass production and be produced instantaneously for mass consumption. For illustration, a radio or TV call-in program may have a financial expert who provides answers to questions called in. The instant answer may serve thousands of people. Similarly, credit card services provide mass services continuously.

High Personal Judgment

In many services, the design of the service is determined by the person who actually provides the service, such as the advisor, the real estate agent, or the beautician. The individual supplier of the service must match the service to the client's desires while providing the service. In some cases, the judgment required by the service provider is very high. For other types of services, such as fast-food restaurants and automatic teller machines, providing the service involves very little discretion.

Judgment is obviously related to the degree of individual customized service. Examples of this relationship are shown in Exhibit 2–6. Education, for example, requires a high degree of personal judgment but is not customized to the individual student. Health care also requires a high degree of judgment on the part of the physician, but it is customized to the patient as well. Public transportation, on the other hand, is low on both measures. Chapter 9 highlights the problems inherent in training a service employee to have "judgment."

Labor Intensiveness

The question of labor intensiveness versus capital intensiveness for service firms has important implications. Capital intensiveness offers a promise of continued increases in productivity, provided the costs of equipment can be kept in line. Although people tend to view services as inherently labor-intensive, this is not always the case. Some are and some aren't. Dentistry is one that offers very little prospect for automation because of the mental and physical requirements of the work, as well as the infinite variability of human subjects and their problems. On the other hand, education, bank services, car rentals, or motel services can become more automated.

Exhibits 2–7 and 2–8 demonstrate that both manufacturing and services may

_____ EXHIBIT 2–6 _____

■ *Customization and Judgment in Service Delivery*

Extent to Which Customer-Contact Personnel Exercise Judgment in Meeting Individual Customer Needs	Extent to Which Service Characteristics Are Customized	
	High	Low
High	Legal services Health care/surgery Architectural design Executive search firm Real estate agency Taxi service Beautician Plumber Education (tutorials)	Education (large classes) Preventive health programs
Low	Telephone service Hotel services Retail banking (excl. major loans) Good restaurant	Public transportation Routine appliance repair Fast-food restaurant Movie theater Spectator sports

Source: Christopher B. Lovelock, *Services Marketing,* © 1984, p. 56. Reprinted by permission of Prentice Hall, Inc., Englwood Cliffs, New Jersey.

vary from capital-intensive (equipment-based) to labor-intensive (labor-based). For example, chemicals are produced in a highly automated manufacturing environment, whereas watchmakers and sculptors rely on their own personal skills for manufacturing their products. Similarly, in services, vending machines represent automated service, while management consultants provide a highly specialized, personalized service.

Equipment and labor intensiveness is not always a dichotomy. Exhibit 2–9 examines the degree of equipment versus people orientation of various services and provides examples of some services that score high or low on both labor and equipment content. For example, five-star hotels and hospitals have extensive facilities but are also people-oriented. On the other end of the scale, ''easy listening'' radio requires little equipment or personal intervention. A college education involves the use of a medium amount of equipment but is high on personal contact. Chapter 10 discusses technology in services, and Chapter 5 gives some advice on selecting equipment.

Decentralized Facilities Near Customers

It is commonly stated that services should be located physically near customers and manufacturing plants should be located near raw materials and suppliers. This has resulted in a proliferation of small, decentralized service units geographically dispersed across the customer service region and large, centralized manufacturing plants located at some distance from the customer.

For services that involve physical contact with customers (lawn care, roof repair, banks, grocery stores, or other retail shops), nearness to customers and the high traffic

EXHIBIT 2–7

- *Classification of Manufacturing Firms by Capital Intensity and Labor Skill*

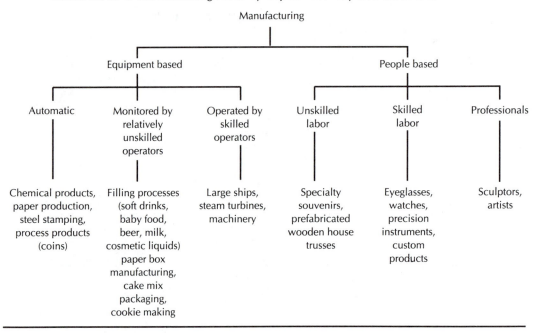

EXHIBIT 2–8

- *Classification of Service Firms by Capital Intensity and Labor Skills*

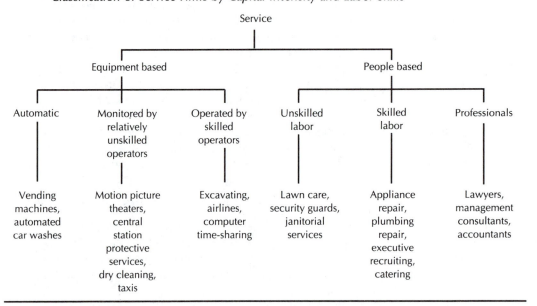

―――― EXHIBIT 2–9 ――――――――――――――――――――――――――――――――――

■ *Understanding the Characteristics of the Service Output*

Extent to Which Equipment/Facility-Based Attributes Form Part of the Service Output[a]	Extent to Which People-Based Attributes Form Part of the Service Output[b]		
	High	Medium	Low
High	Five-star hotel Hospital	Passenger airline Car rental	Subway Retail banking (with ATMs)
Medium	Dentist Live theater College education	Retail banking (with human tellers)	Freight transportation Movie theater
Low	Corporate banking Management consulting Public accounting	Tax preparation	"Easy listening" radio[c]

[a] Could also include such other physical attributes as food and drink.

[b] These could be service personnel, other customers, or both.

[c] Equipment (a radio receiver) is needed to receive broadcasts but is not part of the service itself.

Source: Christopher Lovelock, *Services Marketing,* © 1984, p. 61. Reprinted by permission of Prentice Hall, Inc., Englewood Cliffs, New Jersey.

of potential customers makes adjacent location important. On the other hand, some banking services, retail mail-order businesses, insurance companies, and many other services may be conducted at great distances from the customer entirely by phone or mail.

Chapter 6 is entirely devoted to service location. Chapter 9 discusses some of the problems in managing employees at diverse locations, and Chapter 10 presents some technologies that may facilitate the performance of services at distances physically removed from the customer. Finally, Chapter 13 discusses the problems involved in routing and scheduling vehicles to deliver a service to customers in different geographic locations.

Measures of Effectiveness

Measures of service effectiveness or levels of service are believed by many to be primarily subjective. How should we measure the effectiveness of a professor's lecture, a physician's care, or police protection? As we shall see in Chapter 14, determining the quality of a physical product is much easier than measuring the effectiveness of an intangible service. The problem is aggravated by the difficulty in determining how different customers themselves judge the quality of a service.

Quality Control Primarily Process Control

In manufacturing, quality control occurs in two basic forms: control of the manufacturing process and acceptance sampling of the finished product before shipment to the customer. In contrast, most services involve the customer in some way so that the service is delivered to the customer before it can be inspected and rejected by the producer. Consider a simple bank transaction in which a customer cashes a check. The customer may discover that he or she has been short-changed, at which point the teller makes a correction. To insert a quality-control representative between the teller and the customer would be impractical.

In a more extreme example, consider a plastic surgeon who has reconstructed a person's face. When the bandages come off, the appearance and scars leave the client aghast. In a less serious case, a barber snips off a chunk of hair which the customer feels is too much. In these examples, control of the service has to occur prior to or during the service process.

There are, however, some services that can appropriately use acceptance control and are increasingly doing so. For example, the architect may have several people review a package of drawings to ensure compliance with codes and to catch mechanical errors before distribution to the customer. Chapter 14 discusses quality control in services and process control in particular.

Expanded Price Basis

In manufacturing, a price for a unit is fixed in advance, except in products with a high service content, such as high-technology weapon systems or the custom design and production of wedding dresses. For services, pricing is more difficult and variable. It may be based on

— A *contingency fee,* as in lawsuits where there is a possibility of no return or a very high return

— An *appearance fee,* where the price is negotiated before the service is performed, possibly for a portrait, a book, or a training program

— A *fixed fee,* as for a manicure or a "dial-a-prayer" call

— *Time and materials*

— *Time only,* where only labor is involved

— *Cost plus a fixed fee*

— A *fixed fee or rate minus discounts* for the time a service is received (as in computer processing) and ordered (as in certain air fares)

Airline pricing is probably the best example of complexity in service pricing. Owing to a proliferation of different products and intense competition, airline fares also change frequently. The largest number of airline fare changes recorded in a single day for the industry was 600,000. United Airlines alone routinely changes about 30,000 fares daily.[5]

---

[5] "Competition, Computers Complicate Airline Pricing," *Roanoke Times & World News,* December 4, 1988.

EXHIBIT 2–10

■ *Open Systems View of a Service System*

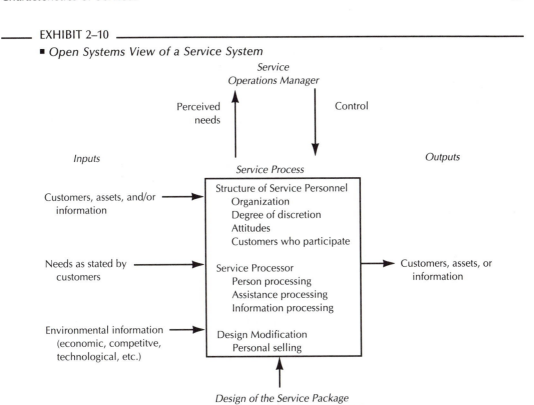

TOTAL VISION OF THE SERVICE SYSTEM
Systems View

For services, the process and the output of the system are the same or closely related. The design, process, and personal sales activities of a service are bound together in what is often termed the **service bundle** or **service package.** A systems view of services was suggested by Fitzsimmons and Sullivan.[6] Drawing on this idea, we constructed the open systems view of a service system shown in Exhibit 2–10. The systems view is designed to fit all types of service systems by identifying key aspects of the service process and service package.

An important input to the service process is the design of the service package. The service package includes specifications on the facility where the service will be

[6] James A. Fitzsimmons and Robert S. Sullivan, *Service Operations Management* (New York: McGraw-Hill, 1982).

provided, designations of any goods that are necessary in providing the service, and descriptions of the physical and/or mental services to be provided for the customer. Chapter 4 discusses service design in more detail. Other inputs to the service process include current customers, assets or information of current customers or businesses, customer needs, and the economic, competitive, and technological environments in which the service is taking place.

The service process depends on the structure of the service personnel, the role of the service processor, and the required degree of modification to the initial service design. Personnel structure is a function of the type of organization, the degree of discretion or judgment allowed the service personnel in completing a service, the attitudes of the service personnel, and the degree of customer participation in the service process. The service processor may process a person through the service system, assist a customer in his or her own servicing, or process information. Customizing a service involves changing the basic service design and may require some degree of personal selling on the part of the service personnel.

The role of the service operations manager is to monitor and control the service process based on feedback from the system to ensure that the perceived needs of the customer and service personnel are being met.

Finally, the outputs of the system may be customers, assets, or information that have increased in value or form because of the service process. Note that the customer is an input as well as an output of the system and also may be a part of the service process.

Managerial View

Another approach to presenting the service process is given by Schmenner,[7] as depicted in Exhibit 2–11. Schmenner's model represents a managerial model of activities rather than a systems model, and in it he identifies current challenges to service managers depending on their service classification.

Two measures are used to classify services:

— The degree of labor intensity, defined as the ratio of labor cost to the value of plant and equipment
— The degree to which the consumer interacts with the service and/or the service is customized for the consumer

Services with a low degree of labor intensity and a low degree of customer interaction/customization, called **service factories,** include airlines, trucking, hotels, and resorts. Services with low labor intensity but high interaction/customization, termed **service shops,** include hospitals and repair services. **Mass services,** such as retailing, wholesaling, banking, and education, have a high labor intensity but low interaction/customization. Finally, **professional services,** such as doctors, lawyers, and accountants, are both highly labor-intensive and customized.

Managers of highly labor-intensive services spend much of their time and efforts managing and controlling the work force. These services also tend to be decentralized,

---

[7] Roger W. Schmenner, "How Can Service Businesses Survive and Prosper?'' *Sloan Management Review,* Vol. 27, No. 3 (Spring 1986), pp. 24–35.

EXHIBIT 2-11

■ *Challenges for Service Managers*

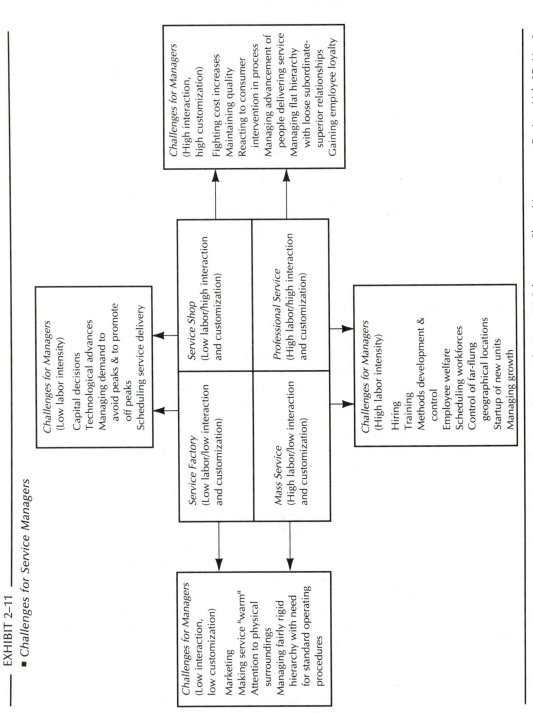

Challenges for Managers
(Low labor intensity)

Capital decisions
Technological advances
Managing demand to
avoid peaks & to promote
off peaks
Scheduling service delivery

Challenges for Managers
(High interaction,
high customization)

Fighting cost increases
Maintaining quality
Reacting to consumer
intervention in process
Managing advancement of
people delivering service
Managing flat hierarchy
with loose subordinate-
superior relationships
Gaining employee loyalty

Service Factory
(Low labor/low interaction
and customization)

Service Shop
(Low labor/high interaction
and customization)

Mass Service
(High labor/low interaction
and customization)

Professional Service
(High labor/high interaction
and customization)

Challenges for Managers
(Low interaction,
low customization)

Marketing
Making service "warm"
Attention to physical
surroundings
Managing fairly rigid
hierarchy with need
for standard operating
procedures

Challenges for Managers
(High labor intensity)

Hiring
Training
Methods development &
control
Employee welfare
Scheduling workforces
Control of far-flung
geographical locations
Startup of new units
Managing growth

Source: Reprinted from "How Can Service Businesses Survive and Prosper" by Roger W. Schmenner, *Sloan Management Review*, Vol. 27, No. 3 (Spring 1986), p. 27, by permission of the publisher. Copyright © 1986 by the Sloan Management Review Association. All rights reserved.

37

often in separate geographic locations, so managers must deal with managing several service locations at once, as well as introducing new locations into the system.

Managers of services with low labor intensity concentrate on a different set of problems. They are more concerned with monitoring their current plant and equipment and evaluating new techniques. Since their equipment-oriented capacity is less flexible than that of labor-intensive services, they also must schedule the delivery of their services more precisely and try to manage demand to smooth out peak periods and promote off-peak times.

If the service has low customer interaction/customization, then the manager must pay close attention to marketing in an effort to make the service appear warm and the service facility attractive. This is also the type of service that lends itself to set operating procedures and strict management hierarchies.

For services with high customer interaction/customization, managers will have difficulty keeping costs down and maintaining high levels of quality. Service employees have a bigger impact on the success of the operation and need to be well trained and treated with care. Management-subordinate relationships also tend to be less stringent.

Strategic View

Still another approach to service operations management involves a strategic view of the service system. Heskett[8] suggests a strategic service vision in which four basic strategic elements—(1) target market segments, (2) service concept, (3) operating strategy, and (4) service delivery system—are brought together by three integrative elements—(1) positioning, (2) value/cost leveraging, and (3) strategy/service integration. These elements are shown in Exhibit 2–12, along with relevant questions to assist in defining the elements for a particular service organization. Determining **target market segments** involves identifying common characteristics of the market, important needs of the market, and strengths of existing competitors. Defining a **service concept** consists of establishing in the minds of customers, employees, shareholders, and lenders perceptions and expectations of the service itself. To integrate the target market with its service concept, the service organization must **position** itself in the competitive environment of the selected market.

Next, an **operating strategy** needs to be developed that addresses such concerns as the role of operations, financing, and marketing and the quality and cost of the service. To integrate the service concept with the operating strategy, differences between the perceived value and cost of a service need to be reconciled. This **value-cost leveraging** can be accomplished by making wise decisions on standardization versus customization, managing supply and demand, and controlling quality. Finally, the **service delivery system** should be established by determining the role of people versus technology; specifying the equipment, layout, and procedures to be used in providing the service; and maintaining quality and delivery standards. For effective service, the design of the service and its operating strategy must be consistent with the service

---

[8] Heskett's book, *Managing in the Service Economy* (Boston, Mass.: Harvard Business School Press, 1986), is organized around the basic and integrative elements of a strategic service vision shown in Exhibit 2–12.

EXHIBIT 2–12

■ *Basic and Integrative Elements of a Strategic Service Vision*

Target Market Segments	Positioning	Service Concept	Value/Cost Leveraging	Operating Strategy	Strategy/System Integration	Service Delivery System
What are common characteristics of important market segments?	How does the service concept propose to meet customer needs?	What are important elements of the service to be provided, stated in terms of results produced for customers?	To what extent are differences between perceived value and cost of service maximized by	What are important elements of the strategy? Operations? Financing? Marketing? Organization? Human resources? Control?	To what extent are the strategy and delivery system internally consistent?	What are important features of the service delivery system, including The role of people? Technology? Equipment? Layout? Procedures?
What dimensions can be used to segment the market? Demographic? Psychographic?	How do competitors meet these needs?	How are these elements supposed to be perceived by the target market segment? By the market in general? By employees as a whole?	Standardization of certain elements? Customization of certain elements? Emphasizing easily leveraged services? Management of supply and demand?	On which will the most effort be concentrated?	Can needs of the strategy be met by the delivery system?	What capacity does it provide? Normally? At peak levels?
How important are various segments?	How is the proposed service differentiated from competition?			Where will investments be made?	If not, what changes must be made in The operating strategy? The service delivery system?	To what extent does it Help insure quality standards?
What needs does each have?	How important are these differences?	How is the service concept perceived?	Control of quality through Rewards? Appeal to pride? Visibility? supervision? Peer group control? Involving the customer? Effective use of data?	How will quality and cost be controlled? Measures? Incentives? Rewards?	To what extent does the coordination of operating strategy and service delivery system insure High quality? High productivity? Low cost? High morale and loyalty of servers?	Differentiate the service from competition? Provide barriers to entry by competitors?
How well are these needs being served? In what manner? By whom?	What is good service? Does the proposed service concept provide it? What efforts are required to bring customer expectations and service capabilities into alignment?	What efforts does this suggest in terms of the manner in which the service is Designed? Delivered? Marketed?	To what extent does this effort create barriers to entry by potential competition?	What results will be expected versus competition in terms of Quality of service? Cost profile? Productivity? Morale/loyalty of servers?	To what extent does this integration provide barriers to entry to competition?	

Basic element

Integrative element

Source: James L. Heskett, *Managing in the Service Economy* (Boston: Harvard Business School Press, 1986), p. 30. Reprinted by permission.

delivery system. Thus, **strategy-systems integration** should verify that the service strategy can be met by the proposed service delivery system. The net result of these basic decisions and their integration is a strategic service vision that should prove profitable to the service provider and valuable to the customer.

TRENDS IN SERVICES

Current trends in the service industry include the following:

1. **Innovative services that consumers are not aware of until they are presented.** Often these are based on new technology. Recent examples are the CAT scan in medicine, cash management accounts, Videotext, home shopping by computer terminal, electronic tellers, teleconferencing on long distance, photo development while you wait, and cellular phones that contact the nearest police station when a car break-in is attempted.

2. **Increased consumer participation in service operations.** Recent examples are self-service gas stations, packaged products to be assembled by the consumer, cleaning of clothes by consumer based on wash-and-wear materials, and use of home videos to replace theater movies.

3. **Prepackaging of services.** This includes self-instruction courses, prepackaged divorce kits, medical services in the form of home instruments to measure blood pressure and test for cancer, and dial-a-message for prepackaged therapy, counseling, or information.

4. **Increased service content of consumer goods.** Examples are touch-to-turn-on lamps, one-stop auto service centers, serve-at-home food outlets and medical services, increased mix of activities at recreational resorts, increased mix of banking services, and increased services from real estate firms (such as computer listings).

5. **Internationalization** of both mass services (new banking services) and small unit services (franchises).

Without a doubt, many more services will be available to society in the future through the introduction of new services (computer programs to draw up contracts and wills or prepare your defense), the automation of existing services (robots to clean our homes and cut our lawns), and greater participation of the consumer in the service process (equipment that allows self-cutting of hair).

—— SUMMARY

This chapter deals with the nature of productive systems in order to point out similarities and differences among systems. Services have been differentiated from manufacturing organizations on the basis of several criteria, including type of output, customer participation, labor intensiveness, measures of effectiveness, and others.

Although each type of service has its own specific characteristics, a study of these criteria helps us to understand the nature of service-dominated organizations versus manufacturing-dominated organizations, as well as to analyze the similarities and differences among various services. It is useful to group services with common characteristics together so that similar operations strategies, management processes, and marketing practices can be applied.

We have presented three perspectives of a service system—systems, managerial, and strategic—that should be of value to managers. These deal with service system processes, as well as managerial problems and strategies for developing and controlling these processes.

The United States, as a service economy, has a vital interest in service innovation. This includes developing new service concepts, increasing the efficiency and productivity of services, introducing new technologies for the service industry, and internationalizing our service businesses. The remainder of the text deals with these and other issues.

____ DISCUSSION QUESTIONS

1. How would you define a service?

2. How would you categorize the output of services?

3. Describe how the following criteria are used to characterize services:

    a. Decentralization
    b. Customer contact
    c. Customer participation

4. How do the following differ for service firms versus manufacturing firms?

    a. Measures of effectiveness
    b. Quality control
    c. Pricing

5. Can services be mass produced? Why or why not?

6. Why are services more labor-intensive than most manufacturing firms? What management problems does this pose?

7. Discuss the role of the service employee. What impact does the individual performance of service employees have on company performance?

8. Define

    a. Service factory
    b. Service shop
    c. Mass service
    d. Professional service

How does the manager's job differ for each type of service?

9. Using your definitions from Question 8, classify the following service organizations:

    a. A hospital
    b. A dry cleaners
    c. A university
    d. A lawyer
    e. A trucking firm

10. What trends in innovative new services do you foresee for the 1990s? How are the trends toward increased consumer participation and prepackaging of services at odds with the trend toward increased service content of consumer goods? What types of services do you think will fall in each category?

—— READING 2.1 ————————————————————————

Moving Money: Citibank's Operating Group Brings Great Efficiency to Bookkeeping Chores

At the foot of Wall Street, near the docks and the heliport and the canvas-domed tennis courts, there is a factory. It is in a tall building sheathed in smoky glass and concrete that from the outside looks like any other 24-story stack of offices. But when the businessmen and stenographers are filing from the other downtown towers at the end of the day, the factory at 111 Wall St. is still rattling away.

Forty-foot-long sorting machines are roaring and hissing like high-speed locomotives. Robot forklift trucks are carrying trays of work from station to storage bin, from storage bin to station. Trucks laden with the night's raw materials are descending on the loading docks. And in several large rooms, workers flailing furiously at electric machines are raising a din equal to a barrage from a hundred burp guns.

MOVING MONEY

The business volume here is high by most factory standards: $20 billion a day. Of course, the factory doesn't make that much money; it moves it. "Money that is not moving," a hurrying worker says, "is useless."

Eighteen billion of those dollars are symbolically shuffled among the world's financial institutions. Two billion are "machined" in the form of 3 million checks and 104,000 corporate documents. Twelve million lines are printed; phones ring and phones are dialed 139,000 times.

In a year, $2.5 trillion ebb and flow through the white corridors of 111 Wall St., where 6500 laborers in the Operating Group of First National City Bank perform the physical acts of the otherwise-ephemeral business of banking. They debit or credit accounts. They send checks drawn on other banks through the clearing houses and back to their original writers. They file checks written by Citibank's own customers and, once a month, wrap them up in a bank statement and drop them in the mail.

"WIN," "PASS," OR "FAIL"

Each Operating Group worker knows precisely what is expected of him. Each job has a standard. Doing better than standard is "a win," meeting the standard is "a pass," falling below standard is "a fail." A worker who fails risks "documentation"— his incapacity is immortalized on a permanent record. The same is true for managers; each has an objective, always intended to pare costs. Forecasts are made and performance is measured—annually, monthly, and, in many instances, daily or hourly. A 2% variation is considered significant. "You sort of expect to meet the forecasts or else," a young manager says.

"No excuses or rationalizations of events 'beyond one's control' are expected," Operating Group Head Bob White said in a three-year-old speech his employees still study. Failing, he said, isn't always an offense, but "hiding a fail is much more serious than a fail itself." Workers at 111 Wall St. all sit at tables, never at desks, because, as Mr. White said, "you can't hide things in tables."

OF PEOPLE AND PAPER

The Operating Group consists of people processing paper. Its managers' ultimate vision is the elimination of people and the elimination of paper. All that will remain is the process: electronic blips coursing through electronic brains.

A unit manager: "I'm not processing paper; I'm processing information. If I could have my way, I'd never see paper at all."

An operations head: "I have 130 people. If I automate the way I want to, there won't be any left."

For the moment, however, there are still people at 111 Wall St. and a great deal of paper. The icy efficiency envisioned in the upper reaches of management isn't achieved without a fair infusion of sweat and muscle.

About 300 of the people and 2500 pounds of the paper pass each day through what is known as the Branch Channel of Check Processing Operations. The Branch Channel is on the eighth floor, a cross-hatching of glass partitions enclosing large, red-carpeted rooms. The rooms are flanked by corridors lined with narrow metal lockers that the workers use—instead of desks—to store their belongings. What happens here, in simplest terms, is this: Checks deposited by customers of the 245 New York area branches of First National City Bank are sorted, credited to the proper accounts, and sent to the banks they were drawn on.

Each day about 1.5 million checks are deposited, worth perhaps $1 billion. The branches stuff them into purple canvas bags, and in late afternoon they are collected by a fleet of 38 trucks and dumped on the loading docks of 111 Wall St. If all goes well, the last check will be put through the mill by 6 A.M. The trick is to send out as many checks as came in.

The check bags are dumped in the encoding rooms where dozens of people sit jabbing the keyboards of noisy machines that translate the amount on every check into a trail of squarish magnetic-ink numbers along the bottom edge of each—a language computers can read. These workers are paid on an "incentive" system, which is another word for piecework. The objective is to encode as many checks as possible. The acceptable standard is 1200 an hour. The record is 2400.

When the encoders are finished, the checks are blocked and batched and placed into "trays" that look like shoe boxes by workers sitting at high tables at the end of each room (they also catch customers' addition errors on deposit slips, 1200 of them a night). Then the checks are "handed off" to the climate-controlled computer room, where four 40-foot "Trace" machines sort them for delivery to dozens of institutions, from Chase Manhattan Bank to the Bank of China.

——— QUESTIONS FOR READING 2.1

1. How is Citibank's Operating Group like a traditional factory, say a plant that produces automobiles?

2. How is Citibank's Operating Group different from a traditional factory?

3. In what terms are the standards for worker performance expressed? Do you see any problems with using standards in this way?

4. Suppose there is an error encoding a check. How can it be tracked down? Who might a customer contact if he or she thinks an error has been made?

5. Think about how Citibank's operations could be further automated. What advances in check processing do you foresee for the banking industry?

——— READING 2.2 ———————————————

A Canadian Hospital Does Brisk Business in Rupture Repairs

On a Thursday morning last year, Arthur J. Remillard, Jr., strolled into an operating room at a small hospital here to undergo major surgery to repair a hernia. After the operation, he gingerly walked back to his room. Later that day he got up for a game of billiards with fellow patients. The following Monday he was back at work.

That case history is typical of the 6000 hernias that are repaired every year by the eight surgeons at the 88-bed Shouldice Hospital, which could be

Source: S. Oliver, "A Canadian Hospital Does Brisk Business in Rupture Repairs," *The Wall Street Journal,* February 7, 1978. Reprinted by permission of *The Wall Street Journal,* © Dow Jones & Company, Inc. 1978. All Rights Reserved Worldwide.

the only institution in the world that does nothing else but treat the common ailment of the hernia.

Because of its unusual specialty, Shouldice has been able to develop techniques that have made it the fast-service expert in the hospital business. It routinely discharges its patients only 72 hours after surgery, compared with the seven-day stay that is normal at other hospitals. And the cost of a routine hernia operation and stay at Shouldice is less than $500, only a third of the cost at a large Toronto hospital.

TAKING A LOCAL

Mr. Remillard, 46, who is the president of Commerce Insurance Co., in Webster, Mass., says he went to Shouldice on the advice of a friend because "I couldn't see why I had to be off work so long to get a hernia fixed." Nor could Mr. Remillard "see any reason for a general anesthetic." Instead, like nearly all the patients at Shouldice, he had a local anesthetic. This not only shortens recovery time and reduces the risks of postoperative complications, but also makes it possible for patients to get in and out of the operating room under their own steam.

Shouldice is able to survive on such a narrow specialty because hernia repair is the most frequently performed major surgery. In the U.S. alone, there are about 50,000 hernia operations a year. The affliction also is painful economically. According to a U.S. government survey, in 1975 Americans spent 18.3 million days in bed and missed 7.4 million days of work because of hernias.

The most common of all hernias, the inguinal, occurs in the groin area. Protrusions elsewhere on the abdominal wall are called femoral and umbilical hernias. Highest up of all is the hiatus hernia, which occurs when part of the stomach pushes through the diaphragm separating the chest and the abdomen. The condition only rarely requires surgery, but Shouldice won't handle such cases because the operation is too complex, involving the opening of the chest and the abdomen.

WEIGHT IS A PROBLEM

Nor will Shouldice accept patients in poor physical condition or who are considerably overweight.

"Overweight people heal much more slowly and much less effectively," says a Shouldice surgeon.

Fast healing is basic to the hospital's philosophy of "early ambulation," which means getting the patient back on his feet and out of the hospital as soon as possible. A few surgeons elsewhere also use these methods, but according to Dr. Blaise Alfano, executive director of the American Society of Abdominal Surgery, they aren't widely practiced. Large hospitals, he says, find it more convenient to wheel patients in and out of operating rooms and to confine them to bed for several days.

Shouldice "doesn't give you a chance to lie in bed," says insurance executive Mr. Remillard. Patients' functional, motel-like rooms are without telephones and television sets, and all meals are served in the communal dining room. "Even the phones are put at a height where you have to stretch to use them," says Mr. Remillard. This doesn't harm the incision because Shouldice surgeons repair hernias by overlapping the three layers of muscle in the abdominal wall with continuous stitches of stainless steel wire.

The hospital keeps in touch with former patients through an annual questionnaire, and every year it hosts a reunion at a Toronto hotel at which ex-patients can be examined by Shouldice doctors. They rarely find any cause for concern because Shouldice says that its annual rate of hernia recurrence is a scant 1%, compared with the average recurrence rate for the condition of 10%.

_____ QUESTIONS FOR READING 2.2

1. How has Shouldice Hospital defined its service?

2. How does Shouldice's environment reflect its service definition? In what ways is it different from a traditional hospital?

3. What differences would you expect in the jobs of doctors, nurses, and staff at Shouldice versus other hospitals?

4. How would you describe the service that Shouldice provides in terms of

  a. Output (tangibility and variability)
  b. Customer contact
  c. Customer participation
  d. Measures of effectiveness

5. Using Schmenner's terminology, would you classify Shouldice as a service factory, a service shop, a mass service, or a professional service? Why?

6. Describe how Shouldice has successfully integrated its strategy and the service it provides according to the integrative elements identified by Heskett.

REFERENCES

Adam, Everett E., Jr. "Towards a Typology of Production and Organizations Management Systems," *Academy of Management Review,* Vol. 8, No. 3 (July 1983), pp. 365–375.

Albrecht, Karl, and Ron Zemke. *Service America!* Homewood, Ill.: Dow Jones–Irwin, 1985.

Chase, R. B. "Where Does the Customer Fit in a Service Operation?" *Harvard Business Review,* Vol. 56, No. 6 (November–December 1978), pp. 138–139.

Clark, C. *The Conditions of Economic Progress.* London: Macmillan, 1940.

Collier, David A. *Service Management: The Automation of Services.* Reston, Va.: Reston Publishing Co., 1985.

"Competition, Computers Complicate Airline Pricing," *Roanoke Times & World News,* December 4, 1988.

Fitzsimmons, James A., and Robert S. Sullivan. *Service Operations Management.* New York: McGraw-Hill, 1982.

Heskett, James L. *Managing in the Service Economy.* Boston: Harvard Business School Press, 1986.

Lovelock, Christopher H. "Classifying Services to Gain Strategic Marketing Insights," *Journal of Marketing,* Vol. 47, No. 3 (Summer 1983), pp. 9–20.

Lovelock, Christopher H. *Services Marketing.* Englewood Cliffs, N.J.: Prentice-Hall, 1984.

Mills, Peter. *Managing Service Industries.* Cambridge, Mass.: Ballinger, 1986.

Mills, Peter K., and Newton Margulies. "Toward a Core Typology of Service Organizations," *Academy of Management Review,* Vol. 5, No. 2 (April 1980), pp. 255–266.

Mills, Peter K. and Dennis J. Moberg. "Perspectives on the Technology of Service Operations," *Academy of Management Review,* Vol. 7, No. 3 (July 1982), pp. 467–478.

Normann, Richard. *Service Management: Strategy and Leadership in Service Businesses.* New York: Wiley, 1984.

Sasser, W. Earl, R. Paul Olsen, and D. Daryl Wyckoff. *Management of Service Operations.* Boston: Allyn and Bacon, 1978.

Schmenner, Roger W. "How Can Service Businesses Survive and Prosper?" *Sloan Management Review,* Vol. 27, No. 3 (Spring 1986), pp. 24–35.

Snyder, Charles A., James F. Cox, and Richard R. Jesse, Jr. "A Dependent Demand Approach to Service Organization Planning and Control," *Academy of Management Review,* Vol. 7, No. 3 (July 1982), pp. 455–466.

Stiff, Ronald, and Julie Pollack. "Consumerism in the Service Sector: Selected Issues and Opportunities," in *Emerging Perspectives on Services Marketing.* Chicago: American Marketing Association, 1983.

Thomas, Dan R. E. "Strategy Is Different in Service Businesses," *Harvard Business Review,* Vol. 56, No. 4 (July–August 1978), pp. 158–165.

Voss, C., C. Armstead, B. Johnston, and B. Morris. *Operations Management in Service Industries and the Public Sector.* New York: Wiley, 1985.

Zeithaml, Valerie, A. Parasuraman, and Leonard L. Berry. "Problems and Strategies in Service Marketing," *Journal of Marketing,* Vol. 49, No. 2 (Spring 1985), pp. 33–46.

3

Forecasting Demand for Services

INTRODUCTION

Every day, managers make decisions without knowing what will happen in the future. Making good estimates is the main purpose of forecasting. In this chapter we explain why forecasting is so important to service operations, what types of service outputs are forecast, and the factors that affect our choice of forecasting methods. We also will present a variety of forecasting models with names such as exponential smoothing, moving averages, time series extrapolation, and linear regression.

Good forecasts are an essential input to all types of productive systems because they form the basis for planning. There are many types of services, however, that would be chaotic without careful forecasting of demand. A few situations that differ widely from manufacturing companies are described briefly below.

Fixed Capacity with Widely Fluctuating Demand

If a service firm has a relatively limited range of capacity and widely fluctuating demand for its services, it must establish policies to prevent idle facilities when demand is normally low. It also must seek means for treating customers when demand exceeds capacities. As an example, tennis clubs in south Florida usually have very little activity during the summer, so that investments of $15,000 per court may be utilized only 25 percent of the time. Policies may establish lower-priced summer memberships, tennis "camps," party-tournaments, corporate tournaments, and short clinics to keep the courts in use. On the other hand, in the winter, when demand usually exceeds court time, policies may include higher prices to reduce demand but increase revenue; activities such as parties, tours, and matches with clubs that have available court capacity; and variable rates to increase night play.

A beauty shop is another example of a service with fixed capacity where demand varies widely by the day of the week, hour of the day, season of the year, and weather conditions. Potential sales, once lost, may not be made up in many cases.

Service Systems That Cannot Carry Inventories

One of the features of manufacturing that allows adjustments for fluctuations to be made more easily is the ability to carry inventory for extended periods of time. Although many "embedded" service outputs such as video tapes, books, maps, and blood for transfusions can be carried in inventory, most services are intangible and are consumed during production. In the case of intangible outputs of services, capacity must be very closely matched to demand. Delays in supplying the service may lead to lost sales or ill-will.

Sharing Capacity

A recent innovation in the service industries is *sharing capacity*. This has long been done by the electric utility industry with plants connected in major interstate grids in the United States. As another example, Service Corporation International of Houston, owner of a chain of 316 funeral homes and 80 cemeteries, has been clustering funeral homes in specific cities so that they can share personnel and automobiles. Their competitors have since developed similar but informal arrangements to do the same.[1] Obviously, realistic forecasting by each funeral home is essential to plan the correct total capacity for the group.

THE DEMAND FORECAST AS THE BASIS FOR OPERATIONS PLANNING

The *demand forecast* is the starting point for all planning. If the product or service is new for the company, the company must estimate whether it should produce such a product or service. It is not necessary to design the product or service for the preliminary demand forecast. The company needs to determine initially if there is a latent demand for a new product or service or what share of an established industry it can reasonably obtain. Therefore, only the product or service concept is needed for this forecast. Once the product or service has been designed in detail, the demand forecast may be revised based on design superiorities or differences from competitors' offerings.

The demand forecast provides estimates of the number of units of services that could be sold by the company, as bounded by the demand for the services and the potential capacity of the company. The number of units that are forecasted to be sold must be based on an approximate price. Therefore, the *total annual revenue* results from the demand forecast. The forecast of revenue is important for making the decision as to whether the service should be marketed. It permits

— An annual budget
— A breakdown analysis

The preliminary annual budget is primarily based on volume of production and marketing plans. Exhibit 3–1 shows income and expense items as components of profit plans for (a) a manufacturing company and (b) a service firm—an airline.

WHAT TYPES OF SERVICE OUTPUTS ARE FORECAST?

In manufactured products, the forecast is clearly in terms of units of product. In the manufacture of intermediate goods, the demand forecast may be in tons (steel), pounds (chemicals), square feet (textiles, wallboard), or other similar physical units, as well as product units (motors, gears, etc.). All these products are clearly defined "countables."

But what of services? The hospital may count emergency operations of accident victims, but these may vary considerably in nature and length of time. The consulting firm may wish to forecast demand for services, but projects may vary in time and complexity. Although the service manager may forecast the number of customers fairly

[1] Jo Ellen Davis, "Bob Waltrip Is Making Big Noises in a Quiet Industry," *Business Week,* (August 25, 1986).

——— EXHIBIT 3–1 ———————————————————————

■ *The Sales Forecast as the Basis for Operations Planning*

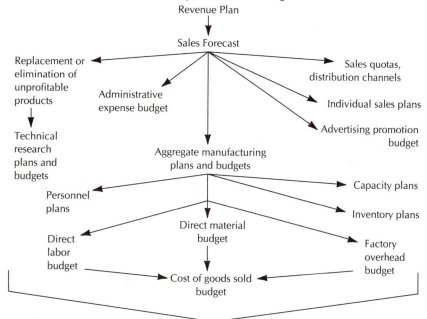

Revenue Plan

Sales Forecast

Replacement or elimination of unprofitable products

Sales quotas, distribution channels

Administrative expense budget

Individual sales plans

Advertising promotion budget

Technical research plans and budgets

Aggregate manufacturing plans and budgets

Personnel plans

Capacity plans

Inventory plans

Direct material budget

Direct labor budget

Factory overhead budget

Cost of goods sold budget

Profit Plan

(a) MANUFACTURING FIRM

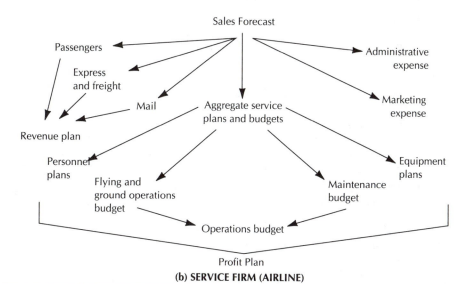

Sales Forecast

Passengers

Administrative expense

Express and freight

Mail

Aggregate service plans and budgets

Marketing expense

Revenue plan

Personnel plans

Equipment plans

Flying and ground operations budget

Maintenance budget

Operations budget

Profit Plan

(b) SERVICE FIRM (AIRLINE)

accurately, the mix of services and the nature of services may vary tremendously. The units of services forecasted therefore are

— Number of customers
— Number of hours of service supplied
— Variety of services supplied and number of each (meals, surgical operations, tailoring, real estate transactions, bank services, financial projects, repair jobs, etc.)
— Units of product supplied (gallons of gasoline, number of dial-a-song calls, number of newspapers sold)

One interesting difference between manufacturing and services forecasting is that net demand in manufacturing involves sales minus returns of goods. In most services (except retail and wholesale sales), the service has disappeared or been used up, so that the only "two-way" transaction is when a customer refuses to pay for unsatisfactory services.

FACTORS THAT AFFECT THE CHOICE OF FORECASTING METHOD

The choice of forecasting method, like most operating decisions, is an economic one. Therefore, each method should be reviewed from a cost-benefit perspective. The factors that should be taken into consideration in forecasting are

1. Time
   a. Span of the forecast
   b. Urgency with which the forecast is needed
   c. Frequency that updates must be made

2. Resource requirements
   a. Mathematical sophistication available to the company
   b. Computer resources
   c. Financial resources

3. Input characteristics
   a. Antecedent data availability
   b. Variability or fluctuation range and frequency
   c. External stability

4. Output characteristics required
   a. Detail or degree of disaggregation
   b. Accuracy

Choosing a Forecasting Method

The output of many services fluctuates widely according to hour of the day, day of the week, week of the month, and month of the year. Other random factors peculiar to demand for services are the weather, special news, items on sale, the economy, some famous personality, the results of a medical study, or changes in interpretations of the law, such as, for example, tax accounting services. Holidays and days before and after holidays also produce surprises many times.

Service forecasting requires, in many cases, forecasts of hour-by-hour and day-to-day activities as well as aggregate forecasts, whereas in manufacturing, weekly, monthly, and aggregate forecasts are more common. This means that in services, very short-range forecasts must be made very frequently.

Basically, all forecasting techniques can be classified under these four groups:

— Judgment
— Counting
— Time series
— Association or causal

Forecasting with **judgment methods,** the manager uses experience, mental estimates of the market, intuition, personal value systems, guesses, and expert opinion to arrive at a forecast.

Counting means just that—counting the number of people who will buy or who *say* they will buy. A *census* is a count of the entire population that is being investigated. A *probability sample* is the counting of a portion of the population in order to estimate some characteristic of the whole population. With such surveys, forecasts may be in error because people change their minds after the survey or did not or could not answer the survey truthfully.

Time series are quantitative models that predict based on the assumption that the future of a data set is a function of the past of that data set. In other words, these models look at what has happened over a period of time and use a series of past data to make a forecast. One weakness of this method is that new factors in the future can throw off the results.

Association or **causal methods,** such as linear regression, are also mathematical models. They incorporate the variables or factors that might influence demand. A causal model for lawn mower sales might include factors such as new housing starts, advertising budget, and competitors' prices.

While many quantitative or mathematical forecasts include some subjectivity, some researchers believe that forecasters should rely more heavily on the output of a quantitative forecast than on their own judgment. Ashton and Ashton have concluded that even simple quantitative techniques outperform the unstructured intuitive assessments of experts in many cases. In addition, using judgment to adjust the values of a quantitatively derived forecast can reduce its accuracy.[2] This is so because judgment methods are susceptible to bias and managers are limited in their ability to process

[2] For survey articles that address this issue, see Essam Mahmoud, ''Accuracy in Forecasting: A Survey,'' *Journal of Forecasting,* Vol. 3, No. 2 (April–June 1984), p. 139; Robin M. Hogarth and Spyros Makridakis, ''Forecasting and Planning: An Evaluation,'' *Management Science,* Vol. 27, No. 2 (February 1981), p. 115; and A. H. Ashton and R. H. Ashton, ''Aggregating Subjective Forecasts,'' *Management Science,* Vol. 31, No. 12 (December 1985), pp. 1499–1508.

EXHIBIT 3–2

■ *Brief Descriptions of Methods*

Judgment Methods		Counting Methods
Naive extrapolation: the application of a simple assumption about the economic outcome of the next time period, or a simple, if subjective, extension of the results of current events. **Sales-force composite:** a compilation of estimates by salespeople (or dealers) of expected sales in their territories, adjusted for presumed biases and expected changes.	**Jury of executive opinion:** the consensus of a group of "experts," often from a variety of functional areas within a company. **Delphi technique:** a successive series of estimates independently developed by a group of "experts," each of whom, at each step in the process, uses a summary of the group's previous results to make new estimates.	**Market testing:** representative buyers' responses to new offerings, tested and extrapolated to estimate the products' future prospects. **Consumer market survey:** attitudinal and purchase intentions data gathered from representative buyers. **Industrial market survey:** data similar to consumer surveys but fewer, more knowledgeable subjects sampled, resulting in more informed evaluations.

Time Series Methods		Association or Causal Methods
Moving averages: recent values of the forecast variables averaged to predict future outcomes. **Exponential smoothing:** an estimate for the coming period based on a constantly weighted combination of the forecast estimate for the previous period and the most recent outcome. **Time series extrapolation:** a prediction of outcomes derived from the future extension of a least squares function fitted to a data series that uses time as an independent variable.	**Time series decomposition:** a prediction of expected outcomes from trend, seasonal, cyclical, and random components, which are isolated from a data series. **Box-Jenkins:** a complex, computer-based iterative procedure that produces an autoregressive, integrated moving average model, adjusts for seasonal and trend factors, estimates appropriate weighting parameters, tests the model, and repeats the cycle as appropriate.	**Correlation methods:** predictions of values based on historic patterns of covariation between variables. **Regression models:** estimates produced from a predictive equation derived by minimizing the residual variance of one or more predictor (independent) variables. **Econometric models:** outcomes forecast from an integrated system of simultaneous equations that represent relationships among elements of the national economy derived from combining history and economic theory.

Source: Reprinted by permission of *Harvard Business Review.* An exhibit from "Manager's Guide to Forecasting" by David M. Georgoff and Robert G. Murdick, Vol. 64, No. 1 (January–February 1986), pp. 110–120. Copyright © 1986 by the President and Fellows of Harvard College; all rights reserved.

information and also to maintain consistent relationships among variables.[3] Reading 3.2, which describes a forecasting model for the performing arts, touches on these concerns further.

Exhibit 3–2 provides a brief listing of the well-known forecasting methods that fall into the four categories noted above. The judgment methods listed are naive extrapolation, sales-force composite, jury of executive opinion, and delphi technique. Counting methods are market testing, consumer market survey, and industrial market survey. The time series methods are moving averages, exponential smoothing, time series extrapolations, time series decomposition, and Box-Jenkins. The association techniques include correlation analysis, regression, and econometric models. Shortly in this chapter a few of the more common time series and association models and techniques such as moving averages, exponential smoothing, extrapolation, and regression will be explored further.

Forecaster's Chart

While each forecasting technique has strengths and weaknesses, every forecasting situation is limited by such constraints as time, funds, competencies, or data. Balancing the advantages and disadvantages of techniques with regard to a situation's limitations and requirements is an important, but tough managerial task.

Georgoff and Murdick developed a chart, published in the *Harvard Business Review*, to help executives decide which technique is appropriate to a particular situation. The part of that chart that groups and profiles the 15 forecasting methods mentioned above is shown as Exhibit 3–3. It arrays the methods against the 11 important evaluative dimensions noted earlier in this chapter. The techniques are listed in columns, and dimensions of evaluation are in the rows.

TIME SERIES FORECASTING MODELS

A **time series** is based on a sequence of evenly spaced (hourly, daily, weekly, monthly, and so on) data points. Examples include weekly sales of IBM PS/2s, quarterly revenue passenger miles on TWA, monthly admissions to General Hospital, and daily ridership on the Washington, D.C. subway. Forecasting time series data implies that future values are predicted *only* from past values and that other variables are incorporated into the past behavior of the time series.

Decomposition of a Time Series

Analyzing time series means breaking down past data into components and then projecting them forward. A time series typically has four components: trend, seasonality, cycles, and random variation.

---

[3] Lennard Sjoberg, "Aided and Unaided Decision Making Improved Intuitive Judgment," *Journal of Forecasting*, Vol. 1, No. 4 (October–December 1982), p. 349.

_____ EXHIBIT 3–3 _____

- *Overview of 15 Forecasting Techniques*

Dimensions/ Questions	JUDGMENT METHODS			
	Naive Extrapolation	Sales Force Composite	Jury of Executive Opinion	Delphi Technique
Time Span: Is the forecast period a present need or a short-, medium-, or long-term projection?	Present need to medium need	Short or medium	Short or medium	Medium or long
Urgency: Is the forecast needed immediately?	Rapid results are a strong advantage of this technique.	Forecast can be assembled, combined, and adjusted relatively quickly.	In-house group forecasts are quicker than outside experts	Urgency seriously compromises quality.
	Dev. short Ex. short	Dev. short Ex. moderate	Dev. short Ex. short to moderate	Dev. moderate Ex. moderate to long
Frequency: Are frequent forecast updates needed?	Can easily accommodate frequent updates.	Forecast can be quickly compiled, but data collection restricts rapidity.	Can accomplish quickly.	Usually used for one-time forecasts, but they can be revised as new information becomes available.
Resource requirements Mathematical sophistication: Are quantitative skills limited?	Minimal quantitative capabilities are required.	⟶	⟶	⟶
Computer: Are computer capabilities limited?	Computer capabilities are not essential.	Nominal processing does not require a computer.	⟶	⟶
Financial: Are only limited financial resources available?	Very inexpensive to implement and maintain.	Inexpensive to implement and maintain.	Financial requirements are nominal for executive groups; they may be higher for outside experts.	Expense depends on makeup and affiliation of participants.
Input Antecedent: Are only limited past data available?	Some past data are required, but extended history is not essential.	Past data are helpful but not always essential.	⟶	⟶
Variability: Does the primary series fluctuate substantially?	Has difficulty adequately handling wide fluctuations.	⟶	Does not handle fluctuations well but can accommodate them if the panel meets frequently.	⟶
External stability: Are significant shifts expected among variable relationships?	Often insensitive to shifts.	⟶	Usually aware of shifts and can reflect them in the forecast.	⟶
Output Detail: Are component forecasts required?	Focus can be readily restricted.	Can often provide useful breakdowns.	Can reflect component forecasts, but is generally concerned with aggregate forecasts.	⟶
Accuracy: Is a high level of accuracy critical?	Often provides a limited practical level of accuracy.	Can be very accurate or subject to substantial bias.	May be most accurate under dynamic conditions.	⟶

COUNTING METHODS		
	Market Survey	
Marketing Testing	Consumer Market Survey	Industrial Market Survey
Medium	Medium	Medium or long

Substantial lag is involved
 	
Dev. moderate
Ex. long to
     extended
Extended, basically used for
  one-time forecasts.
	Method of gathering data
	  may cause a substantial
	  time lag.
	Dev. moderate
	Ex. long to
	     extended
	Depending on methodology,
	  frequent updates are possi-
	  ble, but updates are gener-
	  ally provided at extended
	  intervals.
		⟶

Technical competencies are
  generally needed.
 	
A computer is generally
  needed for data analysis.
Generally very expensive.
	⟶
	
	⟶
	Generally expensive for good
	  controls.
		⟶
		
		⟶
		Moderately expensive, de-
		  pending on controls.

Past data are useful but not
  essential.
Substantial fluctuations limit
  the accuracy of projec-
  tions.
Seriously weak in accommo-
  dating shifts.
	⟶
	Handles fluctuations poorly,
	  but tracking improves per-
	  formance.
	Seldom reflects significant
	  shifts.
		Past data very helpful but not
		  essential.
		Wide fluctuations are fre-
		  quently a significant con-
		  cern.
		If carefully controlled, can
		  handle shifts well.

Handles detail but scope can
  be limited.
Provides highest accuracy in
  new product and limited
  data conditions.
	⟶
	Has limited predictability
	  with durables, somewhat
	  better with nondurables.
		⟶
		Can be most accurate ap-
		  proach in special cases.

(continues)

_____ EXHIBIT 3–3 Continued _____

Dimensions/ Questions	TIME SERIES METHODS				
	Moving Averages	Exponential Smoothing	Time Series Extrapolation	Time Series Decomposition	Box-Jenkins
Time Span: Is the forecast period a present need or short-, medium-, or long-term projection?	Short, medium, or long	Present need to short or medium	Short, medium, or long	Short or medium	Short, medium, or long
Urgency: Is the forecast needed immediately?	Rapid results are a strong advantage of this technique.	⟶	Computation is quick if data are available; data gathering can cause delays.	Program setup and data gathering may cause delays, but once programmed computation is quick.	Operationalizing program can take time, but forecast can be produced quickly.
	Dev. short Ex. short		Dev. short to moderate Ex. short	Dev. moderate Ex. short	Dev. long Ex. moderate
Frequency: Are frequent forecast updates needed?	Forecast can be systematically updated easily.	⟶	⟶	⟶	⟶
Resource requirements Mathematical sophistication: Are quantitative skills limited?	Minimal quantitative capabilities are required.	⟶	⟶	⟶	A high level of understanding is required.
Computer: Are computer capabilities limited?	A computer is helpful for repetitive updating.	⟶	A computer is helpful for repetitive updating.	⟶	A computer is essential.
Financial: Are only limited financial resources available?	If data are readily available, out-of-pocket costs are minimal.	⟶	If data are readily available, out-of-pocket costs are minimal.	Moderately expensive to acquire, develop, and modify.	Acquisition and modification are expensive.
Input Antecedent: Are only limited past data available?	Past history is essential.	Only recent forecasts and current data are required once alpha is determined.	⟶	Past history is essential with some detail required.	Past history is essential with detail required.
Variability: Does the primary series fluctuate substantially?	Can accommodate fluctuations with appropriate averaging period.	Can accommodate fluctuations with suitable alpha.	Wide fluctuations result in decreased confidence in projected outcomes.	Can isolate and determine the level of component effects.	Handles variability effectively.
External stability: Are significant shifts expected among variable relationships?	Cannot validly reflect shifts.	Can only moderately reflect shifts with prior trend.	Cannot validly reflect shifts.	Can only moderately reflect shifts with prior trend.	⟶
Output Detail: Are component forecasts required?	Focus can be readily restricted.	⟶	⟶	⟶	⟶
Accuracy: Is a high level of accuracy critical?	Accurate under stable conditions.	Generally rates high in accuracy for shortterm forecasts.	Normally accurate for trends and stationary series.	Effectively isolates identifiable components.	Frequently the most accurate for short-to-medium-range forecasts.

ASSOCIATION OR CAUSAL METHODS		
Correlation Methods	Regression Models	Econometric Models
Short, medium, or long	Short, medium, or long	Short, medium, or long
Data evaluation may cause delays, but forecast computation is quick. Dev. moderate Ex.　short to 　　moderate ———→	Model formulation takes time, but forecast computation is quick. Dev. moderate 　　to long Ex.　short to 　　moderate ———→	Model building is lengthy, but producing forecast is quick. Dev. long to 　　extended Ex.　short to 　　moderate Forecast can be updated quickly if data are available.
A fundamental competency level is required. A computer is desirable. If data are on hand, development costs are moderate.	———→ A computer is essential for most cases. ———→	A high level of understanding is required. A computer is essential for all cases. Development costs are substantial; operating costs are moderate.
———→ Technique is good if covariation is high; otherwise it is poor. Predictive accuracy is weakened if shifts occur.	———→ May handle large fluctuations well with appropriate independent variables. ———→	———→ ———→ ———→
———→ Predictive accuracy can vary widely.	A restricted focus might substantially compromise technique's predictive accuracy. Can be accurate if variable relationships are stable and the proportion of explained variance is high.	Generally confined to aggregate forecasts. Give spotty performances in dynamic environments.

——— EXHIBIT 3–4 ———

■ *Demand for Services Charted over 4 Years with Trend and Seasonality Indicated*

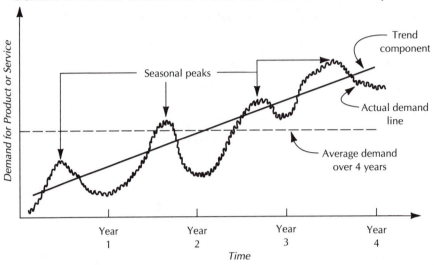

1. **Trend** is the gradual upward or downward movement of the data over time. (See Exhibit 3.4.)
2. **Seasonality** is a pattern of demand fluctuation above or below the trend line that occurs every year.
3. **Cycles** are patterns in the data that occur every several years; they are usually tied into the business cycle.
4. **Random variations** are "blips" in the data caused by chance and unusual situations; they follow no discernible pattern.

In *most* models, forecasters assume that the random variations are averaged out over time. They then concentrate on only the seasonal component and a component that is a combination of trend and cyclical factors.

Moving Averages

Moving averages are useful if we can assume that demand for services will stay fairly steady over time. A 4-month moving average is found by simply summing the demand during the past 4 months and dividing by 4. With each passing month, the most recent month's data are added to the sum of the previous 3 months' data, and the earliest month is dropped. This tends to smooth out short-term irregularities in the data series.

Mathematically, the simple moving average (which serves as an estimate of the next period's demand) is expressed as

$$\text{Moving average} = \frac{\Sigma \text{ demand in previous } n \text{ periods}}{n} \tag{3.1}$$

where n is the number of periods in the moving average—for example, 4, 5, or 6 months, respectively, for a four-, five-, or six-period moving average.

For example, customer demand at We-Haul Movers, Inc., is shown in the following table. A 3-month moving-average forecast appears on the right.

Month	Actual Number of Customers Moved	3-Month Moving Average Forecast
Jan	10	
Feb	12	
Mar	13	
Apr	16	$(10 + 12 + 13)/3 = 11\frac{2}{3}$
May	19	$(12 + 13 + 16)/3 = 13\frac{2}{3}$
Jun	23	$(13 + 16 + 19)/3 = 16$
Jul	26	$(16 + 19 + 23)/3 = 19\frac{1}{3}$

Weighted Moving Averages

When there is a trend or pattern, weights can be used to place more emphasis on recent values. This makes the techniques more responsive to changes, since more recent periods may be more heavily weighted. Deciding which weights to use requires some experience and a bit of luck. Choice of weights is somewhat arbitrary, since there is no set formula to determine them. If the latest month or period is weighted too heavily, the forecast might reflect a large unusual change in the demand or sales pattern too quickly. A weighted moving average may be expressed mathematically as

$$\frac{\text{Weighted moving}}{\text{average}} = \frac{\Sigma \text{ (weight for period } n)(\text{demand for period } n)}{\Sigma \text{ weights}} \tag{3.2}$$

For example, using the demand shown above, We-Haul Movers, Inc., decides to forecast demand for services by weighting the past 3 months as follows.

Weights Applied	Period
3	Last month
2	2 months ago
1	3 months ago

The results of this weighted average forecast are shown in the following table.

Month	Actual Number of Customers Moved	3-Month Weighted Moving Average
Jan	10	
Feb	12	
Mar	13	
Apr	16	$[(3 \times 13) + (2 \times 12) + (10)]/6 = 12\frac{1}{6}$
May	19	$[(3 \times 16) + (2 \times 13) + (12)]/6 = 14\frac{1}{3}$
Jun	23	$[(3 \times 19) + (2 \times 16) + (13)]/6 = 17$
Jul	26	$[(3 \times 23) + (2 \times 19) + (16)]/6 = 20\frac{1}{2}$

In this particular forecasting situation, you can see that weighting the latest month more heavily provides a slightly more accurate projection.

EXHIBIT 3–5

■ *Actual Demand vs. Moving Average and Weighted Moving Average Methods for We-Haul Moving, Inc.*

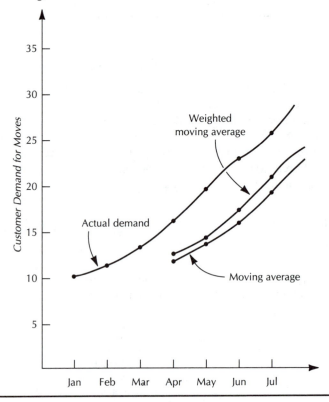

Source: From Jay Heizer and Barry Render, *Production and Operations Management*, p. 130. Copyright © 1988 by Allyn and Bacon. Reprinted with permission.

Both simple and weighted moving averages are effective in smoothing out sudden fluctuations in the demand pattern in order to provide stable estimates. Moving averages are not without problems, however. Increasing the size of *n* (the number of periods averaged) does smooth out fluctuations better, but it makes the method less sensitive to *real* changes in the data. In addition, simple moving averages cannot pick up trends very well. Since they are averages, they will always stay within past levels and will not predict a change to either a higher or lower level.

Exhibit 3–5, a plot of the data in the preceding examples, illustrates the lag effect of the moving average models.

Exponential Smoothing

Exponential smoothing is a moving-average forecasting method that is easy to use and efficiently handled by computers. The basic exponential smoothing formula can be shown as follows:

New forecast = last period's forecast $\qquad\qquad$ (3.3)
$\qquad\qquad$ + α (last period's actual demand − last period's forecast)

where α is a weight, or **smoothing constant,** that has a value between 0 and 1, inclusive. Equation 3.3 also can be written mathematically as

$$F_t = F_{t-1} + \alpha(A_{t-1} - F_{t-1}) \qquad\qquad (3.4)$$

where F_t = the new forecast

$\qquad F_{t-1}$ = the previous forecast

$\qquad \alpha$ = smoothing constant $(0 \le \alpha \le 1)$

$\qquad A_{t-1}$ = previous period's actual demand

The concept is not complex. The latest estimate of demand is equal to the old forecast adjusted by some percentage of forecast error. This error is the difference between the last period's actual demand and the old estimate.

Here is an example. In January, a car dealer predicted a February demand for 142 Ford Tauruses. Actual February demand was 153 autos. Using a smoothing constant of α = 0.20, we can forecast the March demand using the exponential smoothing model. Substituting into the formula, we obtain

New forecast (for March demand) = 142 + 0.2(153 − 142) = 144.2

Thus the demand forecast for Ford Tauruses in March is rounded to 144.

The smoothing constant α can be changed to give more weight to recent data (when it is high) or more weight to past data (when it is low). The closer α is to 0, the closer the forecast will fall to last period's forecast of this period. This contrasts to a regular moving average, in which all data are given equal weight in computing the next period's forecast.

Selecting the Smoothing Constant. The exponential smoothing approach is easy to use, and it has been successfully applied by numerous services industries. The appropriate value of the smoothing constant α, however, can make the difference between an accurate forecast and an inaccurate forecast. In picking a value for the smoothing constant, the objective is to obtain the most accurate forecast. The overall accuracy of a forecasting model can be determined by comparing the forecasted values with the actual or observed values.

The **forecast error** is defined as

$$\text{Forecast error} = \text{demand} - \text{forecast} \qquad (3.5)$$

One measure of the overall forecast error for the model is the **mean absolute deviation (MAD).** This is computed by taking the sum of the absolute values of the individual forecast errors and dividing by the number of periods of data (n).

$$\text{MAD} = \frac{\Sigma |\text{forecast errors}|}{n} \qquad (3.6)$$

Let us now apply this concept with a trial-and-error testing of two values of α.

The Port of Baltimore has unloaded large quantities of a grain from ships during the past eight quarters. The port's operations manager wants to test the use of exponential smoothing to see how well the technique works in predicting tonnage unloaded. He assumes that the forecast of grain unloaded in the first quarter was 175 tons. Two values of α are examined, $\alpha = 0.10$ and $\alpha = 0.50$. Exhibit 3–6 shows actual tonnage, forecasts for both $\alpha = 0.10$ and $\alpha = 0.50$ (each rounded to the nearest ton), and absolute deviations for both forecasts.

Based on this analysis, a smoothing constant of $\alpha = 0.10$ is preferred to $\alpha = 0.50$ because its MAD is smaller. As a matter of fact, values for α typically lie in the range of 0.10 to 0.30. A simple computer program can help evaluate potential smoothing constants and find the best value of α.

EXHIBIT 3–6

■ *Exponential Smoothing MAD Calculations for the Port of Baltimore*

Quarter	Actual Tonnage Unloaded	Rounded Forecast with $\alpha = 0.10$	Absolute Deviations for $\alpha = 0.10$	Rounded Forecast with $\alpha = 0.50$	Absolute Deviation for $\alpha = 0.50$
1	180	175	5	175	5
2	168	176	8	178	10
3	159	175	16	173	14
4	175	173	2	166	9
5	190	173	17	170	20
6	205	175	30	180	25
7	180	178	2	193	13
8	182	178	4	186	4
		Sum of absolute deviations	84		100

$$\text{MAD} = \frac{\Sigma |\text{deviations}|}{n} = 10.05 \qquad\qquad \text{MAD} = 12.50$$

Source: From Jay Heizer and Barry Render, *Production and Operations Management,* p. 133. Copyright © 1988 by Allyn and Bacon. Reprinted with permission.

Besides the mean absolute deviations (MAD), there are three other measures of the accuracy of historical errors in forecasting that are sometimes used. The first, **mean squared error (MSE),** is the average of the squared differences between the forecasted and the observed values. The second, **mean absolute percent error (MAPE),** is the average of the absolute difference between the forecasted and observed values expressed as a percentage of the observed values. The third, the **bias,** tells whether the forecast is too high or too low, and by how much. In effect, bias provides the average total error and its direction.

Exponential Smoothing with Trend Adjustment. As with any moving-average technique, simple exponential smoothing fails to respond to trends. To illustrate a more complex exponential smoothing model, let us consider one that adjusts for trend. The idea is to compute a simple exponential smoothing forecast as above and then adjust for positive or negative lag in trend. The formula is

Forecast including trend (FIT_t) = new forecast (F_t) + trend correction (T_t)

To smooth out the trend, the equation for the trend correction uses a smoothing constant β in the same way the simple exponential model uses α. T_t is computed by

$$T_t = T_{t-1} + \beta(F_t - F_{t-1}) \tag{3.7}$$

where T_t = smoothed trend for period t

T_{t-1} = smoothed trend for previous period

β = trend smoothing constant that we select

F_t = simple exponential smoothed forecast for period t

F_{t-1} = forecast for previous period

There are three steps to compute a trend-adjusted forecast.

1. Compute a simple exponential forecast for time period t (F_t).
2. Compute the trend by using the equation

$$T_t = T_{t-1} + \beta(F_t - F_{t-1})$$

To start step 2 for the first time, an *initial* trend value must be inserted (either by a good guess or by observed past data). After that, trend is computed.
3. Calculate the trend-adjusted exponential smoothing forecast (FIT_t) by this formula:

$$FIT_t = F_t + T_t$$

As an example, we consider a computer disaster recovery firm in Chicago that uses exponential smoothing to forecast demand for its services. It appears that a trend is present.

Month	Demand	Month	Demand
1	12	6	26
2	17	7	31
3	20	8	32
4	19	9	36
5	24		

Smoothing constants are assigned the values of $\alpha = 0.2$ and $\beta = 0.4$. Assume the initial forecast for month 1 was 11 service calls.

1. Forecast for month 2 = forecast for month 1 + α (actual demand for month 1 − forecast for month 1).

   $F_2 = 11 + 0.2(12 - 11) = 11.0 + 0.2 = 11.2$ service calls

2. Compute the trend present. Assume an initial trend adjustment of zero, that is, $T_1 = 0$.

   $$T_2 = T_1 + \beta(F_2 - F_1)$$
   $$= 0 + 0.4(11.2 - 11.0)$$
   $$= 0.08$$

3. Compute the forecast including trend (FIT).

   $$\text{FIT}_2 = F_2 + T_2$$
   $$= 11.2 + 0.08$$
   $$= 11.28 \text{ service calls}$$

We will do the same calculations for the third month also.

1. $F_3 = F_2 + \alpha$ (demand in month 2 $-F_2$)
   $= 11.2 + 0.2(17 - 11.2) = 12.36$
2. $T_3 = T_2 + \beta(F_3 - F_2) = 0.08 + 0.4(12.36 - 11.2) = 0.54$
3. $\text{FIT}_3 = F_3 + T_3 = 12.36 + 0.54 = 12.90$

So the simple exponential forecast (without trend) for month 2 was 11.2 calls, and the trend-adjusted forecast was 11.28 calls. In month 3, the simple forecast (without trend) was 12.36 calls, and the trend-adjusted forecast was 12.90 calls. Naturally, different values of T_1 and β can produce even better estimates.

Exhibit 3–7 completes the forecasts for the 9-month period and compares actual demand, forecast without trend (F_t), and forecast with trend (FIT_t).

The value of the trend smoothing constant β resembles the α constant in that a high β is more responsive to recent changes in trend. A low β gives less weight to the most recent trends and tends to smooth out the trend present. Values of β can be found by the trial-and-error approach, with MAD used as a measure of comparison.

Simple exponential smoothing is often referred to as **first-order smoothing,** and trend-adjusted smoothing is called **second-order,** or **double, smoothing.** Other

——— EXHIBIT 3–7 ———————————————————————————————————————

■ *Comparison of Exponential Smoothing Forecast With and Without Trend for Disaster Recovery Service Calls*

Month	Actual Demand	Forecast, F_t (Without Trend)	Trend	Adjusted FIT$_t$
1	12	11.00	0	—
2	17	11.20	.08	11.28
3	20	12.36	.54	12.90
4	19	13.89	1.15	15.04
5	24	14.91	1.56	16.47
6	26	16.73	2.29	19.02
7	31	18.58	3.03	21.61
8	32	21.07	4.03	25.09
9	36	23.25	4.90	28.15

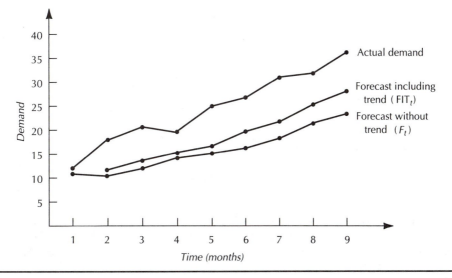

Source: From Jay Heizer and Barry Render, *Production and Operations Management,* p. 135. Copyright © 1988 by Allyn and Bacon. Reprinted with permission.

advanced exponential smoothing models are also in use, including seasonal-adjusted and triple smoothing, but these are beyond the scope of this book.[4]

Time Series Extrapolation and Seasonal Adjustments

Time series extrapolation is a technique that fits a trend line to a series of historical data points and then projects the line into the future for medium- to long-range forecasts. In this section we will look at *linear* (straight-line) trends only.

[4] For more details, see E. S. Gardner, ''Exponential Smoothing: The State of the Art,'' *Journal of Forecasting,* Vol. 4, No. 1 (March 1985); or R. Brown, *Smoothing, Forecasting, and Prediction* (Englewood Cliffs, N.J.: Prentice-Hall, 1973).

If we decide to develop a linear trend line by a precise statistical method, we can apply the **least-squares method.** This approach, described in detail in every introductory statistics textbook, results in a straight line that minimizes the sum of the squares of the vertical differences from the line to each of the actual observations. We can express the line with the following equation.

$$\hat{y} = a + bx \tag{3.8}$$

where $\hat{y}$ = computed value of the demand for services to be predicted (called the **dependent variable**)

a = y-axis intercept

b = slope of the regression line (or the rate of change in y for given changes in x)

x = the independent variable (which is *time* in this case)

The slope b is found by

$$b = \frac{\Sigma xy - n\bar{x}\bar{y}}{\Sigma x^2 - n\bar{x}^2} \tag{3.9}$$

The y intercept, a, is computed as follows.

$$a = \bar{y} - b\bar{x} \tag{3.10}$$

The following example shows how to apply these concepts. Shown below are data on the demand for copies of the software program Lotus 1-2-3 from a Midwestern software retailer over the period 1982–1988. Let us fit a straight-line trend to these data and forecast 1989 demand.

Year	Copies of Lotus 1-2-3 Sold
1982	74
1983	79
1984	80
1985	90
1986	105
1987	142
1988	122

With a series of data over time, we can minimize the computations by transforming the values of x (time) to simpler numbers. Thus, in this case, we can designate 1982 as year 1, 1983 as year 2, and so on.

Year	Time Period	Lotus 1-2-3 Demand	x^2	xy
1982	1	74	1	74
1983	2	79	4	158
1984	3	80	9	240
1985	4	90	16	360
1986	5	105	25	525
1987	6	142	36	852
1988	7	122	49	854
	$\Sigma x = 28$	$\Sigma y = 692$	$\Sigma x^2 = 140$	$\Sigma xy = 3{,}063$

$$\bar{x} = \frac{\Sigma x}{n} = \frac{28}{7} = 4 \qquad \bar{y} = \frac{\Sigma y}{n} = \frac{692}{7} = 98.86$$

$$b = \frac{\Sigma xy - n\bar{x}\bar{y}}{\Sigma x^2 - n\bar{x}^2} = \frac{3{,}063 - (7)(4)(98.86)}{140 - (7)(4^2)} = \frac{295}{28} = 10.54$$

$$a = \bar{y} - b\bar{x} = 98.86 - 10.54(4) = 56.70$$

Hence, the least-squares trend equation is $\hat{y} = 56.70 + 10.54\,x$. To project demand in 1989, we first denote the year 1989 in our new coding system as $x = 8$:

$$\text{Sales (in 1989)} = 56.70 + 10.54(8)$$
$$= 141.02, \text{ or } 141 \text{ copies of the program}$$

We can estimate demand for 1990 by inserting $x = 9$ in the same equation:

$$\text{Sales (in 1990)} = 56.70 + 10.54(9)$$
$$= 151.56, \text{ or } 152 \text{ copies of the program}$$

To check the validity of the model, we plot historical demand and the trend line in Exhibit 3–8. In this case, we may wish to be cautious and try to understand the 1987–1988 swings in demand.

Time series forecasting such as that in the preceding example involves looking at the *trend* of data over a series of time observations. Sometimes, however, recurring variations at certain seasons of the year make a *seasonal* adjustment in the trend-line forecast necessary. Demand for coal and fuel oil, for example, usually peaks during cold winter months. Demand for golf clubs or suntan lotion may be highest in summer. Analyzing data in monthly or quarterly terms usually makes it easy to spot seasonal patterns. Seasonal indices can then be developed by several common methods. The next example illustrates one way to compute seasonal factors from historical data.

Monthly sales of one brand of telephone answering machine at Plane Supplies are shown in Exhibit 3–9 for 1988–1989. Using these seasonal indices, if we expected

—— EXHIBIT 3–8 ——————————————————————————————————

■ *Demand for Lotus 1-2-3 and the Computed Trend Line*

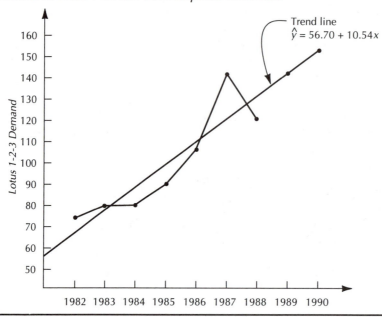

Source: From Jay Heizer and Barry Render, *Production and Operations Management,* p. 138. Copyright © 1988 by Allyn and Bacon. Reprinted with permission.

—— EXHIBIT 3–9 ——————————————————————————————————

■ *Monthly Sales of Answering Machines for a Two-Year Period*

	Sales Demand		Average 1988–1989 Demand	Average Monthly Demand*	Seasonal Index[†]
Month	1988	1989			
Jan	80	100	90	94	0.957
Feb	75	85	80	94	0.851
Mar	80	90	85	94	0.904
Apr	90	110	100	94	1.064
May	115	131	123	94	1.309
Jun	110	120	115	94	1.223
Jul	100	110	105	94	1.117
Aug	90	110	100	94	1.064
Sep	85	95	90	94	0.957
Oct	75	85	80	94	0.851
Nov	75	85	80	94	0.851
Dec	80	80	80	94	0.851
		Total average demand =	1,128		

* Average monthly demand $= \dfrac{1,128}{12 \text{ months}} = 94$

[†] Seasonal index $= \dfrac{\text{Average 1988–89 demand}}{\text{Average monthly demand}}$

the 1990 annual demand for answering machines to be 1200 units, we would forecast the monthly demand as follows:

Jan	$\dfrac{1,200}{12} \times 0.957 = 96$		Jul	$\dfrac{1,200}{12} \times 1.117 = 112$
Feb	$\dfrac{1,200}{12} \times 0.851 = 85$		Aug	$\dfrac{1,200}{12} \times 1.064 = 106$
Mar	$\dfrac{1,200}{12} \times 0.904 = 90$		Sep	$\dfrac{1,200}{12} \times 0.957 = 96$
Apr	$\dfrac{1,200}{12} \times 1.064 = 106$		Oct	$\dfrac{1,200}{12} \times 0.851 = 85$
May	$\dfrac{1,200}{12} \times 1.309 = 131$		Nov	$\dfrac{1,200}{12} \times 0.851 = 85$
Jun	$\dfrac{1,200}{12} \times 1.223 = 122$		Dec	$\dfrac{1,200}{12} \times 0.851 = 85$

For simplicity, trend calculations were ignored in the preceding example. The following example illustrates how indices that have already been prepared can be applied to adjust trend line forecasts.

Hospital Forecasting Example.   As another example of an estimated trend line and seasonality adjustments, we borrow data from a San Diego hospital that used 66 months of adult inpatient hospital days to reach the following equation:[5]

$$\hat{y} = 8091 + 21.5x$$

where $\hat{y}$ = patient days

x = time, in months

Based on this model, the hospital forecasts patient days for the next month (period 67) to be

Patient days = $8091 + 21.5(67) = 9530$ (trend only)

As well as this model recognized the slight upward trend line in the demand for inpatient services, it ignored the seasonality that the administration knew to be present. Exhibit 3–10 provides actual seasonal indices based on the same 66 months. Such seasonal data, by the way, were found to be typical of hospitals nationwide. Note that January, March, July, and August seem to exhibit significantly higher patient days on average, while February, September, November, and December reveal lower patient days.

---

[5] The source of the data for this hospital example is, W. E. Sterk and E. G. Shryock, "Modern Methods Improve Hospital Forecasting," *Healthcare Financial Management*, Vol. 41, No. 3 (March 1987), pp. 96–98.

—— EXHIBIT 3–10 ——————————————

■ *Actual Seasonality Indices for Adult Inpatient Days at San Diego Hospital*

Month	Seasonality Index
Jan	1.0436
Feb	0.9669
Mar	1.0203
Apr	1.0087
May	0.9935
Jun	0.9906
Jul	1.0302
Aug	1.0405
Sep	0.9653
Oct	1.0048
Nov	0.9598
Dec	0.9805

Source: W. E. Sterk and E. G. Shryock, "Modern Methods Improve Hospital Forecasting." Reprinted with permission from the March 1987 issue of *Healthcare Financial Management,* p. 97. Copyright 1987 Healthcare Financial Management Association.

To correct the time series extrapolation for seasonality, the hospital multiplied the monthly forecast by the appropriate seasonality index. Thus, for period 67, which was a January,

$$\text{Patient days} = (9530)(1.0436) = 9946 \text{ (trend and seasonal)}$$

Using this method, patient days were forecasted for January through June (periods 67 through 72) as 9946, 9236, 9768, 9678, 9554, and 9547. This study led to better patient-day forecasts, as well as more accurate forecast budgets.

CAUSAL FORECASTING: REGRESSION ANALYSIS

Causal forecasting models usually consider several variables that are related to the variable being predicted. Once these related variables have been found, a statistical model is built and used to forecast the variable of interest.

Many factors can be considered in a causal analysis. For example, the sales of a product might be related to the firm's advertising budget, the price charged, competitors' prices and promotional strategies, or even the economy and unemployment rates. In this case, sales would be called the **dependent variable** and the other variables would be called **independent variables.** The manager's job is to develop the best statistical relationship between sales and the set of independent variables. The most common quantitative causal forecasting model is **linear regression analysis.**

We can use the same mathematical model we employed in the least-squares method of time series extrapolation to perform a simple linear regression analysis. The dependent variable that we want to forecast will still be $\hat{y}$. But now the independent variable x need no longer be time.[6]

$$\hat{y} = a + bx$$

where $\hat{y}$ = value of the dependent variable, sales in this case

a = y-axis intercept

b = slope of the regression line

x = the independent variable

To illustrate, we consider the case of the Schatz Construction Company, which renovates old homes in Winter Park, Florida. Over time, the company has found that its dollar volume of renovation work is dependent on the Winter Park area payroll. The following table lists Schatz's revenues and the amount of money earned by wage earners in Winter Park during the past 6 years.

Schatz's Sales ($000,000)	Local Payroll ($000,000)
y	x
2.0	1
3.0	3
2.5	4
2.0	2
2.0	1
3.5	7

Using the least-squares regression approach, we find that

$$\hat{y} = 1.75 + 0.25x$$

or   Sales = 1.75 + 0.25 payroll

If the local chamber of commerce predicts that the Winter Park area payroll will be $6 hundred million next year, we can estimate sales for Schatz with the regression equation.

Sales (in $000,000) = 1.75 + 0.25(6) = 1.75 + 1.50 = 3.25

or   Sales = $325,000

---

[6] If there were more than one independent variable introduced, the general form of this *multiple* regression would be

$$\hat{y} = a + b_1x_1 + b_2x_2 + b_3x_3 + \cdots + b_nx_n$$

where the b_i values represent slope coefficients for the respective x-independent variables.

The final part of this example illustrates a central weakness of causal forecasting methods such as regression. Even when we have computed a regression equation, it is necessary to provide a forecast of the independent variable *x*—in this case payroll—before estimating the dependent variable *y* for the next time period. Although not a problem for all forecasts, you can imagine the difficulty in determining future values of *some* common independent variables (such as unemployment rates, gross national product, price indices, and so on).

THE COMPUTER'S ROLE IN FORECASTING

Forecast calculations are seldom performed by hand in this day of computers. Many university and commercial packaged programs are readily available to handle time-series and causal projections.

Several mainframe-oriented packages, such as General Electric's *Time Series Forecasting* (called FCST1 and FCST2), are oriented toward organizations that need to perform large-scale regression and exponential smoothing projections. A large number of corporations also use forecasting programs that incorporate inventory-control routines. Examples are IBM's IMPACT (Inventory Management Program and Control Technique) and COGS (Consumer Goods Program).

Almost every university maintains a library of statistical programs that permit not only forecasts but a wide variety of other statistical analysis methods (such as hypothesis testing, chi-square testing, factor analysis, and so on) as well. Popular packages are SAS, SPSS, BMD, SYSTAT, and Minitab. Some of these, and a wide selection of others, are available for microcomputer use. The microcomputer software package that is available to adopters of this text includes the ability to conduct the following: moving averages, exponential smoothing, trend analysis, and simple linear regression.

GENERAL APPROACHES TO FORECASTING

There are three general approaches to forecasting demand for services that employ various methods just discussed.

Fundamental System-to-Subsystem Approach

The fundamental method of demand forecasting may employ combinations of techniques described in this chapter. It consists of forecasting the economy, then forecasting industry sales (which are dependent on the economy), and finally forecasting company sales (which are dependent on industry sales).

Economic forecast $\longrightarrow$ Industry demand $\longrightarrow$ Company demand
forecast forecast

For example, if the industry demand forecast for next year is $1,222,000 and the company's market share is estimated at 2 percent, the demand forecast is $24,000.

Most companies cannot afford a staff of economists, so their marketing departments either buy economic and industry forecasts when needed or use forecasts of the economy and industry found in *Business Week, The Wall Street Journal, Forbes,* government publications, or forecasting service publications.

Industry demand forecasts may be made by using the past year's demand and adjusting this figure up or down according to predictions about the economy for next year. Industry demand forecasts may be found in *U.S. Industrial Outlook,* published annually by the U.S. Department of Commerce, or in trade publications. In addition, most industries have a trade association (see *Encyclopedia of Associations,* published by Gale Research Co.) that may forecast industry demand. Individual studies of industries are prepared by Predicasts, Inc., in Cleveland, Ohio.

For a new firm, a demand forecast is determined by estimating the market share the company will obtain in its first year of business. This depends on considerations of the value-in-use of the product or service, the degree of differentiation of its product or service, the competitive edge of the new firm, and the marketing program of the new firm. Usually, the initial share of an established market will be very small, and a conservative estimate should be made.

Aggregate-to-Component Forecasts

A restaurant manager may forecast total customers and then estimate the number of dinners, luncheons, and breakfasts. An auto repair shop may estimate the total number of jobs per year and then forecast the number of each type of job. A painting firm may estimate the aggregate of jobs for next month and then forecast the number of residential and the number of commercial jobs. If the total or aggregate number of services can be forecasted, the forecast provides a general bound for the sum of the components and makes component forecasting easier.

Disaggregation into components may be on the following bases:

1. Service disaggregation
   a. Services by classes or types
   b. Services by time of day or week they are supplied
2. Market disaggregation
   a. Geographic disaggregation
   b. Industry, government, and consumer sectors
   c. Industry sectors within the total market
3. Performer disaggregation—a forecast for each person or shop that performs the services

Component-to-Aggregate Forecasts

When an aggregate forecast is desired, it may be more accurate if a forecast of each component of the aggregate is made and then these forecasts added. The preceding section has given the components that make up aggregates.

SUMMARY

Forecasting demand for services is very important in most services because fluctuations in demand cannot usually be taken care of by building inventory. When the service is "embedded" in a physical product, forecasting and meeting demand fluctuations are analogous to the manufacturing situation. In either case, the demand forecast is the basis for all planning.

In manufacturing, demand is forecasted in terms of units of physical product. In services, it is not always clear *what* to forecast and what *can be* forecasted. That is, the outputs of some service firms are of almost infinite variety. Basically, however, service demand is in terms of (1) number of customers and (2) number of services and a number of each anticipated service to be desired.

The selection of a forecasting method depends on four basic factors:

— Time requirements
— Resource requirements
— Input characteristics available or required
— Output characteristics required

There are four basic methods of forecasting:

— Judgment
— Counting
— Time series
— Association or causal

Within these categories there are numerous methods with variations of each. Exhibits 3–2 and 3–3 provided good overviews of the most popular forecasting methods for the service sector.

The strategic approaches to forecasting utilize combinations of these methods. These approaches are

— Economic system to industry system to company system
— Aggregate forecast to component forecast
— Component forecast to aggregate forecast

The technical aspects of actually making a forecast are complex, and a number of books and journals are available that deal with this subject. No forecasting method, as you saw in Exhibit 3–3 and as we learned in this chapter, is perfect under all conditions. And even once management has found a satisfactory approach, it must still monitor and control its forecasts to make sure errors do not get out of hand. Forecasting can often be a very challenging, but rewarding, part of managing.

____ DISCUSSION QUESTIONS

1. What is a time series extrapolation model? Explain why this model is so widely used in service organizations. Name some services in which time series would be the best forecasting model.

2. What is the difference between a causal model and a time-series model?

3. What is a judgmental forecasting model? Give some service-organization examples where judgmental forecasts are appropriate.

4. What is the meaning of least squares in a regression model? What are some independent variables that might be used in service examples?

5. What are some of the problems and drawbacks of the moving-average forecasting model?

6. What effect does the value of the smoothing constant have on the weight given to the past forecast and the past observed value?

7. What is MAD, and why is it important in the selection and use of forecasting models?

8. Why is forecast accuracy so important in service organizations?

____ PROBLEMS

3.1 Judy Smith has developed the following forecasting model:

$$\hat{y} = 36 + 4.3x$$

where $\hat{y}$ = demand for K10 air conditioners
x = the outside temperature (°F).

    a. Forecast demand for K10 when the temperature is 70°F.
    b. What is it for a temperature of 80°F?
    c. What is demand for a temperature of 90°F?

3.2 Data collected on the yearly demand for 50-lb bags of fertilizer at Rhonda's Garden Supply are shown in the following table. Develop a 3-year moving average to forecast sales. Then estimate demand again with a weighted moving average in which sales in the most recent year are given a weight of 2 and sales in the other two years are each given a weight of 1. Which method do you think is best?

Year	Demand for Fertilizer (thousands of bags)
1	4
2	6
3	4
4	5
5	10
6	8
7	7
8	9
9	12
10	14
11	15

3.3 Develop a 2- and a 4-year moving average for the demand for fertilizer in Problem 3.2.

3.4 In Problems 3.2 and 3.3, four different forecasts were developed for the demand for fertilizer. These four forecasts are a 2-year moving average, a 3-year moving average, a weighted moving average, and a 4-year moving average. Which one would you use? Explain your answer.

3.5 Use exponential smoothing with a smoothing constant of 0.3 to forecast the demand for fertilizer given in Problem 3.2. Assume that last period's forecast for year 1 is 5000 bags to begin the procedure. Would you prefer to use the exponential smoothing model or the weighted-average model developed in Problem 3.2? Explain your answer.

3.6 Sales of Cool-Man air conditioners have grown steadily during the past 5 years (see table). The sales manager had predicted in 1985 that 1986 sales would be 410 air conditioners. Using exponential smoothing with a weight of $\alpha = 0.30$, develop forecasts for 1987 through 1991.

Year	Sales	Forecast
1986	450	410
1987	495	
1988	518	
1989	563	
1990	584	
1991	?	

3.7 Demand for patient surgery at Washington General Hospital has increased steadily in the past few years, as seen in the following table.

Year	Outpatient Surgeries Performed
1	450
2	495
3	518
4	563
5	584
6	?

The director of medical services predicted 6 years ago that demand in year 1 would be for 410 surgeries.

a. Use exponential smoothing, first with a smoothing constant of 0.6 and then with one of 0.9, to develop forecasts for years 2 through 6.

b. Use a 3-year moving average to forecast demand in years 4, 5, and 6.

c. Use the extrapolation method to forecast demand in years 1 through 6.

d. With MAD as the criterion, which of the preceding four forecasting approaches is best?

3.8 Consulting income at Kate Walsh Associates for the period February–July has been as follows:

Month	Income (in thousands)
Feb.	70.0
Mar.	68.5
Apr.	64.8
May	71.7
June	71.3
July	72.8

Use trend-adjusted exponential smoothing to forecast August's income. Assume that the initial forecast for February is $65,000 and the initial trend adjustment is 0. The smoothing constants selected are $\alpha = 0.1$ and $\beta = 0.2$.

3.9 Resolve Problem 3.8 with $\alpha = 0.1$ and $\beta = 0.8$. Using MAD, which smoothing constants provide a better forecast?

3.10 Sales of industrial vacuum cleaners at R. Lowenthal Supply Co. over the past 13 months are shown in the following table.

Sales (thousands)	Month
11	Jan.
14	Feb.
16	Mar.
10	Apr.
15	May
17	June
11	July
14	Aug.
17	Sept.
12	Oct.
14	Nov.
16	Dec.
11	Jan.

a. Using a moving average with three periods, determine the demand for vacuum cleaners for next February.

b. Using a weighted moving average with three periods, determine the demand for vacuum cleaners for February. Use 3, 2, and 1 for the weights of the most recent, second most recent, and third most recent periods, respectively. For example, if you were forecasting the demand for February, November would have a weight of 1, December would have a weight of 2, and January would have a weight of 3.

c. Evaluate the accuracy of each of these methods.

d. What other factors might R. Lowenthal consider in forecasting sales?

3.11 Room registrations in the Toronto Towers Plaza Hotel have been recorded for the past 9 years. Management would like to determine the mathematical trend of guest registration in order to project future occupancy. This estimate would help the hotel determine whether a future expansion will be needed. Given the following time-series data, develop a least-squares equation relating registrations to time. Then forecast 1992 registrations. Room registrations are in thousands:

1982: 17	1985: 21	1988: 23
1983: 16	1986: 20	1989: 25
1984: 16	1987: 20	1990: 24

3.12 Quarterly demand for Jaguar XJ6s at a New York auto dealer are forecast with the equation

$\hat{y} = 10 + 3x$

where x = quarters—Quarter I of 1990 = 0

Quarter II of 1990 = 1

Quarter III of 1990 = 2

Quarter IV of 1990 = 3

Quarter I of 1991 = 4

and so on

$\hat{y}$ = quarterly demand

The demand for sports sedans is seasonal and the indices for Quarters I, II, III, and IV are 0.80, 1.00, 1.30, and 0.90, respectively. Forecast demand for each quarter of 1992. Then seasonalize each forecast to adjust for quarterly variations.

3.13 The operations manager of a musical instrument distributor feels that demand for bass drums may be related to the number of television appearances by the popular rock group Green Shades during the previous month. The manager has collected the data shown in the following table.

Demand for Bass Drums	Green Shades TV Appearances
3	3
6	4
7	7
5	6
10	8
8	5

a. Graph these data to see whether a linear equation might describe the relationship between the group's television shows and bass drum sales.

b. Use the least squares regression method to derive a forecasting equation.

c. What is your estimate for bass drum sales if the Green Shades performed on TV nine times last month?

3.14 Dr. Jerilyn Ross, a New York City psychologist, specializes in treating patients who are phobic and afraid to leave their homes. The following table indicates how many patients Dr. Ross has seen each year for the past 10 years. It also indicates what the robbery rate was in New York City during the same year.

Year	Number of Patients	Crime Rate (robberies per 1000 population)
1981	36	58.3
1982	33	61.1
1983	40	73.4
1984	41	75.7
1985	40	81.1
1986	55	89.0
1987	60	101.1
1988	54	94.8
1989	58	103.3
1990	61	116.2

Using trend analysis, how many patients do you think Dr. Ross will see in 1991, 1992, and 1993? How well does the model fit the data?

3.15 Using the data in Problem 3.14, apply linear regression to study the relationship between the crime rate and Dr. Ross's patient load. If the robbery rate increases to 131.2 in 1991, how many phobic patients will Dr. Ross treat? If the crime rate drops to 90.6, what is the patient projection?

3.16 Management of Davis's Department Store has used time series extrapolation to forecast retail sales for the next four quarters. The sales estimates are $100,000, $120,000, $140,000, and $160,000 for the respective quarters. Seasonal indices for the four quarters have been found to be 1.30, 0.90, 0.70, and 1.15, respectively. Compute a seasonalized or adjusted sales forecast.

3.17 Passenger miles flown on Northeast Airlines, a commuter firm serving the Boston hub, are shown for the past 12 weeks below.

Week	Actual Passenger Miles (in 000's)
1	17
2	21
3	19
4	23
5	18
6	16
7	20
8	18
9	22
10	20
11	15
12	22

a. Assuming an initial forecast for week 1 of 17,000 miles, use exponential smoothing to compute miles for weeks 2 through 12. Use α = 0.2.

b. What is the MAD for this model?

3.18 Bus and subway ridership in Washington, D.C. during the summer months is believed to be heavily tied to the number of tourists visiting that city. During the past 12 years, the following data have been obtained.

Year	No. of Tourists (millions)	Ridership (000,000's)
1979	7	15
1980	2	10
1981	6	13
1982	4	15
1983	14	25
1984	15	27
1985	16	24
1986	12	20
1987	14	27
1988	20	44
1989	15	34
1990	7	17

a. Plot these data and decide if a linear model is reasonable.

b. Develop a regression relationship.

c. What is expected ridership if 10 million tourists visit the city?

d. If there are no tourists at all, explain the predicted ridership.

3.19 Emergency calls to Winter Park, Florida's 911 system for the past 24 weeks are shown below.

Week	Calls	Week	Calls
1	50	13	55
2	35	14	35
3	25	15	25
4	40	16	55
5	45	17	55
6	35	18	40
7	20	19	35
8	30	20	60
9	35	21	75
10	20	22	50
11	15	23	40
12	40	24	65

a. Compute the exponentially smoothed forecast of calls for each week. Assume an initial forecast of 50 calls in the first week and use α = 0.1. What is the forecast for the twenty-fifth week?

b. Reforecast each period using an α = 0.6.

c. Actual calls during the twenty-fifth week were 85. Which smoothing constant provides a superior forecast? Explain and justify the measure of error used.

3.20 Using the 911 call data in Problem 3.19, forecast calls for weeks 2 through 25 with a trend-adjusted exponential smoothing model. Assume an initial forecast for 50 calls again for week 1 and an initial trend of zero. Use smoothing constants of α = 0.3 and β = 0.1. Is this mode better than that of Problem 3.19? What adjustment might be useful for further improvement? (Again, assume actual calls in week 25 were 85.)

—— READING 3.1 ——————————————————————————

Managing and Monitoring a Forecasting System: The Chemical Bank Experience

Vincent A. Mabert ▪ Robert L. Stocco

This paper describes Chemical Bank's experience with a daily check volume forecasting system used for planning check processing operations. It presents a case study noting critical monitoring functions, system modifications, and important management issues.

FORECAST SYSTEM

Exhibit 3–11 illustrates the basic structure of the Chemical Bank forecast system, which contains four components: history database, volume-estimation model, forecast review, and system monitoring.

Source: Adapted from *Journal of Bank Research*, Vol. 13 (Autumn 1982), pp. 196–201. Used with permission.

─── EXHIBIT 3–11 ───────────────────────────────

■ *Forecast System Management*

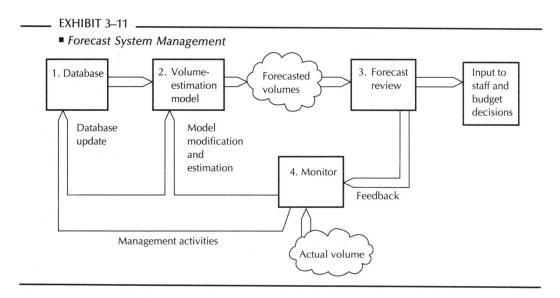

History Database

The system uses two years of history, or about 520 days. At the end of each month, that month is added to the database, and oldest month is removed. This process maintains a 24-month history for estimating future volumes.

Volume-Estimation Model

The system utilizes a two-stage approach to volume estimation. Volume estimates are generated through the use of a multivariable linear regression model for stage one. The independent variables, factors influencing volume, are certain time-oriented events. Since the public and business organizations tend to follow rather regular patterns, it was found that using calendar information—the month (Jan., . . . , Dec.), date (1st, . . . , 31st), weekday (Mon., . . . , Fri.) and holiday (federal or religious)—good daily estimates could be developed. Two years of daily data were used to estimate the model.

Forecast Review

The daily volume estimates are reviewed by bank personnel for reasonableness. All mechanical forecasting systems have a hindsight problem, because future estimates are based on past volumes and relationships. Therefore, a mechanical approach is only able to react after the fact to changes. Members from the user and system departments review and discuss the estimates. In some cases, modifications need to be made to daily forecasts to reflect special events.

Forecasts for days influenced by the presence of holidays are reviewed manually because of their unique nature. The system's forecasts are compared to previous years' actual volumes, and final estimates are made. Approximately 10 to 12 days per year are adjusted due to this review.

Monitoring

Monitoring the forecast system is the joint responsibility of both user and system departments. The user departments keep track of forecast performance on a daily basis and generate monthly summaries. Based on these summary reports, problems are identified. The performance data in these reports are (a) actual monthly volume in pounds; (b) forecasted monthly volume in pounds; (c) average error (AE) for month in pounds; (d) average percent error (APE) for month; (e) average absolute percent error (AAPE) for month; (f) standard deviation of AAPE for month; (g) number of days overforecasted for the month; and (h) number of days underforecasted for the month.

No single criterion is used to measure forecast quality. Rather, the main performance measures,

(d) to (h), are reviewed over time to determine the forecast system's adequacy. The identification of whether the system is in or out of control requires a standard to measure against. In Chemical Bank's case, the *APE, AAPE,* and the days under/over-forecasted are of primary use in evaluating system performance.

The determination of the appropriate standards for the three criteria is based on logic and past history. Since daily forecasting results in both positive and negative errors, a system that is generating unbiased forecasts would have an *APE* that varied around zero.

The final criterion is the number of days over/underforecasted. If the system is creating unbiased forecasts, one would expect around a 50–50 split of over- and underforecasted days.

The importance of using multiple measures should be noted at this point. Using only a single measure by itself may be misleading. Therefore, using multiple measures allows one the opportunity to build solid evidence about system performance.

MANAGING CHANGE

Over the four years the system has been in use, not all has been smooth. At times the forecast users became skeptical of the system because of increased errors. Their confidence had been justifiably shaken, and they were concerned about future performance. However, they began to realize that the dynamics in our society cause change. No mechanical procedure can anticipate every kind of change that can occur or its impact on future volumes. There is no substitute for human judgment. One cannot accept blindly the estimates generated from a mechanical forecasting model. The model's logic and input data must always be monitored to maintain congruency with reality. That is why forecast review is an integral part of the system.

CONCLUSIONS

There is more to a successful forecasting system than its creation. Chemical Bank's forecasting system for predicting daily check volume illustrates that careful evaluation and updating are necessary for useful planning information to be derived. In fact, the daily management over time determines success or failure. Forecasting exists because of the dynamics in our society. Therefore, forecasting is an evolving process, never finished, and always under evaluation.

___ QUESTIONS FOR READING 3.1

1. Briefly describe the four components of Chemical Bank's forecasting system.

2. Why are so many statistical monitoring devices used?

3. Is this a successful forecasting system?

___ READING 3.2 ___

ARTS PLAN: IMPLEMENTATION, EVOLUTION, AND USAGE

Charles B. Weinberg

ARTS PLAN is a user-oriented, decision support system designed to aid a performing arts manager in planning a schedule of performing arts events. First implemented in 1976 by management of the "Lively Arts at Stanford" (LAS) program, the model consists of two major components: (1) a forecasting system to predict attendance at a scheduled event, and (2) an interactive planning model by which the manager can test the impact of scheduling different performing arts events on total attendance for the year. For 5 years, management's use of the model was monitored in order to examine the evolution of this marketing model.

The original ARTS PLAN forecasting model

Source: Reprinted by permission of Charles B. Weinberg, "ARTS PLAN: Implementation, Evolution, and Usage," *Marketing Science*, Vol. 5, No. 2 (Spring, 1986), pp. 143–158. Copyright 1986 The Institute of Management Sciences, 290 Westminster Street, Providence, Rhode Island 02903 USA.

was constructed and estimated using data from 90 performances given over a 3-year period. Based on the type of performing arts event (e.g., dance, jazz, chamber music), the quarter in which it was presented (fall, winter, spring), and other factors, a dummy-variable multiple linear regression was developed. Most important, and somewhat surprising, was the finding that, in general, the name of the individual performer was not needed to forecast attendance accurately. This meant that a forecasting system could be built for performers who had not previously been on campus.

The ARTS PLAN system allows the manager to revise the regression forecasts based on additional information or plans, such as special promotions, that the manager may have. Calling the regression forecast a "model" estimate, we have compared the model estimate to the management's estimate over 3 years to see whether the model or manager (actually the manager plus model) is superior.

The model initially yielded highly accurate forecasts, but became less accurate over time, suggesting a need for revision. However, too frequent revision may erode management confidence in the system. Furthermore, methods that automatically revise forecasts to take account of the most recent data may sometimes produce decreased accuracy due to the incorporation of random error in the prediction and other factors. Consequently, a major issue from both the standpoint of model accuracy and management confidence concerns when and how the model should be revised.

MEASURING ACCURACY

Accuracy, like beauty, may be "in the eye of the beholder." One viewpoint is that of the manager's. When ARTS PLAN was first developed, management was primarily concerned with estimating total annual attendance. This figure was critical for financial planning purposes and for obtaining university approval for implementing a proposed schedule. Consequently, a major criterion in judging the model was the comparison of total predicted to total actual attendance. To facilitate year-by-year comparisons, this figure can be converted to mean error per event. While mean error per event allows over and underestimates to offset each

other, this is a reasonable measure given management's focus on total attendance.

IMPLEMENTATION EXPERIENCE

The ARTS PLAN system has been used as an aid by LAS executives in management of the ongoing season and in the planning of future seasons. Before the start of the one season, attendance forecasts were made for the 26-performance schedule. At the end of the season, the actual and predicted (with managerial revision) attendances were compared. The total attendance prediction of 20,875 was virtually identical to the actual attendance of 20,882.

BOOTSTRAPPING: DOES THE MANAGER IMPROVE THE MODEL'S FORECAST?

In "bootstrapping," linear regression models of judgments are substituted for the judgments themselves. In many repetitive forecasting situations, the bootstrapped judgments are more accurate than the original judgments.

Of course, our situation is not the same; the ARTS PLAN regression model is based on the actual criterion (attendance), not on the manager's forecast of attendance. Rather the issue is: Can the manager improve on the model's forecast? The model forecast overcomes the human inconsistency and the manager just needs to make changes based on knowledge of changed or special circumstances or actions planned to influence (presumably increase) attendance. In other words, can the manager "bootstrap" the model by revising the estimate for factors that the model is "unaware" of?

To review, for each performance the computer program displays a forecast of attendance. The manager can either accept that forecast or revise it upward or downward. The revisions would typically include the input of staff members. Forecasts are made during the winter and spring preceding the year being planned.

Results

In the 15 instances in which management made a large (more than 100-seat) change to the forecast, the revised estimate was closer to the actual attendance 8 times. While the manager accurately judged the direction of change, being correct in 12 of 15 cases, the manager frequently underestimated the magnitude of the change. Management's mean error for the 15 events was considerably lower than the model's. Confining ourselves to the 13 cases in which the manager expected increased attendance, attendance was greater than the model forecast 11 times. In these 11 instances, the manager's estimate exceeded the actual attendance 4 times, but 7 times the revised forecast was between the actual and the model forecast.

Discussion

The limited improvement from the managerial revisions is surprising. Not only does the manager choose the events for which a change in forecast attendance is made, but also the manager controls some factors that can influence attendance. A priori, we expected the manager to consistently outperform the model alone.

In essence, we thought the manager would "bootstrap" the model. The manager would recognize the situations in which unusual circumstances were likely to occur (either due to controllable or uncontrollable elements) and then decrease the errors that would occur because the model could not recognize these unusual situations. In other words, in those situations in which intuitive judgment was most needed, the manager would apply it; in other circumstances, the manager would adopt the model's forecast. While the manager certainly did no worse than the model, and in some years on some measures outperformed the model, an overall, systematic improvement was not achieved.

Why doesn't the manager do better? One reason is that the manager makes revisions in circumstances in which it is most difficult to achieve high forecast accuracy. The model summarizes the available historical information in a systematic manner. For cases in which these historical circumstances appear to hold, the model's forecast is accepted. Consequently, it is only in atypical cases that the manager revises the model forecast, and in these circumstances, the manager has limited previous information on which to base an accurate judgment. Perhaps, then, being directionally

correct is a reasonable achievement for the manager.

The findings in this study appear to be consistent with those reported in Behavioral Decision Theory (BDT). The results in BDT suggest that probabilistic judgments are subject to various types of biases. While several of these biases might apply in the current situation, of particular concern here are those due to availability (i.e., the accessibility or easy retrievability of data) and anchoring. In 7 of the 11 cases in which management correctly predicted that attendance would increase, the revised estimate was between the model forecast and the actual attendance. The model forecast may thus serve as an anchor to the manager's forecast; clearly the forecast value for attendance is easily recalled if not directly seen by the manager. However, more substantial revisions to the forecast may have not been wise on average.

FORECASTING

While the need for periodic review and revision of the ARTS PLAN forecasting equation was recognized, annual updating (or an automatic revision or smoothing approach) of the regression coefficients was rejected for three main reasons. First, the manager, who judged the ARTS PLAN's performance primarily on the basis of mean error (for the manager plus model), considered the ARTS PLAN system to be highly accurate. Whereas before the availability of ARTS PLAN management had spent considerable time trying to generate attendance estimates, now they were generated quickly with relatively little discussion by managers; management was satisfied. Thus, there was no managerial impetus to change.

Second, frequent revision of the model, e.g., by adding the most recent year's data to the database, would likely have had only a small effect on predicted attendance. Management was not interested in small changes in attendance forecasts as these changes would have little impact on planning decisions. Management scientists should be cautious in making changes which are technically appropriate but managerially insignificant.

Third, highly sophisticated forecasting methods (including those in which parameters are automatically revised) do not necessarily produce more accurate forecasts than simpler approaches. While the sophisticated models may fit historical data better, they may not forecast more accurately. Conversely, too simple a model (e.g., omitting seasonal effects when they are present) can result in inaccurate estimates. The goal is to choose an appropriate level of complexity for the situation.

—— QUESTIONS FOR READING 3.2

1. Describe "bootstrapping." How could this affect a forecast?

2. What different methods of measuring forecast accuracy can be employed in forecasting performing arts events?

3. Why was the model not updated annually?

—— CASE 3.1 ————————————————————

The North-South Airline

In 1988, Northern Airlines[1] merged with Southeast Airlines to create the fourth largest U.S. carrier. The new North-South Airline inherited both an aging fleet of Boeing 727-200 aircraft and Stephen Ruth. Ruth was a tough former Secretary of the Navy who stepped in as new President and Chairman of the Board.

Ruth's first concern in creating a financially solid company was maintenance costs. It was commonly surmised in the airline industry that maintenance costs rise with the age of the aircraft. He quickly noticed that historically there had been a significant difference in the reported B727-200 maintenance costs (from ATA Form 41s) both in the airframe and engine areas between Northern Airlines and Southeast Airlines, with Southeast having the newer fleet.

On November 12, 1988, Peg Young, Vice President for Operations and Maintenance, was called into Ruth's office and asked to study the issue. Specifically, Ruth wanted to know (1) whether the average fleet age was correlated to direct airframe maintenance costs, and (2) whether there was a relationship between average fleet age and direct engine maintenance costs. Young was to report back with the answer, along with quan-

titative and graphical descriptions of the relationship, by November 26.

Young's first step was to have her staff construct the average age of Northern and Southeast B727-200 fleets, by quarter, since the introduction of that aircraft to service by each airline in late 1977 and early 1978. The average age of each fleet was calculated by first multiplying the total number of calendar days each aircraft had been in service at the pertinent point in time by the average daily utilization of the respective fleet to total fleet hours flown. The total fleet hours flown was then divided by the number of aircraft in service at that time, giving the age of the "average" aircraft in the fleet.

The average utilization was found by taking the actual total fleet hours flown at September 30, 1987, from Northern and Southeast data, and dividing by total days in service for all aircraft at that time. The average utilization for Southeast was 8.3 hours per day, and the average utilization for Northern was 8.7 hours per day. Since the available cost data were calculated for each yearly period ending at the end of the first quarter, average fleet age was calculated at the same points in time.

The fleet data are shown in Exhibit 3–12. Airframe cost data and engine cost data are both shown paired with fleet average age in that table.

[1] Dates and names of airlines and individuals have been changed in this case to maintain confidentiality. The data and issues described here are actual.

—— QUESTION FOR CASE 3.1

1. Prepare Peg Young's response to Stephen Ruth.

Source: From Jay Heizer and Barry Render, *Production and Operations Management*, p. 159. Copyright © 1988 by Allyn and Bacon. Reprinted with permission.

——— EXHIBIT 3–12 ———————————————————————————

■ *North-South Airline Data for Boeing 727-200 Jets*

	Northern Airline Data			Southeast Airline Data		
Year	Airframe Cost per Aircraft	Engine Cost per Aircraft	Average Age (hrs)	Airframe Cost per Aircraft	Engine Cost per Aircraft	Average Age (hrs)
1981	$51.80	$43.49	6,512	$13.29	$18.86	5,107
1982	54.92	38.58	8,404	25.15	31.55	8,145
1983	69.70	51.48	11,077	32.18	40.43	7,360
1984	68.90	58.72	11,717	31.78	22.10	5,773
1985	63.72	45.47	13,275	25.34	19.69	7,150
1986	84.73	50.26	15,215	32.78	32.58	9,364
1987	78.74	79.60	18,390	35.56	38.07	8,259

REFERENCES

Ashley, R., and J. Guerard. "Applications of Time Series Analysis to Texas Financial Forecasting," *Interfaces,* Vol. 13, No. 4 (August 1983), pp. 46–55.

Ashton, A. H., and R. H. Ashton. "Aggregating Subjective Forecasts," *Management Science,* Vol. 31, No. 12 (December 1985), pp. 1499–1508.

Becker, B. C., and A. Sapienza. "Forecasting Hospital Reimbursement," *Hospital and Health Services Administration,* Vol. 32 (Nov. 1987), pp. 521–530.

Box, G. E. P., and G. Jenkins. *Time Series Analysis: Forecasting and Control.* San Francisco: Holden Day, 1970.

Brown, R. G. *Statistical Forecasting for Inventory Control.* New York: McGraw-Hill, 1959.

Brozovich, J. P., and D. Loftus. "Physician-Administrator Decision Making for High-Technology Purchases," *Health Care Management Review,* Vol. 6, No. 3 (Summer 1981), pp. 63–73.

Bunn, D. W., and J. P. Seigal. "Forecasting the Effects of Television Programming upon Electricity Loads," *Journal of the Operational Research Society,* Vol. 34 (Jan. 1983), pp. 17–25.

Chambers, J. C., C. Satinder, S. K. Mullick, and D. D. Smith. "How to Choose the Right Forecasting Technique," *Harvard Business Review,* Vol. 49, No. 4 (July–August 1971), pp. 45–74.

Claycombe, W. W., and W. G. Sullivan. "Current Forecasting Techniques," *Journal of System Management* (September 1978), pp. 18–20.

Gardner, E. S. "Exponential Smoothing: The State of the Art," *Journal of Forecasting,* Vol. 4, No. 1 (March 1985).

Georgoff, D. M., and R. G. Murdick. "Managers Guide to Forecasting," *Harvard Business Review,* Vol. 64, No. 1 (January–February 1986), pp. 110–120.

Gips, J., and B. Sullivan. "Sales Forecasting—Replacing Magic with Logic," *Production and Inventory Management Review,* Vol. 2, No. 2 (February 1982).

Heizer, J., and B. Render. *Production and Operations Management.* Boston: Allyn and Bacon, 1988.

Holz, B. W., and J. M. Wroth. "Improving Strength Forecasts: Support for Army Manpower Management," *Interfaces,* Vol. 10, No. 6 (Dec. 1980), pp. 31–52.

Lane, D., et al. "Forecasting Demand for Long Term Care Services," *Health Services Research,* Vol. 20, No. 4 (Oct. 1985), pp. 435–459.

Lee, D. R. "A Forecast of Lodging Supply and Demand," *The Cornell HRA Quarterly,* Vol. 25, No. 2 (August 1984), pp. 27–40.

Mabert, V. A., and R. L. Stocco. "Managing and Monitoring a Forecasting System: The Chemical Bank Experience," *Journal of Bank Research,* Vol. 13, No. 3 (Autumn 1982), pp. 195–201.

MacStravic, R. S. "An Early Warning Technique,"

Hospital and Health Services Administration, Vol. 31, No. 1 (Jan.–Feb. 1986), pp. 86–98.

Mahmoud, E. "Accuracy in Forecasting: A Summary," *Journal of Forecasting,* Vol. 3, No. 2 (April–June 1984).

Makridakis, S., S. C. Wheelright, and V. E. McGee. *Forecasting: Methods and Applications,* 2d Ed. New York: Wiley, 1983.

Nandola, K., M. Koshal, and R. K. Koshal. "Forecasting Restaurant Food Sales," *The Cornell HRA Quarterly,* Vol. 23, No. 2 (August 1982), pp. 92–96.

Parker, G. C., and E. L. Segura. "How to Get a Better Forecast," *Harvard Business Review,* Vol. 49, No. 2 (March–April 1971), pp. 99–109.

Plossl, G. W., and O. W. Wight. *Production and Inventory Control.* Englewood Cliffs, N.J.: Prentice-Hall, 1967.

Rao, P. S. "Forecasting the Demand for Railway Freight Services," *Journal of Transportation Economics and Policy,* Vol. 12, No. 1 (Jan. 1978), pp. 7–22.

Render, B., and R. M. Stair. *Quantitative Analysis for Management,* 3d Ed. Boston: Allyn and Bacon, 1988.

Schnaars, S. P., and R. J. Bavuso. "Extrapolation Models on Very Short-Term Forecasts," *Journal of Business Research,* Vol. 14 (1986), pp. 27–36.

Young, M. A., "Sources of Competitive Data for the Management Strategist," *Strategic Management Journal,* Vol. 10, No. 4 (July–August 1989), pp. 285–293.

PART II

The Service System

4

Design of the Service

INTRODUCTION

Design is the creation of a new pattern of relationships among activities, ideas, and/or physical entities. Although all businesses are based on the design of their outputs, not all businesses have formalized procedures for the design process. Design is both an analytical and a creative process. It is also an economic one.

PURPOSES OF DESIGN

Every new business starts with a key idea for a product or service that can be produced and sold for a profit. Basically, the design of products and services is a company's response to competitors, to customers, and to legal changes. For established companies, there is usually a design department or design group that is responsible for creating new products or services. These people may be designated designers (in the apparel industry), engineers (in most manufacturing firms), or service project managers (in banks and financial services). More recently, in both manufacturing and service firms, teams of people from diverse backgrounds (such as marketing, operations, engineering, finance, consumer groups, and supplier goods) have been brought together to design new products and services. This project team approach was used successfully by Ford in the design of its Taurus car and by Marriott in the design of its line of economy hotels.

The purposes of design are many and varied. They include

— Developing new products or services for existing markets
— Developing new products or services for new markets
— Developing new applications for existing products or services
— Improving the quality of existing products or services
— Reducing the cost of an existing product or service
— Minimizing dangers, nuisances, or pollution associated with the use of a product or service
— Reducing or eliminating difficulties associated with the production or use of a product or service
— Standardizing a product or service line
— Adapting a product or service to new legal requirements or opportunities
— Improving customer or public relations
— Specifying and describing the new product or service concepts in sufficient detail for them to be implemented by another person or group

THE ROLE OF MARKETING AND PRODUCTION

In the most general case, the marketing department is responsible for determining customer needs and wants. This activity may range in sophistication from an informal process to a formal market research study. In any case, the marketing department typically serves as the major source of new product or service ideas. Other typical sources of ideas are the R&D group, top management, a formal new product department, suggestion systems, customers, and vendors. Additional external sources of ideas include competitors, the government, and the general public.

Regardless of the idea source, it is usually the marketing department's function to define and refine the new idea so that a commercially profitable product or service can be produced and sold. The description of the needed product or service is called the **performance specification.** It describes what kinds of things (and to what degree) the product or service must do for the customer. For example, the customer may desire transportation for three people about town with a speed of at least 30 mph. These are performance specs. **Design specs** specify what type of service will meet these performance specs. In this example, public transportation, a taxi cab, a rental car, or a limousine are possible alternatives. It is apparent that performance specifications must contain enough information to ensure that the design specifications will yield a product

_____ EXHIBIT 4–1 _____

■ *The Relationship of Design to Marketing and Production*

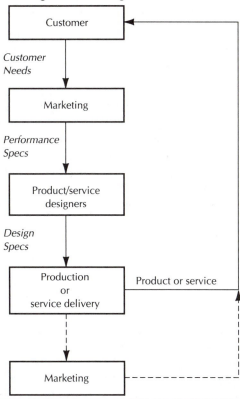

or service satisfactory to the customer at an appropriate price in terms of competitive alternatives.

When the drawings, material specifications, and/or narrative descriptions that constitute the design specs have been completed, the specs are given to the organization or individuals that will produce the product or provide the service. Thus, in the simplest case, the customer is separated from the designer by marketing on the input side and by the productive or conversion system on the output side. Exhibit 4–1 shows this flow. In many types of firms, the marketing organization also appears between the manufacturing or service process and the customer for shipment or transfer of the product or service.

A recent survey of the design process in the service industry reveals some interesting dichotomies.[1] The survey results show that the marketing function is largely responsible for designing new services, but the use of marketing research techniques

_____

[1] E. E. Scheuing, and E. M. Johnson, ''New Product Management in Service Industries: An Early Assessment,'' *Add Value to Your Services* (Chicago, Ill.: American Marketing Association, 1987, pp. 91–95.

is limited. Further, most firms use new "product" evaluation committees and project teams but do not engage in a formal process of new service development. Finally, the primary source of ideas for new services is competitors.

THE SERVICE PACKAGE OR BUNDLE

Whether the outputs of a firm are products or services or a mixture, the product or service alone is only one part of the competitive package the firm offers. As we saw in Chapter 1, every product is accompanied by some aspect of service and most services are associated with some physical items, either in the provision of the service or as part of the service itself. Thus, instead of simply providing a product or a service, firms actually provide a *package* or *bundle* that includes a mixture of physical items, services, images, and experiences.

Sasser, Olsen, and Wyckoff define three components of a service bundle as follows:[2]

— Physical items or facilitating goods
— Sensual benefits or explicit services
— Psychological benefits or implicit services

In the case of a restaurant, the physical items are the facility, food, drinks, tableware, napkins, and other touchable commodities. The sensual benefits include the taste and aroma of the food and the sights and sound of the people. Psychological benefits consist of comfort, status, and a sense of well-being.

The key to an effective design of a service is to recognize and properly define all the items that make up the service bundle. The mix of facilitating goods, explicit services, and implicit services must be appropriate for the customer base and provider resources. Further, each of these components must be specified as part of the service design and not left to chance.

THE DESIGN PROCESS

The product design process has been studied and developed over the years and can be described precisely. The design of services, however, has not received much attention. This is probably due to the misconception that services are more simplistic than manufactured products. Certainly there is no reason why the design of services cannot be approached in the same highly formalized, structured manner as the design of manufactured systems and products. Creativity and control of both time and cost can be achieved for services, too, with proper management planning techniques.

The design process is often controlled by a procedure known as **project management.** Chapter 15 describes project management in more detail. With project man-

---

[2] W. Earl Sasser, R. Paul Olsen, and D. Daryl Wyckoff, *Management of Service Operations* (Boston: Allyn and Bacon, 1978), pp. 8–10.

agement, the design project is broken down into a hierarchy of tasks for the design of subsystems and components. A start date and end date for the project are established. Then dates for the start and conclusion of each task are established. Costs for tasks and times are tightly controlled.

The major advantages of formal project management of the design process are

1. Project purpose, tasks, and subtasks are clearly defined.
2. Responsibilities for the tasks are well defined.
3. There is frequent and complete reporting for coordination and performance/ task/cost evaluation.
4. The development time is shortened.
5. The concentrated team effort produces higher morale.

The major disadvantages are

1. It is difficult to find good project managers.
2. Organizational planning is a complex process and may result in lower utilization of company personnel.
3. Any snag that delays the coordinated design effort may delay the entire project and cause snowballing.
4. Time pressures may stifle creativity.

The process of designing a service involves the following steps: (1) accumulating information, (2) developing conceptual alternatives, (3) designing and testing proto-types, and (4) developing the final design, drawings, and specifications. We discuss each of these steps in the following sections.

Accumulation of Information

The most vital information for design is the performance specification obtained from management or the marketing staff. For many types of intangible services, the per-formance specs closely resemble the design specifications. Other information such as state-of-the-art technology, architectural input, the availability of human skills, and equipment options must be thoroughly researched. It is important at this step to assemble *all* the data and information that can serve as an input to the design process.

The Marriott Corporation is a good example of a company that accumulates volumes of information, mostly from its competitors, when designing new services. When Marriott considered entering the economy hotel business, teams of marketing, finance, human resources, and operations personnel were sent out to nearly 400 com-peting hotels to test their facilities (beds, size of rooms, thickness of walls, restaurants, etc.) and their service (reservations, personal attention, room policies).[3] Hotel managers were interviewed about operations, prices, and morale. In addition, Marriott hired a headhunting team to interview fifteen regional managers from each of the five economy hotel chains across the country. In most cases, the competition was more than willing

---

[3] See B. Dumaine, ''Corporate Spies Stoop to Conquer,'' *Fortune,* November 7, 1988, pp. 68–76.

to share information. As a result, Marriott's line of economy hotels was efficiently designed and well-received by consumers.

Another example of extensive preparation and accumulation of information is the process used by Federal Express in the design of their package delivery service.[4] Faced with limited funds, Federal created the Air Express Buying Power Index to justify demand for the new service and to select an initial target market. The index was developed by examining the correlation between certain Standard Industrial Classification (SIC) codes and the predicted usage of air freight for shipping time-sensitive, high-priority packages. Predictions on usage were derived from such data as the makeup of the industrial base, the number of hospital beds, the number of computer companies, and the number of consulting, architectural, and engineering firms in a metropolitan area. When completed, Federal was able to design an efficient operations plan in which twenty-three target markets were selected that totaled over 60 percent of the air package buying power in the nation.

Development of Conceptual Alternatives

This step converts the performance specifications into alternative service designs. The alternative designs at this stage are called **concepts** because they are essentially ideas that have not yet been implemented or defined in detail. Let us look at a few examples of performance specifications and alternatives for achieving them.

Service	Performance Specs	Alternative Concepts
Movie theater	Waiting in ticket line not to exceed 5 minutes	1. Multiple ticket booths 2. Coin-operated entrance gates 3. Advance ticket purchases by phone with credit cards
Mail-order banking	Supply withdrawal cash to customers within 24 hours	1. Arrange with local bank to supply cash by electronic fund transfer 2. Send cash by overnight express service
Private transportation	Move customers about city rapidly	1. Taxi system 2. Jitney system (i.e., shared rides)

Note that each of the design concepts specifies what the customer experiences, i.e., ticket booths, gates, trips to a bank, riding alone in a taxi, or riding in a group but at a lower price in a jitney. How these designs are to be provided to the customer is the subject of Chapter 5 on process design.

The preceding example represents some relatively mundane alternatives for

---

[4] See R. A. Sigafoos, and R. R. Easson, *Absolutely Positively Overnight* (Memphis, Tenn.: St. Lukes Press, 1988), pp. 129–131, for a complete description of the design process.

meeting performance specifications. In actuality, the development of alternative conceptual designs is the phase in which creativity pays off. It is the time in which blue-sky thinking should be indulged—the time for breaking away from the orthodox, the traditional, and the routine mediocrity so common in large organizations. The conceptual phase is the time when it is most economical to change, rearrange, and try out all types of promising new ideas. Reading 4.2 describes a new type of "service" specifically designed to generate and evaluate *ideas!*

The conceptual design period should be limited to a specified time. Since researchers and designers tend to be perfectionists, they will usually continue to search for the best overall design beyond the point of maximum practicality. If the time is extended, the original burst of creativity may taper off or such a profusion of ideas may flow forth that it will be impossible to develop and/or evaluate them within the resources of the organization. Any excess of ideas or ideas on other subjects that are not used should be recorded so that they do not become lost forever. There may be future design programs where many of them will be used.

The alternative conceptual designs should be worked into a formal presentation. If a design review committee exists—and this is a very desirable and worthwhile approach—it should have the opportunity to evaluate the various approaches. The broad and varied experience of the members can spell the difference between ultimate success or failure. The designs should be evaluated from all angles, and the best three or four should be ranked. The ultimate decision as to which design offers the most promise and is worth pursuing is made by management.

Design and Testing of Prototypes

After the selection of a service design among the conceptual alternatives, a prototype or "sample" service is constructed and tested. In some cases, such as transportation, when the addition of a proposed local bus route or the leasing of buses on a network of routes may be tried on a trial basis, prototyping is feasible. In others, it can be quite expensive to construct a theater, an information-processing network, or other localized delivery system. Fortunately, there are some techniques such as computer simulation (described in Chapter 11) that allow us to view the operation of a proposed system from a hypothetical point of view. Also, many service organizations have multiple outlets (McDonald's, for instance) where different prototypes can be tested.

Final Design, Drawings, and Specifications

The final service design will be affected by the technology of the service process. Nevertheless, the final design must be fitted closely to market preferences. Therefore, research on customer needs, attitudes, and preferences and the results of market tests should bear heavily on the final design decision.

One of the last steps in the design process is to prepare a narrative specification of the bundle of intangibles supplied. Design specifications for the service bundle represent a description of the service in sufficient detail such that the same service experience can be replicated at numerous locations. The individual who reconstructs

───── EXHIBIT 4–2 ──

■ *Narrative Design Specifications of a Multitheater Service*

1. Six-theater complex.
2. A range of general (G) to restricted (R) movies playing at all times.
3. Open seven days a week.
4. Hours of movies 1 P.M. to approximately midnight. Saturday morning children's movies in the summer.
5. Each theater seats 500 patrons on a well-sloped plane.
6. Seats are well-padded, spring-closing, wide, and fabric upholstered.
7. Starting times for movies are staggered and a first-come, first-served queueing system with two ticket clerks keeps waiting time down to 5 minutes maximum.
8. Refreshments are sold up to 30 minutes before closing.
9. All personnel wear uniforms.
10. Ushers are to maintain order and provide security.
11. Theaters will be swept between performances to maintain clean appearance.
12. Prices are competitive with those of better theaters in the area. Discounts for school children and seniors are given during the week.
13. Ambiance includes warm rich colors, open space, and comfort.
14. Smoking is permitted only in the lobby.
15. The location is in a well-lit shopping center with adequate parking and security.

──

the service process, both "backroom" and "front office" segments, is the equivalent to the manufacturing manager in a product firm.

If tangible outputs are part of the service bundle, then drawings and physical models may be required to supplement the narrative description. For instance, a simplified example of the design for a movie theater consists of

— A list of principal features experienced by the customer (shown in Exhibit 4–2), such as times of operation, types of features shown, theater environment, and staff operating procedures
— A layout drawing (only roughly indicated in Exhibit 4–3 without dimensions)
— A three-dimensional model

The layout presents to customers the degree of convenience in getting to and from their seats relative to the entrance and refreshment stand. It also indicates the openness or compact informality of the interior. A three-dimensional model shows the ambiance that customers will experience. The topic of facility layout is discussed in further detail in Chapter 7.

Notice that service design deals only with the bundle of services that the customer *experiences*. The customer is not interested in the process by which the service is produced except as the customer experiences it.[5] For example, the customer at a movie theater has no interest in the type of projector used, whether the projectionist is in a union, whether the theater is part of a chain, or how the films are selected and delivered.

---

[5] This distinction between "backroom" and "front office" activities is noted in C. C. Voss, B. J. Armistead, and B. Morris, *Operations Management in Service Industries and the Public Sector* (New York: Wiley, 1985).

_____ EXHIBIT 4–3 _____

■ *Layout Drawing of Multitheater*

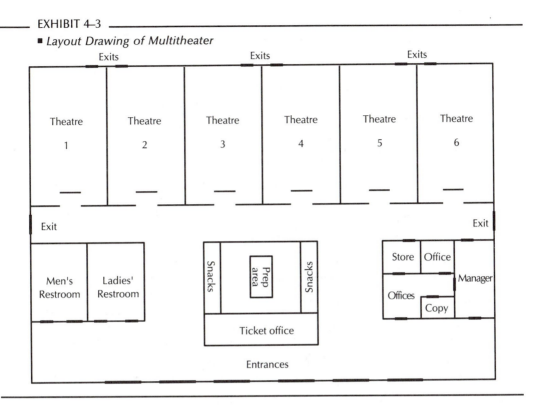

The customer *is* interested in experiences such as the particular film, the convenience of location, the comfort and appearance of the theater, the ticket price, and auxiliary services such as refreshments and crowd noise control.

DESIGNING DIFFERENT TYPES OF SERVICES
Mass Services

Services may be divided into two groups for purposes of describing the design process: (1) those services which are mass delivered or standardized, and (2) those services which involve high customer contact and are more customized. In **mass services,** the technical design of the service and the major work of producing the service are separated from the customer by equipment or by distance. For example, the provision of 24-hour banking with automatic tellers gives the customer little say in the design of the service as the service is being performed. During the presentation of a movie in a theater or the broadcasting of a television program, persons supplying the service are separated from the customer. Public transportation is also impersonal and standardized.

The design and conversion processes are sometimes called the **technical core.** This concept is important because separating the technical core from the customer can allow a business to operate more efficiently. For example, most manufacturing can be planned for and operated without being influenced by the special desires of customers during the production process. Most services are not allowed this luxury. However, some services can be designed to insulate the technical core from the customer by

— Restricting the offerings (a limited-menu restaurant)
— Customizing at delivery (customizing vans at the dealership rather than at the factory)
— Structuring service so customers must go where the service is offered (customer service personnel open new bank accounts, loan officers make loans, and tellers facilitate deposits and withdrawals)
— Self-service so customers can examine, compare, and evaluate at their own pace (a supermarket)
— Separating services that may lend themselves to some type of automation (automatic teller machines)

When the technical core of design and production of a service is such that the customer has essentially no personal contact with the service providers, the design of the service is said to be *mass delivered* or *standardized*. In other words, the design process is independent of day-to-day changes based on customer interaction with designers. For these reasons, the design process for mass services is similar to that of manufactured products and has even been described as a "production-line approach to services."[6] Reading 4.1 describes this approach using the fast-food industry as an example.

High-Contact Services

We now move from the design of services where the customer plays no part in either design or delivery to design where the customer plays a part in one or the other or both. This provides us with the following three cases illustrated simply in Exhibit 4–4.

1. The customer participates in the service design but not in the service delivery (part a).
2. The customer participates in the service delivery but not in the service design (part b).
3. The customer participates in both the service design and the service delivery (part c).

Let us take the first case. A customer may arrange for disposition of his or her body after death in a number of ways. The design process is carried out mainly by undertakers and research hospitals, but the client also makes choices such as burial, cremation, or gift of body parts. Further, the customer can play no part in the postdeath delivery system.

---

[6] Levitt coined this term in his classic article by the same name, "Production-Line Approach to Service," *Harvard Business Review,* Vol. 50, No. 5 (September–October 1972), pp. 41–52.

_____ EXHIBIT 4–4 _____

■ *Customer Participation in the Design of High-Contact Service Bundles*

(a) **Participation in Design** such as pre-arranged funeral services, or cosmetic surgery

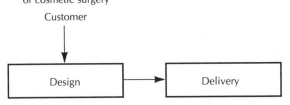

(b) **Participation in Delivery** such as Stress test for cardiac exam, or delivery of a baby

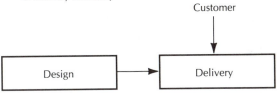

(c) **Participation in Design and Delivery** such as counseling, seminar, financial management of personal affairs, or interior decorating

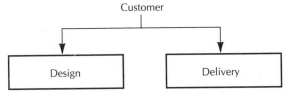

An example of the second case is an electrocardiogram analysis, in which there is high contact between the service provider and the client during the service delivery, but the client has had no input into the design of the test. More dramatically, in the delivery of a baby, the procedure has been established by the provider, but the client is heavily involved in the delivery.

In the third case, counseling services, personal financial management, and interior decorating typify the high-contact simultaneous design and delivery of a service in which the customer participates in both the design and the delivery of the service.

Design and Specification Processes

When the customer participates in the design process only, the service supplier usually has designed a menu of services from which the customer selects options. At this point, the customer also may modify the design of the services he or she is to receive. Design specs may take the form of a contract or a narrative description with photos (e.g., for cosmetic surgery).

When the customer participates in the delivery of the service only, the provider of the service either designs the service or provides a service designed by someone else. The customer has essentially purchased a service that is predesigned to give each customer the same experience. Design specs take the form of well-developed written procedures. Even so, the results of the service process cannot always be predicted because the service *experience* varies by customer. In addition, during the delivery process, either the provider or the customer may modify the service design.

Finally, when the client participates in both design and delivery, the provider of the service typically develops a conceptual design and works with the client in evolving a detailed design as part of service delivery. In this case, the design cannot be specified exactly. For example, in educational seminars, the desired result is agreed on by the provider and the client, possibly in a written contract. Certain aspects of the service design are typically written down in advance, such as the seminar outline, hours and place of meeting, responsibilities of the provider and attendees, and utilization of learning aids, but the content of the seminar or the speed and manner in which it is delivered may change as the service provider (seminar speaker) interacts with the seminar attendees.

SUMMARY

Designing involves developing new patterns or arrangements. It is both a creative and an analytical process. Its output includes methods for communicating the design to those producing the product or providing the service.

The design of a service starts with performance specifications that must be converted into design specifications. The major steps in design are

— Accumulation of information
— Development of conceptual alternatives
— Design and testing of prototypes
— Final design drawings and specifications.

The design of services differs depending on whether the service is standardized or involves high customer contact.

The outputs of service design are design specifications. These differ from product design specifications in that they are primarily narrative and represent the customer's experience with the service process.

DISCUSSION QUESTIONS

1. What is a service bundle?

2. How do performance and design specifications differ?

3. How can project management aid in the design process?

4. Generate several innovative ideas for providing services that will satisfy the customer in each of the following situations:

  a. Increased need for higher education opportunities

  b. Overcrowded prison population

  c. Inadequate health care in rural areas

  d. Low test scores of children in primary grades

5. List several ways that efficiency can be improved by designing a service so that the customer is separated from the service process.

6. What type of information would you gather in designing the following services?
    a. A laundromat
    b. A child care center
    c. A private postal service

7. Describe typical performance specifications for the following services:
    a. A city's refuse service
    b. A seminar on quality assurance
    c. The mathematics program for public kindergarten

8. How does the design process differ for mass services and high-contact services?

9. Using the three elements of a service bundle given by Sasser, classify the following experiences of a restaurant customer:
    a. Menu selection
    b. Size of portions
    c. Quality of cooking
    d. Waiting times
    e. Attitudes of employees
    f. Hours and days of operation
    g. Payment methods
    h. Cleanliness
    i. Entertainment

10. "The most important thing to know about intangible products is that the customers usually don't know what they're getting until they don't get it" (Levitt, 1980). What does this statement imply about the risks of designing new services or improving existing services?

11. Discuss the problems, strategies, and outcomes or prospects for the following companies and their new services.
    a. Federal Express' ZapMail
    b. ServiceMaster's lawncare franchise
    c. Walt Disney World's new hotels, nightclubs, and shopping center
    d. Marriott's line of retirement homes

▬ READING 4.1 ▬

The Technocratic Hamburger

Nowhere in the entire service sector are the possibilities of the manufacturing mode of thinking better illustrated than in fast-food franchising. Nowhere have manufacturing methods been employed more effectively to control the operation of distant and independent agents. Nowhere is "service" better. The thriving nationwide chain of hamburger stands called "McDonald's" is a supreme example of the application of manufacturing and technological brilliance to problems that must ultimately be viewed as marketing problems.

The explanation of McDonald's thundering success is not a purely fiscal one—i.e., the argument that it is financed by independent local entrepreneurs who bring to their operations a quality of commitment and energy not commonly found among hired workers. Nor is it a purely geographic one—i.e., the argument that each outlet draws its patronage from a relatively small geographic ring of customers, thus enabling the number of outlets easily and quickly to multiply. The relevant explanation must deal with the central question of why each separate McDonald's outlet is so predictably successful, why each is so certain to attract many repeat customers.

Entrepreneurial financing and careful size selection do help. But most important is the carefully controlled execution of each outlet's central function—the rapid delivery of a uniform, high-quality mix of prepared foods in an environment of obvious cleanliness, order, and cheerful courtesy. The systematic substitution of equipment for people, com-

---

bined with the carefully planned use and positioning of technology, enables McDonald's to attract and hold patronage in proportions no predecessor or imitator has managed to duplicate. Consider the remarkable ingenuity of the system, which is worth examining in some detail.

To start with the obvious, raw hamburger patties are carefully prepacked and premeasured, which leaves neither the franchisee nor his employees any discretion as to size, quality, or raw-material consistency. This kind of attention is given to all McDonald's products. Storage and preparation space and related facilities are expressly designed for, and limited to, the predetermined mix of products. There is no space for any foods, beverages, or services that were not designed into the system at the outset. There is not even a sandwich knife or, in fact, a decent place to keep one. Thus the owner has no discretion regarding what he can sell—not because of any contractual limitations, but because of facilities limitations. And the employees have virtually no discretion regarding how to prepare and serve things.

Discretion is the enemy of order, standardization, and quality. On an automobile assembly line, for example, a worker who has discretion and latitude might possibly produce a more personalized car, but one that is highly unpredictable. The elaborate care with which an automobile is designed and an assembly line is structured and controlled is what produces quality cars at low prices, and with surprising reliability considering the sheer volume of the output. The same is true at McDonald's, which produces food under highly automated and controlled conditions.

FRENCH-FRIED AUTOMATION

While in Detroit the significance of the technological process lies in production, at McDonald's it lies in marketing. A carefully planned design is built into the elaborate technology of the food-service system in such a fashion as to make it a significant marketing device. This fact is impressively illustrated by McDonald's handling of that uniquely plebeian American delicacy, french-fried potatoes.

French fries quickly become soggy and unappetizing; to be good, they must be freshly made just before serving. Like other fast-food establishments, McDonald's provides its outlets with precut, partially cooked frozen potatoes that can be quickly finished in an on-premises, deep-fry facility. The McDonald's fryer is neither so large that it produces too many french fries at one time (thus allowing them to become soggy) nor so small that it requires frequent and costly frying.

The fryer is emptied onto a wide, flat tray adjacent to the service counter. This location is crucial. Since the McDonald's practice is to create an impression of abundance and generosity by slightly overfilling each bag of french fries, the tray's location next to the service counter prevents the spillage from an overfilled bag from reaching the floor. Spillage creates not only danger underfoot but also an unattractive appearance that causes the employees to become accustomed to an unclean environment. Once a store is unclean in one particular [area], standards fall very rapidly and the store becomes unclean and the food unappetizing in general.

While McDonald's aims for an impression of abundance, excessive overfilling can be very costly for a company that annually buys potatoes almost by the trainload. A systematic bias that puts into each bag of french fries a half ounce more than is intended can have visible effects on the company's annual earnings. Further, excessive time spent at the tray by each employee can create a cumulative service bottleneck at the counter.

McDonald's has therefore developed a special wide-mouthed scoop with a narrow funnel in its handle. The counter employee picks up the scoop and inserts the handle end into a wall clip containing the bags. One bag adheres to the handle. In a continuous movement the scoop descends into the potatoes, fills the bag to the exact proportions its designers intended, and is lifted, scoop facing the ceiling, so that the potatoes funnel through the handle into the attached bag, which is automatically disengaged from the handle by the weight of the contents. The bag comes to a steady, non-wobbling rest on its flat bottom.

Nothing can go wrong—the employee never soils his hands, the floor remains clean, dry, and safe, and the quantity is controlled. Best of all, the customer gets a visibly generous portion with great speed, the employee remains efficient and cheerful, and the general impression is one of extravagantly good service.

MECHANIZED MARKETING

Consider the other aspects of McDonald's technological approach to marketing. The tissue paper used to wrap each hamburger is color-coded to denote the mix of condiments. Heated reservoirs hold pre-prepared hamburgers for rush demand. Frying surfaces have spatter guards to prevent soiling of the cooks' uniforms. Nothing is left to chance or the employees' discretion.

The entire system is engineered and executed according to a tight technological discipline that ensures fast, clean, reliable service in an atmosphere that gives the modestly paid employees a sense of pride and dignity. In spite of the crunch of eager customers, no employee looks or acts harassed, and therefore no harassment is communicated to the customers.

What is important to understand about this remarkably successful organization is not only that it has created a highly sophisticated piece of technology, but also that it has done this by applying a manufacturing style of thinking to a people-intensive service situation. If machinery is to be viewed as a piece of equipment with the capability of producing a predictably standardized, customer-satisfying output while minimizing the operating

discretion of its attendant, that is what a McDonald's retail outlet is. It is a machine that produces, with the help of totally unskilled machine tenders, a highly polished product. Through painstaking attention to total design and facilities planning, everything is built integrally into the machine itself, into the technology of the system. The only choice available to the attendant is to operate it exactly as the designers intended.

_____ QUESTIONS FOR READING 4.1

1. What are the characteristics of the McDonald's "product" that make it successful?

2. Explain how the design of the product and the design of the service delivery are intertwined in the McDonald's example.

3. McDonald's approach to assembly-line service has become the norm for the fast-food industry. There are, however, variations to their approach that competitors emphasize as a marketing tool. How do the design of the product, design of the service, and design of the service delivery system differ for a company such as Wendy's? In other words, how are the marketing strategies of Wendy's versus McDonald's reflected in their product/service/delivery system design?

_____ READING 4.2 _____

What an Idea!

Fresh out of ideas? Why not call TIM? TIM, The Idea Machine, is a unique computer program developed by Virginia Tech professor John Dickey to stimulate thinking and aid in problem solving. He spent six years developing the concept, with assistance from some top thinkers among students and faculty.

"TIM uses the latest in computer, video, and audio technology," said Dickey, a professor who holds joint appointments in the College of Architecture and Urban Studies and the Center for Public

Administration and Policy (CPAP). "It generates ideas through comparisons with other situations and through stimuli of sight, sound, and smell." The program combines research in artificial intelligence, business-decision making, and policy analysis and explores vast data resources to seek new or innovative ideas.

It works something like this: The system is fed several descriptor words, words from a list of 200—Dickey is increasing the number to 1000—that most closely describe the problem. TIM can then

Source: Clara B. Cox, Virginia Tech Public Affairs Officer, in *Virginia Tech*, Vol. 10, No. 1 (Fall 1987), pp. 28–29. Reprinted with permission.

search for these words in 16 sources of concepts. The source could be an electronic encyclopedia or a list of unique facts garnered from such places as Ripley's *Believe It or Not,* Asimov's *Book of Facts,* and *2001 Fascinating Facts.* Or the source could be a list of general concepts—with such offerings as "turn it upside down" or "stretch it"—or a list of synonyms or even Proverbs. Or, maybe, a videodisc on astronomy, earth science, or how to watch pro football.

If your thought processes are stimulated by great works of art, Dickey currently has an artist writing descriptions of the National Gallery of Art inventory so that TIM can show you a painting whose description includes your descriptor words. For those whose mental vision is broadened by music, TIM will play any of a number of unusual selections, providing, of course, that the descriptor words appear in the description of the selection held in memory by TIM. Just for fun, for the time being, anyway, TIM's creator also can titillate your thought processes with a set of aroma discs—roses, gingerbread, or even a candlelight dinner, for example. "Actually, these smells can trigger an idea by bringing out long lost memories, maybe even from your childhood," Dickey notes.

One problem Dickey ran through TIM was how to reduce prison overcrowding. Some of the ideas generated on reducing prison overcrowding came from an electronic encyclopedia. TIM pulled up the concept "electronic funds accounting" from that source, "which suggested to us that overcrowding could be reduced by having prisoners released on their own recognizance but having to wear leg bracelets, which would account for their location, especially relative to other offenders wearing the same device."

Not only does TIM generate ideas, the program also can help in evaluating the ideas and weighing them in importance. According to Dickey, "most individual problems relate to several goals, not just one. In the prison case, for instance, there is a need to keep costs down, protect the public, and both rehabilitate and punish prisoners. TIM helps decision makers decide on the relative importance and likelihood of achieving each of these goals." As if all this were not enough, TIM can even develop reports at each stage of the process. And the reports can include pictures printed from the videodiscs.

Dickey has used TIM in a variety of problem-solving efforts; for example, uses for old railroad ties, scheduling of hospital staffs, builder avoidance of inspection costs, handicapped employability, and business stability in low-income neighborhoods. He is particularly proud of an idea TIM stimulated to develop an inexpensive procedure for fault testing very large scale integrated (VLSI) chips. The idea, to do a CAT or BEAM scan on the chip, had not been used before. "Three weeks after the exercise, *Popular Science* published an article showing infrared scanning for certain chip faults. Since this was similar, we knew we were on the right track."

Dickey is also getting ideas from TIM on how to market his one-of-a-kind product, which probably won't be available outside Dickey's Idea Salon, which now serves as TIM's home, for a few more months. But first, he wants to expand the information bank for the program. And he intends to integrate the various components into one piece of furniture. For now, Dickey will take problems over the phone, or he will let a client use TIM in the Idea Salon. Most problems, he said, can be dealt with in up to six hours.

He expects his creation to revolutionize problem solving, especially in areas where creativity is essential. He also predicts that Idea Salons will one day spring up in every city, much like photocopying services during the last decade. Wonder if he got that idea from TIM?

﹘﹘﹘ QUESTIONS FOR READING 4.2

1. Describe how The Idea Machine might be used to design a service.

2. What advice would you give Dickey for marketing his product/service? In other words, in what *form* should the product/service be offered to the customer?

3. How would technological advances affect the design of TIM? Consider how the information databases should be updated or how new databases should be introduced, the compatibility of TIM software with changing hardware, and the emergence of new hardware that encourages creativity.

4. Discuss how your answers to Questions 2 and 3 support the notion that design of a service and design of service delivery are closely related.

—— CASE 4.1 ————————————————————————————

The Corner Drug Store, Inc.

Despite its name, The Corner Drug Store does not sell drugs or fill prescriptions. Rather its purpose is to help prevent sales and use of illegal drugs by children and young adults. This nonprofit organization was founded in the 1960s in Gainesville, Florida, to provide a place where those who had been caught up in the drug-using customs of the "hippy generation" could go or be taken for professional assistance and counseling. Located in a frame house in a residential area about two blocks from the main entrance to the University of Florida, its clients were mostly students. Over ensuing years, the organization's emphasis has shifted from crisis "handling" to crisis prevention. Because of this shift, plus changing conditions in the community, its clientele consists increasingly of teenage adolescents. The services offered by CDS have been expanded to include, in addition to substance-use intervention, a runaway shelter for youths in crisis and a prevention educational campaign directed toward youths in schools and in the community. It recently acquired more modern and adequate facilities and is coordinating its services with other agencies serving young people and their families within the city, in adjacent counties, in the state of Florida, and throughout the southeastern region of the United States.

CDS derives its operating funds of over $900,000 from a variety of sources: state appropriations—49 percent; federal funds—20 percent; United Way and other contributions from individuals and business firms—7 percent; fees for counseling and other services received from those who can pay—5 percent; and in kind—19 percent. State and federal funds are allocated for specific programs that are carried out by CDS on terms acceptable to the agency giving the grant. "In kind" revenues are the money value of the services received from volunteers and the use of nonowned physical facilities.

The affairs of the Corner Drug Store are the responsibility of a self-perpetuating board of directors. Its members are chosen to be representative of groups or organizations in Gainesville who would be interested in its work and/or could provide advice and assistance. Currently there are representatives from the university faculty; educational, medical and religious communities; and law enforcement agencies. New members are suggested by current members, their qualifications are presented, and if approved, invitations are made. Minority members are sought.

The board appoints the director and associate director, who are in charge of carrying out its stated policies and supervising day-to-day operations. They also select other staff members and volunteers, most of whom are students in appropriate fields at the university. Paid staff members have appropriate degrees and experience. CDS has been fortunate in having had executive directors with genuinely good administrative skills. The planning and executing of programs and the relationships with personnel, clients, funding agencies, and other youth-oriented groups have progressed smoothly over the past few years.

At a recent board meeting, after listening to favorable reports on the achievements of the Corner Drug Store, a board member asked this question: "But how do we know whether or not we are doing the task that is most needed?" He described Theodore Levitt's famous concept of "marketing myopia." Levitt maintained that the railroads lost out to trucks and airlines because their managers forgot that their firms were in the business of supplying transportation not just running trains; the moving picture industry lost to television because it thought its purpose was to make movies not provide the public with entertainment. "Are we," asked the board member, "helping young people to significantly improve the quality of their lives by avoiding crises? Or, perhaps, are we simply running a smooth nonprofit operation that has happy employees, balanced books, professional upwardly mobile managers, and a board of directors who has found a rewarding hobby?" He went on to point out that for a profit-making organization there is the famous "bottom line." If a railroad or a film producer is not meeting some needs of its market, sales and profits will decline. But the revenues of the Corner Drug Store are dependent on

---

Source: This case was prepared by Ralph B. Thompson, Professor Emeritus, The University of Florida.

what someone or some organization thinks it will take to do a stated job. CDS may complete tasks efficiently, but how does it know for sure if the task is needed?

As a "reward" for raising this issue, the outspoken board member was appointed chairman of a program committee to try and evaluate the success of CDS programs in meeting the needs of the community—in other words, to *define the bottom line.*

QUESTIONS FOR CASE 4.1

1. Describe the service bundle that CDS provides to a typical customer. Think of ways to evaluate CDS's performance at each stage of the service experience.

2. Who are the customers of CDS? Whom does CDS serve? Who pays for the services CDS provides?

3. Now put yourself in the place of the newly appointed chairman of the program committee for CDS.

a. Suggest possible definitions of a bottom line for the nonprofit social service agency.

b. What types of internal and external information would you need to determine a bottom line for CDS? How would you go about getting that information?

c. Regardless of whether the findings of the committee are positive or negative, how should they be incorporated into future policymaking at CDS?

REFERENCES

Chase, Richard B., and Nicholas J. Aquilano. *Production and Operations Management,* 5th Ed. Homewood, Ill.: Irwin-Dorsey, 1989.

Dumaine, B. "Corporate Spies Stoop to Conquer," *Fortune,* November 7, 1988, pp. 68–76.

Fitzsimmons, James A., and Robert S. Sullivan. *Service Operations Management.* New York: McGraw-Hill, 1982.

Gillett, Tom F. "New Ways of Understanding Consumers' Service Needs," *Creativity in Services Marketing,* Proceedings Series. Chicago: American Marketing Association, 1986.

Heskett, James L. *Managing in the Service Economy.* Boston: Harvard Business School Press, 1986.

Heskett, James L. "Lessons in the Service Sector," *Harvard Business Review,* Vol. 65, No. 2 (March–April 1987), pp. 118–126.

Horne, David A., John P. McDonald, and David Williams. "Consumer Perceptions of Service Dimensions: Implication for Marketing Strategy," *Creativity in Services Marketing,* Proceedings Series. Chicago: American Marketing Association, 1986.

Jones, J. Christopher. *Design Methods.* New York: Wiley, 1970.

Karger, Delmar W., and Robert G. Murdick. *Managing Engineering and Research,* 3d Ed. New York: Industrial Press, 1980.

Landeard, Eric, Patrick Reffait, and Pierre Eiglier. "Developing New Services," *Creativity in Services Marketing,* Proceedings Series. Chicago: American Marketing Association, 1986.

Lesh, A. Dawn. "Using Consumers To Guide the Way to Design New Services," *Creativity in Services Marketing,* Proceedings Series. Chicago: American Marketing Association, 1986.

Levitt, Theodore. "Production-Line Approach to Service," *Harvard Business Review,* Vol. 50, No. 5 (September–October 1972), pp. 41–52.

Murdick, Robert G., and John J. Smith. *Production/ Operations Management for Small Business.* Worthington, Ohio: Publishing Horizons, 1982.

Northcraft, Gregory B., and Richard B. Chase. "Managing Service Demand at the Point of Delivery," *Academy of Management Review,* Vol. 10, No. 1 (January 1985), pp. 66–75.

Rethans, Arno J., Alissa D. Roberts, and Thomas W. Leigh. "Toward a Research Cycle for New Service Development," *Creativity in Services Marketing,* Proceedings Series. Chicago: American Marketing Association, 1986.

Sasser, W. Earl, R. Paul Olsen, and D. Daryl Wyckoff. *Management of Service Operations.* Boston: Allyn and Bacon, 1978.

Scheuing, E. E., and E. M. Johnson. "New Product Management in Service Industries: An Early Assessment." In *Add Value to Your Services,* Proceedings of the Sixth Annual Services Marketing Conference. Chicago, Ill.: American Marketing Association, 1987, pp. 91–95.

Sigafoos, R. A., and R. R. Easson, *Absolutely Positively Overnight.* Memphis, Tenn.: St. Lukes Press, 1988.

Voss, C., C. Armistead, B. Johnson, and B. Morris. *Operations Management in Service Industries and the Public Sector.* New York: Wiley, 1985.

5

Service Process Planning and Equipment Selection

INTRODUCTION

The service process refers to *how* a service is provided or delivered to a customer. Service systems use various resources, including materials, equipment, and people, to facilitate the service process. Therefore, **service process planning** must consider the selection of conversion processes, materials, equipment, and skills. Specifically, strategic decisions must be made with respect to

—Primary technological process
—Materials and conversion process
—Specific equipment
—Process flow for conversion
—Employee skills and job content
—Site location and selection
—Buildings and facilities
—Facility layout and work flow
—Organizational structure and sociopsychological factors

THE PRIMARY CONVERSION SYSTEM

The first five areas just listed represent the primary conversion system, which is the topic of this chapter. The last four areas are discussed in Chapters 6, 7, and 9, respectively. The primary conversion system is shown in relation to the total service delivery system in Exhibit 5–1. The principal decisions for a primary conversion system are amplified in the following sections.

_____ EXHIBIT 5–1 _____

■ *Decisions for the Design of a Productive System*

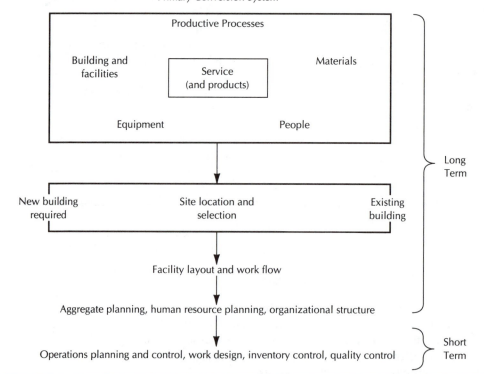

Primary Technological Decision

The primary technological decision involves answering the following question: Is the technology available, or can it be developed, to provide the materials, processes, and equipment to make the product or deliver the service? For example, at one time it was possible to design printed electronic circuits on small chips, but the technology and specific equipment required to produce the chips were beyond the state of the art.

In the case of services, satellite transmission was conceived of long before the capability of constructing the system was available. In the field of medicine, many services such as joint replacements have had to wait for the advance of technology.

In some cases, technology exists, but not in "consumerized" form. Consider that the telephone, invented in 1876, was not widely accepted by the public until 15 years later. What was missing? In 1891, the telephone dial was invented, making the new technology easy for the consumer to use. Telephone "service" could now be provided in the form consumers had envisioned.

Conversion/Materials Decision

The choice of conversion process is complex because it depends on technological and market factors, as well as economic considerations. Typically, there are many alternative processes and materials that will satisfy the design specifications. For example, suppose we need to reproduce some written material. We might select an office copier to reproduce 10 copies of a single page or we might use a letterpress to produce 200,000 copies of a single-page advertising leaflet. As another example, if we need to transfer information to a customer in hardcopy form, we might use overnight delivery services, facsimile transfer, or electronic transfer. Selection among these alternative processes is based on such factors as cost, timeliness of delivery, quality of the delivered service, availability of the technology, ease of using the technology, and customer preference.

An extensive example of conversion process selection at a savings and loan company is described by Northcraft and Chase.[1] The example involves three different service offerings (account transactions, check cashing, and CDs), three service processes (ATM, teller, or branch officer), and three types of customers (A, B, and C). Exhibit 5–2 illustrates how the modes of delivery, services offered, and types of customers may be matched in terms of three possible channels for service delivery. Customer type A uses an ATM for account transactions, customer type B asks a live teller to cash a check, and customer type C invests in a CD with the help of a branch officer. Exhibit 5–3 shows that *efficiency* is achieved when the conversion process is specialized; that is, when each person or machine supplying a service is dedicated to providing that specific service. *Effectiveness,* however, is achieved by flexibility in the conversion process. In other words, service providers should supply the broadest range of services they can. An ATM may only be capable of making account transactions, but a teller should be able to cash checks as well as process account transactions. Similarly, a branch officer should be capable of providing all bank services.

---

[1] See G. B. Northcraft and R. B. Chase, "Managing Service Demand at the Point of Delivery," *Academy of Management Review,* Vol. 10, No. 1 (January 1985), pp. 66–75.

----- EXHIBIT 5–2 --

■ *Managing Demand at the Point of Delivery. Example: Savings and Loan Company*

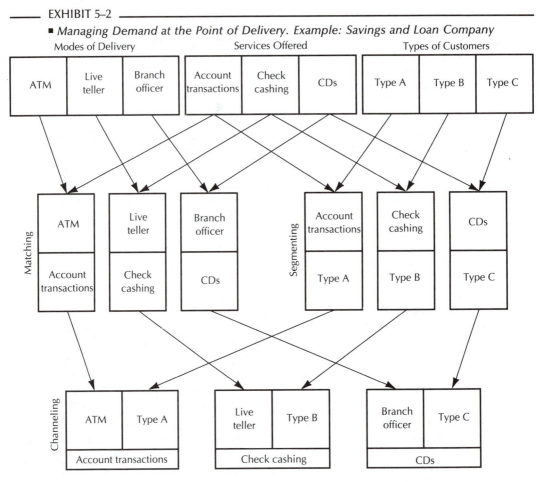

ATM = automatic teller machine; CDs = certificates of deposit; Type A = customers making deposits and withdrawals; Type B = customers cashing checks; Type C = customers purchasing CDs.

Source: G. B. Northcraft and R. B. Chase, "Managing Service Demand at the Point of Delivery," *Academy of Management Review* (January 1985), p. 70. Used with permission of the authors and publisher.

Specific Equipment Decision

The selection of specific equipment is not a decision to be made at the lowest level of management. Investment in capital items is a strategic decision that should be fitted within the guidelines of the strategic plan and approved by top management. Important questions to address when selecting equipment include

- Will this equipment be useful in producing both present and anticipated products and services over the next few years?

—— EXHIBIT 5–3 ——————————————————————

- *Efficiency and Effectiveness Mappings for Managing Demand at the Point of Delivery. Example: Savings and Loan Company*

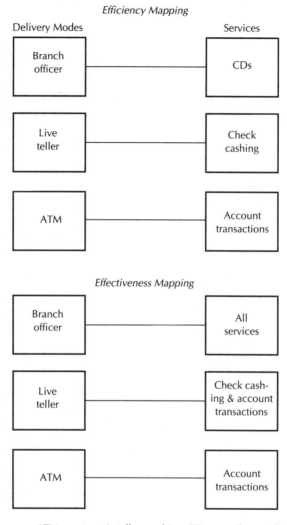

ATM = automatic teller machine; CDs = certificates of deposit.

Source: G. B. Northcraft and R. B. Chase, "Managing Service Demand at the Point of Delivery," *Academy of Management Review* (January 1985), p. 72. Used with permission of the authors and publisher.

- Does this selection match the strategy of utilizing equipment for lowering short-term operating costs?
- Is this equipment compatible with the materials selection and suitable for the tradeoff between capital intensity and labor intensity?
- Do capital investment analyses show that the selection will be profitable?
- Will special training be required for operators or can unskilled operators be used? Who will do the training, the company or the vendor?
- Will spare parts be readily available?
- What maintenance program will be required?
- What is the safety rating of the equipment?

Equipment selection is discussed in more detail later in the chapter.

Process Flow Decision

The process flow decision is obviously related to the conversion/materials decision and specific equipment decision. In fact, it integrates the two decisions. The sequencing of operations is dependent on the functions that particular equipment or people will perform. The mix of people and machines also affects the specification of work flow. An analysis of the proposed process flow, in turn, may lead to a revision in the selection of conversion processes, materials, or equipment. The process flow decision is developed on the basis of flow process charts described later in this chapter.

People Decisions

Decisions regarding people involve determining the number of people, the skills required, and labor cost relative to capital cost *in the long run*. Too often people decisions are made on the assumption that workers may be hired one day, used a few months, laid off, and rehired whenever needed. The need to have a knowledgeable, continuous, involved, and motivated work force is overlooked. People provide ideas, whereas machines do not. Machines have limited adaptability for change, but people can be trained to perform many tasks. Therefore, people decisions must be closely related to equipment and process flow decisions. Chapter 8 on aggregate planning discusses alternatives for planning and utilizing manpower.

Another important aspect of people decisions involves structuring the *content* of people's jobs. This is best illustrated by an example. Jan Carlzon relates this story of job restructuring at SAS airlines:[2]

> Let's say that you've pre-ordered a special vegetarian meal for your SAS flight from Stockholm to New York. Nervously, you approach the check-in counter to find out whether your meal has been delivered to the plane.
>
> "I don't know," the agent sighs. "I'm sorry, but I'm busy, and I'm not familiar with the food service."
>
> "But what can I do?" you ask.
>
> "You'll have to ask at the gate," she replies. "They'll certainly be able to help you there."

[2] Jan Carlzon, *Moments of Truth* (Cambridge, Mass.: Ballinger, 1987), pp. 61–63.

The agent quickly moves on to help the next person in line. Given no alternative, you go to the gate and ask again.

The gate attendant is friendly, but he doesn't know where your meal is either. "I wish I could help, but I don't have anything to do with food service. Just check with the stewardess when you get on board and things should certainly work out."

Reluctantly, you board the plane. When you ask the stewardess about your vegetarian meal, she is bewildered. She hasn't heard anything about special food orders, but the plane is about to take off and nothing can be done now. "You should have contacted us earlier," she reprimands. "There would have been no problem if only we had known in time."

Let's now suppose that the organization has changed [the content of its jobs] by putting a team of people in charge of the Stockholm–New York flight from start to finish.

The team has 15 members, two of whom function as "coaches," one indoors and one out by the plane. The indoor coach sits in on the flight crew's briefing and consults with them about pre-flight information such as the appropriate time to begin boarding, whether any infants . . . are on the passenger list, and whether anyone has ordered a special meal.

In the morning, the indoor team assembles at the check-in counters to solve passengers' ticketing problems, assign seats, handle fragile baggage, and so forth. When a mother arrives with her baby, she is . . . told that a suspended cradle has already been put on board and that the seat beside hers will be kept free if at all possible.

When you arrive at check-in and ask about your vegetarian meal, you won't be hurriedly dismissed by the agent behind the counter. Thanks to the new team arrangement, your meal request becomes that agent's responsibility. She can confirm that it is already on board—or take steps to make sure it's loaded by the time you step into the plane.

As more and more passengers check in, the SAS team gradually moves to the departure gate, where they nod to their passengers in recognition. They are well acquainted with the flight to New York and can answer all the usual questions: how to transfer from JFK to La Guardia, why there is a stopover in Oslo, the actual flight time, and whether the captain will announce when they are flying over Greenland.

Problems are solved on the spot, as soon as they arise. No frontline employee has to wait for a supervisor's permission. No passenger boards the plane while still worried or dissatisfied.

Thus SAS airlines was able to make intelligent people decisions because its management (1) examined the service process from the customer's point of view and (2) redefined the responsibilities of its personnel to support the service process.

FLOWCHARTS TO DESIGN THE PRIMARY CONVERSION SYSTEM

Flowcharts are diagrams consisting of pictorial symbols connected by directed line segments. Their purpose is to show the sequencing of activities, operations, tasks, materials flow, data/information flow, people movement, logic flow, or authority flow in organizations. They are almost essential in designing and describing the design of services and other productive systems. Alternatives to flowcharts include lists of procedures or lengthy narratives. Neither of these alternative methods can compare with the visual portrayal of processing events found in flowcharts, nor can they easily show the parallel operations so common in service systems. For these reasons, a considerable part of this chapter is dedicated to describing different types of flowcharts and their use in service firms.

Flow Process Charts

The flow process chart is the primary tool for developing and describing the conversion system. It provides two essential types of information about the conversion process:

— The actions performed on materials, information, or people in providing the service'
— The relationships among processes

Relationships refer to the order in which actions are performed, what processes have to be performed first, which can be performed in parallel, and what has to be completed before the next step can begin.

For flow process charts, five standardized pictorial symbols are used to describe the processes. These are (1) operations, (2) transportation, (3) inspection, (4) storage, and (5) delay, as shown in Exhibit 5–4. The chart can track the flow of products, customers, or information. An example of a flow process chart for mortgage application and approval is given in Exhibit 5–5. In this example, the flows of information and paperwork for a particular customer are charted.

Flow process charts often include data on the distance a customer or item is moved, the time required to process a customer or item, and the time a customer or item spends waiting. This additional information helps managers to analyze the efficiency of a specified order of operations. Hopefully, tasks can be identified that should be eliminated, combined, resequenced, or simplified. Often the flow process chart is also superimposed on a floor plan of a facility as an aid to improving facility layout and eliminating bottlenecks.

EXHIBIT 5–4

■ *Flow Process Chart Symbols*

Operations, such as performed by a lathe in a machine shop or a hair dryer in a beauty shop

Transportation, such as movement of materials, information, or people

Inspection, such as moisture measurement of paper in a paper mill or a microfilm viewer in a bank for comparing signatures on checks to signatures on file; verification of an object for quality or quantity

Storage, such as refrigeration units in manufacturing or services, vats in chemical processing, or filing cabinets in service firms

Delay, such as papers waiting on a manager's desk to be signed or customers waiting in line at a bank

—— EXHIBIT 5–5 ——————————————————————

■ *Flow Process Chart for Mortgage Application and Approval*

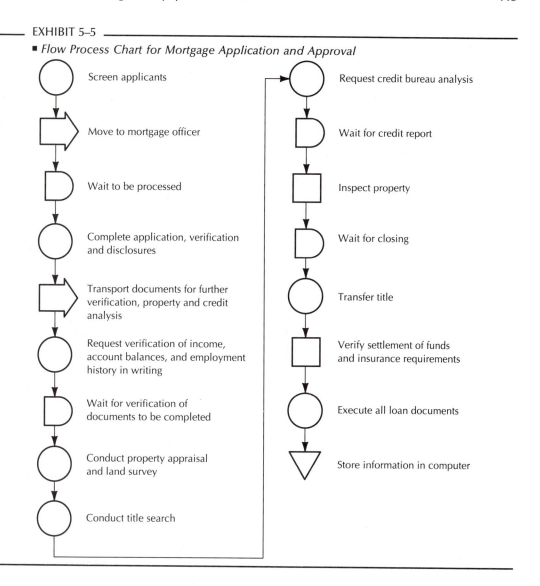

Flow process charting is so popular that standard templates, forms, and computerized versions are available for a manager's use. Less formalized approaches to charting the service process are also common and go by a variety of names. Exhibit 5–6 is such a modified flow process chart dubbed by its author a "blueprint" for discount brokerage operations.[3]

Referring to Exhibit 5–6, the vast majority of these operations are "backroom," that is, invisible to the customer, as denoted by the area beneath the line of visibility.

[3] See G. L. Shostack, "Designing Services that Deliver," *Harvard Business Review*, Vol. 62, No. 1 (January–February 1984), p. 133–139.

EXHIBIT 5–6

■ *Blueprint for Discount Brokerage*

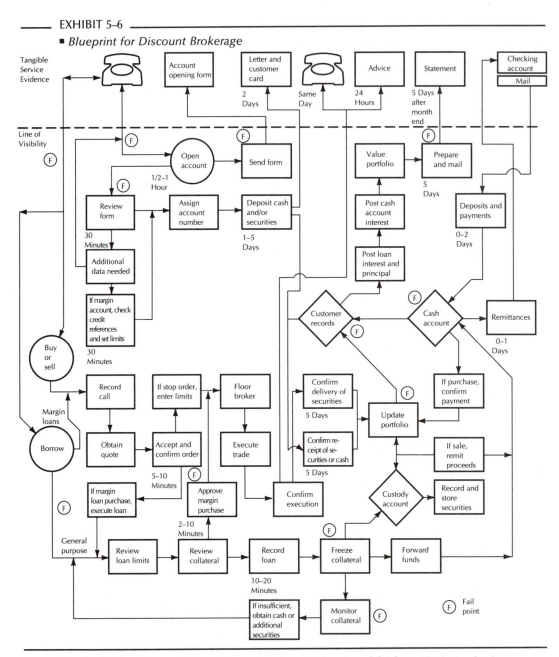

Notice that the chart also includes the expected time to complete various operations and identifies fail points as areas that require special attention or additional resources so that problems may be avoided.

While process charting is not a technique that optimizes the steps in a process, it does present information in a manner that allows the manager to analyze the way a product is being produced or a service is being delivered. After a process has been analyzed thoroughly and is acceptable to management, flow process charts are also useful in standardizing the order of operations for the many employees, often in diverse locations, who must perform that job. Finally, flow process charts are used to train new personnel in the standard operating procedures that have been developed.

Reading 5.1 is a detailed account of how one bank analyzed its process flow and significantly improved its letter-of-credit operations.

Information System Flowcharts

Information system flowcharts present the flow of information in the form of documents, voice, or electronic transmission, as well as actions taken on the information. These information flows may be represented at different levels of detail. Exhibit 5–7 illustrates an information systems flowchart at the conceptual level known as a **block diagram.** In the exhibit, the planning system for a utility company is portrayed as the interactions among eight different planning models.

An example of a detailed system level information flowchart is given in Exhibit 5–8. This exhibit shows the processes and documents involved in accepting, registering, billing, and reporting grades for university students. Standard symbols used for information system flowcharting are shown in Exhibit 5–9.

Examples of Service Flowcharts

Manufacturing consists of changing the form of tangible materials. Therefore, the inputs, process, and outputs may be generalized for the productive system. For services, however, the inputs, processes, and outputs vary so much that there is no representative generalization. For example, an airline produces several diverse *outputs,* including transported people, in-flight services and food, cargo services, and ramp services. On the other hand, a hospital's *inputs* are infinitely variable depending on the people processed for tests, surgery, and other treatments. The output is a ''completed'' patient, either recovered, sent to another health care institution, or deceased.

Flowcharts are helpful in visualizing the various *input-transformation-output* processes of services. Exhibit 5–10 shows a flowchart of some typical bank processes. Banks are unusual in that they process three widely different inputs: people, information (representing transfer of funds), and monetary assets (money and gold). The services they provide serve business, government, and individuals. The flowchart is designed to illustrate how the most common bank services are executed. Specifically, it shows tellers and other bank employees what tasks need to be performed and in what order. It also shows the flow of information and cash between customer and service provider.

Exhibit 5–11 shows the ''front office'' process for a car rental company. The

EXHIBIT 5–7

■ *Block Diagram of Utility Planning System*

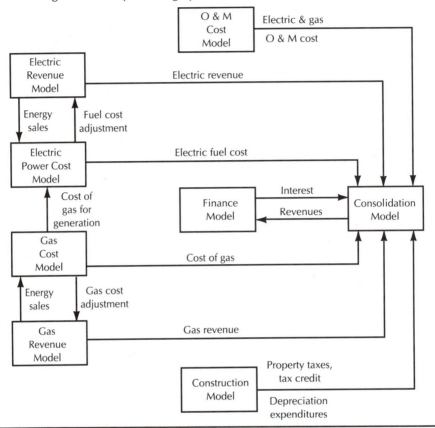

Source: D. H. Swanson, "Planning for Electricity to Avoid Shock," *Planning Review* (November 1986). Used with permission.

principal services in the conversion process are transportation and reservation services. Asterisks on the chart indicate points of customer contact. Notice that the chart follows the processing of both the car and the customer.

We might consider the steps in the conversion process for restaurants, motels, beauty shops, landscapers, express-mail systems, computer service companies, security guard companies, real estate companies, insurance companies, brokerage houses, and others. For each, the conversion process varies widely. A common denominator of many service systems is that people and/or information are the inputs that are processed.

SELECTION OF EQUIPMENT

Equipment selection, or more broadly, technology selection, is an important decision for any firm. It must fully support the design of the product or service, it creates the

───── EXHIBIT 5–8 ───

■ *System-Level Information Flowchart for a University Student System*

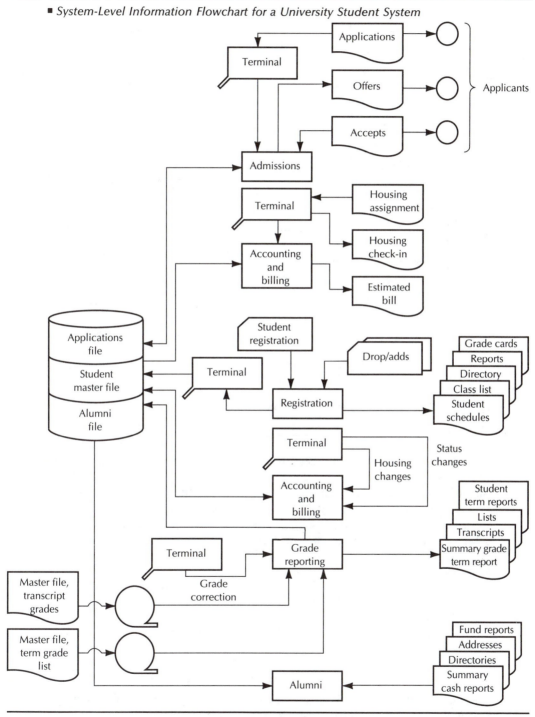

Source: Robert G. Murdick, *MIS: Concepts and Design*, 2d Ed., © 1986, p. 452. Reprinted by permission of Prentice Hall, Inc., Englewood Cliffs, New Jersey.

___ EXHIBIT 5–9 _____

■ *Program and System Flowchart Symbols*

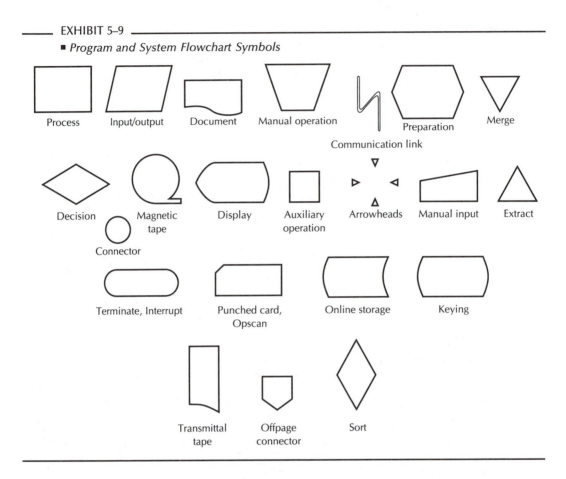

demand and requirements for all other parts of the operating systems, it usually involves a large investment of capital, it is difficult (if not impossible) to reverse, and it may limit and/or reinforce a firm's strategy. Reading 5.2 illustrates why it is essential for a manager to be able to "visualize" the physical process taking place in order to make intelligent decisions about equipment and process technology. Reading 5.3 describes the equipment selection process at Federal Express.

The selection of equipment for a service system should take into account the following:

— The type of basic conversion system
— Operational and strategic tradeoffs
— Equipment capabilities and operational requirements
— Life-cycle cost

Types of Basic Conversion Systems

The selection of equipment is highly dependent on the type of conversion system chosen. We can group conversion systems into three basic categories: (1) fixed-position, (2) process-based, and (3) product- or service-based.

EXHIBIT 5–10

■ *Flowchart of Bank Processes*

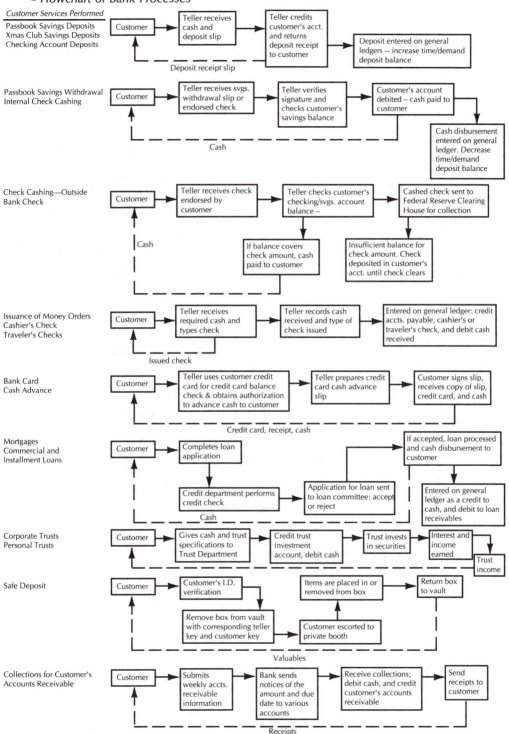

Customer Services Performed

Passbook Savings Deposits
Xmas Club Savings Deposits
Checking Account Deposits

Customer → Teller receives cash and deposit slip → Teller credits customer's acct. and returns deposit receipt to customer → Deposit entered on general ledgers -- increase time/demand deposit balance

Deposit receipt slip

Passbook Savings Withdrawal
Internal Check Cashing

Customer → Teller receives svgs. withdrawal slip or endorsed check → Teller verifies signature and checks customer's savings balance → Customer's account debited – cash paid to customer → Cash disbursement entered on general ledger. Decrease time/demand deposit balance

Cash

Check Cashing—Outside
Bank Check

Customer → Teller receives check endorsed by customer → Teller checks customer's checking/svgs. account balance – → Cashed check sent to Federal Reserve Clearing House for collection

If balance covers check amount, cash paid to customer

Insufficient balance for check amount. Check deposited in customer's acct. until check clears

Cash

Issuance of Money Orders
Cashier's Check
Traveler's Checks

Customer → Teller receives required cash and types check → Teller records cash received and type of check issued → Entered on general ledger: credit accts. payable, cashier's or traveler's check, and debit cash received

Issued check

Bank Card
Cash Advance

Customer → Teller uses customer credit card for credit card balance check & obtains authorization to advance cash to customer → Teller prepares credit card cash advance slip → Customer signs slip, receives copy of slip, credit card, and cash

Credit card, receipt, cash

Mortgages
Commercial and
Installment Loans

Customer → Completes loan application → Credit department performs credit check → Application for loan sent to loan committee: accept or reject → If accepted, loan processed and cash disbursement to customer → Entered on general ledger as a credit to cash, and debit to loan receivables

Cash

Corporate Trusts
Personal Trusts

Customer → Gives cash and trust specifications to Trust Department → Credit trust investment account, debit cash → Trust invests in securities → Interest and income earned → Trust income

Safe Deposit

Customer → Customer's I.D. verification → Items are placed in or removed from box → Return box to vault

Remove box from vault with corresponding teller key and customer key → Customer escorted to private booth

Valuables

Collections for Customer's
Accounts Receivable

Customer → Submits weekly accts. receivable information → Bank sends notices of the amount and due date to various accounts → Receive collections; debit cash, and credit customer's accounts receivable → Send receipts to customer

Receipts

Source: Robert G. Murdick, *MIS: Concepts and Design,* 2d Ed., © 1986, p. 119. Reprinted by permission of Prentice Hall, Inc., Englewood Cliffs, New Jersey.

EXHIBIT 5–11

■ *Flowchart of Car Rental Check-In and Check-Out Process*

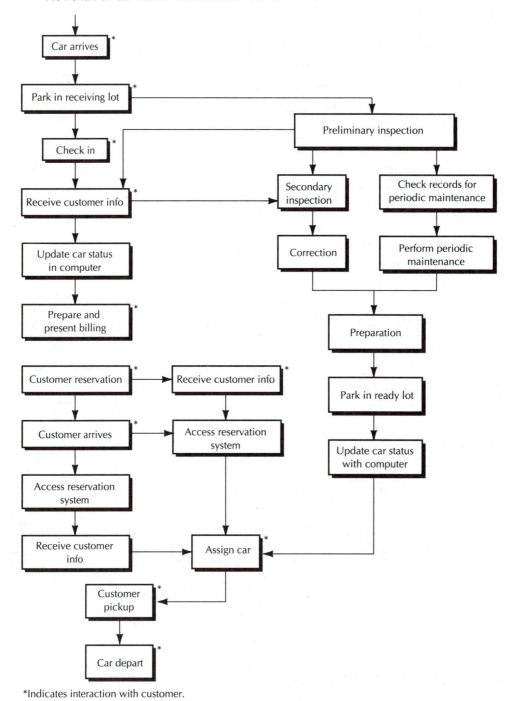

*Indicates interaction with customer.

Source: From W. Earl Sasser, R. P. Olsen, and D. Daryle Wyckoff, *Management of Service Operations,* p. 74. Copyright © 1978 by Allyn and Bacon. Reprinted with permission.

Fixed-Position.   The simplest type of service conversion process is the **fixed-position system.** The customer or item to be serviced remains at one station throughout the service, and materials and labor are brought to that station. In some cases, it is the customer or item being serviced that requires the service to be performed in one location, such as a client's home to be decorated or swimming pool to be cleaned. In other cases, it is the nature of the equipment, such as heavy, expensive hospital equipment for kidney dialysis, that brings the customer, server, and materials to one location. Fixed-position conversion is often characteristic of custom, high-quality, personal service. Beauty treatments, tutoring, landscaping, and psychological therapy are examples.

Equipment selection typically involves choosing between (1) fixed, heavy-duty versus light, portable equipment and (2) general-purpose versus special-purpose equipment items. Although fixed, heavy-duty equipment would seem appropriate for a fixed-position system, light, portable equipment may offer a competitive advantage. For example, portable massage tables allow massages to be performed in offices, homes, and clubs so that customers do not have to travel to a special location. Health examinations, instead of being given in a single office by a general practitioner, could move the patient from room to room where specialists work. This rotation usually improves efficiency, as well as the quality of diagnosis.

The choice between general-purpose and special-purpose equipment depends on the volume and variety of work to be performed. If the *volume* of a special kind of work is high, then it would be worthwhile to invest in special-purpose equipment that can perform that work well. On the other hand, if the *variety* of work is high, general-purpose equipment that can be adjusted to handle many different kinds of work would be more cost-effective.

Process-Based.   In **process-based systems,** similar machines are grouped together to produce batches of services. For example, in a beauty salon, hair dryers may be grouped in one area, chairs where clients have their hair styled in another area, and manicure workstations in another area. Sharing of auxiliary equipment is encouraged. Production is intermittent and variable, such that low-capacity, general-purpose equipment is common. In manufacturing, this type of operation is known as *batch production* or *job-shop production.*

Higher education is a good example of process-based conversion or batch production in services. Students move in batches from class to class. The classes are grouped by discipline and are taught by professors who can teach a variety of courses within their discipline. Class sizes are relatively small, and students take varied paths through the university system in the completion of their degree. The educational process is full of stops and starts (i.e., it is intermittent), including dead time between classes, between semesters, and between drop-out periods.

Service-Based.   If the equipment required to serve a customer is arranged in a sequence according to the steps in the service process, the conversion system is said to be **service-based.** This tailoring of process to customer allows the customer to be served on a continuous basis without interruption. It also encourages the purchase of special-purpose equipment designed to perform a specific task well.

One problem with service-based conversion is its lack of flexibility. For service-based conversion to be efficient, the different types of customers served must be few in number, while the volume of each customer type must be large. Service-based systems are equivalent to manufacturing systems that are product-based, such as the automobile *assembly line,* or *continuous,* such as chemical processing. Examples of service-based conversions are fast-food restaurants, cafeterias, and registration procedures.

Oftentimes, changes in the service design cause changes in the conversion process used to meet demand. For example, many years ago, movie theaters ran feature pictures continuously. It was common for patrons to come in during the early part or middle of a feature and stay until the feature finished and they had watched the part they missed. Continuous production in movies is rare these days, and theaters now use a batch process.

Operational and Strategic Tradeoffs in Equipment Selection

It should be recognized that every specification for equipment involves some tradeoff. For example, the capacity of a piece of equipment represents a tradeoff between building future capacity from a number of small-capacity machines versus having a single large-capacity machine partially idle until demand has expanded. Thus inefficiency is traded off against the cost of an unused capital item. An example is a trucking firm's decision to expand its fleet.

Capacity also can be traded off against cost. A good example can be found in the airline industry in the early 1980s. At that time, airline operating costs could be significantly reduced by purchasing large, wide-bodied aircraft such as McDonnell Douglas DC-10. But to capitalize on these low seat-mile costs, large numbers of passengers had to be routed through central airline "hubs," which sometimes lengthened passenger flight time and the frequency with which certain flights were offered. A better strategic capacity choice may have been to purchase several smaller DC-9s, which, although more costly to operate, provide more options to the customer in terms of flights, destinations, and schedules. Scandinavian Airlines, in fact, followed this latter strategy with much success.[4]

Another type of tradeoff is buying equipment at its present state of the art to lower operating costs and penetrate the current market or waiting for technologically advanced equipment that will make your process superior to your competitors. The first choice may make it unprofitable to update the equipment as it becomes obsolete. The latter choice may make it impossible to enter the market against entrenched competition.

Equipment Capability and Operational Requirements

Equipment capability basically refers to the physical activities a machine can do and how well it can do them. Capability can be measured and described in terms of capacity, materials, range of activities, and quality of output (e.g., specifications, tolerances, and reliability).

---

[4] For more detailed information, see J. L. Heskett, "Lessons in the Service Sector," *Harvard Business Review,* Vol. 65, No. 2 (March–April 1987), pp. 118–126.

Operational requirements include how a machine is started, stopped, operated, changed over from one product to another, speeded up or slowed down, and maintained. In addition, each operating system has certain requirements for human input (number of workers and skills of workers), as well as space, utility, and material input.

Sometimes a detailed understanding of the process leads to the design of new equipment rather than the selection among existing equipment on the market. Consider the Rural/Metro Fire Department located in a growing suburban community and operating under severe budget limitations.[5] Rural/Metro carefully reviewed the community's fire data and discovered that nearly 80 percent of its fires were extinguished with no more than 300 gallons of water, a small percentage of the quantity delivered by large, expensive pumpers. Based on this knowledge, the department designed an ''attack truck'' consisting of a pickup truck painted lime green and equipped with a 300-gallon tank. The truck could be operated by a single firefighter. Rural/Metro also knew that a basic concern in firefighting is being able to deliver enough water quickly to smother a fire in its early stages. Therefore, the department ordered hoses with 4-inch diameters rather than the standard $2\frac{1}{2}$-inch hoses. Service quality improved dramatically.

Rural/Metro understood both its customers' needs and the service process. It also managed the service provision efficiently. Rural/Metro is a good example of the service management concept.

Life-Cycle Cost

Equipment cost includes the initial purchase price of the equipment, installation and debugging costs, and operating costs such as labor, material, maintenance, and utilities. We refer to **life-cycle cost** in order to capture the entire cost over the life of the machine, which may include salvage value, reduction in salvage value due to changes in technology, reduced capacity or operating efficiency as the machine ages, and obsolescence as process requirements or technology change. Investment in equipment and returns from the investment can be discounted for the time value of money and evaluated over the economic life of the equipment. This procedure is straightforward and widely used.[6] The analysis becomes more difficult, however, when investing in new technology that is untested in terms of its physical and economic life span. In other words, it is sometimes hard to predict how new technology will perform or when newer technology will make your current technology obsolete.

—— SUMMARY

Strategic decisions for the design of a service delivery system must be made with respect to

[5] This story is related in J. L. Heskett, *Managing in the Service Economy* (Boston: Harvard Business School Press, 1988), pp. 42–43, and expanded in HBR case no. 9-681-082, ''Rural/Metro Fire Department.''

[6] Capital budgeting commonly involves discounted cash flow methods. Many finance and production textbooks contain examples of net present value, internal rate of return, and more. See for example, R. B. Chase and N. J. Aquilano, *Production/Operations Management*, 5th Ed. (New York: Wiley, 1989), pp. 870–888.

— Primary technological process
— Materials and conversion process
— Specific equipment
— Process flow for conversion
— Employee skills and job content
— Site location and selection
— Buildings and facilities
— Facility layout and work flow
— Organizational structure and sociopsychological factors

The first five areas constitute the primary conversion system and are the subject of this chapter. The flow process chart is the primary tool for developing and describing the conversion system.

Whereas a generic flowchart may be devised for manufacturing systems, services vary so much in structure and process that a *much* wider variety of flowcharts is applicable.[7] This chapter presents a number of examples to illustrate this point.

The selection of equipment for a service depends on

— The type of basic conversion system (fixed-position, process-based, or service-based)
— Operational and strategic tradeoffs
— Equipment capabilities and operational requirements
— Life-cycle cost

Process planning and equipment selection are important decisions for any firm because they define the operating system under which products or services are provided. Further, because of the closeness of the service design to the service process, it is even more essential for services to choose a process for delivery that matches the service design and supports the overall strategy of the firm.

___ DISCUSSION QUESTIONS

1. What is meant by the primary conversion system?

2. Name four factors that affect the process flow decision.

3. Why are people decisions part of process planning?

4. How are flowcharts useful in process planning?

5. What information do flow process charts provide? How are the processes classified?

6. Develop your own flow process chart for

   a. Writing a term paper
   b. Finding employment
   c. Learning how to ski

7. Exhibit 5–12 is a flowchart of the incarceration process at a local jail. Examine the flowchart and answer the following questions.

   a. What factors determine when inmates enter jail?

---

[7] Flowcharts may differ somewhat for each basic type of manufacturing system, that is, whether the system involves project, batch, mass production, or continuous processing. Still, the variation is nowhere near that of service systems.

—— EXHIBIT 5–12 ——————————————————————————————————————

■ *Flowchart of Incarceration Process*

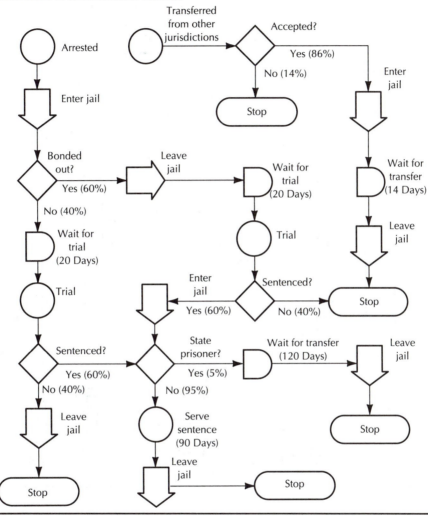

b. What factors determine when inmates are released from jail?

c. What policies might be adjusted to alleviate an overcrowded jail?

8. Explain the differences between fixed-position, process-based, and service-based conversion systems. Give an example of each.

9. Define the following as they relate to equipment selection:

a. Operational and strategic tradeoffs

b. Operational requirements

c. Life-cycle cost

10. Exhibit 5–13 shows the layout of a student cafeteria. Using the standard flow process chart symbols, chart the flow of several students who might be processed through this cafeteria. Then answer the following questions.

—— EXHIBIT 5–13 ——————————————————————————————————

■ *Layout of Student Cafeteria*

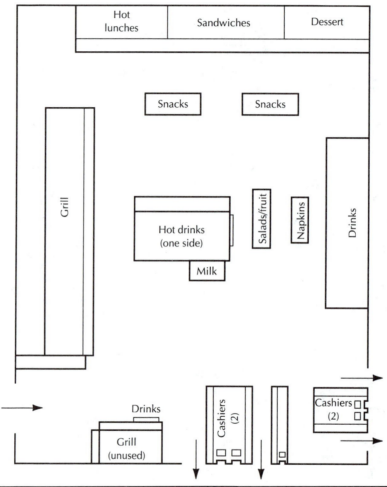

a. How does your chart help in communicating the student's experience?

b. Would the process be clearer if the chart were imposed on the floor plan?

c. Does your diagram help in analyzing the process for possible improvements? Looking at the diagram, what changes would you propose in the layout of the cafeteria? How would these changes improve the "flow" of the student as he or she moves through the cafeteria?

d. What difficulties did you have in performing this exercise? What other information would be helpful in redesigning the system?

READING 5.1

The New Back Office Focuses on Customer Service

A request to issue a letter of credit arrives in the mailroom at Citibank's operations headquarters on Wall Street in New York. The request is from a Citibank correspondent bank in Lyons, France, on behalf of a local company that needs to finance a shipment of machine tools purchased from a company in Michigan.

Sorting clerks in the mailroom check the contents of the envelope and send the item on to the bank's letter of credit department on the building's 24th floor. The item lands on the desk of a pre-processing clerk who determines the source of the item, whether it is from a Citibank branch, a correspondent bank, or a government agency. The clerk shunts the item to the correspondent bank section. There, another clerk has to determine whether the item requests that a letter of credit be issued, amended, or paid or whether it is a customer inquiry. The clerk sends the Lyons item to the issuance unit.

Three days later, the credit for the Lyons company's shipment is issued. At least 14 people—a typist, a log-in clerk, a preparer, a signature control clerk, two checkers, the department manager, a central liabilities clerk at the bank's uptown corporate headquarters, a marketing officer who approves the credit (also from uptown), the accounting department, the files unit, and the customer service clerk—have acted on it.

The original source document from the Lyons correspondent has been read, reread, checked, and rechecked. It has been crumpled, clipped, stapled, unstapled, rubber-banded in bundles of cards and tickets, stuffed into envelopes, copied, copied from, annotated, and preserved in a cardboard file folder.

The processing of the credit issuance has generated a stack of papers maintained in some six files. An offering ticket has gone to central liabilities and to the marketing officer, with a copy for the file; a five-copy fanfold has been typed, split, and its folds dispersed to a variety of destinations; accounting tapes, proof tapes, and MIS tapes have been punched, rolled, and delivered around the bank; special instructions have been duly noted and recorded in duplicate, one set concerning the Lyons customer and the other the beneficiary out in Michigan.

The Diebold files are bulging, and the department requisitions additional forms and paper clips. Yet a week after the credit is issued, the customer requests that it be amended, starting the same process all over again.

When the time comes for payment, the appropriate documents are presented at the letter of credit department, correspondent bank section, payment unit. Tickler files are checked, credit documents are pulled, examiners examine, checkers check, typists type (a nine-part fanfold this time), verifiers verify the accounting entries, a proof clerk stashes the tickets into a pigeonhole on a rolltop desk for action at the end of the day, and a check is made out and mailed—five days after the payment documents were presented.

It is now a year and a half later; the same company requests a similar credit through the same Lyons correspondent. In the Citibank mailroom, a clerk routes the item to "Letter of Credit, 21st floor, European Division." At the division's preprocessing desk, a clerk notes the item's source and puts it in a slot marked "France" on an automatic delivery cart, a mail "robot." As the robot moves along the aisle, the item is plucked from its slot by an individual sitting in a neat, cockpitlike workstation, where she is typing onto a CRT terminal keyboard. As she punches the last key, a printer terminal nearby prints out a formal letter of credit. It is mailed that day. She immediately puts the customer's original request and instructions on microfiche and stores it in a small file case on the flat top of the workstation at her right hand.

Where it once took days, 30-odd separate processing steps, 14 people, and a variety of forms, tickets, and file folders to process a single letter of

---

credit, it now requires one individual less than a day to receive, issue, and mail out a letter of credit—all via a terminal that is fully online to a minicomputer-based system.

Part of the change is dramatically evident. It was a technological leap—from clerks, papers, forms, paper clips, rubber bands, and file folders to workstation professionals, CRT terminals hooked to a minicomputer, and micrographics for record keeping. But part of the change is rooted in the department's basic function of providing financial services to international corporate customers and is less obvious. This is a change in the very approach to services management, a change in the organizational structure to reflect that approach, a change in the work processes, and a change in the jobs themselves.

A letter of credit is a document indicating a guarantee by the bank that it will pay an obligation of its customer to a third party, usually when certain stated conditions have been met. The letter of credit gives a buyer of goods the prestige and financial backing of the issuing bank. And the bank's acceptance of drafts drawn under the letter of credit satisfies the third party and his bank in the handling of the transaction. This is an instrument widely used in the financing of shipments of goods in international trade. Because of the variety of terms and conditions possible, it can be a highly complex financial instrument.

In a letter of credit operation, the basic steps are the issuance of a letter, the amendment of the letter, and payment. The last step involves the bank's receipt and examination of the third party's shipping documents after the goods have been delivered for shipment to ensure that the terms of the letter are met.

The process as a whole involves preparation of the letter of credit itself, checking of credit and terms, examination of documents, and accounting activities. In addition, there is a customer service function: answering written and phone inquiries, advising, and problem handling.

For some time, the bank management had been considering how to automate the process. All attempts had been nipped in the bud as being totally unsatisfactory and unworkable. One set of specifications, for instance, took up five five-inch loose-leaf binders and was so complicated that it would have required an engineer rather than a clerk

to work through the system. The problem underlying all the failures was that the processing operation itself had grown cumbersome and overly complex, and it would have profited us little to automate chaos.

DECENTRALIZING ALONG MARKET LINES

As part of the overall reorganization of customer services, the bulk of letter of credit operations was given over to the division serving the International Banking Group (IBG), whose customer base provides the most letter of credit business. While the IBG Services Management Division's letter of credit department performed work only for the IBG's customer base, it did so on a functionalized, assembly-line basis, with separate units for payment examination, payment processing, files, issuing/amending, customer service, and accounting. All letters of credit, no matter where they came from or what type of customer they served, came into the shop and passed from functional unit to functional unit.

Our first step was to realign the channel around the kinds of customers that provide our letter of credit business: governments, correspondent banks, and our branches. Nevertheless, within each newly aligned customer cut, the functional, assembly-line work flow persisted.

Later, the reorganization would be made wholly market-oriented and, within marketplaces, customer-oriented. First, however, it was necessary to understand the process sufficiently so that we could gear our automation effort to an effective customer design.

ADOPTING THE PROCESSING NETWORK

To build the technological base that would support decentralization, we needed to really understand what happens when a letter of credit is processed. Such understanding was essential if the process was to be shortened—its functions integrated so that a single employee manning a single minicomputer could perform it.

Processing manuals did exist. In three levels of detail, they described exactly how to perform every task of every step along the way. But the management team suspected, indeed assumed, either that the employees had devised their own incidental methodologies or that some tasks had become so automatic one could no longer identify them as steps the automated system should include. The managers assumed, in short, that things in the manual were not in fact being done and that things being done were not in fact in the manual. They decided to find out exactly what was going on. How?

For one thing, the managers just walked around the department scrutinizing the operation, watching people at work, checking what they saw against the manuals. Then they called employees into a conference room and asked them precisely how they did their jobs, and they asked the supervisors how they thought the employees did their jobs. Finally, every morning at 7:00, the letter of credit management team convened to go over what was learned the day before and to match it against the manual.

The end product of this analysis was a book describing the letter of credit operation in full. In this book, the management team charted and described for every step of the processing (1) the inputs to the step, (2) the files required, and (3) the processing tasks.

This guide was then held up for scrutiny and was declared suspect—not as an analysis of what the workers and supervisors were saying, but rather as a mirror of what was actually happening.

Carlos Palomares, vice president and director of letter of credit operations at the time, expressed it this way:

> If we were talking to the supervisor, we weren't 100 percent sure that what he said was really how the clerk was doing the processing. If we were talking to the clerk, we weren't 100 percent sure that he was including every possible form. So we decided that the only way to get down to bottom-level detail was under controlled conditions in a laboratory-like environment.

The management team created the "White Room," which was a separate walled-off area in the letter of credit department, and put in it all the equipment needed to process a letter of credit: typewriter, adding machine, rubber stamps, and forms. The managers selected Betty Matos, a seven-year veteran of various functions of the letter of credit department, and assigned her to the White Room.

The analysis of the process began with the simplest kinds of letter of credit transactions. As Palomares said,

> Different kinds of letters of credit have different levels of complexity. We wanted to be able to dissect the simplest letter of credit and do the processing on that one first so that we understood the most basic processing flow completely before going on to analyze the more complex types.
>
> So we would find the simplest types and bring them into the White Room and have Betty try to process them, given the steps that had been identified in the analysis that we had done, that is, the steps, the file requirements, the forms requirements, the rubber stamp requirements—everything we had learned in our 7:00 A.M. analyses.

In effect, by setting up the White Room, the managers were testing the veracity of their own analysis. They did so, quite simply, by standing next to a seated Betty Matos as she processed a letter of credit step by step.

Several important lessons were learned during this trial in the White Room. For example, some clerks had been keeping redundant files, while others were using forms never mentioned during the initial analysis. One clerk was even using a rubber stamp that had been discontinued in 1970.

The White Room was a testing ground for more than the difference between what was written and what was real. It was an arena to experiment on what should be. As they stood there, watching Betty Matos (and later, an expanding force of workers), the managers would play around with ideas, asking each other and the employees, "What if we combine these two forms or these five forms? What if we eliminate this step altogether?"

In the three months of the White Room's existence, without introducing any new automation, the managers reduced the letter of credit department from 142 to 100 people and the number of steps required to carry out the total processing by half. Yet the figures only reflected the more significant achievement of a clean, efficient operation that was ready to be automated.

Through the downright drudgery of questioning every task, step, and flow, the need for every piece of paper and rubber stamp, management achieved a wholly streamlined operation in the White Room. What was left was bare-bones letter of credit processing; the jargon for it around the department was "plain vanilla." This was the foundation on which change could be built. For the managers, gaining this kind of detailed understanding and control was like learning to walk. It made it possible to run, and so to automate the operation meaningfully.

PROCESS DEFINITION

The thrust of the design process was to meet the service-driven concept that we had defined as our management goal. We retained a software company that had been brought in by one of the hardware vendors, who had earlier tried, unsuccessfully, to automate the letter of credit process. We chose this company to design the new automated system, LOCAS (Letter of Credit Automated System), precisely because it had detailed knowledge of the product, though its experience with our chosen equipment was minimal. The management team set the following five basic guidelines for the design:

First, the system would be modular. That is, the team wanted to automate one step at a time, so it could test and actually use each module as it was designed. Also, the team wanted to follow the experience of the White Room in going from the simple to the complex. Plain vanilla was to be automated first; and even the plain vanilla—the simplest transaction—was to be automated piece by piece, first issuance, then amendment, then payment. In this way, the more complex steps of automation could be looked upon as enhancements to a basic, simplified process.

Second, the system must be totally online with real-time updating of the letter of credit files. Every datum was to be validated at the time it entered the system.

Third, the system should enrich each data element. That is, the managers wanted a capability whereby whenever an employee punched a customer number into the system, he would retrieve all other data about the customer as well.

Fourth, the system's forms were to be designed according to the needs of the computer file; all special-purpose forms would be eliminated. The system itself would supply the appropriate standardized paragraphs for a particular transaction.

Finally, and perhaps most important, the system should fit the managers' concept of the single workstation. A single individual would process the entire letter of credit transaction using the automated system. The system would, therefore, need to integrate functions in such a way that this was possible. In addition, the workstation would contain everything the individual needed to process the transaction.

Given the hookup to the minicomputer, those needs were now simple—a CRT, a microfiche viewer, a box for microfiche files, slots to hold the (now) few pieces of paper needed, and a telephone to handle customer inquiries.

QUESTIONS FOR READING 5.1

1. Citibank's operations were designed after the assembly-line concept in manufacturing. Why does it appear inefficient?

2. Distinguish between back-office and front-office operations in relation to lines of credit. Should these operations be managed differently? Separately?

3. Describe the process Citibank used to improve operations of its letter-of-credit service.

4. How did Citibank approach automating the service? What was the purpose of the White Room?

5. What changes in job descriptions were necessitated by the new processes used? What additional training was necessary? In what ways would a manager's job change?

6. How do customers benefit from Citibank's new operations? How do the employees benefit?

7. What lessons do you think Citibank learned from their experience with the letter-of-credit activity?

READING 5.2

A Manager's Understanding of Technology

A persistent pattern seen in the autopsies of the major operating crises of large corporations and of the final failures of many small companies is the inability of one or more key managers to understand and to manage the technologies of their businesses. Analysis of the careers of executives who topped off their advancement in positions lower than those that their education and basic abilities should have allowed often reveals a similar pattern: lack of knowledge, skills, and/or personal confidence in their competence to deal with and manage the technologies of their firms.

In an age dominated by technology and technological change, technology demands on managers are substantial and growing. But many managers are negative, reluctant, or simply untrained in their attitudes regarding the technologies on which their businesses are often based. Similarly, many managers work toward mastering basic skills and techniques in finance, marketing, control, and human relations, while openly expressing their lack of interest or confidence in building strength in the technology relevant to their work.

The importance of technology to corporations is evident. Corporations that make products or offer services must make decisions involving their technologies when they design products or plan services, choose equipment and processes, and devise operating facilities, distribution, and information systems. Because these decisions involve large commitments of funds and, often more important, large blocks of irreplaceable time, they are some of the most vital and critical of management decisions. Once made, their reversal or even a major shift is apt to be difficult or even impossible. Unwise decisions on technological issues are frequently fatal in a small business.

Although many factors contribute to individual and institutional aversion to technology, at least five assumptions appear significant:

1. It is usually assumed that technological decisions can best be delegated to technical experts, such as engineers.
2. It is often believed that many years of training are required to become competent in a technology.
3. It is often believed that only engineers and scientists can cope with technology-based decisions.
4. Most managers who are neither engineers nor scientists feel somewhat inadequate in matters of technology: they fear to appear stupid or foolish before managers "who know"; they stay away from things they don't understand; they defer to "experts"; they don't try to learn the technology either because others are already too far ahead or they feel it would take too much time to keep up.
5. Conventional wisdom about managing exalts the delegator, the manager who is never caught up in details. Many managers are reluctant to engage in learning technology that may not seem to be part of his or her job.

Such technology-aversive behavior may result in serious business problems and risks of personal obsolescence, and such behavior unfortunately compounds itself because lack of knowledge breeds lack of confidence.

Consider a simple example of equipment technology, a process for cutting grass, a lawn mower.

A lawn mower could be described to a prospective purchaser as follows: "It costs $228. It has a gasoline engine and cuts a 24-inch-wide swath of grass and is well made by a well-known manufacturer."

A technology-aversive prospective buyer might say, "I'll take it," only to get home to the 8-inch grass and find that:

Source: W. Skinner, *Manufacturing: The Formidable Competitive Weapon* (New York: Wiley, 1985), pp. 113–114, 120–121. Copyright © 1985 John Wiley & Sons, Inc. Reprinted by permission of John Wiley & Sons, Inc.

- The cutting technology was based on a reel moving past a cutter bar. It could not handle grass much higher than one-half the reel diameter. It simply pushed the 8-inch crop forward and down.
- It was self-propelled but had no effective free-wheeling device, so that it was not possible to work close to and around a formal garden.
- It took 30 minutes to change the cutting height so that hillside grass could be cut longer (to cut down on erosion) than lawn grass.
- It was not powerful enough to cut wet, thick grass going uphill.
- It did not mulch leaves.
- It had a two-cycle engine, which meant that oil had to be mixed with the gasoline each time the little tank was filled.

This buyer should have purchased an extrapowerful, four-cycle, self-propelled rotary mower with easy handling for tight maneuvering and with a simple height-adjustment mechanism.

Understanding the equipment and process technology of lawn mowing in order to make a wise purchase of machinery would have required the owner-manager to develop an accurate mental concept of the process of cutting grass, with the machine operating on the hillside and on the level, under a variety of conditions, with consideration for the operator's time, money, and skills. The most

crucial mistake, of course, was in the choice of a reel mower rather than one with a rotary blade. But for a house with low, big glass windows and with close-by neighbors' houses that were similarly constructed, the buyer would have also needed to consider the danger from flying stones propelled by the rotary mower. In either case, a reasonably good conceptual approximation of the actual grass-cutting action might have suggested enough of the right questions to lead to other useful questions. Choosing EPTs [equipment and process technologies] in manufacturing or service industry operations has many parallels to the lawn-mower problem.

___ QUESTIONS FOR READING 5.2

1. What questions should the buyer have asked before purchasing the lawn mower? What knowledge of the process of mowing lawns was the buyer lacking?

2. Why do you think many managers are technology-averse?

3. How can a manager be expected to master technologies that engineers, scientists, and other experts have studied for years?

4. Why can't (or shouldn't) technology decisions be delegated to lower-level managers or technical specialists who are nearer to the problem?

___ READING 5.3 ___

Equipment Selection at Federal Express

The Operations Research and Corporate Planning Division of Federal Express was charged with the development of an optimal long-term physical and operational system for the company. Specifically, the group had two major tasks. First, it was to undertake a cost-benefit study investigating the merits of operating with a wholly new network of four to eight regional sorting hubs over the merits of simply expanding the Memphis hub. And second, it was

asked to evaluate the mix of aircraft types needed for the fleet and the quantity of each type of plane.

At the time of Fred Smith's 1978 organizational shakeup, management was committed to a regional hub network. This logistical system appeared to be the most cost-effective means to handle the nightly package volume. Later in 1978, Smith decided to scrap this plan. Subsequent studies showed that the introduction of the fleet of 727s

Source: R. A. Sigafoos and R. R. Easson, *Absolutely, Positively Overnight!* (Memphis, Tenn.: St. Luke's Press, a division of Plaintree Publishers, Ltd., 1988), pp. 158–161. Reprinted with permission.

changed drastically the company's operating model of its system. A regional hub network, company planners concluded, would create heavy fixed-cost commitments in facilities, equipment, and personnel expenses. They concluded that there would not be much savings in variable costs by reducing line haul distance, that is, by requiring all flights to rendezvous at Memphis every night. They also found that the company would have to pay its pilots the same salaries whether they flew in and out of hubs located at Colorado Springs, Colorado, or Newburgh, New York, or any other place, versus flying to and from Memphis every weekday night.

The company also faced the question of how to mix the fleet to attain the payload capacity for the projected nightly package volume. The planners considered a variety of aircraft types, the payloads of different types of aircraft, and their operating characteristics. Fuel efficiency became a primary consideration. Federal's staff looked at Boeing 707s and 727s, 737s and 747s, and at Douglas DC-8s, DC-9s, and DC-10s. After exhaustive cost studies, including expenses associated with aircraft crew training, maintenance, Memphis hub operations and fuel consumption, the conclusion was that Federal's fleet selection had to be a financial compromise between fuel efficiency of particular aircraft on one hand and the capital costs of these aircraft on the other. On these criteria, the 727, 737, and the DC-10 appeared to strike a happy medium for the company.

During the 1978 and 1979 period, used 727-100s in particular were available in quantity. This plane—originally introduced by Boeing in 1964—was the most widely used jet transport in the world. It was fortunate timing for Federal Express that United, Eastern, and Northwest had only recently discontinued use of their "quick change" combination passenger-cargo 727s and designated them surplus.

After extensive study, Federal Express designated the 727-100 as the "right" plane for the company. The first 11 used 727-100s came from United Airlines. The next 20 were purchased from Eastern. This was the start of an acquisition program that brought the fleet of 727-100s up to 38 planes in 1983.

In 1978 and 1979, the company purchased four Boeing 737-200 "quick change" aircraft for about $10 million each. It also leased one 737-200. These aircraft with two turbofan jet engines were more fuel efficient than the three-engined 727-100s, but their payload capacity was some 4000 pounds less. Its "quick change" physical configuration excited the company at the time, because it was seriously considering competing in the daytime commuter airline market.

At the time of the purchase of the new 737s, management believed it had made the correct decision, especially if these aircraft were to be put into daytime scheduled passenger service. But less than two years after acquiring these planes, in a turnabout, management declared the 737s surplus to operations and put them up for sale. Later company studies of the proposed passenger route system pointed to a daytime need for more 737s than could be used economically in the primary business of hauling packages overnight. Fortunately, at the time, some commercial airlines were showing a strong interest in the 737s because of their fuel efficiency. Federal sold them at a profit.

In January 1980, the company bought four used DC-10-10CF aircraft from Continental Airlines for about $26 million each. These three-engine, wide-bodied aircraft had an approximate gross payload of 120,000 pounds and a net payload of 105,000 pounds. The decision to purchase the DC-10s, like the previous decision to purchase the 727s, was heavily influenced by the results of extensive computer simulations examining all physical and operational characteristics, as well as sales prices.

Continental Airlines declared the four DC-10s surplus to its operations because it was desperate for cash after losing over $13 million in 1979. Continental's plight was Federal's good fortune. It permitted the company to stay committed to its successful strategy of buying quality used aircraft at near bargain prices.

Once Federal's negotiators worked out statistically what the company could afford to pay, they were tenacious in holding firm on an offering price. Fortuitous market timing helped them. There was either a surplus of the appropriate types of aircraft available on the open market or a particular commercial airline available wanting to sell off part of its fleet.

Temporarily, Smith had been excited at the prospect of adding Boeing 747s to the fleet. This huge, wide-bodied plane would have given the company a payload per aircraft of some 172,000 pounds. The positive feature as far as Smith was concerned was its fuel efficiency. Its liabilities to Federal were its sheer size and cost. The huge 747 made economic sense on the Newark and Los Angeles routes, but volume projections indicated it would be several years before Boston, Chicago, or any other large metropolitan area would have a nightly package market large enough to justify 747 service.

Management wanted to put DC-10s on the Boston, Chicago, Los Angeles, and Newark nightly routes. The larger plane was the ideal size. Committing the DC-10s to these major routes permitted the release of several of the 727s to other routes. Planners found that the fuel savings from using the DC-10s were substantial, If, for example, three 727s were used nightly on the Los Angeles–Memphis route, the combined fuel use would be 12,700 gallons. But if a single DC-10 were used to cover the same route, the fuel burned would be 7,400 gallons, a considerable savings just on fuel alone. On March 24, 1980, the first DC-10 began pro-viding new service on the Newark–Memphis route.

But Smith made a major strategy decision in 1982, when he opted to reconstitute a large part of the fleet in the latter 1980s. Federal negotiated with Boeing to buy a large number of the 727-200F series of all-cargo aircraft. After that point the fleet grew rapidly, and by 1987 Federal Express's fleet had 8 DC-10-10s, 11 DC-10-30s, 21 727-200s, 39 727-100s, and 66 Cessna 208s. The small Cessnas permitted service to outlying and more remote areas nationwide that were uneconomical to serve with the big planes.

_____ QUESTIONS FOR READING 5.3

1. What factors were considered in selecting aircraft for Federal Express?

2. What analysis techniques and data were employed?

3. Explain briefly the basic aircraft options and why certain selections were made.

4. Describe any constraints that impacted the aircraft purchasing strategy.

_____ CASE 5.1

Ski Limited

Ski Limited, headquartered in Killington, Vermont, owns Killington and Mt. Snow, two of New England's most successful ski resorts. The company earned $5 million on revenues of $56 million in the fiscal year 1985–1986. President and founder Preston Smith is the company's biggest booster. His insistence on gathering information rather than guessing started with his selection of Killington when he opened with one ski lift in 1956. His background in cartography and meteorology led to his analysis indicating that Killington would receive more snow than any other spot within one day's drive of New York and Boston.

Ski has been profitable every year after the first year's loss despite several poor snow years and two gasoline crises. Revenues have grown at a 19 percent compounded rate over the past 20 years. As Vice President Martel Wilson notes, "Everyone else has 52 weeks to make it. We have only 20 to 30 weeks." Wilson points out that the ski business is a conglomeration of enterprises including restaurants, bars, retailing (ski shops), education (ski schools), transportation (shuttle buses), and real estate constructing and leasing (condominiums). The demands for these services are tied to the interrelationship among them. The increasingly complex requirements have led Ski into a growing dependence on automation. Exhibit 5–14 shows a

---

EXHIBIT 5–14

■ *The Killington Resort Area*

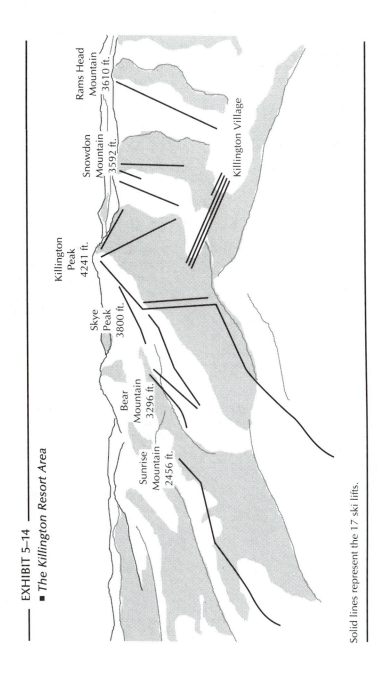

Solid lines represent the 17 ski lifts.

layout of the Killington resort area. The area extends over six mountains with 100 ski trails and 17 ski lift facilities.

Killington attributes much of its revenues to snowmaking operations when nature fails. It conducts its own R&D and manufactures its own snow guns. Information systems play a crucial role in snowmaking operations. Use of trails and chairlifts are monitored, as well.

___ QUESTIONS FOR CASE 5.1

1. Identify opportunities for the application of technology to ski *operations,* including such activities as snow depth prediction, operations planning linking the various businesses, and staff planning.

2. What kinds of projections of skier days would be useful (annual, daily, etc.), and what forecasting methods could be employed?

3. What characteristics of on-site ski operations could Killington monitor to increase the quality and efficiency of operations?

4. What skiing conditions could be visually monitored and displayed on terminals in the lodge for control purposes?

5. How could automation be applied to transportation in this business?

___ REFERENCES ___

Acosta, Dan. "The People Movement," *Detroiter,* May 1982.

Collier, David A. "The Service Sector Revolution: The Anatomy of Services," *Long Range Planning,* Vol. 16, No. 6 (1983).

Heskett, J. L. *Managing in the Service Economy,* Boston: Harvard Business School Press, 1986.

Hoerr, John, Michael A. Pollock, and David E. Whiteside. "Management Discovers the Human Side of Automation," *Business Week* (September 1986), pp. 70–79.

Klatt, Lawrence, A., Robert G. Murdick, and Frederick E. Schuster. *Human Resource Management.* Columbus, Ohio: Merrill, 1985.

Murdick, Robert G. *MIS: Concepts and Design,* 2d Ed. Englewood Cliffs, N.J.: Prentice-Hall, 1986.

Muther, Richard. *Systematic Layout Planning,* 2d Ed. Boston: Cahners, 1974.

Northcraft, Gregory B., and Richard Chase. "Managing Demand at the Point of Delivery," *Academy of Management Review,* Vol. 10, No. 1 (January 1985), pp. 66–75.

Sasser, W. Earl, R. Paul Olsen, and D. Daryl Wyckoff. *Management of Service Operations.* Boston: Allyn and Bacon, 1978.

Sigafoos, R. A., and R. R. Easson. *Absolutely, Positively Overnight!* Memphis, Tenn.: St. Luke's Press, 1988.

Shostack, G. L. "Designing Services that Deliver," *Harvard Business Review,* Vol. 64, No. 1 (January–February 1984), pp. 133–139.

Walton, Richard E. "Quality of Working Life," *Sloan Management Review,* Vol. 15, No. 1 (Fall 1973), pp. 11–21.

Yankee, Herbert W. *Manufacturing Processes.* Englewood Cliffs, N.J.: Prentice-Hall, 1979.

6

Service Location

INTRODUCTION

One of the most important long-term revenue decisions a service organization makes is where to locate its operation. This decision follows the design of the service (the topic of Chapter 4) and service process planning (as seen in Chapter 5) and consists of two parts: finding a *location* and then finding a *site* within it for the service delivery system. Attention in this chapter is focused on the location options available. These options are

1. Enlarge an existing facility at the present site.
2. Close the present facility and construct one or more new ones on new sites.
3. Open a new site or sites.

In essence, we establish a *business,* not just a process, on a particular site.

Location selection is a macro decision involving which countries, regions within a country, and communities (within a region, county or city) are appropriate for locating the service units.

Site selection is a micro decision as to the specific piece of property (or properties) on which to establish the service.

This chapter first examines the location selection decision by describing the effect of

— The business profile
— Dominant location factors
— General selection criteria
— Common mistakes made in selection
— Multiple locations

A variety of quantitative methods for evaluating locations, ranging from factor weighting to several very mathematical models, is examined. Finally, we turn to the site-selection problem and look at criteria for selection, as well as a variety of models and issues that need to be considered.

LOCATION SELECTION
Business Profile

Before considering alternative locations (and sites), a **business profile** should be prepared. The profile describes the nature of the business and the needs of the business in terms of location (and site). It also includes an analysis of the dominant location factors presented in the next section. A comparison is then made of the profile versus the firm's strategic plan, as shown by the model in Exhibit 6–1. The strategy of a firm should serve as the constraining framework and provide the basic direction for locating any business. From the business profile and strategic plan, feasible locations can be generated for consideration.

────── EXHIBIT 6–1 ──

■ *Location and Site Selection Evaluation*

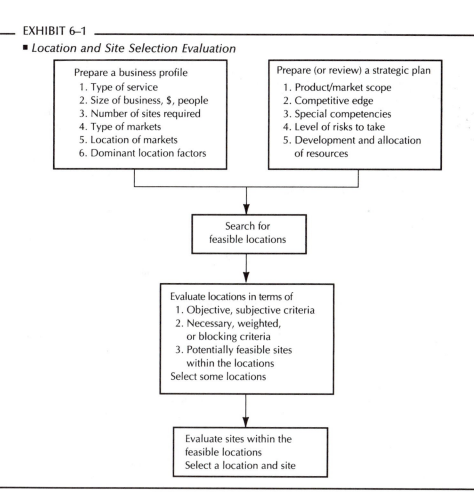

Prepare a business profile	Prepare (or review) a strategic plan
1. Type of service	1. Product/market scope
2. Size of business, $, people	2. Competitive edge
3. Number of sites required	3. Special competencies
4. Type of markets	4. Level of risks to take
5. Location of markets	5. Development and allocation
6. Dominant location factors	of resources

Search for
feasible locations

Evaluate locations in terms of
1. Objective, subjective criteria
2. Necessary, weighted,
   or blocking criteria
3. Potentially feasible sites
   within the locations
Select some locations

Evaluate sites within the
feasible locations
Select a location and site

Dominant Location Factors

The selection of location and site for a service obviously depends on a number of factors and tradeoffs among benefits and costs. However, there may be a particular factor that *dominates* the selection process and limits the number of feasible locations to be evaluated. Below are nine dominant factors relating to location and site selection.

1. *Customer based.* If convenience of location determines where a customer shops, banks, or dines, the service is said to be customer based. Hence, the service should be located in close proximity to its customers. Retail stores, health care and other personal services, theaters, branches of banks and brokerage houses, and restaurants are examples of organizations with customer-based locations.
2. *Cost based.* Most specialty shops, wholesalers, and clerical services find that operating cost is their dominant location factor.

3. *Competitor based.* Some businesses prefer to locate near their competition to observe, share resources, and draw customers from a distance. For example, in manufacturing, we have garment districts, furniture towns, and textile areas. Similarly, in services we see clusters of car dealerships, antique shops, and fast-food restaurants.

4. *Support systems.* Many companies locate in areas where support systems are available. For example, as discussed in Reading 6.3, a hotel may locate near a university medical research center. A bullion firm may locate in a city with good police protection. For Disney World, location at a site with good airline and road support systems, as well as good electric utility service, was essential.

5. *Geographic or environmental factors.* Ocean resorts, ski resorts, and outdoor health ranches or spas illustrate geographic or environmental constraints on location.

6. *Business climate.* When a service business has only minor constraints on its location, the business climate of a state or city may provide the major factor in site location. Insurance companies, private educational institutions, and gaming resorts are likely to fall in this category.

7. *Communication based.* Financial services usually require rapid communication with other companies and perhaps even with governments throughout the world. This is one of the reasons that large banks locate in large, highly developed cities with excellent communications. Further, as telecommunication systems continue to replace transportation of documents by mail, this factor will become more important.

8. *Transportation based.* Mail-order businesses and private express delivery services tend to make location decisions based on entry to a good transportation network.

9. *Personal desires of the CEO.* Despite the preceding factors, many companies have moved their headquarters based on the desire of the president or CEO. When Justin Dart took over Rexall Drug, for example, he moved the headquarters from Boston to Los Angeles because of a personal preference.

Now that we have seen the general relationship between location and site selection and certain dominant factors, we will examine multiple criteria and evaluation processes in more detail.

General Criteria for Location Selection

In addition to dominant location factors, there are many other general criteria that should be considered in selecting a location, as shown in Exhibit 6–2. For example, whether the firm is communication based or transportation based, or whether the personal desires of the CEO are primary in location selection, the criteria listed in Exhibit 6–2, such as labor availability/cost, climate/weather, and state taxes, are still important considerations. Many of the items listed in Exhibit 6–2 apply regardless of the type of service business.

———— EXHIBIT 6–2 ————————————————————————————

■ *General Criteria for Location Selection*

1. Labor availability and costs
2. Labor history and culture
3. Educational centers
4. Recreational and cultural centers
5. Electric power
6. Transportation and road networks
7. Health and welfare system
8. Climate and weather
9. Geography and environmental protection management
10. State business climate and incentives
11. State taxes
12. Health care system
13. Suppliers and supporting service companies
14. Population and population trends
15. Communication systems
16. Preference of management
17. Cost of living
18. Community attitudes
19. Cost of land and construction
20. Potential for expansion

In making comparisons among locations, it is well to group the criteria according to

1. Subjective Criteria
   a. Quantifiable (e.g., management's estimate of risk)
   b. Nonquantifiable (e.g., acceptance by the community, zoning, and legal factors)
2. Objective Criteria
   a. Quantifiable (e.g., cost of construction)
   b. Nonquantifiable (e.g., lower cost of living)

Common Mistakes

Oversights and common mistakes in the location decision have been identified by various writers.[1] Some of these errors are

— Failure to forecast trends. Too often, the long-range location decision is based on factors at the present time without regard to potentially adverse changes or future opportunities. The growth of the Sun Belt in the 1970s and the decay in the North Central states are examples.
— Failure to develop a company profile. In this case, the company simply looks for a place to put a building rather than a place to enhance its business.

[1] See, for example, Richard Muther, *Systematic Layout Planning*, 2d Ed. (Boston: Cahners Books, 1973).

— Paying too much attention to land costs. High land costs *may* accompany a highly desirable area. Also, they *may* indicate the possibility of large growth in value in case the company decides to move its business at some future time.

— Failure to understand the costs of moving people

— Allowing prejudices of executives to override what should be a business decision

— Loss of key people who do not favor the new location

— Failure to take into account the culture of the workers at the location

— Paying too much attention to wage rates rather than productivity

— Failure to coordinate construction and moving with the ongoing operations of the business

Multilocations

Multilocation selection decisions differ in some important respects from single-location selection decisions. For example, a new competitor to Club Med could lay out a plan for locations all over the world taking into account many factors. But when Club Med adds a new location, consideration must be given to its present locations and the specific recreations offered at each. As another example, suppose yet another competitor to Federal Express were to start up. It may wish to limit the first fifty locations of its offices to a specified region of the United States. Federal Express, on the other hand, must take into account present locations served throughout the United States to avoid overlapping and to provide synergy. Banking firms, brokerage firms, resorts, TV networks, motel chains, franchise services, and airlines all face the multilocation as well as the single-location problem.

QUANTITATIVE METHODS FOR LOCATION SELECTION

Quantitative techniques for location selection vary from the simple to the complex. We will give an overview of a few common methods, starting with factor weighting.

Factor Weighting

Factor weighting is a simple numerical method that has six steps:

1. Develop a list of relevant factors.
2. Assign a weight to each factor to reflect its relative importance in the firm's objectives.
3. Develop a scale for each factor (for example, 1 to 5, 1 to 10, or 1 to 100 points).
4. Have management score each location for each factor, using the scale in step 3.
5. Multiply the score times the weights for each factor, and total the score for each location.

EXHIBIT 6-3

■ Factor Weighting in Selection of Ski Resort Location

Factor	Importance Weight	Location Scores			Weighted Scores		
		California	Colorado	New England	California	Colorado	New England
Average snowfall/year	8	5	4	3	(8)(5) = 40	(8)(4) = 32	(8)(3) = 24
Topography	9	4	5	4	(9)(4) = 36	(9)(5) = 45	(9)(4) = 36
Size of nearest market	7	3	2	5	(7)(3) = 21	(7)(2) = 14	(7)(5) = 35
Transportation to ski resort	5	4	4	5	(5)(4) = 20	(5)(4) = 20	(5)(5) = 25
Government incentives	3	3	4	4	(3)(3) = 9	(3)(4) = 12	(3)(4) = 12
Number and size of competitors	3	2	5	5	(3)(2) = 6	(3)(5) = 15	(3)(5) = 15
				Totals	132	138	147

Factor scoring scale: 5 = excellent, 4 = good, 3 = fair, 2 = poor, 1 = unacceptable.

6. Make a recommendation based on the maximum point score, considering the results of qualitative approaches as well.

A simplified illustration is provided in Exhibit 6–3 for location of a new ski resort. The rating sheet in that exhibit provides a list of not easily quantifiable factors that management has decided are important, their weights, and their ratings for three possible sites—California, Colorado, and New England. The factor-weighting analysis indicates that New England, with a total weight of 147, is preferable to both the California and Colorado locations. By changing the weights slightly for those factors about which there is some doubt, we can analyze the sensitivity of the decision.

Cost Comparisons

As seen in Exhibit 6–3, some benefits (such as topography and government incentives) are relatively intangible, while others (such as average snowfall or number of competitors) are more easily quantifiable. Factor rating, as used above, allows for a complete analysis even if all factors are intangible. In situations where intangible benefits and costs play only a *minor* role, strictly objective **cost analysis** can be very useful. As an example, Harding discusses the advantages of moving offices from older urban centers to smaller cities.[2] Some of these benefits appear as measurable cost reductions, as shown in his analysis in Exhibit 6–4.

Center of Gravity Method

The **center of gravity method** is a mathematical technique used for finding a location for a single warehouse that services a number of retail stores. The method takes into account the location of markets, the volume of goods shipped to those markets, and shipping costs in finding a best location for a central warehouse.

By way of an example, consider the case of Sweet Cicely's Garden, a chain of six upscale retail gift shops.[3] The firm's store locations are in Cincinnati, Knoxville, Chicago, Pittsburgh, New York, and Atlanta. They are currently being supplied out of an old and inadequate warehouse in Cincinnati, the site of the chain's first store. Data on demand rates at each outlet are shown in Exhibit 6–5.

The firm has decided to find some "central" location in which to build a new warehouse. Since the number of containers shipped each month affects cost, distance alone should not be the principal criterion. The center of gravity method assumes that cost is directly proportional to both distance and volume shipped. The ideal location is that which minimizes the weighted distance between the warehouse and its retail outlets, where the distance is weighted by the number of containers shipped.

[2] Charles F. Harding, "Why Administrative Offices are Moving to Smaller Cities," *Administrative Management* (September 1981), pp. 40–42, 66.

[3] Modified from an example given by James R. Evans et al., *Applied Production and Operations Management*, 2d Ed. (St. Paul, Minn.: West, 1987), pp. 159–162.

───── EXHIBIT 6–4 ───────────────────────────────────────

▪ *Cost Analysis of Moving from Big City to Smaller City*

Big City Vs. Small City Administrative Office

	Big City Location	Small City Location
Employment		
Clerical	200	188
Managerial	20	22
Salaries		
Average clerical salary	$240 per week	$204 per week
Average managerial salary	$384 per week	$384 per week
Workweek length	37½ hours	40 hours
Annual turnover	30%	20%
Average clerical recruiting cost	10% of salary	5% of salary
Fringe benefit cost	30% of payroll	30% of payroll
Occupancy		
Space requirement	200 square feet per employee	200 square feet per employee
Cost	$15 per square foot	$9 per square foot

Annual Cost Savings in Smaller Cities

		Year 1 ($000)	Year 2 ($000)
Big City			
Salaries			
Clerical		$2,400	$2,798
Managerial		400	447
Fringe benefit costs		840	973
Clerical recruiting costs		72	81
Occupancy costs		660	739
	Total	$4,372	$5,038
Small City			
Salaries			
Clerical		$1,918	$2,229
Managerial		440	493
Fringe benefit costs		707	803
Clerical recruiting costs		19	22
Occupancy costs		378	424
	Total	$3,462	$3,971
Small city advantage			
Dollars		$910	$1,067
Percent		20.8%	21.2%

Source: Charles F. Harding, "Why Administrative Offices Are Moving to Smaller Cities," *Administrative Management* (September 1981), p. 42. Republished with permission from Administrative Management, copyright 1981, by Dalton Communications, Inc., New York.

The first step in the center of gravity method is to place the locations on a coordinate system. This is shown in Exhibit 6–6. The origin of the coordinate system and the scale used are arbitrary, just as long as the relative distances are correctly represented. This can be done easily by placing a grid over an ordinary map. The center of gravity is determined by Formulas 6.1 and 6.2.

_____ EXHIBIT 6–5 _____

▪ *Demand for Sweet Cicely's Garden Stores*

Retail Store Location	Number of Containers Shipped per Month
Cincinnati	400
Knoxville	300
Chicago	200
Pittsburgh	100
New York	300
Atlanta	100

$$C_x = \frac{\sum_i d_{ix} W_i}{\sum_i W_i} \tag{6.1}$$

$$C_y = \frac{\sum_i d_{iy} W_i}{\sum_i W_i} \tag{6.2}$$

where C_x = x coordinate of the center of gravity

C_y = y coordinate of the center of gravity

d_{ix} = x coordinate of location i

d_{iy} = y coordinate of location i

W_i = volume of goods moved to or from location i

For example, location 1 is Cincinnati and, from Exhibits 6–5 and 6–6,

$d_{1x} = 60$

$d_{1y} = 95$

$W_1 = 400$

Using the data in Exhibits 6–5 and 6–6 for each of the other cities, we find

$$C_x = \frac{(60)(400) + (80)(300) + (30)(200) + (90)(100) + (127)(300) + (65)(100)}{400 + 300 + 200 + 100 + 300 + 100}$$

$$= 76.9$$

$$C_y = \frac{(95)(400) + (75)(300) + (120)(200) + (110)(100) + (130)(300) + (40)(100)}{400 + 300 + 200 + 100 + 300 + 100}$$

$$= 98.9$$

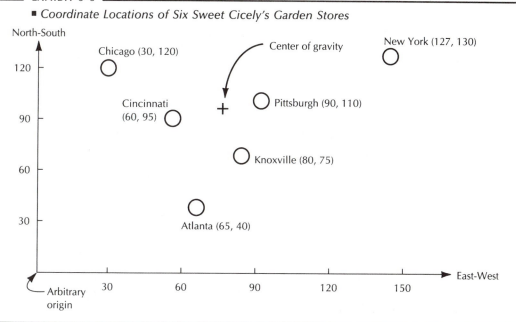

EXHIBIT 6–6

■ *Coordinate Locations of Six Sweet Cicely's Garden Stores*

This location (76.9, 98.9) is shown by the crosshair in Exhibit 6–6. By overlaying a U.S. map on this exhibit, we find that this location is near the border of southern Ohio and West Virginia. The firm may well wish to consider Huntington, West Virginia, or a nearby city as an appropriate location.

Reading 6.1 shows how similar methods have been used in deciding where to locate a blood collection warehouse or "staging area."

Warehouse Multisite Locations and Sizes

Bowman and Stewart developed a warehouse location model that can be readily adapted to a wholesaling service company that desires to set up warehouses to cover a regional area such as New England.[4] Their technique answers the question of how many square miles of area each warehouse should serve. The more warehouses in the system, the smaller is the area served by each and hence the smaller are the warehouses.

Here are the economics of the problem as analyzed by Bowman and Stewart. Warehousing costs per dollar of goods handled tend to decrease with increasing volume (since costs of supervision and other overhead are spread over more units and since labor can usually be used with a lower proportion of idle time). They further reasoned that distance traveled would be the main factor determining costs associated with area and that this cost would tend to vary approximately with the square root of the area. (Radius and diameter vary with the square root of the area of a circle.)

[4] E. H. Bowman and J. B. Stewart, "A Model for Scale of Operations," *Journal of Marketing* (January 1956).

The following terms for the model are defined:

C = total cost per dollar of goods distributed in warehouse region

K = sales density, in dollar volume of goods per square mile handled by a warehouse

A = area in square miles served by warehouse

a = cost, per dollar's worth of goods, which is not affected either by warehouse volume or area served (variable cost per dollar unit)

b = fixed costs associated with warehouse operation

c = costs that vary with the distance from the warehouse

The total costs per dollar of merchandise handled are

$$C = a + \frac{b}{KA} + c\sqrt{A} \tag{6.3}$$

To minimize cost, we take the first derivative of C with respect to A, set it equal to 0 and solve for A. The following formula results:

$$A = \left[\frac{2b}{cK}\right]^{2/3} \tag{6.4}$$

Also dealing with warehouse location and sizing decisions, Effroymson and Ray[5] developed a branch-and-bound algorithm, while Atkins and Shriver[6] tackled the problem through linear programming.

Use of Optimization Criteria

The location of any service facility is strongly influenced by the optimization criterion selected. In private-sector decisions, the optimization criteria could be maximization of profit or minimization of cost. In the public sector, decisions are hopefully more responsive to the needs of society, but the objectives are often more difficult to agree upon and to quantify.

As an example, Abernathy and Hershey dealt with the problem of locating a single health care facility to serve a three-city area.[7] Each city had a population with different health care consumption characteristics. That is, distance barriers and need

[5] M. A. Effroymson and T. L. Ray, "A Branch and Bound Algorithm for Plant Location," *Operations Research* (May–June 1966).

[6] Robert J. Atkins and Richard H. Shriver, "A New Approach to Facilities Location," *Harvard Business Review,* Vol. 46, No. 3 (May–June 1968).

[7] William J. Abernathy and John C. Hershey, "A Spatial Allocation Model for Regional Health Services Planning," *Operations Research,* Vol. 20, No. 3 (May–June 1972), pp. 629–642.

for immediate proximity were higher or lower depending on that city's socioeconomics. The researchers examined three criteria:

1. Maximize the total number of visits (or utilization rate) to the health facility.
2. Minimize the average distance per person in the region to the nearest facility.
3. Minimize the average travel distance per visit to the nearest facility.

Exhibit 6–7 shows a map of the three cities and where the health care facility would be located under each of the preceding criteria. When the first criterion, maximizing utilization rate, is selected, the facility is located at city C—this city had a large number of people for whom distance was a strong barrier. For the second criterion, city B was chosen because of its central location between the two larger cities. And city A, with the largest population base and the most mobile and frequent users of health care, is selected under the third criterion. The final choice of cities would require planners to decide which criterion is most important.

SITE SELECTION

Criteria

Site selection may sometimes be divided into two stages: community (within the location area) and specific site selection. The site chosen should be appropriate to the nature

___ EXHIBIT 6–7 _____

■ *Location of One Health Center for Three Different Criteria*

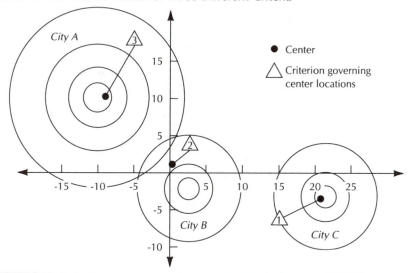

Source: W. J. Abernathy and I. C. Hershey, "A Spatial Interaction Model for Regional Health Services Planning." Reprinted with permission from *Operations Research*, Vol. 20, No. 3 (1972), p. 637, copyright 1972, Operations Research Society of America. No further reproduction permitted without the consent of the copyright owner.

_____ EXHIBIT 6–8 _____

■ *A Guide to Criteria for Site Selection*

1. Area available relative to area required
2. Appropriateness of buildings, if any on site
3. Zoning
4. Traffic, access, and parking
5. City road network
6. Neighborhood character
7. Labor availability, history, and costs
8. Taxes
9. Community attitudes
10. Educational, recreational, and cultural centers
11. Air and water pollution
12. Communications network
13. Banking system
14. Fire and police protection
15. Sewage and waste removal
16. Proximity to airports
17. Local market for the company's services

of the service operation, so clearly the factors involved will differ depending on the type of business. Exhibit 6–8 provides a sample listing of some criteria for site selection. O'Connor and Harris also have developed indicators (called the geo-life index) for site selection in metropolitan areas and communities.[8] The examples in Exhibit 6–9 show the index applied to Alabama as a whole and Mobile specifically.

Locating a Retail Store with the Gravity Model

When deciding where to locate a retail outlet such as a furniture or appliance store, a firm's objective is usually to maximize profits. The size and site of the store are two decision variables. The retailing literature is rich with variations of the so-called gravity or spatial interaction model, first proposed by Reilly in 1929, which can be used to estimate consumer demand.[9] Based on the work of Reilly and many others, a number of empirical observations have been found to affect retail trade:

1. The proportion of consumers patronizing a given shopping area varies with their distance from the shopping area.
2. The proportion of consumers patronizing various shopping areas varies with the breadth and depth of merchandise offered by each shopping area.
3. The distances that consumers travel to various shopping areas vary for different types of product purchases.
4. The "pull" of any given shopping area is influenced by the proximity of competing shopping areas.

[8] M. O'Connor and F. Harris, "Using the Geo-Life Index," *Site Selection Handbook* (July–August 1986).
[9] W. J. Reilly, *The Law of Retail Gravitation* (New York: Putnam and Son, 1931).

————— EXHIBIT 6–9 —————

■ *Geo-Life Index*

Mobile Metro Area	Alabama
Population, 1985: 465,700 (U) Elevation: 211	Population, 1985: 5,124,321 (U)
Growth rate, 1980–85: 5.0 (M)	Population density, 1984: 79 (M)
Counties: Baldwin, Mobile	Population growth rate, 1980–84: 2.5 (M)
Climate	% of population 65 yrs. and older, 1980: 11.9 (M)
Avg. Temps—Jan. Max./Min.: 62 (U) 44 (U)	% housing owner-occupied, 1980: 70.1 (U)
Avg. Temps—July Max./Min.: 92 (U) 73 (U)	Cancer death rate per 100,000, 1984: 186 (M)
Avg. annual heating degree days: 1.560 (L)	Heart disease death rate per 100,000, 1984: 307 (M)
Avg. annual cooling degree days: 2,918 (U)	$ per pupil education expenditures, 1985: 2,241 (L)
Avg. annual precipitation: 65 (U)	Per capita personal income, 1984: 9,961 (L)
Cost of living, 1985:	% of population on welfare, 1984: 7.1 (U)
All items: 96.8 (M) Utilities: 119.3 (U)	Taxes per capita as % of personal income, 1983: 9.4 (L)
Housing: 88.2 (L) Health care: 87.7 (L)	% revenue from federal govt., 1983: 1.58 (M)
% owner occupied homes, 1980: 68.7 (M)	% voting age voting in 1984 presidential election: 50.2 (L)
% of revenues from federal govt., 1982: 5.5 (M)	% graduating from high school, 1983: 67.4 (L)
Unemployment rate, 1986: 9.7 (U)	Violent crime rate per 100,000, 1984: 432 (M)
# of 4-year accredited universities: 6	Property crime rate per 100,000, 1984: 2,572 (L)
Hospital beds per 100,000, 1981: 633 (M)	Per capita aid to the arts, 1984: 0.23 (L)
Days with unhealthful air quality, 1981:	Number of scientists and engineers, 1983: 3,856 (M)
Professional sports teams:	Disaster risks: Earthquakes (M) Tornadoes (H) Land-
Violent crime rate per 100,000, 1984: 777 (U)	slides (L) Hail (L) Floods (M) Nuclear power plants (H)
Property crime rate per 100,000, 1984: 4,881 (M)	Unsafe dams (H) Uranium sites (L) Acid rain (L)
Comments: U. of S. Alabama—medical school.	
Port of Mobile, Tenn—Tom waterway.	

After each of the state and metro entries is a letter indicating whether the value for that entry ranks in the upper third (U), middle third (M) or lower third (L) of all entries for that field.

Source: Michael O'Connor and Freya Harris, "Using the Geo-Life Index," *Site Selection Handbook* (July–August 1986).

The probability that a consumer at a given place of origin i will shop at a particular shopping center j is expressed by David L. Huff in the following model:[10]

$$P_{ij} = \frac{S_j/T_{ij}^{\lambda}}{\sum\limits_{j=1}^{n} (S_j/T_{ij}^{\lambda})} \tag{6.5}$$

where P_{ij} = probability of a consumer at a given point of origin i traveling to a particular shopping center j

    S_j = size of a shopping center j (measured in terms of square footage of selling area devoted to sale of a particular class of goods)

    T_{ij} = travel time involved in getting from a consumer's travel base i to a given shopping center j

[10] David L. Huff, "Defining and Estimating a Trading Area," *Journal of Marketing*, Vol. 28 (1964), pp. 34–38.

λ = a parameter that is to be estimated empirically to reflect the effect of travel time on various kinds of shopping trips.

In Huff's initial pilot study, λ was found to be 2.7 for furniture shopping trips and 3.2 for trips involving clothes purchases. The greater the value of λ, the less time expenditure for a given trip purpose.

The *expected* number of consumers at a given place of origin i that shop at a particular shopping center j is equal to the number of consumers at i multiplied by the probability that a consumer at i will select j for shopping. That is

$$E_{ij} = P_{ij}C_i \tag{6.6}$$

where E_{ij} = expected number of consumers at i likely to travel to shopping center j

$\quad\quad C_i$ = number of consumers at i

The gravity model of Eilon, Tilley, and Fowkes, instead of dealing with the number of consumers, predicted their expenditures at different shopping centers.[11] Assuming the attractive power of the center F_j to be a function of the sales of the center and the accessibility of the center K_{ij} to be an exponential function of distance, their model was

$$S_{ij} = \frac{E_iF_jK_{ij}}{\displaystyle\sum_{j=1}^{n} F_jK_{ij}} \tag{6.7}$$

where S_{ij} = expenditure by residents of zone i in center j

$\quad\quad E_i$ = total expenditure by zone i at all shopping centers

Exhibit 6–10 describes a series of steps used to calculate the size of the expected annual profit for each possible retail site. The end product is a list of potential sites with the size of store at each that would maximize profit. From this list, owners can begin to negotiate real estate deals for the top sites.

The Gravity Model in Nonretail Services

Variations of Huff's and Reilly's gravity models also have been applied to the services supplied by hospitals, recreational facilities, and colleges. For example, the model was used to determine the service areas of existing hospitals in St. Louis by Ault, Bass, and Johnson.[12] Attractiveness of each hospital complex was estimated to be proportional

---

[11] S. Eilon, R. P. R. Tilley, and T. R. Fowkes, "Analysis of a Gravity Demand Model," *Regional Studies,* Vol. 3 (September 1969), pp. 115–122.

[12] David Ault, Stephen Bass, and Thomas Johnson, "The Impact of New Hospital Construction on the Service Areas of Existing Hospital Complexes," *Proceedings of the American Institute for Decision Sciences* (St. Louis, 1971).

EXHIBIT 6–10

■ *Sequential Steps in Determining Optimal Location for a Retail Store*

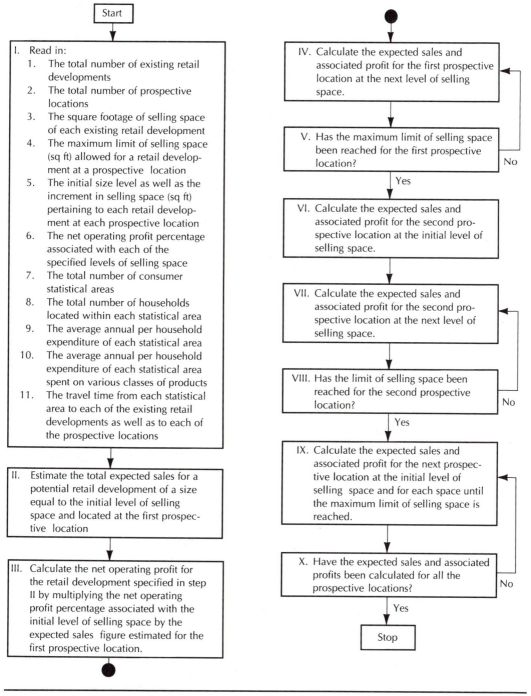

Source: David L. Huff, "A Programmed Solution for Approximating an Optimum Retail Location," *Land Economics* (August 1966), pp. 293–303. Used with permission.

to the total number of services offered there, and cost was measured in minutes to reach the hospital from each sector of the city. Morrill and Kelley used a similar gravity model to study flows of patients to hospitals.[13] Cesario developed a model to measure competition among northeastern Pennsylvania state park facilities in drawing vacationing residents of that state.[14] As a measure of trip cost, he employed road mileages from each county to each park. Finally, Render and Shawhan's model examined the competition among seventy public colleges in Ohio in attracting students from each county to attend their school.[15] All these applications indicate the potential for the use of gravity models in locating a wide variety of service-sector facilities and determining their success in drawing clients away from existing competition.

Factor-Weighting Method

Just as cities and communities can be compared for location selection by the factor-weighting model, as we saw earlier in this chapter, so can actual site decisions be helped. Exhibit 6–11 illustrates four factors of importance to Washington, D.C., health officials charged with opening that city's first public AIDS clinic. Of primary concern (and given a weight of 5) was location of the clinic so it would be as accessible as possible to the largest number of patients. The annual lease cost also was of some concern due to a tight budget. A suite in the new City Hall, at 14th and U Streets, was highly rated because its rent would be free. An old office building near the downtown bus station received a much lower rating because of its cost. Equally important as lease cost was the need for confidentiality of patients and, therefore, for a relatively inconspicuous clinic. Finally, because so many of the staff at the AIDS clinic would be donating their time, the safety, parking, and accessibility of each site were of concern as well.

From the three right-most columns in Exhibit 6–11, the weighted scores are summed. It appears that the bus terminal area can be excluded from further consideration, but that the other two sites are virtually identical in total score. The city may now consider other factors, including political ones, in selecting between the two remaining sites.

Multisites

Within a city or metropolitan area, various services require multiple sites for offices, warehouses, outlets, branches, or service areas for vehicles. Examples range from fire stations to branch banks to auto quick-lube shops. The measures of benefits that arise from an arrangement of sites within a metropolitan area are (1) *distance*, (2) *time*, and (3) *cost*. These three criteria are not necessarily related. For example, a customer may travel a longer distance by bus to reach the service site than traveling by cab. Again,

[13] R. L. Morrill and M. B. Kelley, "The Simulation of Hospital Use and the Estimation of Location Efficiency," *Geographical Analysis*, Vol. 2 (1970), pp. 283–300.

[14] Frank J. Cesario, "A Generalized Trip Distribution Model," *Journal of Regional Science*, Vol. 13 (1973), pp. 233–248.

[15] Barry Render and Gerald Shawhan, "A Spatial Interaction Model for the Allocation of Higher Education Enrollments," *Socio-Economic Planning Sciences*, Vol. 11 (1977), pp. 43–48.

EXHIBIT 6–11

■ *Potential AIDS Clinic Sites in Washington, D.C.*

		Potential Locations*				Weighted Scores		
Factor	Importance Weight	Homeless Shelter (2nd and D, S.E.)	City Hall (14th and U, NW)	Bus Terminal Area (7th and H, NW)		Homeless Shelter	City Hall	Bus Terminal Area
Accessibility for infectives	5	9	7	7		45	35	35
Annual lease cost	3	6	10	3		18	30	9
Inconspicuous	3	5	2	7		15	6	21
Accessibility for health staff	2	3	6	2		6	12	4
				Total scores		84	83	69

* All sites are rated on a 1 to 10 basis, with 10 as the highest score and 1 as the lowest.

a longer route over an expressway may be much quicker than driving through crowded inner-city streets.

The preceding criteria of distance, time, and cost may apply to a service business (1) that delivers goods or services where time is not a factor, (2) that must service people quickly (as in the case of a private ambulance business), or (3) when transportation costs are high and visits to clients frequent. On the other side of the coin, the sites selected may depend on the distance, time, and cost criteria taken from the point of view of the customer who must travel to the service site.

A tradeoff occurs when a service business adds more sites at a greater total cost to the firm. This may reduce the value of one or more of the preceding criteria. Also, the greater the proximity of sites, the more likely it is that some will draw trade from others.

Quantitative methods for finding the minimum number of sites to cover a specified market area are very rough in terms of meeting multiple realistic criteria. For example, geometric distance on a grid is sometimes used as a substitute for actual distance or time of travel. In one method, a table is set up in which markets served and potential sites are matched. When we want to find the minimum number and location of facilities to serve all customers within a specified service time or distance, we face what is called the **location set-covering problem.**

To illustrate, Arlington County, Virginia, which currently has five fire stations, wishes to place highly sophisticated emergency medical vehicles in one or more of those stations. The county's objective is to find a site or sites that will minimize response times to medical emergencies. Although regular firefighters and firetrucks are equipped to deal with minor medical problems, the county now wishes to provide its residents with a higher level and quality of care for severe cases. Exhibit 6–12 identifies the location of each of the current fire stations, its zone of the county, and the distance in time along major roads between zones. The question faced is where the medical vehicle or vehicles should be located. If the objective is to select a site so that maximum response time to any other zone is as small as possible, our analysis in Exhibit 6–13 provides several insights.

For example, if the county is satisfied responding to all medical calls within 30 minutes, then *one* station located in *either* zone B *or* zone D will suffice. If a 15-minute response time is the county's objective, then locating medical units in zones

_____ EXHIBIT 6–12 _____

■ *Zone Connections for Arlington County*

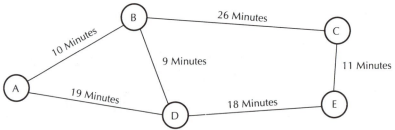

─── EXHIBIT 6–13 ───

■ *Possible Sites for Arlington County Emergency Medical Units*
  with Differing Response Rates

Zone in County	Set of Zones Served from Stations in This Zone		
	Within 10 Minutes	Within 15 Minutes	Within 30 Minutes
A	A, B	A, B	A, B, D
B	A, B, D	A, B	A, B, C, D, E
C	C	C, E	B, C, D, E
D	B, D	B, D	A, B, C, D, E
E	E	C, E	B, C, D, E
Possible locations to meet time constraints	B, C, E	B, C *or* B, E	B *or* D

B and C *or* B and E will suffice. Finally, if a 10-minute response time is desired, the county must place units at three stations, with one each in zones B, C, and E.

Another version of the location set-covering problem is called **maximal covering.** The goal of maximal covering is to maximize the population covered within a desired service distance. First described by Church and Revelle,[16] the approach begins by mapping the population density for a metropolitan area. The first site selected is the one that maximizes the population served within a specified travel distance. Then a second site is selected that serves the maximum of the remaining population. This process is continued until the population served by the last site meets the criterion for level of population to be served.

Geographic Patterns of Service Firms

The geographic patterns of service firms take into account both location and selection of sites. Once again, the diversity of service systems makes classification of firms within patterns difficult. A proposed classification with examples is given in Exhibit 6–14. Such a classification should be helpful in analyzing site selections and making work layouts, the topic of Chapter 7.

─── SUMMARY ───

Part of the design of the service conversion or delivery process consists of location and site selection. Location selection is the macro decision about the general regions or metropolitan areas in which the business is to be established. Site selection is the micro decision as to the specific pieces of property for the business location.

Several methods for evaluating locations, including factor weighting, cost analysis, center of gravity, Bowman and Stewart's warehouse model, and optimization

[16] Richard Church and Charles Revelle, ''The Maximal Covering Location Problem,'' *Papers of the Regional Science Association* (Fall 1974), pp. 101–118.

_____ EXHIBIT 6–14 _____

▪ *Geographic Patterns of Service Firms*

Classification	Examples
1. HQ/SA	Beauty parlor, auto repair, retail store, university, correspondence schools
2. HQ + local SAs	Local retail chains, local restaurant chains, accounting firms, consulting firms, hospital chains
3. HQ + regional offices	National retail chains, restaurant chains, brokerage firms, credit card companies, gasoline distributors
4. HQ + local offices + SAs	Electrical utility firms, telephone companies, brokerage firms, income tax consulting firms, national airlines
5. HQ + mobile telephone cars and trucks/boats/planes	Locksmiths, ambulance services, car towing services, charter boat services, bus companies

HQ = headquarters; SA = service area

criteria were discussed. For the site-selection problem, a variety of gravity or spatial interaction models, along with another factor-weighting example, and the location set-covering approach were presented.

Service location analysis differs in many ways from industrial location analysis. The focus in the industrial sector is usually on minimizing cost, while revenue maximization is the focus of most private-sector service firms. This is so because manufacturing costs tend to vary substantially between locations, but in service firms, costs vary little within a region. The location decision focus for service firms should thus be on determining the volume of business and revenue. Exhibit 6–15 provides a summary of the differences between location strategies for services and industrial organizations.

_____ DISCUSSION QUESTIONS

1. Explain the assumptions behind the center of gravity method. How can the model be used in service facility location?

2. How do service facility location decisions differ from industrial location decisions?

3. What considerations would be important to a police department opening a new station? What information would be useful in making the site-selection decision?

4. Explain the concept of Reilly's gravity model. What is the meaning of λ?

5. Propose an application of the gravity or spatial interaction model other than in retail-store location analysis.

6. Describe the set-covering approach. Why is it popular with public sector organizations?

7. List the factors you think are most important in deciding where to locate

    a. A distribution warehouse

    b. A retail gift shop

    c. A health clinic

    d. A government employment office

_____ EXHIBIT 6–15 _____

■ *Location Strategies: Service versus Industrial Organizations*

Service/Retail/Professional	Industrial
Revenue Focus	*Cost Focus*
Volume/revenue	Tangible costs
Drawing area	Transportation cost of raw material
Purchasing power	Shipment cost of finished goods
Competition	Energy cost per BTU
Advertising/promotion/pricing	Utility costs
Physical quality	Labor
Parking/access	Raw material
Security/lighting	Taxes, etc.
Appearance/image	Intangible and future costs
Associated business	Attitude toward union
Cost determinates	Quality of life
Management caliber	Education expenditures by state
Operation policies	Quality of state and local government
Techniques	*Techniques*
Correlation analysis to determine importance of above factors for a particular type of operation	Linear programming (transportation method)
Traffic counts	Weighted approach to intangibles
Demographic analysis of drawing area	Breakeven analysis
Purchasing power analysis of drawing area	Crossover charts
Factor weighting	
Assumptions	*Assumptions*
Location is a major determinate of revenue	Location is a major determinate of cost
Issues manifesting from high customer contact dominate	Most major costs can be identified explicitly for each site
Costs are relatively constant for a given area: therefore, the revenue function is critical	Low customer contact allows focus on the identifiable costs
	Intangible costs can be objectively evaluated

Source: From Jay Heizer and Barry Render, *Production and Operations Management*, p. 344. Copyright © 1988 by Allyn and Bacon. Reprinted with permission.

_____ PROBLEMS

6.1 A Detroit seafood restaurant is considering opening a second facility in the suburb of West Bloomfield. Exhibit 6–16 shows its ratings of five factors at each of four potential sites. Which site should be selected?

6.2 In placing a new medical clinic, county health offices wish to consider three sites. The pertinent data are given in Exhibit 6–17. Which is the best site?

6.3 The main post office in Tampa, Florida, is due to be replaced with a much larger, more modern facility that can handle the tremendous flow of mail that has followed that city's growth since 1970. Since all mail, incoming or outgoing, travels from the seven regional post offices in Tampa through the main post office, its site selection can mean a big difference in overall delivery and movement efficiency. Using the

EXHIBIT 6–16

Factor	Weight	Site			
		1	2	3	4
Affluence of local population	10	70	60	85	90
Construction and land cost	10	85	90	80	60
Traffic flow	25	70	60	85	90
Parking availability	20	80	90	90	80
Growth potential	15	90	80	90	75

EXHIBIT 6–17

Location Factor	Weight	Scores		
		Downtown	Suburb A	Suburb B
Facility utilization	9	9	7	6
Average time per emergency trip	8	6	6	8
Employee preferences	5	2	5	6
Accessibility to major roadways	5	8	4	5
Land costs	4	2	9	6

data in the following table, calculate the center of gravity for the proposed new facility.

Regional Post Office	X, Y Map Coordinates	Truck Round-Trips per Day
Ybor City	(10, 5)	3
Davis Island	(3, 8)	3
Dale-Marbry	(4, 7)	2
Palma Ceia	(15, 10)	6
Bayshore	(13, 3)	5
Temple Terrace	(1, 12)	3
Hyde Park	(5, 5)	10

6.4 Todd's Video, a major video rental and TV sales chain headquartered in New Orleans, is about to open its first outlet in Mobile, Alabama, and wants to select a site in that city that will place it in the center of the city's population base. Todd examines the seven census tracks in Mobile, plots the coordinates of the center

of each from a map, and looks up the population base in each to use as a weighting. The information gathered appears in the following table. At what center of gravity coordinates should the new store be located?

Census Tract	Population in Census Tract	X, Y Map Coordinates
101	2,000	(25, 45)
102	5,000	(25, 25)
103	10,000	(55, 45)
104	7,000	(50, 20)
105	10,000	(80, 50)
106	20,000	(70, 20)
107	14,000	(90, 25)

6.5 Sweet Cicely's Garden, whose warehouse decision was documented in Exhibits 6–5 and 6–6, has decided its retail outlets are too far-flung geographically. To alleviate the situation, it intends to close the New York store and open a new store in Milwaukee. It is hoped that the demand in Milwaukee, which has coordinates of (31, 140) will equal that of the New York store. To where should the warehouse be relocated?

6.6 The police chief wants to locate enough police stations so that each sector of the city has an average response time of 6 minutes. Using the data in Exhibit 6–18, determine the minimum number of facilities needed and their locations.

<hr/>
EXHIBIT 6–18
<hr/>

City Sector	Response Time in Minutes from this Sector				
	1	2	3	4	5
1	1	2	8	20	15
2		1	3	12	10
3			1	16	5
4				1	4
5					1

6.7 Exhibits 6–12 and 6–13 dealt with the location of emergency medical units at fire stations in Arlington County, Virginia. If the county finds a 25-minute response time is acceptable, how many ambulance sites are needed? What combinations of possible sites will suffice?

6.8 Jeri Ross is proprietress of two exclusive woman's clothing stores in Miami. In her plan to expand to a third location, she has narrowed her decision down to three sites—one in a downtown office building, one in a shopping mall, and one in an old Victorian house in the suburban area of Coral Gables. She feels that rent is absolutely the most important factor to be considered, while walk-in traffic is 90 percent as important as rent. Further, the more distant the new store is from her two existing stores the better, she thinks. She weights this factor to be 80 percent as important as walk-in traffic. Jeri developed Exhibit 6–19, where she graded each site on the same system used in her MBA program in college. Which site is preferable?

<hr/>
EXHIBIT 6–19
<hr/>

	Down-town	Shopping Mall	Coral Gables House
Rent	D	C	A
Walk-in Traffic	B	A	D
Distance from existing stores	B	A	C

<hr/>
READING 6.1
<hr/>

An Application of Warehouse Location Techniques to Bloodmobile Operations

Robert P. Cerveny

Quite often in volunteer, nonprofit organizations, decisions which may have significant effects on the ongoing operational costs of the organization are made without a thorough analysis of the ramifications of the decisions. For example, a warehouse may be poorly located to serve the service area because a benefactor donated the space or the terms of the lease were favorable, etc. Little thought is given to the locational effect on the actual use of the warehouse. Once the lease is signed, the organization is effectively blocked from making changes for a period of time after that.

While not a major determinant of overall blood program efficiency and effectiveness, bloodmobile staging areas (defined here as a warehouse/garage where bloodmobiles are provisioned, re-

<hr/>

Source: Reprinted by permission of Robert P. Cerveny, "An Application of Warehouse Location Techniques to Bloodmobile Operations," *Interfaces*, Vol. 10, No. 6 (December 1980), pp. 88–96. Copyright 1980 The Institute of Management Sciences, 290 Westminster Street, Providence, Rhode Island 02903 USA.

paired, and kept between blood collections) play a significant role in the collection activities for whole blood. In an ongoing program, staging areas are fixed in the short run due to the aforementioned leasing/ownership arrangements. However, as blood programs expand or the demographics of cities change, opportunities arise which allow the location of bloodmobile staging areas to be re-evaluated.

As the two blood centers examined in this study exhibited a mix of urban and rural collection sites, this analysis should be of interest to other organizations which service mixed areas with collection and/or distribution programs.

THE ORIGINAL PROBLEM

Two regional centers of the American Red Cross Blood Program had the option of changing their main warehouse/garage configuration in the near future and therefore wanted to examine the effects of such a change. They were interested in finding a measure which would allow prospective sites to be objectively compared quickly and easily. Total distance traveled by bloodmobiles during a year to collect blood was agreed upon as a reasonable and obtainable measure.

Both centers were interested in considering either a single central site or a combination of a central site with subsites. (A subsite is defined as a satellite staging area which has limited facilities for storage of consumable supplies, vehicle repairs, etc.) It was recognized by all parties concerned that site analysis on the basis of distance traveled is only one facet of a site selection; cost per square foot, availability of sites, highway access, location of processing plants, etc., would ultimately have to be weighed in the evaluation. Therefore, the information provided by the present evaluation would not be the sole determining factor but would be useful input into the decision process.

SPECIAL CONSIDERATIONS

The process of collecting a product like whole blood which is both perishable and has a limited shelf-life places limits on the collection procedures which in turn affect warehouse location. As whole blood is more readily collectable by going to the

donors rather than asking them to come to central collection sites, mobile operations are necessary.

In the regional systems studied, there are three methods of collecting whole blood from donors. The first is at a fixed site or a permanent location. The other two are types of mobile operations; a regular mobile collection vehicle and a buslike collection vehicle. The regular mobile collection vehicle is basically a trailer or van unit which transports all the equipment necessary for blood collection to the remote site where it is set up, operated, and torn down at the end of the collection period. It then returns to the warehouse. This type of operation requires a room and other support facilities at the collection site. The other type of mobile operation is completely self-contained. It requires less site setup and teardown but is limited as to the number of donors it can accept.

Both regions in the study used a mix of regular mobile units and self-contained ones. They attempt to send the self-contained units to collection points which do not have facilities for a regular van, or for which the number of units collected do not warrant sending a regular van.

Finally, one of the regions used five bloodmobile staging areas at the time of the study while the other region operated from a central location. This allowed questions of contraction or expansion of resources to be examined in meaningful context.

After consultations with the managers involved it was decided that the heuristic approach to site selection which is well documented in the literature would be quite satisfactory. This method is both inexpensive and implementable in a short time frame while yielding satisfactory results. Essentially it treats the problem as the minimization of travel distances between points on a plane, where the points represent the staging area and the collection sites.

RESULTS

The warehouse location study examines the following questions:

- What is the present collection pattern for the region; i.e., how many trips were being made from existing site(s) to each collection point?

- If you assigned each collection point to the "nearest" warehouse, what would be the effect on travel distance?
- If you assigned all trips to a single existing warehouse, what would happen to the distance traveled?
- Given some alternative configurations of warehouses (either a single site or up to three sites), how do the distance traveled values change?
- Given the "optimal" location for a single warehouse, what is the minimum travel distance?

The analysis determined that the scheduling practices in the region where multiple warehouses existed were reasonable; i.e., the total mileage was within 14 percent of optimal given the present configuration. A geographic area was then identified as the preferred direction to search for a new site location. If the center deviated too greatly from this direction, the penalties in terms of additional distance traveled increased substantially. This analysis was very useful to this region in that they were able to locate suitable facilities near the "optimal" point and were able to justify the move in part by the results of the study.

The results in the other region showed that moving to the "optimal" location would improve travel distance by a negligible amount, and there were severe penalties for going much further away from that point. This lent credence to the concept that this region's warehouses should expand in the present facility.

This study also allowed a determination of how many bloodmobile collection units should be located at each site. The assignment of each collection point to its nearest warehouse gave the manager a way of determining the number of trips per year each warehouse should support. The number of bloodmobile vehicles necessary was then readily determined and rational decisions could be made as to distribution of bloodmobiles.

CONCLUSIONS

A heuristic method used to assist in the location of bloodmobile staging areas provides useful insight into blood collection patterns and sheds light on a problem that has traditionally been performed by a seat-of-the-pants approach.

This same type of analysis would be of benefit in location of processed blood storage for later distribution to hospitals, and in other process center management.

———— QUESTIONS FOR READING 6.1

1. Name some other organizations that service both urban and rural areas with collection or distribution programs.

2. Describe the differences between bloodmobile staging areas and central operations. What are the advantages and disadvantages of each approach?

3. Search the management science literature and describe some possible heuristics that can be used in site selection. Document and photocopy your source(s).

———— READING 6.2 ————————

The Basics of Branch Site Selection

Robert T. Volk

Rising occupancy costs and retail branching saturation are causing banks to take a hard look at branch sites and how they are selected. More than ever before, site-selection methodologies are being

fine-tuned and made more scientific. Banks, always on the lookout for the next frontier of untapped market share and how to find it, are continuing their relentless search for "the formula"—that pre-

Source: Reprinted with permission from: *The Banker's Magazine* September/October 1987, pp. 68–71, Copyright 1987. Warren Gorham & Lamont, Inc. 210 South Street, Boston, MA 02111.

cise blend of demographic indicators, financial analysis, statistical correlation, and old-fashioned common sense that will shine a bright light on the next successful branch location.

One of the most dramatic reasons for greater focus on the location issue is the escalation in lease expenses. In 1976, when many of the leases coming due this year were first signed, the average lease expense for retail space in New York City was $17 per square foot. Today it is $60.

METHODOLOGY

Senior management uses numerous methodologies to provide a scientific justification for site selection. What these methodologies share is an approach that is primarily made up of three factors:

— Analysis of the bank's position (situation analysis)
— Evaluation of available locations
— Selection of the site

Situation Analysis

This initial phase of site selection can be a subset of the bank's strategic plan. During this process, specific data is developed describing:

— The number of households in a demographic area (using government census tract, ZIP code, or other territorial classification)
— The bank's existing customer totals by demographic area
— The percentage of the bank's total customer base represented by the above totals (This figure identifies the demographic areas that are supplying the most customers.)
— Estimates of the number of core-deposit accounts available in a given area and the number of those accounts already held by the bank

Location Analysis

The next step in the site-determination process is location analysis. In this phase, demographic areas are ranked by criteria selected by the bank, mostly for their market potential within the bank's selected service and product concentrations.

Relevant data here includes the area's population density and housing and income levels, as well as the area's employment distribution, retail trade, industrial base, and banking competition. In order to be considered as a possible site, an area must meet the bank's minimum predetermined levels for all of these factors. The result of this analysis is a list of target areas for consideration as potential branch sites.

Site Selection

Each site identified by the location analysis process must then be subjected to further study to reveal other, more specific geographical strengths and weaknesses such as natural and man-made boundaries (major roads, parks, railroad stations, etc.), traffic patterns, existing and proposed shopping areas, construction plans for new or widened roads, nearby business offices, and location of the competition (along with its proximity to the proposed site).

Once these geographical benefits and disadvantages are determined, the following calculations must be made:

— Current and forecasted economic and demographic data
— Estimated market penetration (the determination of the bank's fair share of the available deposits based on the levels held by the competition)
— Cost of the proposed site, including lease of the building, equipment, occupancy, construction costs, and staffing
— Projected income based on estimated funds, including a break-even analysis to determine the length of time before the branch will begin to be profitable over an established income threshold

The methodology previously summarized can be used to either select branches on an individual basis or to provide an entire list of targets. In both cases, it is crucial to give as much due consideration as any new branch will have on the network as a whole. Branch offices in an extensive network do not operate as islands unto themselves. They are, in fact, part of a carefully planned complement that should be designed for optimum market coverage.

This does not imply, however, that the branches in a network need to be equidistant from one another—indeed, markets, profits, and the availability of space are by no means uniformly distributed. In some cases, creating a presence in an area by establishing one branch location is not as attractive to a bank as dominance in another area by maintaining several locations. In other cases, the opposite scenario may be true.

CONCLUSION

Clearly, the choice of location of a branch and the alternatives for configuring individual branch delivery needs are wide open. Finding the correct "formula" is a more complex process today, but the added complexity has greatly expanded a bank's site-selection methodology. Available tech-nologies have provided banks with some ammunition to reduce the potentially disastrous effects of skyrocketing lease expenses. As a result, banks now have more opportunities to fine-tune methods of delivery until they can satisfy target profitability requirements for each branch.

_____ QUESTIONS FOR READING 6.2

1. Identify the major factors in bank situation and location analysis.

2. What factors influence branch site selection?

3. Identify another service industry. How does site selection differ from banking?

4. Visit your local bank and ask the manager to read this article. What insights did he or she gain? Did your dialogue with the manager add further factors that should be considered?

_____ READING 6.3 _____

How to Pick the Best Hotel Location

Patricia K. Guseman

Real-estate analysts predict that developers will build few new hotels and motels over the next few years, because the hotel market is overbuilt and because changes in the tax code offer little shelter to investors. But opportunities remain in the hotel market, depending on where a business wants to site a hotel.

The revenue estimates for any hotel or motel depend on its location. Investors can make the most money by choosing the right location. One type of location in which there is a continuing demand for hotel rooms is near hospitals and medical centers. Because of the growth of medical complexes in metropolitan areas nationwide, patients and their relatives need nearby hotels. Shorter hospital stays, outpatient care, and the increasing need for diagnostic tests have further contributed to the demand for hospital-area hotels (see Exhibit 6–20).

To find the optimum hospital-area hotel site, a business needs to consider three things: (1) the demographic characteristics of the location, (2) the characteristics of the hospital at the location, and

_____ EXHIBIT 6–20 _____

▪ No Vacancy

Locating a new hotel near a hospital is one way to ensure high occupancy rates. Look for a large metropolitan area where personal income is high and growing rapidly.

Eight most important factors for high occupancy rates in hotels near hospitals, ranked by importance:

1. Large metropolitan area
2. High personal income in area
3. High growth in personal income
4. Existence of a Health Maintenance Organization
5. Fiscal ties between the hospital or medical staff and the hotel
6. Low proportion of hospital beds compared with population
7. Low concentration of medical/health facilities in area
8. Large share of an area's hospital beds at nearest hospital

(3) the characteristics of the proposed hotel. To determine the best mix of these characteristics, Population and Survey Analysts (PASA) analyzed

Source: Excerpted from *American Demographics* (August 1988), pp. 42–43. Reprinted with permission.
© American Demographics, August 1988.

74 existing hospital-area hotels across the nation. PASA measured the success of these facilities using occupancy rates as well as annual revenues, including fees from renting meeting rooms and from other sources.

Eight variables are positively associated with high occupancy rates in hospital-area hotels. Most important is a large metropolitan population size, while second and third are a high personal income and rapid growth in personal income in the metropolitan area. A health maintenance organization (HMO) associated with the hospital also increases the likelihood of high occupancy rates. Joint-venture investments between a hospital or medical staff and a hotel also significantly increase occupancy rates. Occupancy rates are higher in areas that have a small proportion of hotel beds relative to the resident population and that have relatively few medical and health facilities. When the hospital nearest the hotel facility has a disproportionately large share of all hospital beds in the area, the hotel occupancy rates are higher.

While other hospital-specific variables—like the average stay of patients and the number of specialized services provided by the hospital—are important, they rank low compared with these eight factors. Demographic variables, on the whole, prove to be more important than hospital-related variables in determining occupancy rates.

There are six important predictors of financial success for hospital hotels. In some cases these are the same factors that are important for high occupancy rates, but the order of importance

changes. Fiscal ties between a hospital or medical staff and a hotel move up to the number-one position. Growth in personal income in a metropolitan area is the second most important predictor of a hospital-area hotel's financial success.

Once a company analyzes the factors important to the success of a hospital-area hotel, it can then include other characteristics in the design of the hotel that will ensure success. If most of a hotel's customers will be older, the hotel should be designed with their preferences in mind. Older customers typically prefer only one entry to the hotel for security purposes, for example. Rooms should be furnished for those who will be spending time there. The furnishings might include recliners or kitchen facilities.

Using this kind of empirical approach to estimating revenue potential before a hotel is built allows investors and lenders to make a more informed decision in determining the best hotel or motel site. The same approach can be applied to other types of services located near a hospital or medical center, including other medical services and facilities.

_____ QUESTIONS FOR READING 6.3

1. Contact a hospital in your area and ask its administrator to comment on the validity of location selection for a hotel as described in this reading.

2. What factors would a hotel consider if it were *not* interested in locating near a hospital?

_____ CASE 6.1 _____

Red River Blood Center

Red River is a community of 65,000 people in which there are three hospitals with a total of 287 beds. The Red River Blood Center was formed four years ago to provide the needed whole blood and plasma for emergency and surgical use within the three hospitals. The blood center is also part of a

statewide network that shares blood resources. The Center is located downtown next to the largest of the three hospitals. It is on the fourth floor of a doctors' office building.

Given the size of the Red River community, the blood center does relatively poorly in attracting

Source: Jack R. Meredith, *The Management of Operations,* 3d Ed. (New York: Wiley, 1987), pp. 217–218. Copyright © 1987 by John Wiley & Sons, Inc. Reprinted by permission of John Wiley & Sons, Inc.

a sufficient number of blood donors. The administrator of the Red River Blood Center is constantly calling on other members of the network to provide blood needed in emergency cases. On the other hand, Red River is very seldom able to help other members of the network in their emergencies. During the initial two years of operations, the administration believed that newness of the center was the cause for "substandard" donor performance. But, now that the center has been operating for four years, that "excuse" will no longer hold up. Donors have often complained of the horrible traffic conditions downtown and the fact that parking is so scarce.

One of the lab technicians who recently moved from a larger community commented about the use of a mobile blood unit and setting up temporary clinics in meeting halls and other public facilities. She indicated that numerous civic and religious organizations had helped in organizing blood drives through their memberships. The new assistant administrator even commented about the possibility of moving from the downtown location to an outlying shopping center. The administrator argued that the blood center was located where it was to be close to the hospitals.

QUESTIONS FOR CASE 6.1

1. What location/transportation tradeoffs have been made here?

2. Comment on the "demand(s)" made by the blood center's constituents.

3. What factors should be considered in comparing the benefits and costs of mobile or temporary units with a shopping center-based unit?

REFERENCES

Abernathy, William J., and John C. Hershey. "A Spatial Allocation Model for Regional Health-Services Planning," *Operations Research*, Vol. 20, No. 3 (May–June 1972), pp. 629–642.

Borgers, A., and H. J. P. Timmermans. "City Centre Entry Points, Store Location Patterns and Pedestrian Route Choice Behavior," *Socio Economic Planning Sciences*, Vol. 21, No. 1 (1986), pp. 25–31.

Boyer, Richard, and David Savage. *Places Rated Almanac*. New York: Rand McNally & Co., 1981.

Craig, C. Samuel, A. Ghosh, and Sara McLafferty. "Model of the Retail Location Process: A Review," *Journal of Retailing*, Vol. 60, No. 1 (Spring 1984), pp. 5–36.

Davis, Samuel G., et al. "Strategic Planning for Bank Operations with Multiple Check-Processing Locations," *Interfaces*, Vol. 16, No. 5 (November–December 1986), pp. 1–12.

DeSanta, Richard. "All That Glitters Is Not Upscale," *Progressive Grocer* (April 1987), pp. 112–117.

Fitzsimmons, James A., and Lou A. Allen. "A Warehouse Location Model Helps Texas Comptroller Select Out-of-State Audit Offices," *Interfaces*, Vol. 13, No. 5 (October 1983), pp. 40–46.

Ghosh, Avjit, and C. Samuel Craig. "Formulating Retail Location Strategy in a Changing Environment," *Journal of Marketing*, Vol. 47 (Summer 1983), pp. 56–68.

———. "An Approach to Determining Optimal Locations for New Services," *Journal of Marketing Research*, Vol. 23 (November 1986), pp. 354–362.

Goodchild, Michael F. "ILACS: A Location-Allocation Model for Retail Site Selection," *Journal of Retailing*, Vol. 60, No. 1 (Spring 1984), pp. 84–100.

Guseman, Patricia K. "How to Pick the Best Location," *American Demographics* (August 1988), pp. 42–43.

Heizer, Jay, and Barry Render. *Production and Operations Management: Strategies and Tactics*. Boston: Allyn and Bacon, 1988.

Huff, David L. "A Programmed Solution for Approximately an Optimum Retail Location," *Land Economics* (August 1966), pp. 293–303.

Keating, Joseph W. "Facility Planning in a Decentralized Structure: Three Key Areas of Responsibility," *Industrial Development* (July–August 1986).

Khumawala, B. M., and D. C. Whybark. "A Comparison of Some Recent Warehouse Location Techniques," *The Logistics Review*, Vol. 7 (1971).

Kolesar, P., and W. E. Walker. "An Algorithm for Dynamic Relocation of Five Companies," *Operations Research* (March–April 1974).

Lopez, David A., and Paul Gray. "The Substitution of Communication for Transportation: A Case Study," *Management Science,* Vol. 23, No. 11 (July 1977), pp. 1149–1160.

Lord, Dennis J., and Charles D. Lynds. "The Use of Regression Models in Store Location Research," *Akron Business and Economic Review* (Summer 1981), pp. 13–14.

Maas, Michael. "In Offices of the Future: The Productivity Value of Environment," *Management Review* (March 1983).

Mahajan, Vijay, S. Sharma, and D. Srinivas. "An Application of Portfolio Analysis for Identifying Attractive Retail Locations," *Journal of Retailing,* Vol. 61, No. 4 (Winter 1985), pp. 19–34.

Merredew, Clive. "A Model Facility Delivery Process," *Industrial Development* (July–August 1986).

Miller, Darryl. "The Components of a Facility Review," *Industrial Development* (March–April 1986).

Min, Hokey. "A Multiobjective Retail Service Location Model for Fast Food Restaurants," *Omega,* Vol. 15, No. 5 (1987), pp. 429–441.

Molinero, C. Mar. "Schools in Southampton: A Quantitative Approach to School Location, Closure, and Staffing," *Journal of Operational Research Society,* Vol. 39, No. 4 (1988), pp. 339–350.

Pacione, Michael (Ed.). *Progress in Industrial Geography.* London: Croom Helm, 1985.

Price, W. L., and Michel Turcotte. "Locating a Blood Bank," *Interfaces,* Vol. 16, No. 5 (September–October 1986), pp. 17–26.

Render, Barry, and Ralph M. Stair. *Quantitative Analysis for Management,* 3d Ed. Boston: Allyn and Bacon, 1988.

Rudd, Howard F., James W. Vigen, and Richard N. Davis. "The LMMD Model: Choosing the Optional Location for a Small Retail Business," *Journal of Small Business Management* (April 1983), pp. 45–52.

Schmenner, R. *Making Business Location Decisions.* Englewood Cliffs, N.J.: Prentice-Hall, 1982.

Teodorovic, Dusan, et al. "Optimal Locations of Emergency Service Depots for Private Cars in Urban Areas: Case Study of Belgrade," *Transportation Planning and Technology,* Vol. 11 (1986), pp. 177–188.

"The Checklist of Site Selection Factors." In *Site Selection Handbook.* Atlanta, Ga.: Conway, 1978.

Von Hohenbalken, Bolder, and Douglas S. West. "Predation Among Supermarkets: An Algorithmic Locational Analysis," *Journal of Urban Economics,* Vol. 15 (1984), pp. 244–257.

Zarrillo, Mark J. "Strategies for Selecting a Mixed-Use Corporate Site," *Industrial Development* (March–April 1986).

7

Facility Layout

INTRODUCTION

Once the location and site have been selected, as we discussed in Chapter 6, the facility layout must be designed. The layout problem involves finding the best arrangement of the physical components of the service system possible within the time, cost, and technology constraints of the situation.

Portions of this chapter were adapted from Jay Heizer and Barry Render, *Production and Operations Management*. Copyright © 1988 by Allyn and Bacon.

The objectives of designing a good layout are

1. Movement of people, materials, and paperwork the minimum distance possible. One of the largest components of cost in many wholesalers' warehouses is the handling and movement of materials.
2. High ultilization of space, balanced with means for expansion. There should be some space available for growth that will have low utilization, or else the building should be constructed so that a wing or floor may be easily added on.
3. Flexibility for rearrangement, services, and growth. Changes in product or service, changes in output required, and improvements in layout make modification of layout desirable from time to time.
4. Satisfactory physical environment for workers. This includes good lighting, temperature control, low noise, cafeterias, rest rooms, and exits. Fixed equipment, such as boilers, should be external to the work area.
5. Convenience for customers during the service.
6. Attractive appearance of room office arrangements for management and customers. An example is the use of planter boxes and foliage to separate areas in banks and offices.

A variety of layout strategies are available to management depending on whether the firm is dealing with arranging processes, stores, warehouses, assembly lines, or offices. Exhibit 7–1 provides examples of five types of service layouts.

This chapter begins with a brief discussion of six issues that need to be addressed before tackling service layout problems. It then turns to a detailed look at each of the major layout strategies. We will concentrate on

— Product layout
— Process layout
— Office layout
— Retail store layout
— Warehousing and storage layout

_____ EXHIBIT 7–1 _____

▪ *Some Types of Layout Strategies in the Service Sector*

	Product	Process	Office	Retail	Warehouse
Example	Cafeteria serving line	Insurance company	Hospital	Retail store	Distributor
Problem	Balance work from one serving station to the next	Locate workers requiring frequent contact close to one another	Flow to various services differs with each patient	Expose customer to high margin items and impulse items at exit	Lower cost of storage and material handling

In addition, the topic of building layout problems (such as whether to create a ''smart'' building) is also introduced.

INPUTS TO THE LAYOUT PROBLEM

Richard Muther developed a five-item key to unlocking *factory* layout problems in 1976. Exhibit 7–2 shows a six-item service variation called the **OPQRST key.** The inputs are as follows:

O. Objectives of the company. Those objectives related to layout are diversification plans, cost objectives, expansion plans, and so on.

P. People/services—nature and number. Whether the company is providing a single service or a mix of heterogeneous services, the degree of customer contact and personalization will have an impact on the layout.

Q. Quantity demanded. Layout will be affected by whether high volume or low volume throughput is required.

R. Routing—processes, equipment, materials, information, and customer participation in the process.

S. Space and services. The square feet, the cubic feet, and the shape (rectangular, square, L-shaped) of the space available or desired are important to layout decisions. The type and location of services are also inputs.

T. Timing—flexibility for change over time and timing for additional space needed.

Now that these six inputs to the layout decision have been addressed, we shall introduce each of the strategies available to managers. We begin with product layout.

EXHIBIT 7–2

■ *The Key—OPQRST—for Unlocking Layout Problems*

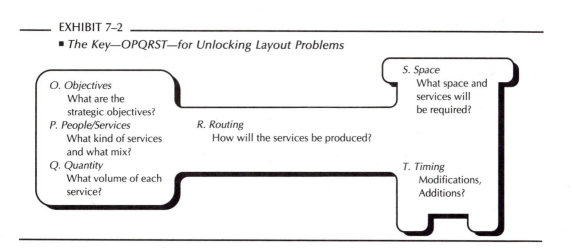

PRODUCT LAYOUT

A **product layout** is one in which a limited number of services is provided, one after the other, to a large number of customers. These services, such as food stations in a student cafeteria, are arranged in the sequence in which they are to be performed. The idea is to maintain a smooth flow of customers through the stations so that bottlenecks can be avoided and the time needed by each individual server or station is equalized. This is the familiar assembly-line layout problem found in the manufacture of cars, toasters, and even jet fighter airplanes.

Assembly lines can be "balanced" by moving tasks from one individual to another. The central problem in product layout planning is to find the ideal balance so a continuous flow of customers is maintained along the service line with a minimum of idle time at each workstation.

To illustrate, assume that you enter your cafeteria, pushing your tray ahead of you, and request various items for your meal. The line is inflexible and some servers may even have specializations that cannot be assigned to others (such as being trained to act as cashier). The ideal (that is, balanced) line is one where each server is assigned tasks that take an equal amount of time. Exhibit 7–3 indicates that there are six service stations in the cafeteria. Exhibit 7–4a illustrates how five workers have currently been assigned to staff the service stations. Workstation (WS) 4 consists of one employee who serves both desserts (15 seconds) and drinks (10 seconds). The problem, however, is that this line is poorly balanced. Workstation 5, the cashier, requires 60 seconds per customer on average, meaning that only 60 customers per hour can be served. The other workers are idle anywhere from 30 to 40 seconds of every minute or customer "cycle."

In Exhibit 7–4b, management has reduced costs by eliminating two workstations (and hence two workers) by merging vegetables and entrees into one station (50 seconds) and soup, dessert, and drinks into a second station (45 seconds) and placing a cashier at the third (still 60 seconds). Although this first alternative lowers costs, service is still slowed to a pace of 60 customers per hour, or one per minute, on average.

If the real problem is the need for increased throughput, alternatives 2 and 3 (see Exhibit 7–4c and d) may be explored. In Exhibit 7–4c, the current layout is retained but for the opening of a second cashier station. With the reduction of that bottleneck, 120 customers may now be served, albeit at a higher labor cost, since there are now six workers.

EXHIBIT 7–3 ───

■ *Cafeteria Service Times*

Sequence	Service Station	Average Service Time
1	Serve vegetables	20 seconds
2	Serve entree	30 seconds
3	Serve soup	20 seconds
4	Serve dessert	15 seconds
5	Serve drink	10 seconds
6	Collect money	60 seconds

EXHIBIT 7–4

- *Cafeteria Line-Balancing Layouts*

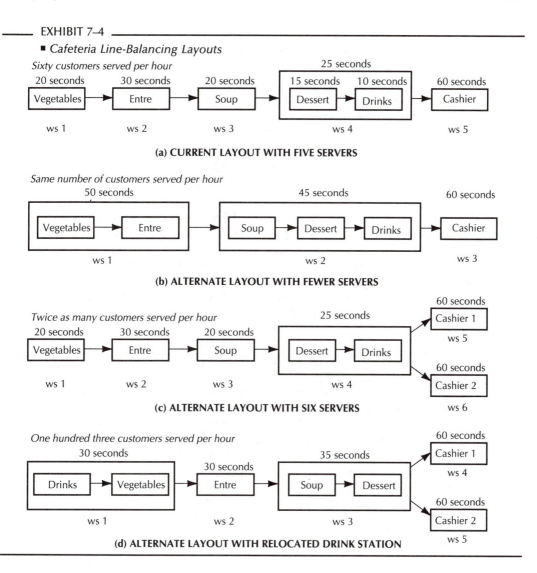

(a) CURRENT LAYOUT WITH FIVE SERVERS

(b) ALTERNATE LAYOUT WITH FEWER SERVERS

(c) ALTERNATE LAYOUT WITH SIX SERVERS

(d) ALTERNATE LAYOUT WITH RELOCATED DRINK STATION

The final alternative shown is one in which the drink equipment is relocated to the beginning of the cafeteria line and assigned to the worker currently serving vegetables. The soup and dessert tasks are assigned to workstation 3, and the freed worker is trained to work as a second cashier. There will be some costs of reconfiguring the service line, but labor costs will not increase. Now 103 customers can be handled per hour. The new bottleneck is workstation 3, which requires 35 seconds per customer.

Many services can be viewed in the context of product layout, even though they are not as rigid as this assembly-line example. Oil change/lube shops, for example, provide well-defined services, require special equipment for different tasks, and work well with a division of labor. Again, the sevice output is limited to the slowest activity.

Another example of assembly-line balancing is provided in Reading 7.1, which describes how Burger King meets changing fast-food product demands at different times of day. Rather than move equipment or machines, Burger King changes the number of personnel and task assignments to meet its varying product volume.

PROCESS-ORIENTED LAYOUT

Whereas product layouts are arranged to deliver a specific product, **process-oriented layouts** are arranged by similar process function. Most service organizations use this approach, for it can simultaneously handle a wide variety of services. It is very efficient when dealing with customers of law offices, insurance companies, or travel agencies, typical situations in which each customer has a different need. Another good example of the process-oriented layout is a hospital or clinic. A continuous inflow of patients, each with his or her own request, requires routing through records areas, admissions, laboratories, operating rooms, intensive care areas, pharmacies, nursing stations, and so on.

A big advantage of process layout is its flexibility in equipment use and in employee assignments. In the hospital example, there may be several obstetricians on duty available to deliver an unexpected baby in a number of similar delivery rooms. However, if a specialist is unavailable, there are other doctors with broad enough skills to step in during an emergency. The service provided is enhanced by the personalization found in the process approach.

In process layout planning, the most common tactic is to arrange departments or service centers in the most convenient locations. This often entails placing departments with large interdepartmental flows of people or paperwork next to one another. Costs in this approach depend on (1) the number of people or documents moving during some period of time between two departments and (2) the distances between departments. The best way to understand the steps of process layout is to look at an example.

North Slope Hospital

The North Slope Hospital is a small emergency-oriented facility located in a popular ski resort area in northern Vermont. Its new administrator decides to reorganize the hospital using the process layout method she studied in business school. The current layout of North Slope's eight emergency departments is shown in Exhibit 7–5.

The only physical restriction perceived by the administrator is the need to keep the entrance and initial processing room in its current location. All other departments or rooms (each 10 ft × 15 ft) can be moved if the layout analysis indicates it would be beneficial.

The first step is to analyze records in order to determine the number of trips made by patients between departments in an average month. The data are shown in Exhibit 7–6. The objective is to lay out the rooms so as to minimize the total distance walked by patients who enter for treatment. The administrator writes her objective as

$$\text{Minimize patient movement} = \sum_{i=1}^{8} \sum_{j=1}^{8} N_{ij} D_{ij}$$

EXHIBIT 7–5

▪ *North Slope Hospital Layout*

Entrance/ Initial Processing	Exam Room 1	Exam Room 2	X Ray	15'
Laboratory Tests/EKG	Operating Room	Recovery Room	Cast-setting Room	15'

← 40' →

where N_{ij} = number of patients (or trips) per month moving from department i to department j and from department j to department i

D_{ij} = distance in feet between departments i and j (which, in this case, is the equivalent of cost per load to move between departments)

i,j = individual departments

Departments next to one another, such as the entrance and examination room 1, are assumed to carry a walking distance of 10 feet. Diagonal departments are also considered adjacent and assigned a distance of 10 feet. Nonadjacent departments such as the entrance and examination room 2 or the entrance and recovery room are 20 feet apart, while nonadjacent rooms such as the entrance and x-ray are 30 feet apart. (Hence

EXHIBIT 7–6

▪ *Number of Patients Moving Between Departments in One Month*

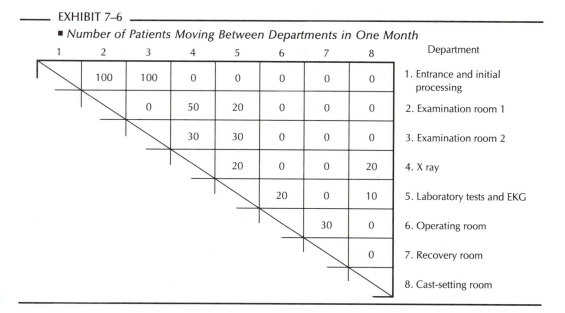

1	2	3	4	5	6	7	8	Department
	100	100	0	0	0	0	0	1. Entrance and initial processing
		0	50	20	0	0	0	2. Examination room 1
			30	30	0	0	0	3. Examination room 2
				20	0	0	20	4. X ray
					20	0	10	5. Laboratory tests and EKG
						30	0	6. Operating room
							0	7. Recovery room
								8. Cast-setting room

───── EXHIBIT 7–7 ──

■ *Current North Slope Patient Flow*

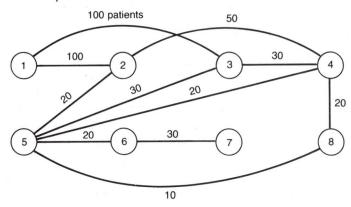

10 feet is considered 10 units of cost, 20 feet is 20 units of cost, and 30 feet is 30 units of cost.)

Given this information, we can redo the layout of North Slope Hospital and improve its efficiency in terms of patient flow. Using North Slope's current layout flow, shown in Exhibit 7–7, the patient movement may be computed.

$$
\begin{aligned}
\text{Total movement} &= \underset{\text{1 to 2}}{(100 \times 10 \text{ ft})} + \underset{\text{1 to 3}}{(100 \times 20 \text{ ft})} + \underset{\text{2 to 4}}{(50 \times 20 \text{ ft})} \\
&+ \underset{\text{2 to 5}}{(20 \times 10 \text{ ft})} + \underset{\text{3 to 4}}{(30 \times 10 \text{ ft})} + \underset{\text{3 to 5}}{(30 \times 20 \text{ ft})} \\
&+ \underset{\text{4 to 5}}{(20 \times 30 \text{ ft})} + \underset{\text{4 to 8}}{(20 \times 10 \text{ ft})} + \underset{\text{5 to 6}}{(20 \times 10 \text{ ft})} \\
&+ \underset{\text{5 to 8}}{(10 \times 30 \text{ ft})} + \underset{\text{6 to 7}}{(30 \times 10 \text{ ft})} \\
&= 1000 + 2000 + 1000 + 200 + 300 + 600 + 600 \\
&+ 200 + 200 + 300 + 300 \\
&= 6700 \text{ feet}
\end{aligned}
$$

It is not generally feasible to arrive at an "optimal" solution, but we should be able to propose a new layout that will reduce the current figure of 6700 feet. Two useful changes, for example, are to switch rooms 3 and 5 (reducing patient movement by 1000 feet) and to interchange rooms 4 and 6 (reducing patient movement by an additional 900 feet). The revised layout is shown in Exhibit 7–8.

———— EXHIBIT 7–8 ————————————————————————————————

■ *Improved Layout*

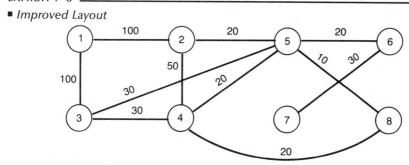

The revised patient movement is calculated as

$$
\begin{aligned}
\text{Total movement} = \ & (100 \times 10 \text{ ft}) + (100 \times 10 \text{ ft}) + (50 \times 10 \text{ ft}) \\
& \quad \text{1 to 2} \qquad\qquad\quad \text{1 to 3} \qquad\qquad \text{2 to 4} \\
& + (20 \times 10 \text{ ft}) + (30 \times 10 \text{ ft}) + (30 \times 20 \text{ ft}) \\
& \quad\ \text{2 to 5} \qquad\qquad \text{3 to 4} \qquad\qquad \text{3 to 5} \\
& + (20 \times 10 \text{ ft}) + (20 \times 20 \text{ ft}) + (20 \times 10 \text{ ft}) \\
& \quad\ \text{4 to 5} \qquad\qquad \text{4 to 8} \qquad\qquad \text{5 to 6} \\
& + (10 \times 10 \text{ ft}) + (30 \times 10 \text{ ft}) \\
& \quad\ \text{5 to 8} \qquad\qquad \text{6 to 7} \\
= \ & 1000 + 1000 + 500 + 200 + 300 + 600 + 200 \\
& + 400 + 200 + 100 + 300 \\
= \ & 4800 \text{ ft}
\end{aligned}
$$

Further improvement *may* be possible. Do you see where it could take place?

Computerized Layout

The graphic approach we have been discussing is adequate for finding a reasonable layout for small service centers.[1] When 20 departments are involved in a layout problem, over 600 trillion (or 20!) different department configurations are possible. Fortunately, computer programs have been written to handle layouts of up to 40 departments. The best-known of these is CRAFT (Computerized Relative Allocation of Facilities Technique),[2] a program that produces "good," but not always "optimal" solutions. CRAFT is a search technique that systematically examines alternative departmental rearrangements to reduce the total movement cost. CRAFT has the added advantage of not only

[1] Also see Richard Muther, *Systematic Layout Planning,* 2d ed. (Boston: Cahners, 1976), for a similar approach to what the author calls simplified layout planning.
[2] E. S. Buffa, G. S. Armor, and T. E. Vollman, "Allocating Facilities with CRAFT," *Harvard Business Review,* Vol. 42, No. 2 (March–April 1964), pp. 136–159.

___ EXHIBIT 7–9 _____

■ *Illustration of the CRAFT Program*

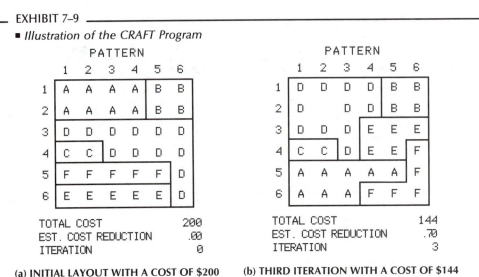

(a) INITIAL LAYOUT WITH A COST OF $200   (b) THIRD ITERATION WITH A COST OF $144

allowing the number of people and distance to be examined, but also introducing a third factor, a difficulty rating.

Exhibit 7–9 illustrates the results of a series of iterations of the CRAFT program. Management's initial layout (on the left) yielded a movement cost of $200. By rearranging the layout in square and rectangular patterns and exchanging locations of departments that yield the largest cost decrease, the program produced the layout on the right (Exhibit 7–9b) at a cost of $144.

Computerized techniques have been developed for both two-dimensional and three-dimensional cases—the two-dimensional case is a one-story facility successfully addressed by CRAFT; the three-dimensional case is a multistory facility addressed by SPACECRAFT.[3] And, as we have discussed, manual as well as computer techniques exist.

OFFICE LAYOUT

Office workers are concerned with the movement of information. Movement of information is carried out by

—Individuals in face-to-face conversations
—Individuals conversing by phone and computers simultaneously

[3] R. V. Johnson, "SPACECRAFT for Multi-Floor Layout Planning," *Management Science,* Vol. 28, No. 4 (1982), pp. 407–417. A discussion of CRAFT, COFAD, PLANET, CORELAP, and ALDEP is available in James A. Tompkins and James M. Moore, *Computer Aided Layout: A User's Guide,* Publication Number 1 in the Monograph Series (Norcross, Ga.: American Institute of Industrial Engineers, 1977), p. 77–1.

—Mail, hard copy documents
—Electronic mail
—Group discussions or meetings
—Intercom speakers

If *all* work were carried out by phone and telecommunications, the layout problem would be greatly simplified. It is the movement of people and hard documents that largely dictates the nature of office facility layouts. A design checklist to consider in laying out office facilities is as follows:

1. Workers within groups usually have frequent contacts with each other.
2. Some groups interact frequently with certain other groups.
3. Some firms require conference rooms, especially those who supply professional services to clients.
4. Some service work is best done in private offices, whereas other work, such as high-volume routine processing of paper forms, is best suited to large open areas (frequently called "bullpens").
5. Areas visited by customers should be more aesthetic than standard work areas.
6. Aisles should be designed so that all offices may be quickly reached, and yet high traffic past private offices should be avoided to the extent possible.
7. Individual offices usually reflect the status of the workers by size, location, and window space.
8. Shared facilities such as computers and files should be convenient for users.
9. Reception areas may be required, and they should be attractive and convenient for customers.
10. Rooms for storage of supplies may be needed.
11. Generally, rest rooms and coat rooms for employees are required. If the service is in a suite of an office building, rest rooms may be provided already.
12. A central computer room or an information center may be required.

Exhibit 7–10 shows a **relationship chart,** one extremely effective way to plan office activities. This chart, prepared for an office of consulting engineers, indicates that Mr. Smith must be (1) near the engineers' area, (2) near the phones to a lesser extent, (3) still less near to the office manager and central files, and (4) not at all near to the duplicating machine or storage area. Reasons are filled in and recorded in the lower half of the appropriate boxes. In charting relationships, it is not usually realistic to include phone or window availability. However, they are included in Exhibit 7–10, mostly to illustrate the degree of detail an office planner can go to if necessary.

General office area guidelines indicate an average of about 100 ft^2 per person (including corridors). A major executive takes up about 400 ft^2, while a conference room area is based on 25 ft^2 per person, up to 30 people. In contrast, restaurants provide from 16 to 50 ft^2 per customer (total kitchen and dining area divided by capacity).

Aisles leading to main exits should be 44 to 66 inches wide. Aisles between rows of desks should be at least 30 to 36 inches wide. Desks should face in the same direction, not face each other.

_____ EXHIBIT 7–10 _____

■ *Office Relationship Chart*

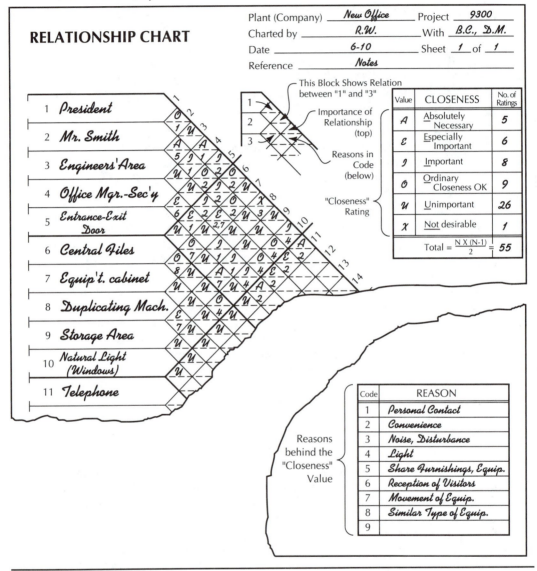

Source: Richard Muther, *Systematic Layout Planning*, 2d Ed. (Kansas City, Mo.: Management & Industrial Research Publications, 1973, p. 5–4. Used with permission.

Workstations

The office layout depends on the total office area, its shape, the process to be performed, and the relationships among the workers. Each worker has a workstation designed for (hopefully) optimal efficiency in terms of the work system as a whole and the tasks of the worker at the station. Different types of jobs require different kinds of working surfaces, equipment, space, and privacy.

Workstation variations are

— Desks packed together in rows in an open area
— Desks or work areas separated by bookcases, foliage, or file cabinets
— Partitions about the work area—metal and glass—varying in height from about 4 to 8 feet, which can be installed in about one day
— Floor-to-ceiling partitions around a group of workstations
— Offices that are built as part of the building construction

By making effective use of the vertical dimension in a workstation, some office designers expand upward instead of outward. This keeps each workstation unit (what designers call the "footprint") as small as possible. Exhibit 7–11 provides sample managerial/executive and clerical/financial workspace layouts.

EXHIBIT 7–11

■ *Sample Workstations*

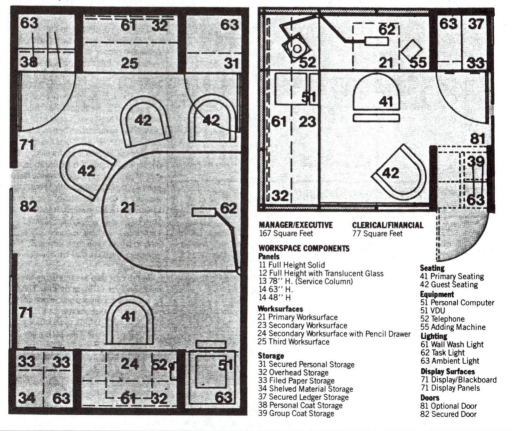

MANAGER/EXECUTIVE
167 Square Feet

CLERICAL/FINANCIAL
77 Square Feet

WORKSPACE COMPONENTS
Panels
11 Full Height Solid
12 Full Height with Translucent Glass
13 78" H. (Service Column)
14 63" H.
14 48" H

Worksurfaces
21 Primary Worksurface
23 Secondary Worksurface
24 Secondary Worksurface with Pencil Drawer
25 Third Worksurface

Storage
31 Secured Personal Storage
32 Overhead Storage
33 Filed Paper Storage
34 Shelved Material Storage
37 Secured Ledger Storage
38 Personal Coat Storage
39 Group Coat Storage

Seating
41 Primary Seating
42 Guest Seating

Equipment
51 Personal Computer
51 VDU
52 Telephone
55 Adding Machine

Lighting
61 Wall Wash Light
62 Task Light
63 Ambient Light

Display Surfaces
71 Display/Blackboard
71 Display Panels

Doors
81 Optional Door
82 Secured Door

Source: Steven Manners, "Optimizing the Cube," *Administrative Management* (October 1986), p. 20. Republished with permission from Administrative Management, copyright 1986, by Dalton Communications, Inc., New York.

EXHIBIT 7–12

- *Examples of Space Utilization*

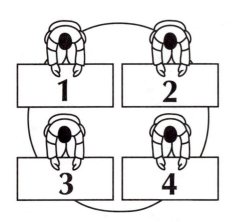

(a) CONVENTIONAL UTILIZATION
OF A SPACE BY FOUR PEOPLE

(b) SAME SPACE UTILIZED BY FIVE PEOPLE
IN AN OPEN OFFICE SYSTEM

Source: M. J. Paznik, "Comfort and Technology to Mesh More Easily in the Office of the Future," *Administrative Management* (October 1986), p. 59. Republished with permission from Administrative Management, copyright 1986, by Dalton Communications, Inc., New York.

Exhibit 7–12 provides an additional unusual arrangement of workstations in which five workers take the same space needed by four (in the layout on the left).

The Electronic (But Not Paperless) Office

The increased use of computer equipment has developed a breed of "electronic office workers" who are more knowledgeable and information-based than their clerical predecessors. Steven Manners writes about such employees:[4]

> They have more stringent requirements for a proper physical environment—heating, lighting, ventilation, privacy—and need adequate ergonomics, such as comfortable seating and positioning to keyboards and terminals, enough access area, leg room, and proper work surface heights. . . .

> The computer has revolutionized the way tasks are performed. Employees are now responsible for generating, updating, circulating, and storing their own documents. The most immediate impact has been a significant increase in paper in the paperless office. . . .

> Managers must reorient their thinking to design space that accommodates electronic data—different seating and lighting, for example. . . . Since glare is a problem, windows—once highly prized in offices—become a hindrance.

---

[4] Steven Manners, "Optimizing the Cube," *Administrative Management* (October 1986), pp. 19–21.

Reading 7.2 examines the concept of layout of the automated office from yet another perspective.

Office Layout Techniques

The recommended scale for office layouts is $\frac{1}{4}$ inch equals 1 foot. Most commercial kits for layouts are based on this scale. A smaller scale leads to inaccuracy and lack of clarity, whereas a larger scale makes many layouts too big to handle easily or to reproduce. With this important concept in mind, let us briefly examine the techniques for actually designing a layout that can be communicated to interested parties. These are

1. Use transparent $\frac{1}{4}$-inch grid paper and templates for office equipment. Draw in dark pencil. Reproduction of the layout may be by office copier or diazo equipment for large layouts.
2. Use transparent Mylar grid sheets and sheets with removable silhouettes of office furniture (as seen earlier in Exhibit 7–11).
3. Use a magnetic layout board with guidelines painted on it. Magnetic models of furniture may be easily moved about such a board. The final layout must be photographed for further reproduction.
4. Use three-dimensional models that attach to a Velcro board. This layout also must be photographed for further reproduction.

BUILDINGS

Other than repair services (such as automobile or aircraft) and processing services (such as dry cleaning or printing), service buildings differ considerably from manufacturing buildings. Manufacturing buildings usually involve storage of raw materials and goods in process. If they are not pure assembly operations, change in form of raw materials tends to produce dirt, scrap, and dust. Floors are often concrete to support heavy machinery.

In services such as offices and stores, there is little movement of heavy packages, and air-conditioning can easily handle air pollutants. Windows offer a view and are usually used for offices and stores (although not in malls). The disadvantages of windows are the same for office buildings as for factories. They are expensive to install, make heating and cooling more difficult, and allow noises to come in or go out. Modern office skyscrapers, in many cases, have treated glass plates that give a mirror-like appearance from the outside. They also reflect light so that heating and cooling are cheaper.

Modern factories are usually found in the suburbs, where land is cheap and zoning laws permit them, where production is carried out on a single floor. The offices may be located on the second or third floor. This is so because the movement of materials from one story to another is expensive.

In contrast, office skyscrapers are found in the centers of large population areas. A particular company may occupy several floors because information is the primary entity being moved. Today, multistory office buildings are being designed as "smart" buildings. As Dorothy Owens wrote in the *Miami Herald* (August 12, 1985):

> Time was when beauty was enough to sell offices. These days it also takes brains. The building must be smart. Intelligent buildings—those with advanced communications and, in some cases, computer-guided security and energy management systems—are becoming the driving force behind office development.

Office buildings built before the concept of "smart" buildings was applied are becoming obsolete, because the cost of installing telecommunication systems and computer-controlled management systems is too high to make them competitive.

RETAIL STORE LAYOUT

In retail organizations, the objective is to maximize the net profit per square foot of display space. Because the retail grocery store is pervasive and widely studied, we will use it as an example. An hypothesis that has been widely accepted for the retail case is that sales vary directly with customer exposure to products. Consequently, a requirement for good profitability is to expose customers to as many products as possible.

Studies do show that the greater the rate of exposure, the greater the sales—hence the higher return on investment. The service manager has two distinct variables to manipulate: the overall arrangement or flow pattern for the store and the allocation of space within that arrangement to various products.

Although Reading 7.3 suggests that there is no longer any set pattern for store layouts, we can still note six ideas that are helpful for determining the overall arrangement of many stores.

1. Locate the high-draw items around the periphery of the store. Thus we tend to find dairy products in one corner of a supermarket and bread and bakery products in another. An example of this is shown in Exhibit 7–13.
2. Use prominent locations such as the first or last aisle for high-impulse and high-margin items such as housewares, beauty aids, and shampoos.
3. Remove the crossover aisles that allow customers the opportunity to move between aisles. Place continuous shelves the length or width of the store. In the extreme case, customers are allowed only one path through the store.
4. Distribute what are known in the trade as "power items"—items that may dominate a purchasing trip—to both sides of an aisle, and disperse them to increase the viewing of other items. This results in a "bounce" pattern of shopping that increases exposure and hence sales of those items located adjacent to the power items.
5. Use end-aisle locations because they have a very high exposure rate.
6. Convey the image of the store by careful selection in the positioning of the lead-off department. Produce remains a popular choice in stores, but managers

—— EXHIBIT 7–13 ——

- *Sample Supermarket Layout*

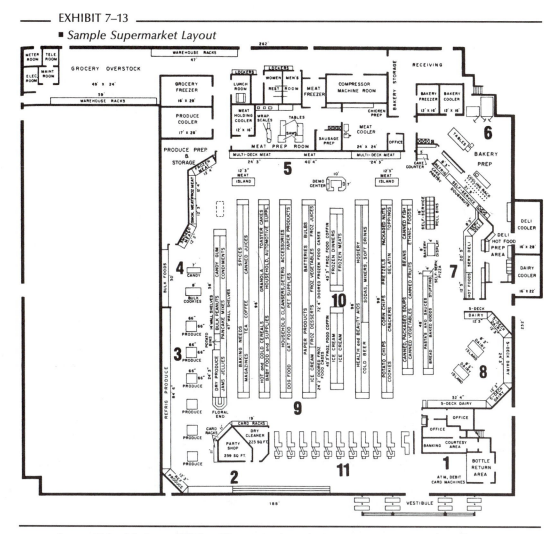

Source: Richard DeSanta, "All That Glitters Is Not Upscale," *Progressive Grocer* (April 1987), p. 117. Copyright 1987 by Progressive Grocer Company. Used with permission.

who want to convey a low-price message may want to start off with a wall of values. Others will position the bakery and deli up front to appeal to convenience-oriented customers who want prepared foods.

With these six ideas in mind, we move to the second phase of retail store layout, which is to allocate space to various products.[5]

The objective is to maximize profitability per product per square foot of shelf space. The criteria may be modified to the needs of the product line by using linear

[5] "Computers Revolutionize Shelf Allocation," *Chain Store Age/Supermarkets* (November 1980), p. 66.

_____ EXHIBIT 7–14 _____

■ *Minimizing Storage and Materials Handling Costs (Note That Both Lines Shift Up or Down Depending on Investment and Variable Costs).*

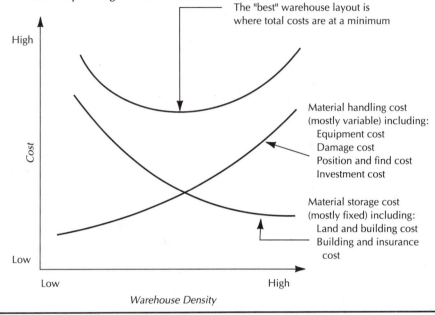

The "best" warehouse layout is where total costs are at a minimum

High

Cost

Material handling cost (mostly variable) including:
    Equipment cost
    Damage cost
    Position and find cost
    Investment cost

Material storage cost (mostly fixed) including:
    Land and building cost
    Building and insurance cost

Low

Low   High

Warehouse Density

foot of shelf space in lieu of square foot of shelf space. "Big-ticket," or expensive, items may yield greater dollar sales, but the profit per square foot may be lower. Additionally, determining actual cost per item means determining spoilage, pilferage, breakage, and returns, as well as the necessary labor to stock and sell. There are, of course, other issues, such as having a full line of merchandise regardless of margin. A drug store selling only high-margin shampoo would have met the criteria, but it would have a different set of problems.

Rapid manipulation of data by means of computers, accurate reports, and the capture of sales data through point-of-sale terminals allow retail store managers an opportunity to find optimal allocation of space. A number of computer programs exist that can assist managers in evaluating the profitability of various merchandise.

One such program is SLIM (Store Labor and Inventory Management), which can assist store managers in determining when shelf space is adequate to accommodate another full case. Sales and restocking information can be collected directly from a point-of-sale terminal, combined with a program such as SLIM, and the profitability can be established per product. This is a strong management tool for retail store layout.

Another software package is COSMOS (Computerized Optimization and Simulation Modeling for Operating Supermarkets). COSMOS matches shelf space with delivery schedules, allocating sufficient space to minimize out-of-stock between loads. A disadvantage of COSMOS is that analysis traditionally has been based on warehouse withdrawal figures rather than on actual store sales. This means that a good bit of the product could still be in the store. Once again, point-of-sale terminals, providing prompt information, can supply comprehensive and current data to aid retail store layout.[6]

WAREHOUSING AND STORAGE LAYOUTS

The objective of warehouse layout is to find the optimal tradeoff between handling cost and warehouse space (Exhibit 7–14). Consequently, management is to maximize the utilization of the total ''cube'' of the warehouse—that is, utilize its full volume while maintaining low materials handling costs. We define **materials handling costs** as all the costs related to the incoming, storage, and outgoing transport of the materials. These costs are related to equipment, people, type of materials, supervision, insurance, obsolescence, shrinkage, spoilage and depreciation. Management minimizes the sum of the resources spent on finding and moving materials plus the deterioration and damage to the materials themselves. The variety of items stored and the number of items ''picked'' have direct bearing on the optimal layout. A warehouse storing a few items lends itself to higher density more than a warehouse storing a variety of items. Modern warehouse management is, in many instances, an automated procedure utilizing automatic stacking and picking cranes, conveyors, and sophisticated controls that manage the flow of materials. Of course, with the recently demonstrated success of Just-in-Time concepts in cutting inventory costs, the whole issue of warehousing costs needs to be reexamined. We suspect, however, that there will always be some situations in which inventory storage is unavoidable.

ADDITIONAL LAYOUT TECHNIQUES

In addition to the approaches discussed so far, other techniques are useful for layout planning. One technique is a two-dimensional template on which people, equipment, aisles, service areas, loading docks, waiting rooms, and so on can be placed to provide the insight not available through other means. One such template is shown in Exhibit 7–15.

Another approach, more three dimensional in nature, is found in the form of isometric drawings, such as that of the employee cafeteria in Exhibit 7–16.

—— SUMMARY

The layout problem is the determination of the most nearly optimal arrangement of the physical components of the service system within time, cost, and technology constraints. Objectives of good layout include

---

[6] See ''There Are Two Kinds of Supermarkets: The Quick and the Dead,'' *Business Week,* August 11, 1986, pp. 62–63; and ''At Today's Supermarket, The Computer Is Doing it All,'' *Business Week,* August 11, 1986, pp. 64–65.

—— EXHIBIT 7–15 ———————————————————————————————————

■ *A Two-Dimensional Template for an Office or Store Layout*

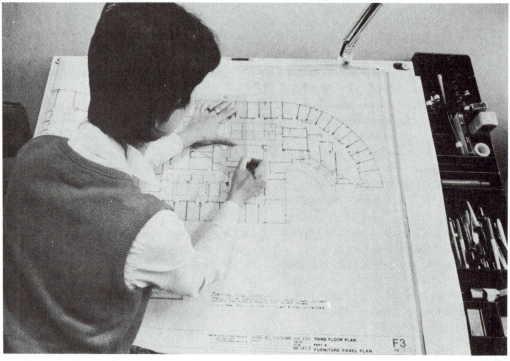

Source: Photo by Robert Harbison.

— Minimum movement of people, materials, and paperwork
— High utilization of space, balanced with future expansion needs
— Flexibility
— Satisfactory physical environment for the workers
— Convenience for customers
— Aesthetic appearance for both workers and customers

Although there are many types of services, various business groups have much in common. Exhibit 7–17 illustrates some classifications for which general principles apply.

A six-point list of inputs to the layout problem (called OPQRST) was given in this chapter, and a number of layout strategies were described. Examples of cafeteria "assembly lines" (product layout), hospital service areas (process layout), electronic offices (office layout), and supermarkets (retail layout) were provided to illustrate how wide-ranging and numerous the variables are in the layout problem. For this reason, layout decisions, while having received substantial research effort, remain something of an art.

_____ EXHIBIT 7–16 _____

▪ *A Typical Employee Cafeteria*

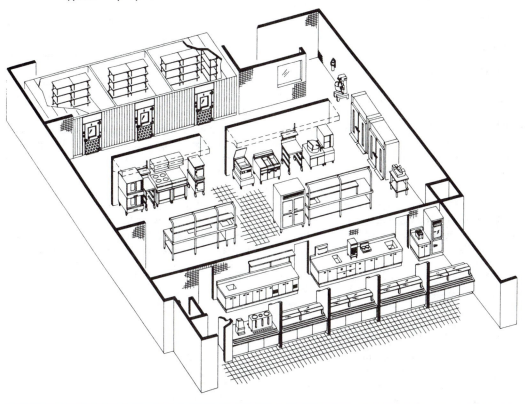

Source: Ira B. Beer, "Efficiency + Productivity = Profit," *Restaurant Business*, November 1, 1987, p. 147. Reproduced with permission.

_____ EXHIBIT 7–17 _____

▪ *Commonalities for Layouts*

1. Retail stores
2. Central warehouse for retail stores, wholesale warehouses, mail order houses
3. Home office and office branches for real estate sales, stock brokerage firms, insurance agencies
4. In-house personal services such as law firms, consultants, doctors, beauty salons, fitness center, bars
5. Office fronts/back office such as drycleaning, photo finishing, restaurants, auto repair shops, printing services, car rental firms, airlines, bus lines, mail/parcel distribution
6. Multiple process centers such as banks, hospitals, educational institutions
7. Mass services such as theaters, TV studios, stadiums
8. Office for field services such as pool and lawn care, sign painting, investigations, industrial services, large appliance repair
9. Hospitality centers such as hotel, motel, nursing homes
10. Resort area firms such as Club Med, tennis resorts, golf resorts, ski resorts

____ DISCUSSION QUESTIONS

1. This chapter concludes with the statement, ". . . layout decisions, while having received substantial research effort, remain something of an art." Explain why this might be the case in

    a. Office layout.
    b. Supermarket layout.
    c. Department store layout.

2. What is the layout strategy of your local "quick copy" or print shop? Draw it on grid paper.

3. How would you go about collecting data to help a small business, such as a print shop, improve its layout?

4. In what service organizations are customer waiting-room aesthetics of major concern? Compare a variety of waiting rooms you have visited by listing the characteristics of each.

5. Describe the objective of each of the major categories of layout discussed in this chapter.

6. Visit the supermarket in which you normally shop, including a tour (with management's permission, of course) of the back rooms. Compare it in detail to the supermarket layout in Exhibit 7–13. How do the vital statistics compare to those in the exhibit? Which design is preferable for your own area?

7. What layout variables might you want to consider as particularly important in an office layout where computer programs are written?

8. Most supermarkets have placed long continuous shelves the length (or width) of the store so that customers will have to pass more items as they shop. Why are some stores rethinking this concept? Talk to a few store managers in your town and ask their opinions about this and other changes in layout.

____ PROBLEMS

7.1 Walters Printing Company's management wants to rearrange the six departments of its print shop in a way that will minimize interdepartmental materials handling costs. Each department is 20 feet by 20 feet, and the building is 60 feet long and 40 feet wide. Exhibit 7–18 shows the current flow of materials (in loads per week) from department to department, while Exhibit 7–19 illustrates the current layout. The cost of moving one load between adjacent departments is estimated to be $1. Moving a load between nonadjacent departments costs $2. Try to improve this layout to establish a reasonably good arrangement of departments.

7.2 You have just been hired as the director of operations for Bellas Chocolates, in Blacksburg, Virginia, a purveyor of exceptionally fine chocolates. Bellas Chocolates has four kitchen layouts under consideration for its recipe making and testing department. The strategy is to provide the best kitchen layout possible so that the food scientists can devote their time and energy to product improvement, not wasted effort in the kitchen. You have been asked to evaluate these four kitchen layouts and prepare a recommendation for your boss, Mr. Bellas, so that he can proceed

with placing the contract for building the testing kitchens. (See Exhibit 7–20.)

7.3 Using the kitchen layouts in Problem 7.2, collect load data (the number of trips between workstations) from an operating kitchen of your choosing, perhaps at home, and determine which is the best layout.

7.4 Using load data (number of trips) collected from an operating kitchen, determine which of the five layouts (the four in Problem 7.2 and the one from which you collected data) is best.

7.5 Georgetown Phone Directory prints and distributes a yellow page phone book for the northwest area of Washington, D.C. Its white-collar staff of clerical and managerial employees currently occupies the first floor of a U-shaped office building in Washington that is configured as shown in Exhibit 7–21. (The firm's warehouse and production facilities are next door.) This organization loses time and money because of unnecessary personnel, information, and materials movements. Without moving the production or shipping departments, see if you can reorganize the facility and create shorter communications distances.

—— EXHIBIT 7–18 ————————————————————————————————

▪ *Walters Printing Company Data*

Number of loads per week

Department	1	2	3	4	5	6
1		50	100	0	0	20
2			30	50	10	0
3				20	0	100
4					50	0
5						0
6						

—— EXHIBIT 7–19 ————————————————————————————————

▪ *Building Dimensions and Current Department Layout for Walters Printing*

Department 1	Department 2	Department 3
Department 4	Department 5	Department 6

40′

60′

—— EXHIBIT 7–20 ——————————————————————

■ *Layout Options*

Number of trips between work centers:

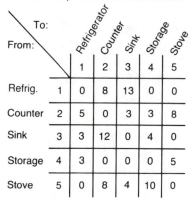

From: \ To:	Refrigerator 1	Counter 2	Sink 3	Storage 4	Stove 5
Refrig. 1	0	8	13	0	0
Counter 2	5	0	3	3	8
Sink 3	3	12	0	4	0
Storage 4	3	0	0	0	5
Stove 5	0	8	4	10	0

Kitchen layout #1

Refrig. ①	Counter ②	Sink ③	Storage ④	Stove ⑤

4   4   4   4

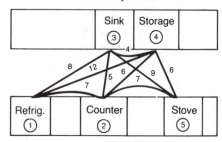

Kitchen layout #2

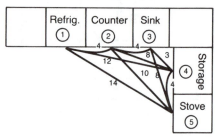

Kitchen layout #3

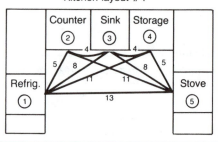

Kitchen layout #4

7.6 The preinduction physical examination given by the U.S. Army involves the following seven activities:

Activity	Average Time (minutes)
Medical history	10
Blood tests	8
Eye examination	5
Measurements (i.e., weight, height, blood pressure)	7
Medical examination	16
Psychological interview	12
Exit medical evaluation	10

These activities can be performed in any order, with two exceptions: the medical history must be taken first and the exit medical evaluation is the final step. At present there are three paramedics and two physicians on duty during each shift. Only a physician can perform the exit evaluation or conduct the psychological interview. Other activities can be carried out by either physicians or paramedics.

    a. Develop a layout and balance the line. How many people can be processed per hour?

    b. What activity is the current bottleneck?

    c. If one more physician and one more para-

EXHIBIT 7–21

■ *Layout for Georgetown Phone*

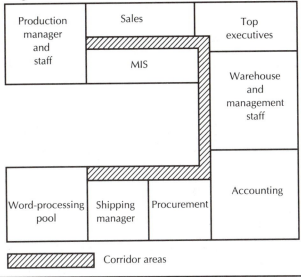

Corridor areas

medic can be placed on duty, how would you redraw the layout? What is the new throughput?

7.7 The cafeteria discussed in this chapter (see Exhibits 7–3 and 7–4) has just decided to eliminate soup from the current servings because of spoilage and demand factors. To compensate, more elaborate desserts can now be ordered, including banana splits and hot fudge sundaes. The average time to serve a dessert is estimated to increase by 33 percent, however. Lay out this line:

    a. With 3 workers
    b. With 4 workers
    c. With 5 workers
    d. With 6 workers

For each of these four cases, identify the throughput per hour and the bottleneck station.

READING 7.1

Competitive Advantage Through Layout and Dynamic Assembly-Line Balancing at Burger King

William Swart ■ Luca Donno

Jim McLamore's original concept in founding Burger King was to serve quality food—quickly and courteously. Speed of service remains the keystone of the fast food hamburger restaurant. The peak service hour is noon luncheon business. For a given facility at a given location, the luncheon business usually can be increased in proportion to the increase in speed of service. Typically, a hamburger

Source: Excerpted by permission of William Swart and Luca Donno, "Simulation Modeling Improves Operations, Planning, and Productivity of Fast Food Restaurants," *Interfaces,* Vol. 11, No. 6 (December 1981), pp. 35–47. Copyright 1981 The Institute of Management Sciences, 290 Westminster Street, Providence, Rhode Island 02903 USA.

—— EXHIBIT 7–22 ——————————————————————————

■ *Positioning Charts: "T" Layout*

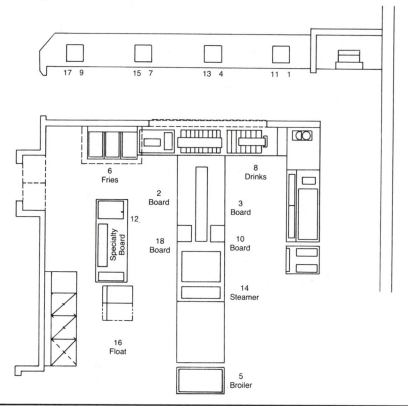

restaurant gains four times as much business a day as it gains for the lunch hour. So, if a Burger King restaurant is to raise sales but cannot, due to competitive pressures, increase prices substantially, it must increase the number of consumers served. And, to do that, the restaurant must increase its speed of service.

The equation is simple. The faster the service, the more people that can be served; therefore, the higher the restaurant's potential sales volume. For this reason the impact of suggested changes on speed of service is the principal criterion for operational decision making not only at Burger King but at most fast food companies.

The first major restaurant concept change was to go to a multichannel service, or "hospitality system." This system allowed for greatly increased sales delivery. To match this, additional production

capacity was required. This was obtained by expanding the building backwards, and placing the sandwich prep board perpendicular to the counter, allowing more sandwich prep employees to work simultaneously. These changes allowed reduced service time which created higher sales capacity to better accommodate peak hour business. An example of one of the restaurant configurations is shown in Exhibit 7–22. Numbers indicate the order in which employees are assigned to handle customer load increases.

Although a restaurant operator cannot control the price of labor, he can control the amount of labor used to operate his restaurant. In establishing staffing levels, the operator has, in the past, been guided by the uniform Burger King Labor Standard, applied to all units.

The Operations Research Department realized that major bottom-line benefits could be achieved by tailoring the amount of labor restaurants required at various sales volumes to the restaurant configuration, product mix, and drive-thru percentage.

Through the use of the model it was possible for the first time to accurately project not only how many crew members were needed, but also the most effective positioning and division of labor within the restaurant.

The results of the simulation modeling are a series of staffing and crew positioning charts. Because staffing and work responsibilities are tailored to individual units, labor savings over the old standard are substantial. For instance, for a standard T

restaurant with drive-thru, the savings occur at both peak and low volume hours and are in excess of 1.5 percent of sales. For a typical restaurant with annual sales of three quarters of a million dollars, this represents an additional profit of $11,250.00.

QUESTIONS FOR READING 7.1

1. How much competitive advantage did Burger King find in its new layout?

2. What technique did Burger King use to model its system?

3. Visit the Burger King closest to your home or campus and develop a layout grid comparing it to the one in Exhibit 7–22.

READING 7.2

Designing for Tomorrow's Office Workers

Rani Lueder

Some say that the future will not be very different because tomorrow's offices already exist. This is only a partial truth: some of today's office workers perform tasks that will be here tomorrow, but in this process, the entire context of work will be transformed.

It is difficult to understand a revolution when we are so close to it. But when a fundamental restructuring of work takes place, it definitely qualifies as a revolution. And this restructuring of the nature of work means that we must completely rethink our old ways of designing the office.

So, what transitions do we face? Probably the most authoritative and thought-provoking answers to this question were provided by a recent report from the Office of Technology Assessment (OTA) titled "The Automation of Tomorrow's Offices 1985–2000."

They indicate that some of the changes that will affect clerical work are that computers will increasingly communicate directly with other computers, such as via modems, PBXs and LANs. Secondly, we will see more firms entering information directly, such as with Automated Teller Machines or direct buying and invoicing. Finally, with the advent of devices such as Optical Character Readers and Speech Recognition, computers will be able to read information directly without keyboarding.

These changes will likely translate into reduced demand for both clerical staff and for lower and middle management who are involved in supervisory capacities.

However, other factors may limit this growth in productivity, such as international competition and whether the costs of the information systems are declining faster than the additional work force can be absorbed.

Yet these changes also indicate that there will be a fundamental restructuring of the work process in the coming years. This transitional period will be painful for those office workers that are not able to or are not allowed to bridge this gap by their organization. Yet for many other workers, work will

Source: Republished with permission from *Administrative Management* October 1986, pp. 58–59, copyright 1986, by Dalton Communications, Inc., New York.

become more meaningful, enriching, and productive.

OTA also suggests that we need to prepare for a new kind of office worker who is operating on a much higher level of effectiveness and creativity than in the past. The open plan was originally designed to support the flow of paper; it will have to increasingly support the flow of ideas.

CHANGE FACTORS IN THE OFFICE

How is the changing context of work reflected in the office?

1. First, our patterns of activity are changing; Peter Ellis of Building Use Studies in London may have been the first to note the blurring between the roles of the clerical, professional and managerial workers. Quite a few of the support staff and professionals are making more decisions formerly made by managers, and management is doing more of the routine work formerly performed at lower levels. Negotiation is taking place at lower levels of the organization.

2. Our communication patterns are changing: We are communicating much more often and at a much more rapid pace.

3. Our patterns of space utilization are becoming much more dynamic: We are using ancillary spaces for training, lounges, machine rooms and all types of meetings much more than in the past. The study found that the ratio of these spaces to work station area was increasing at a rate of 25 percent a year in many organizations.

Our patterns of space usage are also becoming much more group oriented. We are beginning to talk about the work station as an "activity center" which is primarily important for defining territorial boundaries. Dr. Cal Pava of Harvard University indicates that the next generation of hardware will be focused on supporting group activities; perhaps the work environment should reflect this also.

4. The users are changing: Clearly, there are more women, more part time workers, and a new generation of employees with a different set of expectations and values.

With the introduction of information systems, the users are diversifying in other ways as well. One of these is likely to be the disabled person. One out of 11 people in the U.S. and Canada is

disabled and studies have consistently shown that ninety-some percent of these people can be accommodated in the work place if the working conditions allow it.

5. The buildings are changing: We are experiencing a fundamental drop in the quality of many buildings yet the demands introduced by information systems are more stringent. One reason for this is that organizations are diversifying at the same time that buildings are increasingly built on spec for a supposed "average" user. Another is the building shell typically lasts over 35 years, too long to support technological life-cycles.

6. The work environments are changing: Hand in hand with deficiencies of buildings are environmental problems. Lighting requirements for both paper-based and VDT work conflict. Noise is increasing along with the trend toward local printers; although these sources of noise will eventually be replaced by non-impact printers, voice systems introduce new problems. Heat build-ups from concentrations of equipment are not accommodated by central servicing. The open plan is creating pockets of dead air space, and insulation and reductions in air exchanges (in order to conserve energy) are accentuating these problems.

7. The regulatory/union environment is changing: ANSI (American National Standards Institute) and ISO (International Standards Organization) are developing work station guidelines to counter pending (and contradictory) state and national legislations.

The labor environment is also changing. A recent study by Allen Westin found that 750,000 VDT operators are unionized, and unions are increasingly focusing on issues surrounding the implementation of technology.

RESPONDING TO CHANGE

How can the design process be responsive to tomorrow's work and workers?

1. *Identity:* It can provide the user with a sense of identity. In architecture we are seeing a new emphasis on corporate identity, largely resulting from the blurring of roles between individuals, departments and organizations. As a result, it is difficult to figure out who is responsible for what. With the increase in smaller work groups we also

need to better define the boundaries of group spaces and find ways to allow the users of individual and collective work station areas to personalize their work space over time.

2. *Status:* Status is not going away; if anything, it is becoming more important than ever. Yet many of our old indicators don't work anymore. People are becoming more sophisticated than the old school of leather and mahogany. Computers have differentially affected office workers' needs for space; clerical workers need more space than they had before but the manager's needs remain the same. Functional allocation of space is also becoming more important because space is very expensive.

3. *Flexibility:* We are moving more than ever, over both the short and long term. The flexibility that we need in our workstations just is not there. BOSTI (Buffalo Organization for Social and Technical Innovation) found that only one out of five people thought their workstation was oriented correctly. That is a remarkable statement. Four out of five office workers would like to move their work station but they don't because they believe that they can't.

4. *Wayfinding:* We are moving around more than ever. How do we find each other? Electronically it is easy, yet less so on the work station level. We need to start applying the science of wayfinding more systematically.

5. *Privacy:* The research is overwhelming that people need more privacy; with increasingly expensive knowledge workers, we had better figure out how to provide it.

6. *Security:* Security is becoming increasingly important on two levels. For one, we are using more and more expensive equipment that can be more easily carried away. For another, we need to find a way to help prevent leaks of information because in our competitive economic environment it is easy to steal large amounts of information in small forms.

7. *Local Environmental Controls:* Finally, we need to rethink how we can accommodate the office environment. Our old ways of doing things frequently don't work anymore. Local controls will become increasingly important to compensate for existing problems in buildings, and to maximize the effectiveness of energy utilization.

Of course, this list is not comprehensive. What do tomorrow's office workers need? The questions are not simple and the answers are not obvious. But, in the end, the extent that we succeed or fail as an information-based society depends on the extent that we address its human-centered (ergonomic) criteria.

QUESTIONS FOR READING 7.2

1. This article describes several changes in the office environment resulting from automation. Identify how the office of 1990 differs from the office of 1970 because of the new technology.

2. Expand on the concept that space usage patterns are becoming more group-oriented. Why is this so? Provide examples.

3. How is status changing the shape of the office? Will size/style differences between clerical and managerial offices remain?

4. Find out how your local government treats office spacing for employees of different ranks or grades. Is space directly tied to rank or function?

5. Compare tomorrow's office workers with those in a 1980 office.

READING 7.3

The Rethinking of the Supermarket

Robert Dietrich

If all supermarkets looked pretty much alike until recently, one reason was surely the almost carbon-copy sameness of their layouts. This is the first area where the winds of change are sweeping through

---

Source: Excerpted with permission from *Progressive Grocer* (December 1982), pp. 49–67. Copyright 1982 by Progressive Grocer Company.

and leaving evidence of significant differentiation in their wake. Two conceptual schools are fighting it out: the traditionalists, who belong to the service-departments-around-the-perimeter camp; and the revisionists, who seek to transform and reenergize the whole shopping experience by redirecting traffic flow.

With the unveiling of the new Safeway prototype in Arlington, Texas, the revisionists fired a blast which will echo through the industry for some time to come. The store is the crystallization of what Peter O'Gorman, its designer, calls "the need for a change in layout away from the traditional approach which—rather than emphasizing the departments—got customers lost in the linear flow around the walls."

Shoppers in the new Safeway will not find themselves in the basic supermarket box. The store consists of two wide-angled Vs, with the points of the Vs' base widened to create an entrance. An open center-island core—which defines the strong service positioning of the store—is a commanding focal point from anywhere in the store. The island holds bakery, cheese, deli, pharmacy and floral departments, as well as a café and customer service area. The island is located near the store's entrance.

"In a traditional supermarket," O'Gorman explains, "you have only one shot at telling the customer which services you have. If your service departments matter, you should signal you have them as many times as possible. We took sightlines from every position to make sure that every time you turn an aisle you see the island core. This store breaks away totally from traditional design." Height of gondolas is restrained throughout the store to maintain visual access to the service island.

Aside from the core, the store divides into two spheres—one for food and one for nonfood—whose aisles are diagonal to the front of the store. Thus there are variations in the directions in which traffic flows in the store, a relief from the tension and monotony of parallel up-aisle-and-down-aisle flow found in most new superstores.

The merits of such a radical transition in layout theory are, of course, months or years from being proved. Meanwhile, other voices, like that of Stop & Shop's Harold Austin, director of operations and support systems for supermarket operations, make a strong case for the traditionalists. "Our traffic pattern," Austin explains, "starts with florals, a salad bar, produce, our new Food Bazaar, the deli

and service fish. We want to give an immediate and total impression of freshness. Our segments lead to each other. If you look at the total layout you see you can *flow through*. And we have wide aisles to help that flow."

Care was taken to keep the sheer size of the 47,000-square-foot Super Stop & Shop from overwhelming shoppers. "We have no long vistas," Austin says. "We took the sightlines to assure this. Through the center of the store run a large greeting cards section (near the front) and a Barnes & Noble bookstore (to the rear). Austin sees this central zone as an identity point which dramatically signals the break between edibles and nonedibles.

In planning the Stop & Shop layout, care was taken to define the role and placement of store personnel as well as of fixtures and equipment. "In a large store," Austin says, "the customer needs people to talk to—a friendly relationship. That's why we have our Food Bazaar near the front and the bakery near the end. We want to bring our people *out* so customers can see what they're doing for them." Part of that effort is exemplified by The Food Bazaar, a well-staffed rectangular island counter which offers over 150 varieties of cheese plus vitamins, natural foods, coffee beans, tea and gourmet cookies and crackers. "With our people working in the shopper's sight, you know they're there to wait on *you*. It gives the merchandise a just-sliced-for-you aura."

Stop & Shop feels the flow afforded by the perimeter is useful to the service departments but avoids monotony by varying the fixtures by department. "We've broken the departments into shops to give them individuality. This is not quite boutiquing. Boutiquing is a physical breaking up with walls. We have no alcoves or niches but do it with decor."

In planning for the Stop & Shop prototype care was taken all along the line to provide ample room for employees to perform their jobs. "Our employees are very involved. They want to work in a nice pleasant store rather than an uncaring one. This is their home."

QUESTIONS FOR READING 7.3

1. How does the V plan differ from the traditional supermarket layout?

2. How do "superstores" keep from overwhelming customers? Discuss their advantages and disadvantages.

3. Which style of supermarket do you prefer to shop at, and why? Compare the Safeway's design with the layout of your own supermarket.

4. Find a recent copy of the magazine *Progressive Grocer.* Photocopy the "store of the month" feature and compare the layout to the Safeway store described here.

—— CASE 7.1 ———————————————

State Automobile License Renewals

Henry Coupe, the manager of a metropolitan branch office of the state department of motor vehicles, attempted to perform an analysis of the driver's license renewal operations. Several steps were to be performed in the process. After examining the license renewal process, he identified the steps and associated times required to perform each step as shown in the following table.

Step	Average Time to Perform (seconds)
1. Review renewal application for correctness	15
2. Process and record payment	30
3. Check file for violations and restrictions	60
4. Conduct eye test	40
5. Photograph applicant	20
6. Issue temporary license	30

Coupe found that each step was assigned to a different person. Each application was a separate process in the sequence shown above. Coupe determined that his office should be prepared to accommodate the maximum demand of processing 120 renewal applicants per hour.

He observed that the work was unevenly divided among the clerks, and the clerk who was responsible for checking violations tended to shortcut her task to keep up with the other clerks. Long lines built up during the maximum demand periods.

Coupe also found that jobs 1, 2, 3, and 4 were

handled by general clerks who were each paid $6.00 per hour. Job 5 was by a photographer paid $8.00 per hour. Job 6, the issuing of temporary license, was required by state policy to be handled by a uniformed motor vehicle officer. Officers were paid $9.00 per hour, but they could be assigned to any jobs except photography.

A review of the jobs indicated that job 1, reviewing the application for correctness, had to be performed before any other step could be taken. Similarly, job 6, issuing the temporary license, could not be performed until all the other steps were completed.

The branch offices were charged $5 per hour for each camera to perform photography.

Henry Coupe was under severe pressure to increase productivity and reduce costs, but he was also told by the regional director of the Department of Motor Vehicles that he had better accommodate the demand for renewals. Otherwise, "heads would roll."

—— QUESTIONS FOR CASE 7.1

1. What is the maximum number of applications per hour that can be handled by the present configuration of the process?

2. How many applications can be processed per hour if a second clerk is added to check for violations?

3. Assuming the addition of one more clerk, what is the maximum number of applications the process can handle?

4. How would you suggest modifying the process in order to accommodate 120 applications per hour?

—— CASE 7.2 ——————————————————————

The Palm Beach Institute of Sports Medicine

Ronald DeAngelo ▪ R. G. Murdick

INTRODUCTION

Many orthopedic M.D.'s, cardiologists, and sports medicine physicians have recognized the need for implementing diagnoses through physical therapy and fitness programs. Many more people are participating in sports and exercise such as tennis and jogging that may result in some type of injury. As a result, some physicians are forming close connections with quality sports medicine centers or are investing in limited partnerships to develop their own.

The typical sports medicine center (SMC) may provide such services as

— Injury prevention programs
— Athletic training services
— Physical therapy/rehabilitation
— Specialized fitness programs for the athletic competitor
— Physical fitness preparation for the general public
— Stress management
— Nutrition and weight management

The medical profession is the portal provider of many sports medicine center services. Therefore, a referral network is essential among physicians and the SMC. The SMC is differentiated from health or fitness clubs because of this connection and the number of certified employees per member in the center.

BACKGROUND

Mr. Dana Van Pelt opened a physical therapy practice in Pompano Beach, Florida, in 1980. As a registered physical therapist (RPT) and a certified athletic trainer (ATC), Mr. Van Pelt had a deep interest in conditioning and reconditioning of the body. In 1984 he therefore opened a sports medicine and physical therapy center in Boca Raton, north of Pompano Beach. This was so successful that it soon outgrew its quarters. In 1986, Van Pelt had the good fortune to locate about 7600 square feet of floor space in Boca Raton consisting of the entire fourth floor of the Galen Building. This location was within two blocks of the Community Hospital and in the center of a complex of medical buildings surrounding the area.

The organization of the now-named Palm Beach Institute of Sports Medicine (PBISM) consisted of Dana Van Pelt, President; Larry Carlino, Physical Therapist (PT) and Executive Director of Physical Therapy; three other physical therapists; three athletic trainers; one health/fitness instructor; four supporting physical therapy aides; three receptionists; and two business specialists. A number of nearby medical and paramedical specialists were also closely associated with PBISM by virtue of consulting arrangements.

Dana paid particular attention to the business aspects, long-range plans, and physical therapy advances and equipment. Larry Carlino was concerned with the management of day-to-day operations of the physical therapy aspects. Ron De Angelo, one of the athletic trainers managed the fitness operations. Duties were not highly specified, and the three worked as an informal team for the principal goals of the center.

PHILOSOPHY

The philosophy of PBISM is to promote a quality lifestyle for all participating members as well as those utilizing the institute's conditioning and rehabilitation programs. An enhanced membership package of services is shown in Exhibit 7–23.

Source: Used with permission of the authors.

_____ EXHIBIT 7–23 _____

■ *Supplementary Membership Services*

**Palm Beach Institute
of Sports Medicine, Inc.**

```
NEW MEMEBERSHIP PACKAGE INCLUDES:   (As of April 1, 1988)

     *T-shirt
     *Towels
      Blood Chemistry (Smac-26)
      Nutrition Counselling with a R.D.
      Take-Care Book
      Take-care Newsletter (monthly)
      Sportsmedicine Reporter (quarterly)
      Assessment Booklet (computerized)
     *Full Assessment & Evaluation (by Exercise Physiologist)
     *Prescription (exercise)
     *Re-evaluation (every 6 months)

    *All starred items are included in the package before
     April 1, 1988.
```

Source: Used with permission of Palm Beach Institute of Sports Medicine, Inc.

LAYOUT: A CONTINUING CHALLENGE

When Dana was planning his move to the Galen building, the fourth floor was cleared to appear as shown in Exhibit 7–24. This area was to contain three offices, a conference room, examination rooms, treatment areas (partitioned with curtains), a large wet room with underwater treadmill, business office, men's and women's locker rooms, waiting room, reception area opposite the elevator, glass-paneled office overlooking the major equipment areas, and three equipment areas. The equipment areas were planned to be a back treatment area, a large conditioning equipment and stretching area, and an isokinetic equipment area. The items of equipment are listed in Exhibit 7–25. Two or three duplicates of some items of equipment were contemplated because of general heavy usage.

The general pattern for members to follow was to

1. Pick up their exercise plan sheet and clipboard.
2. Warm up on one of the bikes.
3. Stretch.
4. Work out on upper body equipment.
5. Work out on lower body equipment.
6. Work out on abdomen and back machines.

In some cases, members would spend 30 to 45 minutes, or more, on aerobic devices such as bikes, treadmills, UBE, the Versa Climber, the Nordic (ski) Trak, or the rower. The equipment layout would have to be modified at a later date, Dana knew, based on accumulated operating experience with the new SMC.

EXHIBIT 7–24

- *Floor Layout of Gutted Building Area*

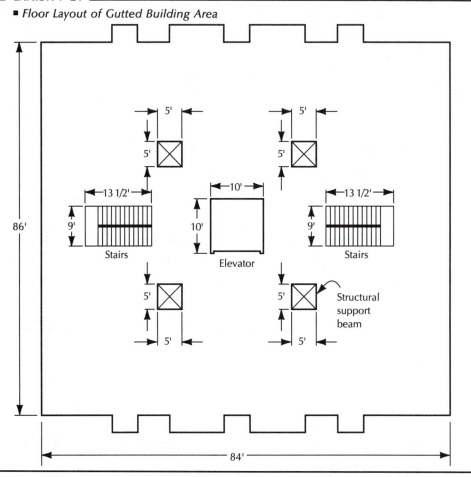

Source: Used with permission of Palm Beach Institute of Sports Medicine, Inc.

EXHIBIT 7–25

- *Equipment*

1. Treadmill	13. (a) Eagle back extension
2. Airdyne bike	(b) Eagle abdominal flexion
3. Life cycle	14. Orthotron
4. Bodyguard bike	15. Cybex
5. Versa climber	16. Cybex II plus
6. Nordic trak	17. SABA
7. Precor skier	18. Cybex back extension
8. Precor rower	19. Cybex back rotation
9. UBE	20. Stair master
10. Fitron	21. Underwater treadmill
11. Kinetron	22. Quinton 3000 stress test unit
12. (a) Keiser (lower body)	23. Abdominal slant board
(b) Keiser (upper body)	24. Bench
	25. Dumbell rack

—— QUESTIONS FOR CASE 7.2

1. Draw an organization chart for PBISM.

2. Suppose you are planning the layout for Dana by following the key to inputs to the layout problem shown earlier in this chapter as Exhibit 7.2. For PBISM, make a brief list of inputs in rough form to indicate your understanding of the key.

3. Prepare a layout of the floor plan of the Institute. Get advice and comments from other students.

4. Lay out the arrangement of equipment within the floor plan.

——————————— REFERENCES ———————————

Ackerman, Kenneth B., and Bernard J. LaLonde. "Making Warehousing More Efficient," *Harvard Business Review,* Vol. 58, No. 2 (March–April 1980), pp. 94–102.

Arcus, A. L. "COMSOAL: A Computer Method for Sequencing Operations for Assembly Line," *International Journal of Production Research,* Vol. 4, No. 4 (1966).

Beer, Ira B. "Efficiency and Productivity Profit," *Restaurant Business* (November 1, 1987), pp. 147–161.

Buffa, E. S., G. S. Armor, and T. E. Vollman, "Allocating Facilities, with CRAFT," *Harvard Business Review,* Vol. 42, No. 2 (March–April 1984), pp. 136–159.

DeSanta, Richard. "All That Glitters is Not Upscale," *Progressive Grocer* (April 1987), pp. 112–117.

Dietrich, Robert. "The Rethinking of the Supermarket," *Progressive Grocer* (December 1982), pp. 49–67.

Donegan, Priscilla. "Breaking the Pattern," *Progressive Grocer* (November 1988), pp. 72–75.

Heizer, Jay, and Barry Render. *Production and Operations Management: Strategies and Tactics.* Boston: Allyn and Bacon, 1988.

Heller, Walter. "Tracking Shoppers Through the Combination Store," *Progressive Grocer* (November 1988), pp. 47–54.

Kaiman, L. "Computer Programs for Architects and Layout Planners," *Proceedings of the 22nd Annual Meeting of the American Institute of Industrial Engineers.* Boston, 1971.

Keating, Joseph W. "Corporate Facility Planning in a Decentralized Structure: Three Key Areas of Responsibility," *Industrial Development* (July–August 1986).

Lambert, Carolyn U., and Karen Marsh Watson. "Restaurant Design: Researching the Effects on Customers," *The Cornell H.R.A. Quarterly* (February 1984), pp. 68–76.

Manners, Steven. "Optimizing the Cube," *Administrative Management* (October 1986), pp. 19–21.

Merredew, Clive. "A Model Facility Delivery Process," *Industrial Development* (July–August 1986).

Miller, Darryl. "The Components of a Facility Review," *Industrial Development* (March–April 1986).

Paznik, M. Jill. "Comfort and Technology to Mesh More Easily in the Office of the Future," *Administrative Management* (October 1986), pp. 56–61.

Stone, Philip J., and Robert Luchetti. "Your Office Is Where You Are" *Harvard Business Review,* Vol. 63, No. 2 (March–April 1985), pp. 102–117.

8

Aggregate Planning

INTRODUCTION

Aggregate planning involves determining the resource capacity that a firm will need to meet its demand. It is rough or approximate planning carried out for an intermediate time span of about one to three years. The role of aggregate planning is to convert the strategic types of marketing plans or demand forecasts associated with long-range planning into overall capacity requirements. These aggregate capacity requirements will subsequently serve as a framework for the short-range allocation (i.e., disaggregation) of overall capacity to individual products and services. Chapter 11 on scheduling discusses short-range capacity allocation.

Exhibit 8–1 indicates the general characteristics of aggregate planning, planning

---

EXHIBIT 8–1

- *Levels of Planning Disaggregation*

Level of Planning	Manufacturing-Like Firms	Service-Like Firms
Level 1 Aggregate planning	Translation of strategic decisions into productive capacity over 1 to 3 years	Translation of strategic decisions into technology and resource planning over 1 to 3 years
Level 2 Disaggregate planning	Decisions on the individual product lines with regard to capacity and timing for each	Decisions on basic service designs and markets to be matched
	Decisions on capacity disaggregated into facilities, equipment, and human resources with timing for each for 1 year ahead	Decisions on how capacity will be expanded or limited and demand will be managed for 1 year ahead
	Make or buy decisions	
Level 3 Scheduling of resources	Weekly, monthly, and quarterly (or rolling 3-month) plans for production to match capacity to short-term fluctuations in demand	Weekly, monthly, and quarterly (or rolling 3-month) plans for production to match capacity with managed demand
	Raw materials and finished goods inventory decisions	Decisions on raw materials inventory
	Decisions on priorities for products, filling of orders, and assignment of work to individual operations	Decisions on assignment of work to individuals

---

disaggregated by resources and outputs, and the short-term scheduling of resources. The distinction between manufacturing-like and service-like firms refers to the tangibility of the output. Manufacturing-like firms are those which have tangible outputs or have distinct front-office/back-office operations.

Aggregate planning is a simple process if demand is relatively stable. Resource capacity can be set to the level of demand, and slight variations in demand can be handled with overtime or undertime. Aggregate planning becomes more difficult when demand varies widely from period to period. Demand fluctuations for products typically follow a seasonal pattern. In addition to seasonality, demand for services also may fluctuate by day of the week and hour of the day. While aggregate planning is not concerned with daily or weekly scheduling decisions, it is concerned with establishing a *strategy* for meeting the variations in demand. Decisions such as the number of full-time workers to employ, whether part-time workers or subcontracting should be used, when services should be offered at which sites or times, and how much capacity is needed are all part of aggregate planning.

Aggregate planning, also known as **capacity planning,** is somewhat different for services than for manufacturing because of the following factors:

1. Most services are perishable and cannot be inventoried. Thus it is impossible to produce the service early in anticipation of higher demand at a later time.
2. Demand for services is often difficult to predict, and demand variations are typically more severe and frequent (i.e., they occur over shorter time periods).
3. Because of the variety of services offered and the individualized nature of services, the capacity required to meet demand is difficult to predict. For example, the time required to serve a customer at a bank can vary considerably depending on the number and type of transactions requested by the customer. *Units* of capacity also may be hard to define. For instance, should a hospital define capacity in terms of numbers of beds, numbers of patients, size of nursing or medical staff, or numbers of patient hours at each level of care?
4. Since most services cannot be transported, service capacity must be available at the appropriate *place* as well as at the appropriate time.
5. In view of these difficulties, it is helpful to note one final difference. Service capacity is generally altered by changes in labor rather than by equipment or space, and labor is a highly flexible resource.

THE DEMAND SIDE OF AGGREGATE PLANNING

If we are considering matching capacity to demand over a period of time, we should first consider the demand curves commonly faced. We can then seek ways to adjust service output along such curves. For the time period of aggregate forecasting, we focus on the broad sweep of demand curves rather than random fluctuations. The basic types of curves are

— Stable, constant demand
— Stable, cyclical demand

—— EXHIBIT 8–2 ——

■ *Typical Curves Representing Forecasts of Demand: Demand vs. Time*

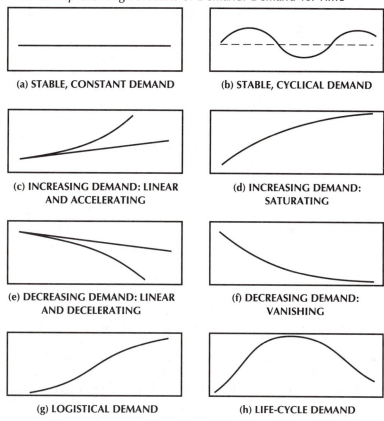

(a) STABLE, CONSTANT DEMAND

(b) STABLE, CYCLICAL DEMAND

(c) INCREASING DEMAND: LINEAR AND ACCELERATING

(d) INCREASING DEMAND: SATURATING

(e) DECREASING DEMAND: LINEAR AND DECELERATING

(f) DECREASING DEMAND: VANISHING

(g) LOGISTICAL DEMAND

(h) LIFE-CYCLE DEMAND

— Increasing demand—linear, accelerating, or saturating
— Decreasing demand—linear, decelerating, or vanishing
— Logistic or S-shaped curves
— Life-cycle curves

The general appearances of such curves are shown in Exhibit 8–2. Although forecasts may be based on judgment and a simple hand-drawn curve, many experts prefer the use of sophisticated forecasting methods and mathematical curve fitting techniques.[1] Case 8.1 illustrates how the curve-fitting technique of regression is used to plan nursing staff levels.

---

[1] The interested reader is referred to R. G. Murdick, "How They Figure the Sales Forecast," *Machine Design* (December 9, 1971); or E. A. Passemier, *New Product Decisions* (New York: McGraw-Hill, 1966), for a detailed description of some common curves and their mathematical representation.

THE GENERAL PROBLEM OF MATCHING CAPACITY AND DEMAND

The basic options in matching capacity to demand depend heavily on underlying strategic decisions. Some options are

1. Increase or decrease capacity both in the strategic and midterm range.
2. Manage demand to fit capacity constrained by resources or limited flexibility.
3. Arbitrarily establish capacity at a level significantly below demand.

Adjusting Capacity

Increasing capacity in labor-intensive firms of large employee size can be carried out in small increments or percentages of the labor force. For small service firms of five or less employees, the addition of one person probably represents a large jump in capacity. By analogy, for capital-intensive firms or firms that use a few very large pieces of equipment, the need to increase capacity may be satisfied only with a large incremental jump. Similarly, many small shops may only expand at some points of time by buying the space next door or moving to a much larger building. In other words, increasing capacity is often only achievable in "lumps."

This lumpiness is shown in Exhibit 8–3. Here capacity is maintained equal to or in excess of forecasted demand. When capacity exceeds forecasted demand, the company is paying for idle equipment, facilities, or labor. In the latter case, one person is hired when, perhaps, only half his or her time is required to meet demand. Part-time help is not always the answer when a specialist or skilled professional is needed.

The size of incremental increases in capacity to match demand can pose a problem for large companies. Exhibit 8–4 shows an option of making one large increase

___ EXHIBIT 8–3 ___

■ *Incremental Increases in Capacity*

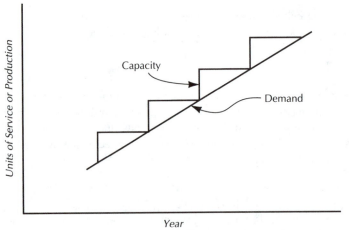

_____ EXHIBIT 8–4 _____

■ *Optional Incremental Increases in Capacity*

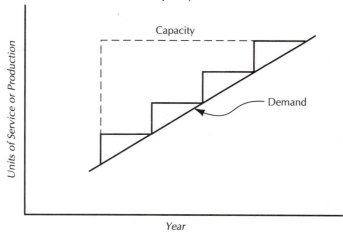

in capacity, such as purchasing a very large efficient machine, versus a number of small increments in capacity, such as purchasing small, less efficient machines. Florida Power & Light (FP&L) faces this type of decision over and over in South Florida. Often when a large development is started outside an established city, it will take 10 years for the development to be completed. FP&L may run large, heavy-duty lines to the development with the prospect that the lines and peripheral equipment will be only partially utilized for years. Alternatively, it may extend smaller lines and then replace the lines every few years with larger lines and more equipment as demand increases. This problem would be a straightforward economic one, except for the uncertainties in the growth of demand, cost of capital, and changes in technology.

As another example, consider the case of the Royal Palm Polo and Sports Club. Its facilities are

— Two polo fields and related stable areas
— Thirteen clay tennis courts
— Four indoor racquet courts
— One Nautilus and fitness room
— One swimming pool and whirlpool area
— One restaurant

In order to attract members, it was considered necessary to present the complete package shown above almost from the beginning, although utilization of some of the facilities initially was marginal. Building in idle capacity was a less costly alternative than adding extra capacity and services at a later date.

Finally, there is the option of expanding capacity beyond demand but only after capacity has fallen below demand as shown in Exhibit 8–5. Here the tradeoff is made

_____ EXHIBIT 8–5 _____

■ *Trading Off Idle Capacity with Lost Sales*

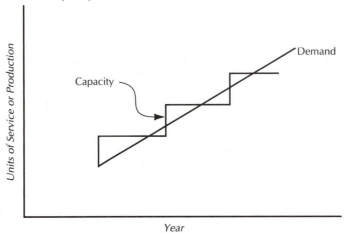

between the costs of overcapacity and the costs of unsatisfied demand in order to minimize total costs for the business as a whole.

Managing Demand

Demand for services is affected by a number of variables other than a basic desire for the service. The time of the service has a value to many clients, and shifting the service time by means of various methods may make is possible to better match demand to supply. Pricing and service extensions also may permit manipulation of demand. Similarly, advertising may increase demand in normally slack periods. During periods of peak demand, complementary services may make the wait for service more bearable for customers and increase the likelihood for their staying in the system or returning at a later date. In this section we discuss three methods for managing demand: complementary services, pricing, and advertising.

Complementary Services.   Loss of patrons because of long waiting lines may be reduced by diverting them to other complementary services. Thus a bar or lounge may hold a surge of patrons for a restaurant. A putting green or driving range may keep golfers occupied when starting times are delayed.

In essence, a complementary service represents one stage of a two-stage queue.[2] The service time for the first stage may stretch out for a considerable time before a client leaves the service stage to exit from the system. An analysis of such a system using restaurant service as an example is shown in Exhibit 8–6.

In Exhibit 8–6, when customers enter the restaurant, one of three things may occur. The customers may be seated immediately in the dining area (principal service

---

[2] Queuing theory is discussed in detail in Chapter 11.

_____ EXHIBIT 8–6 _____

■ *Analysis of a Service with a Complementary Service Stage*

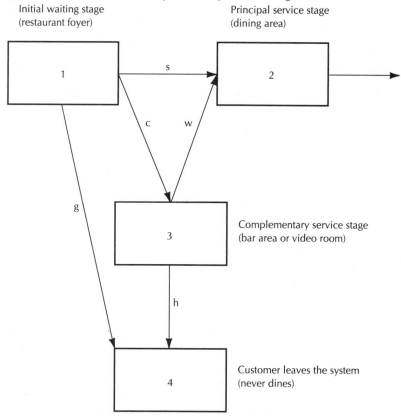

Initial waiting stage
(restaurant foyer)

Principal service stage
(dining area)

Complementary service stage
(bar area or video room)

Customer leaves the system
(never dines)

s = customer is seated immediately
c = no table is available; customer waits in complementary service area
w = table becomes available; customer waiting in complementary service area
    is seated
h = customer waiting in complementary service area leaves before being seated
g = customer sees long line and leaves without service

stage), sent to a bar area or video room to await seating (complementary service stage), or leave the restaurant without dining. From the complementary service stage, customers may wait until they are seated or give up waiting and leave the restaurant.

Obviously, a service firm wants to serve as many customers as possible. Associated with the service system portrayed in Exhibit 8–6 are certain probabilities that a customer will actually be served or that he or she will leave the system at some point without being served. The probabilities may be calculated using the following probability definitions of customer behavior:

$P(s)$ = probability that the customer proceeds directly to the principal service stage

$P(c)$ = probability that a customer enters into the complementary service stage

$P(w)$ = probability that a customer elects to wait in the complementary service stage until he or she can enter the principal. service stage

$P(h)$ = probability that the customer decides to leave the system

$P(g)$ = probability that a customer views a lengthy waiting line and leaves the system upon entering it

Then the probability that a customer reaches the principal service stage may be given by

$$P(s) + P(c)P(w)$$

Similarly, the probability of never reaching the principal service stage is

$$P(g) + P(c)P(h)$$

Pricing.   If demand is too high at certain times of the day, week, month, or year, prices may be raised at the peak times. Also, if demand is too low at certain times, prices may be lowered. Matinees in theaters, early-bird specials in restaurants, out-of-season rates for resorts or air fares, and 24-hour fitness clubs with lower rates after 9:00 P.M. are instances of pricing to shift demand.

When demand is inelastic, the provider of a service may charge high initial fees. For example, in one city, clients must pay $50 in addition to the $35 office fee on their first visit to orthopedic surgeons. This tends to bring the client back to the original surgeon for future needs. Some sports clubs have tried to adopt a similar pricing policy by charging initiation fees with the objective of stabilizing membership rolls. However, the results of this strategy have been mixed. Unlike medical services, people will often seek out or wait for other recreational opportunities where little or no initiation fees are charged.

Pricing, demand, and capacity can be closely related in highly competitive services. For example, since deregulation of the airline industry, shifts in capacity to different markets occur monthly. When capacity is increased, carriers reduce prices in that market to generate traffic. Once traffic goes up or a competitor reduces its capacity, fares go up again. To complicate the pricing process, if a carrier comes into a market with lower fares on their single flight, another airline with more flights may match the low fare on one or two flights close to the discount flight's departure time, but not on all flights!

Advertising and Sales Promotion.   Promotional offers during off-seasons are common. Home insulation service, holiday tours with extended features, promotion of low evening telephone rates, and late-night movie theater showings with prizes are examples.

Setting Capacity Below Demand

For specialized status services such as high-priced conditioning retreats, nonprofit health care centers, addiction treatment centers, vacation islands for the superwealthy, and exclusive clubs, capacity is often set below demand. This is so that a high price may be obtained for them from customers who are essentially bidding for a status item. The management problem is reduced to selecting customers and maintaining the niche that service occupies. Usually the niche is quite stable over the long run, and tradition continues to enhance it.

COMPONENTS OF CAPACITY

In Chapter 3 we discussed the nature of forecasting demand. Now we must look at the components that make up or influence capacity. When we have the concepts of both demand and capacity in mind, we may then discuss the process of aggregate planning. The seven basic components of capacity are human resources, facilities, equipment, tools, money, time, and alternative sources of capacity.

Human Resources

Human resources are directly related to aggregate output. The number of people, the level of skills, and the mix of skills are major factors. Highly skilled people organized into motivated groups and supplied with the best equipment can have an enormous impact on productivity. Further, if the leadership is excellent and the environment is rewarding, the twin factors of leadership and motivation may increase capacity.

Human resources are also a highly flexible capacity component. Workers can be hired and fired easier than equipment can be bought and sold. Labor can work full-time, part-time or overtime. Workers can be cross-trained to perform a variety of jobs. A basic full-time work force can be supplemented with part-timers during peak demand periods. During periods of low demand, permanent workers may be asked to fill multiple positions.

Facilities

Often output may be increased by moving to a new building with a better space pattern or by developing a better layout of equipment in the old building. Better lighting, air-conditioning, and heating improvements also may contribute to productivity and thereby expand capacity. The type of materials handling equipment, such as an electromagnetic crane for an automobile junk yard, may increase the output of a service.

Surplus demand may be handled with multiple facilities, such as retail outlets in various shopping centers throughout a city or half a dozen health care clinics in an urban area.

Equipment and Tools

Although much of equipment planning has already been determined in the capital budgeting stage of the strategic plan, sometimes simple, inexpensive equipment substitutions or modifications may yield increases in productivity and thereby expand capacity. As an example, Sears introduced a computer terminal for order takers in its catalog department to replace hand completion and filing of forms. At the same time, it introduced a terminal stand where customers enter their home phone numbers and the storage location of their packages appears on the screen. Each customer then goes to the storage shelf, picks up the package, and takes it to the cashier. Formerly, the Sears clerk had to retrieve the location number from a desk file. In this example, the work was simplified and shifted to the customer, but customer waiting time was greatly reduced.

Similarly, using multipurpose tools, such as rubber stamps as a substitute for writing repetitive messages, or special tools for mechanical or electronic repair services, also may increase aggregate output. In the Sears example, a computerized telephone operator was installed that would keep calling a residence to inform the customer that his or her order had arrived. This system saved Sears employees countless hours dialing unresponsive numbers.

Money

Money is a component of capacity in services such as credit card firms where the ability to carry receivables is a limit on the primary business. This is quite different than the case of manufacturing companies, where money is only indirectly related to capacity through the purchase of resources.

Where money is a component of capacity as in banks and financial services, aggregate supply focuses on cash flow and short-term credit. Raising capital by issuing stocks, acquiring a company, merging with another company, or selling bonds is considered a strategic (long-term) action.

Time

Time is a component in two ways. First, capacity may be altered by changing the mix between two time periods or shifting output to another time period. This is especially appropriate for services subject to peak demand periods. Second, in a larger sense, increasing the time period to provide the product or service increases the total capacity relative to demand for a specified time period.

Alternative Sources

Alternative sources of capacity may be internal or external. Internal sources may consist of mothballed machines or facilities, extended work hours, or multiple shifts. External sources may consist of subcontracting, acquiring another company, or increasing automation. The leasing of resources also allows for a wide range of capacity expansion alternatives. Reading 8.2 gives an interesting example of an alternative source of capacity for a municipal public safety department.

GENERAL METHODS FOR MATCHING CAPACITY TO DEMAND

Aggregate planning is concerned with matching supply and demand *in total* over an intermediate length of time rather than matching week-to-week fluctuations. Therefore, it is concerned with trends and major fluctuations in demand, such as seasonal changes.

It builds on quarterly and yearly aggregates. Generally, equipment changes are very limited because they represent long-term (three- to five-year) decisions involving sunk costs. The focus of aggregate planning is to determine the aggregate rate of service output for the year and the size of the work force. Other considerations in aggregate planning to meet fluctuating demand include shifting service delivery between time periods, seeking shifts in demand between time periods, subcontracting, and using part-time casual labor.

In order to choose between the many options available for meeting demand, a firm should develop a certain *strategy* for allocating capacity and then support that strategy with specific manpower and production decisions. Some possible strategies for aggregate planning of services are

1. Keep producing at a constant rate and use inventory to absorb fluctuations in demand (if the service can be inventoried).
2. Increase or decrease working hours without changing the size of the work force.
3. Offer service at a later period when capacity is available.
4. Staff for high demand levels.
5. Subcontract work to other firms.
6. Hire and lay off personnel to track demand.
7. Offer additional services with demand patterns countercyclical to current services.
8. Utilize part-time workers.

Not all these strategies are appropriate or feasible for every service. For example, most services cannot be inventoried (it is impossible to inventory seats on an airplane for later use). Similarly, offering a table at a restaurant to hungry customers in "about four hours" when capacity becomes available is not a wise strategy.

Examples of how the addition of new services can potentially balance demand and capacity can be found in several industries. McDonald's and other fast-food chains sell breakfast foods to utilize some of their existing "cooking" capacity during the morning hours. Similarly, many coffee shops and pancake houses offer dinner menus. Hotels catering to business travelers during the week add more luxury services to attract local customers on weekend "minivacations." However appealing these new services may be in utilizing idle capacity, companies that follow this strategy may find themselves involved in services beyond their area of expertise or beyond their target market.[3] For Federal Express, their huge aircraft fleet is used to near capacity for nighttime delivery of packages but is 100 percent idle during the daytime. In an attempt to better utilize their capacity (and leverage their assets), Federal considered two services with opposite or countercyclical demand patterns to their nighttime service—commuter passenger service and passenger charter service. However, after a thorough analysis of these new services, the 12 to 13 percent return on investment was judged insufficient for the risks involved.[4]

Exhibit 8–7 summarizes the associated costs and advantages of each aggregate

---

[3] A good discussion of this is given by W. E. Sasser, "Match Supply and Demand in Service Industries," *Harvard Business Review,* Vol. 54, No. 6 (November–December 1976), pp. 133–140.

[4] This information appeared in R. A. Sigafoos and R. R. Easson, *Absolutely Positively Overnight!* (Memphis, Tenn.: St. Luke's Press, 1988).

EXHIBIT 8–7 ■ Aggregate Planning to Meet Changing Demand

Strategies	Advantages	Disadvantages	Comments
Smooth output to produce inventory in some periods for later demand	Changes in required human resources are gradual or none; no abrupt changes in production are needed.	Inventory holding costs	Not applicable to most services, only to embedded services
Increase working hours without changing the size of the work force	Allows matching of seasonal fluctuations or trends for interim periods without hiring and training costs	Overtime premiums; lower marginal productivity; tired workers; may be insufficient to meet demand	Allows flexibility within the aggregate plan for services with intangible outputs
Offer service at a later period when capacity is available	May avoid overtime; keeps capacity constant	Customer may go elsewhere, as for elective surgery, or customer may have to go elsewhere, as for lifesaving surgery; customer may stay, but goodwill is lost.	Many consumer services as well as industrial services have backlogs and customers are willing to wait a reasonable time; time is, however, a means for gaining competitive edge.
Staff for high demand levels	Overtime is not required; increasing trend for demand is covered; unexpected fluctuations are covered; goodwill is achieved because waiting time for customers is kept near zero.	High idle machine capacity may occur; unless workers can be applied to special projects, idle labor may occur; workers may work more slowly to fill in idle time, thereby antagonizing customers.	Works well when the service is provided by high-level professionals who will generate proposals when not serving customers; also effective when demand may be manipulated to fill normally low demand periods
Subcontract work to other firms	Permits good flexibility and smoothing of the firm's output during an upward trend; may be applied to subassemblies for a buy-vs-make advantage in cost	Loss of quality and time control; reduction in profits; possible permanent loss of future business to the subcontractor	Applicable primarily to industrial services such as painting, repairing, decorating (i.e., work on *things* rather than on *people*), although exceptions such as education exist
Hire and lay off personnel to track demand	Avoids the costs of other alternatives; minimizes consumer waiting time for intangible services	Hiring and layoff costs *may* be significant; training costs may be incurred; poor company image may result.	May be very successful if unskilled personnel are used and the personnel desire only supplementary income
Add services with countercyclical demand patterns	Fully utilizes resources; allows stable work force	May require skills outside firm's areas of expertise; may involve change in strategy or market focus	May be few services with opposite demand patterns that use similar resources; method involves high degree of risk.
Utilize part-time workers	Less costly and more flexible than full-time workers	High turnover; training costs high; quality of service may suffer; scheduling difficult	Works well for unskilled jobs in areas with large temporary labor pools (e.g., students, housewives, retirees)

planning strategy and comments on their applicability to certain services. We must emphasize at this point that in addition to the costs associated with providing a service, the costs associated with failure to meet customer demands adequately also must be taken into account. In addition, firms generally pursue a number of the "pure" strategies listed in Exhibit 8–7 in combination, resulting in a "mixed" aggregate planning strategy for meeting demand.

Approaches to aggregate planning differ by the type of service provided. We consider four service scenarios in the following discussion of aggregate planning: (1) high-volume tangible output, (2) high-volume intangible output, (3) dispersed independent sites, and (4) dispersed interlocking sites. Then a quantitative example of aggregate planning in services is given.

High-Volume Tangible Output

Producing high-volume tangible output using a considerable number of machines is more typical of manufacturing but applies to some services, such as publishing. Aggregate planning in this case is directed toward (1) smoothing the production rate, (2) finding the size of the work force to be employed, and (3) attempting to manage demand to keep equipment and employees working. The general approach for the high-volume tangible output service usually requires building inventory during slack periods and depleting inventory during peak periods.

Since this is very similar to manufacturing, traditional aggregate planning methods may be applied to high-volume tangible services as well.[5] One difference that should be noted is that in services, inventory may be perishable. In addition, the relevant units of time may be much smaller than in manufacturing. For example, in fast-food restaurants, peak and slack periods may be measured in hours and the "product" may be inventoried for only as long as 10 minutes.

High-Volume Intangible Output

Most "miscellaneous" services, many financial services, hospitality services, transportation services, and many communication and recreation services provide high-volume intangible outputs. Aggregate planning for these services rests principally on planning for human resource requirements and managing demand. The goal is to level the demand peak and design methods for fully utilizing labor resources during forecasted low-demand periods. Low-demand periods may occur during the following times.

	Examples of Types of Service
Times of the day	Resorts, recreational, medical
Days of the week	Financial services, recreational, painting, repairing
Times of the month	Financial services
Seasons of the year	Resorts, recreational, home repair, income tax preparation

---

[5] Such as those described in R. B. Chase and N. J. Aquilano, *Production and Operations Management,* 5th Ed. (Homewood, Ill.: Irwin, 1989), Chap. 11.

Low demand during times of the day at resorts or sports facilities can be increased by offering special incentives for members to change their demand patterns. For example, at a tennis facility, special tournaments could be arranged during off times, nearby townspeople could be offered low rates for morning memberships, and retirees could be encouraged to participate through low group morning rates. Low demand during days of the week or seasons of the year can be increased at motels by offering better rooms at lower prices or by including special entertainment features in the lodging package.

Aggregate planning in the motel/hotel industry consists of setting policies that will maximize profits by taking into account such factors as price, vacancies, and demand patterns. The analysis is not always simple, and certain tradeoffs do exist. Price, for instance, can vary by type of customer, time of year, and volume of customers. Obviously, management would prefer to sell all rooms at the highest rate possible, but this strategy may result in empty rooms and lost revenue. On the other hand, filling a hotel with low-rate customers foregoes the revenue that could have been received from higher rates. Uncertainty in demand exists because of customers who do not show up or who cancel their reservations, customers who walk in with no reservations, and customers who are unsure about how long they will stay. To protect themselves from the possibility of vacant rooms, hotel managers typically overbook their rooms and arrange reciprocal agreements with other hotels nearby. Probability distributions are commonly used to predict demand patterns and rates of no-shows by market segment and time of year.

Dispersed Independent Sites

With the advent of national chains of small service businesses such as funeral homes, fast-food outlets, photocopy/printing centers, and computer centers, the question of aggregate planning versus independent planning at each business establishment becomes an issue. One component of aggregate planning for a service chain is centralized purchasing, which has many advantages. Purchase price may be significantly reduced with volume discounts, and volume buying may allow a chain to dictate special quality or design variations for what is usually considered a standardized item. Output also may be centrally planned when demand can be influenced through special promotions. This approach is advantageous because it reduces advertising costs and helps regulate cash flow at the independent sites.

An example of different approaches to managing dispersed independent sites may be found in the supermarket industry.[6] Kroger's is well known among supermarkets for aggressive marketing and efficient operations. Planning is in aggregate terms for the entire chain, decision making is highly centralized, and each store in the huge chain is relatively standardized in terms of layout, product offerings, and operating procedures. This is in sharp contrast to supermarket chains such as Safeway, Winn Dixie, and Food Lion, which allow each store to operate independently. These owner-operated stores are more flexible and can adapt quicker to regional differences and market changes. Their planning, appearance, and operating procedures are also independent. Pretax margins exceed those of Kroger's, too.

---

[6] For an interesting twist to the results of these supermarket strategies, see Lydia Chavez, ''Takeover Shoppers Have Reasons to Go Krogering,'' *The New York Times* (October 1988).

Dispersed Interlocking Sites

Dispersed interlocking sites may be illustrated by a securities brokerage firm head-quartered in New York City but with offices dispersed throughout the United States. The number of employees in each branch office tends to vary with economic conditions. In good times, there are more customers to deal with than in bad times. The "back office," the computer center, is also located in New York. However, as sales volume rises or falls, the number of employees in the computer center changes very little because of the tremendous range of the computer in handling transactions. Aggregate planning in this case is represented by a schedule of the number of transactions to be performed and the number of people required for each branch office for the next year.

A more common example of dispersed interlocking sites may be found in the airline industry. Consider an airline that has its headquarters in New York, two hub sites in cities such as Atlanta and Dallas, and 150 offices in airports throughout the country. Aggregate planning consists of tables or schedules of number of flights in and out of each hub, number of flights on all routes, number of passengers to be serviced in all flights, and number of air personnel and ground personnel required at each hub and airport.

This is considerably more complex than aggregate planning for a single site or a number of independent sites. Even the manufacture of automobiles with component manufacturing sites and multiple assembly sites does not pose such aggregate planning problems. Additional capacity decisions are focused on determining the percentage of seats to be allocated to various fare classes in order to maximize profit or yield. This type of capacity allocation problem is called **yield management.**

A QUANTITATIVE EXAMPLE OF AGGREGATE PLANNING IN SERVICES

This example shows how a city's parks and recreation department could use the al-ternatives of full-time employees, part-time employees, and subcontracting to meet its commitment to provide a service to the city.[7]

Tucson Parks and Recreations Department has an operation and maintenance budget of around $10,000,000. The Parks and Recreation Department is responsible for developing and maintaining open space, all public recreational programs, adult sports leagues, golf courses, tennis courts, pools, and so forth. There are 336 full-time equivalent employees (FTEs) authorized in the department. Of these, 216 are full-time permanent personnel who provide the administration and year-round maintenance to all areas. The remaining 120 positions are all part-time—about three-quarters of them are used during the summer and the remaining quarter are used in the fall, winter, and spring seasons. The three-fourths (or 90 positions) show up as approximately 800 part-time summer jobs. These jobs are as lifeguards, baseball umpires, and instructors in summer programs for children. Currently, the only parks and recreation work sub-

---

[7] This example is taken from Richard B. Chase and Nicholas J. Aquilano, *Production and Operations Management,* 5th Ed. (Homewood, Ill.: Irwin, 1989), pp. 561–567.

contracted amounts to less than $100,000. This is for the golf and tennis pros and for grounds maintenance at the libraries and veterans' cemetery.

The option to hire and fire full-time help daily or weekly in order to meet seasonal demand is pretty much out of the question. However, temporary part-time help is authorized and traditional. Also, it is virtually impossible to have regular employees (non-part-time) staff all the summer jobs. During the summer months, the approximately 800 part-time employees are staffing the many programs that occur simultaneously, prohibiting level scheduling over a normal 40-hour week. Also, a wider variety of skills is required than can be expected from full-time employees (e.g., umpires, coaches, lifeguards, and teachers of ceramics, guitar, karate, belly dancing, and yoga).

There are three options open to the Parks and Recreation Department in their aggregate planning:

1. It can keep its present method, which is to maintain a medium-level full-time staff and schedule work during off-seasons (such as rebuilding baseball fields during the winter months) and to use part-time help during peak demands.
2. It can maintain a lower level of staff over the year and subcontract all additional work presently done by full-time staff (still utilizing part-time help).
3. It can maintain an administrative staff only and subcontract all work, including part-time help. (This would entail contracts to landscaping firms, pool-maintenance companies, and newly created private firms to employ and supply part-time help.)

The common unit of measure of work across all areas is full-time equivalent employees (or FTEs). For example, assume in the same week that 30 lifeguards worked 20 hours each, 40 instructors worked 15 hours each, and 35 baseball umpires worked 10 hours each. This is equivalent to $(30 \times 20) + (40 \times 15) + (35 \times 10) = 1550$ work hours. Then, $1550/40 = 39.75$ FTEs, or full-time-equivalent positions, for that week. Although a considerable amount of workload can be shifted to off-season, most of the work must be done when required.

Full-time employees consist of three groups: (1) the skeleton group of key department personnel coordinating with the city, setting policy, determining budgets, measuring performance, and so forth; (2) the administrative group of supervisory and office personnel who are responsible for, or whose jobs are directly linked to, the direct labor workers; and (3) the direct labor work force of 116 full-time positions. These workers physically maintain the department's areas of responsibility, such as cleaning up, mowing golf greens and ball fields, trimming trees, and watering grass.

Costs required for the determination of the best alternative strategy are

Full-time direct labor employees	Average wage rate $4.45 per hour
Fringe benefits	17% of wage rate
Administrative costs	20% of wage rate
Part-time employees	Average wage rate $4.03 per hour
Fringe benefits	11% of wage rate
Administrative costs	25% of wage rate
Subcontracting all full-time jobs	$1.6 million
Subcontracting all part-time jobs	$1.85 million

EXHIBIT 8–8

■ Actual Demand Requirement for Full-Time Direct Employees and Full-Time-Equivalent (FTE) Part-Time Employees

	Jan	Feb	Mar	Apr	May	Jun	Jul	Aug	Sep	Oct	Nov	Dec	Total
Days	22	20	21	22	21	20	21	21	21	23	18	22	252
Full-time employees	66	28	130	90	195	290	325	92	45	32	29	60	
Full-time days*	1,452	560	2,730	1,980	4,095	5,800	6,825	1,932	945	736	522	1,320	28,897
Full-time-equivalent part-time employees	41	75	72	68	72	302	576	72	0	68	84	27	
FTE days	902	1,500	1,512	1,496	1,512	6,040	12,096	1,512	0	1,564	1,512	594	30,240

Note: Some work weeks are staggered to include weekends, but this does not affect the number of work days per employee.

* Full-time days derived by multiplying the number of days in each month by the number of workers.

Source: R. Chase and N. Aquilano, *Production and Operations Management*, 5th Ed. (Homewood, Ill.: Irwin, 1989). © Richard D. Irwin, Inc., 1989. All rights reserved.

June and July are the peak demand seasons in Tucson. Exhibits 8–8 and 8–9 show the high requirements for June and July personnel. The part-time help reaches 575 full-time-equivalent positions (although in actual numbers, this is approximately 800 different employees). After a low fall and winter staffing level, the demand shown as "full-time direct" reaches 130 in March when grounds are reseeded and fertilized and then increases to a high of 325 in July. The present method levels this uneven demand over the year to an average of 116 full-time year-round employees by early scheduling of work. As previously mentioned, no attempt is made to hire and lay off full-time workers to meet this uneven demand.

Exhibit 8–10 shows the cost calculations for all three alternatives. Exhibit 8–11 compares the total costs for each alternative. From this analysis, it appears that the Parks and Recreation Department is already using the lowest-cost alternative (Alternative 1) and should continue to operate as it has been.

_____ EXHIBIT 8–9 _____

- *Monthly Requirement for Full-Time Direct Labor Employees (Other than Key Personnel) and Full-Time-Equivalent Part-Time Employees*

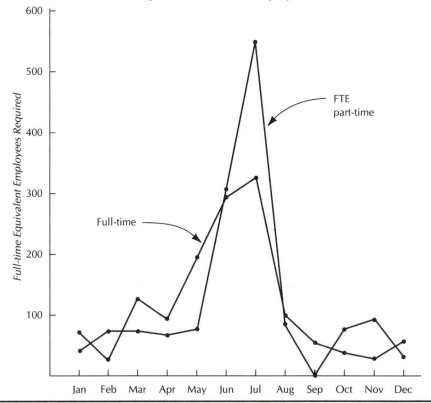

EXHIBIT 8-10

■ *Three Possible Plans for the Parks and Recreation Department*

ALTERNATIVE 1: Maintain 116 full-time regular direct workers. Schedule work during off seasons to level work load throughout the year. Continue to use 120 full-time-equivalent (FTE) part-time employees to meet high demand periods.

Costs	Days per Year (Exhibit 8–8)	Hours[a]	Wages[b]	Fringe Benefits[c]	Administrative Cost[d]
116 full-time regular employees	252	233,856	$1,040,659	$176,912	$208,132
120 part-time employees	252	241,920	974,938	107,243	243,735
Total cost = $2,751,619			$2,015,597	$284,155	$451,867

ALTERNATIVE 2: Maintain 50 full-time regular direct workers and the present 120 FTE part-time employees. Subcontract jobs releasing 66 full-time regular employees. Subcontract cost, $1,100,000.

Cost	Days per Year (Exhibit 8–8)	Hours[a]	Wages[b]	Fringe Benefits[c]	Administrative Cost[d]	Subcontract Cost
50 full-time employees	252	100,800	$ 448,560	$ 76,255	$ 89,712	$1,100,000
120 FTE part-time employees subcontracting cost	252	241,920	974,938	107,243	243,735	
Total cost = $3,040,443			$1,423,498	$183,498	$333,447	$1,100,000

ALTERNATIVE 3: Subcontract all jobs previously performed by 116 full-time regular employees. Subcontract cost $1,600,000. Subcontract all jobs previously performed by 120 full-time-equivalent part-time employees. Subcontract cost $1,850,000.

Cost	Subcontract Cost
0 full-time employees	
0 part-time employees	
Subcontract—full-time jobs	$1,600,000
Subcontract—part-time jobs	1,850,000
Total	$3,450,000

[a] Employees × days × 8 hours
[b] Full-time, $4.45; part-time, $4.03
[c] Full-time, 17 percent; part-time, 11 percent
[d] Full-time, 20 percent; part time, 25 percent

Source: R. Chase and N. Aquilano, *Production and Operations Management*, 5th Ed. (Homewood, Ill.: Irwin, 1989). © Richard D. Irwin, Inc., 1989. All rights reserved.

───── EXHIBIT 8–11 ───

▪ *Comparison of Costs for All Three Alternatives*

	Alternative 1 (116 full-time direct labor employees, 120 full-time-equivalent part-time employees)	Alternative 2 (50 full-time direct labor employees,.120 full-time-equivalent part-time employees, subcontracting)	Alternative 3 (subcontracting jobs formerly performed by 116 direct labor full-time employees and 120 FTE part-time employees)
Wages	$2,015,597	$1,423,498	—
Fringe benefits.	284,155	183,498	—
Administrative costs	451,867	333,447	—
Subcontracting, full-time jobs		1,100,000	$1,600,000
Subcontracting, part-time jobs			1,850,000
Total	$2,751,619	$3,040,443	$3,450,000

───── SUMMARY

The development of a service system proceeds from the design of the service, to aggregate planning of resources, to construction of the system. The basic objective of aggregate planning is to plan a firm's resources so that the firm's capacity and demand for outputs are matched. Thus aggregate planning may alternatively emphasize adjusting the demand side or the supply side to achieve a desired balance.

Initially, our efforts are directed toward selling as many service units as possible. Therefore, we try to increase capacity to match increasing demand or shift capacity to match fluctuations in demand. One problem is that facilities and equipment are acquired by long-run decisions rather than by intermediate-term decisions. Therefore, we have some inherent limitations on these resources in meeting unexpected growth in demand. Further, capacity usually must be added in lumps, whereas demand tends to run more smoothly along some trend. We may also find that providing enough capacity to meet all our customers' demands for a service may be cost-prohibitive. This is especially true if demand fluctuates widely from period to period. At this point, we may set a fixed maximum capacity (which may or may not equal demand) and try to *manage* demand to utilize the facility near capacity at all times.

In manufacturing, aggregate planning consists of planning for resources used in production to match the sales forecast provided by the marketing organization. Services that have tangible outputs deal with aggregate planning in the same manner by building inventory during slack periods, subcontracting, and making limited changes in equipment and facilities. One difference is that some tangible outputs of services such as restaurants and newspapers are highly perishable. Such service companies come closer to intangible service companies in aggregate planning approaches. The matching of supply to demand in this latter situation is carried out more extensively in the short-range scheduling of service operations. This topic is covered in more detail in Chapter 11.

____ DISCUSSION QUESTIONS

1. What is the purpose of aggregate planning?

2. How does aggregate planning differ for services versus manufacturing?

3. Would aggregate planning be more difficult for (a) constant demand, (b) stable, cyclical demand, or (c) increasing linear demand? Why?

4. Discuss some options for *increasing capacity* in the following services.

    a. A university
    b. A copy center
    c. A prison system

5. Discuss some options for *managing demand* in these services.

    a. A hospital
    b. A restaurant
    c. A resort

6. Which of the strategies shown in Exhibit 8–6 would be appropriate for

    a. Secretarial services?
    b. Airlines?
    c. Consulting firms?

7. What are dispersed interlocking sites? How do they complicate the development of an aggregate plan?

8. In what terms would capacity be measured for

    a. A computer center?
    b. Mass transit?
    c. A police force?

____ READING 8.1 ____

Capacity Management in Health Care Services: Future Directions

Health care in this country has undergone dramatic changes in recent years. As health care costs have escalated, existing government programs to improve the availability and quality of health care have come under strict scrutiny to contain costs, and employers have sought alternative forms of health care to reduce their expenditures. This reading presents current trends, as identified by health care managers, that will have an impact on capacity decisions in health care services for the next decade.

VERTICAL INTEGRATION

Vertical integration is an attempt to control the sources of demand and/or to enhance control of the inputs through ownership of supply and distribution channels. A recent trend is the use of forward integration by health care organizations to reduce the uncertainty of demand volume. Hospitals are expanding into the field of ambulatory care to provide a source of inpatients and to in-

crease the utilization of existing facilities and workforce resources. Health care organizations also are developing insurance and HMO plans that guarantee a patient population for a given period (usually one year). It has been projected that vertical integration in the next decade will lead to a situation where health care services will be controlled by twenty to forty companies called the "SuperMeds." The desired result of vertical integration is a balanced health care organization that matches demand with the most appropriate source of care within the vertically integrated system.

MULTIHOSPITAL SYSTEMS

The response of many independent hospitals to an increase in competition has been the formation of multi-institutional hospital systems. Several factors—including increasing capital requirements, new technology, and constrained capital markets—have forced independent hospitals to join systems to improve their ability to compete for fi-

Source: Excerpted with permission from V. L. Smith-Daniels, S. B. Schweikhart, and D. E. Smith-Daniels, "Capacity Management in Health Care Services: Review and Future Research Directions," *Decision Sciences*, Vol. 19, No. 4 (Fall 1988), pp. 889–918. Published by the Decision Sciences Institute at Georgia State University, Atlanta, Ga.

nancial resources. Multihospital systems also present the potential for significant operational savings and downsizing opportunities through the regionalization of services. [There is a] need for an integrative model for facility size, location, and service mix across a multiple-site system. Such a model should incorporate the following factors:

— Economies of scale within specific service types
— Facilitywide economies of scale
— The potential for improved quality when services are delivered at a limited number of facilities, thus increasing patient volume at each delivery site
— The impact of facility decisions on market share potential

Multihospital systems also provide increased opportunities to share common facility and workforce resources.

HOSPITAL DOWNSIZING

Downsizing has been identified as a key strategic alternative for survival in the turbulent hospital industry. The process of downsizing involves reducing the number of hospital beds and related components in the delivery system. However, there is a concern that many health care providers are overlooking the importance of reducing capacity in order to minimize cost. Capacity reduction in inpatient services must simultaneously consider facility and work-force resources. This requires that demand be represented in terms of products rather than only in terms of requirements for a bed and associated nursing services within a specific medical unit. A product-line approach defining demand as a package of services consumed by a patient is necessary for obtaining a well-balanced inpatient delivery system.

SUBCONTRACTING SERVICES

The subcontracting of health care services is a recent innovation that involves contractual agreements between health care provider organizations and HMOs, PPOs, and other insurance plans.[8] For

example, an HMO and a hospital might enter into a contractual affiliation which specifies the amount and types of reimbursement to be provided when HMO subscribers use inpatient services. In general, the motivation for this type of affiliation is (1) to lower costs for the purchaser in exchange for a referral system for the supplier, (2) to offer a more comprehensive range of services to HMO subscribers, and (3) to gain a marketing advantage through affiliation with a well-established provider.

FREESTANDING AMBULATORY CARE CLINICS

There has been tremendous growth in freestanding ambulatory care facilities, such as urgent care clinics and surgicenters, that offer a limited range of services at a low cost and at a convenient location for the patient. These facilities are open for more hours than the typical physician's office; as a result, many consumers are using freestanding clinics for both urgent and primary care needs. Prepaid health organizations are developing agreements with freestanding facilities in order to offer after-hours services to their members and thus eliminate unnecessary visits to hospital emergency rooms. Since freestanding centers are in competition with hospital-based emergency rooms and physician's offices, capacity decisions should concentrate on location and size decisions in a competitive marketplace with a profit-based objective function.

HMOs

HMOs have become a dominant alternative to traditional fee-for-service medicine. The acceptance of HMOs is part of a trend toward capitation to encourage efficiency by limiting payments to a fixed fee per person per year regardless of the quantity of the services delivered. This financial structure requires the HMO to assume the roles of both a comprehensive health care provider and a risk management organization. As a result, HMOs need flexible delivery systems to accommodate the total health needs of subscribers at the lowest possible cost. Flexibility in HMO delivery systems can be gained by moving specialized health care providers between clinics and by hiring a more general-pur-

---

[8] HMO is an acronym for health maintenance organization. PPO stands for preferred provider organization.

pose work force that can substitute for other personnel.

DIAGNOSIS-RELATED GROUPS (DRGs)

Medicare's 1983 decision to use a fixed-price, prospective payment reimbursement system (PPS) for hospital care based on diagnosis-related groups has provided additional impetus for the movement from process to product-line management. DRGs define medically meaningful groups that are predictive of hospital resource consumption. DRGs have the potential for changing the manner in which hospitals are managed and the way in which hospital services are planned and administered. Although PPS/DRG is currently confined to those hospital patients who are reimbursed by Medicare, it is likely that this program, or a similar one, will be expanded to all third-party insurance systems in the future. This shift to predetermined, fixed-price reimbursement for hospital services impacts inpatient facility and work-force allocation decisions.

_____ QUESTIONS FOR READING 8.1

1. Traditionally, health care has been delivered in two types of facilities, a physician's office and a hospital, by some combination of nurses, doctors, and medical technicians. Currently, what mix of service providers and service facilities is available to the consumer of medical services?

2. List several objectives of health care managers in the delivery of their service. What impact does capacity management have on the ability of an institution to reach these objectives? Would the trends in health care presented in this reading change the objectives of typical health care agencies?

3. How do the current trends in health care affect the services offered to the consumer? In what ways are service design and capacity related? What additional capacity decisions are required as a different mix of services is offered?

4. Which trends indicate an enlargement in the size and scope of the health care system? Which trends indicate a reduction in the size and scope of the health care system? What implications do these observations have for the health care manager?

5. Discuss how resources can be shared for each trend. What are the advantages and disadvantages of shared resources?

6. Using health care as an example, discuss how price affects capacity. How does capacity affect price?

7. Examine the trends in health care with regard to resource utilization. How do the new forms of health care make it more difficult to balance (i.e., smooth) the utilization of resources? How do they make it easier?

_____ READING 8.2 _____

A Public Safety Merger in Grosse Pointe Park, Michigan

The city of Grosse Pointe Park has a population estimated at 13,600, of which less than 5 percent are minorities. The city covers a 2.2 square mile area and is northeast of Detroit, with which it shares a common border. In 1986 the police department consisted of thirty sworn officers, and the fire department, which also provided emergency ambulance service, had nineteen firefighters and officers. The budgets were $1.5 million for police

and $800,000 for fire, out of a total city budget of $4.8 million.

For years, city officials had discussed the possibility of merging emergency services as a means of increasing police resources without increasing operating costs. In January 1985, a city commission reported in favor of a merger with a vote of eleven to two. This report coupled with the strong support of the mayor, who had campaigned on a platform

Source: Reprinted by permission of K. Chelst, "A Public Safety Merger in Grosse Pointe Park, Michigan," *Interfaces*, Vol. 18, No. 4 (July–August 1988), pp. 1–11. Copyright 1988 The Institute of Management Sciences, 290 Westminster Street, Providence, Rhode Island 02903 USA.

in support of a merger, provided the momentum to move ahead. By January 1986, a detailed plan for implementing the merger had been developed under the leadership of a new, innovative police chief. The local firefighters' union, backed by the International Association of Firefighters, strongly opposed the merger and succeeded in forcing a citywide referendum. City officials welcomed an "independent expert" to review their plan and comment on it.

THE MERGER PLAN

In the premerged fire department, nineteen people were employed to maintain a staff of five people (three firefighters, a sergeant, and a lieutenant) on duty at the fire station 24 hours a day, seven days a week, including the chief. (The work schedule was 24 hours on-duty and 48 hours off-duty.) A majority but not all of the fire personnel were trained as basic emergency medical technicians (EMTs), and personnel were scheduled so as to have a minimum of three EMTs on duty. They were stationed at the city's only fire station, next door to police headquarters.

The police department had thirty officers and deployment varied by time of day. On average, slightly fewer than four patrol cars (including supervisors) were deployed with an average of 4.5 officers on the road at any time.

The proposed merger called for the fire department staff of nineteen to be reduced to nine first-level firefighters assigned to the fire station. These positions would be filled mainly by current fire personnel who chose not to assume the additional police role, and they would be paid on the current fire salary scale. An average of three firefighters would be on station duty at a time (24 hours on duty followed by 48 hours off duty). Vacations and sick days would be covered by dual-trained patrol officers.

This ten-man reduction from the fire service was used to fund one additional detective and an additional five men assigned to patrol-related activities. The five men would be used to staff one patrol car around the clock.

THE FINDINGS: FIRE AND EMERGENCY MEDICAL SERVICES

The major findings with regard to fire and emergency medical services are listed below:

- The fire and emergency medical services responded to fire and EMS emergencies in an average of 2.2 minutes.
- A merger would result in the first trained person arriving at the scene an average of 1.2 minutes faster.
- Eighty-five percent of the time, the first unit at the scene would be a patrol unit.
- Fire department personnel average 33 minutes a day on calls for service, a total of 2.3 percent of their time.
- On average, once a month three (or four) patrol units will be tied up for more than 45 minutes at the scene of an emergency.

FINDINGS: POLICE SERVICES

The major findings with regard to police services are listed below:

- The police service's average response time was unusually low, only 1.2 minutes for crimes reported in progress.
- A merger would reduce response time an additional 10 percent.
- Patrol units were busy with highest priority noninterruptible calls less than 4 percent of the time.
- A merger could increase crime prevention activities by 20 percent [by adding additional patrol personnel].
- A merger would increase the number of detectives from three to four immediately.

The above data do not indicate a pressing need for additional resources. In contrast, detective resources were stretched thinly. Grosse Pointe Park's staff had to investigate at least 48 percent more Index Crimes[9] and follow through on at least 45 percent more arrests than either of its two neighboring cities.

---

[9] Index crimes are crimes of a serious nature such as murder, forceable rape, robbery, and aggravated assault.

One major immediate benefit of a merger is that it will permit the addition of one detective to assist with this heavy serious crime workload. In the future, if the merged departments assign personnel to standby duty at the stationhouse who are trained police officers, those officers can process some of the detective paperwork and help with the heavy workload.

FINDINGS: COST

The major findings with regard to cost are listed below:

- A merger would save an estimated $110,000 per year, excluding increased pay for public safety officers.
- Each 1 percent increase in salary reduces the savings by $15,000 [i.e., a 7 percent pay raise would consume the entire projected savings].

POSTSCRIPT

On June 12, 1986, the *Grosse Pointe News* published an article that headlined the potential cost savings although city management had emphasized increased patrol coverage. On June 16, the referendum was held. The turnout was the largest in recent memory even though it was a special election for a special ballot. The firefighters proposal was defeated by a margin of 58 to 42 percent. Since then, the city has trained all thirty policemen as firefighters, and eleven of them have also completed emergency medical technician training. Half the firefighters have cross-trained as police-

men, while nine others have decided to remain on fire station assignment. The city has reduced fire station personnel staffing to three and made adjustments in its dispatch strategy.

The city negotiated salary scales with the unions but could not reach an agreement; binding arbitration ensued. The new contract's top pay for a police and fire public safety officer is $31,250 as compared to $29,000 for a single trained officer. This difference in pay overstates the true bonus for switching to public safety. This new contract increased firefighters base pay by $2000. Similarly, the differential between a police officer under the old contract and a public safety officer under the new contract was only $1750. In short, the city held the line on salary raises for public safety officers and should achieve the savings reported earlier.

_____ QUESTIONS FOR READING 8.2

1. Summarize the advantages of the public safety merger. Has the merger increased the *capacity* of the public safety department? Explain.

2. Examine the physical, educational, and psychological requirements of police officers, emergency medical technicians, and firefighters. Discuss their "role" in the community. How are they similar? How are they different? Are they compatible?

3. What kinds of difficulties in training and skill maintenance would you anticipate as a result of the multiple roles of the public safety officers?

4. Summarize the disadvantages of the public safety merger. Can you suggest alternative ways to increase the utilization of public safety personnel?

_____ READING 8.3 _____

Solving the Crisis in the Skies

The uproar about airline problems has grown deafening. But is the U.S. air transportation system really in serious trouble? I'm afraid it is.

According to statistics, the skies are very safe.

But flying is still not as safe as it could and should be. Let's face it: Statistics are no comfort if the plane you happen to be on has a near miss. Besides, we're buying safety with delays and inconvenience. Are these service problems inevitable in a deregulated system that carries nearly 500 million passengers a year? The answer is no.

Curing these safety and service ills won't be easy, quick, or cheap. But remedies must be found. The air transportation crisis of the 1980s, like the energy crisis of the 1970s, demands tough action. For example,

1. To meet the public demand for air travel, we simply must construct more airports and more runways. No major airport has been built since 1974, and it's almost impossible for existing airports to add new runways. The resulting overcrowding causes delays and reduces safety. A major obstacle to airport construction has been public concern about the impact on the environment. We should give transportation needs the same weight as environmental concerns. But that won't happen unless our representatives make air transportation a top priority.

2. Washington must give the underfunded, understaffed Federal Aviation Administration more money. I applaud the government's recent decision to hire almost 1000 more controllers. But that's only a start. Even though traffic has gone up sharply, we have 2500 fewer fully proficient controllers than we did before the 1981 controllers' strike. Of the 15,000 controllers now on the job, some 2500 are eligible for retirement.

3. Money has already been raised to make the system safer and more convenient; we should spend it. The federal government has failed to spend more than $5.5 billion of the levies it has collected from passengers and air-freight shippers. Meanwhile, important technologies such as new radar and additional instrument landing systems wait on the sidelines.

4. The FAA must impose stiff measures to relieve the crowded airspace over many busy airports. This problem is especially acute in some areas. A year ago a private plane collided with an Aeromexico jetliner over Los Angeles. During the past year and a half, a third of American Airlines' near misses happened in the Los Angeles area, although only 3.9 percent of our flights originated there. Nearly 70 percent of those close calls involved private planes. Less than half of all private planes carry a full complement of the altitude reporting devices that can help prevent midair collisions. Private aircraft owners have a right to use the airways, but they also have an obligation not

to jeopardize the lives of other citizens who fly. The planes that share airspace with commercial jetliners should be required to carry the necessary safety equipment to prevent disaster.

5. The FAA should increase the amount of fully controlled airspace. To its credit the FAA recently enlarged the amount of airspace that is fully controlled over Los Angeles. It also proposed the introduction of full control to nine other airports, including Dulles in Washington, D.C. Still more airspace should be controlled.

Until we get more airports, runways, and controllers, and install better technology, the air traffic control system will continue to be overloaded. Allowing all aircraft to fly whenever and wherever they like under current conditions is like trying to cram a size seven foot into a size five shoe. That simply can't be allowed, because safety must never be compromised. The government should limit flights to whatever number the system can safely and reliably accommodate.

I have called on the Department of Transportation to appoint a blue ribbon panel to determine the capacity of our nation's airways and the safest, most effective way to use the capacity we have. I favor a marketplace approach to the allocation of our limited airspace. In my view, the nation's airspace and airport capacity should be divided into time slots and allocated proportionately among airlines, the military, and private and corporate aircraft. Then airlines could buy and sell the slots among themselves just as they now do with gate spaces. A market approach would ease the crowding and delays at peak times such as 7 A.M. and 5 P.M. because those slots would become very expensive. Off-peak slots, when airspace, runways, and terminals are all underutilized, would be relatively cheap. Airlines, like families on a budget, would have to do more orderly planning. This or any other allocation system, however, should continue only until we build the capacity to handle more traffic.

———— QUESTIONS FOR READING 8.3

1. How would an airline define its capacity? How would the FAA define airspace capacity?

2. How has deregulation affected airline and airspace capacity?

3. What are the pros and cons of Mr. Crandall's suggestions for allocating capacity?

___ CASE 8.1 _____

Forecasting Nursing Staffing Requirements by Intensity-of-Care Level

The continuing escalation of health care costs has become a matter of considerable national concern. Research is being conducted throughout the nation on cost containment, and much of this effort has recently been devoted to the macro questions on regulation of health care costs. This case reports the results of a project to develop a micro approach to nursing cost containment at a 220-bed, nonprofit community hospital in an urban setting. The hospital administrator is confident that nursing requirements can be influenced by proper planning and that control over costs can be exerted. Considerable savings can result from reduction or more efficient utilization of nursing personnel-hours. Since payroll expenditures typically account for over 50 percent of the operating budget of most hospitals, this area would seem to provide the greatest potential for savings.

PROJECT DESCRIPTION

The overall goal of this project is to enable hospital management to predict nursing personnel-hour requirements by ward, shift, day of the week, and month of the year. Since the nursing personnel-hours required by ward and by shift for any given day are a function of both the number of patients by care level and the standard hours (for that level of care), the research has focused first on the demand, or patient forecast. The first models are expected to predict required nursing hours by ward and shift with greater accuracy and less effort than is currently being accomplished manually. It is important to note that approximately 50 percent of the nursing hours in the hospital are "variable" costs and can be varied with patient requirements.

METHODOLOGY

In order to obtain estimates of the required nursing personnel-hours, statistical models were developed to predict the number of patients by six intensity-of-care levels for each hospital ward by

month, day, and shift. The magnitude of the distribution of care levels is shown in Exhibit 8–12. Numerous regression runs were made on the data with the following as independent indicator variables:

WARDS:	ICC/CCU	Intensive care, coronary care
	2N	Psychiatric cases
	3N	Medical cases, surgical and orthopedic overflow
	3T	Medical cases
	4T	Surgical cases
	5T	Orthopedic cases
	PEDS	Pediatrics
	OB	Obstetrics—maternity and gynecology cases
	NSY	Nursery
MONTH:	January through December	
DAY:	Sunday through Saturday	
SHIFT:	Day, evening, night	
TIME:	Day of the year, numbered 1 through 365	

The Ward 2N, the month of May, the day of Wednesday, and the day shift were selected as the reference point and set equal to zero (this is reflected in the constant term). The resulting models predict the number of patients by care level, shift, ward, month, and day of the week. The impact of the shift, day of the week, and other independent variables on the workloads can be determined from the model coefficients shown in Exhibit 8–13.

Using the coefficients in Exhibit 8–13, the regression model for care level 1 predicts the number of patients as follows:

No. of patients =
$$1.03 + 0.49(3N) + 0.67(3T) + 1.75(4T)$$
$$+ 0.84(5T) + 0.27(PEDS) + 5.12(OB)$$
$$+ 5.72(NSY) - 0.45(APRIL) - 0.30(JUNE)$$
$$- 0.35(AUGUST) - 0.36(SUNDAY)$$
$$- 0.33(MONDAY) - 0.31(TUESDAY)$$
$$- 0.18(FRIDAY) - 0.34(SATURDAY)$$
$$- 1.31(NIGHT SHIFT) - 0.00097(TIME)$$

Source: Adapted by permission of F. T., Helmer, E. B. Oppermann, and J. D. Surver, "Forecasting Nursing Staffing Requirements by Intensity-of-Care Level," *Interfaces*, Vol. 10, No. 3 (June 1980), pp. 50–56. Copyright 1980 The Institute of Management Sciences, 290 Westminster Street, Providence, Rhode Island 02903 USA.

_____ EXHIBIT 8–12 _____

▪ *Totals by Level of Care*

	Total Census in 1988	Average Patients per Day (Three Shifts)	Average Patients per Shift	Standard Hours of Nursing Care per Patient
CL1	15,226	41.72	13.91	1.5
CL2	94,234	258.18	86.06	2.1
CL3	41,115	112.64	37.55	3.5
CL4	8,131	22.28	7.43	4.7
CL5	1,720	4.71	1.57	6.5
CL6	385	1.05	.35	8.0

For example, if this model were to be used to predict the number of patients requiring level 1 of care in Ward 4T (Surgical Cases) on Monday, July 4, 1988, during the day shift, we would have 4T = 1, Monday = 1, Time = 195, and the following equation:

Estimated no. of CL1 patients
$= 1.03 + 0.175(1) - 0.33(1) - 0.00097(195)$
$= 2.26$ patients

The results of the seven models developed are particularly helpful when compared in the format of Exhibit 8–13. A review of this exhibit by ward clearly shows the distribution of care levels by ward and can be extremely valuable in the distribution of the nursing skill mix (RNs, LPNs, and other) by ward. For example, the care level mix for the surgical ward (4T) reflects the fact that most of the patients require care specified by care level 2 with the following distribution for July 4, 1988, during the day shift.

Care Level	Estimated No. of Patients
CL1	2.26
CL2	24.84
CL3	5.70
CL4	0.05
CL5,6	0.00

An evaluation of the time constant shows that there is relatively little change over time in the number of patients in any care level. However, a review of the monthly data suggests an increase in care level during the later months of the year. The second year of data which has now been collected will be used to clarify these points. Obviously, such information is crucial to the hospital administrator in planning nursing workloads. For weekly scheduling, an evaluation of the daily data is helpful to the administrator. The data clearly show a decreased demand for nursing staff on Fridays, Saturdays, Sundays, and Mondays, which is not unusual. However, the model supports intuition with more precise information. Obviously, with the availability of numerous part-time nurses whose schedules can be a management "variable," management has the ability to bring in this resource as the forecast and actual demand indicate. Predictably, the more acutely ill patients, while showing a seasonal pattern, do not demonstrate any significant daily or by-shift variation.

_____ QUESTIONS FOR CASE 8.1

1. Use the regression model given in Exhibit 8–13 to predict the number of patients requiring care level 2 in Ward 5 on Tuesday, July 18, during the evening shift.

2. Examine Exhibit 8–13 and verify the conclusions of the study in regard to

    a. Number of patients in any care level.
    b. Monthly distributions of care level.
    c. Daily distributions of care level.
    d. Distributions of care level by shift.

_____ EXHIBIT 8–13 _____

■ *Regression (Coefficients) by Care Levels (1988 Data, n = 8687)*

	CL1	CL2	CL3	CL4	CL4,5	CL5,6	CL4,5,6
Constant	1.03	4.99	1.22	0.98	1.07	0.42	1.50
Time	−0.00097	0.00040	0.00209	−0.00250	−0.00279	−0.00283	−0.00601
Shifts							
Day							
Eve		−1.45	0.66		0.06		
Night	−1.31	−0.24	0.65				
Wards							
ICU/CCU			−2.03	3.19	4.44	1.64	4.84
2N*							
3N	0.49	2.30	1.38	−0.66	−0.70	−0.06	−0.72
3T	0.67	18.90	5.89	−0.68	−0.71	−0.06	−0.73
4T	1.75	21.75	3.82	−0.44	−0.46		−0.45
5T	0.84	22.49	4.93	−0.53	−0.57	−0.06	−0.59
PEDS	0.27	−0.136	1.40		−0.42		−0.39
OB	5.12	2.06	−0.31		−0.13	−0.06	−0.15
NSY	5.72	0.64	−1.56	−0.59	−0.62	−0.06	−0.64
Months							
Jan				−0.23	−0.30	−0.36	−0.67
Feb						−0.22	−0.30
Mar			0.21		−0.19	−0.21	−0.36
Apr	−0.45	0.88					
May*							
Jun	−0.30				0.25	0.12	0.38
Jul		−0.45			0.27	0.15	0.54
Aug	−0.35	−1.42	0.38	0.35	0.33	0.26	0.67
Sep		0.21	0.54	0.32	0.31	0.40	0.80
Oct			0.38	0.23	0.29	0.48	0.81
Nov				0.43	0.50	0.62	1.17
Dec				0.58	0.67	0.69	1.43
Days							
Sun	−0.36	−1.79	−0.55				
Mon	−0.33	−1.98	0.25				
Tue	−0.31	−0.98	0.30				
Wed*							
Thr					0.07		0.07
Fri	−0.18	−0.77	0.16	0.07	0.01		0.08
Sat	−0.34	−1.89	−0.17				
R^2	0.61	0.89	0.61	0.64	0.74	0.56	0.77
Std error	1.80	3.51	2.21	0.87	0.93	0.47	0.93

* These variables included in constant term.

3. Use Exhibit 8–12 to calculate the nursing requirements per shift by care level.

4. How can your calculations above aid in determining a nursing skill mix (i.e., how many RNs, LPNs, and Nurses' Aides are required)?

5. Considering the value of the information provided in Exhibit 8–12, why is it necessary to predict number of patients by ward, month, shift, and day?

6. What level of nurse staffing would be considered aggregate planning for this hospital? What aggregate planning strategies for meeting nursing requirements do you suggest for the hospital?

—— **CASE 8.2** ——————————————————————————————————

Developing an Aggregate Capacity Plan for the Campus Police

The campus police chief is attempting to develop a two-year plan for the department that involves a request for additional resources. Recently, the university administration has suggested that the department change its image and operating strategy from that of "policing" to a more comprehensive "public safety" approach.

The department currently has twenty-six sworn officers. The size of the force has not changed over the past fifteen years. Although the size of the student population also has remained stable over that time period, several changes have occurred in the university environment that have prompted the campus police chief to review his operations and request additional resources. These changes include

- The university has expanded geographically. More buildings and other facilities have been added, some in outlying areas miles from the main campus.
- Traffic and parking problems have increased because more students bring their cars to campus.
- More portable, expensive equipment with high theft potential is dispersed across the campus (e.g., there are over 10,000 personal computers on campus).
- Alcohol and drug problems have increased.
- The size of the athletic program and its facilities have increased dramatically.
- The size of the surrounding community has doubled.
- The police need to spend more time on education and prevention programs in an attempt to become more fully integrated into the university community.

The university is located in a small town, thirty-five miles from an urban center. During the summer months, the student population is around 5000. This number swells to 30,000 during fall and spring semesters. Thus demand for police and other services is significantly lower during the summer months. Demand for police services also varies by

- Time of the day (peak time between 10 P.M. and 2 A.M.)
- Day of the week (weekends are the busiest)
- Weekend of the year (on football weekends, 50,000 extra people come to campus)
- Special events (check-in, check-out, Founder's Day, commencement, and so on)

Football weekends are especially difficult to staff. Extra police services are typically needed from 8:00 A.M. to 5:00 P.M. on five football Saturdays. All twenty-six officers are called in to work double shifts. Over forty law enforcement officers from surrounding localities are paid to come in on their own time, and a dozen state police lend a hand free of charge (when they are available). Twenty-five students and local residents are paid to work traffic and parking. During the last academic year (a 9-month period), overtime worked by campus police officers totalled over 2400 hours.

Other relevant data include the following:

- The average starting salary for a police officer is $18,000.
- Work-study, part-time students, and local residents who help with traffic and parking are paid $4.50 an hour.
- Overtime is paid to police officers who work over 40 hours a week at the rate of $13.00 an hour. Extra officers who are hired part-time from outside agencies also earn $13.00 an hour.
- There seems to be an unlimited supply of officers who will work for the university when needed for special events.
- With days off, vacations, and average sick leave considered, it takes five persons to cover *one* 24-hour, 7-day a week position.
- The schedule of officers during fall and spring semesters is typically:

	Week-days	Week-ends
1st Shift (7 A.M.–3 P.M.)	5	4
2d Shift (3 P.M.–11 P.M.)	5	6
3d Shift (11 P.M.–7 A.M.)	6	8

Staffing for football weekends and special events is in *addition* to the preceding schedule. Summer staffing is, on average, half that shown above.

The police chief feels that his present staff is stretched to the limit. Fatigued officers are potential problems for the department and the community. In addition, neither time nor personnel have been set aside for crime prevention, safety, or health programs. Interactions of police officers with students, faculty, and staff are minimal and usually negative in nature. In light of these problems, the chief would like to request funding for four additional officers, two assigned to new programs and two to alleviate the overload on his current staff of officers. He would also like to begin limiting overtime to ten hours per week for each officer.

QUESTIONS FOR CASE 8.2

1. Which variations in demand for police services should be considered in an aggregate plan for resources? Which variations can be handled with short-term scheduling adjustments?

2. In what terms would you define capacity for the department? What additional information do you need to determine capacity requirements?

3. Evaluate the current staffing plan. What does it cost? Are 26 officers sufficient to handle the normal workload?

4. What would be the additional cost of the chief's proposal? How would you suggest that the chief justify his request?

5. How much does it currently cost the university to provide police services for football games? What would be the pros and cons of subcontracting this work completely to outside law enforcement agencies?

6. Can you propose any other alternatives? What suggestions do you have for duties of police officers in nonpeak periods?

REFERENCES

Chase, Richard B., and Nicholas J. Aquilano. *Production and Operations Management*, 5th Ed. Homewood, Ill.: Irwin, 1989.

Fitzsimmons, James A., and Robert S. Sullivan. *Service Operations Management*. New York: McGraw-Hill, 1982.

Harris, Roy D., and Richard F. Gonzalez. *The Operations Manager: Roles, Problems, Techniques*. St. Paul, Minn.: West, 1981.

Levitt, Theodore. "Production Line Approach to Service." *Harvard Business Review*, Vol. 50, No. 5 (September–October 1972), pp. 41–52.

Lovelock, Christopher H. *Services Marketing*. Englewood Cliffs, N.J.: Prentice-Hall, 1984.

Murdick, Robert G. "How They Figure the Sales Forecast," *Machine Design* (December 9, 1971).

Northcraft, Gregory B., and Richard B. Chase. "Managing Service Demand at the Point of Delivery," *Academy of Management Review*, Vol. 10, No. 1 (January 1985), pp. 66–75.

Pessemier, Edgar A. *New-Product Decisions*. New York: McGraw-Hill, 1986.

Rothstein, Marvin. "Hotel Overbooking as a Markovian Sequential Decision Process," *Decision Sciences*, Vol. 5 (1974), pp. 389–394.

Rothstein, Marvin. "Operations Research and the Airline Overbooking Problem," *Operations Research*, Vol. 33, No. 2 (1985), pp. 237–248.

Sasser, W. Earl, R. Paul Olsen, and D. Daryl Wyckoff. *Management of Service Operations; Text, Cases and Readings*. Boston: Allyn and Bacon, 1978.

Sasser, W. Earl. "Match Supply and Demand in Service Industries," *Harvard Business Review*, Vol. 54, No. 6 (November–December 1976), pp. 133–140.

Schonberger, Richard J. and Edward N. Knod. *Operations Management*. 3rd Ed. Plano, Texas: Business Publications, 1988.

Sigafoos, R. A., and R. R. Easson, *Absolutely Positively Overnight!* Memphis, Tenn,: St. Luke's Press, 1988.

Voss, C., C. Armistead, B. Johnson, and B. Morris. *Operations Management in Service Industries and the Public Sector*. New York: Wiley, 1985.

9

Human Resource Management in Service Systems

INTRODUCTION

Human resource management (HRM) consists of all the activities in a company involving the acquisition and utilization of human resources. Good human resource management must meet the needs and rights of employees and at the same time recognize the demands of the community, minorities, governmental concerns, and other parts of society. Line managers are ultimately responsible for managing human resources, but the personnel or HRM department has staff responsibilities for providing technical advice on hiring, firing, training and the like and maintaining services such as record keeping and benefit plans development. The most important activities of human resource management are manpower planning, recruiting and selecting, training and developing, utilizing, and rewarding human resources.

THE NATURE OF HUMAN RESOURCE MANAGEMENT

Manpower Planning

Manpower planning makes sure that a firm has the right number and mix of people at the right times and places. Such planning must be part of the firm's strategic plan, intermediate plan, and operating plan. In large service firms, manpower planning is similar to that of manufacturing firms. In small service firms or small units such as a Burger King outlet, manpower planning is very short range. It may consist largely of tracking employees who are seeking advancement to management positions, those who will return to school or part-time work, or those who regard their job as only a temporary one. Attrition due to retirement or death in small firms is not comparable to that in large companies.

It is apparent, then, that in services, manpower planning varies from long-range planning for large, stable companies to short-range crisis planning for thousands of small companies employing low-paid or transient workers. Exhibit 9–1 suggests a rough classification of the time horizon for manpower planning by type of service.

The length of the planning horizon for manpower planning establishes the forecasting lead time. The choice of forecasting method to be used may be a difficult one, as we saw in Chapter 3. Large companies must forecast both manpower requirements and the supply of people with required skills. Manpower needs must take into account corporate objectives and policies, new hires, training and development, turn-

_____ EXHIBIT 9–1 _____

■ *Manpower Planning in Service Businesses*

	Length of Planning Horizon		
Type of Business	Short (days to months)	Medium (months to 1 year)	Long (years)
Fast-food restaurants	X		
Traditional restaurants		X	
Real estate sales		X	
Colleges			X
Architectural firms			X
Hospitals		X	X
Resorts	X	X	X
Airlines			X
Lawn maintenance		X	
Banks			X
Temporary-help service	X		

EXHIBIT 9–2

■ *Inputs to Forecasting Manpower Requirements*

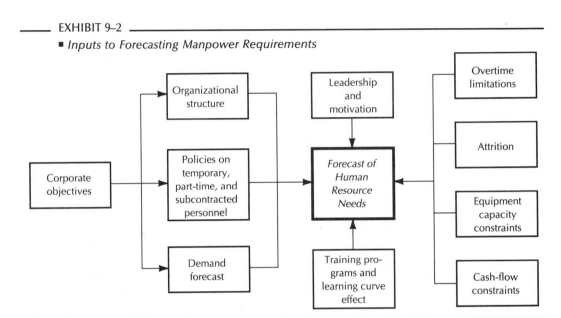

over, promotion, new jobs, and attrition. These factors and others are shown in Exhibit 9–2.

Referring to Exhibit 9–2, corporate objectives help define the organizational structure; establish policies on the use of temporary, part-time, or subcontracted personnel; and develop a framework for forecasting the service demand.[1] These are all inputs into the forecast of human resource needs. Constraints on HR requirements include limitations on overtime, natural attrition, equipment capacity, and cash-flow constraints. Finally, the need for human resources is affected by the leadership and motivation of current personnel and new hires, the effectiveness of training programs, and the efficiency with which employees do their jobs. The efficiency of work and how to measure it is discussed in the supplement to this chapter.

One feature of manpower planning for services that differentiates it from manufacturing is the great number of firms with very few employees. Retail shops, repair shops, personal services firms, and local real estate firms are examples. When a firm's employees consist of highly skilled people such as lawyers, insurance underwriters, physicians, or public accountants, the loss of an individual is serious and the time required to replace such a person may be lengthy. Therefore, the manager of such a firm must know where to go to find good people quickly. He or she must maintain contacts within the profession, with universities, and even with "head hunters."

At the other extreme, many service firms employ unskilled workers. While replacing unskilled workers is usually not a problem, their rapid turnover is a cause for concern. Such employees may tender their resignation by just not showing up one morning, and the loss of an employee will likely affect operations immediately, as in the case of a restaurant. Manpower planning consists largely of having a pool of potential

---

[1] These policies are part of the aggregate planning process discussed in Chapter 8.

employees who appear to be reliable and being able to access them rapidly. Some industries, such as fast-food restaurants and tourism that have traditionally relied on teenage employees, have experienced spot shortages of employees because of the dwindling numbers of 15- to 18-year-olds. One solution: Many have chosen to raise pay above minimum wage and to seek out a new source of employees—senior citizens.

Recruiting and Selecting

Recruiting means identifying and attracting people who could fill positions within the firm and then securing them as applicants. The starting point for recruiting is to prepare a good job description for the position and a specification of skills and abilities the candidate should have. A pool of potential applicants may be developed from replies to newspaper ads, membership lists in professional organizations, government or private employment agencies, walk-ins, "head hunters" who seek and screen for a specific position, friends and relatives of employees, high school and college career offices, and business/professional conventions.

Recruiting managers, professional people, and many white-collar workers for services is similar to that for manufacturing management. In services, however, many white-collar workers and tradespeople are directly concerned with servicing the customer, often while the customer is waiting or is in contact with the employee. There is no buffer between the customer and the surly or shoddy worker. For these reasons, employee recruiting and selection are extremely important for the service firm, and many service firms are highly selective in their employment practices. As J. W. Marriott is fond of saying, "In the service business you can't make happy guests with unhappy employees."[2] Singapore Airlines, for example, hires fewer than 2 percent of the thousands of women who want to become "Singapore Girls" (their name for flight attendants) and Delta Air Lines hires only about 40 of their 20,000 applicants for flight attendants each month.[3]

Employee Selection. The selection of an employee should be based on clearly established criteria for performance of the job. The application form should be designed to uncover the applicant's skills and abilities for job performance. Other selection techniques include testing, interviews, references, and probationary periods of employment. Recent restrictions on the use of lie detector tests for employment purposes have caused a resurgence of psychological testing services that can profile a person's tendency toward honesty and can, in some cases, predict an applicant's "fit" for a particular working environment.[4]

---

[2] G. M. Hostage, "Quality Control in a Service Business," *Harvard Business Review,* Vol. 53, No. 4 (July–August 1975), p. 99.

[3] Bro Uttal, "Companies That Serve You Best," *Fortune* (December 7, 1987), p. 100.

[4] See "Labor Department Restricts Lie Detector Test Use," *Roanoke Times* (October 22, 1988). The tests that detect tendencies toward honesty are known as "pencil polygraphs." Psychological tests such as the MMPI (Minnesota Multiphasic Personality Inventory) can provide a profile of a potential employee. Expert systems, such as Management Edge, can assess subordinate-superior relationships, managerial skills, and the match between an organization and its employees. For more information, see E. Turban, *Decision Support and Expert Systems* (New York: Macmillan, 1988), pp. 534–536.

In personal service firms in particular, it is important that the candidate have a strong customer service and sales orientation. This requires the proper motivation (sometimes called *internalized need*) to provide good service and extend one's self beyond the perfunctory performance of minimum job requirements. Everybody has motivation toward *some* goals. In the selection process, the manager must determine whether the individual's motivation can be compatible with company goals. The hiring of a worker is a psychological contract in which the worker should truly feel committed to the work and its rewards. Disney World has done a masterful job of motivating its employees to provide high-quality, consistent service. Reading 9.1 relates the story of their success.

In those service firms where the pay is low and the work is routine, education is not likely to be a major criterion. In services where manual skills and knowledge are important, the same may be true. Reading 9.2 gives an example of a successful service company, ServiceMaster, that employs unskilled, poorly educated workers but has used their desire to obtain more education as a route to reducing employee turnover and increasing the quality of the service provided.

Service work often requires certification or licenses to be held by the applicant. A **certification** means that a person has passed required course work (as in a teaching certificate) and, in some cases, is also permitted by city or state law to practice in public. A certified public accountant is an occupation in which certification is required to practice, but a license to operate a business also may be required. A licensed barber may be required if a firm is hiring barbers. In contrast, an engineering firm may hire unlicensed engineers to perform work as long as there is a licensed engineer to approve the work. Engineers who are Registered Professional Engineers have taken required formal course work, passed state examinations, and paid the state a registration fee. Exhibit 9–3 gives a number of examples of certification, licensing, and registration requirements for services.

EXHIBIT 9–3

- *Certification, Licensing, and Registration Requirements for Some Occupations and Professions*

Occupation or Profession	Certified	Licensed	Registered
Beautician	X	X	
Bar owner		X	
Airplane mechanic	X	X	
High school teacher	X		X
Real estate broker		X	X
Certified Public Accountant	X		X
Doctor	X	X	X
Lawyer	X	X	X
Physical therapist	X	X	X
Airline pilot	X	X	
Stockbroker		X	X

Training and Development (T&D)

Training is a systematic method for changing an employee's behavior to prepare the employee for a job or upgrade the employee's performance on the job. For example, a new waiter or waitress in a restaurant may be trained to handle difficult customers, or a real estate agent may be trained to organize his or her time better. **Development** is *person-oriented*. It is the preparation of a person for broader responsibilities and higher-level positions within the company. A senior systems analyst in a company may be prepared by on-the-job training, job rotation, and night courses for advancement toward the position of vice president of information systems. In service firms, T&D programs are usually differentiated among the following groups:

— Managers
— Professional personnel
— Office and clerical (including information processors)
— Technicians (such as lab assistants or auto repair mechanics)
— Operative employees (such as mail clerks, janitors, bus drivers, and generally people who do physical work)

Training and development programs can vary significantly from firm to firm, as well as by type or size of service organization. Some firms pay only modest attention to T&D. Personal service firms generally hire specialists who are already trained, certified, or licensed and provide little further training other than in the procedures and services of the company. If unskilled entry-level people are hired, as in both small and large retailing stores and chains, the new employee is usually trained on the job by another employee. The owner or manager may assist with weekly reviews of the employee at first. Development in larger stores, in resort and other hospitality businesses, and in real estate firms is generally limited to encouraging the employee to take outside courses at nearby schools.

Other firms have extensive, long-term T&D programs. Exhibit 9–4 shows some of the types of employee training programs available at Marriott. Electronic Data Systems (EDS) has such an extensive and valuable training program that new employees must pledge a three-year commitment to the company or reimburse the company for training expenses if they leave EDS before the three years are up. Exhibit 9–5 shows Holiday Inn University, a multimillion dollar training facility for managerial employees of the worldwide Holiday Inn hotel chain. It is located on an 88-acre campus outside Holiday Inn's corporate headquarters in Memphis, Tennessee.

The procedures for developing and carrying out T&D programs are covered in numerous human resource management texts.[5] Exhibit 9–6 shows a typical flowchart for the development and execution of a training program. Note that a training program starts with certain objectives and ends with an evaluation of the extent to which the objectives were achieved. If the objectives are not stated clearly in measurable terms,

---

[5] For example, see L. A. Klatt, R. G. Murdick, and F. E. Schuster, *Human Resource Management* (Columbus, Ohio: Merrill, 1985).

EXHIBIT 9–4

■ *Programs for Employees at Marriott*

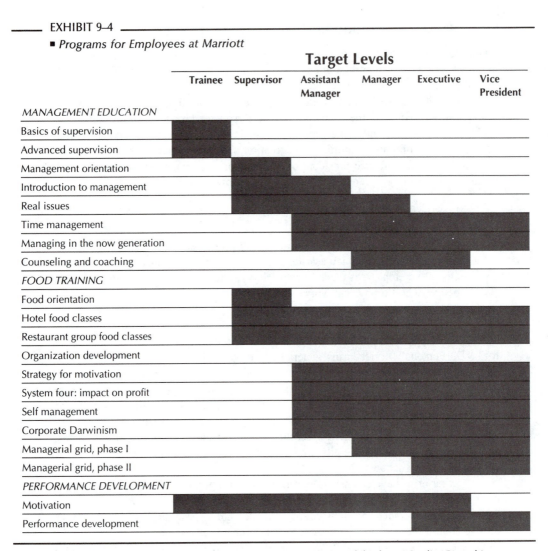

Target Levels

	Trainee	Supervisor	Assistant Manager	Manager	Executive	Vice President
MANAGEMENT EDUCATION						
Basics of supervision	■					
Advanced supervision	■					
Management orientation		■				
Introduction to management		■	■			
Real issues		■	■	■		
Time management			■	■	■	■
Managing in the now generation			■	■	■	
Counseling and coaching			■	■	■	■
FOOD TRAINING						
Food orientation		■				
Hotel food classes		■	■	■	■	■
Restaurant group food classes		■	■	■	■	■
Organization development			■	■	■	■
Strategy for motivation			■	■	■	■
System four: impact on profit			■	■	■	■
Self management			■	■	■	■
Corporate Darwinism			■	■	■	■
Managerial grid, phase I			■	■	■	■
Managerial grid, phase II					■	■
PERFORMANCE DEVELOPMENT						
Motivation	■	■	■	■	■	
Performance development					■	■

then it will be difficult to determine when the training is complete (i.e., has been effective).

In addition to following an organized procedure for training, successful training and development systems should take certain points into consideration.[6]

---

[6] These suggestions are adapted from *Thriving on Chaos: Handbook for a Management Revolution* by Tom Peters (New York: Knopf, 1987), pp. 326–329. Copyright © 1987 by Excel, a California Limited Partnership. Reprinted by permission of Alfred A. Knopf, Inc.

—— EXHIBIT 9–5 ——————————————————————————

■ *Holiday Inn University*

1. *Focus on the particular skills that make the service distinctive.* Entry-level employees have more customer contact than managers. Thus a retail clerk's training should focus on knowledge of the merchandise and communication skills rather than on how to operate a cash register.

2. *Treat all employees as potential career employees.* Federal Express's typical employee is a part-time college student, and yet each receives more extensive training than most skilled workers in America's factories!

3. *Spend time and money generously on training.* One highly successful grocer spends over $1000 for training per employee per year, offering to send anyone— including part-time bag boys—to a full fourteen-week, $600 Dale Carnegie course.[7] Why the expense for menial employees? Because each unhappy customer is a potential loss to the store of $50,000,[8] and cashiers, stockboys, and bag boys are essential to the customer-serving process.

4. *Retrain on a regular basis.* Employees at every level should have their skills broadened and sharpened through training programs that are considered an important part of their job.

5. *Provide training at various levels of skill, regardless of the employee's current position.* ServiceMaster and Embassy Suite Hotels have extensive training programs to accompany their promotion-from-within policies. Through company-sponsored training, a housekeeper at Embassy, for example, can be certified

---

[7] Tom Peters, *Thriving on Chaos* (New York: Knopf, 1987), pp. 98–99.

[8] $50,000 is the "value" of a customer, assuming good customers spend $100 per week on groceries fifty weeks a year over their estimated ten-year lifetime as a customer.

EXHIBIT 9–6

- *The Training and Development System*

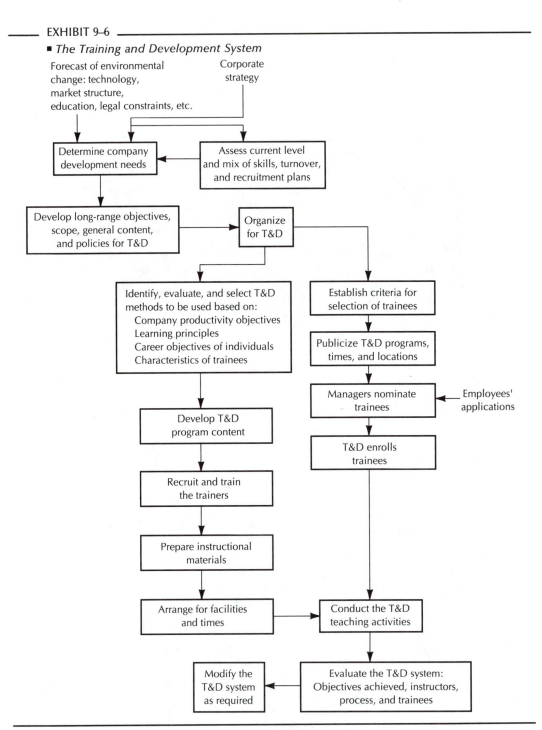

Source: Lawrence Klatt, Robert G. Murdick, and Frederick E. Schuster, *Human Resource Management* (Columbus, Ohio: Merrill, 1985), Exhibit 11.2. Reprinted by permission of the authors.

to run the front desk. This additional training raises the housekeeper's base pay and allows her or him to fill in at the new position whenever needed.[9]

6. *Be line-driven.* This means that training programs should be developed with input from or at the request of the workers actually doing the jobs. Another way of stating this recommendation is that training should be relevant and useful. For example, while it is important that service employees have a good attitude toward the customer they are serving, training must go beyond typical motivational seminars and so-called smile-and-dial courtesy skills. Training should teach how the job is to be done. Employees should be empowered, through proper design, tools, methods, authority, and training to offer the best possible service they can.[10]

7. *Teach the organization's vision and values.* Top management should use every training program as an opportunity to discuss and transmit its vision of the service concept. The best training is by example, and the best examples come from the top. Witness the impact of Bill Marriott, Walt Disney, Fred Smith (Federal Express), Sam Walton (Wal Mart Stores) and Jan Carlzon (SAS Airlines) on their respective organizations.

Employees learn what is expected of them in a job from sources other than training programs; they learn from observing the behavior of other employees and management. **Social learning theory** says that learning and behavior depend on continuous cognitive and behavioral interaction of a person with the environment. Social learning may be illustrated by "socialization" of a new employee. He or she observes the culture and behavior of coworkers. Rewards occur as the new employee bonds with the informal group. Failure to meet group norms may lead to hostility of coworkers.

Cognitive learning theory hypothesizes that people can recognize relationships between signs in the environment and their own goals. As an illustration, a worker wishes to buy a new automobile. She notes that coworkers who do well in a certain training program have a high probability of being promoted. Promotions lead to a series of wage increases with associated probabilities for each. Therefore, the employee's behavior is directed toward learning the most she possibly can from the training program.

Fortunately, no matter what theory we subscribe to, in practice we try to identify the goals of each individual and relate training and development to that individual's goals, as well as to company objectives.

Utilizing Human Resources

Utilizing workers means arranging their work to make them both productive and motivated. The factors that determine the effectiveness of human resource utilization[11] are the following:

---

[9] Bro Uttal, "Companies That Serve You Best," *Fortune* (December 7, 1987), p. 102.

[10] But training alone cannot improve service quality, any more than a dock worker can improve the quality of the product he loads for shipment." See Bro Uttal, "Companies That Serve You Best," *Fortune* (December 7, 1987), pp. 99–100.

[11] From J. E. Ross, *Productivity, People, and Profits* (Reston, Va.: Reston Publishing, 1981).

— Job structure and work that provide an opportunity for "stretch" performance
— Participation in decisions that have a direct effect on the person's job
— Open communications and equitable scheduling of assignments
— Competent supervision and organizational flexibility
— Economic and noneconomic rewards that recognize achievement and equity
— Opportunity for growth
— A culture that encourages caring for both customer and worker needs

Let us first consider the small employee service firms that are successful. Employees may be encouraged to take initiative and be given a variety of tasks and responsibilities. The "shop" operates like a family, with workers participating in decisions and communicating freely with a manager who provides experienced support. Noneconomic rewards, such as flexibility in working hours, time off when needed, and an atmosphere of general caring about other people, are important.

In large, successful service firms, the work may be organized so that small teams share responsibility for key tasks. Here, economic rewards and opportunity for growth are likely to be greater than in the small service firm. The culture of caring about others, both inside and outside the work group, must exist here also.

Perhaps the major difference between utilization of human resources in service and manufacturing firms is the technocratic perspective of the manufacturing firm. Rational organizational structure, subdivision of labor, rigid scheduling based on machines, and a focus on units of output per period are common to American manufacturing firms. Although services firms can be strongly results-oriented, they tend to be strongly people-oriented as well. Attention must be paid to the employees if the employees are expected to pay attention to the customers. Heskett goes so far as to suggest that the service concept be "turned inward to our employees, as well as outward to our customers."[12] Similarly, Albrecht and Zemke consider management itself to be a service to employees.[13] This attention and concern for employees translates into higher employee motivation and higher service quality.

Rewarding Employees

In many service firms, the discretionary content of an employee's job may be large compared with the prescribed content. This is one of the reasons that developing a compensation plan and achieving perceived equity are much more difficult in many service organizations. For example, a teacher may be *required* to present only certain instructional material to the students and to assess their progress in the completion of the material. However, the best teachers also design special materials, programs, or experiences for students at different levels of progress. In addition, they relate to the students on a personal level and engage the help of parents or other professionals in understanding and motivating student performance. Merit pay for teachers has not been

[12] J. L. Heskett, "Lessons in the Service Sector," *Harvard Business Review,* Vol. 65, No. 2 (March–April 1987), pp. 120–124.

[13] K. Albrecht and R. Zemke, *Service America! Doing Business in the New Economy* (Homewood, Ill.: Dow Jones–Irwin, 1985), p. vi.

widely used, in part, because the variability or discretion inherent in teaching makes it difficult to determine what constitutes "merit."

Another problem for many service firms is their low wages relative to those in manufacturing. This makes it difficult to recruit, reward, and hold employees. Thus the standard principles of wage and salary administration in services must be expanded to include an array of low-cost benefits that provide employee satisfactions. Further, candidates who are selected must be those to whom these benefits appeal. Methods for compensating employees in order to attract and retain them may include the following:

1. *Develop a public image of the company such that employees have pride in working for the firm.* Private colleges and college preparatory schools do this quite well. Professions such as teaching, nursing, and law enforcement have to rely on their mission of helping others to attract good people.
2. *Provide flexitime working conditions* so that people may fit their work to their personal needs and lifestyle, including working at other jobs.
3. *Reward employees for participating in suggestions that can make their work more productive* (or that might even eliminate their present jobs without fear of loss of employment). This especially includes ideas for improved methods and automation. Through natural attrition, then, output per worker will increase and employees may share in the monetary gains.
4. *Structure jobs so that employees have control over their work* and responsibilities that challenge them.
5. *Provide first-class facilities,* such as private offices, lounges, cafeterias, and the like. For example, a modern building with carpeting instead of linoleum, modern communications systems, modern conference rooms, an attractive cafeteria, and the name of the employee on the door or entry wall of partitioned areas may be much cheaper than the cost of turnovers due to hiring and training costs.
6. *Reduce the cost of employment for the worker.* For example, uniforms and a cleaning allowance are usually provided for law enforcement and other emergency personnel. This idea could be applied in modified form to dress clothes for store sales personnel (who also may serve as models), receptionists, school teachers, or bank clerks. The cost of such a program is small compared with cumulative wage increases. In addition, the use of well-designed uniforms in companies that do not usually use them (bus drivers, for example) may provide an identity and sense of pride for the employees. Other "perks" of employment include "company" cars; cafeteria compensation plans; transportation tokens; YMCA, health club, or country club memberships; child care facilities or vouchers; vacation packages; and stock options.
7. *Compensate by salary or commission.* This may induce increases in productivity and result in higher income for employees.
8. *Design the service so that the customer does more of the work.* Self-service stores, cafeterias, government agencies, shuttle air lines, and banks (automatic tellers) are examples of services that have increased productivity per employee by this method. Any increase in productivity, of course, offers a firm the

opportunity to share these benefits with employees and to possibly reduce employee turnover.

TYPES OF SERVICE EMPLOYEES

There are many different types of service employees. In this section we examine four categories to help determine how best to utilize, motivate, and compensate different employees. Our classifications are (1) private-profit, not-for-profit, and government workers, (2) full-time versus contingent workers, (3) blue-collar versus white-collar workers, and (4) professional service employees versus consumer service employees.

Private-Profit, Not-for-Profit, and Government Workers

Private, profit-driven service firms cover the gamut of compensation and organizational complexity. Accounting firms, large financial firms such as Bank of America or Sears, small "mom and pop" service businesses, and small outlets of large chains such as Burger King illustrate the variety. There are by far more low-paid positions than high-paid positions in these firms.

Not-for-profit organizations vary from the Salvation Army to the Ford Foundation. In many of these services, we see people who are dedicated to a cause and work for bare subsistence wages. Large philanthropic organizations, however, are likely to pay high salaries. The same is true for not-for-profit research organizations, such as the Institute for Advanced Study in Princeton, the Institute for Defense Analysis in Arlington, Virginia, or the Rand Corporation in Santa Monica, California, and Washington, D.C. The survival of these organizations depends on employing top-notch people and hence paying high salaries. In such organizations, we are likely to find a collegial management style and flexibility in assignments.

Government agencies are mainly information processors, although there are some exceptions (such as the National Park Service). Compensation plans in federal, state, and local governments are rigid and can only be changed by law. More flexibility may appear in quasi-government agencies such as the Postal Service, at the top of some agencies, or in special agencies such as the CIA. Productivity increases paralleling technology gains are difficult to achieve in most government agencies for several reasons, including

— Bureaucratic red tape
— Lack of coordination and standardization among the many agencies of the federal government
— The budgeting process

Couple these difficulties with nonmonetary objectives and you will find that some individuals are unlikely to find satisfaction working for government agencies. Compensation and benefits provided by the federal government for lower-level employees often exceed those for private service firms. At the top levels, however, the reverse tends to be true. City and state governments tend to pay less than federal agencies and may offer less job security.

Full-Time versus Contingent Workers

Large, centralized service companies tend to follow traditional patterns by employing full-time career employees. Large, decentralized service companies such as food chains, retail consumer goods firms, and financial firms tend to fulfill human resource requirements by a combination of full-time employees and contingent employees. **Contingent employees** are part-time people and temporary help who usually do not receive the fringe benefits of full-time employees.[14] In addition, with the proliferation of computers, there has been an increase in people who work full-time at home acting as subcontractors. As such, they do not receive fringe benefits either. There are also a number of firms such as Manpower Temporary Services, Inc., that *lease* people for a variety of jobs. Other firms specialize in subcontracting services such as security, industrial office cleaning, computer services, or accounting.

The growth of the contingent work force in the past few years has been phenomenal. Consider these facts.[15]

- Part-timers have accounted for over 40 percent of the growth in jobs for the retail industry in the past twelve years.
- Since 1983, the number of airline part-timers has more than doubled, to 12 percent of all employees.
- The number of people who "telecommute" to work has increased 400 percent since 1980, to over 8.9 million persons.
- Contingent workers number in excess of 25 million people, accounting for 25 percent of the total work force.
- The number of temporary workers is expected to increase 10 to 15 percent each year until the mid-1990s.
- The federal government can now hire temporary workers.

White-Collar versus Blue-Collar Workers

The terms **white collar** and **blue collar** have generally differentiated between office workers and factory workers. In services, however, there are many people engaged in the productive or conversion process who cannot be clearly put into one of these classes. Is a waiter wearing a tuxedo a blue-collar worker? Is a nurse, a retail salesperson, or a computer service technician a white-collar or blue-collar worker? Additional descriptors such as skilled/unskilled or hourly/salaried/commissioned help to define a new set of categories for managing human resources in services. They suggest a basis for

---

[14] Temporary workers are indeed more flexible and less costly than full-time employees. However, a recent IRS ruling that taxes fringe benefits unless they are offered to all employees, including temporary workers, may force companies to offer benefits to temporary workers, thereby reducing the cost advantage of employing these types of workers.

[15] Drawn in part from Michael A. Pollock, and Aaron Bernstein, "The Disposable Employee Is Becoming a Fact of Corporate Life," *Business Week* (December 15, 1986), pp. 52–53, 56. The federal government was not allowed to hire temporary workers until 1989.

recruiting, selecting, training, and compensating employees. Exhibit 9–7 shows examples of service occupations in terms of white collar, blue collar, skill level, and compensation.

Professional Service Employees versus Consumer Service Employees

Another way to look at different types of service employees is by their background and the level of service provided.[16] A **professional service employee,** for example, refers to doctors, lawyers, accountants, consultants, and other highly skilled customized service providers. This type of employee typically has a higher level of education, a higher level of perceived status, more responsibility and authority, and considerably higher earnings than the normal service employee. He or she is usually self-motivating, with strong ego-gratification needs. Further, it is often difficult to separate the service from the employee providing the service. In other words, the professional service employee *is* the company, and thus retention of good employees is essential.

Consumer service employees, on the other hand, provide relatively standardized services to the public, as typically seen in retail stores, restaurants, and delivery services. These employees perform jobs that are more routine and that require only minimum levels of education. However, consumer service employees must interact with the public and therefore require significant interpersonal skills. Typically, pay is low and advancement is slow. Managers must pay attention to motivating factors to maintain a sufficient level of job satisfaction or face poor service performance and high turnover.

Exhibit 9–8 summarizes the dynamics of human resource management in service organizations with examples by type of service.

_____ EXHIBIT 9–7 _____

- *Three Factors for Characterizing Human Resources in Services*

	White Collar		Blue Collar	
	Hourly	Salaried or Commissioned	Hourly	Salaried or Commissioned
Skilled	Lawyer, accountant, computer service technician, cook	Lawyer, accountant, airline pilot, physical therapist, chef, salesman	Automechanic, tree surgeon, plumber, carpenter	Nurseryman, telephone line repairperson
Semiskilled	Actor, model, sign painter, aerobics instructor	Bus driver, computer word processor, stenographer, nurse's aide	Window-tinter, operator of trench digger in construction	Landscape gardener, building maintenance employee
Unskilled	Department store Santa Claus, babysitter	Clerk, receptionist	Garbage removal person, waitress	Janitor, aircraft cleanup crew

[16] The distinction between professional and consumer service employee is described in W. Earl Sasser, R. P. Olson, and D. Daryl Wyckoff, *Management of Service Operations* (Boston: Allyn and Bacon, 1978), pp. 401–405.

EXHIBIT 9–8

■ *Human Resource Management in Service Organizations*

	Characteristics of the Organization		
Type of Service	Small, custom service	Large, mass service	Professional service
Examples	Beauty parlors, interior decorators, restaurants, travel agencies	Telephone, financial (credit cards, banks), TV, fast food	Law firms, accounting firms, brokerage firms, real estate firms
Geographic Dispersion	Single or multiple local sites	Central headquarters, local sites	Local, regional, national, international
Transaction or Service Rate	Low	High	Low
Value of Transactions	Moderate to low	Low	High
Type of Operating Personnel	Semiskilled	Low-skilled	Professional
Type of Middle Management	None	Professionally trained	Professional
Entry Level Skills	None to certified	Semiskilled	Professional
Training and Development	On-the-job	On-the-job and company T&D	Advanced T&D and on-the-job
Customer Contact	High	Low to none	High
Quality Control	High	Medium to high	High
Customer Loyalty	To the high-quality provider	To the concept and the best price	To the firm
Working Facilities	Small	Large office buildings, small local offices	Luxurious office buildings
Compensation	Low or commission	Low to medium	High

ESTABLISHING A SERVICE CULTURE

The following are some important components of a company culture.[17]

Shared Cultures	Example
Important shared understandings	The company will support you if you are acting in the customer's interest with reasonable costs to the company.
Shared things	Most employees eat in the company cafeteria.
Shared sayings	We live up to our commitments to employees and the community.
Share doings	We all pitch in together to solve a customer's major problem
Shared feelings	If you aren't willing to cooperate by going the extra mile, you don't fit in here.

If there is one value that permeates the culture of successful service organizations, certainly it is the emphasis on serving the customer. The bored, gum-chewing clerk, the argumentative maintenance person, the service representative who conducts personal phone conversations while the customer waits, and the government bureaucrat who knows little and cares less represent a service culture that is rapidly becoming intolerable.

In its place, a service culture is emerging where superlative service is the norm. Consider the phenomenal success of the Seattle-based retailer Nordstrom, Inc. Nordstrom's advertising budget is a small fraction of the industry's average, yet its sales, which have more than doubled in the past five years, are three times higher than the industry norm. Its secret? Customer service and customer loyalty—almost fanatical loyalty. A recent experience by an executive in Portland, Oregon, illustrates the Nordstrom experience. Long hounded by his wife and daughter to try Nordstrom, he finally did with the following results:

> The service in the store was good, he had to admit. And he did find a fine suit on sale, although he also picked up a second suit—at full price. Nordstrom promises same-day alterations. He noted, however, that there was a little asterisk next to the promise—next-day alteration was promised during sales. He chortled at this small chink in the armor.
>
> He came back at 5:45 P.M. the next day to pick up his suits. It was fifteen minutes before closing. He needed the suits for a trip that night.
>
> To his surprise, though he'd only been there once, his salesperson greeted him by name! The fellow then trotted upstairs to pick up the suits. Five minutes passed. The salesperson reappeared—without the goods. They hadn't been finished.
>
> Though he needed the suits, our friend admits to secret glee. Without the suits, he took off for a Monday appointment in Seattle, after which he proceeded to Dallas for the big meeting of the trip.
>
> He checked into his hotel and went up to his room. A message light informed him that a package had arrived for him. A bellhop fetched it—Federal Express, mailing fee $98. Yes, it was from Nordstrom. In it were his two suits. On top of them were three $25 silk ties (which he hadn't ordered) thrown in gratis! There was also a note of apology

---

[17] For a more thorough discussion on corporate culture, see Desmond Graves, *Diagnosis and Change* (New York: St. Martins Press, 1986); and Frederick E. Schuster, *The Schuster Report* (New York: Wiley, 1986).

from the salesperson, who had called his home and learned his travel arrangements from one of his daughters. With a smile of resignation, he admits that he's now a believer.[18]

Such a service culture is not the result of one overzealous employee. The service culture at Nordstrom is created by a CEO with a focused customer orientation (Jim Nordstrom on returns: "I don't care if they roll a Goodyear tire into the store, if they say they paid $200 for it, give them the $200"[19]), an overstaffed sales force providing personalized service (they remember names, send birthday flowers and personal notes, and routinely go out of their way for the customer[20]), salespersons who are multi-functional (they can cash checks, take returns, and gift wrap), and a sparkling store environment (with fresh flowers in the dressing rooms).

Customer Expectations

Service in American firms, on average, is so poor that modest attention to customer needs can yield impressive returns. Typically what customers expect from contacts with personnel in service firms are

1. *Punctuality.* Customers who have made appointments with physicians are often kept waiting over an hour. Some telephone companies still can only estimate within four to eight hours when a service person will appear at the home. When a mechanic promises that the repaired automobile may be picked up, it should be ready.
2. *A caring attitude.* This may be "imperturbability," a smile, or an obvious effort to assist the customer.
3. *Competence.* Customers are more informed and they expect responsive explanations to their questions. Even a high physician's fee may be accepted if the patient is not brushed off without explanation.

Employer Expectations

High-customer-contact services put tremendous pressure on the service provider. Employers, as well as customers, expect service employees to be courteous, competent, and caring *at all times,* even to unruly customers and in unpleasant situations. Whether the job is as a waitress, a bank teller, a teacher, or a sales clerk, the constant requirement to be "on stage" serving the customer creates a stressful situation. Hospital personnel, police officers, and others in similar professions have the added burden of dealing with life-and-death situations and with unsavory "customers" on a day-to-day basis.

The resulting stress is a common cause of *burnout* for service providers, which

---

[18] Excerpts from *Thriving on Chaos: Handbook for a Management Revolution* by Tom Peters (New York: Knopf, 1987), pp. 89–90. Copyright © 1987 by Excel, a California Limited Partnership. Reprinted by permission of Alfred A. Knopf, Inc.

[19] Tom Peters, *Thriving on Chaos* (New York: Knopf, 1987), p. 90.

[20] Says one customer, "When a blouse I wanted wasn't in stock, the clerk volunteered to get one from another store, and drop it by my house." From Amy Dunkin, "How Department Stores Plan to Get the Registers Ringing Again," *Business Week* (November 18, 1985), p. 67.

leads to either high employee turnover or a progression from high absenteeism to deteriorating performance to unresponsive employees for the service firm. Employee health problems due to stress are also common.

Employers should expect that this stress will occur, be able to recognize stress-related problems, and take steps to compensate for stress incurred by high contact service–related jobs. More specifically, in order to preserve the value of their human resources, managers of service firms should provide

1. *Opportunity for positive reinforcement for a job well done,* especially in difficult circumstances. For example, most police officers see only criminals and other undesirables (or even worse, their victims) day and night. It is easy to become skeptical and hardened about the customers they serve. One empathetic lieutenant sent the twenty-five young officers under his command knocking on doors in peaceful neighborhoods. The officers would ring a few doorbells every day, introduce themselves, give out a "business card" with emergency phone numbers, and encourage the citizens to call for any reason. Says the lieutenant, "A lot of people out there are paying our salaries. This is a way to let them know what a good job we're doing, and get a wider base of support and experience for the officer."[21]

2. *Periods of reduced stress,* such as ample breaks during the day, rotating schedules, rotating tasks, or rotating positions. For example, at a university, the student personnel administrator in charge of the judicial system spends each and every day hearing cases of student misconduct and handing down punishment. To give the administrator a different perspective on the student population, he or she might also be assigned as the advisor of a national leadership honor society or other highly motivated, successful student group. In addition, the administrator should not be allowed to serve in such a capacity, as "disciplinarian," for more than two years.

3. *Avenues to alleviate stress,* such as open communication, clear and reasonable expectations of performance, group help sessions, opportunities for physical exercise, and stress avoidance training.

ORGANIZATIONAL STRUCTURE FOR THE SERVICE FIRM

An organization's structure can be defined along the following dimensions:[22]

— Standardization—the degree to which procedures have been established for regular activities
— Formalization—*written* rules and regulations
— Specialization—division of labor
— Centralization—the degree to which authority is concentrated at the top

---

[21] Tom Peters, *Thriving on Chaos* (New York: Knopf, 1987), p. 156.

[22] These dimensions are taken from P. K. Mills, *Managing Service Industries* (Cambridge, Mass.: Ballinger, 1986), p. 56.

— Configuration—span of management, number of levels of management, number of supervisors to nonsupervisors

— Flexibility—the ability of the organization to restructure itself to adapt to external (environmental) changes

In large service firms, departmentalization may be based on function and service lines just as manufacturing or conglomerates are organized. For example, Exhibit 9–9 shows an excerpt from the organization chart of a large retail firm. The chart is similar to a manufacturing firm's organization chart except that the vice president of merchandising position incorporates many of the functions of both the vice president of manufacturing and the vice president of marketing for a primarily manufacturing firm.

If we closely examine the structure of most service firms, however, we would find that they are very different from typical manufacturing firms, and the higher the customer contact of a service, the more different the organizational structure becomes. Consider the following principles on structure from organizational theory, based on studies of manufacturing firms.[23]

1. *As task complexity increases, the span of control decreases.* This makes sense because as tasks become more varied and complex, supervisors have less time to assist their subordinates. However, this is not borne out in service industries. There is no particular relationship between task complexity and the number of people under a manager's supervision. Further, the span of control for services is considerably less than in manufacturing. This is probably due to the fact that even the simplest of jobs in services (e.g., retail clerk) involve relatively complex tasks, a variety of tasks, uncertainty with each different customer, and decision-making responsibilities with each transaction.

2. *As the complexity of technology increases, the number of people responding to the CEO increases.* For manufacturing firms, the increase in technology makes certain groups within the company more self-governing. This means that the CEO has less direct impact on these groups and can therefore supervise more of them, providing general policy guidelines. But the reverse is true for services! The number of people reporting to the CEO actually decreases as the complexity of the customer encounter increases. In services, the more complex interactions are handled by lower levels of employees. CEOs manage at the administrative level, sheltered from direct customer contact, in a more certain, ordered environment. The difference in environment allows the CEO to supervise more people on a regular basis.

3. *As the complexity of technology increases, the number of levels of management increases.* This is primarily due to the number of support systems necessary to protect the technology in manufacturing-oriented firms. Again, in service organizations, the opposite is true. The number of levels of management is inversely related to the complexity of the service encounter. Service organizations tend to be much flatter than manufacturing organizations because customer-contact personnel must be given

[23] This section is a summary of the material presented in P. K. Mills, *Managing Service Industries* (Cambridge, Mass.: Ballinger, 1986), Chapter 4.

EXHIBIT 9-9

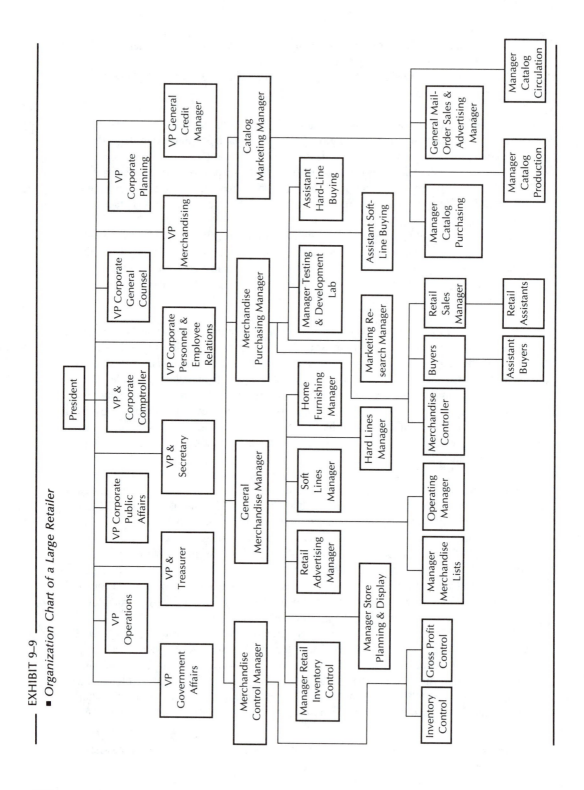

■ *Organization Chart of a Large Retailer*

_____ EXHIBIT 9–10 _____

- *Nordstrom's Organizational Chart*

Customers

Sales & Sales Support People

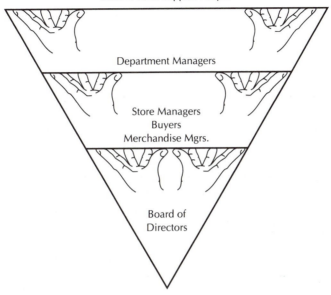

Department Managers

Store Managers
Buyers
Merchandise Mgrs.

Board of
Directors

Source: From *Thriving on Chaos: Handbook for a Management Revolution* by Tom Peters (New York: Knopf, 1987), p. 370. Copyright © 1987 by Excel, a California Limited Partnership. Reprinted by permission of Alfred A. Knopf, Inc.

authority and autonomy to complete the service process. In addition, the more levels of management, the longer it takes to make and implement a decision and, owing to the lapse of time in receiving feedback, the riskier the decision becomes. Services, by their nature, require that decisions be made on the spot and that any feedback on those decisions be immediate.

4. *As organizations increase in size, their organizational structure becomes more complex.* Thus, as the number of people employed increases, there is a tendency in manufacturing-oriented firms to specialize, standardize, and increase the levels of management control. But services (as you might have predicted), regardless of their size, tend toward unbureaucratic forms of organization and a less formal organizational structure.

These contradictions of traditional organizational theory support the contention that to succeed in a service industry, one must "turn the organization chart upside down."[24] Nordstrom's inverted organization chart is shown in Exhibit 9–10.

Peter Drucker, a well-known management expert, further suggests that twenty

_____

[24] D. S. Davidson, "How to Succeed in a Service Industry: Turn the Organization Chart Upside Down," *Management Review* (April 1978), pp. 13–16.

years from now, large businesses of every type will follow the lead of services in drastically reducing their levels of management and their numbers of managers and giving more autonomy to the front-line worker. He predicts that the typical business of the next century is more likely to resemble a hospital, a university, or a symphony orchestra than the manufacturing companies of today.[25]

SUMMARY

Most services are labor-intensive. Further, service personnel tend to have more contacts and interactions with the customers. The management of personnel who employ such discretionary responsibilities on a continuous basis requires different emphases than managing factory or back-office personnel. Therefore, although some human resource management activities (payroll, fringe benefits, and so on) may be the same for all types of employees, the selection, training and development, utilization, and reward of high-contact service personnel requires special treatment.

Recently, international and domestic competition has forced companies to reduce labor costs. Technology has provided some relief. Finding and utilizing lower-cost labor sources have provided more. This has led to a great expansion in the number of *contingency* workers, such as part-time, temporary, and subcontracted workers.

The organizational structure of a service firm must be designed to support a service culture that provides a high level of service quality. Many times this means decentralization of authority, fewer levels of management, and more flexibility than traditional bureaucratic organizations.

DISCUSSION QUESTIONS

1. Name five activities associated with human resource management. Who in a firm is responsible for HRM?

2. How does manpower planning for services differ from that for manufacturing?

3. What are some typical criteria that should be used to select service employees?

4. List and explain several factors involved in successful training and development programs.

5. In general, service firms pay relatively low wages. What other benefits can they provide to attract and retain employees?

6. Differentiate between

    a. White-collar and blue-collar service workers.

    b. Professional service employees and consumer service employees.

7. Discuss the implications of managing a large contingent work force.

8. What is a service culture? Give examples of firms with strong service cultures.

9. What do customers typically expect from service employees? Why are service jobs particularly stressful?

10. Most of the theories on organizational structure are based on studies of manufacturing firms. How does organizational structure differ for service firms?

---

[25] Peter F. Drucker, "The Coming of the New Organization," *Harvard Business Review*, Vol. 66, No. 1 (January–February 1988), pp. 45–53.

___ READING 9.1 _____

What They Teach You at Disney U.

"Just remember: Two d's, two s's and three emotions." Thirty-six pencils record this information in notebooks, ensuring that their owners will know, if asked, the names of the Seven Dwarfs: Doc and Dopey, Sleepy and Sneezy, Happy, Grumpy and Bashful.

The mnemonic for Snow White's friends is an essential element of the curriculum at Disney University at Walt Disney World, whose principal function is to indoctrinate more than 16,000 new employees this year to the unique ways of The Disney Company. The plain office building that serves as a schoolhouse, located on the northern edge of Walt Disney World near Orlando, Florida, swarms with seasonal workers hired for the summer rush. The instructor, identified by his name tag only as Jim, has the blond coiffure, youthful athleticism and breezy confidence of a college fraternity president. The coat of his gray suit hangs as casually from his shoulders as an open beach shirt, and a shock of yellow hair juts straight out over his forehead like a sun visor.

This is an orientation class, but it is not called orientation—nor are the new workers known as employees. They are cast members, and the class is known as Traditions I. Throughout the day the cast members will learn other Disney terms. Ninety percent of the labor force, hourly employees from street sweepers to store clerks to ride operators, wear costumes, not uniforms. They are not on duty but onstage. During breaks they are offstage. Visitors are guests; cast members are hosts and hostesses.

"Working at Disney," Jim had said at the start of the class, "is like going to a foreign country. You have to learn a new language and a new culture." At a time when employees' attitudes, productivity and quality of work are problems throughout corporate America, Disney seems immune to the maladies of the age. America's leading corporations—from General Electric to General Motors—have dispatched executives to Disney University to dis-

cover how Disney inspires its staff to meet the company's exacting standards.

No visitor has to spend much time in the park before he begins to wonder whether Disney feeds some magic potion to its employees, perhaps learned from a certain former sorcerer's apprentice. So confident is Disney that cast members will charm guests that it has devised ways to force contact. One example: Many of the wares in the park's ubiquitous gift shops bear no price tags, requiring shoppers to ask the cost.

If all this frenzied friendliness makes Walt Disney World sometimes seem a bit like Stepford South, its success is beyond dispute. Sixty percent of Walt Disney World's visitors are repeaters. Together, Walt Disney World and its California cousin, Disneyland, accounted for $1.8 billion of the company's almost $2.9 billion in 1987 revenues. The company's ability to retain workers is rare in the service sector which nationally suffers from a 40 percent annual turnover; Disney's is lower by one-third. For white-collar workers, Disney's attrition rate drops to a mere 6 percent.

None of this happens by accident. Disney's hiring policies are designed to find workers who will fit the company mold. Disney takes people who are normally gregarious and trains them to be more so. "Looks don't matter; attitude and personality do," says Valerie Oberle, director of Disney University. The casting department puts more weight on interviews than resumes; Disney wants people who look questioners in the eye. The best bet to fit in: friends of current staffers. Disney offers a $100 bonus to workers who bring in new employees.

Today the pressure on casting is greater than ever. Disney can't be as selective as it once was; the labor pool in Central Florida has shrunk as a result of the boom Walt Disney World started. At one time Disney had ten job seekers for every hourly position; now the ratio is three to one. (For managerial positions the reverse is true: This year

_____

Disney will fill 300 jobs for which it will receive 70,000 resumes.) More and more representatives of Florida's large semiretired population are showing up on Walt Disney World work lines. Disney recruits hourly workers on 130 college campuses and advertises in major markets for positions in hotels and restaurants.

All new employees must attend Traditions I and II classes before starting work, even those hired for a week at spring break. There, in a classroom decorated with posters and pictures depicting great moments in the company's history (Mickey Mouse's first cartoon, *Snow White, Fantasia,* the opening of Disneyland), they are inoculated with the Disney corporate culture. Everything in the room has a purpose: the shape of the table (round, to instill a sense of teamwork), the method of introductions (each person gives not his own name but that of the person to his right, to instill a sense of teamwork), the taking of a test on Disneyana (each table consults on answers, to instill a sense of teamwork). In case someone has somehow missed the point, Jim makes it again: If one employee makes a mistake, a guest goes home unhappy. "We never say, 'It's not my job,' " he warns. "If someone asks us a question, we know the answer. If we see a piece of trash on the ground, we pick it up."

Like all instructors, Jim is not assigned to the university permanently. Nor is he an executive. He is an hourly employee—intended to be a role model—who conducts the class one day a week for one year. Disney puts a time limit on teaching to ensure that its instructors will be fresh and enthusiastic. Some are still in their first year with the company.

More teamwork, "Disney is a first-name company," Jim tells the class. That is tradition No. 1. If the policy promotes informality, it is also meant to reduce individuality. So are the company's strict grooming standards. "Why do we have them?" Jim asks rhetorically. "To make everyone blend in, to promote the whole show, not individuals." Men cannot have mustaches, beards, long sideburns or hair touching the ears or collar. Women may wear one small ring (gold or silver only) on each hand and earrings no larger than a penny (a recent liberalization from previously mandated posts); they cannot have long or brightly painted fingernails, large hair decorations or long necklaces. Thanks

to Walt Disney World, Orlando must be one of the world's principal markets for plain black shoes, which are the required footwear. Acceptable styles are displayed in a glass case near the area where cast members pick up their costumes; twice a month a shoemobile makes the 25-mile drive from town.

The morning session ends with a 26-minute videotape called *Making Magic.* It shows employees volunteering to take pictures of guests, so that the whole family can be in the picture, as well as doing other good deeds. At the end, chairman Michael Eisner and president Frank Wells are joined by Mickey and Donald (Disney's first-name policy extends to omitting even their surnames) while the tune of "When You Wish Upon a Star" swells in the background. When ex-USC football player Nunis first viewed it, it brought tears to his eyes.

Disney manages to Disneyfy its employees despite an hourly pay scale that begins at $4.85 (about $10,000 annually), which company officials describe as competitive for service workers in the Orlando area. There are raises after six months, a year and annually thereafter, but all hourly positions carry a salary cap regardless of longevity. The carrot is that Disney promotes liberally from within. Valerie Oberle, for example, started by typing and opening mail; one of her first management jobs was operations manager at Disney's Polynesian Village Resort Hotel. "I didn't know anything about hotels," she recalls, "but I knew courtesy and I knew Disney."

Disney's low-entry-level-pay but fast-advancement system enables the company to retain employees who have the ability to move up without offering rewards to those who don't. Image-conscious Disney prefers not to fire anyone, since it views every human being on the planet as a potential customer and doesn't want to offend a single one. Instead, it tries to find new positions for problem employees, something that is easy enough to do at a park with 1100 job descriptions and steady turnover. It takes an average of two to three years for a worker to be promoted to lead, a foreman-like position that represents the highest rank for hourly workers. In somewhat less time, leads can move up to line supervisor, joining the management ranks as salaried workers.

Underlying all this is an unflagging companywide obsession with excellence. Disney workers paint every trash can to blend with nearby scenery; they steam-clean every piece of pavement and wash every window in the Magic Kingdom and EPCOT every day. Disney designers stayed in low-budget hotels around the park and then penciled in extra soundproofing and double sinks for the Caribbean Beach resort in order to beat the competition. Disney gardeners have trimmed the oaks on Main Street in the Magic Kingdom to the identical shape every day since the park opened 17 years ago; they have clipped the shrubbery in heavily traveled areas into shapes of penguins, elephants, swans and camels. (The gardeners travel enough miles on lawn mowers each year to circle the earth fourteen times.) Atop EPCOT's Italian pavilion is a four-foot angel; though it is too high for visitors to discern, Disney coats it with the most expensive gold paint available: 14-carat gold leaf.

In all this there ought to be lessons for the rest of corporate America. It sounds so simple: Take the long-term view, insist on quality, recognize that courtesy pays, offer low-level employees incentives for advancement rather than money, hire by giving more weight to personality than credentials and expand by filling the public's needs rather than your own.

_____ QUESTIONS FOR READING 9.1

1. What criteria does Disney use in selecting its employees?

2. How does Disney compensate for its relatively low pay scale?

3. Describe Disney's extensive training program. Why is it necessary?

4. How is Disney's training program supported by its day to day operations?

_____ READING 9.2 _____

Managing the Service Employee

Consider the following two examples of highly successful service companies and how they manage their human resources.

SERVICEMASTER

ServiceMaster is a company based in Downers Grove, Illinois, which manages support services for hospitals, schools, and industrial companies. It supervises the employees of customers' organizations engaged in housekeeping, food service, and equipment maintenance. These are services that are peripheral to the customers' businesses and therefore get little management attention.

Many of the people who ServiceMaster oversees are functionally illiterate. To them, as well as its managers, ServiceMaster directs a service concept centered around the philosophy stated by its CEO, "Before asking someone to do *something* you have to help them be *something*." ServiceMaster provides educational and motivational programs to help these employees "be something."

To its own supervisors the company offers training leading to an ambitious "master's" program taught in part by the chief executive. New responsibilities and opportunities present themselves via the rapid growth of the company, approximating 20 percent per year, nearly all of it from expansion of existing operations rather than acquisition. Elaborate training aids and a laboratory for developing new equipment and materials enhance the employee-managers' "be something" feeling.

For customers' employees ServiceMaster tries to build the "be something" attitude and improve their productivity by redesigning their jobs and by

Source: Reprinted by permission of *Harvard Business Review*. An excerpt from "Lessons in the Service Sector" by James L. Heskett, Vol. 65, No. 2 (March–April 1987), pp. 118–126. Copyright © 1987 by the President and Fellows of Harvard College; all rights reserved. And, condensed from "What Mass-Produced Child Care Is Producing" by Myron Magnet, *Fortune*, November 28, 1983, pp. 157–174. © 1983 Time, Inc. All rights reserved.

developing equipment and pictorial, color-coded instructional material. In most cases it is the first time that anyone has paid attention to the service of which these employees are a part. ServiceMaster holds weekly sessions to exchange ideas and offers educational programs to, among other things, develop literacy. ServiceMaster also recruits up to 20 percent of its own managers from the ranks in jobs it handles. The service concept clearly is improved self-respect, self-development, personal satisfaction, and upward mobility.

Another company slogan, repeated often, is "to help people grow." When a hospital served by the company decided to hire a deaf person, ServiceMaster's local head didn't object. Instead he authorized three of his supervisors to take a course in sign language.

It should be no surprise that the turnover rate among ServiceMaster's 7000 employees is low. Further, the turnover rate in organizations it services is much lower than the averages for their industries. And when ServiceMaster takes a job, the productivity achieved by supervised support workers invariably rises dramatically.

Now a billion-dollar company, ServiceMaster had an average return on equity from 1979 through 1988 that was the highest of all the largest service or industrial companies in the United States, more than 63 percent after taxes. It oversees the support service employees for fifteen hospitals in Japan, which probably makes it the largest exporter of managerial talent to Japan. According to one ServiceMaster executive, "The Japanese immediately recognize and identify with what we do and how we do it."

KINDER-CARE

Kinder-Care's commercial success is truly impressive. The company's stock has been trading at around $20 a share, compared with $2.25 in 1977 and 48 cents in 1972, when Kinder-Care went public. "On Wall Street," founder and President Perry Mendel, 61, boasts, "we are one of the adorables."

This adorability comes partly from the demographic and social changes that have created demand for Kinder-Care's services. Though baby-boomers have small families, they are entering the parental ranks in enough force to raise the total number of preschoolers from 1977's low of 15.6 million to a projected 19.2 million by 1990. Baby-boom mothers have thronged into the labor force: 47 percent of women who have been married and who have preschool-age children now work, vs. 20 percent in 1960. Meanwhile, Grandma has moved to Leisure City and the lady next door has taken a full-time job herself. It's no wonder that the percentage of working mothers who put their preschoolers in group care centers has more than doubled in twenty years.

Perceiving some of these trends in 1969, Mendel, then a Montgomery real estate developer, seized the occasion. "I saw moms and pops operating centers under horrendous conditions," he says. "The opportunity was to bring child care out of antiquity, as McDonald's did with the hamburger or Holiday Inns did with the motel." The managerial challenge was to standardize, rationalize, and centralize, while adding a dash of modern marketing aimed, as Mendel puts it, at "taking the guilt away from the working mother."

To serve this clientele profitably, Kinder-Care must keep its own costs as lean as Oliver Twist. Though its fees are usually among the highest in town, the upper limit is low. The company's bulk-buying muscle wins significant savings—but the key savings come from keeping labor costs low.

Even in this notoriously ill-paying industry, it would be hard to pay less than Kinder-Care. A teacher, including one with a B.A. and teaching certificate, normally starts at or close to the minimum wage, $3.35 an hour. The experienced former director of a Midwestern Kinder-Care center recalls how the 25-cents-an-hour raises she gave two valued teachers were rescinded by headquarters. "You were only allowed to give nickel and dime raises—literally." With such salaries the rule, F. E. Montgomery, vice president of operations, judges, "We shouldn't employ a person who is depending on this for her sole income." Accordingly, many employees—female almost to a person—either live with their parents or have husbands who provide the primary family income. Teachers average just over $7000 for a full year's work; center directors make from $10,000 to $20,000. By comparison, the company's four Kinderoos—mascots in Disneyesque kangaroo suits who clown at grand openings—make $13,000 to over $20,000.

Why do the teachers do it? "There seems to

be a semi-inexhaustible supply of people who like to work with children," says Vice President Hanchrow. "I'm satisfied it's like the Marine Corps—there's a certain number of people who'd pay money to do it." This is hyperbole, but it contains an important grain of truth; the intangible personal rewards do count. For those set on teaching children, the public school employment crunch may make Kinder-Care the only job available. For those already in public school jobs, Kinder-Care offers a chance to shake off government bureaucracy, or to work out flexible part-time schedules, or to keep a new baby in the center with them.

Of course, no one works in a Kinder-Care for pure love of children, and the bad pay and steady corporate pressure on labor costs wear employees down. A sore point is the continual adjustment of working hours to enrollment: when students are out sick or on vacation with their parents, an employee expecting to work forty hours a week may suddenly have only thirty-five, finding herself excused for an unpaid hour in the middle of the next five days while the children nap. Resentment seems the usual response. "The center looked so beautiful on the outside to the public," says the ex-director from the Midwest, "but sometimes inside the employees were just seething."

In a sense the company's financial success makes matters worse. "If you know everybody's getting paid lousy, that's fine," the ex-director says. "But when you hear they made millions in profit, that kind of frosts you." The result is massive employee turnover, a bane of the whole industry. The company keeps no exact statistics on turnover but says it's no higher than in other for-profit child care operations.

A McDonald's burger is basically the same no matter how the girl who serves it to you feels, and Kinder-Care tries to standardize its product too, so that the Kinder-Care experience will as far as possible be independent of the person who administers it. Hence the emphasis on a uniform and generally excellent physical plant—a red bell tower hung with a fiberglass school bell; clean, open classrooms; kiddie-size plumbing fixtures; and rock-solid playground equipment. The decor is cheerful,

the blocks and wooden puzzles a pleasure to handle, the trikes the best you ever saw. Some centers have swimming pools, some home computers with tot-level software—these are the only video screens allowed in Kinder-Care. First-time visitors can't fail to be impressed.

A similar effort at standardization has also molded the educational program that Kinder-Care boasts making it far more than a baby-sitting service, giving your kid a bigger boost toward school than you might be able to provide yourself. Every month the latest installment of the Goal Program arrives at each center. A set of week-by-week brochures, it contains suggested daily activities for the 2- to 5-year-olds relating to the prescribed weekly theme. George Washington got one week in centers from coast to coast, flags got another. On paper it seems a solid if not inspired program. And as an Alabama assistant director says, "If you have never taught, you can do it with this."

The problem with all this is that, while an activities program and a nifty building facilitate good care, they aren't good care in themselves. Most experts on early childhood believe that for children, care is a personal transaction with an individual care-giver, not a product that a succession of strangers can dish out. It matters therefore whether the teachers feel angry and exploited, and it matters whether they quit just when they've learned how to do their job or when the children have learned to trust them.

QUESTIONS FOR READING 9.2

1. Describe how these two companies differ in the management of their human resources. How has each approach helped the respective company be successful?

2. In what ways have the competitive environment, customer expectations, and tangibility of output influenced the development of human resources for each company? Identify other factors that have an impact on the treatment of employees.

3. What trends for the future do you foresee for each company and their respective industries?

_____ CASE 9.1 _____

Pool Delight, Inc.

Pool Delight, Inc., is a small pool service and re-modeling company located on the southwest coast of Florida near Sarasota. It consists of the president of the firm and three permanent "subcontractors," who are individuals roughly equivalent to employees.

The president of Pool Delight, Bill Gordon completed two years of study at Broward Community College. He then worked from 1981 to 1984 for a large pool service company in Sarasota. While employed there, he worked weekends on his own time to develop a list of residential clients south of Sarasota. In 1985, Bill left his employer and founded Pool Delight. Initially, he concentrated on increasing his list of residential clients and taking on some commercial accounts. Florida has a high density of pools in middle- and upper-class areas.

It was apparent to Bill that he could not both service pools and market for Pool Delight if he were to survive and expand. He proposed to a friend, Jim McGuire, that Jim work as an independent contractor by cleaning and servicing pools and working on remodeling of pools with him. He offered to supply Jim with clients to be serviced. Jim would bill Bill. Bill would bill and collect from the customers and give 60 percent to Jim.

Jim was required to supply his own pickup truck, pay about $60 to $80 per week for chemicals used, and pay about $150 per month for health insurance.

Servicing a pool consists of brushing the pool and the walk and taking a chemical count of the water. Once a week the pool must be vacuumed. The service time is about fifteen to twenty minutes including vacuuming. A service contract normally consists of one service per week, for which the monthly charge is $55. One competitor charges only $50 per month and pays his employees a 35 percent commission. If the pool area is surrounded by heavy foliage and trees, $60 is the monthly charge.

In May of 1986, Bill purchased the customer list of a quality competitor who was retiring from business. The customers were being charged only $55 per month for two services per week, and Bill agreed to maintain this rate for three years for them.

As a result of this purchase, Bill had to find another person as a "subcontractor." He knew a number of young men who did lawn maintenance work and selected one named Derek Rohr.

A few months later, Bill received complaints and lost several accounts of wealthy out-of-state people. They had dropped in at their Florida homes and found their pools in bad shape. Bill then severed his contract with Jim McGuire who was responsible for these pools. Bill again had to find a new subcontractor immediately while he worked weekends to maintain Jim's client list. Within two weeks, he had hired Jill Pole.

By the end of 1986, Bill had been operating smoothly for six months. He had taken on a number of pool remodeling jobs, most hinging on remarsiting the pool surface. He used a high-quality subcontractor with three employees to apply the finish after he and Derek did the rough work and acid etch. The three workers took about ten hours to remarsite a standard fifteen- by thirty-foot pool surface. Pool Delight remodels about thirty pools per year.

At the end of 1986, Derek was servicing sixty residential pools and four commercial pools. Jill serviced fifty residential pools and five commercial pools. She also took care of the bookkeeping and sending out bills. Bill handled five commercial pools and did the marketing. Derek and Jill usually worked from 8:00 A.M. to 2:00 P.M. on Monday through Friday on pools. In addition, Jill spent about ten hours per week on bookkeeping for $7.00 per hour.

Bill was considering expanding by opening a pool supply store.

_____ QUESTIONS FOR CASE 9.1

1. Assume that all of Pool Delight's subcontractors are employees. Draw an organizational chart.

2.

a. Assume fringe benefits run about 10 percent of direct labor costs. Make four different assumptions about labor rates ranging from minimum wage to $10 per hour. If Pool Delight hires its subcontractors as employees, paid an hourly rate with benefits, estimate the total labor costs per year for each labor rate assumption.

b. Estimate current annual costs if subcontractors are paid a 35% commission.

c. What conclusions can you draw from comparing your answers to parts a and b?

3. How could Bill go about recruiting employees who are reliable and good workers?

4. What should Bill do to prevent a recurrence of the problem whereby the subcontractor skips servicing of pools? Remember, Bill has very little time to check on pools, and these pools are scattered over a wide area.

5. Evaluate Bill's idea of operating a pool store. Hazardous chemicals for pool work are currently stored at some distance outside the city, while the safer chemicals are stored in a small warehouse.

6. What kind of training for what period of time should be required for this work? Who should conduct the training? Are pool service workers unskilled, skilled, or professional workers?

7. How large do you think this business can grow? What could hinder its growth? What changes in management practices would you anticipate as the business gets larger?

REFERENCES

Albrecht, K., and R. Zemke. *Service America! Doing Business in the New Economy,* Homewood, Ill.: Dow Jones–Irwin, 1985.

Behling, Orlando, and Chester Schriesheim. *Organizational Behavior: Theory, Research, and Application.* Boston, Mass.: Allyn and Bacon, 1976.

Davidson, D. S. "How to Succeed in a Service Industry: Turn the Organization Chart Upside Down," *Management Review* (April 1978), pp. 13–16.

Davis, Steven I. *Excellence in Banking.* New York: St. Martins Press, 1985, Chaps. 2 and 8.

Drucker, Peter F. "The Coming of the New Organization," *Harvard Business Review,* Vol. 66, No. 1 (January–February 1988), pp. 45–53.

Dunkin, Amy. "How Department Stores Plan to Get the Register Ringing Again," *Business Week* (November 18, 1985), pp. 66–67.

"Employees Use New Benefits to Attract Labor in Tight Market," *Roanoke Times and World News* (November 20, 1988).

Georgoff, David M., and Robert G. Murdick. "Manager's Guide to Forecasting," *Harvard Business Review,* Vol. 64, No. 1 (January–February 1986), pp. 110–120.

Gorovitz, Elizabeth. "Employee Training: Current Trends, Future Challenges," *Training and Development Journal,* Vol. 37, No. 8 (August 1983), pp. 24–29.

Graves, Desmond. *Diagnosis and Change.* New York: St. Martins Press, 1986.

Greenlaw, Paul S., and John P. Kuhl. "Selection Interviewing and the Uniform Federal Guide-

lines," *Personnel Administrator,* Vol. 25, No. 8 (August 1980), pp. 74–80.

Heskett, J. L. "Lessons in the Service Sector," *Harvard Business Review,* Vol. 65, No. 2 (March–April 1987), pp. 118–126.

Hostage, G. M. "Quality Control in a Service Business," *Harvard Business Week,* Vol. 53, No. 4 (July–August 1975), pp. 98–106.

Joseph, William. *Professional Service Management.* New York: McGraw-Hill, 1983.

Klatt, Lawrence A., Robert G. Murdick, and Frederick E. Schuster. *Human Resource Management.* Columbus, Ohio: Merrill, 1985.

Knowles, Malcolm. *The Adult Learner: A Neglected Species,* 2d Ed. Houston, Texas: Gulf, 1978.

Kotter, John P., Leonard A. Schlesinger, and Vijay Sathe. *Management of Service Operations,* 2d Ed. Homewood, Ill.: Irwin, 1986.

Latham, Gary P., and Lise M. Saari. "Application of Social-Learning Theory to Training Supervisors Through Behavior Modeling," *Journal of Applied Marketing,* Vol. 64, No. 3 (1979).

Lee, James A. *The Gold and the Garbage in Management Theories and Prescription.* Athens, Ohio: Ohio University Press, 1980, Chap. 11.

Mills, Peter K. *Managing Service Industries.* Cambridge, Mass: Ballinger, 1986.

Mills, Peter K., James L. Hall, Joel K. Leidecker, and Newton Margulies. "Flexiform: A Model for Professional Service Organizations," *Academy of Management Review,* Vol. 8, No. 1 (January 1983), pp. 118–131.

Moore, Michael L., and Philip Dutton. "Training Needs Analysis: Review and Critique," *Acad-*

emy of Management Review, Vol. 3, No. 3 (July 1978), pp. 532–545.

Northcraft, Gregory B., and Richard B. Chase. "Managing Service Demand at the Point of Delivery," *Academy of Management Review,* Vol. 10, No. 1 (January 1985), pp. 66–75.

Peters, Tom. *Thriving on Chaos: Handbook for a Management Revolution.* New York: Knopf, 1987.

Pollock, Michael A., and Aaron Bernstein. "The Disposable Employee Is Becoming a Fact of Corporate Life," *Business Week* (December 15, 1986), pp. 52–53, 56.

Ross, Joel E. *Productivity, People and Profits.* Reston, Va: Reston Publishing, 1981.

Sasser, W. Earl, R. P. Olsen, and D. Daryl Wyckoff. *Management of Service Operations.* Boston: Allyn and Bacon, 1978, Chap. 6.

Schmidt, Frank L., and John E. Hunter. "Employment Testing: Old Theories and New Research Findings," *American Psychologist,* Vol. 36, No. 10 (October 1981), pp. 1128–1137.

Schneider, Benjamin. "The Service Organization: Climate is Crucial," *Organizational Dynamics,* Vol. 9 (Autumn 1980), pp. 52–65.

Schuster, Frederick E. *The Schuster Report.* New York: Wiley, 1986.

Schwartz, Howard, and Stanley Davis, "Matching Corporate Culture and Business Strategy," *Organizational Dynamics,* Vol. 10 (Summer 1981), pp. 30–47.

Sigafoos, R. A., and R. R. Easson. *Absolutely Positively Overnight!* Memphis, Tenn.: St. Luke's Press, 1988.

Uttal, B. "Companies that Serve You Best," *Fortune* (December 7, 1987), pp. 98–116.

9

SUPPLEMENT

Work Measurement in Services

INTRODUCTION

One of the problems faced by human resource managers in Chapter 9 is the effective use of service personnel. Good management means knowing what can be expected from employees, and that requires some sort of labor standards. Such standards are needed to determine

— Labor content of the service performed (labor cost)

— Staffing needs of the organization (how many people are needed on duty to meet customer demands)

— Cost and time estimates prior to performing services (to assist in a variety of decisions)

— Productivity expectations (both supervisor and employee should know what constitutes a fair day's work)

— Basis of wage-incentive plans (what provides a reasonable incentive)

— Efficiency of employees (a standard is needed against which efficiency is determined)

Properly set labor standards represent the amount of time it should take an average employee to perform specific job activities under normal working conditions.

How are labor standards set? There are three major ways:

— Time studies
— Predetermined time standards
— Work sampling

This supplement covers each of these techniques.

TIME STUDIES

The classical stopwatch study, originally proposed by Frederick W. Taylor in 1881, is still a widely used time-study method. A **time-study procedure** involves timing a sample of a worker's performance and using it to set a standard. A trained and experienced person can establish a standard by following these eight steps:

1. Define the job to be studied.
2. Decide how many times to measure the job (the number of cycles or samples needed).
3. Break down the job into precise elements (parts of a job that often take no more than a few seconds).
4. Choose a worker to observe. Time and record how long it takes the worker to complete each element. Rate the worker's performance.
5. Compute the **average cycle time** for *each* job element:

$$\text{Average cycle time} = \frac{\text{sum of the times recorded to perform each element}}{\text{number of cycles observed}} \qquad (S9.1)$$

6. Compute the **normal time** for each job element:

$$\text{Normal time} = (\text{average cycle time}) \times (\text{rating factor}) \qquad (S9.2)$$

The rating factor, based on the performance of the observed worker, adjusts the average cycle time to what a normal worker could expect to accomplish. For example, a normal worker should be able to walk three miles per hour. He or she also should be able to deal a deck of 52 cards into four equal piles in 30 seconds. There are numerous films specifying work pace on which professionals agree, and activity benchmarks have been established by the Society for the Advancement of Management. However, performance rating is still something of an art.

7. Sum the normal times for each element to develop a total normal time for the job.
8. Compute the **standard time** for the job. This adjustment to the total normal time provides for allowances such as personal needs, unavoidable work delays, and worker fatigue.

------ EXHIBIT S9–1 ------

■ *Rest Allowances for Various Classes of Work (in percentage)*

A. Constant allowances
  1. Personal allowance   5
  2. Basic fatigue allowance   4
B. Variable allowances:
  1. Standing allowance   2
  2. Close attention:
    a. Fairly fine work   0
    b. Fine or exacting   2
    c. Very fine or very exacting   5
  3. Noise level:
    a. Continuous   0
    b. Intermittent—loud   2
    c. Intermittent—very loud   5
    d. High pitched—loud   5
  4. Mental strain:
    a. Fairly complex process   1
    b. Complex or wide span of attention   4
    c. Very complex   8
  5. Monotony:
    a. Low   0
    b. Medium   1
    c. High   4
  6. Tediousness:
    a. Rather tedious   0
    b. Tedious   2
    c. Very tedious   5

Source: Excerpted from B. W. Niebel, *Motion and Time Study,* 8th Ed. (Homewood, Ill.: Irwin, 1988), p. 393. Copyright © 1988 by Richard D. Irwin, Inc.

$$\text{Standard time} = \frac{\text{total normal time}}{1 - \text{allowance factor}} \qquad (S9.3)$$

Personal time allowances are often established in the 4 to 7 percent of total time range, depending on nearness to restrooms, water fountains, and other facilities. Delay standards are often set as a result of the actual studies of the delay that occurs. Fatigue standards are based on our growing knowledge of human energy expenditure[1] under various physical and environmental conditions. A sample set of personal and fatigue allowances is shown in Exhibit S9–1.

Time-Study Example

As an example, let us consider Management Science Associates, a firm that promotes its management development seminars by mailing thousands of individually typed letters

[1] Ernest J. McCormick, *Human Factors in Engineering and Design* (New York: McGraw-Hill, 1976), pp, 171–178; also see Haim Gershoni, "Allowances for Heat Stress," *Industrial Engineering* (September 1979), pp. 20–24.

_____ EXHIBIT S9–2 _____

Job Element	Observations (in minutes)					Performance Rating
	1	2	3	4	5	
(A) Type letter	8	10	9	21*	11	120%
(B) Type envelope address	2	3	2	1	3	105%
(C) Stuff, stamp, seal, and sort envelopes	2	1	5*	2	1	110%

to various firms. A time study has been done on the task of preparing the letters for mailing. Based on the observations in Exhibit S9–2, Management Science Associates wants to develop a time standard for the task. The firm's personal, delay, and fatigue allowance factor is 15 percent. The procedure after the data have been collected is as follows:

1. Delete all unusual or nonrecurring observations, such as those marked with an asterisk. (They might be due to an unscheduled business interruption, a conference with the boss, or a mistake of an unusual nature; these are not part of the job.)
2. Compute the average cycle time for each job element.

$$\text{Average time for } A = \frac{8 + 10 + 9 + 11}{4}$$

$$= 9.5 \text{ minutes}$$

$$\text{Average time for } B = \frac{2 + 3 + 2 + 1 + 3}{5}$$

$$= 2.2 \text{ minutes}$$

$$\text{Average time for } C = \frac{2 + 1 + 2 + 1}{4}$$

$$= 1.5 \text{ minutes}$$

3. Compute the normal time for each job element.

$$\text{Normal time for } A = (\text{average time}) \times (\text{rating})$$

$$= (9.5)(1.20)$$

$$= 11.4 \text{ minutes}$$

$$\text{Normal time for } B = (2.2)(1.05)$$

$$= 2.31 \text{ minutes}$$

$$\text{Normal time for } C = (1.5)(1.10)$$

$$= 1.65 \text{ minutes}$$

Normal times are computed for each element because the rating factor may vary for each element, which it did in this case.

4. Add the normal times for each element to find the total normal time (the normal time for the whole job).

$$\text{Total normal time} = 11.40 + 2.31 + 1.65$$

$$= 15.36 \text{ minutes}$$

5. Compute the standard time for the job.

$$\text{Standard time} = \frac{\text{total normal time}}{1 - \text{allowance factor}}$$

$$= \frac{15.36}{1 - 0.15}$$

$$= 18.07 \text{ minutes}$$

Thus 18.07 minutes is the time standard for this job.

Sampling Error

Time study is a sampling process, and the question of sampling error in the average cycle time naturally arises. Error, according to statistics, varies inversely with sample size. In order to determine just how many cycles should be timed, it is necessary to consider the variability of each element in the study.

The easiest means of finding the necessary sample size is to use standard charts such as the one in Exhibit S9–3. Such charts help estimate sample sizes that offer the user 95 or 99 percent confidence that the average cycle time from the sample will be within 5 percent of the true average.[2] To use the chart, we follow four steps.

1. Compute the average cycle time $\overline{X}$.
2. Find the standard deviation s based on the sample data.

$$s = \sqrt{\frac{\Sigma(each\ sample\ observation\ -\ \overline{X})^2}{number\ in\ sample\ -\ 1}} \qquad (S9.4)$$

3. Compute the coefficient of variation, which is just the standard deviation divided by the mean, that is,

$$\text{Coefficient of variation} = \frac{s}{\overline{X}} \qquad (S9.5)$$

[2] The sample size formula on which this chart is based is

$$N = \left(\frac{Zs}{h\overline{X}}\right)^2$$

where Z = standard normal deviate for the desired confidence coefficient
h = desired accuracy level
$s/\overline{X}$ = coefficient of variation

_____ EXHIBIT S9–3 _____

- *Chart for Estimating Sample Size with ±5 Percent Accuracy for Given Coefficient of Variation Values*

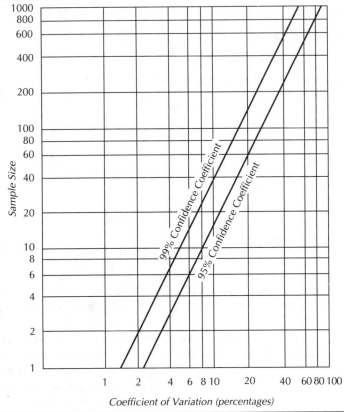

Source: A. Abruzzi, *Work Measurement* (New York: Columbia University Press, 1952), p. 161. Copyright © 1952 by Columbia University Press. Used by permission.

4. Find the appropriate coefficient of variation on the horizontal axis in Exhibit S9–3, proceed up to the curve that gives the confidence coefficient desired, and then read the sample size on the left-hand scale.

As an example, we take a sample of twelve cycles in a study of insurance data entry clerks. The result is an average cycle time of 2.80 minutes with a standard deviation of 0.56 minute. In order to be 95 percent confident that the resultant standard time is within 5 percent of the true average, we need to know whether this sample size of twelve observations is large enough.

To find the answer, we compute the coefficient of variation.

$$\frac{s}{\overline{\overline{X}}} = \frac{0.56}{2.80}$$

$$= 0.20$$

Turning to Exhibit S9–3 for a coefficient of variation of 20 percent, we see that the required sample size is about sixty cycles. Thus the sample of twelve cycles is not large enough and the observation process should continue.

PREDETERMINED TIME STANDARDS

A third way to set service labor standards is to use predetermined time standards. **Predetermined time standards** divide manual work into small basic elements that have established times (based on very large samples of workers). To estimate the time for a particular task, the time factors for each basic element of that task are added together. For any given service firm to develop a comprehensive system of predetermined time standards would be prohibitively expensive. Consequently, a number of systems are commercially available. The most common predetermined time standard is *methods time measurement* (MTM), which is a product of the MTM Association.[3] *Computerized standard data* (CSD) is a product of Rath and Strong, a management consulting firm. Predetermined time standards are an outgrowth of basic motions called **therbligs.** Therbligs include activities such as select, grasp, position, handle, fasten/loosen, move, reach, hold, rest, and inspect. These activities are stated in terms of time measurement units (TMUs), which are each equal to only 0.00001 hours or 0.0006 minutes. MTM values for various therbligs are specified in very detailed tables. Exhibit S9–4 provides, as an example, the set of time standards for the motion GET and PLACE. To use GET and PLACE (which is the most complex in the MTM system), one needs to know what is "gotten," its approximate weight, and where and how far it is placed. Two illustrations will help clarify this concept.

Pouring a Tube Specimen in a Hospital Lab

A simple example of how standard time data are developed is provided in Exhibit S9–5. The sample tube is in a rack, and the centrifuge tubes are in a nearby box. A technician removes the sample tube from the rack, uncaps it, gets the centrifuge tube, pours, and places both tubes in the rack.

The first work element involves getting the tube from the rack. Suppose the conditions for GETTING the tube and PLACING it in front of the technician are

— Weight—less than 2 pounds
— Conditions of GET—easy
— Place accuracy—approximate
— Distance range—8 to 20 inches

---

[3] MTM is really a family of products available from the Methods Time Measurement Association, a nonprofit corporation based in Fairlawn, N.J. All MTM systems are based on original research, and many of these serve specific groups of activities. For example, MTM-HC deals with the health care industry, MTM-C handles clerical activities, MTM-M involves microscope activities, MTM-V deals with machine shop tasks, and so on. In addition to the United States, there are MTM Associations in twelve countries. MTM-UAS, used in setting laboratory standards, was developed by the German MTM Association.

EXHIBIT S9–4

- *Sample MTM Table, for GET and PLACE Motions*

MTM ASSOCIATION®

UNIVERSAL ANALYZING SYSTEM

UAS

JANUARY 1984	IF TRAINING IN MTM AND UAS IS LACKING, USAGE OF THIS TABLE LEADS TO WRONG RESULTS	TIME UNITS			
		TMU	SEC	MIN	HRS
		1	0.036	0.0006	0.00001

TIME VALUES IN TMU

GET AND PLACE			DISTANCE RANGE IN IN.	<8	>8 <20	>20 <32
WEIGHT	CONDITIONS OF GET	PLACE ACCURACY	CODE	1	2	3
<2 LBS	EASY	APPROXIMATE	AA	20	35	50
		LOOSE	AB	30	45	60
		TIGHT	AC	40	55	70
	DIFFICULT	APPROXIMATE	AD	20	45	60
		LOOSE	AE	30	55	70
		TIGHT	AF	40	65	80
	HANDFUL	APPROXIMATE	AG	40	65	80
>2 LBS <18 LBS		APPROXIMATE	AH	25	45	55
		LOOSE	AJ	40	65	75
		TIGHT	AK	50	75	85
>18 LBS <48 LBS		APPROXIMATE	AL	80	105	115
		LOOSE	AM	95	120	130
		TIGHT	AN	120	145	160

PLACE	CODE	1	2	3
APPROXIMATE	PA	10	20	25
LOOSE	PB	20	30	35
TIGHT	PC	30	40	45

Source: Copyright © 1984 by the MTM Association for Standards and Research. No reprint permission without written consent from the MTM Association, 16–01 Broadway, Fair Lawn, N.J. 07410.

Then the MTM element for this activity is AA2 (as seen from Exhibit S9–4). The rest of Exhibit S9–5 is developed from similar MTM tables. Most MTM calculations, by the way, are computerized, so the user need only key in the appropriate MTM codes, such as AA2.

Computer Data Entry Analysis

As a second illustration, we may refer to Exhibit S9–6. This exhibit shows MTM coding to develop standard times for entering a computer system, providing user identification, and requesting a specific program or procedure.

Advantages

Predetermined time standards have several advantages relative to direct time studies. First, they may be established in a laboratory environment, which will not upset service activities (which time studies tend to do). Second, the standard can be set before a

───── EXHIBIT S9–5 ─────────────────────────────────────

■ *MTM-HC Analysis: Pouring Tube Specimen*

Element Description	Element	Time	Frequency	Total
Get tube from rack	AA2	35	1	35
Get stopper, place on counter	AA2	35	1	35
Get centrifuge tube, place at sample tube	AD2	45	1	45
Pour (3 seconds)	PT	1	83	83
Place tubes in rack (simo)	PC2	40	1	40
			Total TMU	238
			Total MIN	.14

Source: A. S. Helms, B. W. Shaw, and C. A. Lindner, "The Development of Laboratory Workload Standards Through Computer-Based Work Measurement Technique, Part I," *Journal of Methods-Time Measurement,* Vol. 12, p. 43. Used with permission of MTM Association for Standards and Research.

───── EXHIBIT S9–6 ─────────────────────────────────────

■ *MTM Standard Data Development for Computer Entry Task*

Code: L4　　Name: computer entry

Description	Element	Time	Frequency	Total
Enter system	UBA1	10	5	50
Password	UBA1	10	4	40
Initials	UBA1	10	4	40
User code	UBA1	10	6	60
Visual	UVA	15	1	15
Lab procedure	UBA1	10	4	40
Department procedure	UBA1	10	4	40
User code	UBA2	25	5	125
Visual	UVA	15	1	15
Work station	UBA1	10	4	40
Work sheet	UBA1	10	4	40
Visual	UVA	15	1	15
			Total TMU	520
			Stnd. minutes	0.3120

Source: A. S. Helms, B. W. Shaw, and C. A. Lindner, "The Development of Laboratory Workload Standards Through Computer-Based Work Measurement Techniques, Part II," *Journal of Methods-Time Measurement,* Vol. 12, p. 48. Used with permission of MTM Association for Standards and Research.

task is done and can be used for planning. In addition, no performance ratings are necessary—and the method is widely accepted by unions as a fair means of setting standards. Predetermined time standards are particularly effective in firms that do substantial numbers of studies where the tasks are similar. In these cases, standard data tables, tailored to the particular firm's procedures may be developed for a group of similar tasks. Some service firms use both time studies and predetermined time standard to ensure accurate labor standards.

WORK SAMPLING

The third method of developing service labor standards, work sampling, was developed by an Englishman, L. Tippet, in the 1930s. **Work sampling** estimates the percentage of time that an employee spends working on various tasks. The method involves random observations to record the activity that the worker is performing.

The work-sampling procedure can be summarized in seven steps.

1. Take a preliminary sample to obtain an estimate of the parameter value (such as percentage of time a worker is busy).
2. Compute the sample size required.
3. Prepare a schedule for observing the employee at appropriate times. The concept of random numbers (discussed in Chapter 11) is used to provide for random observation so that a representative sample of activities can be obtained.
4. Observe and record employee activities; rate the employee's performance.
5. Record the number of units produced (such as paychecks written) or services rendered during the applicable portion of the study.
6. Compute the normal time per service.
7. Compute the standard time per service.

To determine the number of observations required, management must make a statement about the desired confidence level and accuracy. But first the work analyst must select a preliminary value of the parameter under study (step 1 above). The choice is usually based on a small sample of perhaps fifty observations. The following formula then gives the sample size for a desired confidence and accuracy.

$$n = \frac{Z^2 p(1 - p)}{h^2}$$

(S9.6)

where n = required sample size

Z = standard normal deviate for the desired confidence level ($Z = 1$ for 68 percent confidence, $Z = 2$ for 95.45 percent confidence, and $Z = 3$ for 99.7 percent confidence—these values are derived from the normal table in Appendix A)

p = estimated value of sample proportion (of time employee is observed busy or idle)

h = Accuracy level desired, in percent.

Word-Processing Pool Example

To illustrate work sampling, we examine a word-processing typing pool. The head of the unit estimates the operators are idle 25 percent of the time. The supervisor would like to take a work sample that would be accurate within 3 percent and wants to have 95.45% confidence in the results.

In order to determine how many observations should be taken, the supervisor applies the equation

$$n = \frac{Z^2 p(1 - p)}{h^2}$$

where n = sample size required
Z = 2 for 95.45 percent confidence level
p = estimate of idle proportion = 25 percent = 0.25
h = accuracy desired of 3 percent = 0.03

It is found that

$$n = \frac{(2)^2(0.25)(0.75)}{(0.03)^2} = 833 \text{ observations}$$

Thus 833 observations should be taken. If the percentage of idle time noted is not close to 25 percent as the study progresses, then the number of observations may have to be recalculated and increased or decreased as appropriate.

Random Observation

To obtain the random sample needed for work sampling, a manager divides a typical work day into 480 minutes. Using a random-number table to decide what time to go to an area to sample work occurrences, the manager records observations on a tally sheet such as the one that follows.

Status	Talley	Frequency
Productively working	༔ ༔ ༔	16
Idle	||||	4

In this case, the supervisor made twenty observations and found that employees were working 80 percent of the time. So, out of 480 minutes in an office workday, 20 percent, or 96 minutes, was idle time, and 356 minutes was productive. Note that this procedure describes what a worker *is* doing, not necessarily what he or she *should* be doing.

—— SUMMARY

Labor standards are required for efficient service operations. They are needed for manpower planning, costing, and evaluating performance. They can also be used as a basis for incentive systems. Standards may be established by time studies, predetermined time standards, and work sampling. In particular, MTM-HC is gaining acceptance as a tool for setting standards that improve productivity in the health care field. Work sampling is a tool with unlimited potential in most service and white-collar jobs where service output is not easily quantified.

DISCUSSION QUESTIONS

1. What is the difference between normal time and standard time?

2. Consult a production management or reference text and locate a sample of MTM measurement tables. How do tables used in factories differ from those in clerical or hospital jobs?

3. Why do managers need labor standards?

4. Contact a service organization that uses work-measurement techniques and describe the tasks analyzed and results reached.

PROBLEMS

S9.1. An office worker is clocked performing three work elements, with the results shown in Exhibit S9–7. The allowance for tasks such as this is 15 percent.

    a. Find the normal time per cycle.

    b. Find the standard time per cycle.

S9.2. Installing mufflers at the Ross Garage in Queens, New York, involves five work elements. Richard Ross times workers performing these tasks seven times. The times are shown in Exhibit S9–8. By agreement with his workers, Ross allows a 10 percent fatigue and a 10 percent personal time factor. To compute standard time for the work operation, Ross excludes all observations that appear to be unusual or nonrecurring.

    a. What is the standard time for the task?

    b. How many cycles are needed to ensure a 95% percent confidence level?

    c. How many are needed to ensure a 75 percent confidence level?

S9.3. Sample observations of a hospital lab worker made over a 40-hour work week revealed that the worker completed a total of 320 tests. The performance rating was 125 percent. The sample also showed that the worker was busy testing specimens 80 percent of the time. Allowances for work in the hospital total 10 percent. Find the normal time and standard time for this task.

S9.4. A bank wants to determine the percentage of time its tellers are working and idle. It decides to use work sampling, and its initial estimate is that the tellers are idle 30 percent of the time. How many observations should be taken to be 95.45 percent confident that the results will not be more than 5 percent away from the true result?

S9.5. A work operation consisting of three elements has been subjected to a stopwatch time study. The observations recorded are shown in Exhibit S9–9. By

EXHIBIT S9–7

Job Element	Observations (in minutes)						Performance Rating
	1	2	3	4	5	6	
1	13.0	11.0	14.0	16.0	51.0	15.0	100%
2	68.0	21.0	25.0	73.0	26.0	23.0	110%
3	3.0	3.3	3.1	2.9	3.4	2.8	100%

EXHIBIT S9–8

Job Element	Observations (in minutes)							Performance Rating
	1	2	3	4	5	6	7	
1. Select correct mufflers	4	5	4	6	4	15	4	110%
2. Remove old muffler	6	8	7	6	7	6	7	90%
3. Weld/install new muffler	15	14	14	12	15	16	13	105%
4. Check/inspect work	3	4	24	5	4	3	18	100%
5. Complete paperwork	5	6	8	—	7	6	7	130%

EXHIBIT S9–9

Job Element	Observations (in minutes)						Performance Rating
	1	2	3	4	5	6	
A	0.1	0.3	0.2	0.9	0.2	0.1	90%
B	0.8	0.6	0.8	0.5	3.2	0.7	110%
C	0.5	0.5	0.4	0.5	0.6	0.5	80%

union contract, the allowance time for the operation is personal time 5 percent, delay 5 percent, and fatigue 10 percent. Determine the standard time for the work operation.

S9.6. A preliminary work sample of an operation indicates the following:

Number of times operator working	60
Number of times operator idle	40
Total number of preliminary observations	100

What is the required sample size for a 99.7 percent confidence level with ±4 percent precision?

S9.7. Sharpening your pencil is an operation that may be broken down into eight small elemental motions. In MTM terms, each element may be assigned a certain number of TMUs, as shown:

Reach four inches for the pencil	6 TMU
Grasp the pencil	2 TMU
Move the pencil six inches	10 TMU
Position the pencil	20 TMU
Insert the pencil into the sharpener	4 TMU
Sharpen the pencil	120 TMU
Disengage the pencil	10 TMU
Move the pencil six inches	10 TMU

What is the normal time for sharpening one pencil? Convert this time to minutes and seconds.

REFERENCES

Aft, Lawrence S. *Productivity Measurement and Improvement*. Reston, Va.: Reston Publishing, 1983.

Barnes, Ralph M. *Motion and Time Study*. New York: Wiley, 1980.

Denton, D. Keith. "Work Sampling: Increasing Service and White Collar Productivity," *Management Solutions* (March 1987), pp. 36–41.

Helms, Ashley S., et al. "The Development of Laboratory Workload Standards Through Computer-Based Work Measurement Techniques: Part III," *Journal of Methods-Time Measurement*, Vol. 12, pp. 51–54.

Karger, Delmar W. *Advanced Work Measurement*. New York: Industrial Press, 1982.

Konz, Stephen. *Work Design*, Columbia, Ohio: Grid, Inc., 1975.

Lindner, Carl A. "The Application of Computer-Based Work Measurement in a Community Hospital," Working Paper, University Community Hospital, Tampa, Florida, March 10, 1986.

Nadler, Gerald. *Work Design: A Systems Concept*. Homewood, Ill.: Irwin, 1976.

Neibel, Benjamin W. *Motion and Time Study*. Homewood, Ill.: Irwin, 1976.

10

Technology, Information, and Expert Systems

INTRODUCTION

Productivity increases in service industries have traditionally been slow because of the labor intensity of many services. In recent years, however, there has been a growing recognition of the need for research and development to apply technology to service processes. Advances in computer and telecommunication systems have provided the leading edge for this type of thinking. The purpose of this chapter is to highlight the role of technology in services by discussing principal areas where technology is having a major effect. In addition, we look specifically at new technology for information systems and the emergence of expert systems in services.

TECHNOLOGY IN SERVICES

The stereotype of a service firm is a small-scale, labor-intensive establishment with unsophisticated processes that require little or no investment in technology. This dated view of services is not supported by the evidence presented in Exhibit 10–1.[1] Exhibit 10–1a shows that the value added per employee in large service firms is comparable to that of similar manufacturing firms. Thus many services are no more labor-intensive than manufacturing. Exhibit 10–1b shows that services as a whole have the same or greater capital intensity than manufacturing. Finally, Exhibit 10–1c suggests that services have the size and capital to invest in new technology.

And, invest they do. It is estimated that in 1982 the service sector invested nearly $47 billion in new technology, a 145 percent increase over the $19.1 billion spent on new technology in 1975.[2] Further, in a recent sampling of 145 industries, nearly half of the 30 most capital-intensive industries were services.[3] One reason is that services rely heavily on communications and computer technologies, which rapidly become obsolete. This results in a shorter useful life of capital equipment in services versus manufacturing.

It also should be noted that service companies are creators as well as users of new technology. Examples are Citicorp, who helped develop and introduce the first automatic teller machines, and Federal Express, whose technology for package sorting, handling, and tracking is sought after by "sophisticated" manufacturing concerns.

Technology as a Competitive Edge

Technology is the application of scientific research to improve the practical processes of our lives. Everyday we read in our newspapers about advances in technology such as

Artificial organs	Automated language translation
Optical fibers	Space travel
Genetic engineering	Compact disks for entertainment systems

By being the first to use new technology, a firm may gain an important edge over its competitors.

Competitive edge is what distinguishes a firm from its competitors. It is an asymmetry that appeals to prospective buyers of a service. A competitive edge may

---

[1] The data for this exhibit came from the PIMS (Profit Impact of Market Strategy) database and was analyzed by Christopher E. Gagnon. The graphs appeared in James B. Quinn, Jordon J. Baruch, and Penny C. Paquette, "Technology in Services," *Scientific American*, Vol. 257, No. 6 (December 1987), pp. 50–58.

[2] Alissa D. Roberts and Eugene J. Kelley, "Technoservices and the Organizational Encounter," in J. A. Czepiel, M. R. Solomon, and C. F. Surprenant (Eds.), *The Service Encounter* (Lexington, Mass: Lexington Books, 1985), pp. 283–290.

[3] James B. Quinn, Jordon J. Baruch, and Penny C. Paquette, "Technology in Services," *Scientific American*, Vol. 257, No. 6 (December 1987), pp. 50–58.

EXHIBIT 10–1

■ *Technology Utilization by Service Companies*

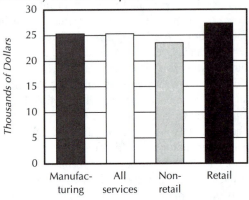

(a) VALUE ADDED PER EMPLOYEE

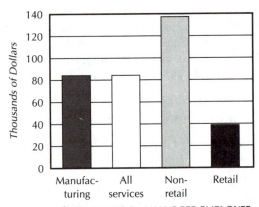

(b) GROSS BOOK VALUE PER EMPLOYEE

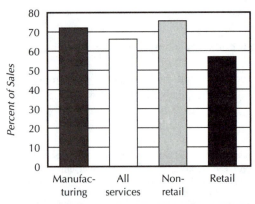

(c) MARKET SHARE OF FOUR LARGEST FIRMS

be the speed of service, increased scope of the service package, lower price for the same quality, or better "fit" to the customer.

Technology may *improve* the process of providing the service to yield a competitive edge. Technology also may change the entire process through *substitution*. In the first case, examples are wide-screen movie theaters, fiber optics to transmit information, or desk-top publishing services. In the latter case, we have electronic mail as a substitute for hard-copy mail, television as a substitute for radio, air travel as a replacement for train travel, automated car washing as a substitute for hand washing, and computer-programmed stock trading as a substitute for judgmental trading.

Companies today aggressively seek competitive advantage by monitoring new technical advances or conducting applied research themselves. Close monitoring of the market is also carried out in parallel.

Application Areas of Technology in Services

Technology applications in service industries are plentiful, as shown in Exhibit 10–2. For example, in banking, which is just one part of financial services, such technologies as EFT (electronic funds transfer), ATM (automatic teller machines), and MICR (magnetic ink character recognition) readers for encoding checks are widely used to increase productivity. Similar advances in technology are evident in government services, communication services, transportation services, education services, restaurant/food services, wholesale/retail trade, hotel/motel services, and leisure services. In health care services, technologies such as CAT scanners and fetal monitors are diagnostic in nature, while technologies such as pacemakers and dialysis machines aid in managing existing illnesses. Unlike most other services, advancements in health care have concentrated on improving the quality of care rather than on reducing its cost.

Technology may be applied at four different points in the service process. These points occur when

— Processing the customer
— Processing the customer's equipment or material
— Processing information
— Creating new services

Processing the Customer.   Processing the customer is typical of personal services such as medical, cosmetics, and entertainment. Consider a beauty shop for which we seek a competitive edge. We first identify the various factors that we can improve. Next, we ask what technology we could use to surpass our competitors. Here are some areas in which technology may be applied. We will call them *degrees of freedom.*

1. Extend hours of answering and appointment service. An answering machine combined with a computer for scheduling might be possible.
2. Improve the benefits to a customer being treated. Why not show videotapes, provide listening tapes to learn a foreign language or obtain health tips, or provide several services simultaneously?
3. Improve the nature of the materials used to provide multiple benefits.

_____ EXHIBIT 10–2 _____

▪ *Applications of Technology in Service Industries*

Service Industry	Example	Service Industry	Example
Financial services	Electronic funds transfer systems, automatic teller machines, Master card II—the electronic checkbook, IBM 3890 encoded check processor machine, pneumatic delivery systems, automated trust portfolio analysis	Education services	Personal/home computers, audio-visual machines, speak and spell/speak and read, electronic calculators, language translation computers, library cataloging systems
Utility/government services	Automated one-man garbage trucks, optical mail scanners, electronic computer-originated mail, mail sorting machines, electric power generating plants, airborne warning and control systems	Restaurant/food services	Optical supermarket checkout scanners, assembly line/rotating service cafeterias, automatic french fryer, vending machines
Communication/ electronic services	Information systems, two-way cable television, teleconferencing/picturephone, telephone switching systems, phone answering machines, word processing, paper copying machines, voice-actuated device, FAX machines, electronic data interchange	Wholesale/retail trade	Telemarketing, point-of-sale electronic terminals, dry cleaner's conveyors, automatic window washers, newspaper dispenser, automatic car wash, automated distribution warehouse, automated security systems
Transportation services	Air traffic control systems, autopilot, Boeing 747, automatic toll booths, space shuttle, containerization, France's RTV trains, ship navigation systems, Bay Area Rapid Transit system	Hotel/motel services	Electronic reservation systems, elevators/escalators/conveyors, automatic sprinkler systems, electronic key/lock system
		Leisure services	Television games, video-disc machines, movie projectors, Disney World (Hall of Presidents, Country Bear Jamboree, Circle-Vision 360), beach surf rake
		Health care services	CAT scanners, pacemakers, fetal monitors, ambulance electronic dispatching systems, electronic beepers, dentists' chair system, medical information systems

Source: David A. Collier, *Service Management: The Automation of Services* (Reston, Va.: Reston Publishing), © 1985, pp. 22–23. Adapted by permission of Prentice Hall, Inc., Englewood Cliffs, New Jersey.

4. Provide music with subliminal messages to make the client more restful when the work is complete.
5. Improve the skills of the workers. Technology such as videotapes and programmed learning may be possible.
6. Substitute equipment or do-it-yourself steps for some treatments.
7. Add gifts as part of the benefits package that extend the treatments, provide additional treatments, or provide gift-satisfactions.

In other words, in our search for degrees of freedom, we try to find all the dimensions of a particular service and then select one or more to improve in order to surpass our competition. Technology can often be applied to keep us ahead.

Technology also can help us process the customer more rapidly by streamlining the beginning stages of the service process. Computer therapists, for example, now replace or supplement the human kind in many workplaces where troubled workers need help in sorting through problems and causes of stress. In one program, the role of a human therapist is limited to evaluating the employee's progress at various stages through ten one-hour computer sessions and recommending treatment alternatives.[4] As another example, shown in Exhibit 10–3, First Nationwide Bank responds to telephone inquiries with a complex switching system that guides the customer to the right service representative. The next step would involve handling customer requests with further automated equipment. Perhaps a change of mailing address could be voice-entered directly into the computer.

Processing the Customer's Materials. The second area on our list of technology applications involves processing a customer's equipment or materials. Photoprocessing, dry cleaning, car washing, or many industrial services are examples. Let us try to develop a set of degrees of freedom to which technology may be applied to photoprocessing.

1. Improve the developing solution to give clearer, better color photographs.
2. Improve the process as a system to develop photos in a shorter time.
3. Improve the process to develop enlarged or reduced photos.
4. Develop new presentations such as photos on the sides of coffee mugs, embedded in clear plastic cubes, embedded in flexible plastic cards, and so on.
5. Lower the cost.

In the abstract, the degrees of freedom for this example are quality, time, size, form of presentation, and cost.

A prominent example of new technology applied to the processing of a customer's "money" is the automatic teller machine. ATMs have revolutionized the handling of cash and other banking transactions. For instance, Girard Bank of Philadelphia was able to close eighteen of its full-service branches by installing 200 ATMs at supermarkets and other stand-alone sites. The closings saved sufficient funds to totally defray the $5.4 million in costs associated with the ATM program and, at the same time, increased the availability of banking services by 50 percent.[5]

ATM-like machines are now available for retail shopping, too. NCR recently unveiled a freestanding computer terminal that shoppers can use to purchase items without having to encounter a sales clerk. The terminal displays on a screen items that

[4] "Troubled Workers Confide in Computer," *Roanoke Times and World News* (January 1, 1989), p. D7.
[5] As reported in J. L. Heskett, *Managing in the Service Economy* (Boston, Mass.: Harvard Business School Press, 1986), p. 161.

EXHIBIT 10–3

▪ *First Nationwide Bank Loan Service Department Self-Service Telephone System*

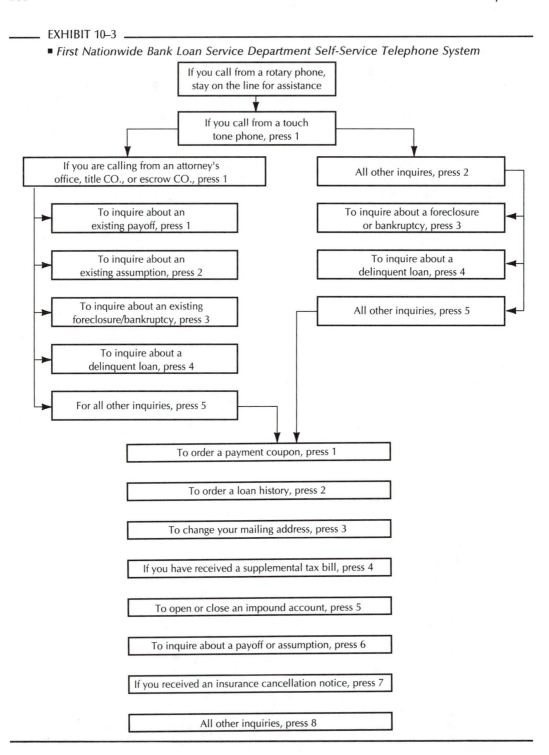

shoppers can purchase by inserting a credit card. The order is automatically shipped to the customer's home.

As another example, the rapid processing of customers' merchandise in the retail industry has gone beyond bar-coded price tags and UPC codes. Imagine wheeling a shopping cart through your local supermarket, picking items off the shelves, and having a device register their price as you put them into the cart. When you get to the checkout counter, all the clerk has to do is add the tax, total your bill, and collect your money. This high-tech shopping cart, also produced by NCR, is now available for your local supermarket![6]

Processing Information.   The third area where technology may be applied to improving services is data and information processing. This topic is so important that we will take it up in more detail later in the chapter. At this point, what degrees of freedom for information processing can you think of that can be improved through the application of technology?

Basically, information comes into a firm, is edited, and is converted to a standard form. Multiple copies are prepared and distributed to different work sequences where operations are performed. The copies finally end up in files, are sent to some outside agency such as a customer or vendor, or are destroyed. Some opportunities for increasing the level of technology are electronic document interchange, computer-to-copier reproduction, and the automatic generation of orders as electronically monitored needs are detected.

Current levels of information technology allow rapid replenishment of goods for retail establishments. For example, the successful Wal-Mart discount chain uses scanners, point-of-sale terminals, computerized inventory and forecasting systems, satellites, and its own trucking fleet to stock its shelves within thirty-six hours of a computer-detected need for an item.[7] K-Mart stores transmit sales information from store cash registers to K-Mart headquarters via satellites 22,300 miles over head. Credit card purchases can be authorized in three seconds.[8]

The impact of information technology on the selling process is further evidenced by the following account:[9]

> I have one client, a distribution outfit, that has issued PCs to all its sales people and put cellular phones in all their cars. Before visiting a client, the sales person taps the PC for up-to-date client information, such as order status, discount levels, order history, names, etc. As soon as the sales rep leaves the client, he or she plugs the PC into the cellular phone and transmits order information while driving to the next customer or back to the office. By the time the sales rep gets to the home office, the orders are made up and ready to check. This is better service than the customer can get anywhere else.

---

[6] The two NCR examples are from Lena H. Sun, "Retailing's High-Tech Revolution," *The Washington Post* (February 12, 1989), pp. H1 and H5.

[7] John Huey, "Wal-Mart, Will It Take Over the World?" *Fortune* (January 30, 1989), pp. 52–53.

[8] Lena H. Sun, "Retailing's High-Tech Revolution," *The Washington Post* (February 12, 1989), pp. H1 and H5.

[9] Excerpted from M. Victor Janulaitis, "Gaining Competitive Advantage," *Infosystems* (October 1984), pp. 56–58.

What *new* developments for information processing can you envision? One that is waiting in the wings is the "smart" credit card.[10] In the 1970s, the magnetic-stripe plastic card was a technological wonder, allowing merchants to verify a cardholder's credit status instantly and banks to replace tellers with automatic cash-giving machines. Now the "smart" credit card is emerging with a built-in microprocessor and memory chip. These cards, coupled with electronic cash registers and communications networks, can record a customer's purchase and debit the customer's bank account automatically, thus eliminating the need for bank checks at point of sale. Eventually, "smart" cards will replace coin-operated public telephones and simplify billing for long distance calls as well.

Another important use of the "smart" card is as a medical record to be carried by an individual. Each card contains a chip that gives a person's entire medical history. In the event of an emergency, the hospital can quickly obtain all data necessary for admission, including insurance information.

Creating New Services.   Finally, technology may create completely new services through development of new products or processes. The development of television created the services of television programming and broadcasting, and, later, cable TV. The invention of VCRs brought with it the era of video rental stores. And think of all the services created by the introduction of the computer! Later in this chapter we discuss new service opportunities in database systems, information systems, and telecommunications.

Levels of Technology

Technology or automation of services can be applied at different levels of sophistication. Progression from a low degree of technology (say, level 0) to a high degree of technology (say, level 4) is not necessarily good or bad in and of itself. A computer program that evaluates consumer loan applications may be highly efficient, but it may also add to the impersonal, uncaring image of a bank and cause it to lose customers. Technology usually improves productivity. A firm just has to make sure the quality of the entire customer service process is improved as well.

Exhibit 10–4 shows how different levels of technology can be applied to washing a car. In Exhibit 10–4a at automation level 0, the car is washed completely by hand. At level 1 in Exhibit 10–4b, automated tools are available to help wash the car. For example, wands are used that can pulsate different amounts of water or soap. In Exhibit 10–4c, technology reaches level 2 when the car is washed completely by an automated car wash. Drying is still manual (or the car can be air-dried and this step eliminated). Payment has been automated.

A more general evaluation of technology levels is provided in Exhibit 10–5. This exhibit describes degrees of sophistication of information technology for three areas of a business: order entry, operations, and administration. Examining adminis-

---

[10] For more information, see Martin Moyer, "Here Comes the Smart Card," *Fortune* (August 8, 1983), pp. 74–79; and "Credit Cards: The U.S. Is Taking Its Time Getting Smart," *Business Week* (February 9, 1987), p. 88.

EXHIBIT 10–4

▪ *Technology Profile for Washing a Car*

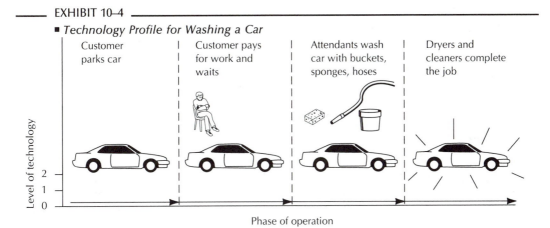

(a) MANUAL WASHING, LEVEL 0

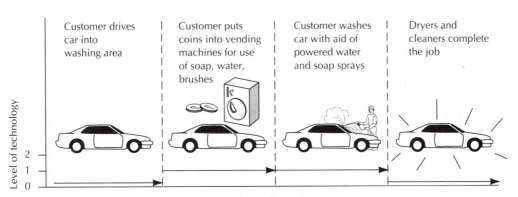

(b) PARTIALLY AUTOMATED WASHING, LEVEL 1

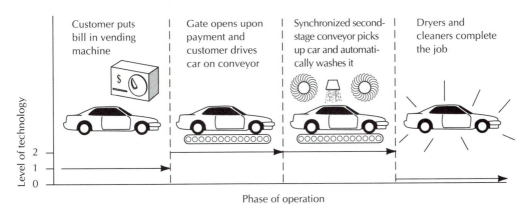

(C) COMPLETELY AUTOMATED WASHING, LEVEL 2

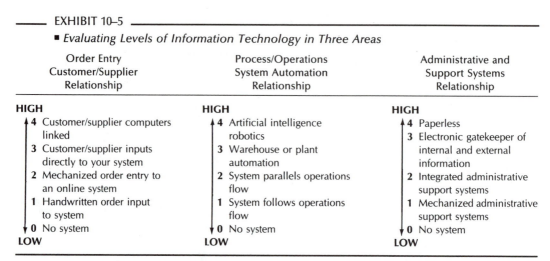

_____ EXHIBIT 10–5 _____

■ *Evaluating Levels of Information Technology in Three Areas*

Order Entry Customer/Supplier Relationship	Process/Operations System Automation Relationship	Administrative and Support Systems Relationship
HIGH	**HIGH**	**HIGH**
4 Customer/supplier computers linked	**4** Artificial intelligence robotics	**4** Paperless
3 Customer/supplier inputs directly to your system	**3** Warehouse or plant automation	**3** Electronic gatekeeper of internal and external information
2 Mechanized order entry to an online system	**2** System parallels operations flow	**2** Integrated administrative support systems
1 Handwritten order input to system	**1** System follows operations flow	**1** Mechanized administrative support systems
0 No system	**0** No system	**0** No system
LOW	**LOW**	**LOW**

Source: Adapted from "ISM Interviews . . . M. Victor Janulaitis." Reprinted from *Journal of Management Information Systems,* Fall 1986 (New York: Auerbach Publishers). © 1986 Warren, Gorham & Lamont, Inc. Used with permission.

trative systems, we can see that the levels of technology vary from a low technology rating of 0 for no system to a rating of 4 for a paperless system.

In assessing opportunities for advancement in technology, service firms should first chart their current processes, identify bottlenecks, and look for steps with low levels of technology as candidates for automation.[11] Then, a careful cost-benefit analysis should be performed taking into account specific pieces of equipment and the impact on both service productivity and service quality.

INFORMATION SYSTEMS

Information systems contain products and services for processing data or information. The product or service may be used to generate, record, store, destroy, manipulate, or transmit information. In Exhibit 10–6 we provide a matrix that classifies information products or services according to whether they are directed toward information content or toward transmitting information. Note the predominance of both products and services that merely transmit information. The information services shown in Exhibit 10–6 may be provided by independent service companies, they may appear as support departments within companies, or they may be an integral part of company operations.

Data versus Information

Data consist of facts or uninterpreted observations. They may take the form of words, numbers, or strings of characters. Although the terms data and information are often

_____

[11] Charting can take the form of process flowcharts, as shown in Chapter 5, or technology profiles, as shown in Exhibit 10–4.

EXHIBIT 10-6

■ *A Classification of Information Services*

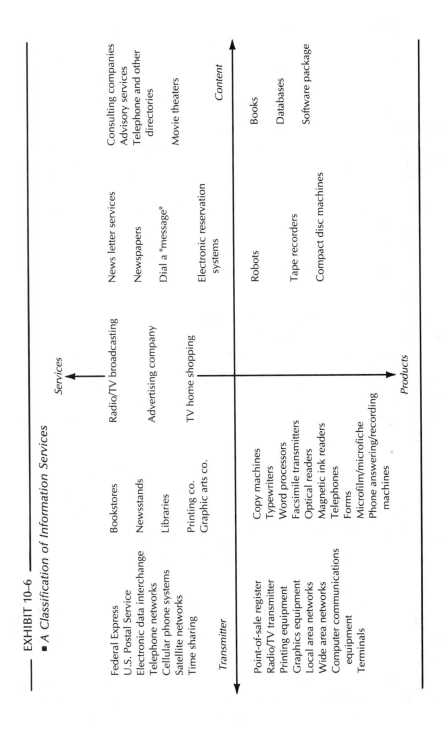

	Services		
Transmitter			
Federal Express	Bookstores	Radio/TV broadcasting	News letter services
U.S. Postal Service	Newsstands		Newspapers
Electronic data interchange	Libraries	Advertising company	Dial a "message"
Telephone networks			
Cellular phone systems	Printing co.		Electronic reservation systems
Satellite networks	Graphic arts co.	TV home shopping	
Time sharing			

Content:
Consulting companies
Advisory services
Telephone and other directories
Movie theaters

Books
Databases
Software package

Products:
Point-of-sale register
Radio/TV transmitter
Printing equipment
Graphics equipment
Local area networks
Wide area networks
Computer communications equipment
Terminals

Copy machines
Typewriters
Word processors
Facsimile transmitters
Optical readers
Magnetic ink readers
Telephones
Forms
Microfilm/microfiche
Phone answering/recording machines

Robots

Tape recorders

Compact disc machines

293

used interchangeably, data are best viewed as raw material that can be processed into useful information for managers or other users. **Information** is therefore data that have been transformed into a useful and meaningful form for decision-making needs.

Database Services

The types and numbers of businesses selling data and information are growing steadily, giving rise to an industry referred to as "the information vending machine."[12] One of the earliest types of databases developed provides financial information on a large segment of publicly owned corporations. COMPUSTAT covers the Standard and Poors listing. COMPUSERVE, Inc. provides information on more than 10,000 publicly owned companies. Dow Jones News Retrieval provides general business and security information to corporate users via AT&T Information Systems' Net 1000. Telerate sells information on commodities and securities prices. Dun & Bradstreet sells credit and miscellaneous business information. Collectors Data Services is an international listing for collectors and connoisseurs of the world's most sought-after collectibles.

The most difficult part of entering the information and database business is determining exactly what will sell. This is no different from introducing any new product or service. However, the cost of introduction may be very high, and the result is usually a clear go or no-go. It is important to identify a clear market segment and then get there first. Customers tend to be very loyal, and there is little room for a new competitor. Once a company has built a database, it can be expanded to customize services for specific market segments. Aggressive selling is required. For example, the Institute for Scientific Information in Philadelphia indexes articles for about 300,000 customers and has access to over 7000 scientific and medical formulas. The company spends at least 15 percent of sales on marketing the service, primarily on seminars for customers.

Forms of Information Systems

Transaction Processing System.   Information systems appear in a number of different forms that may enhance the productivity of services. The most basic form is the computerized **transaction processing system** (TPS). All firms must record economic events within the firm in the various functional areas. When the recording of these events is linked into preplanned systems and supported by computerized processing and storage, we have a computer-based transaction system. To the extent that such systems can be automated beyond those of competitors, a competitive edge such as speed of order processing, speed of actual service, or improvement in accuracy may be achieved. For example, Security Pacific National Bank in Los Angeles was the first to develop a computerized system providing daily automatic reconciliation for automatic banking.

Management Information System.   A second form of information system is the **management information system** (MIS). This system is concerned with getting appropriate information to managers when they need it, in a readable format.

---

[12] A. C. Gross, "The Information Vending Machine," *Business Horizons* (January–February 1988), p. 24.

Both MIS and transaction processing systems appear as internal services. However, it is fairly common for small businesses of all kinds to subcontract portions of their transaction and information systems work. For example, payroll and general accounting functions may be subcontracted to a computer service company. MIS in the form of monthly financial analysis and statements is also commonly performed by outside companies. However, with the development of powerful PCs and the availability of sophisticated software packages, the subcontracting of MIS services is on the decline.

Decision Support System. A third form of information system is the **decision support system** (DSS). A DSS goes one step further than an MIS by aiding the manager in making decisions, rather than simply providing the information. It is an interactive, user-friendly computer-based system that utilizes both data and mathematical models to help solve unstructured or semistructured problems. The ability of the user to query the DSS concerning the effect of different potential scenarios of a decision (called "what if" analysis) is an important attribute of decision support systems.

Consider the following example of a DSS used by the vice president for management services at Florida Power and Light:[13]

> I had a telephone call about a quarter of five on a Tuesday afternoon relative to some information I was going to need at a meeting the next morning. The staff had just left for the evening. I was able to go to the terminal and compare some payroll information from Florida Power and Light with several other companies. From the COMPUSTAT database I had access to 20 years of payroll data from all utilities. I was able to put in parameters on what I wanted to look at—companies with nuclear plants (as we have) and companies that are over a certain size by number of customers and kilowatt hours produced annually. In a few seconds I had a list of 23 utility companies that met the criteria. There was one other company I also wanted to include, so I keyed that company in.
>
> I asked the terminal to do a calculation: I wanted to know what the average payroll was per employee among those utility companies. It takes longer to tell about it than it took to do it. I got back the average figures for as many years as COMPUSTAT had data from the companies. I had the information in my hands in 20 minutes and was able to go home and look it over quietly that evening. There I added the numbers together and produced some averages, which took me another 30 minutes.
>
> The next morning it took me 25 minutes with the manual and interactive facility to produce a new graph of the data. I decided then to plot the data for only five years. On one graph I was able to show Florida Power and Light compared with the average of 24 selected companies, with the average of 8 selected companies, as well as with the high and low companies.
>
> Developing this kind of information would have taken weeks without the system. Moreover, it allowed me to refine my own thinking as I proceeded, depending on the significance of the numbers I generated.

The power of a "what-if" capability is further illustrated in the following unusual application of a DSS:[14]

---

[13] Efraim Turban, *Decision Support and Expert Systems: Managerial Perspectives* (New York: Macmillan, 1988), p. 134.

[14] Efraim Turban, *Decision Support and Expert Systems: Managerial Perspectives* (New York: Macmillan, 1988), p. 11.

Ten years ago, Rachelle Laboratories, Inc. (Long Beach, CA), a competitor of Pfizer, began selling an antibiotic called Doxychel, which was the same drug as Pfizer's Vibramycin. Pfizer contended that its patent had been violated.

The disagreement came to a head in the winter of 1983 in a district court in Honolulu. Throughout the six-week trial, however, Pfizer had an edge over Rachelle. Pfizer had a DSS. Jeffrey Landau, manager of DSS of Pfizer, recalls: "We put together a team of lawyers, system-staff professionals, and others, and built a model." The model, he says, looked at one key "what-if." If Rachelle hadn't started selling Doxychel, how much more money would Pfizer have made? The answer, of course, depended on two assumptions. One was that all Rachelle's sales were at Pfizer's expense. The other was that, without Rachelle as a competitor, Pfizer could have sold its antibiotic at a higher price.

Armed with these assumptions, the Pfizer team set up, three blocks from the courthouse, a DSS war room, complete with terminals, printers, plotters, and high-speed communication to a DEC System-10 mainframe in Connecticut. With the system in place, the opposition could not stall for time by requesting additional information. Pfizer's system accessed the requested information instantly.

When the trial got under way, however, Pfizer's decision-support system was really put to the test. "We could measure the impact of claims witnesses made about the market. Using the information provided, the lawyers would yield on points that were determined to be insignificant. If the other side made a claim that had big monetary implications, our lawyers would fight it." In effect, the Pfizer team used the model to plan its legal tactics.

The result: On June 30, 1983, Judge Martin Pence, who frequently alluded to Pfizer's model, awarded Pfizer $55.8 million. It was the largest judgment on a patent-infringement suit in U.S. history.

Decision support systems have been developed for a wide range of applications, including[15]

— University tuition and fee policy analysis
— Portfolio management
— Strategic planning
— Real estate management
— Airline scheduling, pricing, and fuel usage
— Student financial aid

Expert System.   A fourth type of information system is an expert system (ES). Simply put, an **expert system** is a computer program that mimics the behavior of an expert. Experts can solve difficult problems, explain the result, learn from experience, restructure their own knowledge, and determine the relevance of certain data in making decisions. They also know what they do not know. Current expert systems can do a good job of mimicking an expert's ability to solve problems. Most systems are also able to explain their decisions by backtracking through the logic used to arrive at a conclusion. And some expert systems have limited learning capabilities. The remaining

---

[15] These applications and more are described in Efraim Turban, *Decision Support and Expert Systems: Managerial Perspectives* (New York: Macmillan, 1988).

——— EXHIBIT 10–7 ———————————————————————————————————

■ *Structure of an Expert System*

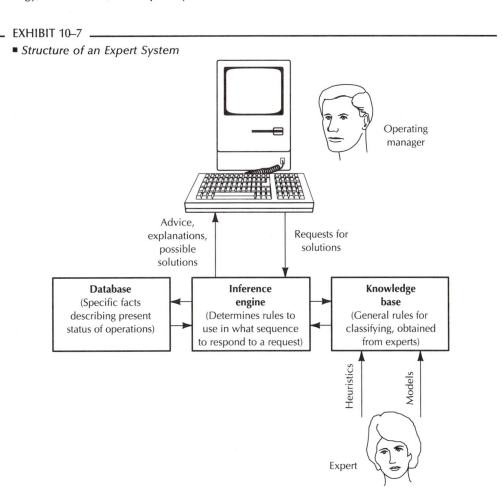

attributes of experts—knowledge restructuring, determining the relevance of data, and recognizing a lack of knowledge—have yet to be incorporated into expert systems.[16]

An expert system generally consists of three elements—a database, a knowledge base, and an inference engine, as depicted in Exhibit 10–7. The database contains facts that are specific to the problem. The knowledge base contains heuristics or ''rules of thumb'' that experts use to solve particular problems. The inference engine is an electronic representation of the expert's thought process. It provides the reasoning strategy that allows problems to be solved by determining when and how to use the facts and rules in the database and knowledge base. Applications of expert systems to services are numerous and are discussed in the next section.

---

[16] From Dorothy Leonard-Barton, and John Sviokla, ''Putting Expert Systems to Work,'' *Harvard Business Review*, Vol. 66, No. 2 (March–April 1988), p. 93.

Exhibit 10–8 lists various attributes of the four types of information systems we have presented. Note that all four information technologies, TPS, MIS, DSS, and ES, are interrelated, and each supports a different aspect of managerial decision making. For instance, as we move from transaction processing systems to expert systems, the focus of each system changes from data to information, to decisions, to inference. The types of problems addressed also progress from no problem to structured problems and from semistructured problems to unstructured problems. The four information technologies serve different levels of management and different purposes (expediency, efficiency, or effectiveness) as well.

_____ EXHIBIT 10–8 _____

■ *Attributes of Computerized Information Systems*

Dimension	Transactions Processing Systems (TPS)	Management Information Systems (MIS)	Decison Support Systems (DSS)	Expert Systems (ES)
Applications	Payroll; inventory; record keeping; production and sales information	Production control; sales forecasting; monitoring	Long-range strategic planning; complex integrated problem areas	Diagnosis; strategic planning; internal control planning; maintenance strategies; narrow domain
Focus	Data transactions	Information	Decisions; flexibility; user-friendliness	Inferencing; transfer of expertise
Database	Unique to each application; batch update	Interactive access by programmers	Database management systems; interactive access; factual knowledge	Procedural and factual knowledge; knowledge base (facts, rules)
Decision capabilities	No decision or simple decision models	Structured routine problems using conventional operations research tools	Semistructured problems; integrated *or* models; blend of judgment and structured support capabilities	Complex decisions, unstructured; use of rules (heuristics)
Manipulation	Numerical	Numerical	Numerical	Symbolic
Type of information	Summary reports; operational	Scheduled and demand reports; structured flow; exception reporting	Information to support specific decisions	Advice and explanations
Highest organizational level served	Submanagerial; low management	Middle management	Top management	Top management and specialists
Impetus	Expediency	Efficiency	Effectiveness	Effectiveness and expediency

Source: Reprinted with permission of Macmillan Publishing Company from *Decision Support and Expert Systems: Managerial Perspectives* by Efraim Turban, p. 16. Copyright © 1988 by Macmillan Publishing Company.

APPLICATIONS OF EXPERT SYSTEMS TO SERVICES

The use of expert systems provides several advantages that are especially appropriate for service industries. An expert system can

1. *Make decisions faster than a knowledgeable employee.* This is important for services trying to minimize customer waiting time. For example, American Express Company (AMEX) uses an expert system to help its credit authorization staff sort through data from as many as thirteen databases. The American Express credit card has no set spending limit. This feature is important for competitive reasons, but determining the credit level for each customer poses a stiff administrative challenge. Each time the customer makes a large purchase, the merchant telephones AMEX to authorize the charge. The AMEX employee then has to make a quick judgment call. Authorization requests outside the normal buying pattern require a search of the databases for more information. Now the Authorizer's Assistant ES performs that search and makes recommendations to the person who makes the authorization decision. The entire process takes only seconds; the merchant is still on the phone.[17]

2. *Make expert advice available to numerous nonexpert employees at geographically dispersed locations.* The decentralization of services and the high cost of "duplicating" experts at numerous locations makes the transferability of ES attractive to many services. Consider the following example.[18]

> Daphne Young, the senior vice president of Western Central Bank, was trying to take advantage of new opportunities in the rapidly expanding eastern suburbs of Los Angeles. The bank just opened many branches, and loan generation opportunities were mounting because of the influx of new businesses. To handle all these loan applications, many of which were complex commercial ones, it was necessary to have experienced loan officers. Such people were just not available at the bank or at its various divisions.
>
> Training local people quickly to become loan officers was out of the question, because the judgment and expertise required to properly evaluate complex loan applications may take years to acquire. Young thought that if she could only provide each outlying branch with an expert loan officer (having about ten years of experience), her problem would be solved.
>
> Said Young, "I need an expert system to diagnose the condition of a company that is requesting a loan. I will then have all the expert diagnosticians [loan officers] I need packaged in a computer disk that can be in all outlying locations. Then the bank would be able to train local people in weeks instead of years."
>
> And that's what happened! An expert system was developed that helped novice loan officers to interpret the meanings of financial ratios and recommend corrective action to qualify for a loan.

3. *Increase the quality and consistency of decisions.* Many service-related decisions involve judgment and subjective evaluations of people and situations. Expert

---

[17] From Dorothy Leonard-Barton and John Sviokla, "Putting Expert Systems to Work," *Harvard Business Review*, Vol. 66, No. 2 (March–April 1988), p. 92.

[18] Efraim Turban, *Decision Support and Expert Systems: Managerial Perspectives* (New York: Macmillan, 1988), pp. 493–509.

systems can work with incomplete information and degrees of uncertainty. For example, in Fairfax County, Virginia, the fire department has an expert system to help diagnose chemical spills on the beltway (I-495). Prior to the ES, the department had to call Atlanta, describe the conditions, and ask for advice.

Often, in emergency situations, high-quality decisions are needed when the human expert is the most stressed or fatigued. Expert systems, in these cases, can be used to verify the quality and consistency of decisions. Reading 10.1 describes such an expert system application to hostage taking.

4. *Be used as an effective training tool.* This is especially appropriate as a substitute for experience when training personnel for tasks that are somewhat ambiguous. Examples are medical diagnosis, criminal investigations, and employee selection and promotion. Expert systems are also used to diagnose deficiencies in employee readiness for certain tasks or positions and to customize computer-aided instruction for an employee or student.

5. *Handle important but routine jobs, thereby freeing up experts for more strategic decisions.* Among the most promising areas of application for expert systems are mundane tasks that are common to many services, especially those processing information. Examples are contracting, negotiating, underwriting, auditing, and any other jobs that currently make use of complex questionnaires. ExperTAX, developed by Coopers and Lybrand, is a well-known expert system described as follows:[19]

> Tax accrual, the process of identifying tax-book differences and explaining differences between statutory and effective tax rates, is an audit task requiring specialized training, great expertise, and considerable time. Tax accrual is executed in connection with tax services provided by a CPA firm. The client's tax strategy, timely filing issues, and planning opportunities are also identified during the course of the audit. Many accounting firms have developed questionnaires, forms, or checklists that facilitate the gathering of information necessary to conduct the tax accrual and tax planning functions. These questionnaires are usually completed by staff accountants in the field and may be brought back to the office or left in the field for analysis. At the client's location, an audit manager conducts the accrual analysis, and a tax manager, either in the office or at the client's location, reviews the analysis and identifies tax planning issues and opportunities. If these issues or opportunities are significant, the case is referred to more experienced personnel, such as the tax and audit partners, for further analysis and/or interaction with the client.
>
> The process as designed seems efficient, but in practice is not. Tax accrual questionnaires are perceived by audit personnel to be long, complicated documents. On the other hand, tax professionals are concerned that such questionnaires attempt to simplify and standardize rather complex situations. Audit staff assigned to the task are concerned primarily with the tax accrual computation and may not be aware of the detailed tax planning implications of some of the information collected. Other questions clearly address tax issues that are beyond their audit expertise and, although perhaps important to the tax function, may not be directly relevant to the task at hand. Reviewing the issues may require several rounds of on-site information gathering to complete the questionnaires and answer follow-up questions. In the process of this review, the tax and audit reviewers

---

[19] Efraim Turban, *Decision Support and Expert Systems: Managerial Perspectives* (New York: Macmillan, 1988), pp. 480–483.

must focus their expert attention on both simple and complex issues. The physical timing of this task creates considerable stress on tax planning efficiency, sometimes necessitating late hours and emergency meetings to meet critical deadlines.

ExperTAX functions as an "intelligent" questionnaire, guiding the user through the information-gathering process. It asks only questions that are relevant to the client situation, is capable of sifting through issues that require clarification, and requests additional information when needed. It is also capable of explaining to the user why a question is being asked and why the response is relevant. In addition, it keeps track of any relevant questions still unanswered and documents all the questions asked, answers given, and user-generated "marginal notes."

6. *Increase productivity.* Services are notoriously inefficient. Expert systems can increase productivity and reduce personnel. American Express's ES, Authorizer's Assistant, increased each authorizer's productivity by 20 percent, as well as significantly reducing losses from overextension of credit.[20] American International Group, Inc., the nation's seventh largest insurance company, developed an expert system for underwriting complex insurance policies at a cost of $2 million. The ES paid for itself in $2\frac{1}{2}$ years by replacing fourteen senior risk managers paid $60,000 per year.[21]

A sample of current expert system applications to different types of services is shown in Exhibit 10–9.[22] It is clear that expert systems have found bountiful applications in service industries.

TELECOMMUNICATIONS

It is generally agreed that the advent of the digital computer signaled the end of the Industrial Revolution and the beginning of the Information Age. As computing science and technology have matured, we have begun to recognize that we may have overvalued the obvious computational capabilities of computing machines and undervalued the informational capacities that they offer.[23] The next revolution in information systems will not occur in computing information, but rather in fields that *distribute* information, such as telecommunications.

Advances in telecommunications are proceeding so rapidly that it is difficult to estimate the effects on society over the next ten years. Business units and people all over the world will be drawn as close together as the people in an old town meeting. Services will appear that we do not even envision at this time. Consider how far we

---

[20] From Dorothy Leonard-Barton and John Sviokla, "Putting Expert Systems to Work," *Harvard Business Review*, Vol. 66, No. 2 (March–April 1988), p. 93.

[21] Efraim Turban, *Decision Support and Expert Systems: Managerial Perspectives* (New York: Macmillan, 1988), pp. 531–533.

[22] The information contained in this exhibit is compiled from several sources, including Efraim Turban, *Decision Support and Expert Systems: Managerial Perspectives* (New York: Macmillan, 1988), pp. 542–543; Hilary Roberts, "Expert Systems and the Personnel Department," *Personnel Management* (June 1988), pp. 52–55; Patricia Higgins, "Continental Insurance Finds a Desk for Expert Systems," *Research Review* (November 1987), pp. 31.46.1–33.29.8; Jennifer Bestor, "Using Expert Systems to Improve Lenders' Performance during Mergers and Acquisitions," *The Journal of Commercial Bank Lending* (March 1987), pp. 10–16; and Mitch Betts, "Retailers May Soon Be Sold on Expert Systems," *ComputerWorld* (October 10, 1988), p. 17.

[23] R. C. Heterick, "An Information Systems Strategy," *CAUSE/EFFECT*, Vol. 9, No. 6 (September 1986).

_____ EXHIBIT 10–9 _____

■ *Expert System Applications in Services*

Financial Services
Claims estimation
Underwriting
Credit analysis
Tax advisor
Financial statement analysis
Financial planning for individuals
Corporate financial planning
Retail bank services
Insurance contract and benefits package generator
Loan application assistant
Portfolio manager
Merger/acquisitions planner

Data Processing
Front-end to statistical analysis package
Front-end to a large software package
Database management system selection
Software services consultant

Education
Problem diagnosis training aid
Speech pathology advisor
Test result interpreter
Worksheet generation based on students' prior performance
Student behavior consultant
Learning disability classification advisor
Textbook selection advisor

Personnel Administration
Personnel evaluation assistant
Leave authorization assistant
Legal advisor
Pension scheme manager
Manager bonus evaluator
Candidate selection assistant
Job requirement/staff availability evaluator
Staff trainer

Operations
Inventory management advisor
Staff scheduler
Vendor selection assistant
Cash flow manager
Facility layout assistant
Site selection assistant
Routing and distribution advisor
Evaluator of price breaks and shipping terms
Capital investment assistant

Sales and Marketing
Expert sales assistant
Advisor on merchandise planning and distribution
Micromarketing advisor
Qualifier of sales leads
Option selection assistant

Public Services
Hazardous material identifier
Criminal psychological profiler
Medical diagnostician
Investigative advisor
Legal defense assistant
Health claims analyzer
Emergency situation advisor

_____

have come since May 24, 1884, when Samuel Morse, a New England portrait painter, tapped out the world's first telegram over a forty-mile iron wire from the U.S. Supreme Court in Washington, D.C., to the Baltimore & Ohio railroad office in Baltimore. Today, a helical wave guide may carry over 1 million or more voice channels simultaneously across the United States.

Telecommunications is the transmission of signals over long distances. These signals can include data, images, or voices. **Data communication** deals with movement of data from computer to computer. New types of service businesses, or internal company services, based on telecommunications may be derived from the following telecommunications concepts:

— Front-end hardware
— Methods channels for communicating over distance

— Common and specialized signal carriers
— Network communication systems

Front-end hardware includes items such as modems, multiplexors, concentrators, and communications controllers. A company considering providing telecommunication as a service needs to purchase such equipment, design a system with these components, and derive a cost schedule for depreciation and transmission costs.

The channels for transmission of data are cable pairs, microwave stations and relays, coaxial cable, optical fibers, and satellites.

Common carriers provide communication transport for anybody at a fee regulated by a government agency. AT&T is the largest common carrier. Specialized carriers provide customer services for certain clients at negotiated fees. The latter offers many opportunities for smaller service companies.

Network communication systems are basically local area networks (LAN) and long-distance or wide-area networks. A LAN is a high-speed data transfer system for a cluster of offices or buildings within the bounds of a single building or site. Such systems may be custom-designed, although a number of companies provide more or less standard systems with equipment.

The technology of telecommunications has been advancing at a very fast rate. This has brought down prices, opened up opportunities for service businesses to find niches between the services supplied by the giant firms, and opened up opportunities for completely new applications and services. Reading 10.2 describes the effect of advances in telecommunications on the emergence of a "global office."

TECHNOLOGY AND FUTURE SERVICES

Technology will certainly have a major impact on the types of services offered in the future. Examples of technology-enhanced services already available include the following scenarios: (1) before setting out on a shopping spree, the customer screens various stores' products and prices from his or her home television set; (2) specialized databases allow clients to sit at home and obtain the latest information or the latest advice; (3) local databases provide information on real estate, advice on stocks, names of government agencies and individuals to contact for help, and how to do home repairs; (4) college education is carried out primarily at home with two-way communication and the use of teleconferencing.

Currently, ten major newspapers, including *The New York Times* and *The Washington Post*, are available to home subscribers in electronic format. In 1982, the U.S. Postal Service began delivering electronic computer-originated mail (E-COM). Messages were sent electronically to the receiving post office, where they were printed, enclosed in envelopes, and put in the regular mail stream. The service cost 26 cents for a two-page letter.[24] Although the Postal Service has since eliminated E-COM, MCI now offers a similar service. It is not farfetched to envision government and private

---

[24] David A. Collier, *Service Management: The Automation of Services* (Reston, Va.: Reston Publishing, 1985), p. 25.

E-COM systems eventually connected to corporate computer and information centers and to any home with cable television. Currently, France is the leader in the widespread use of electronic communications. For example, in most homes in France today, there are no telephone directories. Directory assistance takes place through terminals in the homes.

Nationwide, even worldwide, electronically based information networks will dramatically change the way we communicate. Does this mean the gradual disappearance of mail carriers, mailboxes, newspapers, paper boys, and printed media? In a word—yes!

SUMMARY

Services have traditionally been known for low productivity and the difficulty of substituting machines for humans. The advancement of technology and of information equipment and systems, in particular, promises a revolution in this aspect of service management.

Technology has not only improved the processes of current services, but it has also been a source of many new services. As such, it provides a competitive edge for aggressive and entrepreneurial firms.

Technology in services may be applied to processing a customer, processing a customer's equipment or materials, processing information, or creating new services. An analysis of degrees of freedom in each of these areas is helpful in determining what aspect to exploit with new technology.

Information systems, including telecommunications, deserve special treatment in seeking competitive advantage through technology and automation. Information systems and database systems have opened up a whole new sector of services. Such services as transaction processing systems, MIS, or database resources may be either external independent services or services performed within a corporation. Decision support systems, expert systems, and other forms of artificial intelligence are rapidly being applied to services with encouraging results.

DISCUSSION QUESTIONS

1. In what ways is technology important to services?

2. Give examples of several technology applications in services. At what point in the service process are these technologies applied?

3. What is meant by "levels of technology"? Describe different levels of technology for the following services:

    a. Income tax preparation

    b. Elementary school education

    c. Food service

4. Refer to Exhibit 10–4. How would you evaluate process (a) versus (b) versus (c)? Is the most automated process the best? By what criteria?

5. Define information system. Differentiate between information and data.

6. How is a DSS different from an MIS?

7. In what ways are decision support systems and expert systems different?

8. Can a firm have all four types of information systems (TPS, MIS, DSS, and ES) simultaneously? Support your view with examples.

9. Why are expert systems particularly well-suited to services?

10. What is telecommunications? How are recent advances in telecommunications changing the way we work?

READING 10.1

An Expert System Application for Decision Support in Law Enforcement

Expert systems are developed so that human knowledge and reasoning abilities can be brought to bear on organizational or social problems by means of computers. Two especially promising fields for expert systems development are emergency management and crisis management. This paper relates our efforts to apply this new technology to the management of contemporary social problems (such as hostage taking) and thus to help law enforcement officials make better decisions. We believe that effective expert systems could ameliorate tragic incidents such as the following summarized from a news account.

> On July 23, 1984, near Tucson, Arizona, a 41-year-old woman telephoned her family doctor and threatened to kill herself and her 7-year-old son. When Pima County law enforcement officials arrived at her rural homestead, they surrounded it and tried to negotiate with the distraught mother. Her incoherent responses led officers to request a SWAT team and a psychiatrist. Before they could arrive, a shot was heard from within the home. The son walked out the front door and began to move toward the officers. The woman then came out and leveled a shotgun at the police. She was shot and killed after opening fire on the officers.

This sad story is not unusual. Domestic unrest and armed robberies are the most frequent causes of hostage taking in the United States. In these highly unstructured situations, police officers must make critical, emotionally charged decisions under conditions of high stress and great uncertainty. Furthermore, although a coherent body of knowledge on the subject is available, trained law enforcement personnel who are expert in responding to hostage-taking crises are few. These situations represent the very problems for which the calm, methodical, yet rapid reasoning of an expert system holds great promise.

DEVELOPING THE EXPERT SYSTEM

Currently, HIT (Hostage-Taking Information and Tactics) is a rule-based expert system featuring sharp, terse dialogue based on the scenario model of a hostage-taking incident. It also assists several different decision makers simultaneously. However, the system did not start out with these features.

To become familiar with the problem domain, the first author spent six weeks gathering accounts of hostage taking, most of them concerning international hijacking incidents. From these cases he induced several key situational attributes (such as the type of hijacking; the weapon (if any) used; the number, age, sex, and social status of the hostage(s); the number of hostage takers; and whether or not the hostage taker was motivated politically. These attributes then were correlated with the actions taken by responding law enforcement units

Source: Condensed from Richard G. Vedder and Richard O. Mason, "An Expert System Application for Decision Support in Law Enforcement," *Decision Sciences*, Vol. 18, No. 3 (1987), pp. 400–414. Published by the Decision Sciences Institute at Georgia State University, Atlanta, Ga. Used with permission.

and the outcomes of the incidents. This collection of incident descriptions, situational attributes, actions taken, and outcomes became the knowledge base for HIT Version Alpha. Version Alpha's typical mode of operation was simply to have the user describe the situation by answering a series of questions designed to identify relevant attributes of the incident. The system then retrieved and presented all cases in the database that matched the current situation on all or most attributes.

Although encouraged by the performance of the Version Alpha prototype, we knew that our knowledge engineering was based primarily on secondary information and that we had been relatively uninvolved in the actual processes themselves. Further progress demanded input from a real expert who currently dealt with hostage-taking situations. The expert we chose was Captain Ronald Zuniga, Commander of the Hostage Negotiation Unit of the Tucson Police Department. We asked Zuniga to evaluate HIT Version Alpha. He recommended the following revisions, many of which were incorporated in HIT Version Beta.

1. Law enforcement officials who respond to a hostage-taking incident initially have very little information. By the time they have collected enough information to describe the key situational attributes required by HIT Version Alpha, many of their action options are spent. Our error was to assume that one more-or-less global response was involved rather than a sequence of conditional responses.
2. Because of the intensity of these situations and the need for quick thinking and action, Version Alpha's long paragraphs of auxiliary text were viewed as "too academic."
3. Police procedures in hostage-taking situations establish not one but four decision makers among whom responsibility shifts as the incident unfolds. It is vital that these four decision makers coordinate their activities at all times.
4. It is necessary to provide communication among the four decision makers and to permit redundancies in the knowledge base.
5. It is essential that the system continue to provide advice needed irrespective of how officers dealt with earlier recommendations.
6. Expertise from the other three decision makers

must be added to the stored knowledge of the hostage negotiations unit commander.
7. The system should help police develop psychological profiles of both the hostage(s) and the hostage taker(s).
8. The system should be linked to external police databases such as those available at the National Crime Information Center.
9. It would be useful for HIT to provide the four decision makers with information drawn from other kinds of external databases, such as the color-coded floorplans of banks, convenience markets, and other high-risk sites.

One of our most important findings from developing Version Beta is that some of the rules which "fire" in specific states are counterintuitive and thus likely to be overlooked by typical law enforcement officers without extensive training in hostage-taking incidents. For example, the system recommends that male hostages be released before women and children. Experience shows that this tends to de-escalate the intensity and emotionality of the situation (male hostages tend to put more pressure on the hostage taker(s) who expect some "macho" act). The system urges refusing exchanges of policemen or others for present hostages. Again, experience shows that exchanges of hostages lessen the comparative power advantage of the police. Finally, HIT recommends providing material for food preparation rather than "fast" food. Experience here suggests that the activity of food preparation refocuses the hostage taker's attention, is a calming influence, and helps bind the hostage taker to the hostages in a common communal activity. These three examples represent points in an incident where untrained or forgetful officers under great stress might instinctively make a less-desirable decision. The system cautions against these decisions and explains why. This is one of the strongest potential advantages of an expert system like HIT.

TESTING HIT

We subjected HIT Version Beta to a form of public test by simulating an actual hostage-taking incident that occurred on December 12, 1983, at a Valley National Bank office in Tucson, Arizona. Members of the Tucson Police Department, the Valley National Bank, the press, and the general public were in attendance. Two classes of master's students in business also were present, with several students assuming roles as key actors in the case. All agreed that HIT provided good advice at critical points where needed and dealt adequately with most potential crisis situations as they occurred.

nience stores would benefit from exposure to the system. Thus, HIT could serve as a catalyst for improving communication and cooperation between law enforcement officials and the general public. However, new versions of HIT must be developed before the system can be considered for use in real-life hostage-taking situations.

THE FUTURE

HIT Version Beta is a successful prototype in our opinion. In its current form it can serve as a useful training tool. Both law enforcement and bank personnel believe it has considerable potential as part of a training program in their organizations. Additionally, both parties suggest that operators of retail establishments such as liquor and conve-

———— QUESTIONS FOR READING 10.1

1. Why is hostage taking an appropriate application for expert systems?

2. Why was HIT Version Alpha insufficient as an expert system?

3. List several advantages for using HIT.

4. Can you think of other areas of application in law enforcement for expert systems?

———— READING 10.2 ————

Global Office: A New Spin-Off of Technology

For the New York Life Insurance Company, the office of the future is in this rural Irish market village, where high technology has usually meant a new tractor.

New York Life came here largely because it is having trouble finding enough skilled workers to process insurance claims in the United States. Ireland, on the other hand, has a large pool of well-educated young people who need jobs and are willing to work for wages lower than those that must be paid in the United States. So since July, New York Life has been processing claims from Castleisland, using a computer link to its processing center in New Jersey.

The step puts New York Life in the forefront of the development of the "global office," the movement of office jobs abroad to take advantage of lower pay scales and other costs. The movement could have a sweeping effect on how and where white-collar work is done in the future.

Behind the development are recent improvements in telecommunications and computer tech-

nology that permit many office jobs to be performed thousands of miles from where the work is needed.

With the new technology, service industries could follow the route taken for more than a decade by manufacturing industries, which have large parts of their products made more cheaply abroad.

Corporate executives and business experts say the fast-growing services sector of the economy is ripe for such globalization. They say that the handful of companies that have already set up offices abroad, like New York Life, will be followed by many others.

Ireland has made it national policy to attract American companies seeking foreign locations for office work. In addition to the New York Life operation, which combines data entry with analysis, the Industrial Development Authority of Ireland has focused on luring companies to set up computer software operations.

Last year, for example, the Travelers Corp., a Hartford, Conn.–based insurer, opened an office in Castleroy to write software for its own use. Mc-Graw-Hill, Inc., the New York–based publishing house, last July began processing subscription renewal and marketing information for several of its magazines in Galway. Others, like Boeing and Bechtel, have also set up software development offices for their own use.

But the forces pushing corporations to send white-collar work abroad go well beyond the wage benefits, as shown by the New York Life case. With unemployment low, especially in the New York region, the company found that recruiting workers for low-level jobs like claims processing became more and more difficult. Moreover, employee turnover in claims offices in the industry is high, as much as 30 percent a year. And changing demographic trends will aggravate the problem. In the decade ending in 1995, the number of 18- to 24-year-olds in the American work force will decline by 17.5 percent.

A NATIONWIDE CHALLENGE

"The demographics make this a nationwide challenge," said John Foy, a vice president of New York Life. "American companies will find it much more difficult to find skilled workers at home for the rest of this century."

The development of the global office has been an evolutionary process. For years, many companies have moved some "back office" clerical, accounting and data-processing operations out of urban headquarters sites, where office and housing costs are high. And American executives have begun using portable computers, fax machines and the like to work from home or while traveling so they can stay in touch, electronically, with their offices.

The additional technological advances of satellite communications and transocean fiber optic cables now make it reasonable for corporations to view each of their many service functions separately and ask: Where in the world can a certain task be done most efficiently and at the lowest cost?

EXTENSIONS OF THE U.S.

"More and more, companies are looking at foreign countries as extensions of the U.S.," said Paul Coombes, a principal of McKinsey & Company, the consulting firm. "Technology has enabled corporate managements to make sourcing and location decisions internationally in ways that they could not before."

The office tasks taken abroad range from the rudimentary entering of information into a computer system to the development of software by university-trained computer scientists. The more basic functions went overseas first. For example, Saztech International, Inc., an information conversion concern that has computerized the cataloging systems of the New York Public Library and the Getty Museum, set up an operation in the Philippines in 1979. Today, Saztech employes 300 people in Manila.

"Data entry and coding can be done anywhere in the world today," said Thomas L. Reed, Saztech's chairman.

PROFIT MAKER FOR AIRLINE

Another early entrant, American Airlines, decided four years ago that it could save money by sending its ticket stubs to the Caribbean, where keyboard operators type the flight information into a computer, instead of having more costly workers do that at American's data-processing center in Tulsa, Oklahoma.

American's data-entry operation, Caribbean Data Services, is a subsidiary of the airline's parent company, AMR. Employing 1050 workers in Barbados and the Dominican Republic, Caribbean Data Services is now an independent profit maker for AMR. It handles data entry not only for the airline but also for outside customers.

BREAKING DOWN PREJUDICES

The global offices in Ireland are still in an experimental stage. But the obstacles to growth have more to do with traditional corporate views than with difficulties of adjusting to new technology, executives say.

Still, traditional prejudices often melt when executives are confronted with the economic advantages of the global office. One example: Computer science graduates in Ireland earn an average annual salary of $14,000, according to the Irish Development Authority. Their counterparts on the East or West Coasts of the United States earn twice as much.

Moreover, the unemployment rate in Ireland is at 19 percent, more than three times the level in America.

Foy of New York Life, an Irishman who emigrated to the United States twenty years ago, examined the economics of setting up in Ireland. He estimated that telecommunications charges would be three times as high in Ireland and the bill for shipping the insurance claim forms to Ireland by air would be $50,000 a year. Still, he put the cost of the Castleisland operation at 20 percent below a similar one in the United States.

When New York Life placed an advertisement in an Irish paper for 25 jobs last May, it received 600 applications. The company now employs 52 people in Castleisland, mostly Irish women in their twenties. They work as claims processors.

When the medical claims arrive in Castleis-land, workers enter the information into personal computers linked by a trans-Atlantic line to the company's data processing center in Clinton, N.J. Aided by the company's computer programs, the workers determine claims and amounts—decisions that are transmitted instantly to the United States.

QUESTIONS FOR READING 10.2

1. To date there has been no significant social or political resistance to the globalization of white-collar work. Do you anticipate any resistance in the future?

2. What are the practical limitations of internationalizing service work? What other types of services are appropriate for long-distance processing?

3. What are the disadvantages of work being performed at such a physical distance from its origination?

4. What other indications do you see of the emergence of a global work force?

CASE 10.1

The Central Tracing Agency of the International Committee of the Red Cross

Mr. Francois Perez was appointed head of the Central Tracing Agency (the agency) shortly after he returned from a nineteen-week executive program at a well-known European international management institute.

Mr. Perez had chosen to focus his initial efforts on the activities at the home office in Geneva. The computer was located in Geneva, and improving the effectiveness of the computer use was a high priority. Mr. Perez summed up the task ahead of him by saying, "We're trying to improve the productivity of a group of very skilled professional people who are providing a variety of services to a changing world where there is little prospect for certain planning."

BACKGROUND

The Red Cross is well known as an organization offering humanitarian services all over the world in times of international and noninternational conflicts, internal disturbances, and natural disasters. The founding committee, the International Committee of the Red Cross (ICRC), located in Geneva, Switzerland, provides its services in all locations of conflict. The Central Tracing Agency is part of the ICRC and is charged with the following responsibilities:

— To obtain, record, process, and, if need be, transmit all information required for the iden-

Source: Condensed from D. C. Whybark, "The Central Tracing Agency of the International Committee of the Red Cross," *International Operations Management: A Selection of IMEDE Cases* (Homewood, Ill.: Irwin, 1989, pp. 41–53. © Richard D. Irwin, Inc., 1989.

tification of persons in need of ICRC assistance, in the context of international conflicts, civil wars, and situations of internal unrest and tension.

— To transmit correspondence between captives and their families and between civilians separated from their relatives
— To search for missing persons
— To reunite families, organize transfers and repatriations
— To issue travel documents to persons without identity papers (refugees, displaced persons, political exiles) wishing to travel to a country willing to receive them or repatriate them and to provide capture, sickness, or other certificates to persons who, in order to obtain pensions or assistance, must supply evidence.

CENTRAL TRACING AGENCY ACTIVITIES

In very general terms the agency's primary task is information management. The raw material of the agency is information; it is the inventory of the organization and is the basis for the services performed. Indeed, the first charge to the agency is to gather information. The discharge of all the remaining tasks depends on what information has been gathered. The agency functions break down into three main categories. The first of these, registration, has to do with recording and storing information on prisoners, wounded persons, refugees, etc. The second function is message forwarding for military and civilian prisoners and for civilians in case of breakdown of postal communications. This requires information (on locations), as does the third function of answering requests for information on people or providing documents.

One of the key sources of information is the registration of prisoners, displaced persons, refugees, and so on. In many cases the registration of their names also provides them a guarantee of safety. Many have commented that "The Red Cross gives me hope" or "Now I cannot simply disappear. Someone knows where I am." The registrations are based on official Red Cross delegate visits to the areas of disturbance and lists of POWs provided by the detaining power. In addition to these official sources, the agency occasionally receives informal information from the prisoners, escapees,

returnees, etc. Only formal information (verified) becomes part of the official files, however. The registration file from these field sources is created by the agency.

Historically, the agency prepared registration cards which were then filed. Recently, however, the computer has been used in registration. Data entry clerks feed the information to the computer. In some applications they need to be able to read the language of the countries involved, since the basic registration forms can differ between country, delegate, and government lists. In some cases it is difficult to tell a person's name from a town name or a battlefield from a prison camp without knowing the language. The transcription situation has been helped somewhat by a standardized "capture card" which is used by internment or POW camp officials to register their prisoners. The informal information, however, can arrive at Geneva in virtually any form from scribbles on the back of a cigarette package to neatly typed columns of names.

The file not only needs to be created, but needs to be updated as changes occur. The delegates, on follow-up visits, record status changes (i.e., releases, changes of location, death, sickness, etc.) for the people they are seeing. These changes, and those which may come from the captors, need to be incorporated into the files. This is complicated by identical names, aliases, errors in recording identification numbers, and so on. The agency has developed a great deal of experience with these kinds of problems in Europe, but is faced with new challenges as the activities expand all over the world.

The registration files are the basis for nearly all agency activities. The transmission of detainee lists to the power (country) of origin, determining where to send correspondence, issuing verification certificates, and responding to requests for information all use the files. This means that the files need to be accessible for retrieving and matching information. File organization is complicated because it is difficult to envisage all possible future forms of request for information. The requests may come from inside the ICRC as well as outside. For example, the ICRC delegate's follow-up visits are facilitated when the current status of all the people to be visited is available. Even with the computer, it has not always been possible to provide this because of the shortness of time between the initial and follow-up visits.

The registration files also provide a basis for responding to requests for information from families and others concerned about a possible detainee (tracing). When requests are received, there is a need to acknowledge the request and to check and see if it contains any new information as well as to see if the request can be answered. If the case involves a current situation, then a check is made with the field for any current status changes or to get information if there is nothing in the files in Geneva. The requestor needs to be notified whether or not there is any information available. No information is given to the requestor without the permission of the sought person, however. Files are opened on the requests for which no information is available, in case relevant information is obtained later. The tracing activities can go on for decades after the conflict has ceased.

The forwarding of messages makes use of the files also. When the sender does not know the whereabouts of the prisoner, the file might provide the answer. A check for new information should be made before delivery to the field. If an answer to a message is received, it should be dispatched to the message originator.

A SPECIFIC EXAMPLE

Although the individual activities at each of the geographical subdivisions of the agency are different, there is a common thread that runs through them. The Iran-Iraq conflict will provide a specific example of the activities of the Central Tracing Agency. The Iran-Iraq "desk" is headed by Mr. Martin. A record of some of the Iran-Iraq activity is shown in Exhibit 10–10.

The Iran-Iraq group has both contract and temporary people. The data entry jobs tend to be the ones assigned to temporary persons. As the group has grown, the composition has changed as well. Of the initial eight people, only four remain. Of the four replacements, only two remain. Only some of the people leave the Red Cross; others go to the field, change geographical areas, or leave for training. The current composition of the group is as follows:

1. One desk officer coordinates work from the field and Geneva, prepares budget requests, plans and monitors work flows, and forecasts workloads.
2. Two assistants coordinate computer activity, help manage desk, and perform special projects.
3. Three executive secretaries carry out the tracing activities (case work) and message forwarding.
4. Five data entry clerks perform the computer registration and record status changes.

The data entry clerks can enter about one-hundred new computer registrations per day, but only about twenty changes in status (this results in an average of about forty entries per day, since about three-quarters of the activity concerns changes). The messages are processed about once a week and take about one-half day (largely for gathering statistics) for one executive secretary. The

_____ EXHIBIT 10–10 _____

- *Statistics on Iran-Iraq Desk Activities*

Month	Staff	Computer Registration	Tracing Requests	Messages
Jun	8	6,000	500	53,000
Dec	7	9,500	650	196,000
Feb	8	10,000	700	262,000
Apr	11	25,000	750	331,000

Note: Except for staff, cumulative totals as of month end are shown. Currently, only about 10,000 of the registrations have been entered into the computer.

executive secretaries can process about ten tracing requests per day. The actual volume they process varies greatly, depending on the nature of the requests, number of messages, and what other activities are going on. An executive secretary's effectiveness in tracing improves greatly with practice. The more experienced persons not only perform their tasks more quickly, they can handle more complicated situations.

Communications destined for the Iran-Iraq desk arrive at the main building of the International Committee of the Red Cross in Geneva. An initial screening and distribution of the documents or telephone messages is made there for later distribution to the different departments. When the documents reach the Central Tracing Agency, Miss Pic, the head secretary, reads through them and decides which specific area should receive each. Almost everything in Arabic comes to a secretary for the Mideast and Iran-Iraq desks. The secretary distributes the communications between the two desks.

When the information finally arrives at Mr. Martin's desk, he scans the documents in order to follow the trends for his desk. Somewhat more than 1000 communications related to registration and tracing activities cross his desk a month. The documents will be assigned to an executive secretary or data entry clerk, although currently there is about 1½ months' backlog of tracing requests at Mr. Martin's desk. An important step is the recording of basic statistics on volumes of work. These are used for reporting back to the countries that support ICRC activities and to help organize and estimate workloads for the desk and division.

The tracing requests are entered into a log book that is maintained by everyone in the area, and an acknowledgment letter, prepared on the word processor by the executive secretary, is sent to the requestor. Next, the computer registration list and the manual inquiry file are checked to make sure that no file has already been opened on the

person involved in the request. If not, an index card is made with the information and a file is opened. Whether or not there is any information in the files, the executive secretaries follow up with the field. They check for newer information on anything that they have found in the files, and they request information if nothing is found. They make up request letters to the field, using the word processor. Recently they have had to schedule several days in advance in order to use one of the word processors.

The executive secretaries use the log book to follow up on requests that have been sent to the field. They check the log book periodically to communicate with any requestor that is still waiting and to make sure that no request gets lost in the system. When a response does come back from the field, a letter to the requestor is prepared by the executive secretary for Mr. Martin's signature. Even in cases where the response from the field is "no information available," a letter is sent out. In all instances the log book is closed out at this time, and no other follow-up with the request is made.

_____ QUESTIONS FOR CASE 10.1

1. Examine the tasks performed by the Iran-Iraq desk. Develop a flowchart of typical activities. Can you suggest any improvements in their methods?

2. List the characteristics of an information system that would meet the agency's needs.

3. Assuming that the current activity levels are representative, how well are the Iran-Iraq desk resources utilized? Mr. Perez has requested three additional people for the Iran-Iraq desk. If his request is granted immediately, how long will it take to reduce the current backlog of registrations?

4. Why is it difficult to "plan" at ICRC? What priorities would you suggest to Mr. Perez for tackling the problems facing his agency?

_____ REFERENCES _____

"Banking on Automation," *Infosystems* (September 1984), pp. 116–119.

" 'Big Brother Inc.' May Be Closer Than You Thought," *Business Week* (February 9, 1987), pp. 84–86.

Bestor, Jennifer. "Using Expert Systems to Improve Lenders' Performance During Mergers and Acquisitions," *The Journal of Commercial Bank Lending* (September–October 1987), pp. 89–94.

Betts, Mitch. "Retailers May Soon Be Sold on Expert

Systems,'' *ComputerWorld* (October 10, 1988), p. 17.

Burns, William J., Jr., and F. Warren McFarlan. ''Information Technology Puts Power in Control Systems,'' *Harvard Business Review,* Vol. 65, No. 5 (September–October 1987), pp. 89–94.

Collier, David A. ''The Service Sector Revolution: The Automation of Services,'' *Long Range Planning* (December 1983), pp. 12–27.

Collier, David A. *Service Management: The Automation of Services.* Reston, Va.: Reston Publishing, 1985.

''Credit Cards: The U.S. Is Taking Its Time Getting Smart,'' *Business Week* (February 9, 1987), p. 88.

Field, Anne R., and Catherine L. Harris. ''The Information Business,'' *Business Week* (August 25, 1986), pp. 82–90.

Fitzsimmons, James A., and Robert S. Sullivan. *Service Operations Management.* New York: McGraw-Hill, 1982.

Gross, A. C. ''The Information Vending Machine,'' *Business Horizons* (January–February 1988), pp. 24–33.

Heskett, James L. *Managing in the Service Economy.* Boston, Mass.: Harvard Business School Press, 1986.

Higgins, Patricia. ''Continental Insurance Finds a Desk for Expert Systems,'' *Research Review* (November 1987), pp. 31.46.1–33.29.8.

Huey, John. ''Wal-Mart, Will It Take Over the World?'' *Fortune* (January 30, 1989), pp. 52–53.

Janulaitis, M. Victor. ''Gaining Competitive Advantage,'' *Infosystems* (October 1984), pp. 56–58.

Leonard-Barton, Dorothy, and John Sviokla. ''Putting Expert Systems to Work,'' *Harvard Business Review,* Vol. 66, No. 2 (March–April 1988), pp. 91–98.

Marchand, Donald A., and Forest W. Horton, Jr. *Infotrends.* New York: Wiley, 1986.

Martin, Merle P., and James E. Trumbly. ''Measuring Performance of Automated Systems,'' *Systems Management* (February 1986).

Murdick, Robert G. *MIS: Concepts and Design.* Englewood Cliffs, N.J.: Prentice-Hall, 1986.

Quinn, James B., Jordon J. Baruch, and Penny C. Paquette. ''Technology in Services,'' *Scientific American,* Vol. 257, No. 6 (December 1987), pp. 50–58.

Quinn, James B., and T. L. Doorley. ''Key Policy Issues Posed by Services,'' *Technological Forecasting and Social Change,* Vol. 34 (1988), pp. 405–423.

Roberts, Alissa D., and Eugene J. Kelly. ''Technoservices and the Organizational Encounter,'' in J. A. Czepiel, M. R. Solomon, and C. F. Surprenant (Eds.), *The Service Encounter.* Lexington, Mass.: Lexington Books, 1985, pp. 283–290.

Roberts, Hilary. ''Expert Systems and the Personnel Department,'' *Personnel Management* (June 1988), pp. 52–55.

Strassmann, Paul A. *Information Payoff.* New York: The Free Press, 1985.

Sun, Lena H. ''Retailing's High-Tech Revolution,'' *The Washington Post* (February 12, 1989), pp. H1 and H5.

Tomme, Carol Thiel. ''Reach Out and Touch Someone's Car,'' *Infosystems* (February 1984), pp. 38–40.

Turban, Efraim. *Decision Support and Expert Systems: Managerial Perspectives,* New York: Macmillan, 1988.

Wright, Jan. ''E-Mail and Voice-Mail Systems: Conspirators or Competitors?'' *Infosystems* (June 1986).

Yellowlees, Robert A. ''White Collar Productivity: The Technology Challenge,'' *Industrial Management* (March–April 1986), pp. 14–17.

PART III
Operation and Control of Services

11

Scheduling Capacity

INTRODUCTION

In this chapter we shall explore tactics for improving service by adjusting short-term capacity. Capacity can be altered by such varied techniques as extending hours, using part-time employees, cross-training employees, providing an alternative service location, increasing customer participation in the service, setting up appointment systems, or delaying the service.

FROM AGGREGATE PLANNING TO SHORT-TERM PLANNING

In Chapter 8 we discussed the aggregate scheduling of capacity. This involves establishing gross production requirements to match demand over quarters of years for the next one to three years. It also involves planning for facilities, equipment, and human resources to handle the cumulative demand over time. Exhibit 11–1a illustrates this concept simply.

In the short run—that is, day by day, week by week, and even month by month—long-term capital and human resource adjustments cannot (or should not) be made to meet fluctuations in short-term demand. In the case of intangible or perishable services, service must meet demand or sales may be lost. It is necessary, therefore, to **disaggregate** the rough-cut aggregate plan into the schedules for each type of service provided and into specific time periods. Exhibit 11–1b shows the typical disaggregated plan for a particular service.

Multiple- versus Single-Service Firms

Most service firms supply a variety of services. Restaurants, for example, supply many different meals, often grouped by time of day or night. Aggregate planning is concerned with planning for total number of meals per month. Disaggregation is concerned with scheduling the types of meals for the next day and for the week as a whole. Banks, legal firms, personal and business services, and many other types of service firms are also concerned with scheduling multiple services. In some types of firms, such as financial service suppliers, the services are not separated by time but are carried out simultaneously.

In scheduling multiple-service operations, a main consideration is the mode of delivery. That is, can one person supply all services or does each service require a specialist? In automobile repair shops, for example, a brake specialist may not be trained to do engine repair or electrical system diagnosis. Or one person may be trained to carry out only the word-processing stage of desk-top publishing.

From the preceding we see that disaggregation of total production may vary according to service and according to resources applied to production. The scheduling in each case requires attention to different kinds of things.

——— EXHIBIT 11–1 ———

- *Plans for Matching Production to Demand*

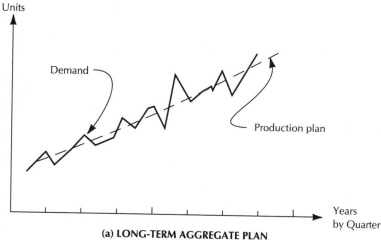

(a) LONG-TERM AGGREGATE PLAN

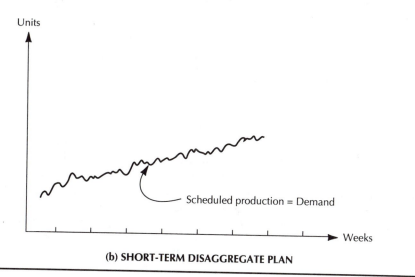

(b) SHORT-TERM DISAGGREGATE PLAN

Service Life and Inventory

Scheduling capacity to meet short-term fluctuations in demand is very similar to dealing with capacity issues for manufactured products. The difference is frequently found in the short life of service products such as newspapers, magazines, investment advisory letters, and so on. Even in short-life services, methods are available that come close to scheduling supply to meet demand while taking into account the short-term inventory.

Disaggregation may be based on the time that the stock has been in inventory. For example, a retail outlet for VCR tape rentals may disaggregate rentals on type of movie and currency of the movie; that is, rentals of recent movies are apt to have a much higher turnover than old movies.

SCHEDULING SHORT-TERM CAPACITY

Once aggregate capacity has been established, the upper limit on the rate of output is physical and the lower limit is economic. Usually only minor changes in output rate may be made in the short term. Scheduling output is therefore dependent on a limited range of system variables.

Capacity Variables

Many services are labor-intensive. And even mechanized services depend on some type of back-office human resource support. Where major fixed equipment is required, capacity is limited by the equipment. In many cases, the size of the facility (building and office space) does not allow extra workers even on a temporary basis. As exceptions, some services such as packing, delivery, and recreational services can sometimes rent or borrow additional facilities on a short-term basis.

Five means of adjusting short-term capacity are

— Increasing customer participation
— Using part-time workers
— Cross-training workers
— Extending service hours
— Providing an alternative service location.

The first, increasing customer participation, is best illustrated in fast-food restaurants such as Wendy's that offer extensive self-service hot/cold salad bars. Many Burger Kings now have self-service soft drink machines, and most fast-food establishments encourage customers to clean their tables when leaving. This concept speeds service, requires fewer employees, and provides extra capacity exactly when it is needed. Self-service gas stations are extending this concept by not only requiring the customer to pump his or her own gas, but also by providing pumps that read and process credit cards as well.

Using part-timers is, of course, a common means of supplementing regular workers during predictable peak periods in banks, restaurants, and retail stores. Especially in retail stores during the Christmas and summer school holidays, students often provide the pool of this source of capacity.

The third way of adjusting capacity is by cross-training employees to perform different tasks to meet peaks in demand. In drug stores and supermarkets, for example, stock clerks can be trained to fill in as cashiers when queues start to build up.

Time is also a variable that allows scheduling to meet peaks. Extension of hours and days of operation, as is done in retailing during the heavy shopping seasons, may be possible.

A fifth means of altering capacity is by considering place as a variable. For example, a ski resort that owns two somewhat close resort areas (say within 100 miles of each other) may handle surplus demand by transferring customers to the lesser-used facility at management's expense.

Delaying Service Delivery

In some services it is possible to introduce short-term delays and still retain the customers. An air-conditioner repairman may not be able to respond for a whole week during the busy August season, while in September repairs may be available immediately. Likewise, a prestigious consulting or law firm may be able to hold onto customers requesting service by convincing the customer that the delay is worth the wait. So when supply must be matched to the short-run demand, delaying delivery of a service encounter into the next day or week, or until capacity becomes available is one means of making the workload more uniform. Obviously, pushing a customer into a future time period is likely to lose a firm some goodwill or lower the quality of service.

Fixed Supply

In many cases, the capacity of services per time period is limited because of a fixed number of personnel supplying the service, fixed capital equipment used, or fixed facilities (such as a restaurant or theater). Two ways of dealing with customers in such cases are by use of appointments or use of queues.

Appointments and Reservations. One of the problems with appointment and reservation systems is that some people do not show up. Airlines handle this by overbooking and paying a premium to volunteers to cancel in the event too many passengers do arrive. Hotels place overbooked guests into similar quality nearby hotels at no cost to the customer. Dentists sometimes make a partial charge to no-shows, but this risks loss of the client. Many dentists and doctors call the patient the day before the appointment to remind the patient and confirm the appointment.

The appointment system is essentially a controlled queuing system. Variations in arrival, waiting, and service times are normally slight, except when overbooking (say, by a doctor) is used, when care of some patients extends beyond expected times, or when emergencies must be handled.

Queuing Systems. Queues occur in many services and in different parts of services. Queuing theory can provide information to help determine the amount of capacity needed so that waiting lines will be reasonable. It also helps establish the amount of space that should be set aside for those waiting. The next section examines queuing systems in some detail.

MANAGEMENT SCIENCE TOOLS FOR SCHEDULING CAPACITY: QUEUING AND SIMULATION

Applications of Queuing Models to Scheduling

The body of knowledge about waiting lines, often called **queuing theory,** is a valuable tool for the service operations manager. Waiting lines are a common situation—they may, for example, take the form of cars waiting for repair at an auto service center, printing jobs waiting to be completed at a print shop, or students waiting for a consultation with their professor. Exhibit 11–2 lists just a few uses of waiting-line models. Analysis of waiting-line length, average waiting time, and other factors helps to understand service system capacity.

Service operations managers recognize the tradeoff that must take place between the cost of providing good service and the cost of customer waiting time. Managers want queues that are short enough so that customers do not become unhappy and either leave without buying or buy but never return. However, managers are willing to allow some waiting if the waiting is balanced by a significant savings in capacity costs. Reading 11.1 describes how the managers of such diverse organizations as Zayre, American Airlines, Chase Manhattan Bank, and Disneyland view these tradeoffs.

One means of evaluating a service facility is to look at total expected cost, a concept illustrated in Exhibit 11–3. Total cost is the sum of capacity costs plus expected waiting costs.

Capacity costs are seen to increase as a firm attempts to raise its level of service. Managers in *some* service centers can vary their capacity by having standby personnel and machines that can be assigned to specific service stations to prevent or shorten excessively long lines. In grocery stores, managers and stock clerks can operate extra checkout counters when needed. In banks and airport check-in points, part-time workers may be called in to help. As service improves (i.e., speeds up), however, the cost of time spent waiting in lines decreases. Waiting cost may reflect lost productivity of workers while their tools or machines are awaiting repairs or may simply be an estimate of the cost of customers lost because of poor service and long queues. In some service systems (e.g., emergency ambulance service), the cost of long waiting lines may be intolerably high.

Basic Queuing System Configurations

Service systems are usually classified in terms of their number of channels (e.g., number of servers) and number of phases (e.g., number of service stops that must be made).

EXHIBIT 11–2

■ *Common Queuing Situations*

Situation	Arrivals in Queue	Service Process
Supermarket	Grocery shoppers	Checkout clerks at cash register
Highway toll booth	Automobiles	Collection of toll at booth
Doctor's office	Patients	Treatment by doctors and nurses
Computer system	Programs to be run	Computer processes jobs
Telephone company	Callers	Switching equipment to forward calls
Bank	Customers	Transactions handled by teller
Machine maintenance	Broken machines	Repairpeople fix machines
Harbor	Ships and barges	Dockworkers load and unload

_____ EXHIBIT 11–3 _____

• *The Tradeoff Between Waiting Costs and Capacity Costs*

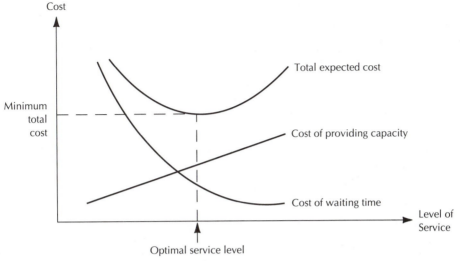

A single-channel queuing system with one server is typified by the drive-in bank that has only one open teller or by a drive-through fast-food restaurant. If, on the other hand, the bank had several tellers on duty and each customer waited in one common line for the first available teller, then we would have a multichannel queuing system at work. Most banks today are multichannel service systems, as are most large barber shops, airline ticket counters, and post offices.

A single-phase system is one in which the customer receives service from only one station and then exits the system. A fast-food restaurant in which the person who takes your order also brings you the food and takes your money is a single-phase system. So is a driver's license agency in which the person taking your application also grades your test and collects the license fee. However, if the restaurant requires you to place your order at one station, pay at a second, and pick up the food at a third service stop, it becomes a multiphase system. Likewise, if the driver's license agency is large or busy, you will probably have to wait in a line to complete the application (the first service stop), then queue again to have the test graded (the second service stop), and finally go to a third service counter to pay the fee. To help you relate the concepts of channels and phases, Exhibit 11–4 presents four possible configurations.

Measuring the Queue's Performance

Queuing models help managers make decisions that balance desirable capacity costs with waiting-line costs. Some of the many measures of a waiting-line system's performance that are commonly obtained in a queuing analysis are

EXHIBIT 11–4

■ *Basic Queuing System Configurations*

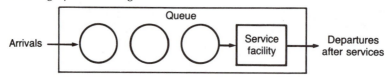

Single-channel, single-phase system

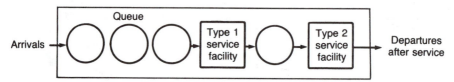

Single-channel, multiphase system

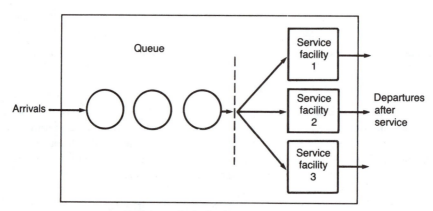

Multichannel, single-phase system

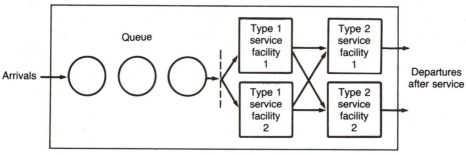

Multichannel, multiphase system

— The average time each customer or object spends in the queue
— The average queue length
— The average time each customer spends in the system (waiting time plus service time)
— The average number of customers in the system
— The probability that the service facility will be idle
— The utilization factor for the system
— The probability of a specific number of customers in the system

A Single-Channel Waiting Line

The most common case of queuing problems involves the single-channel, or single-server, waiting line. In this situation, arrivals form a single line to be serviced by a single station (Exhibit 11–4). It is often possible to assume that the following conditions exist in this type of system:

1. Arrivals are served on a first come, first served (FIFO) basis, and every arrival waits to be served, regardless of the length of the line or queue.
2. Arrivals are independent of preceding arrivals, but the average number of arrivals (arrival rate) does not change over time.
3. Arrivals are described by a Poisson probability distribution and come from an infinite (or very, very large) population.[1]
4. Service times vary from one customer to the next and are independent of one another, but their average rate is known.
5. Service times occur according to the negative exponential probability distribution.[2]
6. The average service rate is faster than the average arrival rate.

When these conditions are met, the equations shown in Exhibit 11–5 can be developed. These equations allow us to calculate the seven measures of a waiting line system's performance mentioned earlier. Note that all of the calculations are based in some way on the average number of *arrivals* per time period (λ) and the average number of customers *served* per time period (μ). The following example illustrates how this single-channel model may be used.

---

[1] The Poisson distribution is established by the formula

$$P(x) = \frac{e^{-\lambda}\lambda^x}{x!} \qquad \text{for } x = 0, 1, 2, \ldots$$

where $P(x)$ = probability of x arrivals per unit of time

      x = number of arrivals per unit of time

      λ = average arrival rate

      e = 2.7183 (which is the base of natural logs)

[2] This distribution takes the form

Probability (service takes longer than x minutes) = $e^{-\mu x}$ for $x \geq 0$

where μ = average number served per minute

―――― EXHIBIT 11–5 ――

▪ *Equations for the Single-Channel Waiting-Line Model*

λ = Mean number of arrivals per time period

μ = Mean number of people or items served per time period

L_s = Average number of units (customers) in the system (waiting line + service)

$$= \frac{\lambda}{\mu - \lambda}$$

W_s = Average time a unit spends in the system (waiting time + service time)

$$= \frac{1}{\mu - \lambda}$$

L_q = Average number of units in the queue

$$= \frac{\lambda^2}{\mu(\mu - \lambda)}$$

W_q = Average time a unit spends waiting in the queue

$$= \frac{\lambda}{\mu(\mu - \lambda)}$$

ρ = Utilization factor for the system

$$= \frac{\lambda}{\mu}$$

P_0 = Probability of 0 units in the system (that is, the service unit is idle)

$$= 1 - \frac{\lambda}{\mu}$$

$P_{n>k}$ = Probability of more than k units in the system, where n is the number of units in the system

$$= \left(\frac{\lambda}{\mu}\right)^{k+1}$$

Golden Muffler Shop. Jones, the mechanic at Golden Muffler Shop, is able to install new mufflers at an average rate of three per hour (or about one every twenty minutes), according to a negative exponential distribution. Customers seeking this service arrive at the shop on the average of two per hour, following a Poisson distribution. The customers are served on a first in, first out basis and come from a very large population of possible buyers.

From this description, we are able to obtain the operating characteristics of Golden Muffler's queuing system:

$$\lambda = 2 \text{ cars arriving per hour}$$

$$\mu = 3 \text{ cars serviced per hour}$$

$$L_s = \frac{\lambda}{\mu - \lambda} = \frac{2}{3 - 2} = \frac{2}{1}$$

$$= 2 \text{ cars in the system, on average}$$

$$W_s = \frac{1}{\mu - \lambda} = \frac{1}{3 - 2} = 1 \text{ hour}$$

= 1-hour average waiting time in the system

$$L_q = \frac{\lambda^2}{\mu(\mu - \lambda)} = \frac{2^2}{3(3 - 2)} = \frac{4}{3(1)} = \frac{4}{3}$$

= 1.33 cars waiting in line, on average

$$W_q = \frac{\lambda}{\mu(\mu - \lambda)} = \frac{2}{3(3 - 2)} = \frac{2}{3} \text{ hour}$$

= 40-minute average waiting time in the queue per car

$$\rho = \frac{\lambda}{\mu} = \frac{2}{3}$$

= 66.6 percent of time mechanic is busy

$$P_0 = 1 - \frac{\lambda}{\mu} = 1 - \frac{2}{3}$$

= 0.33 probability there are 0 cars in the system

$$P_{n>3} = \left(\frac{\lambda}{\mu}\right)^{k+1} = \left(\frac{2}{3}\right)^{3+1}$$

= .198 or a 19.8% chance that more than 3 cars are in the system

Once we have computed the operating characteristics of a queuing system, it is often important to do an economic analysis of their impact. The waiting-line model described above is valuable in predicting potential waiting times, queue lengths, idle times, and so on, but it does not identify optimal decisions or consider cost factors. As stated earlier, the solution to a queuing problem may require management to make a tradeoff between the increased cost of providing better service and the decreased waiting costs derived from providing that service.

A Multichannel Queuing Model

The next logical step is to look at a multichannel queuing system, in which two or more servers or channels are available to handle arriving customers. Let us still assume that customers awaiting service form one single line and then proceed to the first available server. An example of such a multichannel, single-phase waiting line is found in many banks today. A common line is formed, and the customer at the head of the line proceeds to the first free teller. (See Exhibit 11–4 for a typical multichannel configuration.)

The multichannel system presented here again assumes that arrivals follow a Poisson probability distribution and that service times are exponentially distributed. Service is first-come, first-served, and all servers are assumed to perform at the same rate. Other assumptions listed earlier for the single-channel model apply as well.

The queuing equations for this model are shown in Exhibit 11–6. These equations are obviously more complex than the ones used in the single-channel model, yet they

—— EXHIBIT 11–6 ——————————————————————————————————

▪ *Equations for the Multichannel Queuing Model*

M = Number of channels open

λ = Average arrival rate

μ = Average service rate at each channel

P_0 = Probability that there are zero people or units in the system

$$= \frac{1}{\left[\sum_{n=0}^{M-1} \frac{1}{n!} \left(\frac{\lambda}{\mu}\right)^n\right] + \frac{1}{M!} \left(\frac{\lambda}{\mu}\right)^M \frac{M\mu}{M\mu - \lambda}} \qquad \text{for } M\mu > \lambda$$

L_s = Average number of people or units in the system

$$= \frac{\lambda\mu(\lambda/\mu)^M}{(M-1)! \, (M\mu - \lambda)^2} P_0 + \frac{\lambda}{\mu}$$

W_s = Average time a unit spends in the waiting line or being serviced (namely, in the system)

$$= \frac{\mu(\lambda/\mu)^M}{(M-1)! \, (M\mu - \lambda)^2} P_0 + \frac{1}{\mu} = \frac{L_s}{\lambda}$$

L_q = Average number of people or units in line waiting for service

$$= L_s - \frac{\lambda}{\mu}$$

W_q = Average time a person or unit spends in the queue waiting for service

$$= W_s - \frac{1}{\mu} = \frac{L_q}{\lambda}$$

——

are used in exactly the same fashion and provide the same type of information as the simpler model.[3]

Golden Muffler Revisited. The Golden Muffler Shop has decided to open a second garage bay and to hire a second mechanic to handle muffler installations. Customers, who arrive at the rate of about $\lambda = 2$ per hour, will wait in a single line until one of the two mechanics is free. Each mechanic installs mufflers at the rate of about $\mu = 3$ per hour.

To find out how this system compares to the old single-channel waiting-line system, we will compute several operating characteristics for the $M = 2$ channel system and compare the results with those found in the first example.

—————

[3] See either B. Render and R. Stair, *Quantitative Analysis for Management*, 3d Ed. (Boston: Allyn and Bacon, 1988); or J. Heizer and B. Render, *Production and Operations Management: Strategies and Tactics* (Boston: Allyn and Bacon, 1988), for details.

$$P_0 = \cfrac{1}{\left[\displaystyle\sum_{n=0}^{1} \frac{1}{n!}\left(\frac{2}{3}\right)^n\right] + \frac{1}{2!}\left(\frac{2}{3}\right)^2 \frac{2(3)}{2(3) - 2}}$$

$$= \cfrac{1}{1 + \cfrac{2}{3} + \cfrac{1}{2}\left(\cfrac{4}{9}\right)\left(\cfrac{6}{6-2}\right)} = \cfrac{1}{1 + \cfrac{2}{3} + \cfrac{1}{3}} = \frac{1}{2}$$

= 0.50 probability of zero cars in the system

Then $L_s = \cfrac{(2)(3)(2/3)^2}{1![2(3) - 2]^2}\left(\cfrac{1}{2}\right) + \cfrac{2}{3} = \cfrac{8/3}{16}\left(\cfrac{1}{2}\right) + \cfrac{2}{3} = \cfrac{3}{4}$

= 0.75 average number of cars in the system

$W_s = \cfrac{L_s}{\lambda} = \cfrac{3/4}{2} = \cfrac{3}{8}$ hour

= 22.5-minute average time a car spends in the system

$L_q = L_s - \cfrac{\lambda}{\mu} = \cfrac{3}{4} - \cfrac{2}{3} = \cfrac{1}{12}$

= 0.083 average number of cars in the queue

$W_q = \cfrac{L_q}{\lambda} = \cfrac{0.083}{2} = 0.0415$ hour

= 2.5-minute average time a car spends in the queue

We can summarize these characteristics and compare them to those of the single-channel model as follows:

	Single Channel	Two Channels
P_0	0.33	0.5
L_s	2 cars	0.75 car
W_s	60 minutes	22.5 minutes
L_q	1.33 cars	0.083 car
W_q	40 minutes	2.5 minutes

The increased service has a dramatic effect on almost all characteristics. In particular, time spent waiting in line drops from 40 minutes to only 2.5 minutes. This is consistent with the tradeoff curve illustrated earlier in Exhibit 11–3.

Reading 11.2 describes a similar multichannel queuing problem at Wesley Long Community Hospital, in Greensboro, N.C. This organization had to decide how many cardiac monitors to have on hand so that patients would not be kept waiting an unreasonable amount of time to be provided one.

More Complex Queuing Models and the Use of Simulation

Many practical waiting-line problems that occur in service systems have characteristics like the models just described. Often, however, *variations* of this specific case are present in an analysis. Service times in an automobile repair shop, for example, tend to follow the normal probability distribution instead of the exponential distribution. A college registration system in which seniors have first choice of courses and hours over all other students is an example of a first-come, first-served model with a preemptive priority queue discipline. A physical examination for military recruits is an example of a multiphase system, one that differs from the single-phase models discussed earlier. A recruit first lines up to have blood drawn at one station, then waits to take an eye examination at the next station, talks to a psychiatrist at the third, and is examined by a doctor for medical problems at the fourth. At each phase, the recruit must enter another queue and wait his or her turn.

Models to handle these cases have been developed by operations researchers. The computations for the resulting mathematical formulations are more complex than the earlier ones, though. And many real-world queuing applications are too complex to be modeled analytically at all. When this happens, analysts usually turn to computer simulation.

Simulation, our next topic, is a technique in which random numbers are used to draw inferences about probability distributions (such as arrivals and services). Using this approach, many hours, days, or months of data can be developed by a computer in a few seconds. This allows analysis of controllable factors, such as adding another service channel, without actually doing so physically. Basically, whenever a standard analytical queuing model provides only a poor approximation of the actual service system, it is wise to develop a simulation model instead.

Simulation as a Scheduling Tool

When a system contains elements that exhibit chance in their behavior, the **Monte Carlo method** of simulation may be applied. The basis of Monte Carlo simulation is experimentation on the chance (or *probabilistic*) variables through random sampling.

The simulation technique breaks down into five simple steps:

1. Set up a probability distribution for important variables.
2. Build a cumulative probability distribution for each variable.
3. Establish an interval of random numbers for each variable.
4. Generate random numbers.
5. Actually simulate a series of trials using the random numbers to obtain values for the variables.

We will demonstrate a Monte Carlo simulation with the aid of Exhibits 11–7 through 11–9. Assume that a single-channel, single-phase queuing system, such as that at a postal substation, is being analyzed. The analyst makes a number of observations of the number of arrivals per five-minute period and the number of services per five-minute period. The data are classified into frequency distributions and then represented

—— EXHIBIT 11–7 ——————————————————————————

■ *Probabilities for a System Simulation*

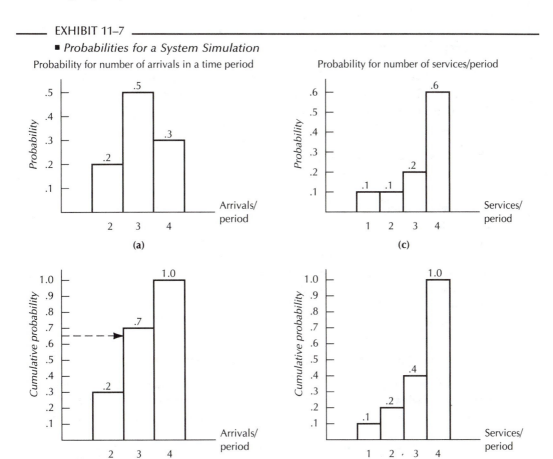

as probability distributions, as shown in Exhibit 11–7a and c. Next, the cumulative probability distributions for Exhibit 11–7a and c are computed as shown in Exhibit 11–7b and d. We now proceed as follows:

1. Set up headings for the time and status of each item in the system, as in Exhibit 11–8. (Items in this case are the number of people arriving or being served.)
2. Obtain a table of random numbers found in management science texts. A portion of such unrelated numbers is shown in Exhibit 11–9.
3. Select a row and column, and then proceed to the random number table. We selected the second column to start and decided to read down. Enter the number 0.63 for the second column and 0.17 for the fourth column in Exhibit 11–8.
4. Go to the first cumulative probability chart (Exhibit 11–7b), and find 0.63 on the vertical scale. Draw a horizontal line to the bar it first meets. This is the

three-arrivals-per-period bar. Enter 3 in the table in Exhibit 11–8 in the appropriate column.

5. Go to the second cumulative probability chart (Exhibit 11–7d), and find 0.17 on the vertical scale. Draw a horizontal line to the bar it first meets. This is the two-units-serviced-per-period bar. Enter 2 in the appropriate column in Exhibit 11–8.

6. Units arriving minus units serviced in the period gives a surplus of one waiting to be served in the next period.

7. Repeat steps 3 through 5, keeping track of units left to be serviced in each following period, if any.

Note that no matter how complex the system may be, simulation consists of examining the inputs, waiting lines, services, and output at one particular time period. Then the "clock" is moved up one time period and the system is examined again. After hundreds (or thousands) of simulations, average waiting periods, or average total service times through many different transactions may be found.

Reading 11.3 provides some interesting examples of how simulation is used at Burger King in analyzing lines at drive-thru service windows, as well as in analyzing other service and capacity problems.

The Role of Computers in Simulation

Computers are critical in simulating complex tasks. They can generate random numbers, simulate thousands of time periods in a matter of seconds or minutes, and provide

---

EXHIBIT 11–8

■ *Simulation of a Postal Substation for Three Time Periods*

Period	Random Number	Units Arriving During the Period	Random Number	Units Serviced During the Period*	Units in Line Waiting to Be Serviced at End of Period
1	—	0	—	0	0
2	0.63	3	0.17	2	1
3	0.87	4	0.03	1	4
4	0.11	2	0.42	3	3

* These would proceed to the next station.

EXHIBIT 11–9

■ *Portion of a Table of Random Numbers*

5497	6317	5736	9468	5707	8576	2614
0234	8703	2454	6094	1760	3195	0985
9821	1142	6650	2749	3677	4451	4959
9681	5613	9971	0081	7249	3016	1385

management with reports that make decision making easier. As a matter of fact, a computer approach is almost a necessity in order for us to draw valid conclusions from a simulation. Since we require a very large number of simulations, it would be a real burden to rely on pencil and paper alone.

Although general-purpose languages such as BASIC, FORTRAN, and PASCAL can be used to help the simulation process, several special-purpose simulation languages are available. They have such names as GPSS (General Purpose System Simulator, developed by IBM), SIMSCRIPT (created by the Rand Corporation), DYNAMO (developed at MIT), and SLAM (developed by Alan Pritsker).

A sample of a microcomputer-based GPSS program is provided in Exhibit 11–10. It represents a queuing simulation in which customers arrive at a bank according to a known arrival pattern. If a teller is free, the deposit is made; if the teller is busy, the customer enters a queue. When the transaction is completed, the customer "gives up" the teller, takes a taxi home, and departs the simulation. Quite similar GPSS programs can be written to handle such diverse queuing analyses as waiting at a barbershop, buying a ticket at a theater, or receiving service at a repair facility.

SLAM (Simulation Language for Alternative Modeling) is a FORTRAN-based language that combines network, discrete event, and continuous modeling capabilities.

EXHIBIT 11–10

■ *GPSS Language Sample Simulation for a Bank Queue*

```
  ;  GPSS/PC Program file TEST24.GPS              02-11-1984   10:03:34
  7 MOTORPOOL STORAGE    3                  ;
  9 LINETABLE TABLE      Q$TELLER,2,2,10     ;
 10 ***********************************************************************
 12 *                                                                    *
 14 *                    Bank Simulation                                 *
 16 *                                                                    *
 18 ***********************************************************************
 20          GENERATE     300,100,,,300        ;Create next customer.
 30          QUEUE        TELLER               ;Begin queue time.
 40          SEIZE        TELLER               ;Own or wait for teller.
 50          DEPART       TELLER               ;End queue time.
 60          ADVANCE      400,200              ;Bank deposit takes a few minutes.
 65          TABULATE     LINETABLE            ;Record waiting line in histogram.
 70          RELEASE      TELLER               ;Deposit done. Give up the teller.
 71          ASSIGN       LINESIZE,Q$TELLER    ;Remember the size of the queue.
 72          SAVEVALUE    CLOCKSAVE,C1         ;Save the clock.
 73          LOGIC S      SWITCH1              ;Set the switch.
 75          JOIN         DEPOSITS,1995        ;Record the deposit.
 76          JOIN         CUSTOMERS            ;Join the group of customers
 77          LINK         TAXILINE,FIFO,EXITDOOR  ;
 79 EXITDOOR ENTER        MOTORPOOL            ;Get a taxi.
 86          ADVANCE      2000                 ;Go home.
 88          UNLINK       TAXILINE,EXITDOOR,1,BACK   ;Leave the taxi queue
 89          LEAVE        MOTORPOOL            ;Give up the taxi.
 90          SPLIT        1,DESTINATION        ;Create a new transaction.
 95          BUFFER
100          TERMINATE    1                    ;Customer leaves the simulation.
102 DESTINATION PRIORITY  200
103          ASSIGN       COLOR,BLUE           ;Initialize a parameter.
104          BUFFER                            ;Let parent terminate.
105          TERMINATE
112          REPORT       TEST24               ;Bank Simulation
115          START        50,,,1               ;
```

Source: GPSS/PC™ sample simulation. Reproduced with permission of Minuteman Software, P.O. Box 171, Stowe, Mass. 01775 USA.

───── EXHIBIT 11–11 ──

■ *Graphic Display of SLAM Process*

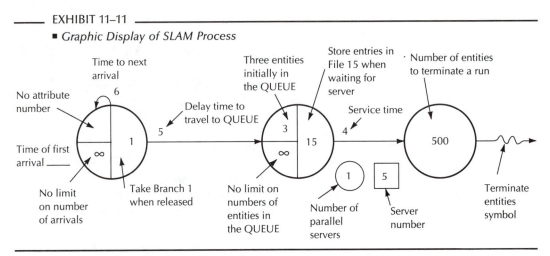

Source: Robert Murdick, *Management Information Systems: Concepts and Design*, 2d Ed., © 1986, p. 469. Reprinted by permission of Prentice Hall, Inc., Englewood Cliffs, New Jersey.

Exhibit 11–11 is a graphic representation of a simple single-server queuing system for processing invoices. In the process, entities (invoices) flow through the system. Entities have attribute values, such as the time of arrival to a process. Attribute values may be constants or take on values from probability distributions. In addition, an entity leaving a node (large circle in Exhibit 11–11) may be directed to one of several branches on a probabilistic basis. Even from this brief description, it is apparent that complex systems may be easily displayed and then specified in relatively few programming statements by means of SLAM.[4]

MATCHING DELIVERY PROCESS TO CUSTOMERS
The General Model

If we assume that the service process has been designed (the topic of Chapters 4 and 5) and that capacity has been adjusted as much as possible to match demand, then a general model for short-term scheduling may be developed (Exhibit 11–12). Whether the service is processing credit card transactions, serving food in restaurants, or supplying home interior decorating, the basic scheduling model is the same. Orders or client requests may appear as a queue at the beginning of the scheduling period, usually of one week's duration. During the week, additional orders may arrive that, in short-processing-time services, must be scheduled in the same week.

Available resources provide upper limits on service capacity, although often materials may be obtained on the same day the need is identified. Each service or job requires certain resources that in some cases can be defined precisely and in others

───

[4] For details see A. A. B. Pritsker, C. E. Sigal, and R. D. Hammesfahr, *SLAM II: Network Models for Decision Support* (Englewood Cliffs, N.J.: Prentice-Hall, 1989).

———— EXHIBIT 11–12 ————————————————————————

■ *A General Model for a Scheduling System*

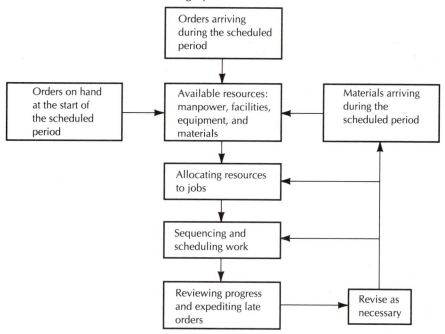

only approximately. Once resources have been allocated to individual services, the services may be sequenced and scheduled. As new orders arrive during the week, reallocation and rescheduling may be required for the remainder of the week. No-show clients, like newly arriving clients, also create the need for continuous rescheduling in some types of services.

Types of Schedules

Four types of schedules are useful. These are

— Job-order, or service schedules
— Manpower schedules
— Material requirements schedules
— Equipment schedules

The **job-order schedule** gives the sequence of job completions and starting times. A Gantt chart or one of many commercial equivalents is typically used (Exhibit 11–13).

The **manpower schedule** is necessary to identify each employee and either the jobs each will be working on *or* the times the employee will be at work each day for the week. In restaurants, for example, identification of workers on each shift is critical,

EXHIBIT 11–13

■ Gantt Chart for an Interior Decorating Firm

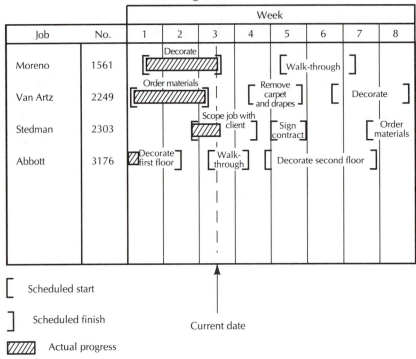

and changes of hours worked must be scheduled formally in advance by the manager. In typical 8 A.M. to 5 P.M. jobs, vacations, medical appointments, and so on must be reflected in the schedule (Exhibit 11–14).

The **material requirements schedule** shows the anticipated material quantities and mix required for the scheduled jobs day by day (Exhibit 11–15).

Equipment schedules take into account two factors—daily requirements and daily availability—in terms of units of capacity or hours of capacity. The daily requirements, when matched with available capacity for the day, indicate if excess capacity is available. If excess capacity *is* available, management may seek alternative uses of the spare time. For example, this extra time may be subcontracted out to other firms. Exhibits 11–16 and 11–17 provide simple examples of equipment schedules.

To further illustrate the important process of manpower scheduling, we present an example of an algorithm used in nurse scheduling in a Colorado hospital.

Nurse Scheduling Case.[5]   Spending nearly one week making up each seven-week schedule for the twenty nurses and nurses' aides in the pediatric ward, the head nurse

[5] Joe D. Megeath, ''Successful Hospital Personnel Scheduling,'' *Interfaces,* Vol. 8, No. 2 (February 1978), pp. 55–59.

—— EXHIBIT 11–14 ————————————————————————

▪ *Labor Schedule*

Position	Name	Week of Aug 1–6					
		M	T	W	TH	F	S
Chef	Lafleur	8–2	1–7	—	1–7	1–7	1–7
Cook	R. Flint	8–2	8–2	10–7:30	8–2	8–2	8–2
	W. Lester	12–7	12–7:30	12–7:30	12–7:30	12–7:30	12–8
Hostess	J. Par	—	5–8	5–8	5–8	5–8	5–8
Waiter/waitress	J. Butler	8–2	1–8	1–8	1–8	1–8	1–6
	T. Loft	8–2	8–2	8–2	8–2	8–2	8–2
	G. Palling	8–2	8–2	—	8–2	8–2	8–5
	F. McGuire	1–8	8–2	11–8	1–8	1–8	1–8
	G. Colton	1–8	1–8	2–8	1–8	1–8	—
	D. Hart	1–8	1–8	1–8	1–8	1–8	2–8
Busperson	R. Aman	8–2	8–2	8–2	8–2	8–2	8–2
	T. Chen	1–8	1–8	1–8	1–8	1–8	1–8
Dishwasher	G. Lynn	10–8	10–8	10–8	10–8	10–8	10–8

—— EXHIBIT 11–15 ————————————————————————

▪ *Materials Schedule*

Material	Week of Aug 1–6					
	M	T	W	TH	F	S
Beef, lbs	175	180	185	185	190	200
Fish, lbs	50	60	60	70	100	90
Vegetables, lbs	120	120	120	120	130	140
Salad oil, qts	15	15	20	20	25	25
Bread, loaves	20	32	32	35	35	40
Detergent, qts	6	6	6	6	6	8

EXHIBIT 11–16

• *Schedule of Equipment Requirements*

Equipment Requirements	Week of Aug 1–6					
	M	T	W	TH	F	S
Oven, hours	4	5	5	5	5	7
Coffee maker, hours	11	11	11	11	11	15
Electric slicer, hours	2	2	2	2	2	2
Dishwasher, hours	7	7	7	7	7	8

EXHIBIT 11–17

• *Schedule of Available Equipment Capacity*

Available Equipment Capacity	Week of Aug 1–6					
	M	T	W	TH	F	S
Oven, hours	10	12	12	12	12	12
Coffee maker, hours	12	12	11	12	12	12
Electric slicer, hours	12	12	12	12	12	12
Dishwasher, hours	10	11	12	12	11	12

at Colorado General Hospital knew he had a problem. His objective was to establish "a procedure that would make up a seven-week schedule for nurses, in a timely and efficient manner, so that adequate health care would be delivered to the patients and the scheduled personnel would be happy with their work hours."

The problem elements that required consideration to achieve a usable solution were as follows:

1. Three shifts required coverage in each 24-hour period (day, evening, night).
2. Evening and night shifts were considered "off" shifts; all personnel were required to work a maximum of two-thirds of their time in an "off" shift.
3. To maintain coordination and personnel-awareness of problems, no one was allowed to work all the time in one shift time period (e.g., all days).
4. Two additional RNs were also "team leaders" and were required to work seven "off" shifts during each seven-week scheduling period.
5. Of the eleven RNs (registered nurses), five worked a day-evening rotation, five worked a day-night rotation, and one worked all three shift periods.
6. A registered nurse could work a maximum of seven shifts without a day off.

7. The LPNs (practical nurses) and the aides were under state labor regulations that required two days off every Sunday through Saturday time period, and no overtime or compensatory time was allowed.
8. The head nurse was also an RN and could work any of the shifts but required principally day-shift work in order to satisfy administrative responsibilities.
9. The minimum required coverage per shift was

2 RNs,	1 LPN		(night shift)
3 RNs,	1 LPN,	1 Aide	(evening shift)
3 RNs,	1 LPN,	1 Aide	(day shift)

10. Each staff member had 50 percent of the weekends off.
11. As an added benefit, the RNs were promised a long weekend each seven-week period.
12. In addition, because of the physical and mental strain, doublebacks were to be kept to a maximum of two per planning period. (A *doubleback* is working an off-shift, then continuing the next day to work the day shift).

Although there are several ways of tackling this problem, including mathematical programming,[6] a workable, yet simple procedure called **cyclical scheduling** was adopted from research by Howell.[7] Cyclical scheduling has seven steps.

1. Plan a schedule equal in length to the number of people being scheduled.
2. Determine how many of each of the least desirable off-shifts must be covered each week.
3. Begin the schedule for one nurse by scheduling the days off during the planning cycle (at a rate of two days per week on the average).
4. Assign off-shifts for that first nurse using step 2. Here's an example of one nurse's 42-day schedule, where X = day off, D = day shift, and E = evening shift:

S	M	T	W	T	F	S		S	M	T	W	T	F	S		S	M	T	W	T	F	S		S	M	T	W	T	F	S		S	M	T	W	T	F	S		S	M	T	W	T	F	S
E	E	E	E	E	X	X		X	X	E	E	E	E	E		E	D	X	D	D	D	D		D	D	X	X	D	E	X		X	E	E	E	E	E	X		D	E	D	D	X	X	E

5. Repeat this pattern for each of the other nurses, but offsetting each one by one week from the previous one.
6. Allow each nurse to pick his or her "slot" or "line" in order of seniority.
7. Mandate that any changes from a chosen schedule are strictly between the personnel wanting to switch.

---

[6] For details regarding the mathematical programming approach, see D. M. Warner, "Scheduling Nursing Personnel According to Nursing Preference," *Operations Research,* Vol. 25, No. 5 (September–October 1976).

[7] J. P. Howell, "Cyclical Scheduling of Nursing Personnel," *Nursing Service,* Vol. 40 (January 16, 1966), pp. 77–85.

The advantages of this approach were

1. No computer hardware, software, or data entry were required.
2. The head nurse saved twenty to thirty hours in preparing each schedule.
3. The nurses were happy with the schedule.
4. The cycles could be changed during different seasons (which accommodated avid skiers).
5. Recruiting was made easier because of predictability and flexibility,

SUMMARY

Scheduling capacity is concerned with matching daily output to daily demand. It deals with the disaggregation of aggregate long-term output and demand and involves the matching of short-term fluctuations in supply and demand. This matching must be considered from the viewpoint of single-service firms and multiservice firms.

We first considered adjusting short-term capacity. The five means of adjusting capacity are (1) increasing customer participation, (2) using part-time workers, (3) cross-training workers, (4) extending hours, and (5) providing additional service sites. In some cases it is possible to delay the service without losing the customer. Maintaining a fixed supply also may be a means of managing capacity.

We then examined two management science tools, queuing theory and simulation, which are often useful in scheduling capacity. They can both provide information about the capacity needed so that customers are not forced to wait an unreasonable length of time. When certain mathematical conditions can be met, a series of queuing formulas may describe the parameters of the wait. When the situation at hand does not fit the assumptions of queuing theory, Monte Carlo simulation can be employed as a scheduling tool.

Specific types of schedules and a general model of short-term scheduling were the final topics of this chapter. Manpower scheduling can be a complex problem that has been addressed by a variety of researchers.

DISCUSSION QUESTIONS

1. Describe how these organizations could increase customer participation in the service process.

   a. Airline
   b. Restaurant
   c. Picture framing shop
   d. Library
   e. Bank

2. What are the components of the following queuing systems? Draw and explain the configuration of each.

   a. Barber shop
   b. Car wash

   c. Laundromat
   d. Small grocery store

3. Do doctors' offices generally have random arrival rates for patients? Are service times random? Under what circumstances might service times be constant (i.e., each service takes the same amount of time)?

4. Why must the service rate be greater than the arrival rate in a single-channel queuing system?

5. Briefly describe three situations in which the first-in, first-out (FIFO) discipline rule is not applicable in queuing analysis.

6. Describe the difference in how the following organizations generally handle no-shows in appointments or reservations.

    a. Hotel
    b. Doctor
    c. Airline
    d. Restaurant
    e. Hair salon

7. Why is a computer necessary in conducting a real-world simulation?

____ PROBLEMS

11.1. The Tengler Electronics Corporation retains a service crew to repair machine breakdowns that occur on an average of $\lambda = 3$ per day (approximately Poisson in nature). The crew can service an average of $\mu = 8$ machines per day, with a repair time distribution that resembles the exponential distribution.

    a. What is the utilization rate of this service system?
    b. What is the average down time for a machine that is broken?
    c. How many machines are waiting to be serviced at any given time?
    d. What is the probability that more than one machine is in the system? Probability that more than two are broken and waiting to be repaired or being serviced? More than three? More than four?

11.2. Barry's Car Wash is open six days a week, but its heaviest day of business is always Saturday. From historical data, Barry estimates that dirty cars arrive at the rate of twenty per hour all day Saturday. With a full crew working the hand-wash line, he figures that cars can be cleaned at the rate of one every two minutes. One car at a time is cleaned in this example of a single-channel waiting line.

    Assuming Poisson arrivals and exponential service times, find the

    a. Average number of cars in line
    b. Average time a car waits before it is washed
    c. Average time a car spends in the service system
    d. Utilization rate of the car wash
    e. Probability no cars are in the system

11.3. Judy Holmes manages a large Montgomery, Alabama, movie theater complex called Cinema I, II, III, and IV. Each of the four auditoriums plays a different film; the schedule is set so that starting times are staggered to avoid the large crowds that would occur if all four movies started at the same time. The theater has a single ticket booth and a cashier who can maintain an average service rate of 280 movie patrons per hour. Service times are assumed to follow an exponential distribution. Arrivals on a normally active day are Poisson distributed and average 210 per hour.

    In order to determine the efficiency of the current ticket operation, Judy wishes to examine several queue operating characteristics.

    a. Find the average number of moviegoers waiting in line to purchase a ticket.
    b. What percentage of the time is the cashier busy?
    c. What is the average time a customer spends in the system?
    d. What is the average time spent waiting in line to get to the ticket window?
    e. What is the probability that there are more than two people in the system? More than three people? More than four?

11.4. A university cafeteria line in the student center is a self-serve facility in which students select the food items they want, then form a single line to pay the cashier. Students arrive at a rate of about four per minute according to a Poisson distribution. The single cashier ringing up sales takes about 12 seconds per customer, following an exponential distribution.

    a. What is the probability there are more than two students in the system? More than three students? More than four?
    b. What is the probability that the system is empty?

8. Why might a manager be forced to use simulation instead of an analytical model in dealing with a problem of

    a. Ships docking in a port to unload
    b. Bank teller service windows

9. Visit your local hospital and compare its nurse scheduling system to that used at Colorado General Hospital.

c. How long will the average student have to wait before reaching the cashier?

d. What is the expected number of students in the queue?

e. What is the average number in the system?

11.5. Jerry's Department Store in Dubuque, Iowa, maintains a successful catalog sales department in which a clerk takes orders by telephone. If the clerk is occupied on one line, incoming phone calls to the catalogue department are answered automatically by a recording machine and asked to wait. As soon as the clerk is free, the party that has waited the longest is transferred and answered first. Calls come in at a rate of about twelve per hour. The clerk is capable of taking an order in an average of four minutes. Calls tend to follow a Poisson distribution, and service times tend to be exponential.

The clerk is paid $5 per hour, but because of lost goodwill and sales, Jerry's loses about $25 per hour of customer time spent waiting for the clerk to take an order.

a. What is the average time that catalogue customers must wait before their calls are transferred to the order clerk?

b. What is the average number of callers waiting to place an order?

c. Jerry's is considering adding a second clerk to take calls. The store would pay that person the same $5 per hour. Should it hire another clerk? Explain.

11.6. The administrator at a large hospital emergency room faces a problem of providing treatment for patients that arrive at different rates during the day. There are four doctors available to treat patients when needed. If not needed, they can be assigned to other responsibilities (for example, lab tests, reports, x-ray diagnoses) or else rescheduled to work at other hours.

It is important to provide quick and responsive treatment, and the administrator feels that, on the average, patients should not have to sit in the waiting area for more than five minutes before being seen by a doctor. Patients are treated on a first-come, first-served basis and see the first available doctor after waiting in the queue. The arrival pattern for a typical day is:

Time	Arrival Rate
9 A.M.–3 P.M.	6 patients/hour
3 P.M.–8 P.M.	4 patients/hour
8 P.M.–Midnight	12 patients/hour

These arrivals follow a Poisson distribution, and treatment times, twelve minutes on the average, follow the exponential pattern.

How many doctors should be on duty during each period in order to maintain the level of patient care expected?

11.7. The number of cars arriving at Jim Harvey's Car Wash during the last 200 hours of operation is observed to be the following:

Number of Cars Arriving	Frequency
3 or less	0
4	20
5	30
6	50
7	60
8	40
9 or more	0
	200

a. Set up a probability and cumulative probability distribution for the variable of car arrivals.

b. Establish random number intervals for the variable.

c. Simulate 15 hours of car arrivals and compute the average number of arrivals per hour. Select the random numbers needed from Exhibit 11–9.

11.8. Blacksburg, Virginia's, General Hospital has an emergency room that is divided into six departments: (1) the initial exam station to treat minor problems or make diagnoses; (2) an x-ray department; (3) an operating room; (4) a cast fitting room; (5) an observation room (for recovery and general observation before final diagnoses or release); and (6) an out-processing department (where clerks check patients out and arrange for payment or insurance forms).

The probabilities that a patient will go from one department to another are presented in the accompanying table.

a. Simulate the trail followed by ten emergency room patients. Proceed, one patient at a time, from each one's entry at the initial exam station until he or she leaves through out-processing. You should be aware that a patient can enter the same department more than once.

b. Using your simulation data, what are the

chances that a patient enters the x-ray department twice?

From	To	Probability
Initial exam at emergency room entrance	X-ray-department	0.45
	Operating room	0.15
	Observation room	0.10
	Out-processing clerk	0.30
X-ray department	Operating room	0.10
	Cast-fitting room	0.25
	Observation room	0.35
	Out-processing clerk	0.30

From	To	Probability
Operating room	Cast-fitting room	0.25
	Observation room	0.70
	Out-processing clerk	0.05
Cast-fitting room	Observation room	0.55
	X-ray department	0.05
	Out-processing clerk	0.40
Observation room	Operating room	0.15
	X-ray department	0.15
	Out-processing clerk	0.70

11.9. Fully loaded barges arrive at night in New Orleans following their long trips down the Mississippi River from industrial midwestern cities. The number of barges docking on any given night ranges from 0 to 5. The probability of 0, 1, 2, 3, 4, and 5 arrivals is displayed below.

Number of Arrivals	Probability
0	0.13
1	0.17
2	0.15
3	0.25
4	0.20
5	0.10

A study by the dock superintendent reveals that because of the nature of their cargo, the number of barges unloaded also tends to vary from day to day. The superintendent provides information from which one can create a probability distribution for the variable *daily unloading rate* (see the following table).

Daily Unloading Rate	Probability
1	0.05
2	0.15
3	0.50
4	0.20
5	0.10
	1.00

Barges are unloaded on a first-in, first-out basis. Any barges that are not unloaded the day of arrival must wait until the following day. Tying up a barge in dock is an expensive proposition, and the superintendent cannot ignore the angry phone calls from barge line owners reminding him that "time is money!" He decides that, before going to the Port of New Orleans's controller to request additional unloading crews, a simulation study of arrivals, unloadings, and delays should be conducted. Develop a fifteen-day simulation.

11.10. Management of the First Syracuse Bank is concerned over a loss of customers at its main office downtown. One solution that has been proposed is to add one or more "drive-through" teller stations to make it easier for customers in cars to obtain quick service without parking. Chris Carlson, the bank president, thinks the bank should only risk the cost of installing one drive-through. He is informed by his staff that the cost (amortized over a 20-year period) of building a drive through is $12,000 per year. It also costs $16,000 per year in wages and benefits to staff each new teller window.

The director of Management Analysis, Anita Greenberg, believes that the following two factors encourage the immediate construction of two drive-through stations, however. According to a recent article in *Banking Research* magazine, customers who wait in long lines for drive-through teller service will cost banks an average of $1.00 per minute, in loss of goodwill. Also, adding a second drive-through will cost an additional $16,000 in staffing, but amortized construction costs can be cut to a total of $20,000 per year if two drive-throughs are installed together, instead of one at a time. To complete her analysis, Mrs. Greenberg collected one month's worth of arrival and service rates at a competing downtown bank's drive-through stations. These data are shown as Observation Analysis 1 and 2 on the next page.

a. Simulate a one-hour time period, from 1 to 2 P.M., for a single-teller drive-through.

b. Simulate a one-hour time period, from 1 to 2 P.M., for a two-teller system.

c. Conduct a cost analysis of the two options. Assume the bank is open 7 hours per day and 200 days per year.

Observation Analysis 1—Interarrival Times for 1000 Observations

Time Between Arrivals (in minutes)	Number of Occurrences
1	200
2	250
3	300
4	150
5	100

Observation Analysis 2— Customer Service Time for 1000 Customers

Service Time (in minutes)	Number of Occurrences
1	100
2	150
3	350
4	150
5	150
6	100

—— READING 11.1 ——————————————————————————————

Conquering Those Killer Queues

N. R. Kleinfeld

Lines are one of Richard Larson's odd fascinations. He is a steadfastly gleeful professor of electrical engineering and computer science at the Massachusetts Institute of Technology, and something of an expert on waiting. Thus the Zayre Corporation, whose discount prices make it something of an expert on making people wait, has hired him to come up with fresh ideas to combat that immemorial bugaboo—customer lines.

Eugene Fram, a professor of marketing and management at the Rochester Institute of Technology, feels that businesses are recognizing that by keeping customers waiting they become "time bandits." They are finding that people will pick one establishment over another because of shorter lines. All this means more pressure on companies— from banks to restaurants, supermarkets to airlines—to solve the waiting problem. There are quick cures: spend more money and provide more service. But most businesses cannot afford to—or do not want to—and so they have been trying harder to find imaginative methods to curtail waiting or at least make it less repugnant.

Those who wrestle with waiting often contact someone like Richard Larson. More and more researchers and consultants are studying lines and, in their efforts to demystify and quantify them, have produced a mathematical discipline. Queuing theory makes heavy use of probability theory and gets into abstruse mathematical equations that gauge such things as how many people will arrive at a drugstore to buy dental floss during the noon hour.

The father of queuing theory is A. K. Erlang, a Danish telephone engineer who, in 1908, began to study congestion in the telephone service of the Copenhagen Telephone Company. A few years later, he arrived at a mathematical approach to assist in designing telephone switches. Queuing theory has grown far more sophisticated. While it continues to have its chief application in telecommunications and computer design, it has seeped elsewhere.

Ideas about lines matter to the people at Zayre, because they have tried to differentiate their stores from competitors in part by how swiftly they take customers' money. For years, Zayre has had a policy that if more than three people are lined up at a checkout register, another register will open.

The system, Zayre admits, has its flaws. Lines do occasionally swell to four or five customers when no one is free to handle another register. At times, every register is open and yet the lines are four deep. "We found the system was difficult to manage, because it was hard to predict when customers would arrive," said Frank Capek, Zayre's manager of operations planning.

Years of listening to howling customers have also taught the airlines some baggage-retrieval lessons. When American designed its baggage-claim area in the Dallas–Fort Worth Airport, it put it close to the gates, so disembarking passengers would not have to trudge too far. But even though passengers reach the area quickly, they must wait for their luggage. At Los Angeles International Airport, passengers have to walk quite some distance to the claim area, but when they arrive, their suitcases are usually there. Even though the Los Angeles travelers spend more total time picking up their baggage, American has found they do not grouse as much about baggage delays as do the Dallas passengers.

Few businesses have taken more hard shots about bad management of lines than banks. "Our research indicates that people don't like to spend time in bank branches," said David Mooney, senior vice president of Chemical Bank. "It's probably second in their disdain to waiting to see the dentist."

To reduce lines, most banks have installed automatic teller machines and tried to persuade employers to alter their check distribution or to directly deposit payroll checks in the bank. The lines, however, persist.

One way to take some of the sting out of waiting is to entertain customers. Since 1959, the Manhattan Savings Bank has offered live entertainment during the frenzied noontime hours. In 13 branches, a pianist performs and one branch has an organ player (Willard Denton, the former Chemical chairman who dreamed up the idea, liked organs, though present management thinks they are a trifle loud for a bank). Occasionally, to make line-waiting even more wonderful, Manhattan Savings has scheduled events such as a fancy-cat exhibit, a purebred dog show and a boat show.

Because of all this, Manhattan Savings believes customers endure long waits better than those who go to banks where the only music is the person in front of you grinding his teeth. "At very hectic times, we get very few complaints," said Jean Madsen, a senior vice president.

At hotels and office buildings, mirrors affixed to elevator doors make people less maniacal during waits. Instead of deciding whom to kill, they can comb their hair. A study done by Russel Ackoff showed that hotels that had mirrors received far less grumbling about elevator delays than ones without mirrors.

Just telling people how long they have to wait often cheers them up. Disneyland is sensitive to waiting, since the line for a hot attraction like Star Tours can run to 1800 people. Like many amusement parks, Disney employs entertainment for waiters, but it is also big on feedback. At various spots along lines, signs give estimated delays from those points. Queuing experts say nothing is worse than the blind waiting familiar to people at bus stops, who don't know if the next bus is one minute or 15 minutes away. Disney's feedback permits parents to weigh odd options: Is it wiser to wait 25 minutes for Mr. Toad's Wild Ride or 30 minutes for Dumbo?

Peter Kolesar, a professor of operations research at the Columbia University Business School, thinks there ought to be more efforts to shift demand by altering pricing. Some rail lines, for example, charge less for offpeak trains and restaurants offer early-bird discounts.

During a whimsical moment, Dick Larson speculated that if the average American waited half an hour a day in one line or another, then the population expended 37 billion hours a year in lines. It strikes him, he said, that businesses ought to consider merchandising products to idle waiters to take their minds off pulling out their hair. "Like those flower peddlers outside tunnels and bridges," he said. "They're very shrewd."

——— QUESTIONS FOR READING 11.1

1. What options might a chain store such as Zayre employ to increase capacity? To influence demand?

2. What techniques can be employed to make a wait seem more pleasant (besides the ones mentioned here)?

3. What products could be realistically merchandised to idle waiters (see the last paragraph of the article)?

____ READING 11.2 _____

Queuing Model Aids Economic Analysis of Health Center

Tom Scott ▪ William A. Hailey

A wide variety of seemingly diverse problem situations have been described by queuing models.
Utilization of these models in the health care field
can assist management by providing more information for the decision-making process. Queues
in a hospital can be found where patients must
wait for radiology exams, admissions, and emergency room visits.

The following application of queuing modeling in the health care environment represents an
effort to analyze the telemetry system at Wesley
Long Community Hospital, Greensboro, NC, and
compare the current system to systems involving
additional telemetry units.

The model 8300 A.O. telemetry system used
here is a completely self-contained, wireless, one-
patient cardiac monitor. It is particularly suitable
for use on ambulatory patients, on patients in progressive care and recovery areas, in operating
rooms and on those undergoing exercise and stress
testing. The system provides radio (wireless) transmission of a patient's ECG to a receiver either at
a central station or at bedside.

The major objective of this study was to analyze the utilization of 16 telemetry units. The following characteristics were considered fundamental to this analysis:

1. Waiting time per patient should be computed
   based on the derived arrival and service
   times. Derived arrivals include all requests
   for service, as opposed to actual arrivals,
   which include only those arrivals which
   request and remain for service.
2. A cost/benefit analysis of additional telemetry
   units should be provided.

QUEUING ANALYSIS

To apply the queuing model to an analysis of the
telemetry system, patient arrival and service times
were required. Actual records were reviewed to
obtain this data.

The arrival rate for a 38-day period, considering 156 patients, was 0.1711 requests/hour. The
service rate, on the other hand, was 0.0106 pa-
tients/hour/machine during this period. These rates
can be converted to average arrival times of one
every 5.8 hours and average service times of 93.6
hours.

With the arrival and service rates, the system
descriptors were calculated. Also, the impact of
adding additional telemetry units was determined.
In these calculations, the derived arrival rate was
used to analyze how the present systems would
handle all requests.

Exhibit 11–18 reveals that the probability of
the present system being busy (that is, all 16 units
simultaneously in use) is 0.87. The expected number in the queue is 29.8; the expected number in
the queue and/or being serviced is 45.3. With respect to time in the queue, the expected time is
174.3 hours.

If the present system is increased with additional telemetry units, a drastic drop in expected
time in the queue would be realized. For example,
the expected time for 18 telemetry units would be
85.5 percent less than that of the current system;
for 19 units it would be 93.2 percent less; for 20
units it would be 96.5 percent less; and for 21 units
it would be 98.1 percent less.

With the foregoing information, the appropriate balance of the number of telemetry units can

_____ EXHIBIT 11–18 _____

System Characteristics	Number of Telemetry Units					
	16	17	18	19	20	21
Derived arrival rate (λ)	0.17100	0.17100	0.17100	0.17100	0.17100	0.17100
Service rate (μ)	0.01068	0.01068	0.01068	0.01068	0.01068	0.01068
Probability of the system being busy (P_{busy})	0.87	0.74	0.54	0.38	0.26	0.17
Expected number of patients in system (queue and service) (L_s)	45.3	28.2	20.4	18.0	17.1	16.6
Expected number of patients in queue (L_q)	29.8	12.1	4.3	2.0	1.0	0.6
Expected time (hours) in queue (W_q)	174.3	70.9	25.3	11.8	6.1	3.2
Percent decrease in expected time in queue from current system of 16 units		59.3%	85.5%	93.2%	96.5%	98.1%

be decided. What is considered appropriate remains a subjective decision for management, but it can be better made considering these results.

The application of management science techniques such as queuing modeling to the health care environment adds another dimension to quantitative analysis for decision-making purposes. The utilization of this model has provided the management of the hospital with a better approach to decision making. It is felt that utilization of the model jointly with subjective managerial experience will provide the appropriate guidelines for the most effective telemetry unit combination.

_____ QUESTIONS FOR READING 11.2

1. Describe, in your own words, the queuing situation at Wesley Long Hospital.

2. What conclusions were drawn from the queuing study of telemetry units?

3. What are some other possible applications of queuing models in hospitals?

___ READING 11.3 _____

Simulation Modeling Improves Operations, Planning, and Productivity of Fast-Food Restaurants

William Swart ▪ Luca Donno

James McLamore opened the first Burger King restaurant in Miami in 1954 with a simple concept; he served a few variations of the basic hamburger, and did not need a traditional kitchen. Because small businessmen could operate such a restaurant even without previous food experience, McLamore began to franchise the units.

Growth was deliberate and controlled. In less

Source: Reprinted by permission of William Swart and Luca Donno, "Simulation Modeling Improves Operations, Planning, and Productivity of Fast-Food Restaurants," *Interfaces*, Vol. 11, No. 6 (December 1981), pp. 35–41. Copyright 1981 The Institute of Management Sciences, 290 Westminster Street, Providence, Rhode Island 02903 USA.

than 15 years, McLamore went from running a restaurant grossing under $100 a day to heading a company with $66 million in annual sales. The chain grew to 274 units by 1967, when it was acquired by The Pillsbury Company. Today the restaurant chain has systems sales worldwide of more than $2 billion. Average unit sales went from $254,000 in 1967 to $700,000 plus in 1980. Annual system sales have increased an average of 36 percent since Burger King's acquisition by Pillsbury.

With a dramatically changing fast-food hamburger restaurant business, it became clear that corporate productivity had to be a top priority.

In late 1977 and early 1978, meat prices began to fluctuate widely. Because beef is the primary component of the food Burger King serves, cost pressure on margins was severe. The Operations Research Department therefore developed a computer model to determine what kind of meat to buy from which supplier so as to have the correct hamburger formulation at minimum cost. The result was a savings of almost $3/4 ¢$ per pound. In a system that buys over three million pounds of hamburger meat a week, that $3/4 ¢$ represents savings in excess of $22,000 each week.

The computer model was subsequently expanded not only to determine least-cost formulations at each individual packing plant, but also the least-cost distribution throughout the system. The new model optimized shipping and distribution costs based on meat availability nationwide and on anticipated demand for processed meat within the entire system. This expanded computer model saves Burger King Corporation at least $2 million annually.

But the impact of productivity improvement effort was most clearly demonstrated on the analysis of the drive-thru system.

Burger King established a standard transaction time of 30 seconds for the drive-thru window, but most units had service times in excess of that. During peak periods it simply was no longer possible for drivers wishing to use the drive-thru to even join the end of the car line. Sales were clearly being lost due to this problem. A system initially devised to provide customers convenience had become an inconvenience. Analysis at a number of units showed drive-thru transaction times were aver-

aging 45 seconds. With a 45-second transaction time, the restaurant could handle a maximum of 80 cars an hour. With an average check of $2.44 per order, drive-thru sales were limited to a maximum of $195 per hour.

If the transaction time could be shortened to 30 seconds, cars served per hour could increase by 50 percent, and maximum sales would rise by almost $100 to $292 an hour. That represents an annual capacity benefit (or sales increase) of over $35,000 per restaurant. Working with franchisees, Operations Research devised a plan to improve speed of service at the drive-thru. The heart of the new system is the separation of drive-thru work into a series of distinct tasks.

The Operations Research Department also recognized that customers waited an average of 11 seconds at the order station before being acknowledged. The rubber bell hose was therefore moved ahead of the order station so that the order taker was alerted to the customer's arrival prior to the car reaching the order station.

Today, all Burger King restaurants with a drive-thru have adopted the efficiency package. These restaurants have increased their annual sales capacity by over $35,000. If each restaurant in the system gained only 50 percent of this, or $18,000 per unit in annual sales increases, the Burger King system would enjoy additional sales of $52 million annually.

Although most of the studies mentioned did involve the use of either simulation, optimization, or statistical models, these models were developed to solve specific problems. However, it soon became apparent that the increasing demands placed on the OR department by management would require the development of a comprehensive general purpose restaurant model which could be used to address a wide variety of issues.

In the past year, over 20 changes have been evaluated with the model. Descriptions of several major changes follow:

1. In an on-going analysis of the drive-thru, Operations Research recognized that in many restaurants the stack size, or distance between the order station and the pick-up window, was too short and accommodated only two or three vehicles. The simulation models were used to determine what stack size gave the optimal lead time

so that when a car reached the window its likelihood of waiting was minimized.

2. The longer stack, by drastically reducing waiting time, allows an additional 12 to 13 customers to be served in an hour. This adds $30 per hour in sales during the peak lunch hour, for an annual benefit of over $10,000 per restaurant. This change has been implemented throughout the system. Taking a conservative estimate of 1500 restaurants in which this change has been implemented, this would provide an additional $15 million in annual sales capacity.

3. The second drive-thru window (placed in *series* to the first as opposed to a two-lane drive-thru), has been proposed as a means of expanding the sales capacity of the drive-thru during peak hours. The simulation model evaluating this modification projected a sales benefit of 15 percent during peak lunch hours. An experimental second window unit was installed in company-owned R&D restaurants. The observed sales benefit in actual operation was 14 percent. Based on average restaurant sales during the lunch hour and average drive-thru percentages, the second window adds $36.40 in sales each day, or more than $13,000 per year per restaurant. This revision has been introduced into the system. Estimating that 10 percent of the 300 new restaurants built each year will be able to implement the second drive-thru window, that represents an additional $390,000 in annual sales capacity.

4. The model has proven especially valuable in examining the operational impact of the introduction of new products. For example, small specialty sandwiches were considered for introduction to supplement sales of the larger sandwiches. The computer simulation showed the introduction of these sandwiches would generate an average delay of 8 seconds per customer. On a yearly basis, this would represent a $13,000 loss in sales capacity for an average restaurant. On this basis, it was recommended that these sandwiches not be introduced. This resulted in the avoidance of a $39 million loss in capacity to the entire system.

Jerry Ruenheck, president of Burger King US, which is the largest of the corporation's three decentralized operating divisions, says

> Our business has undergone dramatic changes. The importance of the simulation modeling program to all areas of operational and productivity planning is almost incalculable. The analytical knowledge and sophistication that simulation modeling gives Burger King, therefore, provides annual savings, or profits, in the millions of dollars for the system of company-owned and franchised restaurants.

QUESTIONS FOR READING 11.3

1. How were simulation models used by Burger King?

2. What were the problems facing the drive-thru systems?

CASE STUDY 11.1

Synergistic Systems Corporation

Mr. Norman Jenkins, manager of office equipment at Synergistic Systems Corporation, one of the top seven government contractors, was reasoning with Mr. George Wilson, manager of the contract typing pool. "George, I can't approve your request for a third copying machine just because you say you see typists waiting in line practically every time you're near your two machines. Back in 1980, I could have approved it without question, but this is 1988. You know that we aren't doing as well these days due to the government cutbacks in aerospace spending. The word has come down from upstairs that we have to cut expenses wherever possible.

Source: Copyright © 1970, 1971 by the President and Fellows of Harvard College. Harvard Business School case 171–266. This case was prepared by Stuart L. Zarembo under the direction of John S. Hammond as the basis for class discussion rather than to illustrate either effective or ineffective handling of an administrative situation. Reprinted by permission of the Harvard Business School.

"As a matter of fact, we have been running a survey on usage of the machines in the building, hoping to reduce costs by eliminating unnecessary machines. Let me show you our results for your machines, George. The first table [Exhibit 11–19] shows that you average 16.17 pages per contract. This second table [Exhibit 11–20] shows that the average time between users arriving at the machines is 16.48 minutes.

"Previous surveys have shown that it takes one minute to make the required twenty copies of each contract page. Therefore, the average user should be on a machine 16.17 minutes. Since secretaries arrive to use the machine an average of 16.48 minutes apart, but only use the machine an average of 16.17 minutes, one machine should be adequate for your copying needs. Each machine costs us $220 per month or $10 per working day. How can

I approve your request for a third machine with these facts in front of me? In fact, I was thinking of taking away one of your machines."

George Wilson puzzled over the tables a bit and then asked, "Why are all the times even numbers? Don't the users arrive three minutes apart, or five minutes apart?"

"Yes, but we found that it was convenient and accurate enough to record the information to the nearest two minutes. Anything up to one minute was recorded a 0, anything from one to three minutes was recorded as 2, etc. By the way here's the form we used to record the results," he added, showing Mr. Wilson the acompanying form. . . . (See Exhibit 11–21.) "We just used two of the machine columns in your case since you only had two machines, and we recorded twenty all the time in the number of copies column. We fitted a smooth

---

EXHIBIT 11–19

Pages	Percentage of Contracts	Pages	Percentage of Contracts	Pages	Percentage of Contracts
6	1	13	6	20	7
7	1	14	8	21	5
8	2	15	9	22	3
9	2	16	11	23	2
10	2	17	12	24	1
11	3	18	11	25	1
12	4	19	9		

EXHIBIT 11–20

Time between Arrivals					
Time since Last Arrival	Percentage of Arrivals	Time since Last Arrival	Percentage of Arrivals	Time since Last Arrival	Percentage of Arrivals
0	17	20	3	40	2
2	8	22	3	42	1
4	7	24	3	44	1
6	6	26	2	46	1
8	6	28	2	48	1
10	5	30	2	50	1
12	5	32	2	52	1
14	4	34	2	54	1
16	4	36	2	56	1
18	3	38	2	58	1
				60	1

curve to what we recorded on both the pages and time between arrivals."

"Well, I don't really care how you recorded that data," said Mr. Wilson. "The important point is that secretaries are waiting in line and that's costing us money.

"You're familiar with our system of assigning each typist to only one contract at a time and having her make her own copies when she finishes the typing. The worst drawback of our present system is that the time anyone spends waiting to use a machine is wasted time, and women who type with the speed and accuracy that we need don't work for peanuts. The fifteen secretaries who work for me cost us about $10 an hour each, including variable overhead, and that's $80 per working day. That's why I worry when I see them waiting in line at the machine."

Mr. Jenkins asked, "Why don't you hire someone just to make copies? You ought to be able to get someone to do that for only $4 an hour. You would save the time your typists spend making copies, eliminate all waiting time, and still get by with only one machine."

"I fought that battle last year with Bob Johnson in Security. He agreed that we could save money by hiring someone just to run the copying ma-

chines, but he won't allow it. Most of the contracts are classified Secret or Top Secret, and he's scared stiff of what the government security inspectors will say about any procedure where extra personnel handle the documents," Mr. Wilson replied. "Now the problem is worse. With the aerospace spending cuts, we've got a hiring freeze. We wouldn't be allowed to hire a Xerox operator, even if we thought it was desirable."

"George, I understand your concerns, but I just can't help you when the numbers show that I should take a machine away from you rather than give you another one. Take this copy of our survey with you. If you can show me that I'm wrong, you'll get your machine."

Mr. Wilson folded the copy of the survey, put it in his shirt pocket and walked out dejectedly.

QUESTIONS FOR CASE 11.1

1. Using the data as collected, determine if another machine can be economically justified by simulating one day for each machine configuration. Use the random numbers in Exhibit 11–9.

2. What are the simulated costs for two machines and three machines?

EXHIBIT 11–21

■ *Data Sheet*

Time of Arrival	Number of Pages	Number of Copies	Machine 1		Machine 2		Machine 3	
			Time On	Time Off	Time On	Time Off	Time On	Time Off

REFERENCES

Bechtold, Stephen E., and Michael J. Showalter. "A Methodology for Labor Scheduling in a Service Operation Room," *Decision Sciences*, Vol. 18 (1987), pp. 89–107.

Byrd, J. "The Value of Queuing Theory," *Interfaces*, Vol. 8, No. 3 (May 1978), pp. 22–26.

Chung, K. H., "Computer Simulation of a Queuing System," *Production and Inventory Management*, Vol. 10, No. 1 (1969), pp. 75–82.

Cooper, R. B., *Introduction to Queuing Theory*. New York: Macmillan, 1972.

Cox, D. R., and W. L. Smith. *Queues*. New York: Wiley, 1965.

Deutsch, Howard, and Vince Mabert, "Queuing Theory and Teller Staffing: A Successful Application," *Interfaces*, Vol. 10, No. 5 (October 1980), pp. 63–67.

Erikson, W. "Management Science and the Gas Shortage," *Interfaces*, Vol. 4, No. 4 (August 1974), pp. 47–51.

Eschcoli, Z., and I. Adiri. "Single-Lane Budget Serving Two-Lane Traffic," *Naval Research Logistics Quarterly*, Vol. 24, No. 1 (March 1977), pp. 113–125.

Foote, B. L. "Queuing Case Study of Drive-In Banking," *Interfaces*, Vol. 6, No. 4 (August 1976), p. 31.

George, J. A., D. R. Fox, and R. W. Canvin. "A Hospital Throughput Model in the Context of Long Waiting Lines," *Journal of the Operational Research Society*, Vol. 34 (January 1983), pp. 27–35.

Gostl, J., and I. Greenberg. "An Application of Queuing Theory to the Design of a Message-Switching Computer System," *Communications of the ACM*, Vol. 28, No. 5 (May 1985), pp. 500–505.

Grassmann, Winfried K. "Finding the Right Number of Servers in Real World Queuing Systems," *Interfaces*, Vol. 18, No. 2 (March–April 1988), pp. 94–104.

Green, L., and P. Kolesar. "The Feasibility of One-Officer Patrol in New York City," *Management Science*, Vol. 30, No. 8 (August 1984), pp. 964–981.

Kaplan, Edward H. "A Public Housing Queue with Reneging and Task-Specific Servers," *Decison Sciences*, Vol. 19 (1988), pp. 383–391.

Lambert, Carolyn U., and Thomas P. Cullen. "Balancing Service and Costs Through Queuing Analysis," *Cornell Quarterly* (August 1987), pp. 60–72.

Morse, Philip M. *Queues, Inventories and Maintenance*. New York: Wiley, 1958.

Northcraft, Gregory B., and Richard B. Chase. "Managing Service Demand at the Point of Delivery," *Academy of Management Review*, Vol. 10, No. 1 (January 1985), pp. 65–75.

Panico, J. A. *Queuing Theory: A Study of Waiting Lines for Business, Economics and Sciences*. Englewood Cliffs, N.J.: Prentice-Hall, 1969.

Paul, R. J., and R. E. Stevens. "Staffing Service Activities with Waiting Line Models," *Decision Sciences*, Vol. 2 (April 1971), pp. 206–218.

Render, B., and R. M. Stair. *Quantitative Analysis for Management*, 3d Ed. Boston: Allyn and Bacon, 1988.

Sasser, W. Earl. "Match Supply and Demand in the Service Industries," *Harvard Business Review*, Vol. 54, No. 6 (November–December 1976), pp. 133–140.

Sasser, W. Earl, R. Paul Olsen, and D. Daryl Wyckoff. *Management of Service Operations*. Boston: Allyn and Bacon, 1978.

Shannon, R. E. *Systems Simulation: The Art and Science*. Englewood Cliffs, N.J.: Prentice-Hall, 1975.

Solomon, S. L. *Simulation of Waiting Lines*. Englewood Cliffs, N.J.: Prentice-Hall, 1983.

Sze, D. Y. "A Queuing Model for Telephone Operator Staffing," *Operations Research*, Vol. 32, No. 2 (March–April 1984), pp. 229–249.

Watson, H. J. *Computer Simulation in Business*. New York: Wiley, 1981.

Welch, N., and J. Gussow. "Expansion of Canadian National Railway's Line Capacity," *Interfaces*, Vol. 16, No. 1 (January–February 1986), pp. 51–64.

Worthington, D. J. "Queuing Models for Hospital Waiting Lists," *Journal of the Operational Research Society*, Vol. 38 (May 1987), pp. 413–422.

12

Service Inventory Systems

INTRODUCTION

To date, operations managers, both practitioners and academicians, have focused on developing the theory and planning of inventory control systems for manufacturing

This chapter was written by Sidhartha R. Das, Department of Decision Sciences, George Mason University.

––––– EXHIBIT 12–1 ––

■ *Input Materials and Output Goods in Services*

Type of Service	Input Materials (What Is Processed)	Output Goods (What Is Sold)
Retailers, wholesalers	Consumer goods, repair parts	Consumer goods, repair parts
Restaurant	Raw food, cooked food, beverages	Prepared food, beverages
Publisher	Paper, ink	Books, magazines, newspapers
Bank	Currency, gold	Currency, gold, coins, legal documents
Consulting and advisory	Forms, paper, ink or ribbons	Reports
Legal firm	Forms, paper	Legal documents, reports
Airline, bus, rail line	Gasoline or oil, food and beverages, tickets	Tickets, food and beverages
Movie theater	Tickets, snack foods	Tickets, food
Real Estate	Forms, real estate	Legal documents, reports, real estate

operations. In this chapter we extend this theory to the area of service inventory management.

If a service is a deed, performance, or effort, as some writers have defined it, why are we concerned with inventory problems? There are several reasons for giving considerable consideration to inventories in service businesses.

First, practically all services utilize some sort of input materials that are kept in inventory. Second, many services supply an output product in addition to some sort of performance. Third, adequate service levels usually mean that performance of service cannot be permitted to be delayed for lack of materials or related products.

Input inventory for services is required for matching service to demand. It is also an operating cost of the system, as in manufacturing. However, the cost of running out of inventory is usually much higher for services because of customer expectations of prompt service. In manufacturing, inventories separate production from customers. In contrast, in services, input materials in inventory are used on customers, provided for customers during the performance of the service, or used up to generate the service.

Many services fall in a classification called the **knowledge industry.** These services usually provide stored rather than oral information. The storage device (book, disk, tape, or report) that contains the information is the unit that is sold. The service is embedded in a low-value container that may be stored. Other services such as retail, wholesale, and restaurants must usually retain some output goods in inventory. In Exhibit 12–1 we show examples of input materials and output goods for services.

CHARACTERISTICS OF SERVICE INVENTORIES
Input and Output Materials

Manufacturing is concerned with changing the form of input materials. In many services, however, the form of input materials remains unchanged. Retailing and wholesaling, for example, usually involve no change in the form of goods. Real estate services usually accept property as the owner supplies it to sell. Even restaurants serve some foods in exactly the form in which they buy it. Banks, of course, deal in currency, so that input and output are identical.

In services, input materials are often a trivial cost of doing business. That is, many services use only blank paper or forms as process input materials. Inventories of these are usually a very small cost of operations.

Output materials may be used on the customer directly, as in the cases of proprietory cosmetics, surgical thread, anesthetics, and prepared food. The customer cannot store such output materials for use at such time as he or she needs them again. In manufacturing, the customer can always store the goods he or she needs and continue uninterrupted production. If the service supplier, however, runs out of raw materials, the service cannot be performed and customers may be lost.

Perishability

Style goods of retailers, input and output food items of restaurants, and newspapers are examples of perishable inventory items of services. Exhibit 12–2 shows examples of input and output goods with different degrees of **perishability.**

Sometimes an item in input inventory may have a long life while the same item in output inventory may have a short life. For example, newspapers keep files on notable living people. Such data are kept for long periods. However, when data from the files are used in a newspaper article, the resale output item (newspaper) has a very short inventory life. Conversely, the input information represented by actors playing in a movie is very short, but the finished film has a very long inventory life.

These examples of perishability are indications that in services the inventory problem varies tremendously and is often quite different from that of manufacturing. In many services, the amount of inventory purchased is heavily weighted by perishability factors. This implies that the cost of holding perishable items beyond a certain period is very high.

EXHIBIT 12–2

▪ *Perishables in Service Inventories*

Life of Items	Items
Very short	Certain transplant organs, tickets for same-day event
Short	Fresh fruit, certain transplant organs, retail items for a commemorative occasion
Medium	Certain retail goods, hospital drugs, seasonal style goods in retailing, credit cards
Long	Postage stamps, books, certain retail and wholesale goods

—— EXHIBIT 12–3 ——————————————————————————

■ *Lumpiness of Input Materials in Services*

Lumpiness	Examples
Smooth	Provision of gas for cooking/heating applications by gas service firms
Minor lumpiness	Office supplies, paint, food supplies, and other locally available items
Moderate lumpiness	Office forms, mail order supplies, textile materials, or lumber cut to order
Major lumpiness	Office forms, clothing, cosmetics, and chemicals requiring months of lead time

Lumpiness of Input Materials

Lumpiness refers to the need to buy in quantities, or "lumps," because of the nature of the input materials, the lead time, and the difficulty or high cost of obtaining small shipments from vendors. It is common in services to have a low degree of lumpiness and a smoother flow of input materials than in manufacturing. Many small services simply pick up input materials locally as needed. Exhibit 12–3 gives examples of materials for various levels of lumpiness. This aspect of services means that holding costs for input inventory tend to be negligible.

THE INPUT MATERIAL DECISION PROBLEM

There is a close relationship between the timing of inventory orders and the size of an order. The greater the frequency of orders, the smaller is the order size.

There is also a decision to be made as to whether orders of variable size are to be placed at regular intervals, whether constant-size orders will be placed at irregular intervals, or whether it is possible to place constant-size orders at regular periods.

Because of random variations in demand for services and in lead time for delivery of input materials, the two variables of order size and timing of purchases may be difficult to specify. The adverse effects of errors in quantity or timing are indicated in Exhibit 12–4. They include excessive carrying costs, poor customer service, and excessive order processing or purchase costs.

The input material decision problem must often take into account a series of inventories through which materials move. In Exhibit 12–5 we see that the service maintains its own inventory. For replenishment, the service calls on its vendor or supplier. The vendor calls on the factory warehouse, which, in turn, calls on manufacturing for replenishment. If any link in the chain runs short, replenishment of the service firm's inventory may be additionally delayed. Such a system, with information loops, has been simulated by distribution requirements planning[1] models.

---

[1] For a complete treatment of distribution requirements planning (DRP), the reader is referred to: Andre Martin, *DRP: Distribution Resource Planning* (Essex Junction, Vt.: Oliver Wight Limited Publications, 1983).

EXHIBIT 12–4

■ *Adverse Effects of Wrong Timing and Quantity*

	Planning Production and Purchase Orders			
	Wrong Timing		Wrong Quantity	
Effects	Order Is Late	Order Is Early	Too Large	Too Small
Customer service	Poor	—	—	Poor
Inventory carrying cost	—	Excessive	Excessive	—
Order-processing cost	Excessive	—	—	Excessive
Capacity control	Poor	—	Poor	Poor

Source: Richard J. Schonberger, *Operations Management* (Homewood, Ill.: BPI/Irwin, 1981), p. 166. Used with permission.

EXHIBIT 12–5

■ *Storage Points for Alternative Channels for Materials Supply*

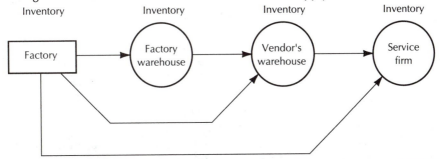

SERVICE INVENTORY CONTROL SYSTEMS

Managers of service operations can establish control systems for managing inventory. The first step in such a system is to classify inventory items by the ABC method of classification.

ABC analysis divides on-hand inventory into three classifications based on annual dollar volume. ABC analysis is an inventory application of what is known as the **Pareto principle.** The Pareto principle states that there are a critical few and trivial many.[2] The idea is to focus resources on the critical few and not the trivial many.

To determine annual dollar volume for ABC analysis, we measure the *annual demand* of each inventory item times the *cost per unit.* Class A items are those on which the annual dollar volume is high. Such items may represent only about 15 percent of total inventory items, but they represent 70 to 80 percent of the total inventory cost. Class B items are those inventory items of medium annual dollar volume. These items may represent about 30 percent of the items and 15 percent of the value. Those with

---

[2] Villefredo Pareto, eighteenth-century Italian economist.

——— EXHIBIT 12–6 ———

■ *Graphic Presentation of ABC*

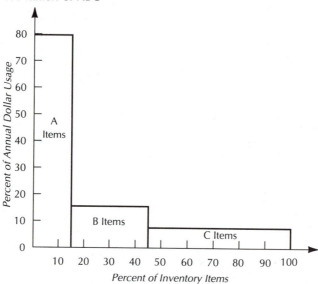

low annual dollar volume are class C, which may represent only 5 percent of the annual dollar volume but about 55 percent of the total items.

Graphically, the inventory of many organizations would appear as presented in Exhibit 12–6. An example of the use of ABC analysis in a health care application is provided in Reading 12.1.

INVENTORY CONTROL SYSTEMS FOR INDEPENDENT DEMAND ITEMS

The inventory models discussed in this section are based on the assumption that demand for a service/service item is *independent* of the demand for another service/service item. These services (or service items) are directly demanded by the customer, usually as a completed service (or service item), which is also known as an **end service** or **end item.** For example, the demand for the services of a dentist may be independent of the demand for the services of a heart surgeon. The demand at your drugstore for a *USA Today* newspaper may be independent of the demand for a copy of the *PC World* magazine. This section is concerned with the application of classical inventory models and systems to an independent service demand situation. The next section will discuss models dealing with dependent service demand situations, where the demand for one service will *depend* on the demand for another. This means that the demand for this service is directly related to or derived from the demand for other end services.

As services subject to independent demand are directly demanded by the customers, they are exposed to demand uncertainty and therefore need to be forecast. Hence it becomes necessary to forecast the number of patients who will require the services of a dentist, as well as the number of daily newspapers that are to be ordered by a newsstand.

An inventory control system has a set of procedures that indicate the quantity of material that should be added to inventory and the time to do so. Control systems for independent demand service inventory can be broadly divided into two classes: fixed-quantity and fixed-period (i.e., periodic) systems.

Fixed-Quantity Systems

A **fixed-quantity system** adds the same amount to the inventory of an item each time it is reordered. Orders are placed when the inventory on hand is reduced to an amount known as the **reorder point.** Hence it is event-triggered, with the event of reaching a reorder point occurring any time, depending on the demand for the specific inventory item. Each time the inventory balance is depleted by a sale, the amount of inventory on hand is compared with the reorder point. If the on-hand balance has dropped to this point, a new order (of a prespecified quantity) is placed. If not, no action is taken by the inventory system until the next sale. (See Exhibit 12–7.)

The advantage of a fixed-quantity system is that sometimes a fixed order size is desirable, as in the case of quantity discounts being offered for an order that exceeds a certain size. This method is also appropriate when an order is constrained by certain physical limitations. For example, one may have to order by the truckload and the capacity of a truck will define the size of the order.

An additional advantage of the fixed-quantity system is that it has lower safety stocks when compared to a fixed-period system. This is because it has to guard against demand uncertainty only during the period between placement of a new order and the receipt of that order. (See our discussion in the next section to comprehend this advantage.)

___

EXHIBIT 12–7

■ *Inventory Level in a Fixed-Quantity System*

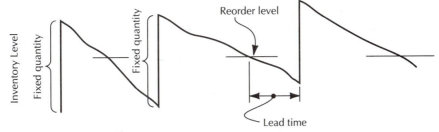

Fixed-Period Systems

In a **fixed-period system,** the inventory level is checked at uniform time intervals. It is time-triggered, with the replenishment of inventory occurring by the passage of a given amount of time. Therefore, there is no tally of the on-hand balance of an item when a withdrawal takes place. The stock on hand is counted only when the ordering date occurs. The quantity ordered is the amount necessary to bring the inventory level up to a prespecified target level. Exhibit 12–8 illustrates this concept.

The advantage of the fixed-period system is that there is no physical count of inventory items after an item is withdrawn—this occurs only when the time for the next review comes up. This procedure is also convenient administratively, especially if inventory control is one of several duties of an employee.

This type of inventory control system and the placement of orders on a periodic basis are appropriate when vendors make routine (i.e., at a fixed time interval) visits to customers to take fresh orders or when purchasers want to combine orders to save ordering and transportation costs (therefore, they will have the same review period for similar inventory items).

The disadvantage of this system is that since there is no tally of inventory during the review period, there is the possibility of a stockout during this time. This scenario is possible if a large order draws the inventory level down to zero right after an order is placed. Therefore, a higher level of safety stock (as compared to a fixed-quantity system) needs to be maintained to provide protection against stockout both during the review period and during the time required for a fresh order to come in.

EXHIBIT 12–8

■ *Inventory Level in a Fixed-Period System*

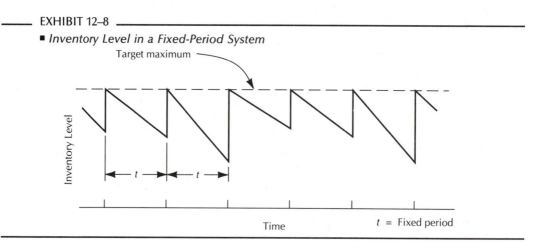

INVENTORY PLANNING
Economic Order Quantity (EOQ) Model

Services may buy and store such items as printed forms, various office supplies, cosmetics (in beauty parlors), medical supplies, consumer goods (in retail and wholesale firms), food (in restaurants), and sporting goods (in resort shops). The service firm's inventory control objective will be to minimize the cost of input inventories.

We will develop a fixed-quantity model in which the **economic order quantity** is used to maintain an inventory of business forms. Such forms may be purchased loose, in pads, or in cartons. It is important to specify the unit whenever calculations are made. In our example we will assume that the forms come in a box of twenty-four pads.

The inventory cost system is made up of two components: holding costs and procurement costs. **Holding costs** are the costs of holding one box for one month of time. These costs consist of such items as rent for space, insurance, obsolescence, utilities, and opportunity cost of money tied up in inventory. (The time period is arbitrary and could be days, weeks, or years, for example.) **Procurement costs** are the costs involved in placing a single purchase order, receiving the goods, moving the goods to storage, and processing payment.[3]

In order to develop the inventory model, we let

Q = number of units purchased at one time

D = demand (usage) rate for the printed forms for one month

P = number of months in a reorder cycle

LT = lead time, that is, the time between placing and receiving an order

ROP = reorder point

The first part of our model is shown in Exhibit 12–9. An order of size Q is used up at rate D. When the inventory reaches zero, a new order arrives. This is so because we placed an order when the inventory reached the ROP to allow for the lead time (LT) that it takes to obtain the goods.

The second part of the model shows the cost side. In selecting the order size, we note that the larger the order that is placed, the larger is the average inventory for the year. Hence total inventory cost for a year is larger for a large order size Q than for a small order quantity. On the other hand, as Q is increased, fewer orders need to be placed during the year. Therefore procurement costs decrease as the order size is increased.

Let H = holding cost for one box of forms for one month

S = cost of placing a single order

---

[3] According to James A. O'Brien, procurement costs can be reduced by information and communications technology such as electronic data interchange (EDI). "This involves the electronic transmission of source documents between the computers of different companies. Source documents representing a variety of business transactions (such as purchase orders, invoices, and shipping notices) are electronically transmitted using standard document message formats. Thus, EDI is an example of the complete automation of the data entry process. Transaction data is transmitted directly between computers, without paper documents and human intervention. Companies in the automotive, chemical, grocery, and transportation industries were the earliest users of this technology, but it has spread to many manufacturing and retailing companies. Some of the benefits of EDI are reductions in paper, postage, and labor costs; faster flow of transactions; reductions in inventory levels; and better customer service" [*Information Systems in Business Management*, 5th Ed. (Homewood, Ill.: Irwin, 1988), p. 187].

_____ EXHIBIT 12–9 _____

■ *Inventory Usage Over Time*

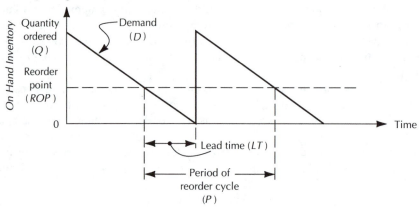

Then $Q/2$ = average inventory (assuming constant demand)

D/Q = the number of purchase cycles per month

The total system cost TC is then

$$TC = S\left(\frac{D}{Q}\right) + H\left(\frac{Q}{2}\right)$$

12.1

In Exhibit 12–10, the component costs and total cost are sketched. The economic order size Q^* occurs when the component costs are equal.

$$S\left(\frac{D}{Q}\right) = H\left(\frac{Q}{2}\right)$$

and therefore,

$$Q^* = \sqrt{\frac{2DS}{H}}$$

12.2

As an example, suppose that the cost of placing an order for business forms is $S = \$20$, the cost of holding one box in inventory for one month is $H = \$0.30$ per month, and the demand for the forms for one month is $D = 3$ boxes per month. Then,

$$Q^* = \sqrt{\frac{2 \times \$20 \times 3}{\$0.30}} = 20 \text{ boxes}$$

EXHIBIT 12–10

■ *Cost Components*

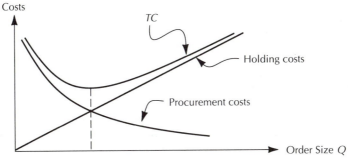

If it takes two months from the time that an order is placed until the forms arrive in the stock room, then the reorder level is

$$ROP = \text{(monthly demand} \times \text{lead time)} = 3 \times 2 = 6 \text{ boxes} \qquad \textbf{12.3}$$

As a safety precaution, a **buffer stock** of two or three extra boxes may be kept in reserve so that if the shipment is delayed, a stockout may be avoided.

Perishable Goods Model

A simple example will illustrate a model for ordering perishable goods. Suppose that a student club has obtained rights to sell brochures for a high school football game. These brochures describe the players of both teams, personalities of the school, and photos of interest. Some local advertising helps pay the publication cost of the number to be published. The brochures sell for $3 and may be ordered from a local printer for a cost of $1 each. The club faces the problem of how many brochures to order from the printer because those which are not sold are worthless. The cost of the unsold brochures must be deducted from the profits of those that are sold.

As a start, the students

— Estimate alternative possible demands for the brochure
— Estimate a probability that each demand will occur
— Compute the conditional profit for stocking an amount equal to each potential demand

Exhibit 12–11 shows these data. To illustrate the computations, we consider a demand of 2100 brochures and an inventory of 2300 brochures. Then we earn $2 × 2100 but have an additional cost of $1 on each of the 200 unsold brochures. Our net profit of $4000 is shown in the right column, second row.

In Exhibit 12–12, we show the computations of expected values for each alternative amount to be ordered. The expected value (or profit) of a particular order

_____ EXHIBIT 12–11 _____

▪ *Conditional Profit for Different Combinations of Demand and Order Quantity*

Alternative Demands	Probability	Order Quantity			
		2000	2100	2200	2300
2000	0.10	$4000	$3900	$3800	$3700
2100	0.30	$4000	$4200	$4100	$4000*
2200	0.40	$4000	$4200	$4400	$4300
2300	0.20	$4000	$4200	$4400	$4600

*[$2 × 2100] − [$1 × (2300 − 2100)] = $4000

_____ EXHIBIT 12–12 _____

▪ *Expected Values for Ordering Different Quantities*

Alternative Demands	Order Quantity			
	2000	2100	2200	2300
2000	$ 400	$ 390	$ 380	$ 370
2100	$1200	$1260	$1230	$1200
2200	$1600	$1680	$1760	$1720
2300	$ 800	$ 840	$ 880	$ 920
Expected profit	$4000	$4170	$4225	$4210

quantity is calculated by multiplying each demand probability in Exhibit 12–11 by its respective conditional profit, then summing over all possible levels of demand. From Exhibit 12–12 we see that ordering 2200 brochures gives us the highest expected profit, $4225. Therefore, the club should order and, hopefully, sell 2200 copies.

REQUIREMENTS PLANNING FOR DEPENDENT DEMAND

The demand for many services or service items may be classified as dependent demand, which requires a different type of inventory control system than previously discussed. Service demand is considered **dependent** when it is directly related to or derived from the demand for other services (known as end services or end items). For example, in a restaurant where bread and vegetables are included in every meal ordered, the demand for bread and vegetables is *dependent* on the demand for meals. The demand for meals may be forecasted. The demand for bread and vegetables is calculated or *derived* from the demand for meals. The meal is an *end* item. The bread and vegetables are *component* items.

A **bill of materials** (BOM) may be created for end items or services, such as a meal, that *lists* the materials and quantity of materials needed to provide the final service in the *order* they are needed. Exhibit 12–13 shows a bill of materials and accompanying product structure tree for veal picante, a top-selling entree in a New

EXHIBIT 12–13

■ *Product Structure Tree and Bill of Materials for Veal Picante*

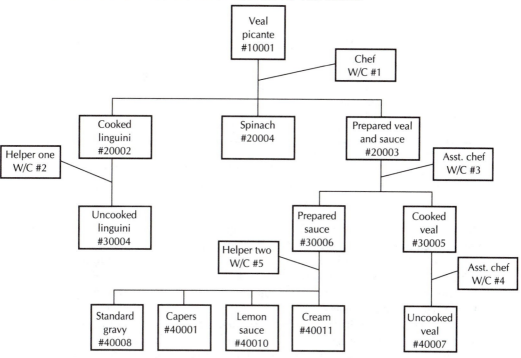

(a) PRODUCT STRUCTURE TREE

Part Number	Description	Quantity	Unit of Measure	Unit Cost
10001	Veal picante	1	Serving	—
20002	Cooked linguini	1	Serving	—
20003	Prepared veal and sauce	1	Serving	—
20004	Spinach	0.1	Bag	0.94
30004	Uncooked linguini	0.5	Pound	—
30005	Cooked veal	1	Serving	—
30006	Prepared sauce	1	Serving	—
40007	Uncooked veal	0.25	Pound	2.15
40008	Standard gravy	1	Serving	0.42
40009	Capers	0.20	Carton	0.80
40010	Lemon sauce	0.050	Bottle	1.15
40011	Cream	0.066	Pint	1.30

(b) BILL OF MATERIALS

Source: John G. Wacker, "Effective Planning and Cost Control for Restaurants," *Production and Inventory Management* (First Quarter 1985), pp. 55–69. Reprinted with permission, American Production and Inventory Control Society, Inc.

———— EXHIBIT 12–14 ——

■ Bill of Labor for Veal Picante

			Labor Hours	
Workcenter	Operation	Labor Type	Set-up Time	Run Time
1	Assemble dish	Chef	.0069	.0041
2	Cook linguini	Helper one	.0005	.0022
3	Cook veal and sauce	Assistant chef	.0125	.0500
4	Cook veal	Assistant chef	.0125	.0833
5	Prepare sauce	Helper two	.0166	.0833

Source: Adapted from John G. Wacker, "Effective Planning and Cost Control for Restaurants," *Production and Inventory Management,* First Quarter, 1985, p. 60. Reprinted with permission, American Production and Inventory Control Society, Inc.

Orleans restaurant. Notice that the various components of veal picante (that is, veal, sauce, and linguini) are prepared by different kitchen personnel (a chef, assistant chef, and helpers). These preparations also require different amounts of time to complete. Exhibit 12–14 shows a **bill of labor** (BOL) for veal picante. It lists the operations to be performed, the order of operations, and the labor requirements for each operation (type of labor and labor hours).

Basically, a **requirements planning system** takes a schedule or forecast of end items or services and, using the bill of materials and bill of labor, determines what component items or services are required and when they are required. It also specifies when an operation should be started or item purchased so that it will be completed or arrive when it is required. Thus, a requirements planning system is both an inventory control system (it decides when to order materials and how much to order) and a scheduling system (it decides when an operation should begin).

Requirements planning systems in manufacturing firms initially were called MRP for Material Requirements Planning. As the name implies, these systems were used to plan for the availability of *materials* as required to manufacture a product. Later, as the systems evolved to include the planning and control of resources other than materials, such as labor hours, machine hours, tooling, and cash, they became known as MRP-II systems for Manufacturing Resource Planning. Exhibit 12–15 defines some terms common to MRP systems. As you can see, many of these terms can be used in services as well as manufacturing. The next section describes in more detail the use of MRP-II systems in services.

MRP-II in the Service Context

Exhibit 12–16 shows how MRP-II logic can be applied to service planning.[4] Referring to the exhibit, the blocks represent plans or schedules at varying levels of detail. The

[4] This section is adapted from B. M. Khumawala, C. Hixon, and J. S. Law, "MRP II in the Service Industries," *Production and Inventory Management* (Third Quarter 1986), pp. 57–63.

—— EXHIBIT 12–15 ——————————————————————————————

■ *Definitions of Terms Used in an MRP Context*

Aggregate Production Planning The planning function of setting the overall level of manufacturing output. Usually stated in broad terms (e.g., product groupings, families of products), its main aim is to establish production rates that will achieve management's objectives (in terms of inventory levels, backlogs, work-force levels, etc.).

Bill of Labor (BOL) or Bill of Resources A statement of the key resources required to produce an item or service. This can be used to predict the impact of the service (or item) scheduled in the master service (or production) schedule.

Bill of Material (BOM) A listing of all the parts, components, and raw materials and the quantities required of each that go into an end item or parent assembly.

Dependent Demand The demand for an item or service when it is directly related to or derived from the demand for other items or services. Dependent demand is calculated from the production plans for parent items.

End Item An item sold as a completed item (i.e., finished product) or repair part. Any item that is subject to a customer order or sales forecast is an end item.

End Service A service that is subject to customer orders or sales forecasts. Often, the service that is directly offered to the customer.

Independent Demand The demand for an item or service when such demand is not related to the demand for other items or services. Independent demand is generated directly by the customers and needs to be forecast.

MRP (Material Requirements Planning) A set of techniques that uses bills of material, inventory data, and the master production schedule to calculate requirements for materials. It is used to efficiently order and schedule the production of dependent demand inventory items.

MRP-II (Manufacturing Resource Planning) A set of techniques for the effective planning of all the resources (and capacities) of a manufacturing company. It includes and links a variety of functions: business planning, aggregate production planning, master production scheduling, materials requirements planning (MRP), capacity requirements planning, shop-floor and production activity control, and so on. Output from MRP-II systems can be integrated with financial reports, shipping budgets, and inventory projection in dollars.

Master Production Schedule (MPS) A statement of what the firm expects to manufacture of end items and service parts. It provides the specific quantities to be produced and dates for producing them.

——

diamonds represent capacity checks to ensure that the resources are available to execute each plan or schedule. Service firms will vary (as do manufacturing firms) in the amount and level of planning for their requirements. Nevertheless, we will discuss all of the planning levels presented in Exhibit 12–16 for completeness.

Business Planning. Both long-term resources (e.g., equipment requirements) and short-term resources (e.g., working capital requirements, inventory costs, wages) are considered at this level, together with their corresponding budgets. Units of service are converted to dollars to keep the business plan up-to-date and are integrated with financial reports. Marketing strategies such as industry variables, competitors' actions, and service mix are also considered in developing the business plan.

Aggregate Service Planning. The aggregate service plan, as discussed in Chapter 8, is a general plan on how the service organization expects to respond to forecasted

EXHIBIT 12–16

- *MRP-II in the Service Context*

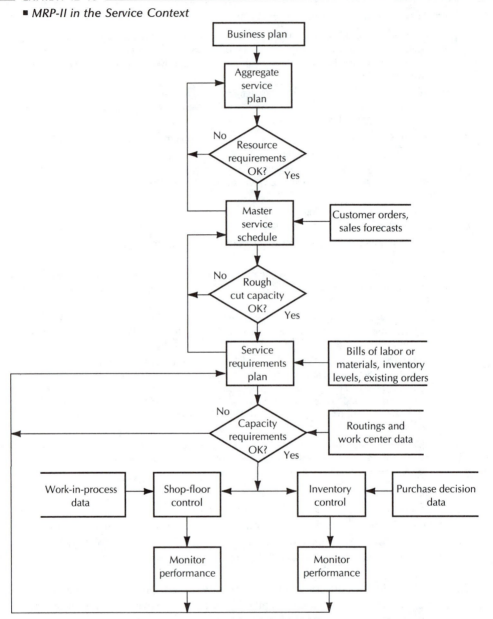

Source: B. M. Khumawala, C. Hixon, and J. S. Law, "MRP-II in the Service Industries," *Production and Inventory Management* (Third Quarter 1986), pp. 57–63. Reprinted with permission, American Production and Inventory Control Society, Inc.

───── EXHIBIT 12–17 ───

■ *Alternatives for Absorbing Variations in Demand*

To Modify Demand	To Control Supply
Vary price—seasonal prices	Specialize tasks during peak
Vary services offered during	demand periods
peaks and troughs	Vary customer participation
Develop alternative services to	Vary available work force
shift peaks	Under/overtime
Smooth demand via reservations	Hire/fire
	Subcontract

demand. It is an overall contract between finance, marketing, and operations, answering questions of what services to provide, how much to provide, and when to provide them. This function should be performed monthly or quarterly and should consider current business conditions along with immediate past company performance. It consists of identifying resources and service rates required to support the business plan in a manner consistent with the overall objectives of the company. These overall objectives include how demand variations are to be absorbed. Exhibit 12–17 shows some alternatives for handling demand variations by modifying demand and/or controlling supply.

Resource Requirements Planning.   Resource requirements planning involves establishing long-term overall levels of capacity. Its purpose is to evaluate the aggregate service plan prior to its implementation. To check its impact on key resources, the aggregate service plan is converted to standard cost dollars, man-hours, and/or equipment hours by using service load profiles and bills of resources. Capacity levels or limits are established, measured, and adjusted so that they are consistent with the aggregate service plan.

Master Service Scheduling.   The master service schedule (MSS) is a realistic, detailed, statement of what the service firm expects to accomplish in terms of services delivered to the customer: what, when, and how many. It is more detailed than the aggregate service plan in terms of timing (hours or days) and the type of service (specifically what the customer has requested).

The master service schedule can vary considerably depending on the type of service. The master schedule is based on *customer orders* if the service can be prepared in advance. However, if demand for the service is immediate, it must be *forecast* for inclusion in the master schedule. For example, a physician uses an appointment calendar as a master schedule. This master schedule includes a number of customer orders (appointments made in advance, such as routine check-ups or nonemergency calls), as well as forecast demand (blocks of time reserved for walk-ins and emergency calls). The master schedule for a beautician would also take the form of an appointment calendar. The master schedule for restaurants may be derived solely from customer orders (when reservations are required), solely from forecast demand (when no reservations are taken), or a combination of the two.

Rough-Cut Capacity Planning.   Rough-cut capacity planning (RCCP) involves short-term capacity considerations that are affected by irregularities in demand. It establishes benchmarks for the proper use of personnel, machines, and shifts.

Bills of capacity and bills of labor for *critical* services or resources are the primary inputs to determine rough-cut capacity. From these bills, the capacity requirements for critical work centers are itemized and evaluated. Any work center that cannot produce the desired output within a given time frame because of capacity limitations is highlighted for adjustment. Such adjustments may include increasing capacity, reassigning services to other work centers if possible, and/or rescheduling planned services. If the RCCP shows that the capacity is available, then the numbers in the master service schedule become the set of planning numbers that "drive" the service requirements plan.

Service Requirements Planning.   Service requirements planning (SRP) determines the relative importance of services: which services should be performed and when. It uses bills of labor, bills of material, and data on existing orders to convert the master service schedule into requirements for component services. As in MRP, it makes recommendations for service releases and for rescheduling when due dates cannot be met. Specifically, the service requirements plan uses the bill of materials to decide how much of what material is needed to meet the demand contained in the master schedule, and the bill of labor to determine how much of what type of labor is needed to meet the master schedule demand. The SRP will take into account when material is needed and how long it takes to receive the material and generate purchase orders. It will examine when an operation must be completed and how long it takes to complete the operation and generate work schedules for particular service operations.

Capacity Requirements Planning.   The SRP generates purchase orders and work schedules sufficient to meet master schedule demand, but it does not consider whether the firm has enough capacity (e.g., workers, space, money) to execute the schedules. The capacity requirements plan (CRP) determines whether labor and other resources exist to accomplish the service requirements plan. Levels of capacity that are consistent with the service plan are established, measured, and adjusted. For services that use appointment calendars to schedule their work, capacity is predefined as the number of "slots" on the calendar and no overloads are typically allowed. Emergency cases can be handled with overtime or by rescheduling existing orders.

Lead times play a major role in CRP. Of the five basic elements of lead time in services (preparation, setup, processing, movement, and queue times), it is queue times that are subject to wide variations. Services are typically more sensitive to lengthy queues than are manufacturing concerns. Thus, most services establish a maximum queue length beyond which they perceive queue time to be excessive. Flexible capacity, such as multi-skilled workers, allows resources to be shifted and queues reduced.

Shop-Floor Control.   This maintains, evaluates, and communicates data such as work-in-process and actual versus planned service requirements. The foundation for good shop-floor control is realistic planning at higher levels (e.g., the master service schedule).

The basis for shop-floor control is a work-in-process file. This file is created when a planned service commences. It states the plan for all existing service orders, operation by operation, as the customer passes through each service. The scheduled completion time is derived from the service requirements planning process. The *appointment calendar* often serves as a dispatch list, showing customer, service(s) to be performed, required setup times, service times, priorities, and expected completion times. Unsatisfactory services can require rework (i.e., reservicing). This can create additional capacity problems if rework time has not been considered during the planning process.

Uncertainty and MRP-II

Services must often deal with indefinite lead times and uncertain bills of materials. Although some services can be based on a time standard (such as an hourly rate), the completion time of many services is difficult to predict. One reason is that a service may involve an undefined parent service. The customer describes the symptoms, from which the service provider determines the problem that needs service (i.e., the end item). If the symptoms described are incomplete or inaccurate, or if the service provider is not aware of all the possible alternative solutions to the problem, then the wrong bill of labor may be derived and the wrong service performed without the desired end results. For example, if an incorrect diagnosis has been made for a patient or until a diagnosis can be correctly made, the bill of material or labor necessary to support the patient's therapy will be uncertain. In case the patient develops other complications, the BOM/BOL has to change accordingly.

One way to alleviate this problem is to split the desired service into common and optional services. The common services will include those services that are always present in the final service configuration. These can be exploded through the requirements planning process without difficulty. The optional services will vary with the customer needs and must be forecast. For example, an automobile repair shop will offer a tune-up as a service. All the basic tune-up procedures will form the common service. The replacement of faulty parts (parts and labor) discovered during the tune-up will be an optional service because it is not possible to know beforehand what parts will need to be replaced.

Applications of MRP-II

Regardless of how unstructured a service is, planning for the service requirements enhances efficiency and accountability. Requirements planning systems are being used increasingly in many service industries. The list now includes health care, educational, and food services.[5] An application of requirements planning systems in a health care environment is provided in Reading 12.2. This reading shows how MRP-II logic has

[5] See J. G. Wacker, "Effective Planning and Cost Control for Restaurants: Making Resource Requirements Planning Work," *Production and Inventory Management* (First Quarter 1985), pp. 55–69, and M. J. Showalter, M. S. Froseth, and M. J. Maxwell, "Production-Inventory Systems Design for Hospital Food Service Operations," *Production and Inventory Management* (Second Quarter 1984), pp. 67–81.

been effectively adopted by a hospital and provides specific examples of the various elements of requirements planning systems that have been discussed in this section.

SUMMARY

Inventory often plays a small role in services because

1. There may be no finished goods inventory.
2. Input inventory such as office supplies may be minimal.
3. Input materials may be immediately obtained from local suppliers so that lead time is very short (e.g., auto repair parts, food, gasoline).

In other cases, major input inventories may be required.

Service systems utilize input and output inventories to meet predetermined service levels. These inventories represent a cost system that must be managed and controlled. Service inventory control systems are classified into two types: independent demand and dependent demand inventory control systems.

Two independent demand inventory control systems have been discussed: they are the fixed-period and the fixed-quantity systems. Other topics addressed include ABC analysis, the EOQ model, and the perishable goods model.

Control of dependent demand inventory items is especially difficult in a service environment, which is characterized by demand variability, on-site production, intermittent processing, low volume requirements, indefinite lead times, and uncertain bills of labor. Concepts derived from manufacturing resource planning (MRP-II) systems, used for similar situations in manufacturing, can be used to control dependent demand inventory items. Effective implementation of MRP-II logic to service industries can contribute to reduced inventory and improved customer service.

DISCUSSION QUESTIONS

1. With the advent of low-cost computing, do you see options for the ABC classification method for service inventory items?

2. What are the main reasons for a service organization to have inventory?

3. What is the difference between independent and dependent demand?

4. Describe the costs associated with ordering and maintaining inventory.

5. How can MRP-II be applied to service inventory management?

6. What are the various functions of the master service schedule?

7. What are the problems associated with inventory planning in a service environment?

PROBLEMS

12.1. Develop the equation for the optimal number of orders per year. Use the symbols developed in this chapter. You should use the following steps.

   a. Determine the annual carrying cost.
   b. Determine the annual ordering cost.

   c. Set the annual ordering cost equal to the annual carrying cost.
   d. Solve for the optimal number of orders per year.

12.2. Develop the equation for the optimal number

of days between orders. Use the same variables that are used in this chapter and the following steps.

a. Determine the annual carrying cost.

b. Determine the annual ordering cost.

c. Set the annual carrying cost equal to the annual ordering cost.

d. Solve for the optimal number of days between orders.

12.3. Lila Battle has determined that the annual demand for number 6 screws is 100,000 screws. Lila, who works in her brother's hardware store, is in charge of purchasing. She estimates that it costs $10 every time an order is placed. This cost includes her wages, the cost of the forms used in placing the order, and so on. Furthermore, it is estimated that the cost of carrying one screw in inventory for a year is one-half of one cent. How many number 6 screws should Lila order at a time?

12.4. It takes approximately two weeks for an order of number 6 screws to arrive once the order has been placed. (Refer to Problem 12.3.) The demand for number 6 screws is fairly constant, and on the average, Lila has observed that her brother's hardware store sells 500 of these screws each day. Since the demand is fairly constant, Lila believes that she can avoid stockouts completely if she only orders the number 6 screws at the correct time. What is the reorder point?

12.5. Lila's brother believes that she places too many orders for screws per year. He believes that an order should be placed only twice per year. If Lila follows her brother's policy, how much more would this cost every year over the ordering policy that she developed in Problem 12.3? If only two orders were placed each year, what effect would this have on the reorder point (ROP)?

12.6. In Problem 12.3 you helped Lila Battle determine the optimal order quantity for number 6 screws. She had estimated that the ordering cost was $10 per order. At this time, though, she believes that this estimate was too low. Although she does not know the exact ordering cost, she believes that it could be as high as $40 per order. How would the optimal order quantity change if the ordering cost were $20, $30, and $40?

12.7. Shoe Shine is a local retail shoe store located on the north side of Centerville. Annual demand for a popular sandal is 500 sandals, and John Dirk, the owner of Shoe Shine, has been in the habit of ordering 100 sandals at a time. John estimates that the ordering cost is $10 per order. The cost of the sandal is $5. For John's ordering policy to be correct, what would the carrying cost as a percentage of the unit cost have to be? If the carrying cost were 10 percent of the cost, what would the optimal order quantity be?

12.8. Pampered Pet, Inc., is a large pet store located in Eastwood Mall. Although the store specializes in dogs, it also sells fish, turtle, and bird supplies. Everlast Leader, which is a leather lead for dogs, costs Pampered Pet $7 each. There is an annual demand for 6000 Everlast Leaders. The manager of Pampered Pet has determined that the ordering cost is $10 per order, and the carrying cost as a percent of the unit cost is 15 percent. Pampered Pet is now considering a new supplier of Everlast Leaders. Each lead would cost only $6.65, but in order to get this discount, Pampered Pet would have to buy shipments of 3000 Everast Leaders at a time. Should Pampered Pet use the new supplier and take this discount for quantity buying?

12.9. Annual demand for the notebook binders at Eck's Stationery Shop is 10,000 units. Mary Eck operates her business 300 days per year and finds that deliveries from her supplier generally take five working days. Calculate the reorder point for the notebook binders that she stocks.

12.10. Your service firm uses a fixed-quantity system where the inventory position of each item is updated after every transaction. The firm operates 52 weeks per year. One of the items has the following characteristics:

Demand D = 19,500 units/year

Ordering cost S = $25/order

Holding cost H = $4/unit/year

Lead time L = 2 weeks

a. Calculate the EOQ for this item.

b. For these policies, what are the annual costs of holding the cycle inventory? Placing the orders?

12.11. Suppose instead that your service firm uses a fixed-period system, but otherwise the data are the same as in Problem 12.10. Calculate the period that gives aproximately the same number of orders per year as the EOQ. Round your answer to the nearest week.

12.12. Blank Brothers Funeral Home maintains five models of caskets in its basement warehouse area.

The item number or stock keeping unit (called the SKU), annual demand, and cost of each casket is as follows:

SKU	Annual Demand	Cost
234	50	$200
179	10	$200
222	100	$800
410	50	$100
160	15	$200

The funeral director, Alfred Blank, asks his son Reid, who just completed his MBA degree, to complete an ABC analysis. What should Reid report back to his father?

12.13. McKenzie Services is considering using ABC analysis to focus attention on its most critical inventory items. A random sample of twenty items has been taken and the dollar usages have already been calculated as shown below. Rank the items and assign them to an A, B, or C class. On the basis of this sample, does it appear that ABC analysis will help management identify the significant few items?

Item	Dollar Usage	Item	Dollar Usage
1	$ 9,200	11	$ 300
2	400	12	10,400
3	33,400	13	70,800
4	8,100	14	6,800
5	1,100	15	57,900
6	600	16	3,900
7	44,000	17	700
8	900	18	4,800
9	100	19	19,000
10	700	20	15,500

▬▬ READING 12.1 ▬▬▬▬▬▬▬▬▬▬▬▬▬▬▬▬▬▬▬▬▬▬▬▬▬

The ABC Method in Hospital Inventory Management: A Practical Approach

Richard A. Reid

APPLYING THE ABC CLASSIFICATION METHOD

The ABC inventory classification is a method of dividing all stocked items into three groups based on total annual dollar usage value. The purpose is to establish unique control policies that will be appropriate for each of the three classes of SKUs. The use of this method allows an inventory manager to establish three sets of procedures that together make a cost-effective inventory policy.

Obviously, different SKU groupings will require different control policies. A comprehensive inventory management policy should include the following considerations.

— Demand forecasting approaches
— Ordering procedures

— Safety stock levels
— Issuing methods
— Inventory verification measures

The ABC classification method was applied to a group of forty-seven disposable SKUs in a hospital-based respiratory therapy unit. The methodology was put into effect through the following ten-step procedure.

1. Select those SKUs to be classified, such as all disposable supply items in the respiratory therapy department.
2. Determine the total number of units issued or utilized during the past fiscal year for each SKU.
3. Determine the average unit cost for each SKU

Source: Reprinted with permission, American Production and Inventory Control Society, Inc., *Production and Inventory Management,* Fourth Quarter, 1987, pp. 67–70.

by dividing total purchase costs by total number of SKUs received during the past fiscal year.

4. Calculate the total annual dollar usage cost by multiplying the number of units used by the average unit cost for each SKU.

5. Sort SKUs according to total annual usage value and place in a descending sequence of total usage value.

6. Label each SKU descriptively and sequentially number the items.

7. Calculate the cumulative percentage associated with the number of each SKU by dividing the sequentially assigned item number by the total number of SKUs (1: 2.1 percent; 2: 4.3 percent; 3: 6.4 percent; . . . ; 47: 100.0 percent).

8. Determine the cumulative total annual dollar usage value for each SKU (1: $5849.64; 2: $11,510.64; 3: $16,547.76; . . . ; 47: $51,684.67).

9. Calculate the percentage of final cumulative total annual dollar usage value for each SKU by dividing the cumulative total amount by the grand cumulative total value for all SKUs (1: 11.3 percent; 2: 22.3 percent; 3: 32.0 percent; . . . ; 47: 100.0 percent).

10. Decide on appropriate divisions for the ABC classes. The percentage of SKUs in each of three groupings depends on the nature of the SKUs being classified and their relationship to the goals of the department. It is important to note that it may be appropriate to use more than three distinct classification categories.

INVENTORY CLASSIFICATION RESULTS

Exhibit 12–18 displays the data elements and resulting computed values for the problem, created on a personal computer with a spreadsheet program. The classification listing of SKUs was rank-ordered in accordance with annual dollar usage.

_____ EXHIBIT 12–18 _____

■ *An ABC Classification Listing of Disposable SKUs for Respiratory Therapy Department*

Sequential SKU Number	Cumulative Percent of All SKUs	Total Annual Usage	Average Unit Cost	Annual Dollar Usage	Cumulative Annual Dollar Usage	Cumulative Annual Percent Usage	ABC Inventory Class
1	2.1	117	$ 49	$5,840	$ 5,840	11.3	A
2	4.3	27	210	5,670	11,510	22.3	A
3	6.4	212	23	5,037	16,547	32.0	A
4	8.5	172	27	4,769	21,317	41.2	A
5	10.6	60	57	3,478	24,796	48.0	A
6	12.8	94	31	2,936	27,732	53.7	A
7	14.9	100	28	2,820	30,552	59.1	A
8	17.0	48	55	2,640	33,192	64.2	A
9	19.1	33	73	2,423	35,616	68.9	A
10	21.3	15	160	2,407	38,023	73.6	A
11	23.4	210	5	1,075	39,098	75.6	B
12	25.5	50	20	1,043	40,142	77.7	B
13	27.7	12	86	1,038	41,180	79.7	B
14	29.8	8	110	883	42,063	81.4	B
15	31.9	12	71	854	42,918	83.0	B
16	34.0	18	45	810	43,728	84.6	B
17	36.2	48	14	703	44,431	86.0	B
18	38.3	12	49	594	45,025	87.1	B
19	40.4	12	47	570	45,595	88.2	B

(continues)

_____ EXHIBIT 12–18 *Continued* _____

■ *An ABC Classification Listing of Disposable SKUs for Respiratory Therapy Department*

Sequential SKU Number	Cumulative Percent of All SKUs	Total Annual Usage	Average Unit Cost	Annual Dollar Usage	Cumulative Annual Dollar Usage	Cumulative Annual Percent Usage	ABC Inventory Class
20	42.6	8	58	467	46,063	89.1	B
21	44.7	19	24	463	46,526	90.0	B
22	46.8	7	65	455	46,981	90.9	B
23	48.9	5	86	432	47,414	91.7	B
24	51.1	12	33	398	47,812	92.5	C
25	53.2	10	37	370	48,183	93.2	C
26	55.3	10	33	338	48,521	93.9	C
27	57.4	4	84	336	48,857	94.5	C
28	59.6	4	78	313	49,171	95.1	C
29	61.7	2	134	268	49,440	95.6	C
30	63.8	4	56	224	49,664	96.1	C
31	66.0	3	72	216	49,880	96.5	C
32	68.1	4	53	212	50,092	96.9	C
33	70.2	4	49	197	50,290	97.3	C
34	72.3	27	7	190	50,480	97.7	C
35	74.5	3	60	181	50,662	98.0	C
36	76.6	4	40	163	50,826	98.3	C
37	78.7	5	30	150	50,976	98.6	C
38	80.9	2	67	134	51,110	98.9	C
39	83.0	2	59	119	51,230	99.1	C
40	85.1	2	51	103	51,333	99.3	C
41	87.2	4	19	79	51,412	99.5	C
42	89.4	2	37	75	51,488	99.6	C
43	91.5	2	29	59	51,547	99.7	C
44	93.6	1	48	48	51,596	99.8	C
45	95.7	1	34	34	51,630	99.9	C
46	97.9	1	28	28	51,659	99.9	C
47	100.0	3	8	25	51,684	100.0	C

A natural break in the sequential decrease of SKU annual dollar usage is apparent between the tenth SKU (Pleural Drainage Bottles—$2407.50) and the eleventh SKU (Croupette Canopy—$1075.20). This discontinuity provides a logical basis for separating class A items from those in class B. Thus the first 10 SKUs in Exhibit 12–18 were designated as class A items. They represent 21.3 percent of all SKUs and account for $38,013.70 of annual usage, or 73.5 percent of the total usage value for all supply items.

The next 13 SKUs, numbers 11 through 23, were assigned to the second category: class B. A visual inspection of the tabular listing shows slight discontinuities occurring in the annual dollar usage

values between items 19 and 20 and again between items 28 and 29. However, informed judgment reflecting the importance of various SKUs in achieving departmental goals was used to identify SKUs 20 through 23 as members of the class B grouping with SKUs 24 through 28 then being labeled, along with the last 20 SKUs, as class C items. Although class C contains over one-half of all inventory items, their total annual usage value amounts to only 8.3 percent of the total expenditures for all disposable supplies during the year. These results are summarized for each of the designated inventory classes in Exhibit 12–19.

The results of the ABC inventory method are further illustrated in Exhibit 12–20. This graphic

_____ EXHIBIT 12–19 _____

■ *Summary Parameter Values for ABC Inventory Classification Method*

ABC Inventory Class	Number of SKU Members	Percent of Total SKUs	Annual Dollar Usage	Percent of Annual Dollar Usage
A	10	21.3	$38,023	73.6
B	13	27.6	9,390	18.1
C	24	51.1	4,270	8.3
Totals	47	100.0	$51,684	100.0

_____ EXHIBIT 12–20 _____

■ *Graphic Results from Application of the ABC Inventory Classification Method*

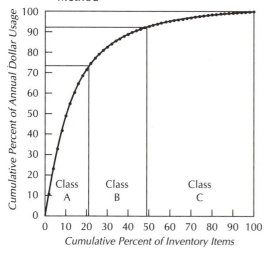

display is a common approach for showing the ABC results. It shows the typical relationship that exists when the cumulative percentage of SKUs is plotted on one axis and the cumulative annual usage value is graphed along the other.

DESIGNING A COMPREHENSIVE INVENTORY MANAGEMENT POLICY

Typically, policy design requires a distinctive approach to each of these five factors within each of the three inventory classes.

Policy for Class A Items

In practice, usage for the 10 class A items was monitored closely and forecasts were updated monthly. Stock replenishment occurred weekly or more frequently, if the reorder point was encountered. Minimum stock levels were established relative to the (1) expected product lead times, (2) availability of substitute SKUs, and (3) SKU criticality. Twice per year these reorder points were reviewed as necessary and revised. A physical inventory was performed weekly to verify recorded stock levels for these SKUs. If several suppliers were available or alternative acceptable products were being distributed, a competitive bidding process was employed.

Policy for Class B Items

The 13 class B inventory items in the respiratory therapy unit were replenished on a biweekly basis. Some emphasis was placed on negotiating price discounts through blanket order commitments with major suppliers. A reevaluation of safety stock levels for the class B items produced some reductions when explicit computations of the trade-offs between stockout risk and additional carrying cost were assessed.

Policy for Class C Items

The ordering of the 24 SKUs in class C was automated. These SKUs were counted and replenished to a preestablished maximum value every two to three months, as time permitted. The two-bin concept was often used to trigger the purchase of an economic order quantity between replenishment points. Limited storage capacity prevented large quantities of C class items from being ordered. Coordination of purchases for these SKUs occurred when class A and B items were being ordered from two major suppliers.

SUMMARY AND CONCLUSIONS

The ABC inventory method provides a straightforward approach that can assist operations managers in developing a cost-effective inventory control policy. Forty-seven disposable supply items for a respiratory therapy unit were partitioned into three classes relative to their total annual dollar usage value and distinct inventory control policies for each class were established. The 10 class A items, representing about 20 percent of the SKUs and accounting for over 70 percent of total annual dollar usage value, received extensive consideration in the design of an effective inventory management policy. By comparison, inventory control procedures for the class C items reflected a more casual managerial approach. This latter attitude reflects

the small inventory investment in these SKUs and thus the minor potential savings that could be expected.

The well-known ABC method provides a simple, yet powerful, approach to managing inventory. It is important to realize, however, that it may be necessary for an operations manager to override SKU class membership assignments or develop alternative operating procedures should informed judgment demand it. There is no substitute for good judgment, even in approaches as simplistic as the ABC method.

——— QUESTIONS FOR READING 12.1

1. Is it possible to get *more* than three classes of inventory items for the SKUs in this reading?

2. What sort of inventory management policy is required for a class C item that is absolutely critical for patients' welfare? (This implies that dollar usage may not be the only factor to be considered.)

——— READING 12.2

Requirements Planning Systems in the Health Care Environment

Earle Steinberg ▪ Basheer Khumawala ▪ Richard Scamell

Expenditures in the surgical operating suite can be separated into two general areas: those that deal with human resources and those that deal with the required equipment, materials and supplies.

This paper addresses the cost reduction of the expenditures relating to the second area. Specifically, we focus on how requirements planning system concepts can be used to improve the management of expensive surgical inventory.

The procedures discussed in this paper were developed for Park Plaza Hospital in Houston, Texas. The objectives of the requirements planning system in the surgical suite at Park Plaza are to accomplish three tasks:

— The conversion of gross to net requirements of equipment, material and supplies essential to meet the demands of the surgical schedule
— An automated purchase order scheme for the required materials and supplies
— Determination of a schedule for surgical supplies that require sterilization

Additionally, these tasks are to be accomplished within four major constraints:

— A short planning horizon for surgical procedures (about seven days)

Source: Reprinted with permission, American Production and Inventory Control Society, Inc., *Journal of Operations Management,* Vol. 2, No. 4 (August 1982), pp. 251–259.

— A sterilization process that can require up to sixteen hours for certain instruments
— A limited supply (in some instances only one) of high-technology surgical instruments
— An environment where the supplies (particularly instruments) required for a specific operation often vary from physician to physician

THE SURGICAL SUITE ENVIRONMENT

Park Plaza Hospital is a privately owned 374-bed facility with a surgical suite of nine operating rooms. These operating rooms are reserved at least one week in advance by physicians with surgery privileges at the hospital. Thus, at any point in time, the schedule of planned operations for the next seven days is known with some certainty, while anything beyond this horizon is far less certain. After an operation has been entered on the surgical schedule, it must be confirmed on two other occasions: first, 72 hours beforehand and second, 48 hours prior to the actual operation. This scheduling process permits the assignment of staff (nursing, orderlies, etc.) and the selection of the necessary supplies and equipment for the specific procedure. The patient is generally admitted to the hospital some 12 hours prior to the operation.

Surgery is, for the most part, performed during normal working hours (i.e., 7 A.M. to 5 P.M.), Monday through Friday and some Saturdays. As for the operations themselves, they generally average about 45 minutes. Obviously, however, different operations take different amounts of time and furthermore, there is no set time for any procedure as they differ from case to case and physician to physician. This lack of definitive durations for the procedures is further complicated by evidence that physicians perceive that they work more quickly than they actually do.

As a result, the surgical schedule, for any given operating room on any given day (and hence, for the seven day planning horizon) is not entirely fixed. A typical surgical schedule is shown in Exhibit 12–21. The schedule includes such information as date, operating room number, scheduled time, patient name, patient room number, operation, physician, estimated time, and anesthesia.

Supplies for any operation fall into three general categories:

— Disposable items that can be used only once (see Exhibit 12–22)
— Reusable instruments that are recycled and used again, i.e., they are cleaned, sterilized, and placed back into inventory (e.g., pickups, clamps, etc.)

───── EXHIBIT 12–21 ─────────────────────────────────────

■ *Surgical Schedule File*

Time	Patient	Rm	Operation	Surgeon	Time
Room 1					
7:30			Meatotomy; cysto; cystogram		45 min
TF			C. & P.		45 min
TF		517	T.U.R.P.		1 hr
TF		504	T.U.R.-B.N.		1 hr
Room 2					
7:30			Tonsillectomy		1 hr
8:30			Left breast biopsy; FS; poss. mastectomy		2 hr
TF		533	Left femoral-popliteal bypass		2 hr
TF			L. breast BX; FS; Poss. Mastectomy		2 hr
TF		412	Hiatal herniorraphy; cholecystectomy; sphincterotomy		2 hr

_____ EXHIBIT 12–22 _____

■ *One-Time Use Items: Disposables*

Surgical drapes	Nontextile towels
Surgical gowns	Needles
Varieties of dressing materials	Syringes
Sutures	Razors
Gloves	

— A limited number of high-technology instruments—this limited supply results from the prohibitive costs of these instruments (e.g., a CAT scan, heart-lung machine, etc.)

In addition, the required stock for any operation not only differs with the particular procedure, but also by physician—each having their preference as to the instruments and disposable supplies to be used for a given procedure (e.g., gown, gloves, etc.).

The system will therefore be concerned with the process of having these required supplies arrive at the proper place (i.e., the correct operating room), at the proper time, correctly assigned by surgical procedure and physician preference, and with the maintenance of appropriate and accurate inventory levels.

THE REQUIREMENTS PLANNING SYSTEM

In order to demonstrate the application of Requirements Planning to the surgical suite, a nomenclature that relates to the hospital environment is required. Exhibit 12–23 shows the nomenclature used in this paper and indicates how it parallels the terminology employed in manufacturing applications. The remainder of this section defines

each system component in the context of the surgical suite and describes the role of each in the system.

Surgical Schedule

The first component of the system is the seven day horizon surgical schedule, the analog of a master production schedule. In this case, however, each product is defined as a specific physician performing a specific procedure. This definition is necessary since two physicians performing identical procedures may desire different surgical kits. Therefore, each may fill out his physician preference sheet differently. If, then, we have k physicians, each performing n procedures, we may identify as many as $k \times n$ separate products.

Unlike the conventional master production schedule where the end items are physical products, here the end items represent procedures performed by a specific physician and each end item has a quantity of only one. However, in both cases, the end item remains the target of the material flow and the output of the process.

Surgical Requirements File

The surgical requirements file—the analog of the bill of materials contains the materials and supplies needed for the various procedures (or level 0 end items). In the traditional MRP system, the bill of materials file defines the final product in terms of its components—in the surgical suite such components are the supplies required for a particular surgical procedure in accordance with physician preference. Thus, the items on the Physician's Preference Sheet are defined as level 1 components that must be ready for use (i.e., sterilized if appropriate) in the procedure.

Extending this concept one step further, all

_____ EXHIBIT 12–23 _____

■ *MRP Terminology*

Categories of Requirements	Application	
	Manufacturing	Health Care
Demand	Master production schedule	Surgical schedule
Materials requirements	Bill of materials	Surgical requirements file
Inventory	Inventory	Inventory item file

items that require sterilization are considered level 2 subassemblies with lead times equal to their required time for sterilization (this time ranges from five minutes to, as mentioned, 16 hours) and recycling. While this concept means that inventory records must be kept on two levels, such a scheme provides an effective method for handling items that must be sterilized. Sterilization units may be viewed as machine centers with limited capacity. One of the outputs of the system is a projected load for sterilization and a schedule of release of sterilized items to projected inventory.

The procedure for systems operation is shown in Exhibit 12–24. The system operation begins with an inquiry to the surgical schedule. If capacity is available in the surgical schedule, the procedure is to update the schedule by inserting the operation in the appropriate spot. The schedule is then exploded through the surgical requirements file to generate gross requirements for all necessary materials and supplies. Note that a specific product (i.e., a particular physician performing a specified procedure) is identified which is traceable to a single physician preference sheet. The gross requirements thus generated are netted against the pro-

jected on hand inventory for all items required. Note that in Exhibit 12–25 a sample record for a reusable component is shown.

Note the similarity to the normal gross to net calculations in a standard MRP system. There are, however, a few significant differences. In the current period, the inventory record shows a balance of fifteen blades. Normal sterilization capacity for this item is ten blades per period. Projected on hand balances are calculated as follows:

$$OH_t = OH_{t-1} + S_t + SR_t + POR_t - GR_t$$

where OH_t = on hand at the end of period t

S_t = completed sterilization at end of period t

SR_t = scheduled receipts by end of period t

POR_t = planned order receipts due by end of period t

GR_t = gross requirements by end of period t

Whenever OH_t becomes negative, a net requirement is generated, resulting in a planned order

---

EXHIBIT 12–24

▪ *System Logic*

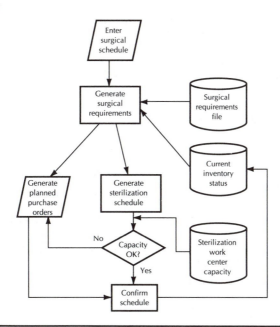

_____ EXHIBIT 12–25 _____

■ *Item Record for Reusable Part*

Item: Blade, #10   Sterilization lead time: 2 periods   Procurement lead time: 1 period

Period

	0	1	2	3	4	5	6	7	8	9	10	11	12
Gross requirements		5	5	10	10	10	15			5	10		
Scheduled receipts													
Projected sterilized				5	5	10	10	10	10	5		5	10
Projected on-hand	15	10	5	0	0	0	0	10	20	20	10	15	25
Net requirements					5		5						
Planned order receipts					5		5						
Planned order release				5		5							

release for the item. In the example shown in Exhibit 12–25, note that all items, once used, are immediately scheduled for sterilization so that they may be returned to inventory as soon as possible. Therefore, given a sterilization lead time of two periods, the gross requirements of five for period one are due out of sterilization in period three. Also note that of the gross requirements for fifteen in period six, only ten are due out of sterilization in period eight and another five in period nine. This results directly from the sterilization capacity constraint of ten for this item.

With the demand pattern shown for the reusable item in Exhibit 12–25, the system will quickly increase inventory to the minimum stable level required to support the surgical schedule. As long as demand does not exceed twenty-five for any two adjacent periods (recall the sterilization lead time is two periods), inventory will remain at that level. If, however, demand were to increase to forty in any two adjacent periods, one of two decisions could be made.

1. Stabilize inventory at forty.
2. Increase sterilization capability to a minimum of twenty parts per period.

Since technology dictates the total sterilization lead time, only a decision regarding increased capacity or inventory is possible. The choice, of course, depends on cost considerations and projection of future demand patterns.

SYSTEMS DATABASE

Over the course of a year, the surgical suite ordinarily has to schedule hundreds of different operations as well as control the flow of thousands of disposable and reusable inventory items. This section outlines the key data elements required to implement the system in the surgical suite.

The Surgical Schedule File

The Surgical Schedule File should contain all posted surgeries for a specific day and time in each operating room. It includes such data as

— Operation number
— Scheduled date and time
— Operating room number
— Patient room number
— Patient name
— Procedure(s)
— Anesthesia
— Physician name

Inventory Item File

The Inventory Item File is a time-phased inventory record of surgical supplies and instruments required by one or more procedures. Particular care must be taken in this file to distinguish between disposable and reusable items. Data contained in this file include

— Unique item number
— Description of the item
— Level

— Gross requirements
— Quantity on hand (current, allocated, projected available)
— Scheduled receipts
— Planned order releases
— Standard inventory ordering data (i.e., lot size, order point, lead time, vendor information)
— Recycling time (if applicable)

Surgical Requirements File

The Surgical Requirements File is the functional equivalent to a single item bill of materials for a procedure. This file identifies quantities of each item that are needed for a procedure as well as the specific size and/or brand of the item. The file is divided into two parts: the common items and the preference items. The common items represent the materials used by *all* physicians when performing a procedure. On the other hand, the preference items reflect physician differences in surgical material requirements. Collectively, these items establish the inventory requirements of a specific procedure in the following manner:

— Level 0 element number (i.e., procedure identifier)
— Lower-level element numbers of common items
— Lower-level element numbers of preference items (for each physician associated with level 0 element number)

Exhibit 12–26 outlines the two parts of the surgical requirements file for a bronchoscopy. Observe that the upper portion shows the common inventory items used and the lower portion depicts the additional inventory items *preferred* by a specific physician.

OPERATION OF THE SYSTEM

In the environment for which the system was developed, the chief nurse of the surgical suite operates as the medical analog to the materials manager. The chief nurse is in charge of all surgical scheduling and equipment sterilization activities, as well as responsible for inventory management of all required medical supplies for the surgical suite, including all tools, instruments, and equip-

---

EXHIBIT 12–26

■ *Surgical Requirements for a Bronchoscopy*

Common Materials
Bronchoscopy set, rigid
Suction tubing
Telescope, right angle
Telescope, forward oblique
Glass slides
Fixative
Specimen trap
Table cover
Towels

Preference Items
Dr. _____
Flexible bronchoscope
Gloves, size 6½ brown
Dr. _____
Gloves, size 7½
Local set

---

ment, (excluding medication) required for all procedures.

The storeroom, sterilization facilities, and operating rooms themselves are located in one contiguous area under her control. In this area, an inventory of more than 2000 items (equivalent to SKUs) used in conjunction with the various surgical procedures is maintained. Inventory balances are updated by an on-line transaction-driven batch processing system that provides a complete inventory status report for the 2000 items each week. In addition, a query-driven system provides access to the current level of inventory on hand for each item.

The system operation is initiated by a physician request for use of a surgical suite. A query is made to the Surgical Schedule (Master Production Schedule) by a nurse whose responsibility it is to maintain the integrity of the data in the system. If available capacity can be matched to customer requirements, then that portion of the calendar is "consumed" and the surgical procedure is scheduled. In the event no capacity (operating room capacity) is available at the time requested, the schedule is searched for a time and date which the physician finds convenient. Obviously, in this environment, overloading the master schedule is not acceptable since two patients arriving for simultaneous surgery in the same operating room would generate considerable consternation.

Once a procedure is scheduled, a specific product is identified (a physician performing a designated operation) and surgical material requirements are generated for level 1 and level 2 items identified on the Physician Preference Sheet. Recall that level 2 items require a sterilization lead time. A two-step procedure is then utilized for determining availability of required inventory.

Step 1

Examine inventory records for required items. All items available in the storeroom which are needed for the procedure are "kitted" (gathered together in a sterile kit and labeled for the date, physician, operating room, and procedure) and set aside.

Step 2

Items which are not currently available because they are being used for other procedures and require sterilization before being used again are identified. Item records for these parts are of the type shown in Exhibit 12–25. When such a requirement is identified, it is added to Gross Requirements for that item which immediately forces a new gross-to-net calculation and an update of Net Requirements and Planned Order Releases or Sterilization Schedule. Of course, the protocol here is to attempt to sterilize first, then order if such capacity is not available.

If level 1 components are not available, a purchase order request is generated. Because the Surgical Schedule (MPS) usually has a horizon of seven days or more (made possible because of the elective nature of most procedures) coupled with the very short lead time for resupply, the hospital rarely experiences material shortages in this category.

Final confirmation of the schedule is made by the customer (physician) 48 hours prior to each operation. This represents the "planning time fence" within which the schedule is regarded as rigid and cannot be changed except in the event of dire emergency. It also represents the last opportunity for a final check of inventory kits for each procedure. Such a check includes level 1 components obtained from the storeroom or outside purchases as well as level 2 components which,

if not out of sterilization, should at least be in process.

The entire system is designed to be operated by nursing personnel. Its success and acceptance stem from two factors.

1. *Generation of reliable schedules and insurance of adequate supplies.* The reduction of problems in this area leads to greater physician satisfaction and a more harmonious relationship with nursing personnel.

2. *Simplicity of operation.* The system outputs are a daily schedule of surgical procedures, a list of items to be picked from storeroom, a list of items for outside purchase, and a sterilization schedule.

IMPLEMENTATION CONSIDERATIONS

The key to implementing effective materials management systems in health care applications of this type is system performance as measured in two areas.

1. *Customer service*—Does it give the physician what he wants when he needs it? It is our experience that unless the physician is convinced that the system will not endanger the lives or well-being of his patients by saving on what he perceives as "nickel and dime" items, the system has little chance of success. Instead, customer service must be sold to physicians in the guise of a system that assures availability of needed supplies, tools, and instruments.

2. *Cost-effectiveness*—Does the hospital administrator believe the system will save money while still meeting customer service objectives? Elimination of costly excessive safety stocks (especially of short shelf life items), better inventory record accuracy, and more reliable schedules which tend to eliminate bothersome last minute crises are important features, *if* these enhancements are coupled with real cost reductions.

CONCLUDING REMARKS

The application of requirements planning to the surgical suite demonstrates how job shop related techniques can be employed in a nonmanufacturing environment with resource and time constraints but without a physical final product. It furnishes hospital administrators a vehicle to better understand and control the investment in material and supplies in this rapidly increasing cost area. Furthermore, the use of MRP-based technology insures that materials will be available when needed, protects against the overcapitalization of inventory,

and aids in formulating and adjusting reordering policies.

_____ QUESTION FOR READING 12.2

Apply the planning procedure developed in this reading to law firms, automobile repair shops, and consulting firms.

_____ CASE 12.1 _____

Western Ranchman Outfitters

Sharon Veta Snyder

Western Ranchman Outfitters (WRO) is a family owned and operated mail order and retail store business in Cheyenne, Wyoming. It bills itself as "The Nation's Finest Western Store" and carries high-quality western apparel and riding supplies. Its catalog is mailed all over the world; the store and its president, John Veta, have appeared in a short article in *Fortune* magazine; and clothes from WRO were featured in the August 1980 *Mademoiselle*.

One of WRO's most staple items is the button front, shrink-to-fit blue jean made by Levi Strauss (model no. 501). This is the original riveted denim pant that cowboys shrunk by sitting in a tub of hot water. It is the epitome of durability and fit and is still a popular jean. When Mr. Veta was asked his stockout philosophy for this item, he answered, "Would you expect a drugstore to have aspirin?" Further, Mr. Veta has had a pleasant relationship with Levi Strauss for all the years of his business career.

Don Randell, director of merchandising, takes a physical inventory of this item once a month. His records show annual usage, amount on hand, quantity ordered, and quantity received (which has been averaging 185 pairs per month, except in January–March when it averages 150 pairs per month), all dated by the month. The store attempts to keep a safety stock adequate for 60 days for two reasons: production problems of the supplier and a hedge against unusually large orders.

Mr. Randell described the problems of ordering. "The rag business," as it is known, "is made up of the most disorganized group of people I've ever had the opportunity to be associated with," according to Randell. The problems he cited include not specifying a delivery date, unexplained late deliveries, a general lack of productivity, and lead times of up to six months.

Randell contrasted this situation with his experience in the flexible packaging industry, where reliability was a hallmark, and a delay of a single day warranted notification to the customer.

The most recent eight-month period is used to illustrate WRO's ordering difficulties. While the sample figures in Exhibit 12–27 may seem peculiar, they reflect WRO's philosophy of offering a full range of sizes and Mr. Randell's attempts to predict Levi Strauss' delivery pattern so that the store is close to obtaining the stock it needs. For example, in the last eight months, no one bought a pair sized 27 × 36. Nevertheless six were ordered and received so that should such a customer appear, he would be able to satisfy his needs. For size 27 × 34, 33 were ordered, but only 21 were received, which is very close to the 18 sold in the eight months of the previous year. The 27-inch and 28-inch waist sizes shown in the exhibit are but two of the many available waist sizes, of course—waist sizes up to 60 inches are produced and sold.

Randell places an order for Levi blue jeans every month, doing his best to ensure an adequate

Source: From Barry Render and Ralph M. Stair, *Cases and Readings in Management Science,* 2nd Ed. (Boston: Allyn and Bacon, 1990). Used with permission.

—— EXHIBIT 12–27 ————————————————————————————

• *Usage and Ordering of the Levi 501 for Selected Sizes*

Size (in Inches), Waist × Length	Usage	Number Ordered	Number Received
27 × 28	11	—	—
27 × 29	1	—	—
27 × 30	6	—	—
27 × 31	0	—	—
27 × 32	4	—	—
27 × 33	—	—	—
27 × 34	18	33	21
27 × 36	—	6	6
28 × 28	—	—	—
28 × 29	—	—	—
28 × 30	—	—	—
28 × 31	—	3	3
28 × 32	4	—	—
28 × 33	7	—	—
28 × 34	8	21	12
28 × 36	27	30	18
	86	93	50*

* Approximately 54 percent of the number ordered were received.

supply for the business. Normally, WRO customers are not disappointed when requesting the Levi 501. However, in the past two months, the Wyoming Game and Fish Department has been requiring extra pairs of this jean, and WRO has not always had this exact jean in stock. Since there are at least four styles that satisfy the state requirements, the problem is usually overcome with other styles or brands.

Annual demand at WRO for the Levi 501 is 2000 pair. The cost of placing an order is about $10, the carrying cost is 12 percent, and the cost of the Levi to WRO is $10.05 per pair.

—— QUESTION FOR CASE 12.1

Evaluate Randell's ordering policy. How does it compare with formal mathematical approaches?

—— CASE 12.2 ████████████████████████████████████

Touro Infirmary

John J. Fedorko

Touro Infirmary is a medium-sized teaching hospital located in New Orleans. The department of dietetics must meet the varying needs for the feeding of patients, staff, and visitors of the facility. The nutritional requirements of the patients are diverse, necessitating a complex menu structure. Diet options include sodium-restricted, bland, calorie-restricted, and numerous other regimes.

Source: From Barry Render and Ralph M. Stair, *Cases and Readings in Management Science*, 2nd Ed. (Boston: Allyn and Bacon, 1990). Used with permission.

The bed capacity for the institution is 500, indicating a maximum of approximately 1500 meals daily. Since Touro has a large number of Jewish patients, a unique demand is the frequent serving of kosher food. Kosher food must be prepared and served in accordance with strict religious rules. For example, the food must be blessed by a rabbi and prepared with equipment that is used exclusively for kosher products. Additionally, there are restrictions placed upon the food combinations that can be offered in a kosher meal and certain types of meats and fishes may not be served.

Approximately 1825 kosher meals are served to Touro patients over a one-year period. Because the hospital cannot prepare these meals in its kitchens, all kosher meals are ordered from Schreiber Foods in New York, and are shipped by air mail. The cost per dinner is $3.50. If more than 150 dinners are ordered at once, the price is reduced to $3.25 per dinner. The order is placed by telephone and shipment can be expected to be received in three working days. The cost of placing an order is $10. It is estimated that carrying costs are 25 percent of the meal cost; the many additional requirements of religious laws, including special silverware, are part of the reason for this high cost.

A problem arises when a patient orders a kosher meal and the hospital has run out of stock. An alternative source is available in New Orleans but at a premium of $10. Another unusual problem is storage. A separate freezer must be used to store the kosher food. The present freezer has a capacity of 75 dinners. Patton Industries offers a commercial freezer that has a capacity of 225 dinners. The cost of the freezer is $1,800 and it has a useful life of ten years.

The head of the dietary department, Mrs. Kathy Fedorko, has requested an inventory analysis to determine a method for inventory control that will minimize costs.

QUESTIONS FOR CASE 12.2

1. What is the optimal amount to be ordered and how often? At what point should the hospital reorder?

2. Besides quantitative methods to determine proper inventory control, what other considerations should be taken into account? Is there an alternative method that will minimize costs?

3. Should the hospital purchase the larger freezer?

REFERENCES

Aft, L. S. *Production and Inventory Control.* Orlando, Fla.: Harcourt, 1987.

Chase, R. B., and N. J. Aquilano. *Production and Operations Management.* Homewood, Ill.: Irwin, 1985.

Fogarty, D. W., and T. R. Hoffman. *Production and Inventory Management.* West Chicago, Ill.: South Western Publishing Company, 1983.

Heizer, J., and B. Render. *Production and Operations Management: Strategies and Tactics,* Boston: Allyn and Bacon, 1988.

Khumawala, B. M., C. Hixon, and J. S. Law. "MRP-II in the Service Industries," *Production and Inventory Management* (Third Quarter 1986), pp. 57–63.

Krajewski, L. J., and L. P. Ritzman. *Operations Management: Strategy and Analysis.* Reading, Mass.: Addison-Wesley, 1987.

Orlicky, J. *Material Requirements Planning.* New York: McGraw-Hill, 1975.

Showalter, M. J., M. S. Froseth, and M. J. Maxwell. "Production-Inventory Systems Design for Hospital Food Service Operations," *Production and Inventory Management* (Second Quarter 1984), pp. 67–81.

Steinberg, E., B. Khumawala, and R. Scamell. "Requirements Planning Systems in the Health Care Environment," *Journal of Operations Management,* Vol. 2, No. 4 (August 1982), pp. 251–259.

Vollmann, T. E., W. L. Berry, and D. C. Whybark. *Manufacturing Planning and Control Systems.* Homewood, Ill.: Irwin, 1988.

Wacker, J. G. "Effective Planning and Cost Control for Restaurants: Making Resource Requirements Planning Work," *Production and Inventory Management* (First Quarter 1985), pp. 55–69.

Wallace, T. V. (Ed.). *APICS Dictionary,* 5th Ed. Falls Church, Va.: American Production and Inventory Control Society, 1986.

13

Vehicle Routing and Scheduling

This chapter was written by Joanna R. Baker, Department of Management Science, Virginia Polytechnic
Institute and State University.

INTRODUCTION

The scheduling of customer service and the routing of service vehicles are at the heart of many service operations. For some services, such as school buses, public health nursing, and many installation or repair businesses, service delivery is critical to the performance of the service. For other services, such as mass transit, taxis, trucking firms, and the U.S. Postal Service, timely delivery *is* the service. In either case, the routing and scheduling of service vehicles has a major impact on the *quality* of the service provided.

This chapter introduces some routing and scheduling terminology, classifies different types of routing and scheduling problems, and presents various solution methodologies. Although every effort has been made to present the topic of vehicle routing and scheduling as simply and as straightforward as possible, it should be noted that this is a technical subject and one of the more mathematical topics in this text. We begin the chapter with an example of service delivery to illustrate some of the practical issues in vehicle routing and scheduling.

A Service Delivery Example: Meals-for-ME

A private, nonprofit meal delivery program for the elderly called Meals-for-ME has been operating in the state of Maine since the mid-1970s.[1] The program offers home delivery of hot meals, Monday through Friday, to ''home-bound'' individuals who are over 60 years of age. For those individuals who are eligible (and able), the program also supports a ''congregate'' program that provides daily transportation to group-meal sites. On a typical day within a single county, hundreds of individuals receive this service. In addition, individuals may be referred for short-term service because of a temporary illness or recuperation. Thus, on any given day, the demand for the service may be highly unpredictable. Scheduling of volunteer delivery personnel and vehicles as well as construction of routes is done on a weekly to monthly basis by regional site managers. It is the task of these individuals to coordinate the preparation of meals and to determine the sequence in which customers are to be visited. In addition, site managers must arrange for rides to the ''group meals'' for participating individuals.

Although these tasks may seem straightforward, there are many practical problems in routing and scheduling meal delivery. First, the delivery vehicles (and pickup vehicles) are driven by volunteers, many of whom are students who are not available during some high-demand periods (Christmas, for example). Thus the variability in available personnel requires that delivery routes be changed frequently. Second, because the program delivers hot meals, a typical route must be less than 90 minutes. Generally, twenty to twenty-five meals are delivered on a route, depending on the proximity of customers. Third, all must be delivered within a limited time period, between 11:30 A.M. and 1:00 P.M. daily. Similar difficulties exist for personnel who pick up individuals served by the congregate program. Given the existence of these very real problems, the solution no longer seems as simple. It is obvious that solution approaches and

---

[1] Gail Ward of Meals-for-ME provided the information contained in this section.

techniques are needed that allow the decision maker to consider a multitude of variables and adapt to changes quickly and efficiently.

OBJECTIVES OF ROUTING AND SCHEDULING PROBLEMS

The objective of most routing and scheduling problems is to minimize the total cost of providing the service. This includes vehicle capital costs, mileage, and personnel costs. But other objectives also may come into play, particularly in the public sector. For example, in school bus routing and scheduling, a typical objective is to minimize the total number of student-minutes on the bus. This criterion is highly correlated with safety and with parents' approval of the school system.[2] For dial-a-ride services for the handicapped or elderly, an important objective is to minimize the inconvenience for all customers. For the Meals-for-ME program, the meals must be delivered at certain times of the day. For emergency services, such as ambulance, police, and fire, minimizing response time to an incident is of primary importance. Some companies promise package delivery by 10:30 A.M. the next morning. Thus, in the case of both public and private services, an appropriate objective function should consider more than the dollar cost of delivering a service. The "subjective" costs associated with failing to provide adequate service to the customer must be considered as well.

CHARACTERISTICS OF ROUTING AND SCHEDULING PROBLEMS
Routing and Scheduling Terminology

Routing and scheduling problems are often presented as graphical **networks.** The use of networks to describe these problems has the advantage of allowing the decision maker to visualize the problem under consideration. As an example, refer to Exhibit 13–1. The figure consists of five circles called **nodes.** Four of the nodes (nodes 2 through 5) represent pickup and/or delivery points, and a fifth (node 1) represents a **depot node,** from which the vehicle's trip originates and ends. The depot node is the "home base" for the vehicle or provider.

Connecting these nodes are line segments referred to as **arcs.** Arcs describe the time, cost, or distance required to travel from one node to another. The numbers along the arcs in Exhibit 13–1 are distances in miles. Given an average speed of travel or a distribution of travel times, distance can be easily converted to time. However, this conversion ignores physical barriers, such as mountains, lack of access, or traffic congestion. If minimizing time is the primary goal in a routing and scheduling problem,

---

[2] See Lawrence Bodin, Bruce Golden, Arjang Assad, and Michael Ball, "Routing and Scheduling of Vehicles and Crews: The State of the Art," *Computers and Operations Research,* Vol. 10, No. 2 (1983), pp. 70–71.

_____ EXHIBIT 13–1 _____
■ *Routing Network Example*

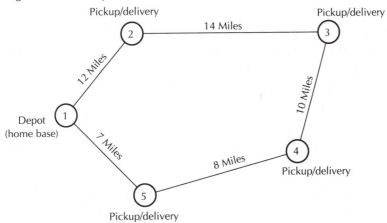

Pickup/delivery

Pickup/delivery

14 Miles

12 Miles

10 Miles

Depot
(home base)

7 Miles

8 Miles

Pickup/delivery

Pickup/delivery

then historical data on travel times are preferable to calculations based on distances.

Arcs may be directed or undirected. **Undirected arcs** are represented by simple line segments. **Directed arcs** are indicated by arrows. These arrows represent the direction of travel in the case of routing problems (e.g., one-way streets) or precedence relationships in the case of scheduling problems (where one pickup or delivery task must precede another).

The small network in Exhibit 13–1 can be viewed as a route for a single vehicle. The route for the vehicle, also called a **tour,** is $1 \rightarrow 2 \rightarrow 3 \rightarrow 4 \rightarrow 5 \rightarrow 1$ or, because the arcs are undirected, $1 \rightarrow 5 \rightarrow 4 \rightarrow 3 \rightarrow 2 \rightarrow 1$. The total distance for either tour is 51 miles.

The tour described in Exhibit 13–1 is a solution to a simple routing problem where the objective is to find the route that minimizes cost or any other criterion that may be appropriate (such as distance or travel time). The minimum-cost solution, however, is subject to the tour being **feasible.** Feasibility depends on the type of problem, but, in general, implies that

1. A tour must include all nodes.
2. A node must be visited only once.
3. A tour must begin and end at a depot.

The output of all routing and scheduling systems is essentially the same. That is, for each vehicle or provider, a route and/or a schedule is provided. Generally, the **route** specifies the sequence in which the nodes (or arcs) are to be visited, and a **schedule** identifies when each node is to be visited.

Classifying Routing and Scheduling Problems

The classification of routing and scheduling problems depends on certain characteristics of the service delivery system, such as size of the delivery fleet, where the fleet is housed, capacities of the vehicles, and routing and scheduling objectives. Exhibit 13–2 lists some typical characteristics of service delivery systems. In the simplest case, we begin with a set of nodes to be visited by a single vehicle. The nodes may be visited in any order, there are no precedence relationships, the travel costs between two nodes are the same regardless of the direction traveled, and there are no delivery-time restrictions. In addition, vehicle capacity is not considered. The output for the single-vehicle problem is a route or a tour where each node is visited only once and the route begins and ends at the depot node (see Exhibit 13–1, for example). The tour is formed with the goal of minimizing the total tour cost. This simplest case is referred to as a **traveling salesman problem** (TSP).

An extension of the traveling salesman problem, referred to as the **multiple traveling salesman problem** (MTSP), occurs when a fleet of vehicles must be routed

---

EXHIBIT 13–2

■ *Classifying Routing and Scheduling Problems*

Characteristics	Options
Size of the fleet	One Multiple
Housing of the fleet	Single depot Multiple depots
Type of demand	At the nodes On the arcs On the nodes and the arcs
Network type	Undirected Directed Mixed
Vehicle capacity	All the same Different Unlimited
Maximum route time	Same for all vehicles Different for all vehicles Not present
Types of operations	Pickups only Deliveries only Mixed
Objectives	Minimum total routing costs Minimum fixed and variable costs Minimum number of vehicles Minimum response time Minimum customer inconvenience

Source: Reprinted with permission from *Computers and Operations Research,* Vol. 10, No. 2, 1983, p. 73, Laurence Bodin, B. Golden, A. Assad, M. Ball, "Routing and Scheduling of Vehicles and Crews: The State of the Art." Copyright 1983, Pergamon Press plc.

_____ EXHIBIT 13–3 _____

■ *Characteristics of Four Routing Problems*

Type	Demand	Arcs	No. of Depots	No. of Vehicles	Vehicle Capacity
Traveling salesman problem (TSP)	At the nodes	Directed or undirected	1	= 1	Unlimited
Multiple traveling salesman problem (MTSP)	At the nodes	Directed or undirected	1	>1	Unlimited
Vehicle routing problem (VRP)	At the nodes	Directed or undirected	1	>1	Limited
Chinese postman problem (CPP)	On the arcs	Directed or undirected	1	≥1	Limited or unlimited

from a single depot. The goal is to generate a set of routes, one for each vehicle in the fleet. The characteristics of this problem are that a node may be assigned to only one vehicle, but a vehicle will have more than one node assigned to it. There are no restrictions on the size of the load or number of passengers a vehicle may carry. The solution to this problem will give the order in which each vehicle is to visit its assigned nodes. As in the single-vehicle case, the objective is to develop the set of minimum-cost routes, where "cost" may be represented by a dollar amount, distance, or travel time.

If we now restrict the capacity of the multiple vehicles and couple with it the possibility of having varying demands at each node, the problem is classified as a **vehicle routing problem** (VRP).

Alternatively, if the demand for the service occurs on the arcs, rather than at the nodes, or if demand is so high that individual demand nodes become too numerous to specify, we have a **Chinese postman problem** (CPP). Examples of these types of problems include street sweeping, snow removal, refuse collection, postal delivery, and paper delivery. The Chinese postman problem is very difficult to solve, and the solution procedures are beyond the scope of this text.[3] Exhibit 13–3 summarizes the characteristics of these four types of routing problems.

Finally, let us distinguish between **routing** problems and **scheduling** problems. If the customers being serviced have no time restrictions and no precedence relationships exist, then the problem is a pure routing problem. If there is a specified time for the service to take place, then a scheduling problem exists. Otherwise we are dealing with a combined routing and scheduling problem.

Solving Routing and Scheduling Problems

Another important issue in routing and scheduling involves the practical aspects of solving these types of problems. Consider, for example, the delivery of bundles of

[3] For more information on the Chinese postman problem the reader is referred to Lawrence Bodin et al., "Routing and Scheduling of Vehicles and Crews: The State of the Art," *Computers and Operations Research,* Vol. 10, No. 2 (1983), pp. 111–112. The problem name derives from the fact the original paper was published in the *Chinese Journal of Operations Research.*

newspapers from a printing site to dropoff points in a geographic area. These dropoff points supply papers to newspaper carriers for local deliveries. The dropoff points have different demands, and the vehicles have different capacities. Each vehicle is assigned a route beginning and ending at the printing site (the depot). For a newspaper with only ten dropoff points there are 2^{10} or 1024 possible routings. For fifty dropoff points, there are 2^{50} or over 1 trillion possible routings. Realistic problems of this type may have over 1000 drop points! It is evident that problems of any size quickly become too expensive to solve optimally even with supercomputers. Fortunately, some very elegant heuristics or "rules of thumb" solution techniques have been developed that yield "good," if not optimal, solutions to these problems. Some of the more well-known of these heuristic approaches are presented in this chapter.

ROUTING SERVICE VEHICLES
The Traveling Salesman Problem

The traveling salesman problem (TSP) is one of the most studied problems in the discipline called management science. Optimal approaches to solving traveling salesman problems are based on mathematical programming (see Chapter 16). But in reality, most TSP problems are not solved optimally. When the problem is so large that an optimal solution is impossible to obtain, or when approximate solutions are good enough, heuristics are applied. Two commonly used heuristics for the traveling salesman problem are the **nearest neighbor procedure** and the **Clark and Wright savings heuristic.**

The Nearest Neighbor Procedure. The nearest neighbor procedure (NNP) builds a tour based only on the cost or distance of traveling from the last-visited node to the closest node in the network. As such, the heuristic is simple, but it has the disadvantage of being rather shortsighted, as we shall see in an example. The heuristic does, however, generate an "approximately" optimal solution from a distance matrix. The procedure is outlined as follows:[4]

1. Start with a node at the beginning of the tour (the depot node).
2. Find the node closest to the last node added to the tour.
3. Go back to step 2 until all nodes have been added.
4. Connect the first and the last nodes to form a complete tour.

Example of the Nearest Neighbor procedure. We begin the nearest neighbor procedure with data on the distance or cost of traveling from every node in the network to every other node in the network. In the case where the arcs are undirected, the distance from i to j will be the same as the distance from j to i. Such a network with undirected arcs is said to be **symmetrical.** Exhibit 13–4 gives the complete distance matrix for the symmetrical six-node network shown in Exhibit 13–5.

---

[4] The outline of the nearest neighbor procedure is taken from Lawrence Bodin et al., "Routing and Scheduling of Vehicles and Crews: The State of the Art," *Computers and Operations Research*, Vol. 10, No. 2 (1983), p. 87.

--- EXHIBIT 13–4 ---

■ *Symmetric Distance Matrix*

From Node	To Node (distances in miles)					
	1	2	3	4	5	6
1	—	5.4	2.8	10.5	8.2	4.1
2	5.4	—	5.0	9.5	5.0	8.5
3	2.8	5.0	—	7.8	6.0	3.6
4	10.5	9.5	7.8	—	5.0	9.5
5	8.2	5.0	6.0	5.0	—	9.2
6	4.1	8.5	3.6	9.5	9.2	—

Referring to Exhibit 13–6, the solution is determined as follows:

1. Start with the depot node (node 1). Examine the distances between node 1 and every other node. The closest node to node 1 is node 3, so designate the **partial tour** or **path** as 1 → 3. (See Exhibit 13–6a. Note that the → means that the nodes are connected, not that the arc is directed.)
2. Find the closest node to the last node added (node 3) that is not currently in the path. Node 6 is 3.6 miles from node 3, so connect it to the path. The result is the three-node path 1 → 3 → 6. (See Exhibit 13–6b.)
3. Find the node closest to node 6 that has not yet been connected. This is node 2, which is 8.5 miles from node 6. Connect it to yield 1 → 3 → 6 → 2. (See Exhibit 13–6c.)
4. The node closest to node 2 is node 5. The partial tour is now 1 → 3 → 6 → 2 → 5. (See Exhibit 13–6d.)
5. Connect the last node (node 4) to the path and complete the tour by connecting node 4 to the depot. The complete tour formed is 1 → 3 → 6 → 2 → 5 → 4 → 1. The length of the tour is 35.4 miles. (See Exhibit 13–6e.)

--- EXHIBIT 13–5 ---

■ *Traveling Salesman Problem*

_____ EXHIBIT·13–6 _____

■ *Nearest Neighbor Procedure*

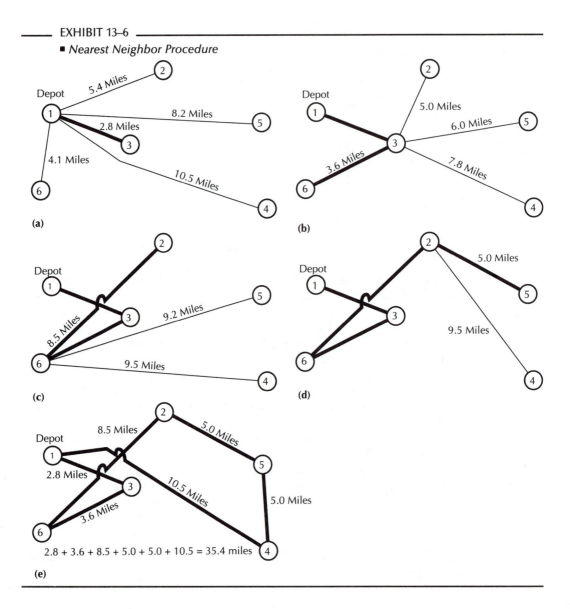

(a)

(b)

(c)

(d)

2.8 + 3.6 + 8.5 + 5.0 + 5.0 + 10.5 = 35.4 miles

(e)

But is this the best-possible route? Examine the network again and try to come up with a better tour. How about $1 \rightarrow 2 \rightarrow 5 \rightarrow 4 \rightarrow 3 \rightarrow 6 \rightarrow 1$? The total distance of this tour is 30.9 miles versus 34.5 miles for the nearest neighbor–constructed tour. This result points to the limitation of heuristics; they cannot guarantee optimality. For this small a network, it would be possible to enumerate every possible tour. However, for large problems with 100 to 200 nodes, enumerating every combination would be impossible.

Before leaving the nearest neighbor heuristic, it should be noted that, in practice, the heuristic is applied repeatedly by assigning every node to be the depot node, re-solving the problem, and then selecting the lowest-cost tour as the final solution. For example, if we repeat the procedure using node 6 as the depot node, the tour that results is $6 \rightarrow 3 \rightarrow 1 \rightarrow 2 \rightarrow 5 \rightarrow 4 \rightarrow 6$ with a total length of 31.3 miles.

Clark and Wright Savings Heuristic. The Clark and Wright savings heuristic (C&W) is one of the most well-known techniques for solving traveling salesman problems. The heuristic begins by selecting a node as the depot node and labeling it node 1. We then assume, for the moment, that there are $n - 1$ vehicles available, where n is the number of nodes. In other words, if we have six nodes in the network, then there are five vehicles available. Each vehicle travels from the depot directly to a node and returns to the depot. Exhibit 13–7 shows this for a three-node network where the miles are shown on the arcs and the arcs are undirected. The distance from node 2 to node 3 is 5 miles. The total distance covered by the two vehicles in Exhibit 13–7 is 36 miles: 20 miles for the trip from the depot to node 2 and return, and 16 miles for the trip from the depot to node 3 and return.

But this is not a feasible solution because the objective of a traveling salesman problem is to find a tour in which all nodes are visited by *one* vehicle, rather than by two vehicles, as shown in Exhibit 13–7. To reduce the number of vehicles needed, we now need to combine the $n - 1$ tours originally specified.

The key to the C&W heuristic is the computation of savings. **Savings** is a measure of how much the trip length or cost can be reduced by "hooking up" a pair of nodes (in the case of Exhibit 13–7, nodes 2 and 3) and creating the tour $1 \rightarrow 2 \rightarrow 3 \rightarrow 1$, which can then be assigned to a single vehicle. The savings is computed as follows. By linking nodes 2 and 3, we *add* 5 miles (the distance from node 2 to node 3), but we *save* 10 miles for the trip from node 2 to node 1 and 8 miles for the trip from 3 to 1. The total tour length for the complete tour, $1 \rightarrow 2 \rightarrow 3 \rightarrow 1$, is 23 miles.

—— EXHIBIT 13–7 ——————————————————————

▪ *Initial C&W Network Configuration: Three-Node Problem*

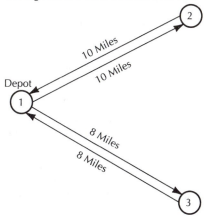

_____ EXHIBIT 13–8 _____

■ *Initial C&W Network: Four-Node Problem*

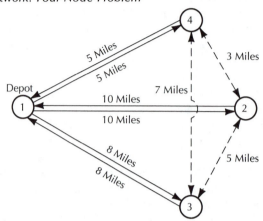

The savings obtained, over the configuration shown in Exhibit 13–7, is 13 miles. For a network with n nodes, we compute the savings for every possible pair of nodes, rank the savings gains from largest to smallest, and construct a tour by linking pairs of nodes until a complete route is obtained.

A statement of the C&W savings heuristic is as follows:[5]

1. Select any node as the depot node (node 1).
2. Compute the savings, S_{ij}, for linking nodes i and j:

$$S_{ij} = c_{1i} + c_{1j} - c_{ij} \quad \text{for } i \text{ and } j = \text{nodes } 2, 3, \ldots, n \qquad \textbf{13.1}$$

where c_{ij} = the cost of traveling from node i to node j.

3. Rank the savings from largest to smallest.
4. Starting at the top of the list, form larger **subtours** by linking appropriate nodes i and j. Stop when a complete tour is formed.

Example Using the C&W Savings Heuristic. To demonstrate how the C&W heuristic is used to solve a TSP problem, consider the network shown in Exhibit 13–8. Here, as in Exhibit 13–7, we assume that there is one vehicle for every node (excluding the depot) in the network. The solid lines show arcs that are in use as we begin the C&W procedure. The dashed lines show arcs that *may* be used but are not in use currently. Distances, in miles, are shown on the arcs. The savings obtained from linking nodes 2 and 3 is 13 miles. This is computed as (10 miles + 8 miles) − (5 miles). The 10- and 8-mile distances are the lengths of the return trip from nodes 2 and 3, respectively, to the depot; 5 miles is the distance from node 2 to node 3. Similarly, the savings of linking nodes 2 and 4 is 12 miles: (5 miles + 10 miles) − (3 miles). The last pair

[5] The outline of the Clark and Wright savings heuristic is taken from Lawrence Bodin et al., ''Routing and Scheduling of Vehicles and Crews: The State of the Art,'' *Computers and Operations Research,* Vol. 10, No. 2 (1983), p. 87.

of nodes to be considered for linking is [4, 3], which yields a savings of 6 miles: (5 miles + 8 miles) − (7 miles).

We next rank the savings for every pair of nodes not yet linked. In order of savings, the pairs are [2, 3], [2, 4] and [3, 4]. The first step in specifying a tour is to link the nodes with the highest savings, nodes 2 and 3. The resulting path is shown in Exhibit 13–9a. Proceeding to the next highest savings, nodes 2 and 4 are linked as shown in Exhibit 13–9b. The tour is now complete—the last pair, nodes 3 and 4, cannot be linked without "breaking" the tour. The complete tour is 1 → 4 → 2 → 3 → 1, which has a total tour length of 21 miles. The total savings obtained over the "one vehicle per node" configuration shown in Exhibit 13–8 is 25 miles.

In general, since C&W considers cost when constructing a tour, it yields better-quality solutions than the nearest neighbor procedure. Both the Clark and Wright savings

_____ EXHIBIT 13–9 _____

■ *First and Second Node Hookups: C&W Heuristic*

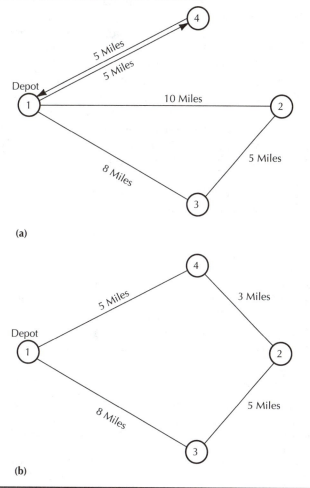

(a)

(b)

heuristic and the nearest neighbor procedure can be easily adjusted to accommodate problems with directed arcs.

Multiple Traveling Salesman Problem

The multiple traveling salesman problem is a generalization of the traveling salesman problem where there are multiple vehicles and a single depot. In this problem, instead of determining a route for a single vehicle, we wish to construct tours for all M vehicles. The characteristics of the tours are that they begin and end at the depot node. Solution procedures begin by "copying" the depot node M times. The problem is thus reduced to M single-vehicle TSPs, and it can be solved using either the nearest neighbor or Clark and Wright heuristics.

The Vehicle Routing Problem

The classic vehicle routing problem (VRP) expands the multiple traveling salesman problem to include different service requirements at each node and different capacities for vehicles in the fleet. The objective of these problems is to minimize total cost or distance across all routes. Examples of services that show the characteristics of vehicle routing problems include United Parcel Service deliveries, public transportation "pick-ups" for the handicapped, and the newspaper delivery problem described earlier.

The vehicle routing problem cannot be fully solved with the same procedures as the multiple traveling salesman problem. Consider the simple example illustrated in Exhibit 13–10. Suppose we have a single depot and two buses, 1 and 2. Vehicle 1 has a capacity of twenty people and vehicle 2 a capacity of ten. There are three nodes where travelers are to be picked up. The number of travelers to be picked up is shown in brackets beside each node.

Ignoring for the moment the capacity of the buses and the demand at each node, the Clark and Wright heuristic would construct a tour for each vehicle as follows:

— Bus 1's tour: $1 \rightarrow 2 \rightarrow 3 \rightarrow 1$
— Bus 2's tour: $1 \rightarrow 4 \rightarrow 1$

This assignment, however, sends twenty-one passengers on bus 1, which violates the capacity constraints of bus 1. Thus this type of problem cannot be solved as a multiple traveling salesman problem. The characteristics of the vehicle routing problem also make it a difficult problem to solve optimally. However, a good heuristic solution can be obtained with the cluster first, route second approach.[6]

---

[6] The cluster first, route-second approach is most appropriate for situations characterized by isolated "clumps" of demand points. However, there is another heuristic called the **route first, cluster second approach** that is more appropriate for areas in which demand points are evenly dispersed across a region. The procedure begins by constructing a large single tour using, for example, the Clark and Wright heuristic, but this first tour is infeasible because all the vehicles are not in use. The next step is to partition the single tour into smaller feasible tours such that all vehicles are used and the tours are constructed from nodes that are grouped in some natural fashion, if possible. A description of these approaches is given in Lawrence Bodin et al., "Routing and Scheduling of Vehicles and Crews: The State of the Art," *Computers and Operations Research*, Vol. 10, No. 2 (1983), p. 98.

EXHIBIT 13–10

■ *Four-Node Vehicle Routing Problem*

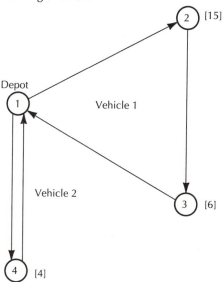

Cluster First, Route Second Approach

The **cluster first, route second approach** is best illustrated by an example. Exhibit 13–11 shows a twelve-node problem in which two vehicles must deliver cargo to eleven stations and return to the depot. Cargo demand is bracketed at each node, and distances, in miles, are shown on the arcs. The twelve nodes have been clustered initially into two groups, one for each vehicle. Nodes 2 through 6 are assigned to vehicle 1 and nodes 7 through 12 to vehicle 2. Node 1 is the depot node. In practice, clustering takes into account physical barriers such as rivers, mountains, or interstate highways, as well as geographic areas such as towns and cities that form a natural cluster. Capacity restrictions are also taken into account when developing the clusters. For this example, the capacities of vehicles 1 and 2 are 45 and 35 tons, respectively.

From the initial clustering, vehicle 1 must carry 40 tons and vehicle 2 must carry 34 tons. Both assignments are feasible (i.e., the demands do not exceed either vehicle's capacity). Using the C&W heuristic, a tour is constructed for vehicle 1 (tour 1), $1 \rightarrow 2 \rightarrow 3 \rightarrow 4 \rightarrow 5 \rightarrow 6 \rightarrow 1$, with a total tour length of 330 miles. Vehicle 2's tour (tour 2) is $1 \rightarrow 7 \rightarrow 8 \rightarrow 9 \rightarrow 10 \rightarrow 11 \rightarrow 12 \rightarrow 1$. Its length is 410 miles.

The next phase of the procedure is to determine whether a node or nodes can be switched from the longest tour (tour 2) to tour 1 such that the capacity of vehicle 1 is not exceeded and the sum of the two tour lengths is reduced. This step is referred to as **tour improvement.** We first identify the nodes in tour 2 that are closest to tour 1. These are nodes 7 and 8. Node 8 has a demand of 6 tons and cannot be switched to tour 1 without exceeding vehicle 1's capacity. Node 7, however, has a demand of 3 tons and is eligible to switch. Given that we wish to consider a switch of node 7,

EXHIBIT 13–11

- *Vehicle Routing Problem: Initial Solution*

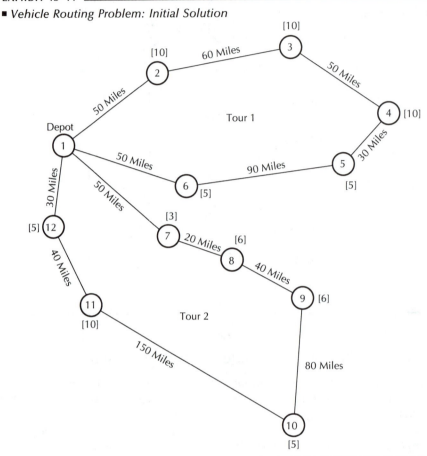

how can we evaluate where the node should be inserted into tour 1 and whether it will reduce the distance traveled? Both these questions can be answered by means of the **minimum cost of insertion technique.**

The minimum cost of insertion is calculated in the same way as the Clark and Wright heuristic. If all distances are symmetrical, then the cost of insertion, I_{ij}, can be calculated as follows:

$$I_{ij} = c_{i,k} + c_{j,k} - c_{ij} \quad \text{for all } i \text{ and } j, \ i \neq j \qquad \textbf{13.2}$$

where c_{ij} = the cost of traveling from node i to node j. Nodes i and j are already in the tour, and node k is the node we are trying to insert. Referring to Exhibit 13–11, node 7 is a candidate for insertion because it is near tour 1. Node 7 could be inserted between nodes 6 and 1 or between nodes 5 and 6. Both alternatives will be evaluated. In order to calculate the cost of inserting node 7 into tour 1, we require the additional distance information provided in the following table. In practice, this information would be available for all pairs of nodes.

From Node	To Node	Distance
1	7	50 miles
6	7	30 miles
5	7	60 miles
1	5	130 miles
1	8	60 miles

The cost of inserting node 7 between nodes 1 and 6 is 30 miles: (30 + 50 − 50). The cost of inserting the node between nodes 5 and 6 is 0: (60 + 30 − 90). The lowest cost is found by inserting node 7 between nodes 5 and 6, resulting in a completed tour for vehicle 1 of 1 → 2 → 3 → 4 → 5 → 7 → 6 → 1. Exhibit 13–12 shows the revised solution. The total length of tour 1 is now 330 miles, and the length of tour 2 is 400 miles. The distance traveled by the two vehicles has decreased from 410, to 400 miles.

EXHIBIT 13–12

■ *Vehicle Routing Problem: Revised Solution*

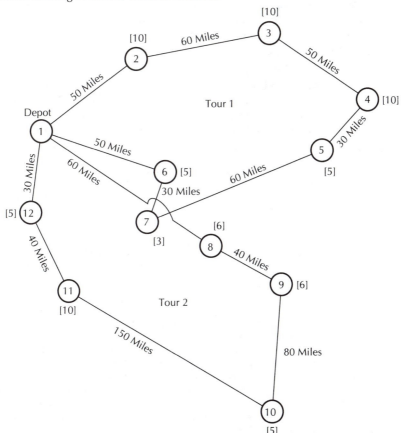

SCHEDULING SERVICE VEHICLES

Scheduling problems are characterized by delivery-time restrictions. The starting and ending times for a service may be specified in advance. Subway schedules fall into this category in that the arrival times at each stop are known in advance and the train must meet the schedule. Time windows bracket the service time to within a specified interval. Recall that in the Meals-for-ME program described earlier, meals had to be delivered between 11:30 A.M. and 1 P.M. This is an example of a **two-sided window.** A **one-sided time window** either specifies that a service precede a given time or follow a given time. For example, most newspapers attempt to have papers delivered before 7 A.M. Furniture delivery is usually scheduled after 9 A.M. or before 4:30 P.M. Other characteristics that further complicate these problems include multiple deliveries to the same customer during a week's schedule.

The general input for a scheduling problem consists of a set of tasks, each with a starting and ending time, and a set of directed arcs, each with a starting and ending location. The set of vehicles may be housed at one or more depots.

The network in Exhibit 13–13 shows a five-task scheduling problem with a single depot. The nodes identify the tasks. Each task has a start and an end time associated with it. The directed arcs mean that two tasks are assigned to the same vehicle. The dashed arcs show other feasible connections that were not used in the schedule. An arc may join node i to node j if the start time of task j is greater than the end time of task i. An additional restriction is that the start time of task j must include a user-specified period of time longer than the end time of task i. In this example, the time is 45 minutes. This is referred to as **deadhead time** and is the nonproductive time required for the vehicle to travel from one task location to another or return to the depot empty. Also, the paths are not restricted in length. Finally, each vehicle must start and end at the depot.

To solve this problem, the nodes in the network must be partitioned into a set of paths and a vehicle assigned to each path. If we can identify the minimum number of paths, we can minimize the number of vehicles required and thus the vehicle capital costs. Next, if we can associate a weight to each arc that is proportional or equal to the travel time for each arc (i.e., the deadhead time), we can minimize personnel and vehicle operating costs as well as time.

The Concurrent Scheduler Approach

This problem may be formulated as a special type of network problem called a **minimum-cost-flow problem.**[7] Alternatively, a heuristic approach may be used. One that

---

[7] The minimal-cost-flow problem is a special type of network problem that consists of a depot node, a set of intermediate nodes, and a set of demand nodes. The depot node has a supply of materials to be delivered to the demand nodes, each of which has a known demand. The intermediate nodes do not have demand. For example, an intermediate node could be a train stop where material is not removed from the cars. The network also consists of a set of arcs that may or may not have a limited capacity. For example, an arc may be able to "carry" between 0 and 20 tons of material. In addition, the per-unit cost of transporting material over an arc is known. The objective of the problem is to find the least-expensive means (routing) of transporting materials from the depot to the demand nodes. A description of this problem may be found in S. P. Bradley, A. C. Hax, and T. L. Magnanti, *Applied Mathematical Programming* (Reading, Mass.: Addison-Wesley, 1977).

_____ EXHIBIT 13–13 _____

■ *Schedule for a Five-Task Network (S = Start Time, E = End Time)*

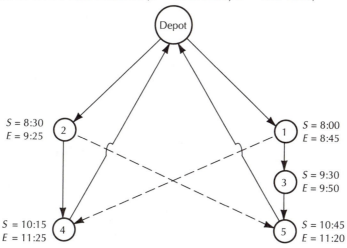

	Task	Start Time
Vehicle 1	1	8:00
	3	9:30
	5	10:45
Vehicle 2	2	8:30
	4	10:15

is simple to use is the **concurrent scheduler approach.** The concurrent scheduler proceeds as follows:[8]

1. Order all tasks by starting times. Assign the first task to vehicle 1.
2. For the remaining number of tasks, do the following. If it is feasible to assign the next task to an existing vehicle, assign it to the vehicle that has the minimum deadhead time to that task. Otherwise, create a new vehicle and assign the task to the new vehicle.

Exhibit 13–14 presents start and end times for twelve tasks. The deadhead time is 15 minutes. The problem is solved using the concurrent scheduler approach. Initially, vehicle 1 is assigned to task 1. Because task 2 begins before vehicle 1 is available, a second vehicle is assigned to this task. Vehicle 2 finishes task 2 in time to take care of task 3 also. In the meantime, vehicle 1 completes task 1 and is available for task 4. A third vehicle is not required until task 5, when vehicles 1 and 2 are busy with tasks 4 and 3, respectively. Continuing in a similar fashion, the schedule for vehicle 1 is $1 \rightarrow 4 \rightarrow 7 \rightarrow 10 \rightarrow 12$, for vehicle 2 the schedule is $2 \rightarrow 3 \rightarrow 6 \rightarrow 9$, and for vehicle 3 the schedule is $5 \rightarrow 8 \rightarrow 11$.

[8] This outline of the concurrent scheduler approach is taken from Lawrence Bodin et al., "Routing and Scheduling of Vehicles and Crews: The State of the Art," *Computers and Operations Research,* Vol. 10, No. 2 (1983), p. 133.

_____ EXHIBIT 13–14 _____

■ *Task Times and Schedule for the Concurrent Scheduler Example*

Task	Start	End	Assign to Vehicle
1	8:10 A.M.	9:30 A.M.	1
2	8:15 A.M.	9:15 A.M.	2
3	9:30 A.M.	10:40 A.M.	2
4	9:45 A.M.	10:45 A.M.	1
5	10:00 A.M.	11:30 A.M.	3
6	11:00 A.M.	11:45 A.M.	2
7	1:00 P.M.	1:45 P.M.	1
8	1:15 P.M.	2:45 P.M.	3
9	1:45 P.M.	3:00 P.M.	2
10	2:00 P.M.	2:45 P.M.	1
11	3:00 P.M.	3:40 P.M.	3
12	3:30 P.M.	4:00 P.M.	1

		Schedule
	Task	Start Time
Vehicle 1	1	8:10 A.M.
	4	9:45 A.M.
	7	1:00 P.M.
Vehicle 2	2	8:15 A.M.
	3	9:30 A.M.
	6	11:00 A.M.
Vehicle 3	5	10:00 A.M.
	8	1:15 P.M.

OTHER ROUTING AND SCHEDULING PROBLEMS

Scheduling workers is often concerned with staffing desired vehicle movements. The two are of necessity related in that vehicle schedules restrict staffing options, and vice versa. In general, vehicle scheduling is done first, followed by staff scheduling. This approach is appropriate for services such as airlines, where the cost of personnel is small in comparison to the cost of operating an airplane. It is less appropriate, however, for services such as mass transit systems, where personnel costs may account for up to 80 percent of operating costs. For such systems it is more appropriate to either schedule personnel first, then schedule vehicles, or to do both at the same time. Chapter 11 discussed issues in personnel scheduling.

Problems that have elements of both routing and scheduling are numerous. Examples include school bus routing and scheduling, dial-a-ride services, municipal bus transportation, the Meals-for-ME program and other meals-on-wheels programs. Certain routing problems also may take on the characteristics of a combined problem. For example, snow plows must clear busier streets prior to clearing less-traveled streets. In addition, there are usually repeated visits depending on the rate of snowfall. These components introduce a scheduling aspect to the routing problem. Considering the fact that there may be literally thousands of variables involved in the formulation of such problems, it becomes apparent that an optimal solution is impossible to obtain. In order to solve real-world problems of this type, management scientists have developed some elegant solution procedures. With rare exception, the procedures use heuristic approaches to obtain "good" but not optimal routes and schedules.

The delivery of emergency services, such as ambulance, police, and fire, is not usually considered a routing or scheduling problem.[9] Rather, emergency services are more concerned with resource allocation (how many units are needed) and facility location (where the units should be located). These issues were covered in Chapters 11 and 6, respectively.

SUMMARY

Effective routing and scheduling of service vehicles are two important and difficult problems for managers of services. The consequences of poor planning are costly, and a decision maker must frequently fine-tune the system to ensure that the needs of the customer are being met in a timely and cost-effective fashion. The criterion used to measure the effectiveness of service delivery depends on the type of service. Although minimizing total cost is an important criterion, for some services, criteria such as minimizing customer inconvenience and minimizing response time may be equally if not more important.

Solution of routing and scheduling problems begins with a careful description of the characteristics of the service under study. Characteristics, such as whether demand occurs on the nodes or the arcs, whether there are delivery-time constraints, and whether the capacity of the service vehicles is a concern, determine the type of problem being considered. The type of problem then determines the solution techniques available to the decision maker.

In this chapter we discussed the characteristics of routing problems, scheduling problems, and combined routing and scheduling problems. Optimal solution techniques for these types of problems are generally based on mathematical programming. However, in practice, a good but perhaps nonoptimal solution is usually sufficient. To obtain a good solution, several heuristic solution approaches have been developed. We presented two well-known heuristics for solving the traveling salesman problem, the nearest neighbor procedure, and the Clark and Wright savings heuristic. Also presented, was the minimum cost of insertion technique for use in solving the vehicle routing problem.

DISCUSSION QUESTIONS

1. Compare the characteristics of the following types of problems:

   a. Routing problems
   b. Scheduling problems
   c. Combined routing and scheduling problems

2. Describe the differences between and give an example of

   a. A traveling salesman problem
   b. The Chinese postman problem
   c. A vehicle routing problem

[9] For a complete discussion of emergency service delivery, see R. C. Larson and A. R. Odoni, *Urban Operations Research* (Englewood Cliffs, N.J.: Prentice-Hall, 1981).

3. A mail carrier delivers mail to 300 houses in Blacksburg. The carrier also must pick up mail from five drop boxes along the route. Mail boxes have specified pickup times of 10 A.M., 12 noon, 1 P.M., 1:30 P.M., and 3 P.M. daily. Describe the characteristics of this problem using the information provided in Exhibit 13–1. What types of service-time restrictions apply?

4. Define each of the following:
   a. Deadhead time
   b. Depot node
   c. Undirected arc

5. Describe what is meant by
   a. A feasible tour for a vehicle routing problem
   b. A feasible tour for a traveling salesman problem
   c. A two-sided time window
   d. A node precedence relationship

_____ PROBLEMS

13.1 Use the Clark and Wright savings heuristic procedure, and the data that follow, to compute the savings obtained by connecting
   a. 2 with 3
   b. 3 with 4
   c. 2 with 5

	To Node (distances in miles)			
From Node	2	3	4	5
1	10	14	12	16
2	—	5	—	18
3	5	—	6	—

13.2 Assume that a tour $1 \rightarrow 3 \rightarrow 5 \rightarrow 1$ exists and has a total length of 23 miles. Given the distance information that follows and using the minimum cost of insertion technique, determine where node 2 should be inserted.

From Node	To Node	Distance
1	3	6
1	5	9
3	5	8
1	2	5
2	3	7
2	6	5
2	5	8

6. Discuss the differences between the nearest neighbor procedure and the Clark and Wright savings heuristic procedure for constructing a tour.

7. Discuss under what circumstances a distance or cost matrix in a routing problem would be asymmetrical.

8. What are some objectives that might be used to evaluate routes and schedules developed for
   a. School buses
   b. Furniture delivery trucks
   c. Ambulances

9. What are some practical problems that might affect the routing and scheduling of
   a. A city's mass transit system
   b. A national trucking fleet
   c. Snow plows

10. What is the "savings" in the Clark and Wright savings heuristic?

13.3 A vehicle routing problem has twenty nodes and two vehicles. How many different routes could be constructed for this problem?

13.4 Given the distance matrix for a traveling salesman problem shown in Exhibit 13–15,
   a. Assume node 1 is the depot node, and construct a tour using the nearest neighbor procedure.
   b. Assume the depot is node 4, and construct a tour using the nearest neighbor procedure.

13.5 Using the Clark and Wright savings heuristic, construct a tour for the data given in the distance matrix for Problem 13.4. Assume node 1 is the depot node.

13.6 You have been asked to route two vehicles through a ten-node network. Node 1 is the depot node; nodes 2 through 5 have been assigned to vehicle 1 and nodes 6 through 10 to vehicle 2. The cost matrix for the network is given in Exhibit 13–16.
   a. Construct the two tours using the nearest neighbor procedure and state the total cost of the tour.
   b. Construct the two tours using the Clark and Wright savings heuristic and state the total cost of the tour.

13.7 Referring to Problem 13.6, assume vehicle 1 has a capacity of 35 passengers and vehicle 2 a capacity of 55 passengers. The number of passengers to be picked up at each node is

Node	Number of Passengers
2	10
3	10
4	5
5	5
6	5
7	5
8	20
9	10
10	5

Using the tours constructed in Problem 13.6, attempt to improve the total cost of the two tours using the minimum cost of insertion technique.

13.8 Convert the distance matrix given in Problem 13.4 to a cost matrix using the following information. The cost of routing a vehicle from any node i to any node j is $100. This is a fixed cost of including a link in a tour. The variable cost of using a link (or arc) is $3.30 per mile for the first 5 miles and $2.00 for the remainder of the arc distance. After computing the cost matrix, resolve the problem using the Clark and Wright savings heuristic.

13.9 Using the task times provided below, determine the number of vehicles required and the task sequence for each vehicle using the concurrent scheduler approach. The deadhead time is 30 minutes.

Task	Start	End
1	8:00 A.M.	8:30 A.M.
2	8:15 A.M.	9:15 A.M.
3	9:00 A.M.	9:30 A.M.
4	9:40 A.M.	10:20 A.M.
5	10:10 A.M.	11:00 A.M.
6	10:45 A.M.	11:30 A.M.
7	12:15 P.M.	12:40 P.M.
8	1:30 P.M.	1:50 P.M.
9	2:00 P.M.	2:40 P.M.
10	2:15 P.M.	3:30 P.M.

─── **EXHIBIT 13–15** ───────────────

From Node	Distance To Node (in miles)							
	1	2	3	4	5	6	7	8
1	—	2.2	5.8	4.0	5.0	8.5	3.6	3.6
2	2.2	—	4.1	3.6	5.8	9.4	5.0	5.8
3	5.8	4.1	—	3.2	6.1	9.0	6.7	9.2
4	4.0	3.6	3.2	—	3.0	6.3	3.6	6.7
5	5.0	5.8	6.1	3.0	—	3.6	2.0	6.0
6	8.5	9.4	9.0	6.3	3.6	—	3.6	8.5
7	3.6	5.0	6.7	3.6	2.0	3.6	—	4.0
8	3.6	5.8	9.2	6.7	6.0	8.5	4.0	—

─── **EXHIBIT 13–16** ───────────────

From Node	Cost To Node ($)									
	1	2	3	4	5	6	7	8	9	10
1	—	22	22	32	32	14	45	56	51	35
2	22	—	32	22	54	36	67	78	67	41
3	22	32	—	22	36	41	42	67	70	64
4	32	22	22	—	56	51	71	86	83	63
5	32	54	36	56	—	32	10	32	45	54
6	14	36	41	51	32	—	40	45	32	32
7	45	67	42	71	10	40	—	20	42	71
8	56	78	67	86	32	45	20	—	32	71
9	51	67	70	83	45	32	42	32	—	45
10	35	41	64	63	54	32	71	71	45	—

____ READING 13.1 ____

Routing Special-Education School Buses

Federal law requires that equal opportunity for an education be given to all students by public school systems. Public school systems are therefore required to supply bus transportation for special-education students as well as non-special-education students. The smaller number of special-education students in a school district tend to make bus routes longer for these students. In addition, whereas non-special-education students are usually picked up and returned to a "central" location, special-education students are usually picked up and dropped off at their home. In addition, special-education students usually attend schools which specialize in their disability. As a result, a bus may have to stop at more than one destination.

The Tulsa, Oklahoma, public school system has approximately 850 special-education students who attend 66 different schools. Severely handicapped students who require buses equipped with hydraulic lifts number 148. The maximum daily total ride for a student is limited to 3 hours, but the school system strives for a 45-minute ride-time per trip. One bus may transport secondary and elementary students even though secondary schools open 45 minutes later than elementary schools in the area. The school system supports two types of routes for special-education students. The first type is used for severely handicapped students who attend a specialized school. Most students who fall into this category are of elementary school age and require buses with lifts to carry wheelchairs. Fourteen percent are emotionally disturbed secondary students who require a route different from the elementary school students. The second type of route transports elementary and secondary students who are less physically disabled but require transportation to a school which specializes in their needs. In total, Tulsa requires 35 routes for transporting all special-education students. Eleven of these routes are devoted to transporting severely-handicapped students.

The special-education routing problem is a special case of the vehicle routing problem where "many" students are delivered to "several" destinations. Thus special-education student transportation is characterized by several vehicles, all with limited capacity, and some which are specialized to carry severely handicapped students. Further, not all students have the same destination and special sequencing or precedence relationships exist for a bus route.

The school system currently generates bus routes manually. An experienced planner typically spends two weeks developing routes prior to the opening of school. During the year, any changes in the routes, such as may be caused by a student moving, must be made manually. During 1985, the Tulsa special-education routing problem became the subject of a faculty-student research project. The school system became interested in determining ways in which operations could be improved and costs reduced. In particular, the school system wished to determine whether smaller routes could be developed for buses transporting the severely handicapped. Also in 1985, a "shuttle" system was developed to help reduce the ride time for students. In this system, students were picked up and delivered to one of two special-education schools. Those students who attended either school were unloaded. Other students were transferred to a bus whose next destination was the student's destination. As a result, no bus had to travel to more than two schools and the routes were shorter.

Prior to introducing the shuttle system, the total manually generated route distance for severely handicapped, special-education student transportation was 509 miles. This distance included total travel on 11 routes. To solve the problem, each of the 11 buses was assumed to have a capacity of 18 students. Reducing the number of buses was of less concern than reducing the ride

Source: Reprinted by permission of R. Russell and R. Morrel, "Routing Special-Education School Buses," *Interfaces*, Vol. 16, No. 5 (September–October 1986), pp. 56–64. Copyright 1986 The Institute of Management Science, 290 Westminster Street, Providence, Rhode Island 02903 USA.

time and improving the level of service. Using the Clark and Wright heuristic to generate routes via computer, a 19.7 percent reduction in total route distance was achieved. Using a modified Clark and Wright heuristic along with the shuttle system, the computer generated routes yielded a 28.5 percent reduction in travel distance.

Following the results of the study, the school system decided to implement the shuttle system. In addition, the planners determined that the two routes for severely handicapped and emotionally disturbed students be left intact. The problem was reduced to determining the best routing sequences for the remaining 9 special-education routes. New data were collected on the route distances and durations of the old routes. The modified Clark and Wright heuristic was used to route the remaining 9 buses using the shuttle system. The computer-generated routes predicted a 12.4 percent reduction in total route time.

The change in bus routing was implemented in midyear. Drivers were given the names and addresses of students, the sequence in which to pick them up, and no further directions. Some drivers resisted the shorter routes, which reduced their driving times and their wages. Other drivers had

special pickup arrangements with some parents which accommodated their work schedules. A few of the computerized routes failed to consider natural barriers, such as rivers and dead-end streets. The drivers, however, were allowed to fine-tune their routes in order to accommodate some of these problems. After the transition problems were resolved, the computerized routes reduced the routing distance by 10.9 percent over the manual routes developed.

——— QUESTIONS FOR READING 13.1

1. What are the scheduling characteristics of this problem?

2. What are the routing characteristics of this problem?

3. Discuss how the use of a travel-time matrix instead of a distance matrix would effect the results obtained.

4. Discuss how a new student would be included in an existing route.

5. In your opinion, did the shuttle system simplify or complicate the routing of special-education school buses?

——— READING 13.2 —————————————————

A Decision Support System for Ambulance Scheduling

Emergency services such as ambulance, police, and fire units operate in an environment where demand for service is variable, revenues and resources are limited, and the costs associated with failing to provide adequate service in a timely fashion are often inestimable. In such an environment, the need for meticulous, informed planning is critical. Frequently, however, the tools and decision aids that would allow a decision maker to plan effectively are unavailable to the practitioner. Horry County, South Carolina, operates an ambulance service which typifies these characteristics. Horry County is a resort area in which the population, and consequently the need for ambulances, doubles during the spring and summer months. In addition, demand for ambulances varies systematically during the day and over the days of the week. Thus, demand quadruples from 3:00 A.M. to 5:00 P.M. during the day and may double from Thursday, the least busy day of the week, to Saturday, the busiest day. This varying pattern of demand makes scheduling of ambulances a difficult task for planners.

Of primary concern to ambulance and other

Source: This is adapted from J. R. Baker and R. T. Sumichrast, "A DSS for Ambulance Allocation and Scheduling," *Proceedings of the Decision Sciences Institute,* Las Vegas, November 1988, pp. 157–158. Published by the Decision Sciences Institute at Georgia State University, Atlanta, Ga. Used with permission.

emergency service planners is how to schedule available units during the course of a 24-hour day and over the days of the week such that the best level of service possible is provided. That is, a manager or planner for an emergency service must make decisions which are cost-effective while allocating available resources efficiently and effectively. Traditional approaches to the problems of allocation and scheduling of emergency services, such as queuing and linear programming, are of limited use to decision makers in two respects. First, planners operate in an environment where there is more than one goal under consideration and these goals are often in conflict. Second, with traditional approaches the decision maker cannot evaluate the effect changes in demand or service level would have on a schedule or how a new schedule might affect the cost of operation or the level of service provided. The usefulness of a decision aid would be enhanced if the traditional models could be integrated into a decision support system which could provide the ambulance service with the ability to evaluate "what if" questions during the planning process.

THE DECISION SUPPORT SYSTEM

Such a system, called DSS-AMB, was built for the Horry County Ambulance Service. DSS-AMB sequentially accesses three databases that contain values for (1) cost, (2) timing and service level, and (3) demand and service data, as inputs to the scheduling model.

Costs are categorized as fixed (those which are incurred regardless of whether a call is or is not made) and variable (those which are dependent on a call being made or a unit being in operation). Fixed costs include wages per hour. The user may specify the number of attendants per unit. The variable costs include a cost per call to the service. The cost-per-call figure is offset in the solution algorithm by an average revenue per call, which enters the model as "lost" revenue.

The last variable cost relates to the cost of failing to provide a minimal (as prescribed by the decision maker or the community) level of service. This cost is subjective owing to such factors as risk of litigation and loss of goodwill and relates directly to the probability that a call must wait.

The heuristic developed by the authors for the short-range model relies on a marginal analysis of the costs. Costs that increase as the number of ambulances scheduled for a particular time period increases include wages and other operating expenses. Costs that decrease as the number of scheduled ambulances increases include lost revenue and possibly the service penalty cost (which increases if the minimum level of service is not provided). The service penalty cost would decrease as long as the probability that a call must wait is greater than the allowed probability of waiting for the N ambulances already scheduled. Ambulances are added to the schedule until either all ambulances are being used or until the marginal increase in cost is greater than the decrease in cost. While the heuristic is simple and may yield a suboptimal solution, limited testing with real data has shown it to consistently provide good-quality solutions.

HORRY COUNTY DATA AND ANALYSES

The DSS is demonstrated for ambulance run data for Horry County, South Carolina. Historical data on demand and service times were obtained, by hour, for the year 1985. Data were obtained on the average call rate for each hour of a seven-day week for each of the four seasons. In this manner, an "average" week of demand by season was captured.

The average wage rate was $10 per hour with two attendants per unit. The estimated revenue per call was $75, which includes an estimated $50 charge per call and a $25 average mileage charge. The minimal service level was 0.05, which is the maximum allowable probability of a call having to wait longer than 10 minutes as mandated by the EMSS Act of 1974. The service cost coefficient and power are 100.0 and 2, respectively. An average service time of 50.5 minutes was used. Beginning with the fall quarter, the average demands per hour were 1.25, 1.02, 1.47 and 1.50, respectively. These demand figures represent average peak demand for the quarter in question.

The maximum number of units available per quarter was three in the fall and winter quarters and four in the spring and summer quarters. The minimum number of units available was two in each quarter. The planning horizon chosen was 24 hours with a minimum 8-hour shift and a shift lag of 4 hours. The average hourly demand rate was 0.63 calls per hour. Seasonality factors were obtained by quarter, day, and hour. For the quarterly demand, the seasonality varied from 0.820 (winter) to 1.19 (summer). Interday seasonality varied from a low of 0.918 (Thursday) to a high of 1.29 (Saturday). Within a given day, demand is lowest from 3 to 7 A.M. (factors less than 0.35) and highest from 10 A.M. to 5 P.M. (factors from 1.3 to 1.5). Demand, in general, is at its maximum on Friday and Saturday during the late morning and early afternoon.

BEST SOLUTION RESULTS

Analyses were run for seven 24-hour days (Sunday–Saturday) for each of the four quarters. A chart of the scheduling results is shown in Exhibit 13–17. The results shown are optimal. The minimum number of units available on all days was two. The model schedules the minimum number of units for the length of the planning horizon (24 hours). For the 28 schedules generated, the average daily total cost was $1376.96, with a standard deviation of $142.42. The average daily cost figures ranged from $1291.95 (Sunday during fall and winter) to $1786.35 (Saturday during the summer). The average probability of a call waiting was 0.0438, with a standard deviation of 0.0091. The fall and winter quarters each required that 64 unit-hours be scheduled per day. No service cost was incurred, indicating that, overall, the probability of waiting was less than 0.05. During the spring quarter, the minimum number of unit-hours scheduled per day range from 64 (Monday–Thursday) to 88 (Saturday). A service cost was incurred if fewer than 72 unit-hours were scheduled. During the summer, a

---

EXHIBIT 13–17

■ *Ambulance Scheduling Results (Legend: a = 00:00 hours, b = 07:00 hours, c = 15:00 hours, d = 24:00 hours)*

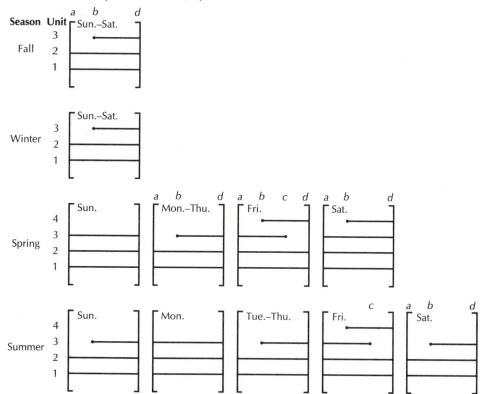

minimum of 64 unit-hours were needed on Sunday and a maximum of 88 on Saturday. In this quarter, a service cost was incurred when fewer than 80 unit-hours were scheduled.

—— QUESTIONS FOR READING 13.2

1. The objective of the scheduling model is to minimize total cost. However, what other factors are included in this objective?

2. Why is it unlikely that the marginal increase in the cost of adding an ambulance will exactly equal the marginal decrease in cost?

3. How would reducing the minimum service level to 0 percent (i.e., all calls would be answered immediately) affect the number of ambulance-hours scheduled?

4. What inputs to the problem can actually be affected by the planner?

—— CASE 13.1 ——————————————————————

Routing and Scheduling of Phlebotomists

Phlebotomists are clinical laboratory technicians who are responsible for drawing blood specimens from patients in the hospital. Their routine responsibilities include drawing samples for laboratory tests ordered that are to be completed on that day by the day crew. A 500-bed medical center usually employs five to seven technicians in this capacity. The morning pickups are made between 6:30 A.M. and 8:00 A.M. On a given morning there may be requests to draw blood samples from 120 to 150 patients. The time required to draw the blood necessary to complete a physician's order varies depending on the age, physical condition, and the number of different types of tests required of a patient. For example, a single phlebotomist may be able to draw samples from twenty maternity patients in 90 minutes, since most of these women are healthy and do not require "unusual" types of blood work. However, that same phlebotomist may only be able to draw blood from eight critically ill patients, who usually require more varied tests and may, because of their physical condition, require more time. The same limitation is true for infants and small children who require special collection techniques due to their size.

In addition to their routine pickups, which must be completed within the 90-minute preshift interval, there are routine specimens that must be drawn at a specific time. These timed specimens include fasting specimens (such as blood glucose tests), which must be collected before the patient eats, and blood gases, which are collected 30 minutes after a patient has received a respiratory treatment. With either of these tests, there is a margin for "error" of 15 minutes. Generally, more routine tests are also collected along with the timed specimens.

The medical center has five floors, each of which specializes in a particular type of patient. For example, one floor may handle surgical patients and another orthopedic patients. In addition, there are special sections, including the nursery, the pediatric floor, and the intensive care unit. Because of the location of the respiratory equipment and monitors, all patients requiring daily blood gases are located in intensive care.

It is the task of the chief phlebotomist to estimate the number of phlebotomists needed on a given day and to assign patients to technicians such that all deliveries are made before the start of the day shift and timed specimens are collected within a 15-minute window of the specified time.

—— QUESTIONS FOR CASE 13.1

1. What characteristics of routing and scheduling are exhibited in this problem?

2. What type of data would you need to collect in order to most effectively schedule technicians?

3. Does a deadhead time exist in this situation? If so, where?

4. If you were to view this as a cluster first, route second situation, based on what criteria would you form clusters?

5. Suggest how you would solve the problem if the timed specimens and routine pickups were considered separately.

REFERENCES

Baker, J. R., M. A. McKnew, T. R. Gulledge, and J. R. Ringuest. "An Application of MAUT to the Planning Emergency Medical Services," *Socio-Economic Planning Sciences,* Vol. 18, No. 4 (1984), pp. 273–280.

Baker, J. R., and R. T. Sumichrast. "A DSS for Ambulance Allocation and Scheduling," in *Proceedings of the Decision Sciences Institute.* Las Vegas, Nev.: Decision Sciences Institute, November 1988, pp. 157–158.

Bondin, Lawrence, Bruce Golden, Arjang Assad, and Michael Ball, "Routing and Scheduling of Vehicles and Crews: The State of the Art," *Computers and Operations Research,* Vol. 10, No. 2 (1983), pp. 63–211.

Bradley, S. P., A. C. Hax, and T. L. Magnanti. *Applied Mathematical Programming.* Reading, Mass.: Addison-Wesley, 1977.

"Emergency Medical Service Systems Act," *Federal Register,* Vol. 39, No. 62, Part 3 (March 29, 1974), pp. 11758–11766.

Fitzpatrick, K. E. "Predicting Demand for Emergency Transportation Services in South Carolina," in R. G. Flood (Ed.), *Proceedings of the Southeast Decision Sciences Institute.* Williamsburg, Va., 1984, pp. 207–209.

Fitzsimmons, J. A., and R. S. Sullivan. "Service Vehicle Scheduling and Routing," in *Service Operations Management.* New York: McGraw-Hill, 1982, pp. 312–336.

Larson, R. C., and A. R. Odini. *Urban Operations Research.* Englewood Cliffs, N.J.: Prentice-Hall, 1981.

Russell, R., and R. Morrel. "Routing Special Education School Buses," *Interfaces,* Vol. 16 (September–October 1986), pp. 56–64.

14

Quality, Productivity, and Excellence

INTRODUCTION

For Harry Hapless, it was a rough day in the service economy. His car, a Fiasco 400, started sputtering on the highway, so Harry pulled into a gas station for help. "Sorry, no mechanics, only gas!" shouted the attendant. "How can you call this a service

—— EXHIBIT 14–1 ————————————————————————————————

▪ *Pul-eeze! Will Somebody Help Me?*

Source: George Russell, "Pul-eeze! Will Somebody Help Me?" *Time* (February 2, 1987), pp. 48–49. Illustration © 1987 Patrick McDonnell.

station?" yelled Harry. He went to the bank to get some emergency cash for a tow truck, only to find the automatic teller machine out of order, again. "Real nice service!" he muttered. Then Harry decided to use a credit card to buy a tool kit at the Cheapo discount store, but he couldn't find anyone to wait on him. "Service! Anyone, please! Help me!" was his cry.

It had been a trying day indeed, Harry thought as he rode a bus home, but at least he could look forward to a trip to Florida the following week with his wife Harriet. That is, until Flyway Air called: "Sorry, Mr. Hapless. Due to our merger with Byway Air, your Florida flight has been canceled." Harry got so angry he was going to call the Federal Aviation Administration immediately. But just then his phone went dead—no doubt because the Bell System had been split up, he imagined. Well, that was the last straw. A few minutes later a wild-eyed Harry burst into the newsroom of his local newspaper. "I've got a story for you!" he cried. "There is no more service in America!"[1] (See Exhibit 14–1.)

---

[1] From George Russell, "Pul-eeze! Will Somebody Help Me?" *Time* (February 2, 1987), p. 49.

A little dramatic? Perhaps, but not far from current opinion on the quality of service in America. Thomas Peters, coauthor of *In Search of Excellence,* says unabashedly, "In general, service in America stinks."[2] Buck Rogers, IBM's marketing vice president states, "If you get satisfactory service in this country from your grocery store, local hardware store, or friendly computer company, it's darn near a miracle."[3]

In the month of January alone in 1988, the Department of Transportation (DOT) received almost 4000 consumer complaints about airline service. Such shoddy service prompted the DOT to require that airlines issue comprehensive reports on the quality of their service. Included are statistics on each airline's on-time performance, luggage lost, connections missed, and reservations not honored. With this information, consumers can compare the quality of the trip as well as the price of the tickets.[4]

Recent industry surveys in financial institutions, insurance, and health care bemoan poor service quality as well. How comforting is it to know that the majority of medicine dosages in nursing homes across the country are administered in error?[5]

We are critical of product companies that typically spend 20 percent or more of their sales dollars doing things wrong and doing them over. And yet service companies, on average, spend *35 percent or more of their operating costs* doing things wrong and doing them over.[6]

The purpose of this chapter is to examine the implications of service quality and to provide suggestions, techniques, and strategies for its systematic improvement. The relationship between quality and productivity is also explored, with an aim toward achieving true *service excellence.* The supplement to this chapter, entitled "Process Control Charts," explores statistical techniques for controlling quality.

REASONS FOR POOR QUALITY IN SERVICES

The reasons for the emergence and tolerance of poor quality in service industries are many and varied.[7]

- The economic upheaval of the 1970s, including inflation and deregulation, caused businesses in general to cut back on service to cut costs. Many have not restored their previous levels of service.
- Labor shortages have fueled the trend toward self-service and automation. Although this may be considered "high-tech" service, it can go too far. Sears, for example, floundered when it reorganized its stores to group salesclerks

---

[2] From George Russell, "Pul-eeze! Will Somebody Help Me?" *Time* (February 2, 1987), p. 49.

[3] Y. K. Shetty and J. E. Ross, "Quality and Its Management in Service Businesses," *Industrial Management* (November–December 1985), p. 8.

[4] Robert L. Crandall, "Solving the Crisis in the Skies," *Fortune* (September 28, 1987), p. 204.

[5] W. Edwards Deming, "Quality and Productivity in Service Organizations," Videotape 13 in the series, *Quality Productivity and Competitive Position* (Cambridge, Mass.: MIT Center for Advanced Engineering Studies, 1984).

[6] C. W. Trim, "Zero Defect," *Mortgage Banking* (January 1987), p. 19.

[7] The various examples in this section are taken from George Russell, "Pul-eeze! Will Somebody Help Me?" *Time* (February 2, 1987), pp. 49, 51, 52, 55.

around fancy cash registers for fast checkout. This left few employees in the aisles to answer questions and a service void for the customer.

- Service workers are often viewed as short-term and service work as "servitude." Consequently, service labor is typically undertrained and overworked, not to mention unmotivated. Examples are abundant—flight attendants, salespersons, teachers, waitresses, police officers.

- The emphasis on increasing efficiency and productivity of services has taken its toll on quality. A prime example is the telephone operator whose performance is monitored by a computer that beeps when the operator has spent too much time with one customer. Another example is a cashier who must type in a 25-digit inventory code to sell a 50 cent birthday card. The process may reduce the number of accountants needed at corporate headquarters, but it does nothing to help the customer or the salesperson.

- Customers typically expect less of services and do not demand more. Studies show that out of 100 dissatisfied customers, only about 4 will complain about service.[8] Moreover, services often have captive markets because of government regulations or low levels of competition within a small geographic area.

- There are more chances of making errors because of the variability inherent in services provided to a number of different customers, by a number of different people, in a number of geographically dispersed locations. In other words, it's more difficult to standardize providing a service than producing a product.

- The customer typically consumes the service as it is produced, leaving no time to test the service quality, correct mistakes, or rework or recall the service.

- The nature of services does not lend itself to quality control. Services produce intangibles. The quality of intangibles are rated by opinion, perceptions, and expectations. Intangibles, by definition, cannot be quantified. Many people believe that what cannot be quantified cannot be measured and what cannot be measured cannot be controlled. (Do you agree with this view?)

DEFINING QUALITY

The **quality** of a service or product is determined by the user's perception. It is the degree to which the bundle of service attributes as a whole satisfies the user. This is called **expectations-to-perception match.** Quality therefore comprises (1) the degree to which attributes of the service desired by the users are identified and incorporated in the service, and (2) the degree to which desired levels of these attributes are perceived by the users to be achieved.

In manufacturing, product quality is often defined as (1) grade, (2) fitness for use, and (3) consistency. **Grade** classifies some major characteristics making up the product into groupings such as high, medium, or low or 1, 2, 3, 4, and so on. In services, such as a hotel, we could grade rooms on the basis of square feet, completeness of furnishings, quality of furnishings, and years that the carpeting has been in place. We could grade banks on the basis of variety of services, capital available, and speed

---

[8] Jacques Horovitz, "How to Check the Quality of Customer Service and Raise the Standard," *International Management* (February 1987), p. 34.

—— EXHIBIT 14–2 ——————————————————————————

■ *Inspection Points in Three Service Organizations*

Inspection Points	Issues to Consider
Bank	
Teller stations	Shortages, courtesy, speed, accuracy
Loan accounts	Collateral, proper credit checks, rates, terms of loans, default rates, loan ratios
Checking accounts	Accuracy, speed of entry, rate of overdraws
Department store	
Stock rooms	Clean, uncluttered, organized, level of stockouts, ample supply, rotation of goods
Display areas	Attractive, well-organized and stocked, visible goods, good lighting
Sales counters	Neat, courteous, knowledgeable personnel; waiting time; accuracy in credit checking and sales entry
Restaurant	
Kitchen	Clean, proper storage, unadulterated food, health regulations observed, well organized
Cashier station	Speed, accuracy, appearance
Dining areas	Clean, comfortable, regular monitoring by personnel

of service. Exhibit 14–2 lists other factors to consider in inspecting or grading the quality of banks, department stores and restaurants.

Fitness for use is the degree to which the service satisfies the user or customer. The user's satisfaction depends on many attributes and characteristics of the service itself as well as the user's perception of these relative to his or her needs and his or her expectations of the service. In order to measure fitness for use, we must have a clear idea of the attributes and characteristics of a service that are important to the customer. These are discussed in the next section.

Consistency refers to a lack of variability in the service provided. McDonald's, for example, is known for the consistency of its service. The hamburger, french fries, and Coke served in Tokyo taste much the same as those served in New York City or Blacksburg, Virginia. Similarly, Holiday Inn rooms across the world are virtually identical. Consumers may prefer the predictable quality of a Holiday Inn to the range of quality (from superb to terrible) of other hotel chains.

Characteristics and Attributes of Service Quality

If we can measure the customer's perception of a service relative to a set of characteristics important to him or her, we may uncover ways to improve the quality of the service as a whole. Quality is more difficult for consumers to measure for services than for manufactured goods. Generally though, a user of a service has a few characteristics and attributes in mind that he or she uses as a basis for comparison among alternatives. Lack of one attribute may eliminate a specific service firm from consideration. Quality also may be perceived as a whole bundle of attributes where many lesser characteristics are superior to those of competitors.

Professors Berry, Zeithaml, and Parasuraman[9] conducted extensive, indepth interviews with twelve consumer focus groups to try to identify general attributes or determinants of service quality. They found that customers assess service quality in terms of

— Reliability
— Responsiveness
— Competence
— Access
— Courtesy
— Communication
— Credibility
— Security
— Understanding/knowing the customer
— Tangibles

Exhibit 14–3 describes and gives examples of these ten determinants of service quality. The same professors also drew the following conclusions from their study:

1. *Consumers' perceptions of service quality result from a comparison of their expectations before they receive service to their actual service experience.* In other words, service quality is judged on the basis of whether it meets expectations.
2. *Quality perceptions are derived from the service process as well as from the service outcome.* The way the service is performed can be a crucial component of the service from the consumer's point of view.
3. *Service quality is of two types, normal and exceptional.* First, there is the quality level at which the regular service is delivered, such as the bank teller's handling of a transaction. Second, there is the quality level at which "exceptions" or "problems" are handled. This implies that a quality control system must recognize and have prepared a set of "plan B's" for less-than-optimal operating conditions. In addition, when a problem occurs, the low-contact service firm may suddenly become a high-contact service firm. Thus good customer relations is important in maintaining quality, regardless of the type of service.

As a result of the study's conclusions and subsequent follow-up interviews with service managers, Berry and his colleagues formulated a service quality model as shown in Exhibit 14–4. The model identifies five gaps between perceptions and expectations that can account for service quality. This research suggests that service quality can be measured by how effectively a service can close the gaps.

[9] L. Berry, V. Zeithaml, and A. Parasuraman, "Quality Counts in Services, Too," *Business Horizons* (May–June 1985), pp. 45–46.

—— EXHIBIT 14–3 ————————————————————————————————————

■ *Determinants of Service Quality*

Reliability involves consistency of performance and dependability. It means that the firm performs the service right the first time and also means that the firm honors its promises. Specifically, it involves

— Accuracy in billing
— Keeping records correctly
— Performing the service at the designated time

Responsiveness concerns the willingness or readiness of employees to provide service. It involves timeliness of service, such as

— Mailing a transaction slip immediately
— Calling the customer back quickly
— Giving prompt service (e.g., setting up appointments quickly)

Competence means possession of the required skills and knowledge to perform the service. It involves

— Knowledge and skill of the contact personnel
— Knowledge and skill of operational support personnel
— Research capability of the organization (e.g., securities brokerage firm)

Access involves approachability and ease of contact. It means

— The service is easily accessible by telephone (lines are not busy and you aren't put on hold)
— Waiting time to receive service (e.g., at a bank) is not extensive
— Convenient hours of operation
— Convenient location of service facility

Courtesy involves politeness, respect, consideration, and friendliness of contact personnel (including receptionists, telephone operators, etc.). It includes

— Consideration for the consumer's property (e.g., no muddy shoes on the carpet)
— Clean and neat appearance of public contact personnel

Communication means keeping customers informed in language they can understand and listening to them. It may mean that the company has to adjust its language for different consumers—increasing the level of sophistication with a well-educated customer and speaking simply and plainly with a novice. It involves

— Explaining the service itself
— Explaining how much the service will cost
— Explaining the tradeoffs between service and cost
— Assuring the consumer that a problem will be handled

Credibility involves trustworthiness, believability, honesty. It involves having the customer's best interests at heart. Contributing to credibility are

— Company name
— Company reputation
— Personal characteristics of the contact personnel
— The degree of hard sell involved in interactions with the customer

Security is the freedom from danger, risk, or doubt. It involves

— Physical safety (Will I get mugged at the automatic teller machine?)
— Financial security (Does the company know where my stock certificate is?)
— Confidentiality (Are my dealings with the company private?)

Understanding/knowing the customer involves making the effort to understand the customer's needs. It involves

— Learning the customer's specific requirements
— Providing individualized attention
— Recognizing the regular customer

—— EXHIBIT 14–3 *Continued* ————————————————————

Tangibles include the physical evidence of the service, such as

— Physical facilities
— Appearance of personnel
— Tools or equipment used to provide the service
— Physical representations of the service, such as plastic credit card or a bank statement
— Other customers in the service facility

Source: A. Parasuraman, Valerie A. Zeithaml, and Leonard L. Berry, "A Conceptual Model of Service Quality and Its Implications for Future Research," *Journal of Marketing* (Fall 1985), p. 44.

Quality Defined as Gaps Between Perceptions and Expectations

Exhibit 14–4 suggests that the problem of establishing measurements of service quality is more complicated than finding measureable attributes. We must measure *perceptions* and *expectations* as well. Moreover, we must match differences in service *customer* and service *provider* perceptions of quality service. A close examination of the gaps shown in Exhibit 14–4 provides us with clues for approaching the monumental task of defining service quality.[10]

Gap 1: Consumer Expectation–Management Perception Gap. Service managers do not always understand what features of a service connote high quality to the consumer. For instance, in a study of hotel services in Britain, the hotel staff judged the quality of the coffee breaks they provided for conference attendees in terms of the quality of the brew offered, while the customers also looked at factors such as the speed of delivery, appropriateness of the timing for the coffee break, sufficient space around the coffee table for conversation, and the availability of restroom facilities. It never dawned on management that restrooms would have anything to do with coffee breaks![11]

Gap 2: Management Perception–Service Quality Specifications Gap. Management does not always include in the service specifications all the quality attributes it perceives consumers want. This is sometimes due to lack of sufficient resources or unreasonableness of consumer expectations. It also may be characteristic of firms that are not wholly committed to the prospect of service quality.

Gap 3: Service Quality Specifications–Service Delivery Gap. Even when appropriate quality guidelines exist, quality service may not be delivered to the customer. Consider this example from a senior marketing officer with the U.S. Postal Service:

> The Postal Service has an enormously profitable business called stamps. If you sell a stamp for collection purposes, that's all profit, period. However, in taking that business

[10] The examples and general discussion of gaps were adapted from A. Parasuraman, Valerie A. Zeithaml, and Leonard L. Berry, "A Conceptual Model of Service Quality and Its Implications for Future Research," *Journal of Marketing* (Fall 1985), pp. 44–46.
[11] Carol A. King, "A Framework for a Service Quality Assurance System," *Quality Progress* (September 1987), p. 29.

EXHIBIT 14–4

- ▪ *Service Quality Model*

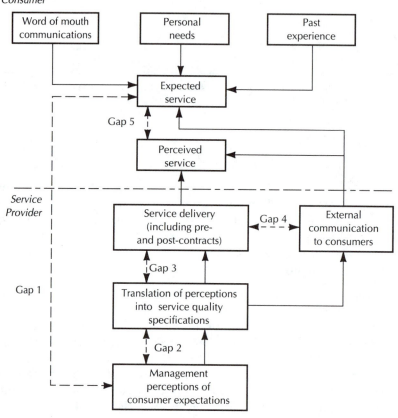

Source: A. Parasuraman, Valerie A. Zeithaml, and Leonard L. Berry, "A Conceptual Model of Service Quality and Its Implications for Future Research," *Journal of Marketing* (Fall 1985), p. 44. Reprinted from *Journal of Marketing,* published by the American Marketing Association.

into competition in the leisure time category, eyeball to eyeball with Parker Bros. and with bowling and other hobbies, we have a very different situation than that faced by product marketers. We have to grasp the fact that all the brilliant marketing, product development, and financial leverage planning comes to a screeching halt if Mrs. Jones goes to buy $10 worth of stamp collecting products and she meets a clerk who says, "I'm sorry, I'm closed. Go to the other window."[12]

Gap 4: Service Delivery–External Communications Gap. Media advertising and other communications by a firm can affect consumer expectations. If expectations are

---

[12] Gary Knisely, "Listening to Consumer is Key to Goods or Service Marketing," *Advertising Age* (February 19, 1979), pp. 54–60.

too high, the service as delivered may receive a poor quality rating. In other words, it is unwise to promise something "absolutely, positively" unless you can do it *every time*. It is better to underpromise and overdeliver.

Gap 5: Expected Service–Perceived Service Gap. The key to ensuring good service quality is meeting or exceeding customer expectations. For example, one customer rated service quality particularly high when a repairman not only fixed her broken appliance, but also explained what had gone wrong and how she could fix it herself if a similar problem occurred in the future. Conversely, a bank customer rated service quality particularly low when his bank would not cash his payroll check from a nationally known employer because it was postdated by one day. The fact that the bank was prevented by law from cashing the check had never been explained to the customer. He perceived the bank to be "unwilling" rather than "unable" to cash the check.

ENSURING QUALITY

How can we close the quality gaps and assure ourselves and our customers of quality service? We can pay attention to quality from the design of the service, to the training of our employees, to the delivery of the service, to the customer evaluation of its quality. CEOs, managers, and all levels of employees must concentrate on maintaining and monitoring quality every day in every transaction, proposal, or plan. This total concept of quality involvement is called **quality assurance.** Here are some suggested steps in the systematic development of quality assurance for a firm.

1. Identify customer expectations.
2. Design the service to meet customer expectations of quality.
3. Develop and implement a quality appraisal program.
4. Design and implement a quality training program.
5. Design and implement a quality control program.

Let us examine the five steps, one at a time.

Identify Customer Expectations

Identifying customer expectations is critical to good service because design of the service must be based on customer expectations. There are several approaches to identifying these expectations, all of which may be used if the cost is not too high. One method is the use of a probability sample survey design that queries the respondents about their expectations relative to a specific service. The second method is simply to discuss with a number of people who might use the service what they would hope for in such a service. In some companies this process is formalized into consumer *focus groups*. For an ongoing business, another method is to obtain comments from customers informally or by means of *suggestion cards,* or call-backs. Exhibit 14–5 shows a typical evaluation/suggestion card for a furniture store.

—— EXHIBIT 14–5 ——

■ *The Cargo Report Card*

Please check the appropriate response and return.

Please Rate Our Delivery Personnel

	Excellent	Good	Acceptable	Unacceptable
1. Was the person who called you from the delivery service center professional and courteous?	□	□	□	□
2. Did your furniture arrive as scheduled?	□	□	□	□
3. Were the delivery drivers professional, courteous and helpful?	□	□	□	□
4. How would you rate our delivery personnel compared to other companies' delivery personnel you have experienced?	□	□	□	□

Please Rate Cargo Furniture

	Excellent	Good	Acceptable	Unacceptable
1. Please rate your level of satisfaction with the Cargo furniture you purchased.	□	□	□	□
2. Finally, most importantly, please give us your overall impression of our company from sales representative to delivery.	□	□	□	□

Would you like someone to call you? Please indicate your phone number below.

(   )_____

Please Rate Our Sales Personnel

	Excellent	Good	Acceptable	Unacceptable
1. Were you greeted in a professional and timely manner at the store?	□	□	□	□
2. Were the sales representatives knowledgeable and informative about product and delivery?	□	□	□	□
3. How would you rate our sales representatives compared to other companies' sales personnel you have experienced?				
4. How would you rate the sales representative who served you?	□	□	□	□
5. What was your overall impression of the showroom?	□	□	□	□

Comments:_____
_____
_____
_____
_____
_____

Thank You!

Source: Courtesy of Cargo Furniture Company, Fort Worth, Texas. Used with permission.

Design the Service to Meet Expectations of Quality and to Maintain Quality

The best opportunity to build the basis for customer satisfaction is when the service is originally designed. If the service is not designed well initially, major costs for modification or redesign may be incurred. Moreover, if the quality of service does not come close to meeting customer expectations originally, the service may never be able to recover.

Because of the large number of consumer outlets typical of most service firms, changes in service design can frequently be field tested at a few sites to measure customer response. Holiday Inn, for example, uses "test inns" and McDonald's boasts of 10,000 "laboratories" available to test new product and service ideas.

Services also must be designed from an operational point of view so that quality is easier to maintain. Methods should be standardized as much as possible, expectations of employee performance should be reasonable, and employee training and monitoring should be designed so that the service can be "done right the first time."

Other approaches to service design, such as *down-loading,* are sometimes appropriate. Down-loading refers to allowing the customer to perform much of the service himself or herself, thereby lowering costs and ensuring that the service is performed to suit the individual customer.

Develop and Implement a Quality Appraisal Program

Management should develop a system for continually appraising the degree to which the service is meeting customer expectations. Expectations are likely to change over time as customers compare services supplied by different companies in the same field, as consumer tastes and preferences change, or as the customers themselves come and go. A turnover in service employees also can affect service quality. Ensuring service quality, as L. L. Bean President Leon Gorman puts it, is "just a day-in, day-out, ongoing, never-ending, unremitting, persevering, compassionate type of activity."[13]

Design and Implement a Quality Training Program

Quality begins with training and ends with training. All new employees should receive training to meet the design and performance specifications for a service, whether the service is personal contact, remote, or mass service. Regardless of the amount of technical training given, employees should be indoctrinated with taking the customer's viewpoint in all transactions and taking whatever action allowed by company policy to retain the customer's goodwill.

Service contact positions involve so much variability that company policies and training manuals cannot possibly prepare employees for every situation they must face. That's when the existence of a company attitude toward service, or **service culture**, is important. The $1.9 billion Nordstrom retailer, for example, has a one-sentence policies and procedures manual: "Use your own best judgment at all times."[14]

In addition to technical and interpersonal training, employees should be trained in methods for assessing and controlling quality. These methods, involving problem-solving analysis, rudimentary statistical process control, and group interaction techniques, are discussed in more detail in the next section.

Design and Implement a Quality Control Program

Quality control involves a set of procedures used by the service provider to measure and control selected aspects of the service process so that acceptable quality criteria are met. Quality control in services consists, for the most part, of the systematic use of the following techniques:

— Histograms
— Process flowcharts
— Pareto charts
— Fishbone diagrams
— Process control charts

These techniques involve the recording of data in various forms. Recording measurements and nonconformities should be a natural part of every worker's job. The

---

[13] B. Uttal, "Companies that Serve You Best," *Fortune* (December 1987), p. 98.
[14] Tom Peters, *Thriving on Chaos: Handbook for a Management Revolution* (New York: Knopf, 1987), p. 378.

EXHIBIT 14–6

■ *Time Required by Two Airlines to Perform Similar Services*

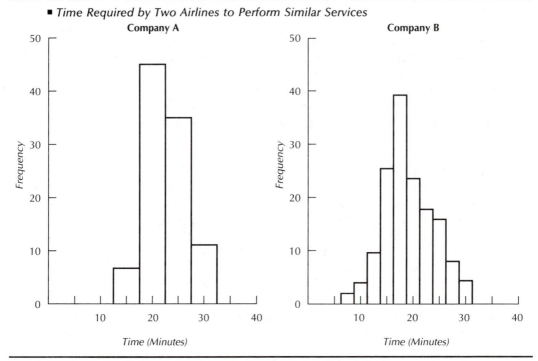

Source: Virgil Rehg, "SPC for White Collar Organizations," *Journal for Quality and Participation*, Vol. 9, No. 4 (December 1986), p. 37. Used with permission.

importance of this task is clearly stated by Richard Schonberger, a prominent management consultant: "The person who records data is inclined to analyze and the analyzer is inclined to think of solutions."[15]

Reading 14.1 is an excerpt from a speech given by W. Edwards Deming, the American quality guru who revolutionized quality systems in Japan. Deming suggests that it is management's responsibility to equip workers with the knowledge and methods necessary to control quality. We will now describe some of the methods he proposes.

Histograms. Exhibit 14–6 shows two **histograms** of the time required by different airlines to perform a similar ticketing service. From the histograms we can tell that the variation of Company A's service process is smaller than Company B's.[16] Possible reasons are

- A's equipment is better.
- A's employees have had more thorough training.

[15] Richard Schonberger, *World Class Manufacturing: The Lessons Applied* (New York: Free Press, 1986), pp. 18–19.

[16] This example is taken from Virgil Rehg, "SPC for White Collar Organizations," *Journal for Quality and Participation*, Vol. 9, No. 4 (December 1986), pp. 37–38.

- A's procedures are more effective.
- A's forms are less complicated.
- A provides fewer services.
- A offers fewer routes.
- Some other factor is more consistent in A's process than it is in B's process.

Now that we have identified that Company B has a problem with service variability, we can investigate the possible causes and take corrective action.

Process Flowcharts. Various flowcharts, including **process flowcharts,** were discussed in Chapter 5. They help analyze quality by identifying problem areas in the service process. Exhibit 14–7 shows a process flowchart for a package delivery service. Suppose the company is unhappy with the time it takes to pick up a package for delivery. The flowchart of the delivery process helps us to identify parts of the process that could cause delays and on which more data should be gathered. For example, we might look at the delay from when a customer telephones an order to when the driver receives the order, or we might analyze the driver's progress on individual orders.

_____ EXHIBIT 14–7 _____

- *Partial Flowchart of Package Pickup and Delivery Process*

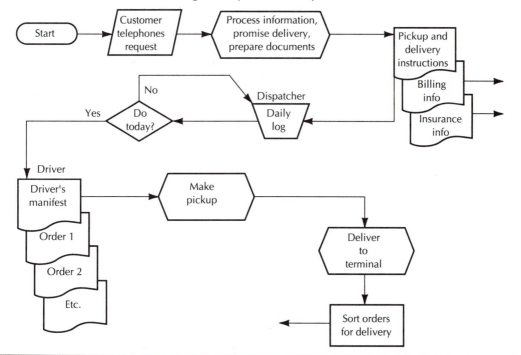

Pareto Charts.   **Pareto charts** are an ordered form of histograms that attempt to isolate the few dominant factors affecting a situation from the many insignificant ones. Exhibit 14–8 shows a Pareto chart that categorizes the average time spent by drivers in picking up packages by customer order. The data represented are ordered from the customer who requires the most time to pick up packages to the customer who requires the least time. From this chart, it is apparent that three customer orders, B, D, and E, account for 90 percent of the time the driver spends picking up packages. Suppose that further examination reveals that these customers are a university, a corporate office, and a major manufacturer. What do these customers have in common? Possibly, their size and geographic dispersion make it difficult to locate package pickup points quickly or the persons requesting service are not explicit enough in their instructions.

Fishbone Diagrams.   To dig deeper into the problem of finding pickup or delivery locations, a cause-effect diagram, or **fishbone diagram,** could be constructed. Exhibit 14–9 shows such a fishbone diagram. The "spine" of the diagram is the problem of finding the customer quickly. The elements of the problem include the customer, the dispatcher, and the driver. Influencing the dispatcher's effectiveness is how busy he or she is, whether the files are maintained properly, and how well the communication system works. Similar analyses can be made for the role of the customer and the driver in the process. The diagram simply helps us to walk through the process and identify potential problem points.

—— EXHIBIT 14–8 ——————————————————————————————

▪ *Pareto Chart of Package Pickup Times by Customer*

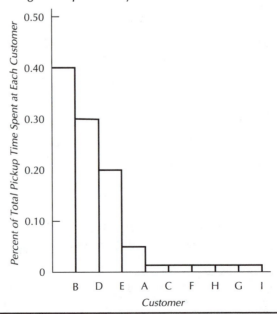

EXHIBIT 14–9

■ *Fishbone Diagram for Finding Customer Quickly*

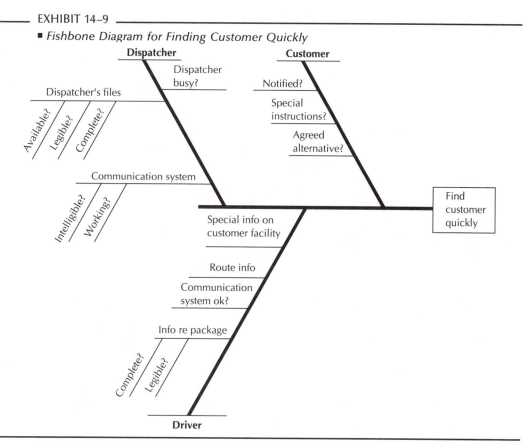

Source: Reprinted from "Quality, Productivity, and Competitive Position," by Myron Tribus, Deming Videotapes, by permission of MIT. Published by MIT, Center for Advanced Engineering Study, Cambridge, Mass. 02139. Copyright 1984.

Process Control Charts. Process control is concerned with monitoring standards, making measurements, and taking corrective action as products are being produced or services are being provided. Periodic samples of process outputs are examined, and if they are within acceptable limits, the process is permitted to continue. If they fall outside certain specified ranges, corrective action may be necessary. In our package delivery example, average pickup or delivery times could be charted and times that exceed the control limits could be investigated. The investigation, in turn, could involve the use of flowcharts, fishbone diagrams, Pareto charts, or similar problem-solving techniques.

Control charts are statistical devices that set upper and lower limits on the process we want to control. A control chart is basically a graphic presentation of data over time. One of the most important quality control tools, it is constructed in such a way that new data can be quickly compared to past performance. Upper and lower limits in a control chart can represent three types of values:

—*Measurable data,* such as time spent in a service or time spent waiting for service

—*Percentages,* such as the percent of goods damaged or the percent of customers complaining

—*Counting data,* such as number of typos in a report or number of mistakes in a claim

We take samples of the process output and plot the average of these samples on a chart that has control limits on it. Exhibit 14–10 graphically reveals the useful information that can be portrayed in control charts. When the average of the samples falls within the upper and lower control limits and no discernible pattern is present, the process is said to be in *control;* otherwise, the process is *out of control* and we need to find out why.

Normally, there is some degree of variation in all processes. A control chart that appears to be in control means that variations in samples of the service process taken over time are for the most part random. In building control charts, averages of small service samples (often of five accounts or customers or daily averages) are used, as opposed to data on individual service encounters. Individual measurements tend to be too erratic to make trends quickly visible. The purpose of control charts is to help distinguish between natural variations and variations due to assignable causes. **Natural variations** affect almost every service process to some degree and are to be expected. As long as output precision remains within specified limits, this fact of life can be tolerated.

Assignable variation in a service process can usually be traced to a specific reason. Factors such as misadjusted equipment, fatigued or untrained employees, or new procedures are all common sources of assignable variations. Control charts identify when a problem is occurring and help the employee pinpoint where a problem may lie.

The determination of control limits for process control charts is a somewhat lengthy statistical process that is described in the supplement to this chapter.

Quality Circles.   It should be apparent at this point that the quality control tools and techniques just presented are best utilized together as a system for solving service quality problems. Quality control methods may be employed by individuals or by groups. One successful group approach to controlling quality involves the use of **quality circles.**

Exactly what is a quality circle? Basically, it is a group of between six and twelve employees who volunteer to meet regularly to solve work-related problems. The members, all from the same work area, receive training in group planning, problem solving, and statistical quality control. The circles discuss and recommend ways to improve the quality of their service, the service process, the working environment, and employee involvement. Circles generally meet about four hours per month (usually after work, but sometimes on company time), and although the members are not rewarded financially, they do receive recognition from the firm. A specially trained worker, called the *facilitator,* usually helps train the circle members and keeps the meetings running smoothly.

EXHIBIT 14–10

■ *Patterns to Look for on Control Charts*

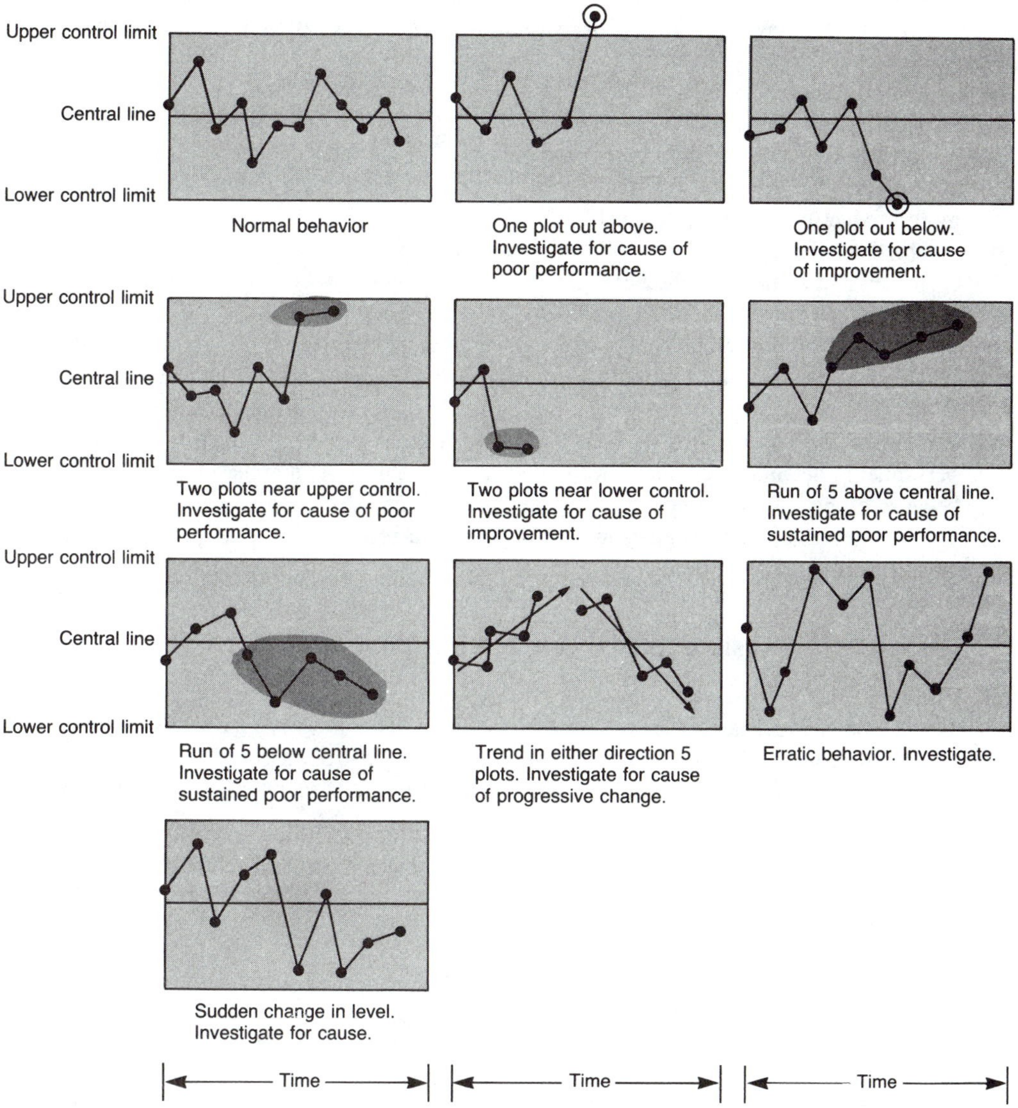
Upper control limit
Central line
Lower control limit
Normal behavior
One plot out above. Investigate for cause of poor performance.
One plot out below. Investigate for cause of improvement.
Two plots near upper control. Investigate for cause of poor performance.
Two plots near lower control. Investigate for cause of improvement.
Run of 5 above central line. Investigate for cause of sustained poor performance.
Run of 5 below central line. Investigate for cause of sustained poor performance.
Trend in either direction 5 plots. Investigate for cause of progressive change.
Erratic behavior. Investigate.
Sudden change in level. Investigate for cause.
Time
Time
Time

Source: Bertrand L. Hansen, *Quality Control: Theory & Applications,* © 1963, p. 65. Reprinted by permission of Prentice Hall, Inc., Englewood Cliffs, New Jersey.

Quality circles have been used successfully in a wide variety of services, including banks, retailing, hospitals, insurance firms, police departments, data processing, education, municipal government, and transportation. Reading 14.2 describes the use of quality circles in supermarkets.

PRODUCTIVITY

Productivity is the ratio of output to input. Unfortunately, this simplistic definition does not tell us how to evaluate different mixes of inputs (except in dollars) or outputs (except in dollars). For example, what if prices decline due to competitive conditions so that an increase in units of output brings in fewer dollars? Suppose two hospitals provide patient care at $300 per day. Can their productivity be compared if the mix of services is different? Suppose two secretaries turn out the same number of reports. In one case, the reports are perfect; in the other, 100 errors were found. Which is the more productive and by how much?

Consider a bank that uses a computer to perform various services offered to customers. At some point the bank purchases a new powerful computer that has come on the market at about the same price as the old one (i.e., there is basically no change in input cost). But now the bank can provide additional services at no additional cost. If the customer base (i.e., output) does not change, has productivity increased?

Is a police department with a high arrest record more productive than one of similar size with a low arrest record? If number of arrests represents the skill of police personnel in detaining criminals, we would say yes. But if the number of arrests is up because crime has increased, we certainly wouldn't call that productive!

From the preceding instances, it appears that productivity, like quality, is not always easy to measure.

Basic Factors Underlying Productivity

The basic factors that affect productivity are both internal and external. In Exhibit 14–11, the external factors are shown as government and industry regulation, unions, and innovations. Industry regulation tends to be derived from association standards, professional ethics (e.g., law and medicine), and established practices. Innovation

EXHIBIT 14–11

■ *Factors that Affect Productivity*

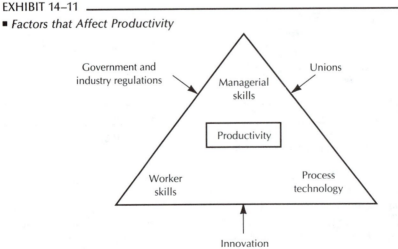

refers to technical advances and new processes developed outside the particular service industry but applicable to the industry.

The internal influences on productivity are managerial abilities, employee skills, and motivation of workers, along with process technology and capital investment. The managerial processes include organizational structure, leadership style, and reward systems. Process technology includes the level of technology applied, degree of automation, degree of internally developed innovations, and information systems support.

Many managers think only of lowering labor costs to increase productivity. As indicated in Exhibit 14–11, all the basic factors underlying productivity change should be examined. In particular, the internal factors that are under the control of management should receive the most attention.

Productivity Measurement

As we pointed out earlier, defining productivity, especially in services, can be difficult. One approach is to define indices that measure some aspect of productivity and then measure the change in those indices over time. For example, in a large retail store, productivity could be measured by sales per employee, sales per asset, sales per square foot of space, frequency of employee absence, and frequency of employee idle time. For an engineer, the number of patents per year, the number of projects finished on time and within budget, and the number of designs accepted might be considered. In the case of a creative pop band, the percentage of seats filled in an auditorium per performance might be one criterion.

When productivity measurement was first applied in service industries, services made the same mistakes as manufacturing. They assumed that measuring something makes it better, and they viewed increased output as a goal in itself. For instance, banks and hospitals spent huge amounts of time and money developing work methods and standards that promoted increasing the *quantity* of work, as measured by the number of checks processed or number of meals served or number of patients treated. No consideration was given to the number of checks processed in error, or the number of dietary errors in meals served, or the number of released patients who would choose not to return to this hospital because of poor service.

Rather than a simple ratio of output to input, then, perhaps productivity should be defined as

$$\text{Productivity} = \frac{\text{units of output} \times \text{quality level}}{\text{units of input}}$$

where quality level ranges from 0.0 to a maximum of 1.0. Producing services at a quality level of 0.5, say, will lead to a rejection of the service half the time by consumers and will effectively lower productivity. That is, poor service is essentially no service and must be provided again, properly done, or not charged to the customer. Low quality, because it often leads to repeating the work of the service, lowers productivity. "Doing it right the first time," even if it takes a little longer, means not only higher productivity but greater strength in the market place.

EXCELLENCE

Recently, attention has been drawn to companies described as "excellent." We hear people speak of a service company as supplying excellent service, that is, service that surpasses that of other companies. We have provided examples of such excellence throughout this text. Excellence of service must include quality at the top of its list, but it also should include productivity.

In their popular book, *In Search of Excellence,* Peters and Waterman studied America's excellent companies and found that these companies worked hard to keep things simple and focused. In particular, the managements were characterized by

— A bias toward action
— Simple form and lean staff
— Continued contact with customers
— Productivity improvement via people
— Operational autonomy to encourage entrepreneurship
— Stress on one key business value
— Emphasis on doing what they know best
— Simultaneous loose-tight controls

These characteristics apply to service firms as well as to manufacturing firms and to small firms as well as large ones. One final note, achieving excellence is an ongoing process. Some of the firms described initially in Peters and Waterman's book have since performed less than admirably in the face of increased competitive pressures.

⎯⎯ SUMMARY

We may see the quality of a product or even test it before we buy. With most services, we experience a service's quality after the service process has already begun, when it's too late not to buy! Further, although the basic service may be of high quality, the personal delivery of it may be abrasive. When we seek quality in a service, we are looking for a total package of characteristics and attributes, some intangible and some tangible.

Quality can be measured by identifying gaps in the perception of the service and customer's expectations of the characteristics and attributes of the service. Quality programs are based on reducing the gaps between what managers believe and perceive as quality and what users expect as quality and perceive has been delivered. Quality assurance, the effort toward quality that everybody in the company makes, is a continuous process for building quality in services. It starts with the identification of customer expectations and carries through every transaction and contact that the service provider has with the customer.

Tools for analyzing quality include histograms, Pareto charts, process flowcharts, fishbone diagrams, and process control charts. Quality can be improved by paying attention to customer feedback (from customer surveys and complaints) and employee feedback (from quality circles).

Productivity means efficiency in operations, the ratio of output to input. Productivity is determined primarily by the internal factors of workers, technology, and managerial systems. External factors that influence productivity are govenment and industry regulations, unions, and innovations in technology and management. Productivity should be considered hand in hand with quality. Only when both productivity and quality are maintained can a service achieve excellence.

—— DISCUSSION QUESTIONS

1. Why is quality so hard to define for services? What is *your* definition of quality?

2. Which of the determinants of service quality listed in Exhibit 14–3 are most important to you in evaluating the quality of

    a. A restaurant
    b. A health care facility
    c. A course taught at a university
    d. A retail store

3. How are perceptions and expectations a part of quality?

4. Explain the different gaps shown in Exhibit 14–4. Why are they important?

5. In what ways does training affect service quality?

6. Give specific examples of how you would *measure* the quality of

    a. An airline service
    b. A repair service
    c. A banking service

7. What quality control techniques are most applicable to services? How do they differ? Explain how they can be used together.

8. Develop a fishbone diagram for each of the following problems.

    a. Low test scores
    b. Lengthy service at a restaurant
    c. Poor image of a public official

9. What is process control? How are control limits used in process control? What does service process variability have to do with process control? What types of data can be used in process control?

10. Use the quality-circle approach (with appropriate quality analysis tools) to suggest and implement improvements in the quality of this course.

11. Define productivity. Why is productivity sometimes difficult to measure? Why is it difficult to interpret?

12. What is the relationship between quality, productivity, and excellence?

—— READING 14.1

We Must Do More Than Our Best

The biggest problem that most any company in the Western world faces is not its competitors, nor the Japanese. The biggest problems are self-inflicted, created right at home by managements that are off course in the competitive world of today. Systems of management are in place in the Western world that for survival must be blasted out; new construction commenced. Patchwork will not suffice.

Everyone doing his best is not the answer. Everyone *is* doing his best. It is necessary that people understand the reason for the changes that are necessary. Moreover, there must be consistency of understanding and of effort. There is much talk about the need to improve quality and productivity. Moreover, everyone knows exactly how to go about it. It is for other people to accomplish, not

---

Source: W. Edwards Deming, "Drastic Changes for Western Management," presented at the TIMS meeting at Gold Coast City, Australia, July 1986. Used with permission.

for me. In the eyes of many people in management, the big trouble is that a lot of employees in operations, and in management as well, are careless and neglectful on the job. One writer has the solution—hold all employees accountable for job behavior as well as for the results expected of them. The fact is that performance appraisal, management by the numbers, M.B.O., and work standards, have already devastated Western industry. More of the same could hardly be a solution. The annual rating of performance has devastated Western industry. Work standards double the cost of the operations that they are applied to.

Other writers see information as the solution. Anyone can improve his work, they say, if he has enough information. The fact is that a figure by itself provides no information, has no meaning, no interpretation, in the absence of theory. In short, there is no substitute for knowledge, and a figure by itself is not knowledge. Other people put their faith in gadgets, computers, new machinery, and robotic machinery. Solving problems is not the answer, nor improvement of operations. They are not the transformation required.

It will not suffice to match the competition. He that declares his intention to meet the competition is already licked, his back to the wall. Likewise, zero defects are a highway down the tube. The sad truth is that all the parts of an apparatus may meet the specifications, yet the apparatus may be unsatisfactory or may even be a total failure. It is necessary in this world to outdo specifications, to move continually toward better and better performance of the finished product.

Likewise, it will not suffice to have customers that are merely satisfied. Satisfied customers switch, for no good reason, just to try something else. Why not? Profit and growth come from customers that can boast about your product or service—the loyal customer. He requires no advertising or other persuasion, and he brings a friend along with him.

Western management has for too long focused on the end product—get reports on people, productivity, quality, sales, inventory. It is necessary

that management shift the focus to management's responsibility for the source of quality and service, *viz.*, design of product and of the processes that turn out the product and service. Management in the Western world have too long been driving the automobile by keeping an eye on the rear view mirror.

Recognition of the distinction between a stable system and an unstable one is vital for management. A stable system is one whose performance is predictable; it appears to be in statistical control. For example, if a plot of points shows that a number of fires per month on the premises over two or three years has been stable, then only fundamental changes by the management will reduce the frequency of fires.

It is instructive to look at a plot of proportion of people absent from the job week by week over the past two years. Does the plot show a stable system? If yes, then only the management can reduce it. Other helpful plots might be the number of accidents week by week over the past year or two years; number of complaints of customers, costs of warranty, sales, outgoing quality, costs, scrap, rejections, accounts overdue by four weeks or more.

Such plots make clear the futility and fallacy of management by the numbers. A goal that lies beyond the capability of the system can not be achieved except at the destruction of other systems in the company. What is needed is not numerical goals, but constant improvement of design and of processes at the source, the responsibility of management.

_____ QUESTIONS FOR READING 14.1

1. What are Mr. Deming's criticisms of Western management?

2. How can statistical process control aid management?

3. Do you agree that "everyone doing his best" and "satisfying the customer" are not sufficient measures of performance?

4. What's wrong with numerical goals?

─── READING 14.2 ───

Productivity: Quality Circles for Supermarkets

Broken eggs, wasted meat, wilted vegetables—these are the special nightmares in the 28,680 supermarkets across the country that haul in sales of $171.6 billion each year but rely on a razor-thin 1 to 2 percent of gross sales for net profits.

Source of the problem: usually, disaffected employees. Possible solution: quality circles, the Japanese management concept that has become popular among American management experts.

The quality circle, more often associated with manufacturing, is moving into such labor-intensive service industries as banks, hospitals—and supermarkets. The food chains, which have been experimenting with the concept in warehousing for some time, are now promoting it in the stores themselves.

"We've got quality circles for store managers, our front-end clerks (cashiers), our meat departments, and so on," said Frank Lennon, vice-president of human resources for the 55-store Price Chopper chain in upstate New York.

"We had one situation where a few of our employees were so upset with their jobs that they would 'accidentally' destroy a fair percentage of dairy products, eggs in particular," added another supermarket executive. Having come up with no solution, he turned to the circle. "A member of the quality circle approached the disgruntled employees and told them to knock it off," he said, "Amazingly, they did."

Harvey Davis, assistant executive director of the International Association of Quality Circles, a nonprofit professional organization, said that perhaps 500 companies were using quality circles just a year ago, while between 1500 and 2000 are doing so now. And most of the growth is appearing in service industries.

The standard supermarket industry quality circle consists of eight to twelve store employees who meet every week or two to attempt to identify problems and implement solutions in a wide range of productivity-related areas.

Problems range from absenteeism to inventory shrinkage, according to Paul Gibson, vice-president of human resources for the Cincinnati-based 1200-store Ralphs Grocery chain, in Compton, California, who brought back the idea after a visit to Japan in the spring of 1980.

"We're in the process now of determining our return-on-investment," Mr. Gibson said, "but I can tell you that in our seven test stores—and we're going to be expanding to include many more—attitude surveys indicate that the hourly employees were less committed, less involved and less interested before we implemented our team-building plan. Our turnover was higher, too. Now our employees are much more committed to their jobs and to the success of the stores."

Not everyone is entranced with the concept. "We think quality circles are worth our effort for the repetitive types of jobs in our warehouses," said Byron Allumbaugh, chairman and chief executive of the 101-store Kroger chain which instituted retail-level quality circles just over a year ago.

"But we haven't made a decision as to whether or not we're going to use them in our retail outlets," he said. "To be honest, we're a little disappointed. Some of the quality circles have turned into nothing groups. That's not to say we had some minor successes; but we're still looking for a success."

Despite some discouraging experiences, most supermarket chains are looking closely at the concept, according to *Progressive Grocer* magazine, an industry trade journal. Any cost-saving or morale-boosting technique will surely be implemented, according to most executives.

"The basic psychological concept of using quality circles to improve productivity is so sound that it's surprising more supermarkets aren't using them," Mr. Davis said. "It's simply a matter of recognizing the dignity of the worker," he added.

Sometimes that's not so easy. "One of the biggest problems in developing successful Q.C.s," Mr. Davis said, "is getting management to accept the fact that their employees care about what have been management problems for so long."

_____ QUESTIONS FOR READING 14.2

1. Identify several quality issues for supermarkets.

2. Why do you think quality circles have been effective for some retailers and ineffective for others?

3. How would you determine the "return on investment" for a program such as quality circles?

___ READING 14.3 _____

Quality in Computer Services

The customer service division of TRW is an independent supplier of maintenance, repair, and customer support services for computers and other information-handling systems. This division has built customer support capabilities for over fourteen hundred different equipment models built by seventy different manufacturers. Through its network of 150 service centers in the United States, TRW employs approximately 2400 service professionals. This reading describes TRW's approach to quality in computer services.

TRW is part of the growing third-party maintenance industry. Third-party maintenance service firms are different from manufacturer service organizations. The third-party suppliers do not, as a rule, sell hardware or software products, except as a product-life extension service when the original manufacturer has discontinued support of such products. They serve customers by providing maintenance, repair, and related support services alone. As such, these third-party maintenance service companies compete with manufacturers such as IBM and DEC.

At the same time, much of the third-party maintenance service business is developed in response to manufacturer and customer need. Some smaller manufacturers do not have the resources to build nationwide service operations for their customers. Some manufacturers have gone out of business or discontinued product lines. Many customers have elected to purchase different types of hardware and software products to enable them to take full advantage of available technology and to minimize costs. Many manufacturers have refused to support such mixed-vendor systems. Still, some other customers simply have not been satisfied with a manufacturer's service program, its personnel, or its cost. All these causes have contributed to the growth of the third-party maintenance services industry during the last decade.

TRADITIONAL MEASURES OF QUALITY: THE CUSTOMER'S CRITERIA

Service itself has long been recognized as a key differentiator among manufacturers of information-handling systems. Delivering a high-quality package of support services is part of the formula for long-term success for many major manufacturers.

Ever since computer systems and automated office equipment were introduced to the business world, there has been a need for organizations to repair equipment. Part of the fear involved in automating business operations has been that office operations would get out of control when data were kept on magnetic storage devices rather than in file drawers. There was the fear of computerization—that business could not be conducted efficiently because information would be lost.

As manufacturers of automatic data process-

Source: Condensed from Jack Smith, "Quality in Computer Services: Maintenance, Repair, and Support Services," in Jay W. Spechler (Ed.), *When America Does It Right* (Norcross, Ga.: Industrial Engineering and Management Press, 1989, pp. 133–143. Copyright Institute of Industrial Engineers, 25 Technology Park/Atlanta, Norcross, Ga: 30092.

ing equipment encountered this customer fear, their strongest ally was their service organization, the people who would be on-call at any hour of the day or night to fix problems with the computer. They were the save-the-day heroes who would straighten out confusion caused by automatic data processing systems and automated offices. A strong customer-support program overcame the fear of computerizing a business operation. Early adapters of computer systems had to have the assurance that they would not be risking their business operations to the computer. They had to have a comfort factor; they had to know that service people were available to find lost information, restore system operations, and keep the productivity high. To ensure this safety factor, they would gladly sign maintenance contracts even if they were not included as part of the system purchase.

Customers learned quickly how to recognize a quality service operation. They had only a few things to count among the criteria for a quality-oriented service operation. The first was *response time*. When a customer had a problem, how long did it take a service representative to get to the customer site? If the time was low—let's say one hour—the service company earned a high score for quality. The service person was responsive; he or she came when it was necessary. That the service person came quickly demonstrated concern for the customer.

The second criterion was *repair time*. If the service representative came to the customer's site quickly and fixed the problem immediately, the service organization was considered a quality provider. If a service representative did not have the knowledge to fix the problem or if the service person did not have the necessary replacement parts, the points won for a quick response would be lost.

DEFINING NEW QUALITY STANDARDS

There have been many changes during the past decade that have made it more difficult for service providers to meet their customers' expectations for *quality* as defined by traditional measurement standards. New expectations and measurement standards have emerged.

First, customers and equipment operators have changed. Older systems used to be installed in large businesses or data centers with proper elec-

trical power and environmental controls. Operators were highly trained and fully experienced. Today there is a computer on almost every business desk, and it is connected to the nearest wall outlet. There are no special environmental controls. Operators of these systems often receive little or no formal training and are far less experienced. Still, these are customers who expect prompt resolution to any and all problems. Whatever the cause, it is up to the successful servicer to correct the situation and get the customer back on-line. This may mean doing much more than fixing the equipment. It might include preparing a customized preventive maintenance program or a recommendation to minimize the problem situation that a customer site is experiencing. It may include recommendations for new software or a totally new environment. It may require spare parts and training so that the customer can service his or her own equipment.

Adding to this complexity of servicing tasks is the tremendous increase in the number of different hardware and software providers and products that customers can select from. Customers are more apt to purchase mixed hardware and software products from various suppliers to enable them to take full advantage of available technology and cost savings. But they do not want to work with a wide number of service suppliers and their many different programs. They prefer to have one service provider for all products. To further complicate the servicer's task, these same customers are installing these products across local and wide-area networks. This often results in lower density of a given product in a specific location—making it more difficult for the service provider to support the investments required to ensure the availability of technical expertise and materials for all products in all locations.

With the advancements in technology comes an increased reliability of information-handling systems. As a result, some customers are less quick to insure their systems investment with maintenance contracts. This is true especially when system downtime does not seriously impact the operation of a business. Instead, customers often are willing to risk a failure and secure service on an as-needed basis. Others are interested in a self-service approach. Still, because they are paying for service on a time-and-materials basis, they are not tolerant with extended repair times, repeat service calls, or unnecessary replacement of parts. Even though they may not have a maintenance contract, these customers expect a reasonable response time when they do have a problem. Customers want a simple service program tailored to their needs.

Providing traditional service quality to customers would be easy if costs did not enter into the picture. However, with the costs of service rising—due to the high *people costs* of the service business and the reduction of price in software and hardware—services are becoming a more significant portion of the costs of ownership. Over the useful life of the product, the cost of service may be greater than the original purchase price of the product. As a result, customers are not only more sensitive to the cost of service, they expect more from it.

Fast response time and fast repair time will always lead the list of quality standards within the computer services industry. Equally important, however, are a number of communication standards that are becoming increasingly important. John Naisbitt, in his bestseller *Megatrends,* foresaw that a *high-tech* society will be balanced by *high-touch* human interactions. This has become fact in the computer services area. Customers want the person-to-person interaction that ensures answers, builds confidence, and reduces worry. Current customers judge their service programs and service providers on the amount and quality of *communications* that take place when problems occur and after they are resolved. All these people-oriented services are costly for the service provider, but since they are key determinants of quality, they cannot be understated and definitely cannot be ignored.

An important component in a quality service program is a steady focus on the customer's business, not on the customer's equipment. Understanding how a customer has applied technology to a business operation will provide the focus necessary to develop a quality service program. Treating each customer as having a unique situation helps the servicer focus on quality standards. Whatever services make up the program, customer and servicer must agree on preestablished performance standards so there is no ambiguity in measurement methods. In the case of on-site maintenance services, exact standards should be developed for the

following components and should be part of the service program:

— Response time
— Repair time
— System availability or uptime
— Protocols for calling the servicer
— Protocols for communicating with the customer
— Emergency repairs
— Preventive maintenance activities
— Protocols for reporting service activities to the customer
— Calendar to review service program with the customer
— Problem-escalation procedures
— Customer responsibilities

APPLYING TECHNOLOGY

In response to the many changes that continue to unfold in the marketplace, TRW has placed increasing emphasis on the application of technology in its service delivery systems. This is needed not only to maintain and improve quality, but also to address increasing costs of people and materials.

One of TRW's early applications, driven by the need to support complex nationwide data communications networks, was the development of a centralized data communications test center. This center is used to assist both customer personnel and TRW service engineers in diagnosing data communications problems. It has all but eliminated the delays, frustration, and expense that often result when the customer attempts to work with telephone companies, data centers, and service providers to resolve data communication problems. The real proof is that problems are often resolved without even having to dispatch a service engineer to a customer's location.

A later application, driven by the rapid growth in the microcomputer systems market, was the development of a multipurpose system and assembly tester called SLEUTH. Equipped with this highly versatile tester and proprietary operating system and diagnostic software, TRW service engineers can service a wide variety of mixed-vendor systems without the difficulties and costs associated with carrying vast amounts of technical documentation and specialized test equipment. It enables prompt, accurate fault diagnosis without the costly *shot-gunning* approach of swapping assemblies, a method used by many other service providers. In addition, the tester is used to test and screen assemblies received at TRW service centers, prior to adding them to local spare parts inventories.

While the SLEUTH tester is an intelligent device, its intelligence must be updated or supplemented if the complexity of the problems exceeds its capabilities. To address this feature, TRW has undertaken the development of two additional technology applications. The first is an on-line technical information system called SLATE. This system provides all TRW service engineers access to the latest technical information pertaining to products they are servicing, and it updates the SLEUTH testers with current diagnostics and support software. The system consists of a central database and a communications controller that allows access via dial-up telephone lines. Contained in the database is the latest product information received from hardware and software providers as well as technical information developed by TRW's own engineering department.

In addition, the SLATE database contains a file of problems and related solutions for the products serviced by TRW. Based on analyses of the thousands of service activities completed by TRW daily and the input received from service engineers, who enter their data directly to SLATE via the dial-up communications link, an extensive file of product problems, symptoms, causes, and solutions is maintained and made available to all TRW's service engineers. All the information and capabilities of SLATE are available to all TRW service engineers and authorized customers twenty-four hours a day, seven days a week.

Further enhancing its own ability to deliver consistently high quality across a wide range of products, TRW is installing *Fieldwatch,* an integrated software package developed by the DATA Group, to manage its complete service operation. The package includes six modules titled as follows:

dispatch, technical assistance center (TAC), billing, logistics, repair center, and scheduling.

The *dispatch module* contains customer records pertaining to the site, equipment, contract provisions, and the complete service history. It also includes information on the training and locations of technicians and service engineers. The *TAC module* allows product-line technical experts to screen calls for service and provide technical assistance to service engineers at customer locations.

The *billing module* handles all billing and recordkeeping to ensure that invoices are filled out accurately and are based either on contract terms or actual expenses for time and material. The *logistics module* handles the spare parts inventory. Instant access to part numbers, prices, and stocking locations makes the service call faster and more productive. The *repair center module* contains information to track repairable assemblies by part number and serial number. The repair center module works in concert with the *scheduling module,* so that repaired parts are available when and where they are needed.

_____ QUESTIONS FOR READING 14.3

1. Describe how customer expectations and measurements of quality have changed in the computer services industry.

2. Explain this statement, "Customers do not think about maintenance or repair services. They think about uptime and their businesses." What implications does this have for establishing an effective computer services program?

3. How has TRW used technology to enhance its service quality? What specific needs do SLEUTH, SLATE, and Fieldwatch address?

4. Currently, what is the tangible evidence of quality in computer services? As diagnostic software becomes more advanced, it is likely that service programs will become almost invisible from the customer's perspective. How will this affect customer expectations and perceptions of quality?

___ CASE 14.1 _____

Falls Church General Hospital

Founded in 1968, the Falls Church General Hospital (FCGH) is a privately owned 615-patient bed facility in the incorporated township of Falls Church, Virginia.[17] Falls Church is four miles from downtown Washington, D.C., and is surrounded by the counties of Arlington, Fairfax, and Alexandria, Virginia, all affluent urban/suburban communities with a highly educated population composed largely of employees of the U.S. government and high tech engineering firms.

THE HOSPITAL

Falls Church General Hospital, with 895 employees, provides a broad range of health care services, including drug/alcohol abuse wards, emergency rooms, x-ray and laboratory facilities, maternity wards, intensive and cardiac care units, and outpatient facilities. With strong competition from other comprehensive facilities such as George Washington University Hospital, Georgetown University Hospital, Fairfax General, and Arlington Hospital, FCGH has had to concentrate on offering high-quality treatment at reasonable prices. FCGH has not attempted to obtain all of the latest up-to-date diagnostic equipment (such as $350,000 CAT scans) because its board felt it would not be cost effective to try to compete with the more research-oriented university hospitals such as Georgetown or George Washington (the latter being where former President Reagan was taken when he was shot by John Hinkley in 1981). Even though FCGH is considered a "medium-to-large" hospital, it has attempted to stress personal attention to each patient. In January 1990, the hospital began a series of ads in the *Washington Post* highlighting its concerned doctors and nurses, its friendly support staff, and its overall philosophy that its employees care about their work and their patients.

THE ISSUE OF ASSESSING QUALITY HEALTH CARE

Quality health care is a goal all hospitals profess, but few have developed comprehensive and scientific means of asking customers to judge the quality of care they receive. A tremendous amount of effort has been devoted to assessing the clinical quality of hospital care; books, journals, and papers on the topic abound. The problem, however, is that past efforts to measure hospital quality have largely ignored the perceptions of customers—the patients, physicians, and payers. Instead of formally considering customer judgments of quality, the health care industry has focused almost entirely on internal quality assessments made by the health professionals who operate the system. In effect, a system for improving health care has been created that all but ignores the voice of the customer.

The board of FCGH believes that all hospitals need to make the transformation from the current practice of attempting to ensure quality to actually measuring and improving the quality of care from both the external, customer perspective and the internal, provider perspective. Fueled by concerns in recent years about costs and medical practice variation and by the demand for greater social accountability, there is an emerging demand by patients and payers that quality health care be provided at best value.

As board president Dr. Irwin Greenberg recently stated at the annual FCGH meeting,

"As the prices people pay in the future for given levels of service become more similar, hospitals will be distinguished largely on the basis of their quality and value as assessed by customers. We must have accurate information about how our customers, not just the health care professionals who work here, judge the quality of care in this institution. Many hospitals already have some methods for measuring

---

[17] Some background information for this case was taken from quotes in T. R. Gillem and E. Nelson "Hospital Quality Trends" in J. W. Spechler (ed.) *When America Does It Right: Case Studies in Service Quality* (Norcross, Ga.: Industrial Engineering and Management Press, 1989), pp. 117–122.

patient satisfaction. A recent survey of more than two hundred hospitals showed that two-thirds routinely conduct patient satisfaction surveys. Typically, the surveys are distributed at discharge to patients who are free to respond or not. The main value of such surveys is to gain quick knowledge of problems experienced by patients, many of whom often fill out questionnaires because they are disgruntled about some specific aspect of the care they received."

In response to Dr. Greenberg's statement, and in light of the advertising campaign, hospital administrator Carla Kimball called a meeting of her department heads to discuss the issue of quality. "Can we really deliver on our promises? Or are we in danger of failing to live up to the level of health care our patients expect, and do we risk losing them?" Ms. Kimball asked.

Frances Pruitt, head of nursing, continued the debate.

"I argue that surveys, such as the one Dr. Greenberg mentioned in his speech, are valuable. But how do we measure the quality of our health care? Some patients who leave FCGH happy may have actually received poor treatment here. If we are serious about improving the quality of care, we need more *valid* and *reliable* data on which to act. We need answers to specific, quality-related questions about activities in areas that affect patients—admission, nursing, medical staff, daily care, and ancillary staff."

"I have an idea," said Merrill Warkentin, Kimball's staff director. "I just finished reading a book by John Groocock. He's the Vice-President for Quality at TRW, a big manufacturer. He says there are 14 steps in TRW's internal quality audits. I made a photocopy of those steps (see Exhibit 14–12). Why don't we consider his approach?"

When the meeting ended, Ms. Kimball read Groocock's list again and began to think about the whole issue of quality control in U.S. firms. It had worked in many manufacturing companies, but could the concepts of quality control really be used in a hospital?

QUESTIONS FOR CASE 14.1

1. Why is it important to get the patient's assessment of health care quality? Does a patient have the expertise to judge the health care he or she receives?

2. How might a hospital measure quality?

3. Using the steps in Exhibit 14–12, discuss how each might apply to FCGH.

4. How can the value of a human life be included in the cost of quality control?

5. There are certain parallels between the evaluation of health care quality and educational quality. How are customer surveys used to evaluate the quality of teaching at your institution? How are the results used? Are any other measures available to assess educational quality? What improvements would you suggest to the current system?

EXHIBIT 14–12

- *Steps in TRW's Quality Audit*

1. *Quality to the customer.* Is conformance of the product to established quality standards measured? Is quality of the organization's product compared with that of competitors' products?
2. *Quality costs.* Have the costs of quality been measured and have areas for possible cost savings been identified?
3. *Design review.* Do procedures exist to review designs for quality? Are these procedures being carried out?
4. *Product qualification.* Have procedures been established and followed to qualify new products before any deliveries to customers?
5. *Product liability.* Has each product been scrutinized regarding safety and are appropriate records kept? Does a written plan exist for dealing with a major product liability problem?
6. *Process capability.* Has the capability of all processes been measured and is that information used in product design and development? *(continues)*

—————— EXHIBIT 14–12 *Continued* ————————————————————————————

7. *Incoming inspection.* Are incoming lots inspected in an efficient manner and are appropriate records kept?

8. *Supplier quality.* Are suppliers made aware of their quality responsibilities? Are records kept on nonconformance?

9. *Process control.* Has the company developed policies for controlling processes? Have employees been trained to follow those policies?

10. *Inspection and test planning.* Do inspection and test plans exist for all products and are records maintained on the results? Is all test equipment calibrated regularly?

11. *Quality performance indicators.* Are quality performance indicators regularly published throughout the organization and made available to employees?

12. *Employee involvement program.* Are employees involved in quality improvement through some process such as quality circles?

13. *Multifunctional quality improvement team.* Has a quality improvement team covering all functional areas been established to monitor quality and work to improve it?

14. *Quality business plan.* Has quality been integrated into the organization's business plan—and from there into the overall strategic plan?

Source: John M. Groocock, *The Chain of Quality* (New York: Wiley, 1986) p. 250. Copyright © 1986 John Wiley & Sons, Inc. Reprinted by permission of John Wiley & Sons, Inc.

———————————————— REFERENCES ————————————————

"A Productivity Revolution in the Service Sector," *Business Week* (September 5, 1983), p. 106.

Alexander, David C. *The Practice and Management of Industrial Economics.* Englewood Cliffs, N.J.: Prentice-Hall, 1986.

"America's Leanest and Meanest," *Business Week* (October 5, 1987).

Bain, David. *Service Management Prescription.* New York: McGraw-Hill, 1982.

Berry, Leonard L., Valerie A. Zeithaml, and A. Parasuraman. "Quality Counts In Services, Too," *Business Horizons* (May–June 1985), pp. 44–52.

Buehler, Vernon M., and Y. Krishna Shetty (Eds.). *Productivity Improvement: Case Studies of Proven Practice.* New York: AMACOM, 1981.

Collier, David A. *Service Management: Operating Decisions.* Englewood Cliffs, N.J.: Prentice-Hall, 1987.

Crandall, Robert L. "Solving the Crisis in the Skies," *Fortune* (September 28, 1987), p. 204.

Davis, Herbert W. "Save Consulting Fees: Do-it-Yourself Measures of Customer-Services Effectiveness," *Advanced Management Journal* (Spring 1984), pp. 41–52.

Drucker, Peter. *Management: Tasks, Responsibilities, Practices.* New York: Harper & Row, 1974.

Gaither, Norman. *Production and Operations Management,* 3d Ed. New York: Dryden Press, 1987.

Gregerman, Ira B. *Knowledge Worker Productivity.* New York: AMACOM, 1981.

Guzzo, Richard A., and Jeffrey S. Bondy. *A Guide to Worker Productivity Experiments in the United States 1976–81.* New York: Pergamon, 1983.

Hansen, Bertrand L. *Quality Control: Theory & Applications.* Englewood Cliffs, N.J.: Prentice-Hall, 1963.

Heizer, Jay, and Barry Render. *Production and Operations Management.* Boston: Allyn and Bacon, 1988.

Heskett, James L. "Lessons in the Service Sector," *Harvard Business Review,* Vol. 65, No. 2 (March–April, 1987), pp. 118–126.

Hobbs, James B. *Corporate Staying Power.* Lexington, Mass.: Lexington Books, 1987.

Horovitz, Jacques. "How to Check the Quality of Customer Service and Raise the Standard," *International Management* (February 1987), pp. 34–35.

Johnson, Eugene M., Eberhard E. Scheuing, and Kathleen A. Gaida. *Profitable Service Marketing.* Homewood, Ill.: Dow Jones–Irwin, 1986.

King, Carol A. "A Framework for a Service Quality

Assurance System,'' *Quality Progress* (September 1987), pp. 27–32.

Marchand, Donald A., and Forest W. Horton, Jr. *Infotrends.* New York: Wiley, 1986.

Nightingale, Michael. ''Defining Quality for a Quality Assurance Program—A Study of Perceptions,'' in R. Lewis et al. (Eds.), *The Practice of Hospitality Management II.* Darien, Conn.: AVI Publishing, 1986, pp. 37–53.

Parasuraman, A., Valerie A. Zeithaml, and Leonard L. Berry, ''A Conceptual Model of Service Quality and Its Implications for Future Research,'' *Journal of Marketing* (Fall 1985), pp. 41–50.

Peters, Tom. *Thriving on Chaos: A Handbook for a Management Revolution.* New York: Knopf, 1987.

Peters, Thomas J., and Robert H. Waterman, Jr. *In Search of Excellence: Lessons from America's Best-Run Companies.* New York: Warner Books, 1982.

Quinn, James Brian, Jordan J. Baruch, and Penny Cushman Pagnette. ''Technology in Services,'' *Scientific American* (December 1987), pp. 50–58.

Rehg, Virgil. ''SPC for White Collar Organizations,'' *Journal for Quality and Participation,* Vol. 9, No. 4 (December 1986), pp. 37–41.

Russell, George. ''Pul-eeze! Will Somebody Help Me?'' *Time* (February 2, 1987), pp. 48–57.

Sasser, W. Earl, R. Paul Olsen, and D. Daryl Wyckoff. *Management of Service Operations.* Boston, Mass.: Allyn and Bacon, 1978.

Sherman, H. David. ''Improving the Productivity of Service Businesses,'' *Sloan Management Review* (Spring 1984), pp. 11–23.

Shetty, Y. K., and Joel E. Ross. ''Quality and Its Management in Service Businesses,'' *Industrial Management* (November–December 1985), pp. 7–12.

Slade, Bernard N., and Raj Mohindra. *Winning the Productivity Race.* Lexington, Mass.: Lexington Books, 1985.

Spechler, Jay W. (Ed.). *When America Does It Right: Case Studies in Service Quality.* Norcross, Ga.: Industrial Engineering and Management Press, 1989.

Tribus, Myron. ''Quality, Productivity, and Competitive Position.'' Deming Videotape Series. Cambridge, Mass.: MIT Center for Advanced Engineering Study, 1984.

Trim, C. W. ''Zero Defect,'' *Mortgage Banking* (January 1987), pp. 19–24.

Walton, Mary. *The Deming Management Method.* New York: Dodd, Mead, 1986.

Zemke, Ron, and Dick Schaaf. *The Service Edge.* New York: New American Library, 1989.

14

SUPPLEMENT

Process Control Charts

INTRODUCTION

In many cases, production and consumption of a service occur simultaneously. This leaves little opportunity for the service provider to test or inspect the quality of the service before it is delivered to the customer. For this reason, quality control in services concentrates on the service *process*.

All processes are subject to a certain degree of variability. This is especially true for service processes because of the variety of customers served, the array of possible tasks involved in providing a service, and the impact of different service employees on the quality of the service provided. Statistical process control uses various control charts to detect unacceptable levels of variability in a process that could adversely affect the quality of the service.

This supplement discusses the concept of control charts, and presents techniques for constructing two categories of charts: (1) control charts for variables (measurable qualities of a service) and (2) control charts for attributes (characteristics which a service may or may not possess).

CONTROL CHARTS FOR VARIABLES

Two types of control charts, one for the sample mean $\overline{X}$ and another for the range R are used to monitor processes that are measured in continuous units. For example, these control charts may monitor the time that it takes to serve a customer or the length of time that a customer waits before being served. The $\overline{X}$ (X-bar) chart would tell us whether significant changes have occurred in the average service time or waiting time.

The *R*-chart values would indicate a steady increase or decrease in service time or waiting time. The two charts go hand in hand when monitoring variables.

$\overline{X}$ Charts

The theoretical foundation for $\overline{X}$ charts is the **central limit theorem.** In general terms, this theorem states that regardless of the distribution of the population of all parts or services, the distribution of $\overline{X}$'s (each of which is a mean of a sample drawn from the population) will tend to follow a normal curve as the sample size grows large. And fortunately, even if *n* is fairly small (say 4 or 5), the distributions of the averages will still roughly follow a normal curve. The theorem also states that (1) the mean of the distribution of the $\overline{X}$'s (called $\overline{\overline{X}}$) will equal the mean of the overall population (which is called μ), and (2) the standard deviation of the sampling distribution $\sigma_{\overline{x}}$ will be the population standard deviation σ_x divided by the square root of the sample size *n*. In other words,

$$\overline{\overline{X}} = \mu \quad \text{and} \quad \sigma_{\overline{x}} = \frac{\sigma_x}{\sqrt{n}} \qquad\qquad \textbf{S14.1}$$

Exhibit S14–1 shows three possible population distributions, each with its own mean μ and standard deviation σ_x. If a series of random samples ($\overline{X}_1$, $\overline{X}_2$, $\overline{X}_3$, $\overline{X}_4$, and

EXHIBIT S14–1

■ *Population and Sampling Distributions*

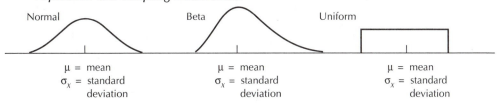

(a) **SOME POPULATION DISTRIBUTIONS**

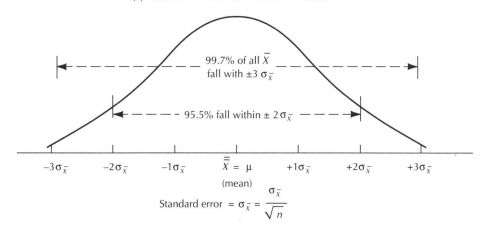

(b) **SAMPLING DISTRIBUTION OF SAMPLE MEANS (ALWAYS NORMAL)**

so on) each of size n is drawn from any of these, the resulting distribution of $\bar{X}_i$ will appear as in the bottom graph of the exhibit. Because this is a normal distribution, we can state that if the process has only random variations

1. 99.7 percent of the time the sample averages will fall within $\pm 3\sigma_{\bar{x}}$.
2. 95.5 percent of the time the sample averages will fall within $\pm 2\sigma_{\bar{x}}$.

In other words, if a point on the control chart falls outside of the $\pm 3\sigma_{\bar{x}}$ control limits, then we are 99.7 percent confident that the process has changed. Similarly, if a point on the control charts falls outside of the $\pm 2\sigma_{\bar{x}}$ control limits, we are 95.5 percent sure that the process has changed. This is the theory behind control charts.

In practice, the standard deviation of the service process may be difficult to determine, but it can be estimated by the **range** of the service process. The range is the difference between the highest and lowest measurement in a sample.

An $\bar{X}$ chart is simply a plot of the means of the samples taken of a process. $\bar{\bar{X}}$ is the average of the sample means. To set upper and lower control limits for the $\bar{X}$ chart, we use the following formulas:

$$\text{UCL}_{\bar{x}} = \bar{\bar{X}} + A\bar{R} \quad \text{and} \quad \text{LCL}_{\bar{x}} = \bar{\bar{X}} - A\bar{R}$$

where $\bar{\bar{X}}$ = the average of the sample means

$\bar{R}$ = the average range of the samples

A = a factor taken from Exhibit S14–2 to establish $3\sigma_{\bar{x}}$ control limits

$\text{UCL}_{\bar{x}}$ = upper control limit for the mean

$\text{LCL}_{\bar{x}}$ = ower control limit for the mean

_____ EXHIBIT S14–2 _____

▪ *Control Limit Factors* ($\pm 3\sigma$)

Sample Size n	A (Mean Factor)	B (Upper-Range Factor)	C (Lower-Range Factor)
2	1.880	3.267	0
3	1.023	2.575	0
4	0.729	2.282	0
5	0.577	2.115	0
6	0.483	2.004	0
7	0.419	1.924	0.076
8	0.373	1.864	0.136
9	0.337	1.816	0.184
10	0.308	1.777	0.223
11	0.285	1.774	0.256
12	0.266	1.716	0.284
13	0.249	1.692	0.308
14	0.235	1.671	0.329
15	0.223	1.652	0.348
20	0.180	1.586	0.459
25	0.153	1.541	0.459

R Charts

In addition to being concerned with the process average, managers are interested in the process variability. Even though the process average is under control, the variability of the process may not be. The theory behind control charts for ranges is the same as for the process average. Limits are established that contain ± 3 standard deviations of the distribution for the average range $\overline{R}$. With a few simplifying assumptions, we can set the upper and lower control limits for ranges as follows:

$$\text{UCL}_R = B\overline{R} \quad \text{and} \quad \text{LCL}_R = C\overline{R}$$

where UCL_R = upper control chart limit for the range

$\quad\quad \text{LCL}_R$ = lower control chart limit for the range

$\quad\quad B$ and C = values from Exhibit S14–2

$\quad\quad \overline{R}$ = average range of the samples

Mail Order Business Example. A mail ordering business wants to measure the response time of their operators in taking customer orders over the phone. Listed below is the time recorded in minutes from five different samples of the ordering process with four customer orders per sample. We will construct 3 standard deviation $\overline{X}$ and R control charts for this process and determine if any points are out of control.

Sample	Observations				Sample Average $\overline{X}$	Sample Range R
1	5	3	6	10	24/4 = 6	10–3 = 7
2	7	5	3	5	20/4 = 5	7–3 = 4
3	1	8	3	12	24/4 = 6	12–1 = 11
4	7	6	2	1	16/4 = 4	7–1 = 6
5	3	15	6	12	36/4 = 9	15–3 = 12
					$\Sigma\overline{X} = 30$	$\Sigma R = 40$

$\overline{\overline{X}} = 30/5 = 6$

$\overline{R} = 40/5 = 8$

$\text{UCL}_{\overline{X}} = 6 + 0.729(8) = 11.832$

$\text{LCL}_{\overline{X}} = 6 - 0.729(8) = .168$

The $\overline{X}$ chart is shown in Exhibit S14–3.

$\text{UCL}_R = 2.282(8) = 18.256$

$\text{LCL}_R = 0(8) = 0$

The R chart is shown in Exhibit S14–4.

Examining Exhibits S14–3 and S14–4, we see that no $\overline{X}$ or R points are out of control. The operators are performing their work within reasonable time limits.

EXHIBIT S14–3 _____

- $\bar{X}$ Chart for Operator Response Time

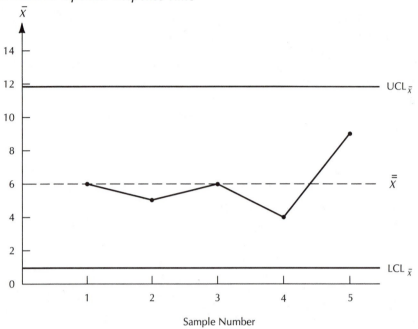

EXHIBIT S14–4 _____

- R Chart for Operator Response Time

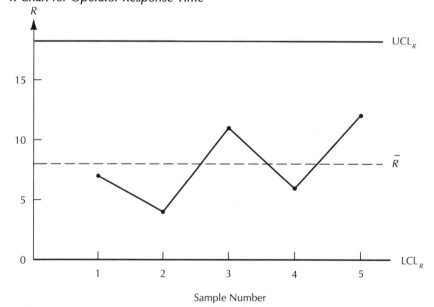

What other measures of service quality would you recommend for this process? How about percentage of orders taken correctly or number of mistakes per order? For this type of quality assessment, we need two new types of control charts.

CONTROL CHARTS FOR ATTRIBUTES

Control charts for $\overline{X}$ and R do not apply when we are sampling attributes, in which items are typically classified as defective or nondefective. Measuring defects involves counting them (e.g., number of bad light bulbs in a given lot or number of data entry records typed with errors), whereas variables are usually measured for length, weight, or time. There are two kinds of attribute control charts: (1) those which measure the percent defective in a sample—called *p* **charts,** and (2) those which count the number of defects—called *c* **charts.**

p Charts

The principal means of controlling attributes are *p* charts. Although attributes that are either good or bad follow the binomial distribution, the normal distribution can be used to calculate *p* chart limits when sample sizes are large. The procedure resembles the $\overline{X}$ chart approach, which also was based on the central limit theorem.

The formulas for *p* chart upper and lower control limits are

$$\text{UCL}_p = \bar{p} + Z\sigma_p \qquad \qquad \textbf{S14.2}$$

$$\text{LCL}_p = \bar{p} - Z\sigma_p \qquad \qquad \textbf{S14.3}$$

where $\bar{p}$ = mean percent defective in the samples

Z = number of standard deviates ($Z = 2$ for 95.5 percent control limits,

$Z = 3$ for 99.7 percent control limits)

σ_p = standard deviation of the sampling distribution

σ_p is estimated by the formula

$$\sigma_p = \sqrt{\frac{\bar{p}(1 - \bar{p})}{n}} \qquad \qquad \textbf{S14.4}$$

where n = size of each sample.

p Chart Example. Using a popular database software package, twenty data entry clerks at ARCO key in thousands of insurance records each day. A sample of one hundred records entered by each clerk was carefully examined to make sure they contained no errors. The percent defective in each sample was then computed as shown in Exhibit S14–5.

_____ EXHIBIT S14–5 _____

■ *Data Entry Errors*

Sample Number	Records with Errors	Percent Defective	Sample Number	Records with Errors	Percent Defective
1	6	0.06	11	6	0.06
2	5	0.05	12	1	0.01
3	0	0.00	13	8	0.08
4	1	0.01	14	7	0.07
5	4	0.04	15	5	0.05
6	2	0.02	16	4	0.04
7	5	0.05	17	11	0.11
8	3	0.03	18	3	0.03
9	3	0.03	19	0	0.00
10	2	0.02	20	4	0.04
			Total	80	

n = size of each sample = 100

We will develop a p chart that plots the percent defective and sets control limits to include 99.7 percent of the random variation in the entry process when it is in control.

$$\bar{p} = \frac{\text{total number of errors}}{\text{total number of records examined}} = \frac{80}{(100)(20)} = 0.04 \qquad \textbf{S14.5}$$

$$\sigma_p = \sqrt{\frac{(0.04)(1 - 0.04)}{(100)}} = 0.02$$

$$UCL_p = \bar{p} + Z\sigma_p = 0.04 + 3(0.02) = 0.10$$

$$LCL_p = \bar{p} - Z\sigma_p = 0.04 - 3(0.02) = -0.02 \text{ or } 0 \qquad \text{(since we}$$
cannot have a negative percent)

The control limits and percent defective are plotted in Exhibit S14–6. Notice that only one data entry clerk (number 17) is out of control. The firm may wish to examine that individual's work a bit more closely to see if a serious problem exists. In addition, it might be interesting to investigate the working habits of clerks 3 and 19. Do they make no errors because they work too slowly or have they developed a superior procedure?

c Charts

In the preceding example we counted the number of defective database records entered. A defective record was one that was not exactly correct. A bad record may contain more than one defect, however. We use c charts to control the number of defects per unit of output (or per insurance record in the preceding case).

▪ *Example p Chart for Data Entry*

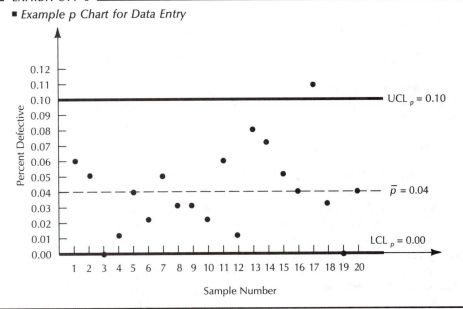

Control charts for defects are helpful for monitoring processes where a large number of potential errors can occur but the actual number that do occur is relatively small. Defects may be typographical errors in newspapers, blemishes on a table, or missing pickles on a fast-food hamburger.

The **Poisson probability distribution,** which has a variance equal to its mean, is the basis for *c* charts. Since $\bar{c}$ is the mean number of defects per unit, the standard deviation is equal to $\sqrt{\bar{c}}$. To compute 99.7 percent control limits for $\bar{c}$, we use the formula

$$\bar{c} \pm 3\sqrt{\bar{c}} \qquad\qquad\qquad \textbf{S14.6}$$

c Chart Example. Red Top Cab Company receives several complaints per day about the behavior of its drivers. Over a nine-day period (where days are the units of measure), the owner received this number of calls from irate passengers: 3, 0, 8, 9, 6, 7, 4, 9, 8, for a total of 54 complaints.

To compute 99.7 percent control limits, we take

$$\bar{c} = \frac{54}{9} = 6 \text{ complaints per day}$$

Thus

$$UCL_c = \bar{c} + 3\sqrt{\bar{c}} = 6 + 3\sqrt{6} = 6 + 3(24.5) = 13.35$$

$$LCL_c = \bar{c} - 3\sqrt{\bar{c}} = 6 - 3\sqrt{6} = 6 - 3(2.45) = -1.35 \text{ or } 0$$

After plotting a control chart summarizing this data and posting it prominently in the drivers' locker room, the number of calls received dropped to an average of three per day. Can you explain why this may have occurred?

SUMMARY

The process control chart is a quality control technique constructed to detect unacceptable levels of variability in a process. $\bar{X}$ and R charts are used together to measure changes in the central tendency and uniformity of a process. The percent defective in a sample of the process is measured by p charts, and c charts count the number of defects.

Service employees can monitor the quality of the service they are providing by sampling their work and recording such data as the time it takes to process a customer, the number of errors made, or the percentage of customers who are satisfied. If the data recorded fall outside prespecified control limits, corrective action needs to be taken.

PROBLEMS

S14.1 City Council has asked the local police department to investigate the problem of slow response time to citizen calls for police service. The department randomly sampled the response time to five calls from the dispatcher's weekly logs over the past three months. Using the data provided below, develop 3σ $\bar{X}$ and R charts for police response time. Then prepare a report for city council based on your findings. Can you think of any possible problems with the data on which your report is based? What other quality control techniques might be useful for this problem?

Sample	Response Time (minutes)				
1	4	12	63	10	20
2	30	8	16	5	26
3	53	32	10	15	24
4	5	2	17	20	9
5	18	25	4	7	10
6	6	5	10	30	5
7	8	4	27	12	10
8	4	16	6	42	16
9	8	33	15	6	13
10	10	20	27	23	5
11	17	32	4	42	27
12	12	5	16	20	50

S14.2 A popular restaurant in town routinely records on customer tickets the time of each customer's arrival to the restaurant (i.e., when they asked to be seated) and the time of each customer's departure (i.e., when they paid the bill). The tickets are then placed in a large fish bowl-type container and a sample of the "time in the restaurant" for five customers is randomly drawn each night of the week. Using the data from last week provided below, develop 3σ $\bar{X}$ and R charts for customer time at the restaurant. Comment on the results. How could the restaurant use this information to control the quality of their service?

Sample	Time in Restaurant (minutes)				
1	20	35	62	43	75
2	50	38	72	92	24
3	44	36	75	54	25
4	90	48	32	71	46
5	27	52	17	68	39
6	54	39	49	35	65
7	79	53	65	72	90

S14.3 An established hospital in an urban area is trying to improve its image by providing a positive experience for its patients and their relatives. Part of the "image" program involves providing tasty, inviting patient meals that are also healthy. A questionnaire accompanies each meal served, asking the patient, among other things, whether he or she is satisfied or unsatisfied with the meal. A 100-patient sample of the survey results over the past seven days yielded the following data:

Day	No. of Unsatisfied Patients	Sample Size
1	24	100
2	22	100
3	8	100
4	15	100
5	10	100
6	26	100
7	17	100

Construct a *p* chart that plots the percentage of patients unsatisfied with their meals. Set the control limits to include 99.7 percent of the random variation in meal satisfaction. Comment on your results.

S14.4 In order to monitor the allocation of patrol cars and other police resources, the local police department collects data on the incidence of crime by city sector. The city is divided into ten sectors of 1000 residents each. The number of crime incidents reported last month in each sector is as follows:

Sector	Crime Incidence
1	6
2	25
3	5
4	11
5	20
6	17
7	10
8	22
9	7
10	33

Construct a *p* chart that plots the rate of crime by sector. Set the control limits to include 99.7 percent

of the random variation in crime. Is the crime rate in any sector out of control? Do you have any suggestions for the reallocation of police resources? What other information might be helpful in your analysis?

S14.5 The school board is trying to evaluate a new math program introduced to second graders in five elementary schools across the county this year. A sample of the student scores on standardized math tests in each elementary school yielded the following data:

School	No. of Test Errors
A	52
B	27
C	35
D	44
E	55

Construct a *c* chart for test errors and set the control limits to contain 99.7 percent of the random variation in test scores. What does the chart tell you? Has the new math program been effective? Should the second graders be allowed to proceed to the next math level?

S14.6 Telephone inquiries of 100 IRS "customers" are monitored daily at random. Incidents of incorrect information or other nonconformities (such as impoliteness to customers) are recorded. The data for last week are

Day	No. of Nonconformities
1	5
2	10
3	23
4	20
5	15

Construct a 3 standard deviation *c* chart of nonconformities. What does the control chart tell you about the IRS telephone operators?

CASE S14.1

The Morristown Daily Tribune

In July 1987, the Morristown *Daily Tribune* published its first newspaper in direct competition with two other newspapers—the Morristown *Daily Ledger* and the *Clarion Herald,* a weekly publication. Presently, the *Ledger* is the most widely read newspaper in the area, with a total circulation of 38,500. The *Tribune,* however, has made significant inroads into the readership market since its inception. Total circulation of the *Tribune* now exceeds 27,000.

Wilbur Sykes, editor of the *Tribune,* attributes the success of the newspaper to the accuracy of its contents, a strong editorial section, and the proper blending of local, regional, national, and international news items. In addition, the paper has been successful in getting the accounts of several major retailers who advertise extensively in the display section. Finally, experienced reporters, photographers, copy writers, typesetters, editors,

and other personnel have formed a "team" dedicated to providing the most timely and accurate reporting of news in the area.

Of critical importance to quality newspaper printing is accurate typesetting. To ensure quality in the final print, Mr. Sykes has decided to develop a procedure for monitoring the performance of typesetters over a period of time. Such a procedure involves sampling output, establishing control limits, comparing the *Tribune*'s accuracy with that of the industry, and occasionally updating the information.

First, Mr. Sykes randomly selected 30 newspapers published during the preceding 12 months. From each paper, 100 paragraphs were randomly chosen and were read for accuracy. The number of errors in each paper was recorded, and the fraction of errors in each sample was determined. Exhibit S14–7 shows the results of the sampling.

EXHIBIT S14–7

■ *Sample of Errors in Thirty Newspapers*

Sample	Errors in Sample	Fraction of Errors (per 100)	Sample	Errors in Sample	Fraction of Errors (per 100)
1	2	0.02	16	2	0.02
2	4	0.04	17	3	0.03
3	10	0.10	18	7	0.07
4	4	0.04	19	3	0.03
5	1	0.01	20	2	0.02
6	1	0.01	21	3	0.03
7	13	0.13	22	7	0.07
8	9	0.09	23	4	0.04
9	11	0.11	24	3	0.03
10	0	0.00	25	2	0.02
11	3	0.03	26	2	0.02
12	4	0.04	27	0	0.00
13	2	0.02	28	1	0.01
14	2	0.02	29	3	0.03
15	8	0.08	30	4	0.04

Source: Written by Professor Jerry Kinard (Francis Marion College) and Joe Iverstine (deceased).

—— QUESTIONS FOR CASE S14.1

1. Plot the overall fraction of errors ($\bar{p}$) and the upper and lower control limits on a control chart using a 95.45 percent confidence level.

2. Assume the industry upper and lower control limits are 0.1000 and 0.0400, respectively. Plot them on the control chart.

3. Plot the fraction of errors in each sample. Do all fall within the firm's control limits? When one falls outside the control limits, what should be done?

15

Project Management

INTRODUCTION

Most service organizations have to take on large, complex projects at one point or another. For example, an airline opening new routes or pulling a jumbo jet out of service for major maintenance faces large expenses if these tasks are delayed for any reason. A department store chain installing a new inventory control system can suffer lost sales and painful ordering costs if timetables are unmet. A government agency installing and debugging an expensive computer spends months preparing details for a smooth conversion to new hardware. NASA completes thousands of individual activities in its extensive overhaul of a space shuttle after each flight. A hospital modernizing its operating rooms can endure not only inconvenience, but a loss of life if the many technical steps involved are not properly controlled.

Large, often one-time projects are difficult challenges to service managers. The stakes are high. Millions of dollars in cost overruns have been wasted due to poor planning on projects. Unnecessary delays have occurred due to poor scheduling. And companies have gone bankrupt due to poor controls.

Special projects that take months or years to complete are usually developed outside the normal operations system. Project organizations within the firm are set up to handle such jobs and are often disbanded when the project is complete. The management of large projects involves three phases (see Exhibit 15–1):

— Planning
— Scheduling
— Controlling

We will begin this chapter with a brief overview of these functions. Two popular techniques to allow managers to plan, schedule, and control—PERT and CPM—will then be described in some detail.*

PROJECT PLANNING

Projects can usually be defined as a series of related tasks directed toward a major output. A new organization form, developed to make sure existing programs continue to run smoothly on a day-to-day basis while new projects are successfully completed, is called **project organization.**

A project organization is an effective way of pooling the people and physical resources needed for a limited time to complete a specific project or goal. It is basically a temporary organizational structure designed to achieve results by using specialists from throughout the firm. For many years, NASA successfully used the project approach to reach its goals. You may recall Project Gemini and Project Apollo. These terms were used to describe teams NASA organized to reach space exploration objectives.

The project organization works best when

1. Work can be defined with a specific goal and deadline.
2. The job is somewhat unique or unfamiliar to the existing organization.
3. The work contains complex interrelated tasks requiring specialized skills.
4. The project is temporary but critical to the organization.

When a project organization takes on a more permanent form, it is usually called a **matrix organization.** This structure can be used when it is critical for the

* This chapter is adapted from Jay Heizer and Barry Render, *Production and Operations Management,* Chapter 16. Copyright © 1988 by Allyn and Bacon. Reprinted with permission.

EXHIBIT 15–1

■ *Project Planning, Scheduling, and Controlling*

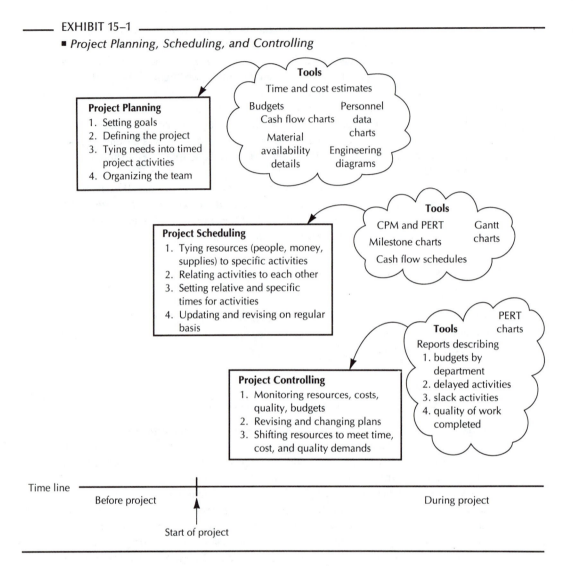

Project Planning
1. Setting goals
2. Defining the project
3. Tying needs into timed project activities
4. Organizing the team

Tools
Time and cost estimates
Budgets   Personnel
  Cash flow charts   data
              charts
   Material
   availability   Engineering
   details   diagrams

Project Scheduling
1. Tying resources (people, money, supplies) to specific activities
2. Relating activities to each other
3. Setting relative and specific times for activities
4. Updating and revising on regular basis

Tools
CPM and PERT   Gantt
Milestone charts   charts
Cash flow schedules

Project Controlling
1. Monitoring resources, costs, quality, budgets
2. Revising and changing plans
3. Shifting resources to meet time, cost, and quality demands

Tools   PERT
Reports describing   charts
1. budgets by department
2. delayed activities
3. slack activities
4. quality of work completed

Time line

Before project   During project

Start of project

firm to be highly responsive to external pressures. The firm might find that a matrix structure allows quicker responses to the environment while maintaining continuity and competence in the functional area. Some industries employing matrix project management include chemical, banking, and electronics.

The project management team begins its task well in advance of the project, so that a plan can be developed. One of its first steps is to set carefully the project's objectives, then define the project and break it down into a set of activities and related costs. Gross requirements for people, supplies, and equipment are also estimated in the planning phase.

PROJECT SCHEDULING

Project scheduling is determining the project's activities in the time sequence in which they have to be performed. Materials and people needed at each stage of production are computed in this phase, and the time each activity will take is also set.

One popular project scheduling approach is the Gantt chart (named after Henry Gantt). As seen in Exhibit 15–2, **Gantt charts** reflect time estimates and can be easily understood. The horizontal bars are drawn for each project activity along a time line. The letters to the left of each bar tell the planner which other activities have to be completed before that one can begin.

Gantt charts are low-cost means of helping managers make sure that (1) all activities are planned for, (2) their order of performance is accounted for, (3) the activity time estimates are recorded, and (4) the overall project time is developed.

Activity progress is noted, once the actual project is underway, by shading the horizontal bars as an activity is partially or fully completed. For example, we see in Exhibit 15–2 that activities *a, b, c,* and *d* are on schedule because their bars have been shaded up to the vertical status date line. The date line, July 1 in this case, is a status-reporting period that lets participants see which tasks are on time, which are ahead of time, and which have fallen behind schedule. Activities *e, f,* and *g* are all behind schedule; their bars are not shaded in their entirety or up to the status date line.

—— EXHIBIT 15–2 ——

- *Sample Gantt Chart (Circled Items Represent Precedence Relationships (For Example, Activity* c, *Test/Debug Hardware, May not Begin until Activity* a, *Which Is Circled, Is Completed)*

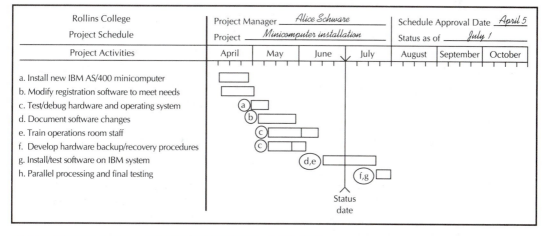

EXHIBIT 15–3

■ *Service Activities for a Boeing 747 Jumbo Jet*

Passengers	Deplaning	
	Transportation	
	Baggage claim	
Crew-operating/F.S.	Deplane	
Baggage	Container offload	
	Container transport	
	Delivery claim belt	
Fueling	Position, connect	
	Pumping	
	Load verification	
	Disconnect, deposition	
	Engine injection water	
Cargo and mail	Container offload	
	Container transport	
	Bulk compt. offload	
Galley servicing	Main cabin door, 4L	
	Main cabin door, 1R	
	Main cabin door, 2R	
Lavatory servicing	Aft	
	Center	
	Forward	
Drinking water	Loading	
Cabin cleaning	First-class section	
	Economy section	
	Lounge	
	Flight deck	
Cargo and mail	Container/bulk loading	
Flight service	Aboard	
	Galley/cabin check	
	Receive passengers	
Operating crew	Aboard	
	Aircraft check	
	Engine start	
Baggage	Container transport	
	Container loading	
Weight and balance	Preparation	
	Aboard	
Passengers	Transportation	
	Boarding	

Time, minutes: 0 5 10 15 20 25 30 35 40 45 50

Source: James Fitzsimmons and Robert Sullivan, *Service Operations Management* (New York: McGraw-Hill, 1982), p. 342. Copyright © 1982, McGraw-Hill Publishing Company. Used with permission.

Scheduling charts such as this one can be used alone on simple projects. They permit managers to observe the progress of each activity and to spot and tackle problem areas. Gantt charts are not easily updated, though. And more importantly, they don't adequately illustrate the interrelationships between the activities and the resources.

A second example of a Gantt chart is shown in Exhibit 15–3. This illustration of a routine servicing of a Boeing 747 airplane during a fifty-minute layover shows that Gantt charts also can be used for scheduling repetitive operations. In this case, the chart helps point out potential delays.

PERT and CPM, the two widely used network techniques that we shall discuss shortly, *do* have the ability to consider precedence relationships and interdependency of activities. On complex projects, the scheduling of which is almost always computerized, PERT and CPM thus hold an edge on the simpler Gantt charts. Even on huge projects, though, Gantt charts can be used as a summary of project status and may complement the other network approaches.

To summarize, whatever the approach taken by a project manager, project scheduling serves several purposes.

1. It shows the relationship of each activity to others and to the whole project.
2. It identifies the precedence relationships among activities.
3. It encourages the setting of realistic time and cost estimates for each activity.
4. It helps make better use of people, money, and material resources by identifying critical bottlenecks in the project.

PROJECT CONTROLLING

The control of large projects, like the control of any management system, involves close monitoring of resources, costs, quality, and budgets. It also usually means using a feedback loop to revise and update the project plan and schedule and having the ability to shift resources to where they are needed most. Computerized PERT/CPM reports and charts are widely available today on mainframes and even on microcomputers. Exhibit 15–4 illustrates several project control reports generated through a popular micro software package called *Harvard Total Project Manager*.

There are a wide variety of other recommended reports as well. Here is a summary and brief description of eight that are commonly available in microcomputer packages.

— Detailed cost breakdown for each task
— Total program manpower curves showing each department's resource contribution
— Cost distribution table listing yearly or quarterly costs by task (it resembles a project cash flow summary for each activity)
— Functional cost and hour summary of how manhours and dollars will be spent by each department
— Raw material and expenditure forecast showing a cash flow based on vendor lead times, payment schedules, and commitments
— Variance report using a percent complete figure for each activity, including planned versus actual costs to date, estimated costs to date, total cost at completion, earned value of work in progress, and a cost performance index
— Time analysis reports related to PERT/CPM schedules, giving estimated completion times, slack and float time, project calendars.
— Work status reports giving weekly task analyses for submission to the project manager for aggregation

EXHIBIT 15–4

■ *Sample Project Control Report.* (a) *Loading Graph, Overallocated Resource.* (b) *Task Form, Actual Start and Finish.* (c) *Project Cost Graph.*

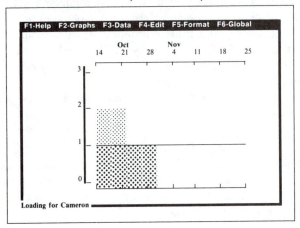

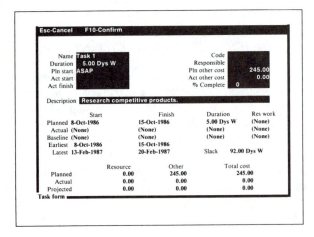

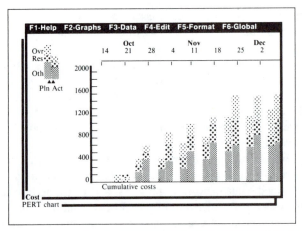

Source: *Harvard Project Manager 3.0 Manual,* pp. 2–32, 2–33, 2–34. Reprinted with permission of SPC Software Publishing, Mountain View, Calif.

PROJECT MANAGEMENT TECHNIQUES:
PERT AND CPM

Program Evaluation and Review Technique (PERT) and the **Critical Path Method** (CPM) were both developed in the 1950s to help managers schedule, monitor, and control large and complex projects. CPM arrived first, in 1957, as a tool developed by J. E. Kelly of Remington Rand and M. R. Walker of DuPont to assist in the building and maintenance of chemical plants at DuPont. Independently, the Special Projects Office of the U.S. Navy, working with Booz, Allen, and Hamilton, developed PERT in 1958 to plan and control the Polaris missile program. That project involved the coordination of thousands of contractors, and PERT was credited with cutting eighteen months off the project length. Today PERT is still required in many government contract schedules. If a person were to walk into the office of a project manager working on a defense department contract, it would not be unusual these days to find a wall covered with a 20-foot-long PERT printout.

The Framework of PERT and CPM

There are six steps common to both PERT and CPM. The procedure is as follows:

1. Define the project and all its significant activities or tasks.
2. Develop the relationships among the activities. Decide which activities must precede and which must follow others.
3. Draw the network connecting all the activities.
4. Assign time and/or cost estimates to each activity.
5. Compute the longest time path through the network; this is called the **critical path.**
6. Use the network to help plan, schedule, monitor, and control the project.

Step 5, finding the critical path, is a major part of controlling a project. The activities on the critical path represent tasks that will delay the entire project if they are delayed. Managers derive flexibility by identifying noncritical activities and re-planning, rescheduling, and reallocating resources such as manpower and finances.

Although PERT and CPM differ to some extent in terminology and in the construction of the network, their objectives are the same. Furthermore, the analysis used in both techniques is very similar. The major difference is that PERT employs three time estimates for each activity. Each estimate has an associated probability of occurrence, which, in turn, is used in computing expected values and standard deviations for the activity times. CPM makes the assumption that activity times are known with certainty, and hence only one time factor is given for each activity.

For purposes of illustration, this section concentrates on a discussion of PERT and PERT/Cost. **PERT/Cost** is a technique that combines the benefits of both PERT and CPM. Most of the comments and procedures described, however, apply just as well to CPM.

PERT, PERT/Cost, and CPM are important because they can help answer questions such as the following about projects with thousands of activities.

- When will the entire project be completed?
- What are the critical activities or tasks in the project, that is, the ones that will delay the entire project if they are late?
- Which are the noncritical activities, that is, the ones that can run late without delaying the whole project's completion?
- What is the probability that the project will be completed by a specific date?
- At any particular date, is the project on schedule, behind schedule, or ahead of schedule?
- On any given date, is the money spent equal to, less than, or greater than the budgeted amount?
- Are there enough resources available to finish the project on time?
- If the project is to be finished in a shorter amount of time, what is the best way to accomplish this at the least cost?

Activities, Events, and Networks

The first step in PERT is to divide the entire project into events and activities. An **event** marks the start or completion of a particular task or activity. An **activity,** on the other hand, is a task or subproject that occurs between two events. Exhibit 15–5 restates these definitions and shows the symbols used to represent events and activities.

Any project that can be described by activities and events may be analyzed by a PERT **network.** Given the following information, for example, we can develop the network shown below.

Activity	Immediate Predecessors
A	—
B	—
C	A
D	B

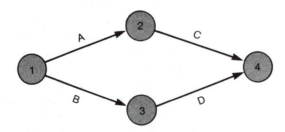

You will note that we assigned each event a number. As you will see later, it is possible to identify each activity with a beginning and an ending event or node. For example, activity A above is the activity that starts with event 1 and ends at node, or event, 2. In general, we number nodes from left to right. The beginning node, or event, of the entire project is number 1, while the last node, or event, in the entire project bears the largest number. The last node shows the number 4.

_____ EXHIBIT 15–5 _____

■ *Events and Activities*

Name	Symbol	Description
Event	○ (node)	A point in time, usually a completion date or a starting date
Activity	→ (arrow)	A flow over time, usually a task or subproject

We also can specify networks by events and the activities that occur between events. The following example shows how to develop a network based on this type of specification scheme. Given the following table, we can develop the network illustrated below.

Beginning Event	Ending Event	Activity
1	2	1–2
1	3	1–3
2	4	2–4
3	4	3–4
3	5	3–5
4	6	4–6
5	6	5–6

Instead of using a letter to signify activities and their predecessor activities, we can specify activities by their starting event and their ending event. Beginning with the activity that starts at event 1 and ends at event 2, we can construct the following network.

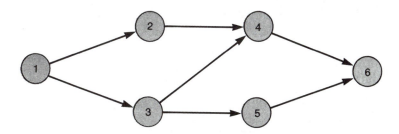

All that is required to construct a network is the starting and ending event for each activity.

Dummy Activities and Events

You may encounter a network that has two activities with identical starting and ending events. **Dummy activities** and **events** can be inserted into the network to deal with this problem. The use of dummy activities and events is especially important when computer programs are to be employed in determining the critical path, project completion time, project variance, and so on. Dummy activities and events also can ensure that the network properly reflects the project under consideration. To illustrate, we develop a network based on the following information.

Activity	Immediate Predecessors	Activity	Immediate Predecessors
A	—	E	C,D
B	—	F	D
C	A	G	E
D	B	H	F

Given these data, the following network might result.

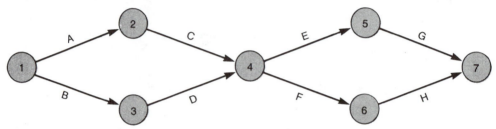

continued

Look at activity *F*. According to the *network*, both activities *C* and *D* must be completed before we can start *F*, but in reality, only activity *D* must be completed (see the table). Thus the network is not correct. The addition of a dummy activity and a dummy event can overcome this problem, as shown below.

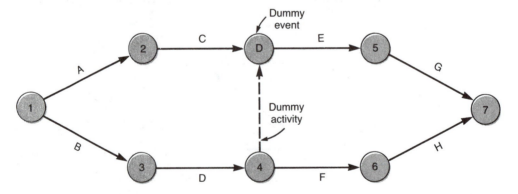

Now the network embodies all the proper relationships and can be analyzed as usual. A dummy activity should have completion time *t* of zero.

PERT and Activity Time Estimates

As mentioned earlier, one distinguishing difference between PERT and CPM is the use of three **activity time estimates** for each activity in the PERT technique. Only one time factor is given for each activity in CPM.

For each activity in PERT, we must specify an **optimistic time,** a **most probable** (or most likely) **time,** and a **pessimistic time** estimate. We then use these three time estimates to calculate an expected completion time and variance for each activity. If we assume, as many researchers do, that activity times follow a **beta probability distribution,** we can use the formulas[1]

$$t = \frac{a + 4m + b}{6} \quad \text{and} \quad v = \left(\frac{b - a}{6}\right)^2 \qquad \textbf{15.1}$$

where a = optimistic time for activity completion
b = pessimistic time for activity completion
m = most likely time for activity completion
t = expected time of activity completion
v = variance of activity completion time

In PERT, after we have developed the network, we compute expected times and variances for each activity. For example, consider the following time estimates:

Activity	a	m	b
1–2	3	4	5
1–3	1	3	5
2–4	5	6	7
3–4	6	7	8

In the table below we compute expected times and variances of completion for each activity above.

Activity	$a + 4m + b$	t	$\frac{b - a}{6}$	v
1–2	24	4	$\frac{2}{6}$	$\frac{4}{36}$
1–3	18	3	$\frac{4}{6}$	$\frac{16}{36}$
2–4	36	6	$\frac{2}{6}$	$\frac{4}{36}$
3–4	42	7	$\frac{2}{6}$	$\frac{4}{36}$

Critical Path Analysis

The objective of **critical path analysis** is to determine the following quantities for each activity:

[1] Although the beta distribution has been widely used in PERT analysis for thirty years, its applicability has been called into question in a recent article. See M. W. Sasieni, "A Note on PERT Times," *Management Science,* Vol. 32, No. 12 (December 1986), pp. 1662–1663.

ES = earliest activity start time. All *predecessor* activities must be completed before an activity can be started. This is the earliest time an activity can be started.

LS = latest activity start time. All *following* activities must be completed without delaying the entire project. This is the latest time an activity can be started without delaying the entire project.

EF = earliest activity finish time.

LF = latest activity finish time.

S = activity slack time, which is equal to (LS − ES) or (LF − EF).

For any activity, if we can calculate ES and LS, we can find the other three quantities as follows:

$$EF = ES + t \hspace{4cm} \textbf{15.2}$$

$$LF = LS + t \hspace{4cm} \textbf{15.3}$$

$$S = LS - ES \hspace{0.5cm} \text{or} \hspace{0.5cm} S = LF - EF \hspace{2cm} \textbf{15.4}$$

Once we know these quantities for every activity, we can analyze the overall project. Typically this analysis includes

1. The **critical path**—the group of activities in the project that have a slack time of zero. This path is *critical* because a delay in any activity along this path would delay the entire project.
2. *T*—the total project completion time, which is calculated by adding the expected time *t* values of those activities on the critical path.
3. *V*—variance of the critical path, which is computed by adding the variance *v* of those individual activities on the critical path.

Critical path analysis normally starts with the determination of ES and EF. The following example illustrates the procedure.

Sample Calculations. Given the following information, we will determine ES and EF for each activity.

Activity	t
1–2	2
1–3	7
2–3	4
2–4	3
3–4	2

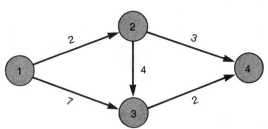

We find ES by moving from the starting activities of the project to the ending activities of the project. For the starting activities, ES is either zero or the actual starting date, say, August 1. For activities 1–2 and 1–3, ES is zero. (By convention, all projects start at time zero.)

There is one basic rule. Before an activity can be started, *all* of its predecessor activities must be completed. In other words, we search for the *longest* path leading to an activity in determining ES. For activity 2–3, ES is 2. Its only predecessor activity is 1–2, for which $t = 2$. By the same reasoning, ES for activity 2–4 also is 2. For activity 3–4, however, ES is 7. It has two predecessor paths: activity 1–3 with $t = 7$ and activities 1–2 and 2–3 with a total expected time of 6 (or 2 + 4). Thus ES for activity 3–4 is 7 because activity 1–3 must be completed before activity 3–4 can be started. We compute EF next by adding t to ES for each activity. See the following table.

Activity	ES	EF
1–2	0	2
1–3	0	7
2–3	2	6
2–4	2	5
3–4	7	9

The next step is to calculate LS, the latest activity starting time for each activity. We start with the last activities and work backward to the first activities. The procedure is to work backward from the last activities to determine the latest possible starting time (LS) without increasing the earliest finishing time (EF). This task sounds more difficult than it really is.

To illustrate, we will determine LS, LF, and S (the slack) for each activity based on the following data:

Activity	t	ES	EF
1–2	2	0	2
1–3	7	0	7
2–3	4	2	6
2–4	3	2	5
3–4	2	7	9

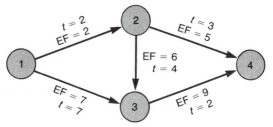

The earliest time by which the entire project can be finished is 9 because activities 2–4 (EF = 5) and 3–4 (EF = 9) *both* must be completed. Using 9 as a basis, we now will work backward by subtracting the appropriate values of t from 9.

The latest time we can start activity 3–4 is at time 7 (or 9 − 2) in order still to complete the project by time period 9. Thus LS for activity 3–4 is 7. Using the same reasoning, LS for activity 2–4 is 6 (or 9 − 3). If we start activity 2–4 at 6 and it takes 3 time units to complete the activity, we can still finish in 9 time units. The latest we can start activity 2–3 is 3 (or 9 − 2 − 4). If we start activity 2–3 at 3 and it takes 2 and 4 time units for activities 2–3 and 3–4, respectively, we can still finish on time. Thus LS for activity 2–3 is 3. Using the same reasoning, LS for activity 1– 3 is zero (or $9 - 2 - 7$). Analyzing activity 1–2 is more difficult because there are two paths. Both must be completed in 9 time units.

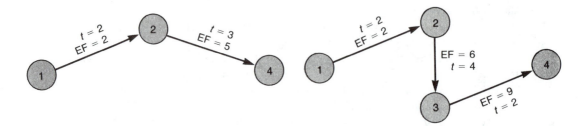

Since both the preceding paths must be completed, LS activity 1–2 is computed from the most binding, or slowest, path. Thus LS for activity 1–2 *is 1* (or $9 - 2 - 4 - 2$) and *not 4* (or $9 - 3 - 2$). Noting the following relationships, we can construct a table summarizing the results.

$$LF = LS + t$$
$$S = LF - EF \quad \text{or} \quad S = LS - ES$$

Activity	ES	EF	LS	LF	S
1–2	0	2	1	3	1
1–3	0	7	0	7	0
2–3	2	6	3	7	1
2–4	2	5	6	9	4
3–4	7	9	7	9	0

Once we have computed ES, EF, LS, LF, and S, we can analyze the entire project. Analysis includes determining the critical path, project completion time, and project variance. Consider the following example.

Project Analysis. We wish to find the critical path, total completion time *T,* and project variance *V,* of the following network.

Activity	t	v	ES	EF	LS	LF	S
1–2	2	$\frac{2}{6}$	0	2	1	3	1
1–3	7	$\frac{3}{6}$	0	7	0	7	0
2–3	4	$\frac{1}{6}$	2	6	3	7	1
2–4	3	$\frac{2}{6}$	2	5	6	9	4
3–4	2	$\frac{4}{6}$	7	9	7	9	0

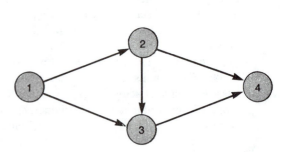

The critical path consists of those activities with zero slack. These are activities 1–3 and 3–4.

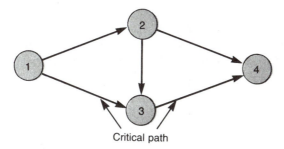

Critical path

The total project completion time is 9 (or 7 + 2). The project variance is the sum of the *activity variances* along the *critical path,* which is 7/6 (or 3/6 + 4/6).

Knowing a network and values for activity times and variances (*t* and *v*) makes it possible to perform a complete critical path analysis, including the determination of ES, EF, LS, LF, and S for each activity as well as the critical path, *T*, and *V* for the entire project.

The Probability of Project Completion

Having computed the expected completion time *T* and completion variance *V*, we can determine the probability that the project will be completed at a specified date. If we make the assumption that the distribution of completion dates follows a normal curve, we can calculate the probability of completion as in the following example.

Let us say that the expected project completion time *T* is 20 weeks and the project variance *V* is 100. What is the probability that the project will be finished on or before week 25?

$T = 20$

$V = 100$

σ = standard deviation = $\sqrt{\text{project variance}} = \sqrt{V}$

   = $\sqrt{100}$ = 10

C = desired completion date

   = 25 weeks

The normal curve would appear as follows:

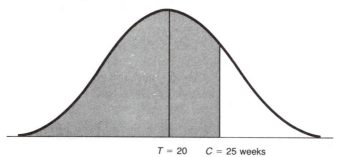

$T = 20$ $C = 25$ weeks

$$Z = \frac{C - T}{\sigma} = \frac{25 - 20}{10} = 0.5 \qquad \qquad \textbf{15.5}$$

where Z equals the number of standard deviations from the mean. The area under the curve, for $Z = 0.5$, is 0.6915. (See the normal curve table in the Appendix.) Thus the probability of completing the project in 25 weeks is approximately 0.69, or 69 percent.

PERT/COST

Until now, we have assumed that it is not possible to reduce activity times. This is usually not the case, however. Perhaps additional resources can reduce activity times for certain activities within the project. These resources might be additional labor, more equipment, and so on. Although it can be expensive to shorten activity times, doing so might be worthwhile. If a company faces costly penalties for being late with a project, it might be economical to use additional resources to complete the project on time. There may be fixed costs every day the project is in process. Thus it might be profitable to use additional resources to shorten the project time and save some of the daily fixed costs. But which activities should be shortened? How much will this action cost? Will a reduction in the activity time in turn reduce the time needed to complete the entire project? Ideally, we would like to find the least expensive method of shortening the entire project. This is the purpose of PERT/Cost.

In addition to time, the service manager is normally concerned with the cost of the project. Usually it is possible to shorten activity times by committing additional resources to the project. Exhibit 15–6 shows cost-time curves for two activities. For activity 5–6, it costs $300 to complete the activity in eight weeks, $400 for seven

EXHIBIT 15–6

■ *Cost-Time Curves Used in PERT/Cost Analysis*

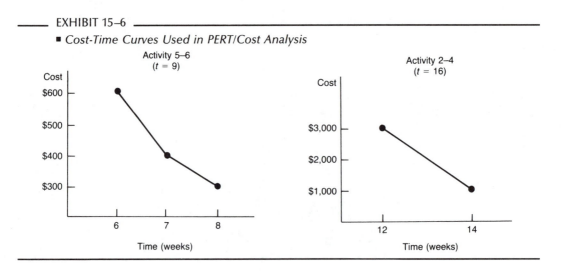

weeks, and $600 for six weeks. Activity 2–4 requires $3000 of additional resources for completion in twelve weeks and $1000 for fourteen weeks. Similar cost-time curves or relationships can usually be developed for all activities in the network.

The objective of PERT/Cost is to reduce the entire project completion time by a certain amount at the least cost. Although there are several good computer programs that perform PERT/Cost, it is useful to understand how to complete this process by hand. To accomplish this objective, we must introduce a few more variables. For each activity, there will exist a reduction in activity time and the cost incurred for that time reduction. Let

M_i = maximum reduction of time for activity i

C_i = additional cost associated with reducing activity time for activity i

K_i = cost of reducing activity time by one time unit for activity i

$K_i = C_i/M_i,$

With this information, it is possible to determine the least cost of reducing the project completion date.

Reducing Completion Time Example.   As an illustration, we use the following information to determine the least cost of reducing the project completion time by one week.

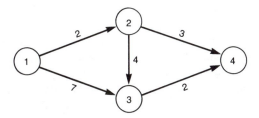

Activity	t (weeks)	M (weeks)	C	Activity	ES	EF	LS	LF	S
1–2	2	1	$ 300	1–2	0	2	1	3	1
1–3	7	4	2000	1–3	0	7	0	7	0
2–3	4	2	2000	2–3	2	6	3	7	1
2–4	3	2	4000	2–4	2	5	6	9	4
3–4	2	1	2000	3–4	7	9	7	9	0

The first step is to compute K for each activity.

Activity	M	C	K	Critical Path
1–2	1	$ 300	$ 300	No
1–3	4	2000	500	Yes
2–3	2	2000	1000	No
2–4	2	4000	2000	No
3–4	1	2000	2000	Yes

The second step is to locate that activity on the critical path with the smallest value of K_i. The critical path consists of activities 1–3 and 3–4. Since activity 1–3 has a lower value of K_i, we can reduce the project completion time by one week, to eight weeks, by incurring an additional cost of $500.

We must be very careful in using this procedure. Any further reduction in activity time along the critical path would cause the critical path also to include activities 1–2, 2–3, and 3–4. In other words, there would be two critical paths and activities on both would need to be "crashed" to reduce project completion time.

OTHER SERVICE APPLICATIONS OF PERT

To further illustrate the potential for project management techniques in services, this section provides three larger illustrations. The first deals with the installation of a financial computer system, the second with the relocation of a hospital, and the third with the planning and control of an audit by a CPA firm.

Implementing a Computerized Information System[2]

Exhibits 15–7 and 15–8 describe the steps involved in replacing one computer system with another at a large Denver consulting firm. The present computer is at capacity and no longer adequate for all financial applications. The current software systems must all be modified before they can be run on the new computer. In addition, new applications that the firm would like to have developed and implemented have been identified and ranked according to priority. The specific activities and their estimated completion times are shown in Exhibit 15–7. A PERT network diagram to aid in coordinating these activities is provided in Exhibit 15–8. Problem 15.15 at the end of this chapter asks you to use these data in answering several management questions.

Relocating a Hospital with Project Networks

When St. Vincent's Hospital and Medical Center moved from a 373-bed facility in Portland, Oregon to a new 403-bed building in the suburbs five miles away, a large variety of planning considerations had to be taken into account. Army vehicles and private ambulances had to be used to move patients; police escorts would be needed; local stores would be affected by the move, among many other concerns. To coordinate all the activities, a project network was developed and used as a basic planning tool eight months before the move. Although the actual network contained dozens of activities, a portion of it is provided in Exhibit 15–9 to illustrate how valuable project management tools can be in planning and carrying out a complex project.

---

[2] Adapted from S. A. Moscove and M. G. Simkin, *Accounting Information Systems*, 3d Ed. (New York: Wiley, 1987), p. 555.

—— EXHIBIT 15–7 ————————————————————————————

■ *Activities of the Consulting Firm for Installing a New Computer System*

Activity	Description	Expected Time Required to Complete (weeks)
AB	Wait for delivery of computer from manufacturer	8
BC	Install computer	2
CH	General test of computer	2
AD	Complete an evaluation of work-force requirements	2
DE	Hire additional programmers and operators	2
AG	Design modifications to existing applications	3
GH	Program modifications to existing applications	4
HI	Test modified applications on new computer	2
IJ	Revise existing applications as needed	2
JN	Revise and update documentation for existing applications as modified	2
JK	Run existing applications in parallel on new and old computers	2
KP	Implement existing applications as modified on the new computer	1
AE	Design new applications	8
GE	Design interface between existing and new applications	3
EF	Program new applications	6
FI	Test new applications on new computer	2
IL	Revise new applications as needed	3
LM	Conduct second test of new applications on new computer	2
MN	Prepare documentation for the new applications	3
NP	Implement new applications on the new computer	2

Source: S. A. Moscove and M. G. Simkin, *Accounting Information Systems*, 3d Ed. (New York: Wiley, 1987), p. 556. Copyright © 1987 by John Wiley & Sons, Inc. Reprinted by permission of John Wiley & Sons, Inc.

Audit Planning and Control with PERT

As a final example, we turn to the use of PERT and PERT/Cost in an audit application. These tools have proven to be of practical value to auditors in scheduling audit work, in allocating personnel resources, in predicting engagement completion time, in anticipating work bottlenecks, and in guiding audit acceleration. Exhibit 15–10 shows an engagement network for one firm. Since auditors are usually familiar with the conditions of a client's book, internal controls, and problem areas and have actual work times from previous audits, reasonably good time estimates are usually available for each activity. In an audit case, completion deadlines are often imposed by clients or regulators. If the probability of finishing the audit after the deadline is too high, the firm may decide to add more personnel to shorten the critical path's duration.

A CRITIQUE OF PERT AND CPM

It has been more than three decades since PERT and CPM were first introduced as project management tools. This is just enough time to step back and examine their

EXHIBIT 15–8

■ PERT Network Diagram for the Consulting Firm

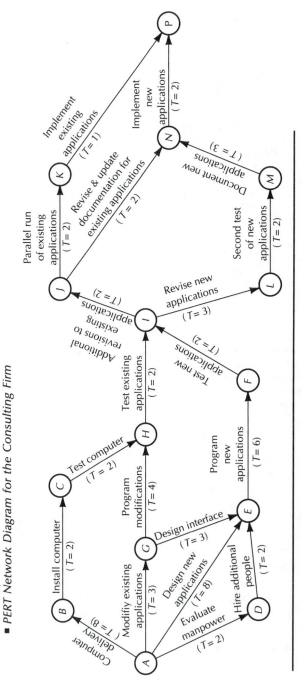

Source: S. A. Moscove and M. G. Simkin, *Accounting Information Systems*, 3d Ed. (New York: Wiley, 1987), p. 556. Copyright © 1987 by John Wiley & Sons, Inc. Reprinted by permission of John Wiley & Sons, Inc.

EXHIBIT 15–9

■ *A Portion of St. Vincent's Hospital Project Network: Critical Activities*

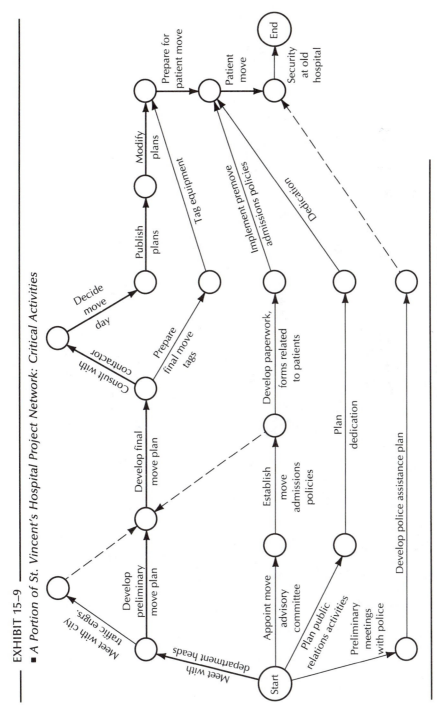

Source: Adapted from R. S. Hanson, "Moving the Hospital to a New Location," *Industrial Engineering* (November 1982). Copyright Institute of Industrial Engineers, 25 Technology Park/Atlanta, Norcross Ga. 30092.

481

EXHIBIT 15–10

- *Engagement for a Sample Audit*

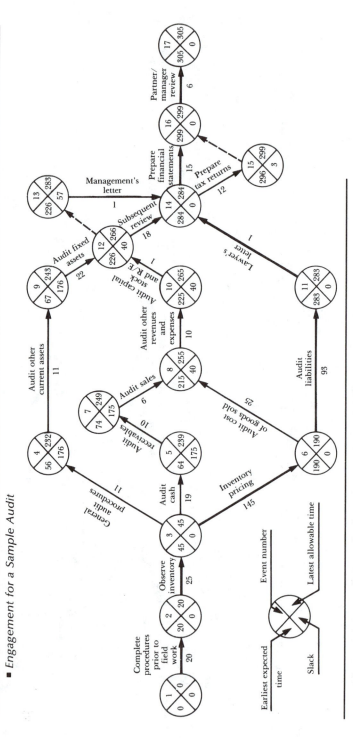

Source: J. L. Krogstad, G. Grudnitski, and D. W. Bryant, "PERT and PERT/Cost for Audit Planning and Control," *Journal of Accounting*, Vol. 144, No. 5 (1977), pp. 82–91. Copyright 1977 by the American Institute of Certified Public Accountants, Inc.

strengths and limitations objectively—a process that helps us understand the role of critical path scheduling today.

Because the Department of Defense (DOD) overwhelmingly adopted PERT and made its use a requirement for all defense contractors, PERT's first 10 years were its zenith. Many managers, professors, computer professionals, and magazine and journal editors became converts (and "experts"). With enthusiasm and interest strong, PERT even became a verb, and all good projects were "perted out." This sometimes meant wall-to-wall computer-generated and updated charts and a tendency to trust PERT as a solution to solve all project management problems.

As was probably inevitable, PERT's fashionability dropped off during the 1970s. As some converts became critics, others who had long resented the forced burdens of the PERT and CPM approach became vocal in their scorn of the tool.[3]

Now critical path analysis appears to be leveling out and even increasing once again in popularity. Project managers are more knowledgeable about the pluses and minuses of PERT use and are aided by the spread of powerful but easy-to-use microcomputer-based software packages. As a summary of our discussions of PERT, here are some of its features about which operations managers need to be aware.

Advantages

1. PERT is useful at several stages of project management, especially in the scheduling and control of large projects.
2. It is straightforward in concept and not mathematically complex. Although projects with hundreds or thousands of activities are usually computerized, smaller ones can be tackled easily by hand.
3. The graphical displays using networks help to perceive quickly relationships among project activities.
4. Critical path and slack time analyses help pinpoint activities that need to be closely watched. This provides opportunity for resource reallocation when the project needs to be shortened ("crashed").
5. The networks generated provide valuable project documentation and graphically point out who is responsible for various activities.
6. PERT is applicable to a wide variety of service projects and industries.
7. It is useful in monitoring not only schedules, but costs as well. This helps avoid cost overrun penalties and facilitates "early finish" bonuses.

Limitations

1. Project activities have to be clearly defined, independent, and stable in their relationships. In spite of our focus on the techniques of project management, this step is typically the most difficult.

---

[3] Two articles describing these new attitudes both candidly and humorously are M. Krakowski, "PERT and Parkinson's Law," *Interfaces,* Vol. 5, No. 1 (November 1974); and A. Vazsonyi, "L'Historie de la grandeur et de la decadence de la methode PERT," *Management Science,* Vol. 16, No. 8 (April 1970). Both articles make interesting reading (and are both written in English).

2. Precedence relationships must be specified and networked together. Sometimes precedences are hard to clarify and are not shown correctly.
3. Time activities in PERT are assumed to follow the beta probability distribution. It is difficult for users to verify whether or not this really holds true for each activity. There is now some question about the validity of this assumption.
4. Time estimates tend to be subjective and are subject to fudging by managers who fear the dangers of being overly optimistic or not pessimistic enough.
5. There is the inherent danger of too much emphasis being placed on the longest, or critical, path. Near-critical paths need to be monitored closely as well.

SUMMARY

PERT, CPM, and other scheduling techniques have proven to be valuable tools in controlling large and complex projects. A wide variety of software packages to help managers handle network modeling problems is also available for use on both large and small computers. Some of the more popular of these programs are Harvard Total Project Manager (by Harvard Software, Inc.), Primavera (by Primavera Systems, Inc.), Project (by Microsoft Corp.), MacProject (by Apple Computer Corp.), PertMaster (by Westminster Software, Inc.), and VisiSchedule (by Paladin Software Corp.). Reading 15.1 illustrates how PertMaster was used by British Airways to implement a new corporate image.

PERT, CPM, and PERT/Cost will not, however, solve all the project scheduling and management problems in the service industry. Good management practices, clear responsibilities for tasks, and straightforward and timely reporting systems are also needed. It is important to remember that the models we described in this chapter are only tools to help service managers make better decisions.

DISCUSSION QUESTIONS

1. What are some of the questions that can be answered with PERT and CPM?

2. What is an activity? What is an event? What is an immediate predecessor?

3. Describe how expected activity times and variances can be computed in a PERT network.

4. Briefly discuss what is meant by critical path analysis. What are critical path activities and why are they important?

5. What are the earliest activity start time and latest activity start time and how are they computed?

6. Describe the meaning of slack and discuss how it can be determined.

7. How can we determine the probability that a project will be completed by a certain date? What assumptions are made in this computation?

8. Briefly describe PERT/Cost and how it is used.

9. What is crashing and how is it done by hand?

10. Select a service industry with which you are familiar and describe how a Gantt or PERT chart could be used to improve the operation.

PROBLEMS

15.1 Sally Rider is the personnel director of Babson and Willcount, a company that specializes in consulting and research. One of the training programs that Sally is considering for the middle-level managers of Babson and Willcount is leadership training. Sally has listed a number of activities that must be completed before a training program of this nature could be conducted. The activities and immediate predecessors appear in the accompanying table. Develop a network for this problem.

Activity	Immediate Predecessor	Activity	Immediate Predecessor
A	—	E	A,D
B	—	F	C
C	—	G	E,F
D	B		

15.2 Sally Rider was able to determine the activity times for the leadership training program. She would like to determine the total project completion time and the critical path. The activity times appear in the accompanying table. (See Problem 15.1.)

Activity	Time (Days)
A	2
B	5
C	1
D	10
E	3
F	6
G	8
Total	35 days

15.3 Insert dummy activities and events to correct the following network:

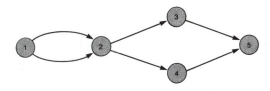

15.4 Calculate the critical path, project completion time T, and project variance V based on the following information.

Activity	t	v
1–2	2	2/6
1–3	3	2/6
2–4	2	4/6
3–5	4	4/6
4–5	4	2/6
4–6	3	1/6
5–6	5	1/6

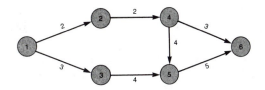

15.5 Given the following information, perform a critical path analysis.

Activity	t	v	Activity	t	v
1–2	2	$\frac{1}{6}$	4–5	4	$\frac{4}{6}$
1–3	2	$\frac{1}{6}$	4–6	3	$\frac{2}{6}$
2–4	1	$\frac{2}{6}$	5–7	5	$\frac{1}{6}$
3–4	3	$\frac{2}{6}$	6–7	2	$\frac{2}{6}$

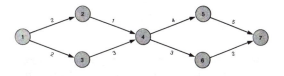

15.6 Zuckerman Computing provides computer services to business and government. The company is bidding on the replacement of a mainframe system and has identified the following activities and time estimates (in hours) for the activities that will make up the project. Determine the expected completion time and variance for each activity.

Activity	a	m	b	Immediate Predecessors
A	3	6	8	
B	2	4	4	
C	1	2	3	
D	6	7	8	C
E	2	4	6	B,D
F	6	10	14	A,E
G	1	2	4	A,E
H	3	6	9	F
I	10	11	12	G
J	14	16	20	C
K	2	8	10	H,I

15.7 Jane Zuckerman would like to determine the total project completion time and the critical path for replacing the old computer system. See Problem 15.7 for details. In addition, determine ES, EF, LS, LF, and slack for each activity.

15.8 What is the probability that Zuckerman will finish the project described in Problems 15.7 and 15.8 in 40 hours or less?

15.9 Using PERT, Jan Ross was able to determine that the expected project completion time for the overhaul of a pleasure yacht is 21 weeks, and the project variance is 4 weeks.

    a. What is the probability that the project will be completed in 17 weeks?

    b. What is the probability that the project will be completed in 20 weeks?

    c. What is the probability that the project will be completed in 23 weeks?

    d. What is the probability that the project will be completed in 25 weeks?

15.10 The following information has been computed from a project:

$$T = 62 \text{ weeks}$$
$$V = 81$$

What is the probability that the project will be completed 18 weeks *before* its expected completion date?

15.11 Determine the least cost of reducing the project completion date by three months based on the following information:

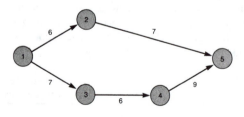

Activity	t (months)	M (months)	C
1–2	6	2	$400
1–3	7	2	$500
2–5	7	1	$300
3–4	6	2	$600
4–5	9	1	$200

15.12 Getting a degree from a college or university can be a long and difficult task. Certain courses must be completed before other courses may be taken. Develop a network diagram, where every activity is a particular course that must be taken for a given degree program. The immediate predecessors will be course prerequisites. Don't forget to include all university, college, and departmental course requirements. Then try to group these courses into semesters or quarters for your particular school. How long do you think it will take you to graduate? Which courses, if not taken in the proper sequence, could delay your graduation?

15.13 The Bender Construction Company is involved with constructing municipal buildings and other structures that are used primarily by city and state municipalities. This requires developing legal documents, drafting feasibility studies, obtaining bond ratings, and so forth. Recently, Bender was given a request to submit a proposal for the construction of a municipal building. The first step is to develop legal documents and to perform all necessary steps before the construction contract is signed. This requires approximately 20 separate activities that must be completed. These activities, their immediate predecessors, and time requirements are given in Exhibit 15–11. As you can see, optimistic (*a*), most likely (*m*), and pessimistic (*b*) time estimates have been given for all of the activities described in the above table. Using these data, determine the total project completion time for this preliminary step, the critical path, and slack time for all activities involved.

15.14 Using the information in Exhibits 15–7 and 15–8, provided earlier in this chapter,

    a. Determine the number of weeks that will be needed to fully implement the new information system.

    b. Identify the actual tasks.

    c. Determine the slack for each activity.

_____ EXHIBIT 15–11 _____

■ *Developing Documents for Bender Construction*

Activity	Time Required (weeks)			Description	Immediate Predecessor(s)
	a	m	b		
1	1	4	5	Drafting legal documents	—
2	2	3	4	Preparation of financial statements	—
3	3	4	5	Draft of history	—
4	7	8	9	Draft demand portion of feasibility study	—
5	4	4	5	Review and approval of legal documents	1
6	1	2	4	Review and approval of history	3
7	4	5	6	Review feasibility study	4
8	1	2	4	Draft final financial portion of feasibility study	7
9	3	4	4	Draft facts relevant to the bond transaction	5
10	1	1	2	Review and approval of financial statements	2
11	18	20	26	Firm price received of project	—
12	1	2	3	Review and completion of financial portion of feasibility study	8
13	1	1	2	Draft statement completed	6, 9, 10, 11
14	0.10	0.14	0.16	All material sent to bond rating services	13
15	0.2	0.3	0.4	Statement printed and distributed to all interested parties	14
16	1	1	2	Presentation to bond rating services	14
17	1	2	3	Bond rating received	16
18	3	5	7	Marketing of bonds	15, 17
19	0.1	0.9	0.2	Purchase contract executed	16
20	0.1	0.14	0.16	Final statement authorized and completed	19
21	2	3	6	Purchase contract	19
22	0.1	0.1	0.2	Bond proceeds available	20
23	0.0	0.2	0.2	Sign construction contract	21, 22

_____ READING 15.1 _____

PertMaster Helps Change the Face of British Airways

It has been three years since British Airways decided to rejuvenate its image using international design consultants to undertake development of the new identity. Serious implementation of the new designs began early in 1984. To transform each component that goes to make up the corporate image is a huge task. Aircraft, check-in desks, lounges, shops, ground vehicles, all printed

Source: Excerpted from *Industrial Management and Data Systems* (March/April 1986), pp. 6–7. Used with permission of MCB University Press Limited.

material—including company stationery, timetables, tickets, baggage tags—and, of course, uniforms were all to be changed. To help the British Airways team plan the exercise, a computerised project management package—PertMaster from Abtex Software—was used.

Key members of BA's marketing department were to be the front runners in co-ordinating the program because the establishment of a corporate image is basically a marketing exercise. Help was brought in from the internal consulting branch of BA's Marketplace Performance Department in the form of Joe Garratt, a senior internal management consultant.

Garratt already had experience of critical path analysis, as his work at BA had taken him into various planning departments over the years. While he was in the airport planning department for Heathrow, he had a group of staff using network analysis to plan aircraft turnarounds on a short time scale or aircraft introductions over longer periods.

BA has 167 aircraft and serves about 150 airports with 180 shops and public offices around the world. Eventually, they will all be fitted out in the new colors. The company has over 20,000 staff in uniform—captains, stewards, stewardesses, ground staff and people in the workshops.

The biggest and most prominent representation of an airline is the aircraft itself. A launch date for the new livery was fixed for December 4, 1984. As many other items as possible were to be ready for that date.

BA's first thought was to have a Boeing 747 refurbished for the launch, with new livery and a completely new interior. The 747s were already undergoing a program of interior upgrading to improve passenger amenities, and perhaps the programs could be linked.

Garratt set about finding the earliest possible date that an aircraft from this production line could be fully fitted out. All the items had to be identified—ordering, procuring and applying the new paint, ordering new upholstery fabrics and new carpets, obtaining all the trim for the interior, stripping out the old interior and fitting the new. The information was fed into the PertMaster program and the critical path established. PertMaster revealed what had been feared. The first that could have been fitted out was "November Fox"—but not before the middle of January. "November Os-

car," however, could be ready in new exterior finish only, by the December 4 deadline.

Therefore, they had to use a smaller aircraft than they had wanted. A new 737, "Yankee Fox" was available at the Boeing plant in Seattle in early November. They focused on this plane and obtained just sufficient material to change the livery and interior on the one aircraft for the launch date.

In the end, it was a good thing that a smaller aircraft was used because it was possible to make it the star of the launch. A production company that specialised in razzamatazz launches was hired to build an auditorium inside one of the hangars at Heathrow. The 737 appeared on the stage amid a brilliant light show. Meanwhile "November Oscar" provided a backdrop on the tarmac outside.

It was decided in September that ground vehicles should also appear on December 4. PertMaster was used to plan the schedule, and this time it was found that the vehicles could be ready by the end of November, in time for the launch.

The launch would feature an aircraft and vehicles—what else could BA have ready in time? PertMaster was used to demonstrate that uniform designs could not be ready for that date.

A separate launch at the end of May 1985 introduced the designs for the new uniforms—the work of British designer Roland Klein. The range includes pilots', stewards' and stewardesses' outfits, and work-wear for maintenance and ground staff.

PertMaster came into use again to establish how soon the uniforms could be issued to staff. Alternative plans were drawn up according to whether, for instance, new central issue premises would be available. An optimistic and pessimistic time frame has been established, making it likely that issue will begin in spring this year. Until then, the designs have been made up into prototype garments to be worn by members of BA's publicity staff. Various manufacturers will tender for supply of materials and the purchase and control will be performed using the PertMaster plan as a guide.

During the time he has had PertMaster, Garratt has proved the flexibility and adaptability of the package. He has planned the refitting and painting of aircraft, the equipping of vehicles and scheduling of uniform manufacture and issue.

Having the plan on paper when it has to be presented at meetings is very useful—in fact it is the major benefit. In the cases of the uniforms and the fitting of the 747, it proved that it was impossible to meet the December 4 deadline. It enables decisions to be made concerning what can be done in the frame and provides an agenda for items to be discussed.

Garratt believes that there would be wide applications within the airport if the package could be enhanced to allow different time frames. Instead of working in days and weeks, it would be useful if the time interval could be minutes—aircraft turn-rounds at the airport, for example, could then be plotted.

—— QUESTION FOR READING 15.1

Describe two other possible applications of PERT at British Airways besides the image-change project described in this reading.

—— CASE 15.1 ——

Bay Community Hospital

The staff of the Bay Community Hospital had committed itself to introduce a new diagnostic procedure in the clinic. This procedure required the acquisition, installation, and introduction of a new medical instrument. Dr. Ed Windsor was assigned the responsibility for assuring that the introduction be performed as quickly and smoothly as possible.

Dr. Windsor created a list of activities that would have to be completed before the new service could begin. Initially, three individual steps had to be taken: (1) write instructions and procedures, (2) select techniques to operate the equipment, and (3) procure the equipment. The instructions and selection of the operators had to be completed before the training could commence. Dr. Windsor also believed it was necessary to choose the operators and evaluate their qualifications before formally announcing the new service to the local medical community. Upon arrival and installation of the equipment and completion of the operators' training, Edward Windsor wanted to spend a period checking out the procedures, operators, and equipment before declaring the project was successfully completed. The activities and times are listed in Exhibit 15–12.

Jack Worth, a member of the Bay Community Hospital staff, reported that it would be possible to save time on the project by paying some premiums to complete certain activities faster than the normal schedule listed in Exhibit 15–12. Specifically, if the equipment were shipped by express truck, one week could be saved. Air freight would save two weeks. However, a premium of $200 would be paid for the express truck shipment and $750 would be paid for air shipment. The operator training period could also be reduced by one week if the trainees worked overtime. However, this would cost the hospital an additional $600. The time required to complete the instructions could be reduced by one week with the additional expenditure of $400. However, $300 could be saved if this activity was allowed to take three weeks.

—— QUESTIONS FOR CASE 15.1

1. What is the shortest time period in which the project can be completed using the expected times listed in Exhibit 15–12?

2. What is the shortest time in which the project can be completed?

3. What is the lowest cost schedule for this shortest time?

Source: From W. E. Sasser, R. P. Olsen, and D. D. Wyckoff, *Management Service Operations,* pp. 97–98. Copyright © 1978 by Allyn and Bacon. Reprinted with permission.

───── EXHIBIT 15–12 ───

▪ *Bay Community Hospital Activities Required to Introduce a New Diagnostic Procedure*

Activity	Duration (weeks)	Immediately Preceding Activities	Immediately Following Activities
A. Write instructions	2	Start	C
B. Select operators	4	Start	C,D
C. Train operators	3	A,B	F
D. Announce new service	4	B	End
E. Purchase, ship, and receive equipment	8	Start	F
F. Test new operators on equipment	2	C,E	End

─────────────────────────────── REFERENCES ───────────────────────────────

Ameiss, A. P., and W. A. Thompson. "PERT for Monthly Financial Closing," *Management Advisor* (January–February 1974).

Clayton, E. R., and L. J. Moore. "PERT vs. GERT," *Journal of Systems Management,* Vol. 23 (February 1972), pp. 11–19.

Cleland, D. I., and W. R. King. *Project Management Handbook.* New York: Von Nostrand Reinhold, 1984.

Dusenbury, W. "CPM for New Product Introductions," *Harvard Business Review,* Vol. 45, No. 4 (July–August 1967).

Heizer, J., and B. Render. *Production and Operations Management.* Boston: Allyn and Bacon, 1988.

Kefalas, A. G. "PERT Applied to Environmental Impact Statements," *Industrial Engineering,* Vol. 8, No. 10 (October 1976), pp. 38–42.

Kerzner, H., and H. Thamhain. *Project Management for Small and Medium Size Business.* New York: Van Nostrand Reinhold, 1984.

Krogstad, J. L., G. Grudnitski, and D. W. Bryand. "PERT and PERT/Cost for Audit Planning and Control," *The Journal of Accountancy* (November 1977).

Levy, F., A. Thompson, and J. Weist. "The ABC's of Critical Path Method," *Harvard Business Review,* Vol. 41, No. 5 (September–October 1963), pp. 98–108.

Moder, J., and C. Phillips. *Project Management with CPM and PERT.* New York: Van Nostrand, 1970.

Render, B., and R. M. Stair. *Quantitative Analysis for Management,* 3d Ed. Boston: Allyn and Bacon, 1988.

Ryan, W. G. "Management Practice and Research— Poles Apart," *Business Horizons* (June 1977).

16

Linear and Goal Programming Applications for Services

INTRODUCTION

Many service operations management decisions involve trying to make the most effective use of an organization's resources. Resources typically include labor, money, storage space/capacity, or materials. These resources may be used to produce services such as schedules for shipping and production, advertising policies, investment decisions, or hospital meal plans. **Linear programming** (LP) and **goal programming** (GP) are widely used mathematical techniques designed to help operations managers in planning and decision making relative to the tradeoffs necessary to allocate resources.[1]

Just a few examples of problems in which LP and GP have been applied successfully in service management are

— Improving bank scheduling operations at Banc Ohio[2]
— Allocating police patrol units to high-crime areas[3]
— Developing long-range manpower planning in the U.S. Army[4]
— Scheduling school buses in New Haven, Connecticut[5]
— Controlling the fleet of 3300 trucks at North American Van Lines[6]
— Planning the repairs of boxcars at Chesapeake and Ohio rail yards.[7]

This chapter stresses the importance of *formulating* linear programming problems; it leaves the mathematical details of solving such problems to management science texts.[8] Since computer programs are readily available to conduct the mechanics of LP (and are illustrated in this chapter), most operations managers can avoid the complex manual algorithms associated with LP and GP. Most of the chapter looks at the more common linear programming formulation, in which a service organization has but one objective to be attained (such as minimizing labor costs). Later, the chapter concludes with an extension of LP known as **goal programming** (GP). GP is capable of handling decision problems having multiple goals, some of which may be contradictory.

---

[1] Portions of this chapter are adapted from Jay Heizer and Barry Render, *Production and Operations Management,* pp. 77–111, and Barry Render and Ralph M. Stair, *Quantitative Analysis for Management,* 3d Ed., pp. 408–436. Copyright © 1988 by Allyn and Bacon. Reprinted with permission.

[2] V. A. Mabert and J. P. McKenzie, "Improving Bank Operations: A Case Study at Banc Ohio/Ohio National Bank," *Omega,* Vol. 8, No. 3 (1980), pp. 345–354.

[3] K. Chelst, "An Algorithm for Deploying a Crime Directed Patrol Force," *Management Science,* Vol. 24, No. 12 (August 1978), pp. 1314–1327.

[4] S. Gass, et al., "The Army Manpower Long-Range Planning System," *Operations Research,* Vol. 36, No. 1 (January–February 1988), pp. 5–17.

[5] A. J. Swersey and W. Ballard, "Scheduling School Buses," *Management Science,* Vol. 30, No. 7 (July 1984), pp. 844–853.

[6] D. Avramovich et al., "A Decision Support System for Fleet Management," *Interfaces,* Vol. 12, No. 3 (June 1984), pp. 1–6.

[7] L. C. Brosch, et al., "Boxcars, Linear Programming, and the Sleeping Kitten," *Interfaces,* Vol. 10, No. 6 (December 1980), pp. 53–61.

[8] See B. Render and R. M. Stair, *Quantitative Analysis for Management,* 3d Ed. (Boston: Allyn and Bacon, 1988); or B. W. Taylor, *Management Science,* 3d Ed. (Boston: Allyn and Bacon, 1990).

OVERVIEW OF LINEAR PROGRAMMING

All LP problems have four properties in common.

1. All problems seek to *maximize* or *minimize* some quantity (usually profit or cost). We refer to this property as the **objective function** of an LP problem. The major objective of a typical firm is to maximize dollar profits in the long run. In the case of a trucking or airline distribution system, the objective might be to minimize shipping costs.

2. The presence of restrictions, or **constraints,** limits the degree to which we can pursue our objective. For example, deciding how many units of each product in a firm's warehouse should be stocked in one retail outlet is restricted by space, available labor, and budgets. We want, therefore, to maximize or minimize a quantity (the objective function) subject to limited resources (the constraints).

3. There must be *alternative courses of action* to choose from. For example, if a store stocks three different products, management may use LP to decide how to allocate among them its limited display space and advertising budget. If there were no alternatives to select from, we would not need LP.

4. The objective and constraints in linear programming problems must be expressed in terms of *linear* equations or inequalities.

The best way to illustrate these properties and how to formulate an LP problem is through an example. Let's consider the case of a small furniture retailer.

Dixon Furniture Store

Dixon Furniture is planning for its Labor Day weekend special sale. The two items that have been selected for promotion, because of the time of year, are folding tables and chairs; both are ideal for backyard parties. The store has only 100 square feet of space available for displaying and stocking these items. Each table has a wholesale cost of $4, takes up 2 square feet of space, and will retail for $11. The wholesale price of a chair is $3; each requires 1 square foot to stock and will sell for $8. The manager believes that no more than sixty chairs can possibly be sold, but that the demand for the $11 tables is almost unlimited. Finally, Dixon's budget for procuring the tables and chairs is $240. The question facing the store manager is to decide how many tables and chairs to stock so as to maximize profit.

'We begin to formulate this situation as an LP problem by introducing some simple notations for use in the objective function and constraints. Let

X_1 = number of tables to stock

X_2 = number of chairs to stock

Now we can create the LP *objective function* in terms of X_1 and X_2

Maximize net profit = retail price − wholesale cost = $7X_1$ + $5X_2$

Our next step is to develop mathematical relationships to describe the three constraints in this problem. One general relationship is that the amount of a resource *used* is to be less than or equal to the amount of resource *available*.

First constraint: Budget used $\leq$ budget available

$4X_1 + 3X_2 \leq 240$ dollars available for purchases

Second constraint: Space used $\leq$ space available

$2X_1 + 1X_2 \leq 100$ square feet of floor space

Third constraint: Chairs ordered $\leq$ anticipated chair demand

$X_2 \leq 60$ chairs that can be sold

All three of these constraints represent stocking restrictions and, of course, affect the total profit. For example, Dixon Furniture cannot order 70 tables for the sale because if $X_1 = 70$, the first two constraints will be violated. It also cannot order $X_1 = 50$ tables and $X_2 = 10$ chairs. Hence we note one more important aspect of linear programming. That is, certain interactions will exist between variables. The more units of one product that the store orders, the less it can order of other products.

GRAPHICAL SOLUTION TO A LINEAR PROGRAMMING PROBLEM

The easiest way to solve a small LP problem such as that of the Dixon Furniture Store is the graphical solution approach. The graphical procedure is useful only when there are two decision variables (such as number of tables to order, X_1, and number of chairs to order, X_2) in the problem. When there are more than two variables, it is *not* possible to plot the solution on a two-dimensional graph, and we must turn to more complex approaches or to the use of a computer (which we shall do shortly). But the graphical method is invaluable in providing us with insights into how other approaches work.

Graphical Representation of Constraints

In order to find the optimal solution to a linear programming problem, we must first identify a set, or **region,** of feasible solutions. The first step in doing so is to plot each of the problem's constraints on a graph.

The variable X_1 (tables, in our example) is usually plotted as the horizontal axis of the graph, and the variable X_2 (chairs) is plotted as the vertical axis. The complete problem may be restated as

Maximize profit $= \$7X_1 + \$5X_2$

subject to the constraints:

$4X_1 + 3X_2 \leq 240$ (budget constraint)

$2X_1 + 1X_2 \leq 100$ (space constraint)

$X_2 \geq 60$ (chair demand constraint)

$X_1 \geq 0$ (number of tables ordered is greater than or equal to 0)

$X_2 \geq 0$ (number of chairs ordered is greater than or equal to 0)

We would like to represent graphically the constraints of this problem. The first step is to convert the constraint *inequalities* into *equalities* (or equations); that is,

Constraint 1: $4X_1 + 3X_2 = 240$

Constraint 2: $2X_1 + 1X_2 = 100$

Constraint 3: $1X_2 = 60$

The equation for constraint 1 is plotted in Exhibit 16–1.

To plot the line in Exhibit 16–1, all we need to do is to find the points at which the line $4X_1 + 3X_2 = 240$ intersects the X_1 and X_2 axes. When $X_1 = 0$ (the location where the line touches the X_2 axis), it implies that $3X_2 = 240$ or that $X_2 = 80$. Likewise,

EXHIBIT 16–1

■ *Plotting the Budget Constraint for Dixon*

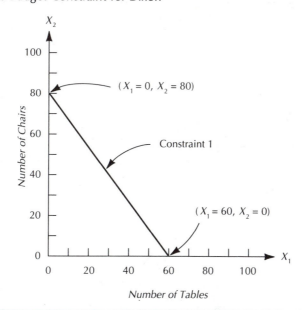

when $X_2 = 0$, we see that $4X_1 = 240$ and that $X_1 = 60$. Thus constraint 1 is bounded by the line running from $(X_1 = 0, X_2 = 80)$ to $(X_1 = 60, X_2 = 0)$. The shaded area represents all points that satisfy the original *inequality*.

Constraints 2 and 3 are handled similarly. Exhibit 16–2 shows all three constraints together. Note that the third constraint is just a straight line, which does not depend on the values of X_1.

The shaded region in Exhibit 16–2 is the part that satisfies all three restrictions. This region is called the area of feasible solutions, or simply the **feasible region.** This region must satisfy *all* conditions specified by the program's constraints and thus is the region where all constraints overlap. Any point in the region would be a **feasible solution** to the Dixon Furniture Store problem. Any point outside the shaded area would represent an **infeasible solution.** Hence it would be feasible to order three tables and two chairs ($X_1 = 30$, $X_2 = 20$), but it would violate the constraints to order 70 tables and 40 chairs. This can be seen by plotting these points on the graph of Exhibit 16–2.

Iso-Profit Line Solution Method

Now that the feasible region has been graphed, we may proceed to find the optimal solution to the problem. The mathematical theory behind linear programming states that an optimal solution to any problem (i.e., the values of X_1, X_2 that yield the maximum profit) will lie at a *corner point,* or *extreme point,* of the feasible region. The optimal solution is then the corner point lying in the feasible region that produces the highest profit.

EXHIBIT 16–2

▪ *All Constraints Plotted to Produce the Feasible Region for Dixon*

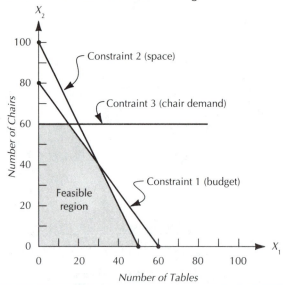

There are several approaches that can be taken in solving for the optimal solution once the feasible region has been established graphically. The speediest one to apply is called the **iso-profit line method.**

We start by letting profits equal some arbitrary, but small, dollar amount. For the Dixon Furniture problem, we may choose a profit of $210. This is a profit level that can easily be obtained without violating any of the three constraints. The objective function can be written as $210 = 7X_1 + 5X_2$.

This expression is just the equation of a line; we call it an **iso-profit line.** It represents all combinations of (X_1, X_2) that would yield a total profit of $210. To plot the profit line, we proceed exactly as we did to plot a constraint line. First, let $X_1 = 0$ and solve for the point at which the line crosses the X_2 axis.

$$\$210 = \$7(0) + \$5X_2$$

$$X_2 = 42 \text{ chairs}$$

Then let $X_2 = 0$ and solve for X_1.

$$\$210 = \$7X_1 + \$5(0)$$

$$X_1 = 30 \text{ tables}$$

We can now connect these two points with a straight line. This profit line is illustrated in Exhibit 16–3. All points on the line represent feasible solutions that produce a profit of $210.

EXHIBIT 16–3

■ *A Profit Line of $210 Plotted for Dixon*

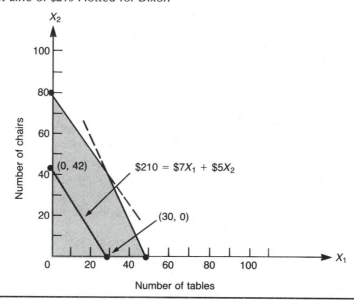

_____ EXHIBIT 16–4 _____

■ *Optimal Solution for the Dixon Furniture Problem*

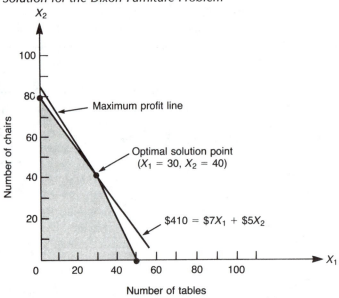

Now, obviously, the iso-profit line for $210 does not produce the highest possible profit to Dixon. In Exhibit 16–4 we try graphing a new line, one yielding a higher profit. Note that the further we move from the 0 origin, the higher the profit will be. Another important point to note is that these iso-profit lines are parallel. We now have two clues as to how to find the optimal solution to the original problem. We can draw a series of parallel profit lines (by carefully moving our ruler away from the origin parallel to the first profit line). The highest profit line that still touches some point of the feasible region will pinpoint the optimal solution.

The highest possible iso-profit line touches the tip of the feasible region of Exhibit 16–4 at the corner point $(X_1 = 30, X_2 = 40)$ and yields a profit of $410.

COMPUTER SOLUTION TO A LINEAR PROGRAMMING PROBLEM

As we mentioned earlier, it is not possible to solve any LP problem graphically that has more than two variables. Microcomputer software available with this text, as well as commercial packages such as LINDO, can easily tackle any size problem, however. They operate by using an algebraic technique known as the **simplex algorithm.** The simplex method systematically examines corner points, always searching for the point that yields a higher value for the objective function. It not only provides the optimal solution to any LP problem, but also provides valuable economic information, in the form of **shadow prices** and **sensitivity analysis.**

The input to our microcomputer LP package is shown in Exhibit 16–5. The

—— EXHIBIT 16–5 ——

■ *Computer Input for Dixon Furniture*

```
ENTER PROBLEM TITLE ? DIXON FURNITURE

DO YOU WISH TO:
1 - MINIMIZE
2 - MAXIMIZE
ENTER YOUR CHOICE (1-2)


ENTER THE NUMBER OF CONSTRAINTS ? 3
ENTER THE NUMBER OF VARIABLES ? 2
ENTER THE NUMBER OF <= EQUATIONS ? 3
ENTER THE NUMBER OF = EQUATIONS ? 0
ENTER THE NUMBER OF >= EQUATIONS ? 0


   FOR OBJECTIVE FUNCTION
-----------------------------------------------------------------------
ENTER COEFFICIENT # 1  OF THE OBJECTIVE FUNCTION? 7
ENTER COEFFICIENT # 2  OF THE OBJECTIVE FUNCTION? 5



         FOR (<=) CONSTRAINT #  1

ENTER THE VALUE OF COEFFICIENT  1 ? 4
ENTER THE VALUE OF COEFFICIENT  2 ? 3
ENTER THE RIGHT HAND SIDE VALUES ? 240

         FOR (<=) CONSTRAINT #  2

ENTER THE VALUE OF COEFFICIENT  1 ? 2
ENTER THE VALUE OF COEFFICIENT  2 ? 1
ENTER THE RIGHT HAND SIDE VALUES ? 100

         FOR (<=) CONSTRAINT #  3

ENTER THE VALUE OF COEFFICIENT  1 ? 0
ENTER THE VALUE OF COEFFICIENT  2 ? 1
ENTER THE RIGHT HAND SIDE VALUES ? 60
```

user needs only to answer a series of questions regarding the problem data. All places where we entered a response to a computer prompt are highlighted.

As a first step in analyzing these data, the computer software automatically restates each of the three inequality ($\leq$) constraints as equalities, or equations. It does this by adding a unique **slack variable** to each constraint. Slack variables represent unused resources; these may be in the form of time on a machine, labor hours, money, or space, just to name a few.

In the Dixon Furniture case, we can let

S_1 = slack variable representing unused budget

S_2 = slack variable representing unused floor space

S_3 = slack variable representing number of chairs that could have been sold

The three constraints are now rewritten as equalities.

$$4X_1 + 3X_2 + S_1 = 240$$
$$2X_1 + 1X_2 + S_2 = 100$$
$$1X_2 + S_3 = 60$$

When the computer output appears (see Exhibit 16–6), we see that the final solution is $X_2 = 40$, $X_1 = 30$, and $S_3 = 20$. (Any variable that does not appear under the word "ANSWERS," by the way, has a value of zero. Thus $S_1 = 0$ and $S_2 = 0$.) So 40 chairs and 30 tables should be ordered. Slack variable $S_3 = 20$ means that 20 more chairs *could* have been ordered without violating the third constraint. Slack variables S_1 and S_2 are both zero because the full \$240 of the budget resource and 100 square feet of the space resource have been utilized in ordering 40 chairs and 30 tables.

_____ EXHIBIT 16–6 _____

▪ *Computer Results for Dixon Furniture*

```
                        *** LINEAR PROGRAMMING ***

                            -- DATA ENTERED --



        PROBLEM TITLE = DIXON FURNITURE

        MAX Z = 7X1 + 5X2

        SUBJECT TO:

        4X1 + 3X2 <= 240
        2X1 + 1X2 <= 100
        0X1 + 1X2 <= 60
```

```
AFTER 2 ITERATIONS THE FINAL OPTIMAL SOLUTION IS:
**********************************************************************************
                            ANSWERS
                VARIABLE                VALUE
                   x 2                   40.000
                   x 1                   30.000
                   s 3                   20.000


                       SHADOW PRICES:

                CONSTRAINT #             VALUE
                     1                   1.500
                     2                   0.500
                     3                   0.000

                    OPTIMAL Z =    410
**********************************************************************************
```

Shadow Prices

This printout also leads us to the important subject of shadow prices. Exactly how much should Dixon Furniture be willing to pay to make one additional unit of each resource (that is, the number on the right-hand side of each constraint) available? Is renting one more square foot of floor space worth $1 or $5 or 25 cents to Dixon? Will an extra dollar of budget increase profit by more than $1, or will it not be worthwhile to seek additional funding for the sale?

We see in Exhibit 16–6 that each additional unit of the first resource, that is, budget dollars, will increase Dixon's overall profit by $1.50. This **shadow price** is valuable information for management. Furthermore, each additional square foot of display area (above the 100 square feet currently fully utilized) would increase the current $410 profit by $0.50. There is clearly no value to the third shadow price. Increasing the upper restriction on the number of chairs ordered, from 60 to 61, will not increase profit at all. This is so because there are $S_3 = 20$ slack units currently available. A shadow price will always be zero if its constraint's corresponding slack variable is not zero.

Sensitivity Analysis

Shadow pricing is actually one form of **sensitivity analysis,** that is, the study of how sensitive the optimal solution would be to errors or changes in inputs to the LP problem. For example, if the store manager at Dixon Furniture had been off by 10 percent in setting the net profit per table at $7, would that drastically alter the decision to order 30 tables and 40 chairs? What would be the impact of a budget of $265 instead of $240?

Exhibit 16–7 is part of the computer-generated output available to help a decision

––––– EXHIBIT 16–7 –––

■ *Sensitivity Analysis for Dixon Furniture*

```
                    SENSITIVITY ANALYSIS
                    ********************


                    RIGHTHAND SIDE RANGES

      CONSTRAINT    LOWER            RHS           UPPER
      NUMBER        LIMIT            VALUE         LIMIT
      ===========================================================
         1          200.00           240.00        260.00
         2           90.00           100.00        120.00
         3           40.00            60.00        NO LIMIT
      -----------------------------------------------------------


              OBJECTIVE FUNCTION COEFFICIENT RANGES

                    LOWER            CURRENT       UPPER
      VARIABLE      LIMIT            VALUE         LIMIT
      ===========================================================
         x 1          6.67            7.00         10.00
         x 2          3.50            5.00          5.25
      -----------------------------------------------------------
```

maker know whether or not a solution is relatively insensitive to reasonable changes in one or more of the parameters of the problem. First, let us consider changes to the right-hand side of a constraint. In doing so, in Exhibit 16–7, we assume changes are made in only one constraint at a time; the other two remain fixed at their original values. **Right-hand side ranging** tells us over what range of right-hand side values the shadow prices for that constraint will remain valid. In the Dixon example, the $1.50 shadow price for the budget constraint will apply even if the current budget of $240 drops as low as $200 or increases as high as $260.

This concept that the right-hand side range limits the shadow price is important in sensitivity analysis. Suppose Dixon Furniture could obtain additional funding at a cost less than the shadow price. The question of how much to obtain is answered by the upper limit in Exhibit 16–7; that is, secure $20 more than the current $240.

Now let us look at changes in one of the objective function coefficients. Sensitivity analysis provides, for each decision variable in the solution, the range of profit values over which the answer will be the same. For example, the net profit of $7 per table (X_1) in the objective function could range from $6.67 to $10.00 without the final solution of $X_1 = 30$, $X_2 = 40$ changing. Of course, if a profit coefficient changed at all, the total profit of $410 would change, even if the optimal quantities of X_1 and X_2 do not.

FORMULATING LINEAR PROGRAMMING MODELS

The purpose of this section is to show how a large number of real-life problems can be tackled using LP. We do this by presenting applications in the areas of ingredient blending, transportation/shipping, employee scheduling, labor planning, and media planning. Although some of these problems are relatively small numerically, the principles developed here are definitely applicable to larger problems.

Ingredient Blending Applications: The Diet Problem

The **diet problem,** one of the earliest applications of linear programming, was originally used by hospitals to determine the most economical diet for patients. Known in agricultural applications as the **feed mix problem,** the diet problem involves specifying a food or feed ingredient combination that satisfies stated nutritional requirements at a minimum cost level.

The Whole Food Nutrition Center uses three bulk grains to blend a natural cereal that it sells by the pound. The store advertises that each 2-ounce serving of the cereal, when taken with $\frac{1}{2}$ cup of whole milk, meets an average adult's minimum daily requirement for protein, riboflavin, phosphorus, and magnesium. The cost of each bulk grain and the protein, riboflavin, phosphorus, and magnesium units per pound of each are shown in Exhibit 16–8.

The minimum adult daily requirement (called the *U.S. Recommended Daily Allowance,* or *USRDA*) for protein is 3 units; for riboflavin, 2 units; for phosphorus, 1 unit; and for magnesium, 0.425 units. Whole Food wants to select the blend of grains that will meet the USRDA at a minimum cost.

───── EXHIBIT 16–8 ─────────────────────────────────

▪ *Whole Food's Natural Cereal Requirements*

Grain	Cost per Pound	Protein (units/lb)	Riboflavin (units/lb)	Phosphorus (units/lb)	Magnesium (units/lb)
A	33¢	22	16	8	5
B	47¢	28	14	7	0
C	38¢	21	25	9	6

We let X_A = pounds of grain A in one 2-ounce serving of cereal

X_B = pounds of grain B in one 2-ounce serving of cereal

X_C = pounds of grain C in one 2-ounce serving of cereal

Objective function:

Minimize total cost of mixing a 2-ounce serving
$$= \$0.33X_A + \$0.47X_B + \$0.38X_C$$

Constraints:

$$22X_A + 28X_B + 21X_C \geq 3 \qquad \text{(protein units)}$$

$$16X_A + 14X_B + 25X_C \geq 2 \qquad \text{(riboflavin units)}$$

$$8X_A + 7X_B + 9X_C \geq 1 \qquad \text{(phosphorus units)}$$

$$5X_A + 0X_B + 6X_C \geq 0.425 \qquad \text{(magnesium units)}$$

$$X_A + X_B + X_C = \tfrac{1}{8} \qquad \text{(total mix is 2 ounces or } \tfrac{1}{8} \text{ pound)}$$

$$X_A, X_B, X_C \geq 0$$

The solution to this problem requires mixing together 0.025 lb grain A, 0.050 lb grain B, and 0.050 lb grain C. Another way of stating the solution is in terms of the proportion of the 2-ounce serving of each grain, namely, $\frac{2}{5}$ ounce grain A, $\frac{4}{5}$ ounce grain B, and $\frac{4}{5}$ ounce grain C in each serving. The cost per serving is $0.05075, a little over $0.05 per serving.

Transportation Applications: The Shipping Problem

The **transportation** or **shipping problem** involves determining the amount of goods or items to be transported from a number of origins to a number of destinations. The objective is usually to minimize total shipping costs or distances. Constraints in this type of problem deal with capacities at each origin and requirements at each destination. The transportation problem is a very specific case of linear programming.

The Top Speed Bicycle Company markets a line of ten-speed bicycles nationwide. The firm has warehouses in two cities, New Orleans and Omaha. Its three retail outlets are located near the large market areas of New York, Chicago, and Los Angeles.

The sales requirements for the next year at the New York store are 10,000 bicycles, at the Chicago store 8000 bicycles, and at the Los Angeles store 15,000 bicycles. The capacity at each warehouse is limited. New Orleans can store and ship 20,000 bicycles, while the Omaha site can warehouse 15,000 bicycles per year.

The cost of shipping one bicycle from each warehouse to each retail outlet differs, and these unit shipping costs are

	To		
From	New York	Chicago	Los Angeles
New Orleans	$2	$3	$5
Omaha	$3	$1	$4

The company wishes to determine a shipping schedule that will minimize its total annual transportation costs.

To formulate this problem using LP, we employ the concept of double-subscripted variables. For example, we can let X_{11} = number of bicycles shipped from New Orleans to New York. We let the first subscript represent the origin (warehouse) and the second subscript the destination (retail outlet). Thus, in general, X_{ij} refers to the number of bicycles shipped from origin i to destination j. We could instead denote X_6 as the variable for origin 2 to destination 3, but we think you will find the double subscripts more descriptive and easier to use. So we also let

X_{12} = number of bicycles shipped from New Orleans to Chicago

X_{13} = number of bicycles shipped from New Orleans to Los Angeles

X_{21} = number of bicycles shipped from Omaha to New York

X_{22} = number of bicycles shipped from Omaha to Chicago

X_{23} = number of bicycles shipped from Omaha to Los Angeles

The objective function and constraints then become

Minimize total shipping costs
$$= 2X_{11} + 3X_{12} + 5X_{13} + 3X_{21} + 1X_{22} + 4X_{23}$$

Subject to:

$$X_{11} + X_{21} = 10,000 \qquad \text{(New York demand)}$$

$$X_{12} + X_{22} = 8,000 \qquad \text{(Chicago demand)}$$

$$X_{13} + X_{23} = 15,000 \qquad \text{(Los Angeles demand)}$$

$$X_{11} + X_{12} + X_{13} \leq 20,000 \qquad \text{(New Orleans warehouse supply)}$$

$$X_{21} + X_{22} + X_{23} \leq 15,000 \qquad \text{(Omaha warehouse supply)}$$

Why are transportation problems a special class of linear programming problems? The answer is that every coefficient in front of a variable in the constraint equations is always equal to 1. This special trait is also seen in another special category of LP problems, the assignment problem.

The computer-generated solution to Top Speed's problem is shown below. The total shipping cost is $9600.

From	To		
	New York	Chicago	Los Angeles
New Orleans	10,000	0	8000
Omaha	0	8000	7000

Employee Scheduling Applications: An Assignment Problem

Assignment problems involve determining the most efficient assignment of people to jobs, machines to tasks, police cars to city sectors, salespeople to territories, and so on. The objective might be to minimize travel times or costs, or to maximize assignment effectiveness. Assignment problems are unique because they not only have a coefficient of 1 associated with each variable in the LP constraints, but also because the right-hand side of each constraint is always equal to 1 also. The use of LP in solving this type of problem yields solutions of either 0 or 1 for each variable in the formulation. The following is an example situation.

The law firm of Ivan and Ivan maintains a large staff of young attorneys who hold the title of junior partner. Ivan, concerned with the effective utilization of his manpower resources, seeks some objective means of making lawyer-to-client assignments.

On March 1, four new clients seeking legal assistance come to Ivan. While the current staff is overloaded, Ivan would like to accommodate the new clients. He reviews current case loads and identifies four junior partners who, although busy, could possibly be assigned to the cases. Each young lawyer can handle at most one new client. Furthermore, each lawyer differs in skills and specialty interests.

Seeking to maximize the overall effectiveness of the new client assignments, Ivan draws up the following table in which he rates the estimated effectiveness (on a 1-to-9 scale) of each lawyer on each new case.

Lawyer	Client's Case			
	Divorce	Corporate Merger	Embezzlement	Insider Trading
Adams	6	2	8	5
Brooks	9	3	5	8
Carter	4	8	3	4
Darwin	6	7	6	4

To solve using LP, we again employ double-scripted variables.

$$\text{Let } X_{ij} = \begin{cases} 1 & \text{if attorney } i \text{ is assigned to case } j \\ 0 & \text{otherwise} \end{cases}$$

where $i = 1, 2, 3, 4$ stands for Adams, Brooks, Carter, and Darwin,
respectively

$j = 1, 2, 3, 4$ stands for divorce, merger, embezzlement,
and insider trading, respectively

The LP formulation follows.

$$\text{Maximize effectiveness} = 6X_{11} + 2X_{12} + 8X_{13} + 5X_{14}$$
$$+ 9X_{21} + 3X_{22} + 5X_{23} + 8X_{24}$$
$$+ 4X_{31} + 8X_{32} + 3X_{33} + 4X_{34}$$
$$+ 6X_{41} + 7X_{42} + 6X_{43} + 4X_{44}$$

Subject to:

$$X_{11} + X_{21} + X_{31} + X_{41} = 1 \quad \text{(divorce case)}$$
$$X_{12} + X_{22} + X_{32} + X_{42} = 1 \quad \text{(merger)}$$
$$X_{13} + X_{23} + X_{33} + X_{43} = 1 \quad \text{(embezzlement)}$$
$$X_{14} + X_{24} + X_{34} + X_{44} = 1 \quad \text{(insider trading)}$$
$$X_{11} + X_{12} + X_{13} + X_{14} = 1 \quad \text{(cases assigned to Adams)}$$
$$X_{21} + X_{22} + X_{23} + X_{24} = 1 \quad \text{(cases assigned to Brooks)}$$
$$X_{31} + X_{32} + X_{33} + X_{34} = 1 \quad \text{(cases assigned to Carter)}$$
$$X_{41} + X_{42} + X_{43} + X_{44} = 1 \quad \text{(cases assigned to Darwin)}$$

The law firm's problem is solved with a total effectiveness rating of 30 by letting $X_{13} = 1$, $X_{24} = 1$, $X_{32} = 1$, and $X_{41} = 1$. All other variables are therefore equal to 0.

Labor Planning

Labor planning problems address staffing needs over a specific time period. They are especially useful when managers have some flexibility in assigning workers to jobs that require overlapping or interchangeable talents. Large banks frequently use LP to tackle their labor scheduling.

Arlington Bank of Commerce and Industry is a busy bank that has requirements for between ten and eighteen tellers depending on the time of day. The lunch time, from noon to 2 P.M., is usually heaviest. Exhibit 16–9 indicates the workers needed at various hours that the bank is open.

───── EXHIBIT 16–9 ───

▪ *Arlington Bank of Commerce and Industry*

Time Period	Number of Tellers Required
9 A.M.–10 A.M.	10
10 A.M.–11 A.M.	12
11 A.M.–Noon	14
Noon–1 P.M.	16
1 P.M.–2 P.M.	18
2 P.M.–3 P.M.	17
⁻3 P.M.–4 P.M.	15
4 P.M.–5 P.M.	10

The bank now employs twelve full-time tellers, but many women are on its roster of available part-time employees. A part-time employee must put in exactly four hours per day, but can start anytime between 9 A.M. and 1 P.M. Part-timers are a fairly inexpensive labor pool, since no retirement or lunch benefits are provided them. Full-timers, on the other hand, work from 9 A.M. to 5 P.M. but are allowed one hour for lunch. (Half the full-timers eat at 11 A.M., the other half at noon.) Full-timers thus provide 35 hours per week of productive labor time.

By corporate policy, the bank limits part-time hours to a maximum of 50 percent of the day's total requirement.

Part-timers earn $4 per hour (or $16 per day) on average, while full-timers earn $50 per day in salary and benefits on average. The bank would like to set a schedule that would minimize its total manpower costs. It will release one or more of its full-time tellers if it is profitable to do so.

We can let

F = number of full-time tellers

P_1 = number of part-timers starting at 9 A.M. (leaving at 1 P.M.)

P_2 = number of part-timers starting at 10 A.M. (leaving at 2 P.M.)

P_3 = number of part-timers starting at 11 A.M. (leaving at 3 P.M.)

P_4 = number of part-timers starting at noon (leaving at 4 P.M.)

P_5 = number of part-timers starting at 1 P.M. (leaving at 5 P.M.)

Objective function:

Minimize total daily manpower cost

$$= \$50F + \$16(P_1 + P_2 + P_3 + P_4 + P_5)$$

Constraints: For each hour, the available man-hours must be at least equal to the required man-hours.

$$F + P_1 \qquad\qquad\qquad\qquad\qquad \geq 10 \text{ (9 A.M. to 10 A.M. needs)}$$
$$F + P_1 + P_2 \qquad\qquad\qquad\qquad \geq 12 \text{ (10 A.M. to 11 A.M. needs)}$$
$$\tfrac{1}{2}F + P_1 + P_2 + P_3 \qquad\qquad\qquad \geq 14 \text{ (11 A.M. to noon needs)}$$
$$\tfrac{1}{2}F + P_1 + P_2 + P_3 + P_4 \qquad\qquad \geq 16 \text{ (noon to 1 P.M. needs)}$$
$$F \qquad\quad + P_2 + P_3 + P_4 + P_5 \geq 18 \text{ (1 P.M. to 2 P.M. needs)}$$
$$F \qquad\qquad\quad + P_3 + P_4 + P_5 \geq 17 \text{ (2 P.M. to 3 P.M. needs)}$$
$$F \qquad\qquad\qquad\quad + P_4 + P_5 \geq 15 \text{ (3 P.M. to 4 P.M. needs)}$$
$$F \qquad\qquad\qquad\qquad\quad + P_5 \geq 10 \text{ (4 P.M. to 5 P.M. needs)}$$

Only twelve full-time tellers are available so,

$$F \leq 12$$

Part-time worker hours cannot exceed 50 percent of total hours required each day, which is the sum of the tellers needed each hour.

$$4(P_1 + P_2 + P_3 + P_4 + P_5) \leq 0.50(10 + 12 + 14 + 16 + 18 + 17$$
$$+ 15 + 10)$$

or $4P_1 + 4P_2 + 4P_3 + 4P_4 + 4P_5 \leq 0.50(112)$
       $F, P_1, P_2, P_3 \, P_4, P_5 \geq 0$

There are two alternative optimal schedules that Arlington Bank can follow. The first is to employ only ten full-time tellers ($F = 10$) and to start two part-timers at 10 A.M. ($P_2 = 2$), seven part-timers at 11 A.M. ($P_3 = 7$), and five part-timers at noon ($P_4 = 5$). No part-timers would begin at 9 A.M. or 1 P.M.

The second solution also employs ten full-time tellers, but starts six part-timers at 9 A.M. ($P_1 = 6$), one part-timer at 10 A.M. ($P_2 = 1$), two part-timers at 11 A.M. and noon ($P_3 = 2$ and $P_4 = 2$), and three part-timers at 1 P.M. ($P_5 = 3$). The cost of either of these two policies is $724 per day.

Marketing Applications: Media Selection

Linear programming models have been used in the advertising field as a decision aid in selecting an effective media mix. Sometimes the technique is employed in allocating a fixed or limited budget across various media, which might include radio or television commercials, newspaper ads, direct mailings, magazine ads, and so on. In other applications, the objective is taken to be the maximization of audience exposure. Restrictions on the allowable media mix might arise through contract requirements, limited media availability, or company policy. An example follows.

The Win Big Gambling Club promotes gambling junkets from a large midwestern city to casinos in the Bahamas. The club has budgeted up to $8000 per week for local advertising, the money to be allocated among four promotional media: TV spots, newspaper ads, and two types of radio advertisements. Win Big's goal is to reach the largest possible high-potential audience through the various media. The following table presents the number of potential gamblers reached by making use of an advertisement in each of the four media. It also provides figures regarding the cost per advertisement placed, and the maximum number of ads that can be purchased per week.

Medium	Audience Reached per Ad	Cost per Ad	Maximum Ads per Week
TV spot (1 minute)	5000	$800	12
Daily newspaper (full-page ad)	8500	$925	5
Radio spot (½ minute, prime time)	2400	$290	25
Radio spot (1 minute, afternoon)	2800	$380	20

Win Big's contractual arrangements require that at least five radio spots be placed each week. To ensure a broad-scoped promotional campaign, management also insists that no more than $1800 be spent on all radio advertising every week.

The problem can now be stated mathematically as follows. Let

X_1 = number of 1-minute TV spots taken each week

X_2 = number of full-page daily newspaper ads taken each week

X_3 = number of 30-second prime-time radio spots taken each week

X_4 = number of 1-minute afternoon radio spots taken each week

Objective function:

$$\text{Maximize audience coverage} = 5000X_1 + 8500X_2 + 2400X_3 + 2800X_4$$

Subject to:

$$X_1 \leq 12 \quad \text{(maximum TV spots per week)}$$

$$X_2 \leq 5 \quad \text{(maximum newspaper ads per week)}$$

$$X_3 \leq 25 \quad \text{(maximum 30-second radio spots per week)}$$

$$X_4 \leq 20 \quad \text{(maximum one-minute radio spots per week)}$$

$$800X_1 + 925X_2 + 290X_3 + 380X_4 \leq 8000 \quad \text{(weekly advertising budget)}$$

$$X_3 + X_4 \geq 5 \quad \text{(minimum radio spots contracted)}$$

$$290X_3 + 380X_4 \leq 1800 \quad \text{(maximum \$ spent on radio)}$$

The solution to this LP formulation, using our microcomputer software package, was found to be

$X_1 = 1.9$ TV spots

$X_2 = 5$ newspaper ads

$X_3 = 6.2$ 30-second radio spots

$X_4 = 0$ 1-minute radio spots

This produces an audience exposure of 67,240 contacts. Since X_1 and X_3 are fractional, Win Big would probably round them to 2 and 6, respectively. Problems that demand all-integer solutions are discussed in detail in most management science textbooks.

GOAL PROGRAMMING

In today's business environment, profit maximization or cost minimization are not always the only objectives that a service organization sets forth. Often maximizing total profit is just one of several goals, including such contradictory objectives as maximizing market share, maintaining full employment, providing quality ecologic management, minimizing noise level in the neighborhood, and meeting numerous other noneconomic goals.

Linear programming has the shortcoming that its objective function is measured in one dimension only. It is not possible for linear programming to have *multiple goals* unless they are all measured in the same units (such as dollars), a highly unusual situation. An important technique that has been developed to supplement linear programming is called **goal programming.**

In typical decision-making situations, the goals set by management can be achieved only at the expense of other goals. It is necessary to establish a hierarchy of importance among these goals so that lower-priority goals are tackled only after higher-priority ones are satisfied. Since it is not always possible to achieve every goal to the extent the decision maker desires, goal programming attempts to reach a satisfactory level of multiple objectives. This, of course, differs from linear programming, which tries to find the best possible outcome for a *single* objective.

How, specifically, does goal programming differ from linear programming? The objective function is the main difference. Instead of trying to maximize or minimize the objective function directly, with goal programming we try to minimize **deviations** between set goals and what we can actually achieve within the given constraints. In the LP simplex approach, such deviations are called **slack variables** and they are used only as dummy variables. In goal programming, these slack terms are either positive or negative, and not only are they real variables, but they are also the only terms in the objective function. The objective is to minimize these deviational variables.

Once the goal programming model is formulated, the computational algorithm is almost the same as for an LP problem solved by the simplex method.

Goal Programming Example: Dixon Furniture Revisited

To illustrate the formulation of a GP problem, let's look back at the Dixon Furniture Store case, presented earlier in this chapter as an LP problem. That formulation, you recall, was

$$\text{Maximize net profit} = \$7X_1 + \$5X_2$$

Subject to:

$$4X_1 + 3X_2 \le 240 \quad \text{(\$ of budget constraint)}$$
$$2X_1 + 1X_2 \le 100 \quad \text{(space constraint)}$$
$$X_2 \le 60 \quad \text{(chair demand constraint)}$$
$$X_1, X_2 \ge 0$$

where X_1 = number of tables ordered

X_2 = number of chairs ordered

We saw that if Dixon management had a single goal, say profit, linear programming could be used to find the optimal solution. But let's assume that the store is breaking in a whole new staff of sales clerks on the Labor Day weekend and feels that maximizing profit is not a realistic goal. The store manager sets a profit level, which would be satisfactory during the training period, of $380. We now have a goal programming problem in which we want to find the mix of tables and chairs that achieves the goal as closely as possible, given the budgetary and space constraints. This simple case will provide a good starting point for handling more complicated goal programs.

We first define two deviational variables:

d_1^- = the underachievement of the profit target

d_1^+ = the overachievement of the profit target

Now we can state the Dixon Furniture problem as a *single-goal* programming model.

$$\text{Minimize under- or overachievement of target profit} = d_1^- + d_1^+$$

Subject to:

$$7X_1 + 5X_2 + d_1^- - d_1^+ = 380 \quad \text{(profit goal constraint)}$$
$$4X_1 + 3X_2 \le 240 \quad \text{(budget constraint)}$$
$$2X_1 + 1X_2 \le 100 \quad \text{(space constraint)}$$
$$X_2 \le 60 \quad \text{(chair demand constraint)}$$
$$X_1, X_2, d_1^-, d_1^+ \ge 0$$

Note that the first constraint states that the profit made, $\$7X_1 + \$5X_2$, plus any underachievement of profit minus any overachievement of profit has to equal the target of \$380. For example, if $X_1 = 10$ tables and $X_2 = 60$ chairs, then \$370 profit has been made. This misses the \$380 target by \$10, so d_1^- must be equal to 10. Since the profit goal was *underachieved*, Dixon did not overachieve and d_1^+ will clearly be equal to 0. This problem is now ready for solution by a goal programming algorithm.

If the target profit of \$380 is exactly achieved, we see that both d_1^+ and d_1^- are equal to zero. The objective function will be minimized at 0. If Dixon's manager was only concerned with *underachievement* of the target goal, how would the objective function change? It would be

$$\text{Minimize underachievement} = d_1^-$$

This is also a reasonable goal, since the store would probably not be upset with an overachievement of its profit target.

In general, once all goals and constraints are identified in a problem, management should analyze each goal to see if under- or overachievement of that goal is an acceptable situation. If overachievement is acceptable, the appropriate d^+ variable can be eliminated from the objective function. If underachievement is okay, the d^- variable should be dropped. If management seeks to attain a goal exactly, both d^- and d^+ must appear in the objective function.

An Extension to Equally Important Multiple Goals

Let's now look at the situation in which Dixon's manager wants to achieve several goals, each equal in priority.

— *Goal 1:* To produce as much profit above \$380 as possible during the Labor Day sale
— *Goal 2:* To fully utilize the available budget of \$240
— *Goal 3:* To avoid using more than the allotted floor space
— *Goal 4:* To avoid overstocking chairs

The deviational variables can be defined as follows:

d_1^- = underachievement of the profit target

d_1^+ = overachievement of the profit target

d_2^- = underspending of the allotted budget (underutilization)

d_2^+ = overspending of the allotted budget (overutilization)

d_3^- = underuse of the floor space allotted (underutilization)

d_3^+ = overuse of the floor space allotted (overutilization)

d_4^- = underachievement of the chair goal

d_4^+ = overachievement of the chair goal

Dixon is unconcerned about whether there is overachievement of the profit goal, overspending of the allotted budget, underuse of the floor space, or whether less than

60 chairs are ordered; hence d_1^+, d_2^+, d_3^-, and d_4^- may be omitted from the objective function. The new objective function and constraints are

$$\text{Minimize total deviation} = d_1^- + d_2^- + d_3^+ + d_4^+$$

Subject to:

$$7X_1 + 5X_2 + d_1^- - d_1^+ = 380 \qquad \text{(profit constraint)}$$
$$4X_1 + 3X_2 + d_2^- - d_2^+ = 240 \qquad \text{(budget constraint)}$$
$$2X_1 + 1X_2 + d_3^- - d_3^+ = 100 \qquad \text{(space constraint)}$$
$$X_2 + d_4^- - d_4^+ = 60 \qquad \text{(chair constraint)}$$
$$\text{All } X_i, d_i \text{ variables} \geq 0$$

Ranking Goals. In most goal programming problems, one goal will be more important than another, which in turn will be more important than a third. The idea is that goals can be ranked with respect to their importance in management's eyes. Lower-order goals are considered only after higher-order goals are met. Priorities (P_i's) are assigned to each deviational variable—with the ranking that P_1 is the most important goal, P_2 the next important, then P_3, and so on.

Let's say Dixon Furniture sets the priorities shown in the accompanying table.

Goal	Priority
Reach a profit as much above $380 as possible	P_1
Fully use budget available	P_2
Avoid using more space than available	P_3
Ordering less than 60 chairs	P_4

This means, in effect, that the priority of meeting the profit goal (P_1) is infinitely more important than the budget goal (P_2), which is, in turn, infinitely more important than the space goal (P_3), which is infinitely more important than ordering no more than 60 chairs (P_4).

With ranking of goals considered, the new objective function becomes

$$\text{Minimize total deviation} = P_1 d_1^- + P_2 d_2^- + P_3 d_3^+ + P_4 d_4^+$$

The constraints remain identical to the previous ones.

The GP solution to this problem turns out to be $X_1 = 15$ tables, $X_2 = 60$ chairs, $d_1^+ = \$25$ profit above the $380 target, and $d_3^- = 10$ square feet of floor space unused. All other deviational variables have values of zero and all goals are fully attained.

____ SUMMARY

Linear programming has proven to be a popular tool that can handle a wide variety of service operations management problems. Although a graphical method can be used to actually solve small problems, most organizations have access to LP software that runs on either microcomputers or larger systems and uses a solution procedure known as the **simplex algorithm.** LP not only finds optimal solutions to problems that can be formulated mathematically, but it also provides valuable management information in the form of shadow pricing and sensitivity analysis.

In this chapter we saw how to formulate LP problems with marketing, shipping, labor scheduling, assignment, ingredient blending, and retail ordering applications. Many of the problems at the end of the chapter involve extending the skills you have developed so far and tackling yet more complex service problems.

The final section introduced an extension of LP known as goal programming. GP helps the service manager who is faced with multiple goals. It tries to satisfy goals in priority order rather than maximize or minimize a single objective. The simplex method of LP can be manipulated to also solve goal programming problems, but special software is available specifically for the GP technique.

—— DISCUSSION QUESTIONS

1. It has been said that each linear programming problem that has a feasible region has an infinite number of solutions. Explain.

2. Is sensitivity analysis a concept applied to linear programming only, or could it also be used when analyzing other techniques? Provide examples to prove your point.

3. What is a shadow price?

4. The mathematical relationships that follow were formulated by an operations research analyst at the Smith-Lawton Chemical Company. Which ones are invalid for use in a linear programming problem, and why?

Maximize profit
$$= 4X_1 + 3X_1X_2 + 8X_2 + 5X_3$$

Subject to:
$$2X_1 + X_2 + 2X_3 \le 50$$
$$8X_1 - 4X_2 \ge 6$$

$$1.5X_1 + 6X_2 + 3X_3 \ge 21$$
$$19X_2 - \tfrac{1}{3}X_3 = 17$$
$$5X_1 + 4X_2 + 3\sqrt{X_3} \le 80$$
$$-X_1 - X_2 + X_3 = 5$$

5. What is the value of the computer in solving linear programming problems today?

6. Compare the similarities and differences between linear and goal programming.

7. What are deviational variables? How do they differ from decision variables in traditional linear programming problems?

8. If you were the president of the college you are attending and were employing goal programming to assist in decision making, what might your goals be? What kinds of constraints would you include in your model?

9. What does it mean to rank goals in goal programming? How does this affect the problem's solution?

—— PROBLEMS

16.1 Solve the following linear programming problem using the graphical method.

Maximize profit $= 4X_1 + 4X_2$

Subject to:
$$3X + 5X \le 150$$

$$X_1 - 2X_2 \le 10$$
$$5X_1 + 3X_2 \le 150$$
$$X_1, X_2 \ge 0$$

16.2 Consider the following linear programming formulation:

Minimize cost $= \$1X_1 + \$2X_2$

Subject to:

$$X_1 + 3X_2 \geq 90$$
$$8X_1 + 2X_2 \geq 160$$
$$3X_1 + 2X_2 \geq 120$$
$$X_2 \leq 70$$

Graphically illustrate the feasible region. Indicate which corner point produces the optimal solution. What is the cost of this solution?

16.3 The famous Y. S. Chang Restaurant is open 24 hours a day. Waiters and busboys report for duty at 3 A.M., 7 A.M., 11 A.M., 3 P.M., 7 P.M., or 11 P.M., and each works an eight-hour shift. The following table shows the minimum number of workers needed during the six periods into which the day is divided.

Period	Time	Number of Waiters and Busboys Required
1	3 A.M.– 7 A.M.	3
2	7 A.M.–11 A.M.	12
3	11 A.M.– 3 P.M.	16
4	3 P.M.– 7 P.M.	9
5	7 P.M.–11 P.M.	11
6	11 P.M.– 3 A.M.	4

Chang's scheduling problem is to determine how many waiters and busboys should report for work at the start of each time period in order to minimize the total staff required for one day's operation. (*Hint:* Let X_1 equal the number of waiters and busboys beginning work in time period i, where $i = 1, 2, 3, 4, 5, 6$.)

16.4 The advertising director for Diversey Paint and Supply, a chain of four retail stores on Chicago's North Side, is considering two media possibilities. One plan is for a series of half-page ads in the Sunday *Chicago Tribune* newspaper, and the other is for advertising time on Chicago TV. The stores are expanding their lines of do-it-yourself tools, and the advertising director is interested in an exposure level of at least 40 percent within the city's neighborhoods and 60 percent in northwest suburban areas.

The TV viewing time under consideration has an exposure rating per spot of 5 percent in city homes and 3 percent in the northwest suburbs. The Sunday newspaper has corresponding exposure rates of 4 percent and 3 percent per ad. The cost of a half-page *Tribune* advertisement is $925; a television spot costs $2000.

Diversey Paint would like to select the least costly advertising strategy that would meet desired exposure levels. Formulate this using LP.

16.5 The Krampf Lines Railway Company specializes in coal handling. On Friday, April 13, Krampf had empty cars at the following towns in the quantities indicated.

Town	Supply of Cars
Morgantown	35
Youngstown	60
Pittsburgh	25

By Monday, April 16, the following towns will need coal cars.

Town	Demand for Cars
Coal Valley	30
Coaltown	45
Coal Junction	25
Coalsburg	20

Using a railway city-to-city distance chart, the dispatcher constructs a mileage table for the preceding towns. The result is shown in Exhibit 16–10.

a. Formulate as a linear programming problem to minimize total miles over which cars are moved to new locations.

EXHIBIT 16–10

| From | To | | | |
	Coal Valley	Coaltown	Coal Junction	Coalsburg
Morgantown	50	30	60	70
Youngstown	20	80	10	90
Pittsburgh	100	40	80	30

—— EXHIBIT 16–11 ——

From	W	X	Y	Z	Excess Supply
A	12¢	4¢	9¢	5¢	55
B	8¢	1¢	6¢	6¢	45
C	1¢	12¢	4¢	7¢	30
Unfilled power demand	40	20	50	20	

(To spans columns W, X, Y, Z)

b. Compute the best shipment of coal cars using a linear programming computer program.

16.6 The state of Missouri has three major power-generating companies (*A, B,* and *C*). During the months of peak demand, the Missouri Power Authority authorizes these companies to pool their excess supply and to distribute it to smaller independent power companies that do not have generators large enough to handle the demand.

Excess supply is distributed on the basis of cost per kilowatt-hour transmitted. Exhibit 16–11 shows the demand and supply in millions of kilowatt hours and the costs per kilowatt hour of transmitting electric power to four small companies in cities *W, X, Y,* and *Z.*

a. Formulate an LP model for this problem.

b. Find the least cost distribution system using an LP computer program.

16.7 The hospital administrator at St. Charles General must appoint head nurses to four newly established departments: urology, cardiology, orthopedics, and obstetrics. In anticipation of this staffing problem, he had hired four nurses: Hawkins, Condriac, Bardot, and Hoolihan. Believing in the quantitative analysis approach to problem solving, the administrator has interviewed each nurse, considered her background, personality, and talents, and developed a cost scale ranging from 0 to 100 to be used in the assignment. A 0 for Nurse Bardot being assigned to the cardiology unit implies that she would be perfectly suited to that task. A value close to 100, on the other hand, would imply that she is not at all suited to head that unit. Exhibit 16–12 gives the complete set of cost figures that the hospital administrator felt represented all possible assignments. Which nurse should be assigned to which unit?

16.8 The Gleaming Company has just developed a new dishwashing liquid and is preparing for a national television promotional campaign. The firm has decided to schedule a series of 1-minute commercials during the peak housewife audience viewing hours of 1 to 5 P.M. To reach the widest possible audience, Gleaming wants to schedule one commercial on each of four networks and to have one commercial appear during each of the four 1-hour time blocks. The exposure ratings for each hour, which represent the number of viewers per $1000 spent, are presented in the table at the top of the next page. Which network should be scheduled each hour in order to provide the maximum audience exposure?

—— EXHIBIT 16–12 ——

Nurse	Urology	Cardiology	Orthopedics	Obstetrics
Hawkins	28	18	15	75
Condriac	32	48	23	38
Bardot	51	36	24	36
Hoolihan	25	38	55	12

(Department spans columns Urology, Cardiology, Orthopedics, Obstetrics)

	Networks			
	A	*B*	*C*	Inde-pendent
1–2 P.M.	27.1	18.1	11.3	9.5
2–3 P.M.	18.9	15.5	17.1	10.6
3–4 P.M.	19.2	18.5	9.9	7.7
4–5 P.M.	11.5	21.4	16.8	12.8

16.9 The Arden County, Maryland, superintendent of education is responsible for assigning students to the three high schools in his county. He recognizes the need to bus a certain number of students, for several sectors of the county are beyond walking distance to a school. The superintendent partitions the county into five geographic sectors as he attempts to establish a plan that will minimize the total number of student miles traveled by bus. He also recognizes that if a student happens to live in a certain sector and is assigned to the high school in that sector, there is no need to bus him since he can walk from home to school. The three schools are located in sectors *B*, *C*, and *E*.

Exhibit 16–13 reflects the number of high-school-age students living in each sector and the distance in miles from each sector to each school.

Each high school has a capacity of 900 students. Set up the objective function and constraints of this problem using linear programming so that the total number of student miles traveled by bus is minimized.

16.10 Harris Segal, marketing director for North-Central Power and Light, is about to begin an advertising campaign promoting energy conservation. In trying to budget between television and newspaper advertisements, he sets the following goals in order of importance:

1. The total advertising budget of $120,000 should not be exceeded.
2. There should be a mix of TV and newspaper ads, with at least ten TV spots (costing $5000 each) and at least twenty newspaper ads (costing $2000 each).
3. The total number of people to read or hear the advertisements should be at least 9 million.

Each television spot reaches approximately 300,000 people. A newspaper advertisement is read by about 150,000 persons. Formulate Segal's goal programming problem to find out how many of each type of ad to place.

16.11 Major Bill Bligh, director of the Army War College's new six-month attaché training program, is concerned about how the twenty officers taking the course spend their precious time while in his charge. Major Bligh recognizes that there are 168 hours per week and thinks his students have been using them rather inefficiently. Bligh lets

X_1 = number of hours of sleep needed per week

X_2 = number of personal hours (eating, personal hygiene, handling laundry, etc.)

X_3 = number of hours of class and studying

X_4 = number of hours of social time off-base (dating, sports, family visits, etc.)

He thinks that thirty hours per week should be enough study/class time for students to absorb the material and that this is his most important goal. Bligh feels that students need at most seven hours sleep per night on average and that this goal is number 2. He believes that goal number 3 is to provide at least twenty hours per week of social time. Formulate this as a goal programming problem.

───── EXHIBIT 16–13 ─────

	Distance to School			
Sector	School in Sector B	School in Sector C	School in Sector E	No. of Students
A	5	8	6	700
B	0	4	12	500
C	4	0	7	100
D	7	2	5	800
E	12	7	0	400
			Total	2,500

16.12 New Orleans's Mt. Sinai Hospital is a large, private, 600-bed facility complete with laboratories, operating rooms, and x-ray equipment. In seeking to increase revenues, Mt. Sinai's administration has decided to make a 90-bed addition on a portion of adjacent land currently used for staff parking. The administrators feel that the labs, operating rooms, and x-ray department are not being fully utilized at present and do not need to be expanded to handle additional patients. The addition of 90 beds, however, involves deciding how many beds should be allocated to the medical staff (for medical patients) and how many to the surgical staff (for surgical patients).

The hospital's accounting and medical records departments have provided the following pertinent information. The average hospital stay for a medical patient is eight days, and the average medical patient generates $2280 in revenues. The average surgical patient is in the hospital five days and receives a $1515 bill. The laboratory is capable of handling 15,000 tests per year more than it *was* handling. The average medical patient requires 3.1 lab tests and the average surgical patient takes 2.6 lab tests. Furthermore, the average medical patient uses one x-ray, while the average surgical patient requires two x-rays. If the hospital were expanded by 90 beds, the x-ray department could handle up to 7000 x-rays without significant additional cost. Finally, the administration estimates that up to 2800 additional operations could be performed in existing operating room facilities. Medical patients, of course, require no surgery, while each surgical patient generally has one surgery performed.

Formulate this problem so as to determine how many medical beds and how many surgical beds should be added in order to maximize revenues. Assume that the hospital is open 365 days per year.

16.13 South Central Utilities has just announced the August 1 opening of its second nuclear generator at its Baton Rouge, Louisiana, nuclear power plant. Its personnel department has been directed to determine how many nuclear technicians need to be hired and trained over the remainder of the year.

The plant currently employs 350 fully trained

technicians and projects the following manpower needs:

Month	Manpower Needed (in hours)
August	40,000
September	45,000
October	35,000
November	50,000
December	45,000

By Louisiana law, a reactor employee can actually work no more than 130 hours per month. (Slightly over one hour per day is used for check-in and check-out record keeping and for daily radiation health scans.) Policy at South Central Utilities also dictates that layoffs are not acceptable in those months when the nuclear plant is overstaffed. So, if more trained employees are available than are needed in any month, each worker is still fully paid, even though he or she is not required to work the 130 hours. Training new employees is an important and costly procedure. It takes one month of one-on-one classroom instruction before a new technician is permitted to work alone in the reactor facility. Therefore, South Central must hire trainees one month before they are actually needed. Each trainee teams up with a skilled nuclear technician and requires 90 hours of that employee's time, meaning that 90 hours less of the technician's time are available that month for actual reactor work.

Personnel department records indicate a turnover rate of trained technicians at 5 percent per month. In other words, about 5 percent of the skilled employees at the start of any month resign by the end of that month.

A trained technician earns an average monthly salary of $2000 (regardless of the number of hours worked, as noted earlier). Trainees are paid $900 during their one month of instruction.

a. Formulate this staffing problem using LP.

b. Solve the problem. How many trainees must begin each month?

READING 16.1

United Airlines Station Manpower Planning System Using Linear Programming

Thomas J. Holloran ■ Judson E. Byrn

In 1982, upper management of United Airlines initiated the station manpower planning project as part of cost-control measures associated with the airline's 1983–1984 expansion. Expanded flight schedules and increased passenger volumes would require substantial planning to control labor costs and still maintain desired customer service levels.

A manpower planning group was established directly under United's senior vice president of corporate services. The group targeted for attention those airports and reservations offices where work loads would be greatly increased by expansion. In a single month of 1984, for example, United would add 67 departures to its operation at Chicago's O'Hare Airport.

PROBLEM DEVELOPMENT

Historically, shift schedules at airports and reservations offices were prepared by hand. The coverage for each half-hour period was based either on the shift's peak requirement during the week or on its average requirement over the week. Peak-based schedules were costly and left employees underutilized on nonpeak workdays. On the other hand, schedules based on the average failed to provide adequate coverage on peak days. While workload patterns differ from one day of the week to the next, both processes staffed to a "representative" day.

Shift scheduling problems like United's have been solved by using integer and linear programming techniques to solve single-day models. Full work schedules including days off and schedule period transitions are then handled separately. The size implications of combining daily and weekly scheduling are formidable. In average schedules,

United's airports and reservations offices have combinations of shift types, starting times, lunch and break assignment times, and days off which result in an integer LP matrix containing over 20,000 activities (variables) and millions of matrix elements (coefficients). Using only IBM's MPSX and MIP/370 optimization software, the Station Manpower Planning System combines both daily and weekly scheduling into a single model.

STATION MANPOWER PLANNING SYSTEM (SMPS)

SMPS is accessed through United's time-sharing computer system and is available at virtually all United operating locations. SMPS requires no sophisticated knowledge of computers or mathematics to operate. Local schedulers at airports, reservations offices, and field offices, as well as corporate planning groups, have been trained to use SMPS.

The first work schedules developed by SMPS were not accepted with enthusiasm. Although they were economically optimal, they did not incorporate other considerations deemed essential by reservations managers. Whether these other considerations were in fact important (and many were not) was not the point; rather, the perception that these considerations were ignored became the central issue. The cardinal rule for earning the trust and respect of operating managers and support staffs—"getting them involved in the development process"—had been violated.

Subsequent reservations work schedules were developed with substantially increased user participation, thereby overcoming this resistance. In the process we realized that SMPS needed to be

Source: Reprinted by permission of Thomas Holloran and Judson Byrn, "United Airlines Station Manpower Planning System," *Interfaces*, Vol. 16, No. 1 (January–February 1986), pp. 39–50. Copyright 1986 The Institute of Management Sciences, 290 Westminster Street, Providence, Rhode Island 02903 USA.

more flexible. Satisfying the group culture at each office was essential in garnering field support. As a result, office-specified input variables, such as the number of start times, the preferred shift lengths, the length of breaks, preferred days off combinations, and so forth, became an integral part of SMPS. This versatility gave office managers the luxury of evaluating schedules incorporating different input parameters but identical manpower requirements.

BENEFITS

The SMPS has been an overwhelming success at United. Benefits it has provided include

— Significant labor cost savings
— Improved customer service
— Improved employee schedules
— Quantified manpower planning and evaluation

In addition, while SMPS is currently used to schedule around 4000 employees on a regular basis, it will eventually be used to schedule up to 10,000 employees (20 percent of United's work force).

United's key operations managers believe that the intangible benefits of SMPS may outweigh the tangible cost savings. This is particularly apparent in the area of improved customer service. Recently,

at United's eastern regional station manager's meeting, one manager described the model to the gathering as "magical, . . . just as the (customer) lines begin to build, someone shows up for work; and just as you begin to think you're overstaffed, people start going home."

Operating managers and United's stockholders are not the only ones to benefit from the SMPS. Many employees want part-time work in reservations offices and airports and prefer to work less hours than had usually been required by the manually developed schedules. New short tours were scheduled by SMPS and, in combination with United's 1983–1984 expansion, the result was that all labor cost savings were attained without layoffs or other forced employee reductions.

In the course of 18 months, use of SMPS has completely changed United's perception and approach to scheduling manpower. SMPS has introduced new scheduling practices at airports and reservations offices without disrupting operations or personnel relations.

——— QUESTIONS FOR READING 16.1

1. Why was the new scheduling system needed?

2. Why is it important for local managers to have input into a model such as SMPS?

——— CASE 16.1 ———————————

Northwest General Hospital

Northwest General, a large hospital in Providence, R.I., has initiated a new procedure to ensure that patients receive their meals while the food is still as hot as possible. The hospital will continue to prepare the food in its kitchen, but will now deliver it in bulk (not individual servings) to one of three new serving stations in the building. From there, the food will be reheated, meals will be placed on individual trays, loaded onto a cart, and distributed to the various floors and wings of the hospital.

The three new serving stations are as efficiently located as possible to reach the various hallways in the hospital. The number of trays that each station can serve are as follows:

Location	Capacity (meals)
Station 5A	200
Station 3G	225
Station 1S	275

——— EXHIBIT 16–14 ———————————————————————————————————

From	To					
	Wing 1	Wing 2	Wing 3	Wing 4	Wing 5	Wing 6
Station 5A	12	11	8	9	6	6
Station 3G	6	12	7	7	5	8
Station 1S	8	9	6	6	7	9

There are six wings to Northwest General that must be served. The number of patients in each follows:

Wing	Patients
1	80
2	120
3	150
4	210
5	60
6	80

The purpose of the new procedure is to increase the temperature of the hot meals that the patient receives. Therefore, the amount of time needed to deliver a tray from a serving station will determine the proper distribution of food from serving station to wing. Exhibit 16–14 summarizes the distribution time (in minutes) associated with each possible distribution channel.

——— QUESTION FOR CASE 16.1

What is your recommendation for handling the distribution of trays from the three serving stations?

——— CASE 16.2 ———————————————————————————————————————

Schank Marketing Research

Schank Marketing Research has just signed contracts to conduct studies for four clients. At present, three project managers are free for assignment to the tasks. Although all are capable of handling each assignment, the times and costs to complete the studies depend on the experience and knowledge of each manager. Using his judgment, John Schank, the president, has been able to establish a cost for each possible assignment. These costs, which are really the salaries each manager would draw on each task, are summarized as follows:

Project Manager	Client			
	Hines Corp.	NASA	General Foundry	CBT Television
Gardener	$3200	$3000	$2800	$2900
Ruth	2700	3200	3000	3100
Hardgraves	1900	2100	3300	2100

Source: From Barry Render and Ralph M. Stair, *Quantitative Analysis for Management,* 3rd Ed., p. 539. Copyright © 1990 by Allyn and Bacon. Reprinted with permission.

Schank is very hesitant about neglecting NASA, which has been an important customer in the past. (NASA has employed the firm to study the public's attitude toward the Space Shuttle and proposed Space Station.) In addition, Schank has promised to try to provide Ruth a salary of at least $3000 on his next assignment. From previous contracts, Schank also knows that Gardener does not get along well with the management at CBT Television, so he hopes to avoid assigning her to CBT. Finally, as Hines Corporation is also an old and valued client, Schank feels it is twice as important to immediately assign a project manager to Hines' task as it is to provide one to General Foundry, a brand new client. Schank wants to minimize the total costs of all projects while considering each of these goals. He feels that all these

goals are important, but if he had to rank them, he would put his concern about NASA first, his worry about Gardener second, his need to keep Hines Corporation happy third, his promise to Ruth fourth, and his concern about minimizing all costs last.

Each project manager can handle, at most, one new client.

QUESTIONS FOR CASE 16.2

1. If Schank were not concerned about noncost goals, how would he formulate this problem so that it could be solved quantitatively?

2. Develop a formulation that will incorporate all five objectives.

REFERENCES

Anderson, A. M., and Earle, M. D. "Diet Planning in the Third World by Linear and Goal Programming," *Journal of Operations Research Society,* Vol. 34 (1983), pp. 9–16.

Balbirer, Sheldon D., and David Shaw. "An Application of Linear Programming to Bank Financial Planning," *Interfaces,* Vol. 11, No. 5 (October 1981), pp. 77–82.

Bres, E. S., D. Burns, A. Charnes, and W. W. Cooper. "A Goal Programming Model for Planning Officer Accessions," *Management Science,* Vol. 26, No. 8 (August 1980), pp. 773–781.

Brosch, Lee C., Richard J. Buck, William H. Sparrow, and James R. White. "Boxcars, Linear Programming and the Sleeping Kitten," *Interfaces,* Vol. 10, No. 6 (December 1980), pp. 53–61.

Buffa, Frank P., and Wade M. Jackson. "A Goal Programming Model for Purchasing Planning," *Journal of Purchasing and Material Management* (Fall 1983), pp. 27–34.

DeKluyver, Cornelis A., and Herbert Moskowitz. "Assessing Scenario Probabilities Via Interactive Goal Programming," *Management Science,* Vol. 30. No. 3 (March 1984), pp. 273–278.

Holloran, Thomas, and Judson Byrn. "United Airlines Stationed Manpower Planning System," *Interfaces,* Vol. 16, No. 1 (January–February 1986), pp. 39–50.

Ignizio, J. P. *Goal Programming and Extensions.* Lexington, Mass.: D. C. Heath, 1976.

Jackson, Bruce L., and John M. Brown. "Using LP for Crude Oil Sales at Elk Hills," *Interfaces,* Vol. 10, No. 3 (June 1980), pp. 65–70.

Jones, Lawrence, and N. K. Kwak. "A Goal Programming Model for Allocation of Human Resources for the Good Laboratory Practice Regulations," *Decision Sciences,* Vol. 13. No. 1 (1982), pp. 156–166.

Lee, S. M. *Goal Programming for Decision Analysis.* Philadelphia: Auerbach Publishers, 1972.

Lee, Sang M., and Marc J. Schniederjans. "A Multicriterial Assignment Problem: A Goal Programming Approach," *Interfaces,* Vol. 13, No. 4 (August 1983), pp. 75–79.

Leff, H. Stephen, Maqbool Dada, and Stephen C. Graves. "An LP Planning Model for a Mental Health Community Support System," *Management Science,* Vol. 32, No. 2 (February 1986), pp. 139–155.

Marsten, Roy E., and Michael R. Muller. "A Mixed Integer Programming Approach to Air Cargo Fleet Planning," *Management Science,* Vol. 26, No. 11 (November 1980), pp. 1096–1107.

Render, Barry, and Ralph M. Stair. *Quantitative Analysis for Management,* 3d Ed. Boston: Allyn and Bacon, 1988.

Ruth, R. Jean. "A Mixed Integer Programming Model for Regional Planning of a Hospital Inpatient Service," *Management Science,* Vol. 27, No. 5 (May 1981), pp. 521–533.

Schniederjans, Marc J., N. K. Kwak, and Mark C. Helmer. "An Application of Goal Programming to Resolve a Site Location Problem," *Interfaces,* Vol. 12, No. 3 (June 1982), pp. 65–72.

Taylor, B. W., et al. "An Integer Nonlinear Goal Programming Model for the Deployment of State Highway Patrol Units," *Management Science,* Vol. 31, No. 11 (November 1985), pp. 1335–1347.

Tingley, Kim M., and Judith S. Liebmen. "A Goal Programming Example in Public Health Resource Allocation," *Management Science,* Vol. 30, No. 3 (March 1984), pp. 279–289.

INTRODUCTION

Marketing is the analysis, planning, and implementation of carefully formulated programs designed to communicate with and satisfy an organization's target market. The marketing of *services,* as distinct from the marketing of products, is receiving increased attention from marketing scholars and practitioners. This change in emphasis is due to many factors other than the obvious growth of the service economy.

With the deregulation of such industries as airlines, trucking, financial services, and telecommunications, marketing strategies are needed to address issues previously under government control, such as service offerings, pricing, and promotion. With new competitors entering the marketplace, markets for some firms are narrowing and becoming increasingly segmented. For others, market opportunities are rapidly expanding.

Marketing has lost its negative connotation for professional services, as demonstrated by the fact that many of the professions have dropped their restrictions on advertising. In addition, the overabundance of professional services, health care services, and hospitality services has significantly increased the level of competition in these industries, has intensified marketing efforts, and has led to service specialization for focused markets.

New technologies, especially in information processing, have given rise to new service concepts. Marketing is needed to communicate these new concepts to the customer and educate the public on how to use them (ATMs, for example). Finally, the increasing number of women in the work force, changing family structures, and the aging of the U.S. population are examples of some of the social changes that have precipitated the marketing of new services or refocused the marketing of existing services.

Many issues currently discussed in the field of services marketing—such as service design, service delivery, and service quality—have previously been addressed in this text. This overlap (or integration) of topics is due to the closeness that the marketing and operations functions enjoy in services. The purpose of this chapter is to explore the integration of marketing and operations, examine the differences between product and services marketing, expand the traditional marketing mix to incorporate service-oriented concerns, discuss consumer behavior in services, and consider the specialized case of marketing professional services.

INTEGRATION OF MARKETING AND OPERATIONS

Neither marketing nor operations should dominate the service function. They should, in fact, be balanced and supportive of one another. Consider the following example of a service that was guilty of **undermarketing** by failing to properly position itself in its market.[1]

---

[1] Excerpted from Penny Merliss and Christopher Lovelock, ''Health System, Inc.,'' a case study at Harvard Business School, 1980.

Health Systems, Inc., was founded in 1970 by Robert DeVore, an architect, and Robert Bland, a venture capitalist, who had been classmates at college. DeVore and Bland were convinced that project and operating cost models and elaborate forecasting could be applied to public and nonprofit health care projects as well as private-sector construction. Health Systems, Inc., was organized to offer design, engineering, construction, and financial expertise in a single package; unfortunately, such broad positioning resulted in a severe competitive handicap, since HSI, which was not a contractor, found itself competing against both architects and contractors for jobs. As DeVore himself remarked, describing the company's early struggles: "We made the classical marketing error of running in twenty different directions at twenty different times."

Typical of these early days was a project management job for a hospital in Vero Beach, Florida. The stakes were high: a $10,000 job at a time when the company's total annual income was about $40,000. HSI threw all its resources into the proposal and came out second best. Afterward, the chairman of the board of trustees commented frankly to DeVore: "We know you boys can do a better job. But if I pick you, and you fail, I'll be killed for giving the job to a small, unknown firm. If the other guys fail, no one can blame us for choosing them."

In desperation, DeVore and Bland decided to reposition HSI. Rather than competing for projects at major medical centers across the nation, they decided to concentrate on the design and construction of doctors' office buildings and ambulatory care (outpatient) centers in the Northeast, an area they knew well. Their reasoning was that a small company could defeat the "big boys" for small jobs by putting its best people into the project and assimilating more information about the client's needs, objectives, and environment than large competitors were willing to pursue for a proposal. Almost immediately the new strategy paid off, as HSI won contracts for medical office buildings in Marlborough, Massachusetts, and Rochester, New York, defeating much larger design firms.

Undermarketing is a common problem in services, but a firm can make the mistake of **overmarketing,** too. Overmarketing occurs when a firm spends so much time and money on the marketing function that it jeopardizes the operations on which marketing claims are based. That's what happened in this example.[2]

The major objective of a particular management consulting firm was to achieve rapid billings growth. The firm's management developed a long-range plan incorporating strong marketing activity. Marketing was recognized as a firm-wide activity. Staff personnel were expected to work on expanding services to existing clients. Officers were expected to develop new clients and to close sales leads initiated by the staff. The entire program was under the personal direction of the president.

There was a carefully planned and vigorous program for building referral sources. Frequent meetings were held to coordinate and plan new business development activities. A public relations consultant was retained to obtain favorable newspaper and trade paper publicity. Every effort was made to motivate new business development activity. Staff personnel received bonuses for successful leads. Ability to generate new business was

---

[2] From Philip Kotler and Paul Bloom, *Marketing Professional Services* (Englewood Cliffs, N.J.: Prentice-Hall, 1984), pp. 161–162.

made a significant element in promotion. Officers' compensation was based almost entirely on the volume and rate of growth of the client assignments under their supervision.

This program initially produced outstanding results. In two years, annual fee billings had risen to over $12 million from offices located in six major cities. However, this represented a high point from which the firm began to decline, at first slowly and then precipitously. As the billings of the firm declined, it fell into disarray. All the branch offices were closed. Several officers resigned to establish their own consulting firms. At the present time, the firm is still in existence but is no longer a major competitor.

What happened? The original objective was for a sustained growth rate of 15 percent a year. This was achieved, but the effort did not leave sufficient time for the acquisition, training, and development of the professional staff. The firm was developing business at a faster rate than its capacity to deliver quality work.

The staff perceived that high awards were given for business development but not for professional excellence. A number of staffers with great professional promise but little interest in selling left the firm to join competitors. In addition, because officers were selected primarily for their ability to develop new business, several lacked the technical background to properly supervise the assignments handled by their staff. Since the difference in compensation between officers and staff was substantial, this led to poor morale and increased turnover. Further, the high financial rewards for new business development led to intense competition and infighting among officers and created an unhealthy atmosphere in the firm.

The firm's decline was not the result of adverse conditions in the marketplace. Rather, it was paying a deferred penalty for long-term overemphasis on hard selling. Having committed itself to rapid growth, it neglected other things. Specifically, it neglected operations.

Marketing and operations in services should be viewed as two sides of the same coin.[3] Some firms, such as Federal Express, have been successful in doing so. Case 17.1 tells the Federal Express story of balance and support between marketing and operations.

DIFFERENCES IN PRODUCT AND SERVICES MARKETING

Goods typically are first produced, then sold, and then consumed. Most services, on the other hand, are first sold, then produced and consumed simultaneously.[4] The location of the selling function (i.e., prior to production) and the inseparability of the production of a service (an operations function) from the consumption of a service (a marketing function) significantly change the role of marketing in a service firm.

---

[3] This is the view of many, but was explicitly stated by Christopher Lovelock of Harvard Business School. See Christopher Lovelock, *Managing Services: Marketing, Operations, and Human Resources* (Englewood Cliffs, N.J.: Prentice-Hall, 1988).

[4] This idea was first put forth by W. J. Regan, "The Service Revolution," *Journal of Marketing*, Vol. 27 (July 1963), pp. 57–62.

This difference is verified by marketing managers who have transferred from goods-producing firms to service-performing firms. Reading 17.1 is an excerpt from an interview with a marketing executive who made the switch from product to services marketing and survived.

The differences between product and services marketing may be viewed in terms of

— Output tangibility
— Organizational features
— Ownership, use, and consumption
— The scope of marketing activities
— The consumer's role
— Advances in marketing

Tangibility

In several chapters throughout this text we have discussed the difficulties in dealing with the intangible nature of services. The problem is no less serious for the marketing of intangibles. In fact, the greater the presence of intangible elements in a service, the greater will be the divergence from product marketing principles and approaches.[5]

For example, consumer product marketing attempts to enhance a physical object through abstract association. Coca-Cola is associated with authenticity and youth. Dr. Pepper suggests originality and risk-taking. 7-Up is light, clean, and buoyant. Tangible products are given intangible images.

For service marketing, however, the opposite strategy should be used. Services are already intangible. Abstractions are not needed. What the marketer can do is provide tangible evidence as to the reality of the service. Thus an investment management service described in terms of "sound analysis," "careful portfolio monitoring," and "strong research capability" does not achieve the credibility or the customer draw of Merrill Lynch's bull charging through an advertisement. Other good examples of making the intangible tangible can be found in the insurance industry.

- "You're in good *hands* with Allstate."
- "I've got a piece of the *rock.*"
- "Under the Traveler's *umbrella.*"
- "Nationwide's *blanket* of protection."

Firms with a mixture of product and service offerings can follow a mixed marketing strategy. McDonald's, for instance, markets its food product as *nutritious* (two all-beef patties, etc.), *fun* (Ronald McDonald), and *helpful* ("We Do It All For You," "You Deserve a Break Today," etc.). Its service, in contrast, is marketed through a tangible uniformity of environment, including color, style of graphics, apparel, and those golden arches.

---

[5] This view is strongly expressed in G. Lynn Shostack, "Breaking Free From Product Marketing," *Journal of Marketing* (April 1977), pp. 73–80. Many of the examples in this section are from the Shostack article.

—— EXHIBIT 17–1 ——————————————————————

- *Organizational versus Informal Marketing*

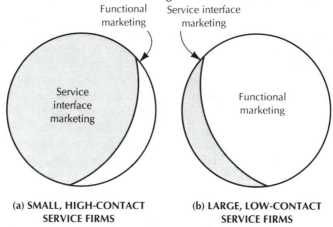

(a) SMALL, HIGH-CONTACT
SERVICE FIRMS

(b) LARGE, LOW-CONTACT
SERVICE FIRMS

Organizational Features

In product firms, manufacturing personnel are not normally engaged in marketing the products, except in rare cases of custom-made items. The marketing department is a separate department within the company. In contrast, any service that has personal contact with the customer conducts marketing activities as it provides the service. In addition, many services companies, particularly the larger ones, have a separate marketing department that carries out traditional marketing functions. These two marketing components may be identified respectively as *service interface marketing* (SIM) and *functional marketing* (FM).

In Exhibit 17–1, the contrast between the marketing of high-contact services (i.e., personal services) and low-contact services (i.e., impersonal or mass services) is depicted. In personal services, the marketing organization may be small or nonexistent. The owner-manager may perform these promotional activities informally on a part-time basis. Service interface marketing is more predominant. For impersonal services, such as utilities and credit card systems, as well as for manufacturing companies, the formal marketing department carries out practically all marketing activities. Marketing is well established in the organizational structure.

The need for the integration of marketing and operations in services has already been suggested. To formalize this integration, several researchers have promoted the idea of reorganizing service firms so that marketing, human resources, and operations can work more closely together.[6]

---

[6] See Christian Gronroos, ''Innovative Marketing Strategies and Organization Structures for Service Firms,'' in *Emerging Prospectives on Services Marketing,* Proceedings of the 1983 Conference on Services Marketing (Chicago: American Marketing Association, 1983); and Christopher H. Lovelock, *Managing Services: Marketing, Operations and Human Resources* (Englewood Cliffs, N.J.: Prentice-Hall, 1988).

Ownership, Use, and Consumption

In manufacturing companies, the firm is essentially selling a product, even though the promotional technique may imply a service. For example, IBM does not picture itself as selling hardware but rather a system that is a service to the customer. Perfume firms don't emphasize the perfume as a product but rather as a producer of fantasies.

For services, the central item in the marketing transaction is always the service itself. Even in embedded services, it is the service, not the package, that is more important. If the service is immaterial to the package, then the transaction item is a product. There are many different options in owning, using, and consuming services.

We may purchase a service and own the service, as in the case of an airline ticket, an insurance policy, or a pension plan. Alternatively, we may obtain *use* of a service for limited time periods. For example, we may borrow a book from a library, rent a videotape, or buy a ticket to enter Disney World. In other words, the basic service is not purchased by us or consumed by us; it is merely lent to us. Finally, we may purchase a service for consumption as the service is produced—a meal, a boat trip, a movie showing, or an appliance repair. These different consumption options present additional opportunities for services marketing.

Scope of Marketing Activities

The *scope* of marketing activities is defined by a basic marketing concept called **marketing mix.** An organization's marketing mix consists of all the variables that are controllable by the organization in communicating with and satisfying its target market.

The traditional, goods-oriented marketing mix can be categorized into four elements: product, price, place, and promotion. With some adjustment, these elements are important to service marketing as well. However, there are other variables in the service environment that can be controlled and coordinated to communicate with and satisfy service customers.[7] These include the service employee, the physical environment in which the service is provided, and the service process itself. Thus the four P's of product marketing currently incorporated in the marketing mix need to be expanded to the seven P's for services to include

— *Participants* (employees and customers)
— *Physical evidence* (building, uniforms, and other tangible evidence)
— *Process* (the actual procedures and flow of activities involved in providing the service)

This expanded marketing mix for services is discussed in more detail later in the chapter.

---

[7] This discussion of expanded product mix is adapted from M. J. Bitner and V. A. Zeithaml, "Fundamentals in Services Marketing," in *Proceedings of the 1988 Conference on Services Marketing* (Chicago: American Marketing Association, 1989), pp. 7–11. The original idea for an expanded marketing mix appeared in B. H. Booms and M. J. Bitner, "Marketing Strategies and Organization Structures for Service Firms," in *Marketing of Services,* Proceedings of the 1981 Conference in Services Marketing (Chicago: American Marketing Association, 1983), pp. 47–52.

The Consumer's Role

Consumer behavior is a more difficult process to study for services than for products because the customer may be involved in the service process itself. In addition, since consumer purchasing and consumption of the service may occur simultaneously, consumer behavior *during* the service encounter must also be considered.

Consumers evaluate services differently from products. Most goods are relatively easy to evaluate because we can base our evaluations mainly on visible, touchable, quantifiable qualities that can be searched *prior* to purchase and back up our evaluations with the qualities we experience *after* purchase. Most services, however, are more difficult to evaluate because we base our evaluations on qualities we experience and even on some qualities that we believe are present in the service but of which we cannot be sure. We can thus categorize product or service qualities as[8]

- *Search qualities*—attributes that a consumer can determine prior to purchasing a product or service, such as color, style, price, fit, feel, hardness, and smell
- *Experience qualities*—attributes that can only be determined after purchase or during consumption, such as taste, wearability, and purchase satisfaction
- *Credence qualities*—attributes that the consumer may be unaware of or lack the technical knowledge to evaluate even after consumption, such as appendix operations and brake relinings

Exhibit 17–2 views consumer evaluations of goods and services on a continuum from easy to evaluate to difficult to evaluate and includes the three quality categories.

Marketing of experience qualities and credence qualities is a more difficult task than marketing search qualities. These different evaluative qualities also imply that prepurchase and postpurchase behavior of service consumers may differ from product consumers. The need for marketing activities may actually be greater after the purchase of a service than *before* the purchase!

Advances in Marketing

In discussing the differences between product and service marketing, we have suggested that the marketing of services is a more complicated task, involves more interrelationships, and includes a broader marketing mix than the marketing of products. Unfortunately, the current level of marketing expertise in most service firms is much lower than in product firms, and the marketing concept is narrower. Viewing marketing in broad terms as being responsible for all the factors that ensure customer satisfaction is radically different and will produce different results from the predominant view of marketing in services as primarily advertising and selling.

Market research is different for services, too. The service marketer usually has

---

[8] This material is adapted from V. A. Zeithaml, "How Consumer Evaluation Processes Differ Between Goods and Services," in *Marketing of Services,* Proceedings of the 1981 Conference on Services Marketing (Chicago: American Marketing Association, 1981), pp. 186–190.

___ EXHIBIT 17–2 _____

■ *Continuum of Consumer Evaluation of Goods and Services*

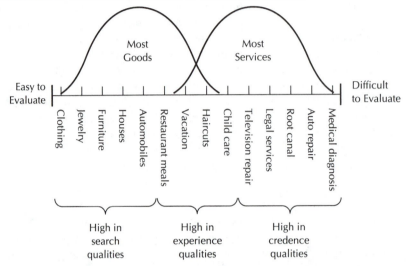

Source: Valarie A. Zeithaml, "How Consumer Evaluation Processes Differ Between Goods and Services," in James Donnelly and William George (Eds.), *Marketing of Services,* Proceedings of the 1981 Conference on Services Marketing (Chicago: American Marketing Association, 1981), p. 186. Used with permission.

to undertake more market research than is common in product marketing, and the existing market database may not be as extensive. Further, the data gathered typically have a different orientation. The service marketer must acquire a high tolerance for subjective, "soft" data, combined with a rigidly objective attitude toward analyzing those data. Also, the tools and skills of the marketer may rely more heavily on psychology and other behavioral sciences.[9]

MARKETING MIX

As presented earlier, the marketing mix for services consists of seven elements: product (service), price, place, physical evidence, participants, promotion, and process. These elements and examples of their activities are shown in Exhibit 17–3. We will now discuss each element.

Product (Service)

The "product" element of marketing mix for services refers to the variety and depth of *services* offered within a particular service area. It is concerned with the matching

_____

[9] From G. L. Shostack, "Breaking Free From Product Marketing," *Journal of Marketing,* Vol. 41 (April 1977), p. 42.

—— EXHIBIT 17–3 ——————————————————

■ *The Marketing Mix for Services*

Product (Service)	*Physical Evidence*
Target markets	External appearance of the site
Services	Internal appearance and ambiance
Service level	Appearance of employees
Rent, lease, or sell	Credentials of employees
After-sales service	Equipment
Warranties	Materials
Price	*Participation*
Rent, lease, or sell	Interpersonal behavior
Structure and time	Skills
Discounts	Attitudes
Payment terms	Commitment
Flexibility	Discretion used
Customer's perceived value	Frequency of customer contacts
Place	Duration of customer contacts
Location	Selling activities
Accessibility	Training
Channels of distribution	*Process*
Distribution coverage	Customer needs and wants
Promotion	Customer involvement
Advertising	Demand control
Publicity	Quality control
Public relations	Customer followup
Selling by salespeople	Policies and procedures
Selling by service providers	Flow of activities
Employee training in customer relations	

of services to target markets. The quality of service to be supplied is determined by market demand and competitive positioning. Also part of this element are the performance specifications of rent, lease, or sell; after-sales service; and warranties. Much of the material discussed in Chapter 4 on service design is relevant to this aspect of marketing mix.

Price

Pricing policy is much more complex for services than for products. To manage demand, the price for the same service may be different for different times of the day (at theaters) or seasons of the year (for resorts). Price may be scaled to match the steps of a service versus the entire service (upper body massage versus total body massage). Discounts for services tend to be promotional, whereas product discounts may be promotional, volume-oriented, and trade-oriented.

The price of a service must be adjusted to reflect whether the service is rented, leased, or sold. The decision concerning whether service should be rented, leased, or sold depends greatly on the type of service. For example, a movie ticket is sold because the price is low and nobody is likely to lease the theater and film for one person. On

------ EXHIBIT 17–4 ------

▪ *A Sample of Pricing Practices in Services*

Professional/Consultants	*Education*
Retainer	Tuition
Hourly and daily rate	Salary/wage
Per consultation	Honorarium
Fixed fee per job	Fee
Contingency fee	Admission
Cost plus fixed fee	Registration fee
Insurance/Finance	*Miscellaneous Services*
Per service	Fare
Commissions	Subscription
Charge	Membership fee
Premium	Initiation fee
Retail/Wholesale	Toll
Odd number pricing ($3.95, $1.99)	Tariff
Discount pricing	Trade differential
Price lining (limited set of prices)	
Promotional pricing (cents off, coupons)	
Loss leader pricing	
Trade discounts	
Volume discounts	

the other hand, the theater and personnel might be rented for a day to a group. Leasing is more typical of an intermediary in a channel of distribution such as a franchised restaurant or laundromat. Pricing for a lease is a longer-term decision and is not as simple as a short-term admission sale.

A complex pricing structure may be illustrated by club memberships. There may be a general membership fee, a golf membership fee, a tennis membership fee, and so on. Memberships for off-season or off-times also may be offered. Other optional pricing practices are listed in Exhibit 17–4.

For services, pricing not only affects the level of customer demand, but also sends a message to customers concerning their expectations of a service.[10] This is especially important for intangible and professional services. And because price is an indicator of value, service firms typically use factors other than the cost of a service to set prices.

Federal Express provides a good example of a service pricing strategy.[11] The pricing decisions at Federal are worked out jointly between the marketing staff and the corporate financial staff. The trick is to set prices at a high enough level to protect company profit margins while at the same time making absolutely certain that the

---

[10] See V. A. Zeithaml, "How Consumer Evaluation Processes Differ Between Goods and Services," in *Marketing of Services,* Proceedings of the 1981 Conference on Services Marketing (Chicago: American Marketing Association, 1981), pp. 186–190.

[11] This example is taken from Sigafoos, R. A., and R. R. Easson, *Absolutely, Positively Overnight!* (Memphis, Tenn.: St. Luke's Press, 1988), p. 154.

company is not pricing itself out of the market. Marketing strategy must then convince customers that Federal Express charges the prices it does because it is rendering a superior type of service.

Place

Place basically refers to the location and distribution of services. Some services are delivered right to the home or business. Such delivery may be optional, such as in the case of a music teacher or a business consultant. In other services, delivery is essential, such as for cleaning a house or servicing a pool. The decision to bring a customer to a fixed location or the service to the customer depends on the market for each type of service, the price, the cost, and the competition.

Services may be transportable, location-bound, or a combination, depending on the degree to which the service or parts of it may be separated from its production. [12] Thus a computer database service may serve anyone anywhere there are telephone lines. On the other hand, a restaurant is location-bound, although a franchised chain reduces this limitation somewhat. A financial service may require local representatives, but the major part of the service production may be performed anywhere. Channels of distribution for services include agents (insurance) and franchises (U-Haul, restaurants).

As discussed in Chapter 6, the location decision is extremely important for a service firm because accessibility can ultimately determine whether a service succeeds or fails. Is it true that the three most important elements for success in a service business are location, location, and location? It seems so in the following example of two Philadelphia lawyers who run a legal service center. [13]

> After three and one-half years in operation, with more than 20,000 clients, lawyers Peter Levin and Steven Arkans decided they needed a new branch office.
>
> They leased a big recreational vehicle, spent $4000 to put in carpets and a desk, and sent their newly created mobile law office into shopping centers. "We had reservations as to how the public would receive it," Mr. Levin said. "But the reaction has been unbelievably good. When the van is right there when people are shopping, they don't have any hesitancy about knocking on the door."
>
> The overhead on the van is about $1500 a week, not counting gas. In the first two weeks the mobile office handled 25 clients, who could pay by MasterCharge or Visa. "There's no mystery about how much the fees will be, because they are clearly posted right on the outside of the van," said Mr. Arkans. An uncontested divorce goes for $245 plus costs, a will runs $45, a real estate settlement costs $245, and a first arrest for drunk driving costs $245.
>
> The mobile office location schedule will vary until client demands set a more permanent one.

---

[12] See J. J. Boddewyn, Marsha Baldwin Halbrich, and A. C. Perry, "Service Multinationals: Conceptualization, Measurement, and Theory," *Journal of International Business Studies* (Fall 1986).

[13] Adapted from *National Law Journal* (February 16, 1981), p. 39.

Physical Evidence

Physical evidence is an important element of the marketing mix because the customer is usually in contact with at least some part of the service production facilities, equipment, and personnel. In addition, since services are intangible and thus difficult to evaluate, physical evidence provides clues as to service quality. A simple example is the "gold" credit card that promotes a superior package of credit services. The grade of paper and print, form, and language of letters and statements also affect the perception of service quality. Similarly, credentials indicated by diplomas hung on the wall or certification initials in advertisements are physical evidence of service quality.

Airlines are well known for their ability to create service identity through consistency in the decor of their planes, their graphics, their advertising, and their uniforms. As another example, Fred Smith of Federal Express does not want anyone to have a neutral reaction to the brazen purple, orange, and white emblem on his planes, delivery trucks, and advertising material. He also stresses personal grooming of his employees—cleancut, no beards, no trendy hairstyles. Even the selection of courier uniforms is a major corporate event.[14]

Physical evidence adds substance to the service concept. Service marketers should therefore be involved in the design, planning, and control of such physical evidence.

Participants

Participants refers to any and all people who play a role in the service encounter. This includes both employees and other customers. The attitudes and actions of employees can certainly affect the success of a service encounter. It is also likely that the behavior of other customers, in a movie theater, restaurant, or classroom, can affect an individual's service experience.

Employee behavior must be strongly customer-oriented in services. Employees in contact with the customers should truly be considered salespeople. Throughout its development, AT&T has been noted for the friendliness of its telephone operators. Florida Power & Light is another example of a company where the employees do their utmost to answer queries and assist customers. In contrast, most of us have had contact with uncaring sales people, rude service people, and discourteous managers.

In services, marketing is everyone's job. Thus it is important to have employees with the skills, attitudes, commitment, and ability to use discretion in dealing with customers. Sometimes employees are even called on to subdue unruly or out-of-place customers so that the service experience may remain positive for the rest of the customers.

Promotion

Services utilize the traditional methods of **promotion,** including advertising, publicity, sales promotion, and personal selling. However, because of the interactive and intangible

---

[14] R. A. Sigafoos and R. R. Easson, *Absolutely, Positively Overnight!* (Memphis, Tenn.: St. Luke's Press, 1988), p. 154.

nature of services, there are some differences in how promotions are carried out. Reading 17.2 provides an example of promotion in a professional service.

Determining a message content for a promotion is more difficult in services. Tangible clues of service quality are needed. Customer expectations have to be determined and put into words. Personal selling is by far the most commonly used promotion for services. Everyone in the organization who has contact with the customer "sells" the service. Employees must be trained in customer relations to promote the service while the service process is on-going.

Nordstrom, the highly successful retailer that we discussed in Chapters 9 and 14, does little advertising. The money it saves goes into employee training, which, in turn, improves service quality and increases its word-of-mouth reputation.

An important part of service promotion takes place *after* the sale and delivery of the service. Since many services are dependent on repeat business, maintaining relationships with existing customers is important. "Reselling" service benefits, customizing services, rewarding existing customers with special attention or promotions, and quickly and effectively resolving problems are all part of the after-sale marketing activities known as **relationship marketing.**[15]

Process

A major objective of marketing is to identify the needs and wants in the marketplace, so that the service may be designed to fulfill these needs. This includes the design of the service **process** and how the service is delivered. Ultimately, it reflects how all the marketing mix elements are coordinated to provide consistent, quality service for the customer.

Poor attention to the service process leads to poor service quality. Overworked salesclerks, whose jobs include inventory management, difficult paperwork, sales-floor maintenance, and many other operational tasks, cannot be expected to respond warmly and proactively to customers. The system does not allow them to do so, nor reward them for doing so. Speed, not interaction quality, is the prime performance criterion. Bank tellers operate under similar conditions. In these examples, the design of the service process, which dictates the design of the job, does not support service quality.[16]

It is one of marketing's tasks to ensure that the service encounter is a positive one and that service quality is maintained. Thus marketing must be involved in designing the service process and is often involved in, or responsible for, quality control in services.

---

[15] See Theodore Levitt, "After the Sale is Over . . . ," *Harvard Business Review,* Vol. 62, No. 5 (September–October 1983), pp. 87–93; Leonard Berry, "Relationship Marketing," in *Proceedings of the 1983 Conference on Services Marketing* (Chicago: American Marketing Association, 1983), pp. 25–28; and M. J. Bitner and V. A. Zeithaml, "Fundamentals in Services Marketing," in *Proceedings of the 1988 Conference on Services Marketing* (Chicago: American Marketing Association, 1988), pp. 7–11.

[16] This material is from G. L. Shostack, "Planning the Service Encounter," in John Grepiel, Michael Solomon, and Carol Suprenant (Eds.), *The Service Encounter* (Lexington, Mass.: Lexington Books, 1985), pp. 243–253.

CONSUMER BEHAVIOR

Consumer behavior in services can be quite complex because every service encounter is potentially different. Some elements of consumer behavior that have an impact on the marketing of services include

— Time budgeting
— Consumer socialization as a producer
— Dramatic states
— Consumer evaluations of services
— Attitudes towards service alternatives

Time Budgeting

Time budgeting refers to the situation in which consumers make time the major variable in their service selection process. For example, if your car is immobilized, you would certainly like to have the car fixed immediately, not next week. Further, you would like to have it repaired within an hour or the same day rather than leave it for several days. In recent times, the complexity of everyday life has put such demands on our time that we never seem to have enough of it, and time budgeting has become an important decision factor. Thus, in determining consumer needs and wants, service marketers need to take into account time budgeting as an indication of service quality.

Consumer Socialization as Coproducer

Another service trend is that of the consumer as **coproducer** of a service. When self-service gas stations were first introduced, only money-conscious people took advantage of them. Gradually the majority of drivers have been ''socialized'' to save both time and money by serving themselves. This consumer socialization as part of the service process has extended to how a customer evaluates the service he or she has received.

Consumers tend to attribute some of their dissatisfaction with services to their own inability to specify or perform their part of the service. Similarly, due in part to the belief that they themselves may be somewhat responsible for their dissatisfaction, consumers complain less frequently about services than products.[17] A recent study revealed that twenty-six out of every twenty-seven customers who are dissatisfied with the service they received will *not* report it to the service provider.[18]

Dramatic States

A **dramatic state** refers to the development of a ''mental script'' by consumers for often-repeated experiences. Consumers will only be satisfied if the service conforms

---

[17] This hypothesis and the discussion on consumer evaluations and consumer attitudes in the next few sections are based on V. A. Zeithaml, ''How Consumer Evaluation Processes Differ Between Goods and Services,'' in *Marketing of Services,* Proceedings of the 1981 Conference on Services Marketing (Chicago: American Marketing Association, 1981), pp. 186–190.

[18] Tom Peters, *Thriving on Chaos* (New York: Knopf, 1987), p. 91.

to their "script" for that service. The script may be based on their own experiences, their friends' experiences, or expectations from advertising promises and images—one reason that services should not promise more than they can deliver. The quick demise of Holiday Inn's television campaign promising "no surprises" is a case in point. In a company as complex as Holiday Inn, in which thousands of people are involved in the operations of facilities spread throughout the world, surprises, no matter how small, are bound to occur.

Consumer Evaluations

As stated previously, consumers evaluate services differently than they do products. When evaluating services prior to purchase, they seek and rely more on information from personal sources, such as word of mouth, than from nonpersonal sources, such as advertising. Of nonpersonal sources, the main determinants of service quality prior to purchase are price and physical facilities. Plumbing, housecleaning, and lawn care are examples of services of which price may be the only prepurchase indicator of quality. Higher price in this instance indicates higher quality. With other services, such as counseling, legal aid, hair care, and dental services, consumers may evaluate the offices, personnel, equipment, and paraphernalia to assess service quality.

Consumers of services engage in more postpurchase evaluation and information seeking with services than with products. They also engage in more postpurchase evaluation than prepurchase evaluation when selecting and consuming services. This makes sense because many qualities of a service cannot be evaluated until after the service is experienced.

The predominance of postpurchase evaluations, evaluations based on consumer experiences and perceptions, and the reliance on personal recommendations to assess service quality sends a strong signal to service marketers: *Pay attention to the customer throughout the service process and after the service has been completed.* This attention includes

— Communicating information about the service received *during* and *after* the service process (even if the information is highly technical or seems redundant)
— Making sure the customer is satisfied with the service (even if he or she doesn't complain)
— Reducing any dissonance between service expectations and service delivery (even if the service is delivered according to plan by the service provider)

Consumer Attitudes

Consumer attitudes toward services are different from their attitudes toward products. To begin with, the consumer's perceived set of alternatives for services is smaller than for products. This perception may be related to the difficulty in locating, evaluating, and differentiating similar services. For many nonprofessional services, consumers consider self-provision of the service as one alternative. Thus the standards for these services are probably quite high.

Consumers also perceive greater risks when buying services than when buying products. Services tend to be nonstandardized, do not come with warranties, and are difficult to evaluate prior to the service being performed. These uncertainties imply risk.

Perhaps because of the risk involved, consumers adopt innovations more slowly in services than in goods and switch brands less frequently with services than with physical products. These consumer attitudes basically say, "You can't afford mistakes in marketing services." A former vice president at Chase Manhattan puts it this way:[19]

> You can back away from bad product positioning. You've seen it happen. Somebody brings out a cosmetic, prices it at 89 cents and it dies. Take the same formula, charge $1.89, put it in a different package and bring it out again under a different name, and it goes.
>
> You can't do that with a bank. The bank's got the same brand name on everything it sells. That's not to say you can't change a bank's positioning or image. You can. But, it takes longer. For that very reason—the longer time element involved in changing basic consumer perceptions and images of a service business—I think marketing is all the more important to those businesses.

Consumers may be hesitant to complain about a service to the service provider, but not to their friends and neighbors. Customers tell twice as many people about their bad experiences as good ones. Moreover, dissatisfaction with a service may not surface until the consumer has discussed the service experience with other recipients of similar services. On average, unhappy customers will tell nine or ten colleagues about their plight. Thirteen percent of dissatisfied customers will spread the news to twenty or more people.[20] These are disturbing statistics, considering that services are evaluated primarily from personal sources.

Making sure the customer understands what service he or she has received, ensuring that the customer is satisfied, and reconciling any dissatisfaction requires an aggressive program of quality assurance. Chapter 14 discussed quality assurance programs and techniques. One aspect of quality assurance that we will expand on in this chapter is quality feedback in terms of customer complaints.

Customer Complaints

Customer complaints can be a significant source of marketing information for services and can provide opportunities for a marketing edge over competing services. The average return on company dollars invested in handling customer complaints for makers of consumer durables (such as appliances) is 100 percent, for banks as much as 170 percent, and for retailing even higher.[21]

Among shoppers dissatisfied with products or services worth more than $100, over half of those whose complaints are resolved will be return customers and buy

---

[19] Gary Knisely, "Listening to the Consumer in Service Marketing," *Advertising Age* (February 1979), pp. 47–50.

[20] Tom Peters, *Thriving on Chaos* (New York: Knopf, 1987), p. 91.

[21] Patricia Sellers, "How to Handle Customers' Gripes," *Fortune* (October 24, 1988), p. 92.

again. Almost 20 percent will buy again if the company just listens to their complaints! To receive complaints, questions, and suggestions, toll-free 800 numbers are used by over half of U.S. companies with more than $10 million in sales. British Airways goes one step further, by giving disgruntled travelers the opportunity to tape their grievances as soon as they get off the plane in the airline's new Video Point booths.[22]

Personal contact in an increasingly impersonal world can go a long way toward turning critics into supporters. Turning away a complainer by telling him "It's our policy" enrages him. It's the corporate equivalent of the parental response, "Because I said so." A complainer who is denied a request over the phone is 30 percent more likely to remain brand-loyal than a customer who receives the same message in a letter.[23] The owner of Domino's Pizza's top franchise attributes much of his success to calling 100 customers per week. He insists that call-backs be given priority over the shop's nightly accounting closeout. His explanation: "Nobody's ever bought a pie from us because we had a great closeout."[24]

MARKETING PROFESSIONAL SERVICES

The marketing of professional services has long been considered different from the marketing of other services. Exhibit 17–5, based on a study by Hill and Neely,[25] differentiates professional services from generic (i.e., nonprofessional) services on the basis of the consumer decision process. The decision of selecting a professional service includes problem recognition, search process, evaluation of alternatives, choice, use and postpurchase evaluation. Basically, the material in Exhibit 17–5 confirms previous accounts of consumer behavior in services. Where differences exist in consumer behavior between products and services, they also exist between generic services and professional services.

In the past, marketing of many professional services was based mainly on obtaining clients through contacts in social and civic organizations. In recent years, social, economic, and competitive changes have led to much more planned and aggressive marketing by professionals such as lawyers, dentists, architects, consultants, and accountants.

Lawyers, once forbidden from advertising by methods other than listing their names, have been freed from professional constraints by court decisions. Now, lawyers appear on TV avidly soliciting accident and malpractice business. Chiropractors advertise their businesses in newspapers, often offering free consultations. Other professionals send mailings and proposals. The new "deregulation" opens the door for sophisticated marketing programs using tasteful advertising and pricing policies.

Law and medical professions, among others, have become overcrowded. Those willing to press to the limits in advertising, pricing, and service put pressure on the

---

[22] Patricia Sellers, "How to Handle Customers' Gripes," *Fortune* (October 24, 1988), p. 92.

[23] Patricia Sellers, "How to Handle Customers' Gripes," *Fortune* (October 24, 1988), pp. 92, 96.

[24] Tom Peters, *Thriving on Chaos* (New York: Knopf, 1987), p. 95.

[25] From C. Jeanne Hill, and Sue E. Neeley, "Differences in the Consumer Decision Process for Professional vs. Generic Services," *Journal of Services Marketing* (Winter 1988).

EXHIBIT 17-5

■ *Differences in the Consumer Decision Process for Generic versus Professional Services*

Decision Process	Generic Services	Professional Services
Problem recognition	Buyer defines problem Little (if any) advisor role by provider	Buyer dependent on provider to define problem and advise
Search process	Relatively little willingness to expend effort Sufficient information available Use of advertising Buyer has experience	Willingness to expend great effort Insufficient information available Little use of advertising Buyer uses personal info sources such as referrals
Evaluation of alternatives	Many alternatives to evaluate Relatively easy comparison Evaluative criteria are known	Fewer alternatives to evaluate Difficult comparison Evaluative criteria not known
Choice	Relatively clearcut	More uncertain
Use and postpurchase evaluation	Outcome is uncertain but consequences are minimal "Redo" is possible	Outcome is uncertain but consequences are serious "Redo" may not be possible or desirable

Source: Jeanne C. Hill and Sue E. Neeley, "Differences in the Consumer Decision Process for Professional vs. Generic Services," *Journal of Services Marketing,* (Winter 1988). Used with permission of Grayson Associates, Inc., Santa Barbara, Calif.

more traditional professionals to develop marketing programs. Professions are learning how to specialize for focused markets.

Malpractice suits against doctors, engineers, architects, and lawyers themselves have resulted in a declining public image for these professions. Positive marketing is required for individual professionals to overcome this poor image. A more educated public wants more information before selecting a professional service. Thus marketing communication is replacing secrecy and arrogance among the progressive professions.

More and more, market niches are being carved out so that professional firms are not placebound. Doctors and lawyers may have offices in two cities with planned days in each. Universities may have campuses in several cities and use TV to reach distant cities. The promotion, pricing, and mix of services then become complex.

SUMMARY

The special aspects of marketing of services are gaining attention from researchers and practitioners as services occupy a major role in our economy. Product marketing views the tools of management as establishing (1) product, (2) price, (3) place, and (4) promotion. The marketing mix for services, however, can be expanded to include (5) physical evidence, (6) participants, and (7) process.

Management must develop a good understanding of the service encounter in order to design and market its service. This involves a knowledge of the customer decision process and consumer behavior. Studies of service customers have produced some interesting observations in terms of prepurchase and postpurchase behavior. These observations give credence to the expanded role of the marketing mix for services.

Marketing of services varies according to the nature of the service and the nature of the customer. Recent legal, ethical, and competitive changes have produced a major restructuring of professional services. This has made the marketing of professional services more important, more sophisticated, more aggressive, and more complex.

DISCUSSION QUESTIONS

1. How does the marketing of services differ from the marketing of products?

2. Why is it especially important that the marketing and operations functions be integrated for services?

3. Identify the search qualities, experience qualities, and credence qualities of the following services.

    a. A pizza parlor

    b. The fire department or other emergency services

    c. A management seminar

4. To what does the marketing mix refer? Why is the marketing mix for services larger than the marketing mix for products?

5. Describe the seven elements of marketing mix for services.

6. What do the following concepts have to do with consumer behavior in services?

    a. Time budgeting

    b. Consumer as co-producer

    c. Dramatic states

7. Discuss the issue of postpurchase evaluations and the marketing of services. Give several recommendations on handling customer complaints.

8. How do consumer attitudes differ for products versus services? What implications do these differences have for services marketing?

9. How is the marketing of professional services different from the marketing of other services?

10. What trends do you foresee in the marketing of services in the next decade?

READING 17.1

Greater Marketing Emphasis at Holiday Inn Breaks the Mold

This is an interview conducted by consultant Gary Knisely with James L. Schorr, executive vice president of marketing at Holiday Inns, Inc. Mr. Schorr previously held positions in account management with Ogilvy & Mather and in brand management with Procter & Gamble. Prior to joining Holiday Inn, he served in a succession of senior marketing positions with the U.S. Postal Service and as a special consultant to the president of the United States on energy communications. Mr. Schorr's responsibilities at the time of the interview included planning, product development, sales, advertising and promotion activities of the Holiday Inn system of hotels throughout the world.

Knisely: You've marketed soap, postal services, and now hotel rooms. What's the difference between what you were doing five years ago and now, in terms of managing the marketing process?
Schorr: Well, I suppose a major difference between product marketing and service marketing is that we can't control the quality of our product as

Source: Excerpted from Gary Knisely, "Greater Marketing Emphasis by Holiday Inn Breaks Mold," *Advertising Age* (January 15, 1979), pp. 47–50. Used with permission of Crain Communications, Inc., Detroit, Mich.

well as a P&G control engineer on a production line can control the quality of his product. When you buy a box of Tide, you can reasonably be 99 and $^{44}/_{100}$ percent sure that this stuff will work to get your clothes clean. When you buy a Holiday Inn room, you're sure at some lesser percentage that it will work to give you a good night's sleep without any hassle, or people banging on the walls and all the bad things that can happen to you in a hotel.

Holiday Inns really brought the brand name into the hotel business. Back in the fifties, the only brand name in the business was Hilton with a lot of downtown aging properties. Today, Holiday Inns is ten times bigger than the Hilton chain. We brought the brand name concept to the business by providing a uniformity of experience and certain standards that the customer can depend on.

But that's still a far cry below the kind of quality control that manufacturers can put on their products.

Knisely: What exactly are you "selling" at Holiday Inn? By that I mean, what is your product?
Schorr: What I am really selling, in terms of what people are buying, is a hotel experience. I'm selling the room, the way they treat you at the front desk, the way the bellman treats you, the way the waitress treats you—it's all mixed together in a consumer's mind when he makes a hotel decision. I could go out and convince everybody in the world that I had the world's most superior rooms and it probably wouldn't have much impact on my business, even though that's obviously the most important thing I've got. My sale is much more a service sale and much more a people-on-people sale.

Knisely: How do you sell people-on-people? Are advertising and some of the standard marketing tactics of selling a package goods product as applicable to this business as they are to P&G or General Foods?
Schorr: No. Such tactics are not as directly efficient for us as for somebody who can control the quality of their product or service better than we can. Half of our efforts are in product development, which is part of the marketing organization here. Very unusual. Even in a sophisticated company like P&G, product development is not part of the marketing operation.

I am famous here for what's called the Bucket

Theory of Marketing in the service business. I say you've got to think of marketing as a big bucket. It's what the sales programs, the advertising programs, and the other programs do that shovels business into the top of that bucket. When the bucket's full, that's 100 percent occupancy. And we keep building new programs and accelerating existing programs to shovel more and more business into that bucket.

There's only one problem. There's a hole in the bottom of the bucket. When we run our business really well, when we control the quality of our product, then the hole is very small and the business falls out much more slowly than I throw it in at the top.

But when we run weak operations, when our experience, our people contact, our systems, or our rooms degrade or deteriorate, then that hole gets bigger. When I'm in a period of declining occupancy, what's happening is I'm losing them out of the bottom of that bucket faster than I can bring in new ones at the top. Those two functions—product quality and selling—that is marketing.

DIFFICULT TO TEST

Knisely: Is market research more difficult in this business than when you're selling a product in a box?
Schorr: Much more difficult. Also much more rewarding. No one else does much of it in the industry but us. You have most competitors flying by the seat of their pants. We are taking the techniques that have been developed in the package goods industry and then putting those techniques to work in the industry.

Knisely: Do you have to fiddle with them to make them work here?
Schorr: Invariably. Things that are applicable to the package goods business are only somewhat applicable here.

The best example would be something we run called "travel audit." That would be this industry's version of a Nielsen, except that only Holiday Inns has it.

Knisely: What about more attitudinal marketing research—qualitative? Are you looking at demographics and psychographics?
Schorr: We don't do much qualitative research.

Most of it is quantitative, even the attitudinal re-search.

We do something annually here that basically splits our market down into whether or not people are traveling to a property as a destination or as an overnight pit stop. Then that splits out by business versus leisure travel. Then we go into the usage of hotel chains by these categories and the attitudinal reasons why. It's very similar to national brand usage studies conducted by a major package goods company.

Knisely: What about the functional linkages? In the classic package goods terms, there are certain relationships between manufacturing, R&D, distribution, etc. What about your linkages?
Schorr: In a service business, marketing and operations are more closely linked than they are in a manufacturing business. My eye is on the same target as the eye of the guy who runs operations. As a result, we tend to walk hand-in-hand.

There's an awareness in the company about marketing. Marketing is not subservient to operations and neither is operations subservient to marketing. If there is a conflict, theoretically the president of the company resolves it.

In the structure of this corporation, there tend not to be the conflicts between operations and marketing. I may go into operations, for example, and say, "Hey, listen, I've got this idea on something we ought to do." His response to me may be, "Sounds nifty, but it would be a nightmare if I did that." My response is, "I know it would be a nightmare, but let's see if we can figure out a way to do it. Put it in our test inns and we'll see if everybody stumbles over themselves and what the customer thinks of it, and what he's going to pay for it."

That's a very easy way to work things out, so you quickly find out first of all if it is a good marketing idea, and secondly if it is an operational infeasibility—if it just can't be done.

THEY'RE PIONEERS

Knisely: You've worked in two organizations now where you've had to recruit a lot of people from the package goods industry. Did you find that there are certain mind sets that might have come along that make it difficult for them to adapt to this way of thinking? Were there certain surprises that hit a

lot of people that they just never thought about?
Schorr: That's the best question you've asked. There definitely are certain kinds of people who should never make the move. There are some that certainly could make it, and should. After all, the service industries are the growth sectors of the U.S. economy.

The biggest difference is that—let's go back to package goods companies. There are essentially two kinds of people. There is the kind who gets his marketing plan from last year, who gets an assignment to ship 8 percent more cases next year and who develops the marketing plan to do that. And that's a certain mind set that functions very well inside of P&G. That person should probably never leave the package goods industry.

On the other hand, there is a kind of person who is somewhat more pioneering, a person who wants to take those skills that heretofore have not been applied to that industry and to see something dramatic happen, more dramatic than 8 percent.

I think every one of the persons [from package goods] we attracted to Washington when I was there [and now here at Holiday Inns] really comes because his mind set is a little more pioneering, more innovative, more of "I don't want to do that same thing for the next thirty years of my life," and "I want to have a little more fun" and "innovate a little more," to be a builder of things at least as much as a manager.

Knisely: Are there more surprises here than in package goods?
Schorr: Yes. One of the things I've learned is the difference between our kinds of businesses—tactical, not strategic, but it makes a big difference.

In the process of learning differences about the hotel business, there have been a lot of surprises. I came in believing the classical marketing tactics and I've learned that only about half of the so-called classical beliefs are immutable truths. For example, I was taught by Procter that in marketing you fish where the fish are: In periods of high consumption, that's when you advertise the most.

Well, that's ridiculous in this industry. For example, in periods of high consumption, I'm full. I don't have any rooms to sell. This is not the time that I want to spend all my marketing money. Yet, classical theory would have me spend 40 percent of my marketing effort in that three-month period to stimulate that activity; I have a capacity problem, so I don't spend any of my marketing funds during that period of time.

There have been, I suppose, a dozen little surprises like that where you can't operate out of rote. It means a little more open mindedness, a little less moving by rote.

1. How do product and services marketing differ? How are they similar?

2. According to Mr. Schorr, which is more difficult? Why?

——— READING 17.2 ———

The Footman Runneth

You might call Myles Schneider the running footman.

You also might call him up on Tuesday nights for some free foot (and related leg, knee, hip, and back) advice.

Any other time you might call him up and hear one or another of eight taped footnotes—he calls it his "Foot Facts" program.

Myles Schneider, podiatrist, is into public service with almost as much passion as he devotes to his running, and his practice. Besides the foot line he conducts Tuesdays with his partner Paul Ross, at their Bethesda office, and the tapes (he's currently preparing eight more), he also

— Offers free examinations of children's feet— "We now know a lot of problems—even back problems—are sports injuries, a lot of these things are predictable, and if you can catch it early enough, you can prevent it."
— Lectures (for free) to PTA groups or running groups on how to avoid sports injuries and what to do about them when they do happen
— Talks (for free) to grade-school classes (complete with slides) about good "footsie" techniques, even for the youngest athletes
— Conducts free courses for trainers and coaches on how to evaluate injuries and help teams as well
— Conducts a program in which high school track teams may come in (with their coach) for individual evaluations—for about $10 a head (or pair of feet). Each youngster gets a

full half-hour diagnostic session, complete with treadmill and "whatever else needs to be done" to discover what problems there may be or are likely to be.

Backed up by his doctor of podiatry degree from the Ohio College of Podiatric Medicine, Schneider's sophistication in the field led to his first book (with colleague, Dr. Mark Sussman), *How to Doctor Your Feet Without the Doctor*, a valuable self-help syllabus with photographs, diagrams, and a lot of common sense. This experience in turn led to a section on sports medicine in a forthcoming book on biking and a second book of his own that provides do-it-yourself formulas for amateur sportspeople, be they swimmers, runners, skiers, or tennis players, to determine how much, how fast, and how long each individual can push him or herself without getting hurt.

——— QUESTIONS FOR READING 17.2

1. What types of promotional tools does Myles Schneider use?

2. Why are they effective for his business?

3. How can a layman who has no technical or specialized knowlege in a field evaluate a professional service? How did you select your doctor? Your college?

4. What is your opinion of professionals who advertise their services?

Source: Excerpted from Sandy Rovner, "Health Talk: The Footman Runneth," *Washington Post* (February 27, 1981), p. C5. © 1981 The Washington Post.

—— CASE 17.1 ——————————————————————

The Marketing/Operations Strategy at Federal Express

Fred Smith, owner, operator, and creator of Federal Express, knew that if he were to attract interest from investors and customers for his proposed service, he would need to successfully differentiate his service from the general hauling of air freight. Smith told the business world:

> Federal Express is in the transportation, communication, and logistics business.
>
> We're a freight service with 550-mile per hour delivery trucks.
>
> We're an intermodal transportation system using jet cargo planes.

But the business world was skeptical that anyone could successfully combine an airline and a trucking company. And they didn't understand why Federal would transport just small packages.

Smith responded

> This company is nothing short of being the logistics arms of a whole new society that is building up in our economy—a society that isn't built around automobile and steel production, but that is built up instead around service industries and high-technology endeavors in electronics and optics and medical science. It is the movement of these support items that Federal Express is all about.
>
> Transporting small packages represents a clear, unambiguous image to the public. We have found our niche in the market. We're not carrying mice and elephants on the same plane like a lot of cargo outfits such as Airborne Freight, Emery Air Freight and Flying Tigers. We carry what a person can lift.

To make his new service a reality, Fred Smith had to support his *marketing vision* with an equally strong *operations vision*. Federal's management knew from their extensive market research that throughout the United States each day there was a quantifiable demand for so many computer parts, for so many pieces of diagnostic medical equipment, and for so many sets of architectural plans. Of course, the mystery—that is, the source of the demand—was the unknown. The demand was quantifiable, but the distribution random. They borrowed from the telephone company's switching system to come up with its "hub and spokes" concept. All packages and documents would be flown nightly, Monday through Friday, to a central sorting hub before being transshipped to their ultimate destination. As far as the customer was concerned, it really made no difference that his package was not flown in a linear fashion, or directly, from City A to City B. Since the package was an inanimate object which could not complain during its journey between pickup and delivery, the only concern originated with the customer who wanted Federal Express to deliver it to the consignee the next day on time.

The nonlinear system permitted service to a far greater number of points with fewer aircraft. And in addition, the central hub system helped reduce mishandling and delay in transit, because Federal Express kept total control over the packages from the pickup point through delivery. The system also permitted Federal Express the opportunity each night to match aircraft flights with package loads and reroute flights when the load volume required it. This flexibility permitted considerable savings in operating costs.

Smith located the sorting hub at the Memphis International Airport. His radial distribution system was unique, effective, and visionary. He could now describe Federal Express operationally as "a special expedited service where the packages never stop moving with the primary conveyer being the airplane."

Source: Adapted from Robert A. Sigafoos and Roger R. Easson, *Absolutely, Positively Overnight! The Unofficial Corporate History of Federal Express* (Memphis, Tenn.: St. Luke's Press, a division of Plaintree Publishing, Ltd., 1988), Chaps. 5, 10, 11 and 12 (Reprinted by permission of the publisher); and Christopher H. Lovelock, "Developing and Managing the Customer-Service Function in the Service Sector," in John Grepiel, Michael Solomon, and Carol Suprenant (Eds.), *The Service Encounter* (Lexington, Mass.: Lexington Books, D. C. Heath & Co., 1985), p. 270 (Reprinted by permission of the publisher, copyright 1985 D. C. Heath & Co.).

A MARKETING PLAN

Vince Fagan was Federal's top marketing executive, and he was a masterful man. In developing
a marketing plan, he stressed that the company
needed to address the question of a two-tiered market. One market was the traditional distribution
sector. These were the shipping departments and
the mail rooms and loading docks of business and
industry—what the company called the "back door
market." The other market was called the "front
door market," since it consisted of executive offices
or what are sometimes called the "papermills of
America." In this front door market were the ad
agencies, architectural firms, banks, consultants,
law firms, and similar business and financial services.

In the first tier market, or back door business,
Federal Express had to compete head-to-head with
Emery, Airborne, United Parcel Service, and the
whole gamut of air freight forwarders and commercial airlines. The other tier was a nontraditional
market, and a market that few people had precisely
identified or understood very well. Within this first
tier of potential customers were those in the business and professional service industries. At best,
those in the second tier may have shipped by air
on rare occasions. But Vince Fagan felt these front
office groups might constitute a strong customer
base if given a sufficient reason to use air express
overnight service. His strategy was to get the attention of the people in the mailroom or the shipping departments as well as the secretaries who

daily make decisions about what mode of transportation will be used to ship packages and documents and which air express company will be
called.

Fagan recognized soon after his arrival in
Memphis that the company needed to identify precisely what marketing approach should be taken
to build volume quickly. His choice was to use
advertising to reach a mass market versus the traditional direct "cold call" approach to reach individual accounts. He saw little use for a separate
sales force and recommended that Federal spend
another $1 million on advertising and do away
with its salesmen.

This was quite a controversial and risky recommendation, especially when the details of Fagan's plan were revealed. He proposed that heavy
emphasis be given to television advertising with
secondary support from print media advertising.
No one in the air freight industry had ever used
TV before—it was a radical plan.

Over the years 1974–1983, Federal's marketing department, in collaboration with the New
York advertising agency Ally and Gargano,
launched five basic campaigns. Each was well-
planned and memorable. (See Exhibit 17.6.)

Federal's media campaign was enormously
successful in building business volume. But as one
marketing executive said, "You could probably
overdo it, if you relied solely on this strategy. The
ability to deliver service is really the main determinant of how well you do."

EXHIBIT 17–6

▪ *Federal's Five Basic Campaigns*

Campaign Purpose	Campaign Slogan
Build public awareness	America, You've Got a New Airline. But Don't Get Excited Unless You're a Package. No First Class, No Meals, No Movies. In Fact, No Passengers. Just Packages
Dominate competition (Emery, specifically)	Twice As Good As The Best In The Business
Stress service efficiency	Take Away Our Planes and We'd Be Just Like Everybody Else
Stress dependability of service	Absolutely, Positively Overnight
Reinforce customer recognition of Federal	Various humorous ads, including Dingbat Air Freight, Untouched by Civil Servants, Fast Paced World, and The Paper Blob

NEW COMPETITION

In 1982, Federal Express faced its toughest competitive challenge—UPS decided to enter the overnight air service market. Smith had always admired UPS because of its financial success and its efficient management. During Federal's startup in 1973, it relied heavily on the technical help of ex-UPS employees. It adopted many of UPS's administrative procedures and selling techniques until Federal had time to devise its own. Privately, it wished that it did not have to meet head-to-head competition from UPS.

Federal's counterattack was based again on differentiating itself from its competitor, but this time differentiation was based on the *quality* of service. Smith sent out this message:

> UPS is the best in the business at what they do—moving low priority, consumer-oriented parcels where emergency is not a factor. But Federal, in turn, is best at what it does—movement of the most vital and time-sensitive parcels and documents. We want to dispel in the minds of the customers the idea that competitors are the equal of us when in fact they are not. We are not going to let competitors equal Federal Express. We will offer 10:30 A.M. delivery, more service options, Saturday pickups, package tracing, and call-backs to shippers informing them that the packages have been delivered.

To support this strategy, operations had to become even more streamlined and efficient. New technology was added. Modern computer technology enabled the company to develop a professional customer-service function located at four interlinked call centers across the country. Electronic "order blanks" on cathode-ray tube (CRT) screens replaced paper records, and a sophisticated information and retrieval system allowed customer service agents (CSAs) to call up data on a regular customer simply by keying in that customer's account number. Since all packages were now computer coded and passed through optical scanners at each stage in the transportation and sorting process, information on package movements could be entered in the central computer and was easily accessible to CSAs for tracing purposes. Problems beyond the capabilities of a CSA to solve were transferred promptly to specialist personnel.

_____ QUESTIONS FOR CASE 17.1

1. Summarize in your own words how Federal Express integrates its marketing and operations strategies.

2. Which parts of the marketing mix does Federal use successfully?

3. What aspects of Federal's marketing plan are unique?

4. What factors differentiate Federal's operations from its competitors?

5. In your opinion, does the marketing function or operations function play a bigger role in Federal's success?

_____ REFERENCES _____

Assael, Henry. *Consumer Behavior and Marketing Action*, 3d Ed. Boston: Kent, 1987.

Berry, Leonard L. "Big Ideas in Services Marketing," *The Journal of Services Marketing* (Summer 1987), pp. 5–9.

Berry, Leonard L. "Relationship Marketing," in *Emerging Perspectives on Service Marketing*. Proceedings of the 1983 Conference on Services Marketing. Chicago: American Marketing Association, 1983, pp. 25–28.

Berry, Leonard L. "Services Marketing is Different," *Business* (May–June 1980), pp. 24–29.

Bitner, Mary Jo, and V. A. Zeithaml. "Fundamentals in Services Marketing," in *Proceedings of the 1988 Conference on Services Marketing*. Chi-

cago: American Marketing Association 1988, pp. 7–11.

Bloom, Paul N. "Effective Marketing for Professional Services," *Harvard Business Review*, Vol. 62, No. 5 (September–October 1984), pp. 102–110.

Booms, Bernard H., and M. J. Bitner, "Marketing Strategies and Organization Structures for Service Firms," in *Marketing of Services*, Proceedings of the 1981 Conference in Services Marketing. Chicago: American Marketing Association, 1983, pp. 47–52.

Boddewyn, J. J., Marsha Baldwin Halbrich, and A. C. Perry. "Service Multinationals: Conceptualization, Measurement, and Theory," *Journal of International Business Studies* (Fall 1986), pp. 41–57.

Cowell, Donald. *The Marketing of Services*. London: Heinemann, 1984.

Denney, Robert W. "How to Develop—and Implement—a Marketing Plan for Your Firm," *Practical Accountant* (July 1981), pp. 18–29.

Fisk, Raymond P., Patriya S. Tansuhaj, and Lawrence A. Crosby (Eds.). *SERVMARK:The Electronic Bibliography of Services Marketing Literature*. Tempe, Ariz.: First Interstate Center for Services Marketing, Arizona State University, 1987.

Gronroos, Christian. "Innovative Marketing Strategies and Organization Structures for Service Firms," in *Emerging Prospectives on Services Marketing*, Proceedings of the 1983 Conference on Services Marketing. Chicago: American Marketing Association, 1983.

Gronroos, Christian. "Designing a Long Range Marketing Strategy for Services," *Long Range Planning* (April 1980), pp. 36–42.

Guiltinan, Joseph P. "The Price Bundling of Services: A Normative Framework," *Journal of Marketing* (April 1987), pp. 74–85.

Hill, C. Jeanne, and Sue E. Neeley. "Differences in the Consumer Decision Process for Professional vs. Generic Services," *Journal of Services Marketing* (Winter 1988).

Hill, C. Jeanne, and William R. Fannin. "Professional Service Marketing Strategies in the 80s," *Journal of Professional Services Marketing* (Fall-Winter 1986).

Knisely, Gary. "Greater Marketing Emphasis by Holiday Inn Breaks Mold," *Advertising Age* (January 15, 1979), pp. 47–50; "Listening to the Consumer in Service Marketing," *Advertising Age* (February 19, 1979), pp. 54–60; "Financial Services Marketing Must Learn Package Goods Selling Tools," *Advertising Age* (March 19, 1979), pp. 58–62; "Services Business is Dealing with Other People," *Advertising Age* (May 14, 1979), pp. 57–58.

Kotler, Philip, and Paul Bloom. *Marketing Professional Services*. Englewood Cliffs, N.J.: Prentice-Hall, 1984.

Levitt, Theodore. "After the Sale is Over . . . ," *Harvard Business Review*, Vol. 61, No. 5 (September–October 1983), pp. 87–93.

Levitt, Theodore. "Marketing Intangible Products and Product Intangibles," *Harvard Business Review*, Vol. 59, No. 3 (May–June 1981), pp. 94–102.

Light, Donald H. "A Guide for New Distribution Strategies for Service Firms," *Journal of Business Strategy* (Summer 1986).

Lovelock, Christopher H. "Developing and Managing the Customer-Service Function in the Service Sector," in John Grepiel, Michael Solomon, and Carol Suprenant (Eds.), *The Service Encounter*. Lexington, Mass.: Lexington Books, 1985, pp. 266–280.

Lovelock, Christopher H. *Managing Services: Marketing, Operations and Human Resources*. Englewod Cliffs, N.J.: Prentice-Hall, 1988.

Lovelock, Christopher H. *Services Marketing*. Englewood Cliffs, N.J.: Prentice-Hall, 1984.

Peters, Tom. *Thriving on Chaos*. New York: Knopf, 1987.

Rathmell, John M. *Marketing in the Service Sector*, Cambridge, Mass.: Winthrop, 1974.

Sigafoos, R. A., and R. R. Easson. *Absolutely, Positively Overnight!* Memphis, Tenn.: St. Luke's Press, 1988.

Sellers, Patricia. "How to Handle Customers' Gripes," *Fortune* (October 24, 1988), pp. 88–100.

Shostack, G. Lynn. "Breaking Free From Product Marketing," *Journal of Marketing*, Vol. 41 (April 1977), pp. 73–80.

Shostack, G. Lynn. "Planning the Service Encounter," in John Grepiel, Michael Solomon, and Carol Suprenant (Eds.), *The Service Encounter*. Lexington, Mass.: Lexington Books, 1985, pp. 243–253.

Tierno, David. "How to be Market-Driven: A Step-by-Step Guide for Service Firms," *Journal of Business Strategy* (Winter 1987), pp. 92–96.

Webster, Cynthia. "Strategies for Becoming Market-Oriented in the Professional Services Area," *Journal of Professional Services Marketing* (Summer 1987).

Zeithaml, Valarie A. "How Consumer Evaluation Processes Differ Between Goods and Services," in *Marketing of Services*, Proceedings of the 1981 Conference on Services Marketing. Chicago: American Marketing Association, 1981, pp. 186–190.

Zeithaml, Valarie, A. Parasuramon, and Leonard Berry. "Problems and Strategies in Services Marketing," *Journal of Marketing*, Vol. 49 (Spring 1985), pp. 33–46.

PART IV

Applying the Concepts of Service Operations Management

18

Integrated Project and Cases

INTRODUCTION

Throughout this book we have attempted to challenge and excite you with readings from leading journals and magazines, case studies, discussion questions, and mathematical problems to be solved. Each of these learning techniques was intended to strengthen your understanding of the material covered in a specific chapter. Although the cases, problems, and questions were by no means trivial, you at least had an idea what the basic issue at hand was (e.g., layout or location or forecasting).

The purpose of this final chapter is to stretch your knowledge and skills one step further. One term project and two case studies are presented here; they all require the application of common sense and the integration of material from the various chapters. The term project is intended as a team effort investigation of the operations functions of a service firm in *your* community. The cases represent real-world problems that have been summarized for your analysis, interpretation and suggestions.

━━ SERVICE OPERATIONS MANAGEMENT TERM PROJECT ━━

DESCRIPTION OF TERM PROJECT

The purpose of the term project is to have you explore, in modest depth, the operations function of an existing service organization of your choosing. On completion of the project you should

— Understand how a service is generated and delivered to the customer using one service delivery system.

— Have explored in depth the operations management activities in the organization.

Source: Professor Asoo J. Vakharia, Karl Eller Graduate School of Management, University of Arizona.

In order to achieve these goals, your group is expected to select a service organization (a firm, the service function in a manufacturing organization, government entity, health service organization, etc.) and complete the following activities:

1. *Document current operations.* Using flowcharts, job analyses, job descriptions, verbal explanations, or similar methods, you should explain the operations activities and technology for the firm. Specifically, the various inputs, transformation processes, and several outputs must be identified.
2. *Detail OM activities.* Carefully and in depth, tell how the following activities are performed in the firm:
   a. Capacity planning
   b. Manpower planning, acquisition, and control
   c. Scheduling
   d. Managing for quality
   e. Material control (inventory, supplies, etc.)
   f. Cost control
   g. Training and development for employees
   h. Facility location and layout planning
3. *Identify a problem and propose a solution.* For each of the activities discussed in activity 2, identify at least one operating problem in the firm, describe the problem as you best understand it, and suggest one or more tentative solutions to the problem.
4. *Prepare a written report.* Report your findings to the rest of the class. You also may be required to submit a copy of your report to the firm, and hence you should use professional standards in preparing your report (see guidelines for report preparation that follow).

As a group, you are to identify your organization, seek permission to do your project with the firm, and turn in a one page summary about the firm chosen and the proposed work that is to be carried out.

GUIDELINES ON REPORT PREPARATION

General Format

1. The report must be typed and double spaced.
2. Report covers are a choice of the group but must allow the report to lie flat when open.
3. Use subheadings within the report and when necessary.
4. A table of contents page is necessary.
5. Plan the report carefully so as to develop an organized and nonredundant report. It should be organized and assembled as a continuous report and should *not* be several independent segments bound together.

Tentative Outline of the Report

1. *Executive abstract* The report must begin with a 1- to 2-page abstract that orients the reader as to the contents as well as the major sections of the report. The abstract, by itself, must provide enough information about the project so that the reader can judge simply by reading this portion if he or she wants to read further.

2. *Introduction* This first segment should present a *brief* history of the organization and its local operations. Be brief and succinct but make sure that the reader can obtain a perspective of the organization.

3. *Environmental background* In this section discuss the following two aspects. First, briefly outline the nature of the organization's external environment, examining the critical factors influencing its operations and policies as well as its overall operations strategy. Second, in more detail, examine the firm's internal environment. This involves consideration of customers, suppliers, distributors, and competitors that comprise the industry. Your analysis should focus on how the micro environment affects the tactical and operational decisions made by the organization. To complete this section of the report, you will need to do some library research, as well as have several meetings with the organizational representative(s).

4. *Organizational analysis* This part of the report should focus on activities 1 and 2 as outlined in the description of the term project. In particular, be specific when writing up this section. *Do not make open-ended statements.*

5. *Problem identification and solution* In this segment of the report, each team should focus on activity 3 in the description of the term project. When identifying a problem, be specific and also make sure that the problem relates to the activities you are to study. Further, when developing a solution(s), *do not be open-ended.* If you are recommending changes in the current method(s), you need to estimate the costs, if any, of such changes. As before, be thorough about solutions that are proposed; that is, make sure that you consider all aspects of the problem.

6. *Summary* In 2 to 3 pages, you must summarize your project, including what you did, how you did it, the major problems, and the solutions proposed.

7. *Exhibits, tables, and figures* All calculations, figures, and other information should be summarized in this section. Additionally, any appendix, exhibit, table, and/or figure attached to the report must be typed and referred to in the report.

━━ CASE 18.1 ━━━━━━━━━━━━━━━━━━━━━━━━━━━━━━━━━━━━━━

William T. Gambo, D.D.S.

It was 7:00 P.M. when Dr. Bill Gambo left his dental office. He had arrived in the office at 7:00 A.M., started with patients at 7:30 A.M., and had worked such a full schedule that he had not even had time for lunch. He had not finished with his last patient until 5:30 P.M. and then spent 90 minutes on paperwork. Dr. Gambo did not mind the hard work; in fact, he loved it.

What bothered him was that after all the work, he was still not meeting his revenue goals. Dr. Gambo had set his revenue goal at $26,000 per month and the dental hygienist's goal at $40 per hour. The dental hygienist easily met her goal, but Dr. Gambo frequently had difficulty meeting his.

BACKGROUND

After graduating from the Medical College of Virginia's Dental School, Dr. Gambo had done a two-year general practice residency at the University of Virginia in Charlottesville, Virginia, so that he could broaden his dental skills. During his residency, he had participated in many of the activities available around Charlottesville (including sky diving and hiking in the nearby mountains) and had become very fond of the area. Therefore, upon completing his residency, he purchased a dental practice from a retiring dentist in Charlottesville. The practice had about 1750 patients and was growing rapidly; during the past July, 30 new patients were added.

Dr. Gambo described himself as a "restorative" dentist. He concentrated on restoring the mouth to good condition by means of crowns, bridges, partial dentures, and fillings. He referred patients whose needs were not of a restorative nature to other specialists.

He believed that dental practices were either characterized by service or volume and that these two attributes were mutually exclusive. He was determined to provide his patients with quality care and had no interest in conducting a high-volume practice. He believed that spending an extra 10 minutes with a patient would give them a longer-lasting crown or filling and a better feeling about the quality of care received. This additional service was important for repeat business and word-of-mouth advertising.

Dr. Gambo believed that his professional practice was quality oriented and that "people who

Source: This case was written by Janis A. Ericksen and Professor David A. Collier, Faculty of Management Sciences, The Ohio State University. Copyright © 1984 by the Colgate Darden Graduate School of Business Administration, Sponsors Case Research Program, University of Virginia.

are looking for cheap dentistry should not come here." He estimated that 75 percent of the residents of Charlottesville were "bargain hunters" and the remainder were "quality seekers." Dr. Gambo guessed that 12 percent of the 70 dentists practicing in Charlottesville catered to patients able and willing to pay a premium for quality care. He considered his patients to be from this 12 percent and reasoned that he would attract additional patients if he satisfactorily served his affluent clientele. He did not treat welfare or Medicaid patients.

Dr. Gambo was in a "people business" and considered his best attribute to be an ability to talk and relate effectively to people. He thought himself the best advertisement for his dental practice and relied totally on word-of-mouth to get new patients. He called this method "internal marketing," and it has thus far proven very successful. To implement this "internal marketing" program, Dr. Gambo kept a patient referral box. This box contained the number of new patients that each of his old patients had referred. After a patient made five referrals, he or she received a complimentary dinner at a local restaurant from Dr. Gambo.

THE OFFICE

Dr. Gambo had four employees: a receptionist, a chairside assistant, a floater, and a dental hygienist. The receptionist was the patients' first contact with the dental practice; therefore, this person was expected to be cheerful and friendly at all times and to make patients feel comfortable and important. The receptionist was also responsible for answering the phone, scheduling appointments, confirming appointments, and the books. The chairside assistant helped Dr. Gambo during dental procedures and sterilized instruments during free periods. The floater helped out wherever needed in the office—assisting Dr. Gambo at chairside, sterilizing instruments, cleaning up, working in the lab, or helping the dental hygienist and receptionist. The dental hygienist cleaned patients' teeth, performed oral exams, and educated patients about oral hygiene. New patients saw the dental hygienist before seeing Dr. Gambo.

On Monday through Friday of each week, every member of the staff was in the office except the floater, who did not work on Mondays and Fridays. Dr. Gambo's appointment system assumed that demand was fairly constant throughout the week. The office was closed on Saturdays and Sundays.

CURRENT APPOINTMENT SYSTEM

Two categories of patients were treated in the office. One category would see the dental hygienist for a regular checkup and cleaning before being looked over by the dentist. The second category consisted of patients who had seen the hygienist in a previous appointment and were returning for restorative work.

Ideally, Dr. Gambo wanted to spend a total of 32 hours with patients each week. Monday through Thursday, he usually began with patients at 7:30 A.M. and finished with them at 3:30 P.M. He started at 7:30 A.M. because he wanted to accommodate patients who needed to have dental work completed in time to work a full day. He preferred these hours because he feared that the quality of his work might suffer if he saw patients more than seven or eight hours a day. On occasion, however, he would schedule a patient earlier than 7:30 A.M. or later than 3:30 P.M. to satisfy a special request. He believed that Tuesdays and Wednesdays were his best days because he started to burn out toward the end of the week. On Fridays he started at 7:30 A.M. and completed his work by 11:30 A.M. He would spend the remainder of Friday on record keeping, lab work, financial management—the details necessary to maintain the effective performance of his practice.

Dr. Gambo scheduled an hour-long lunch break each day but rarely had time for it. Furthermore, he seldom had any idle time even though a 10 minute "breather" was scheduled for each morning.

Normally, Dr. Gambo did not make appointments any farther in advance than two weeks. This policy enabled him to schedule the procedures that would group together most efficiently in any one day. It also allowed him to take advantage of any sudden opportunities that would require him to be out of the office. These opportunities included dental seminars and conventions and sky diving and ski trips and accounted for 45 of the working days in the past year.

Dr. Gambo thought continuing education was critical to the quality and success of his practice.

In his opinion, dentists learned only the fundamentals in dental school and needed further education on an ongoing basis if they were to keep up with their ever-changing field. He estimated that a one-week seminar cost approximately $8100 (including lost practice-opportunity costs, seminar expenses, and staff salaries). He thought he recovered this cost as a result of additional learning within two months after attending the seminar.

Dr. Gambo believed his appointment policy enhanced the quality and efficiency of his practice. He could "construct a nice day" for the patient by scheduling an appointment long enough to deliver personal service of high technical quality. A long appointment for multiple dental procedures meant only one numbing, which pleased the patient, and also reduced the number of appointments and set-ups necessary for treatment.

The receptionist kept a call list of the names of patients to be scheduled for appointments. She would attempt to group similar appointments together and to maximize the use of Dr. Gambo's time by avoiding scheduling any idle time other than lunch and the regular break period in the morning.

Dr. Gambo's shortest appointment was around 20 minutes; his longest was all day. The time allotted for each appointment was based on Dr. Gambo's estimates of the time he spent on each procedure. (Exhibit 18–1 shows these estimates and the fees for each procedure; Exhibit 18–2 shows a typical week's schedule using these as standards.) In addition, 30 minutes were set aside after lunch on Monday through Thursday for emergencies.

Because of patients' preferences and availability, however, blocks of idle time often appeared in the schedule (note unused times in Exhibit 18–2). On those occasions, Dr. Gambo wondered whether he should try to reschedule patients to utilize his time more effectively. So far, however, he had not attempted to reschedule patients once they had been given an appointment time.

The dental hygienist was scheduled to see from 10 to 12 patients a day. These appointments were scheduled separately from Dr. Gambo's ap-

----

EXHIBIT 18–1

■ *William T. Gambo, D.D.S.: Dental Procedures, Standard Times, and Fees*

Code	Procedure	Appointment No.	Standard Time per Appointment (min)	Fee ($)
A	Silver filling	1	30	45
B	Pin-reinforced silver filling	1	40	70
C	Tooth-colored filling	1	30	35
D	Bridge	1	180	330/unit*
		2	40	
E	Single crown	1	90	330
		2	30	
F	Partial denture	1	30	475–500
		2	20	
		3	30	
G	Partial denture with precision attachments	1	40	800–1200
		2	30	
		3	80	
H	Full denture	1	10	900
		2	60	
		3	60	
		4	30	
		5	40	
I	Occlusal analysis	1	30	35
J	Cast post	1	60	125

* The bridge fee was $330 for the bridge itself. An average bridge replaced three teeth.

----- EXHIBIT 18–2 -----

- **William T. Gambo, D.D.S.: Typical Weekly Appointment Schedule**

Monday, Oct. 24	Tuesday, Oct. 25	Wednesday, Oct. 26	Thursday, Oct. 27	Friday, Oct. 28
7:30 MARTHA RAGLAND — C,C,B	7:30 JAMES PAYNE — C,C,C,C,C,A,A	7:30 KEEY HUSTED — A — CARMEN GAETHE — A,B	7:00 STEVE HANEY A,A — JAY FARRAR — A,A,A	7:00 ED SWINDLER — C,B — CAROL ROADES — B,E1
9:00 BREAK / IDLE / IDLE / IDLE / SUSAN HESTER — B — F1(3 TEETH)	9:00	9:00 JOE COLLIER — A,A,A,A,B	9:00 BREAK / LEE FARRAR — A,A,I	9:00 BREAK / SAM VERDUCI — E2
11:00	11:00 BREAK / JOYCE BROUSH — A / IDLE / IDLE	11:00	11:00 BREAK / MARY COLEMAN — I / IDLE	11:00 WALLACE WEST — C / IDLE / IDLE / IDLE
12:00 LUNCH	12:00 LUNCH	12:00 LUNCH	12:00 LUNCH	12:00 LUNCH
1:00 MARY TAYLOR (EMERGENCY) — A / TAMMY SMITH — A,A,A	1:00 EMERGENCY— UNUSED / RUTH GIANAROS — E1	1:00 EMERGENCY— UNUSED / WAYNE POOR — A,A,A,A	1:00 EMERGENCY— UNUSED / JAMES MERGNER — E1	1:00 LINDA PARKER — B / JOHN BRESHNER — A
2:00	2:00	2:00 (To 4:00 PM)	2:00	2:00
3:00 IDLE / IDLE	3:00 PHILLIS BRUHL — I / JAMES STEINE (TO 4:00 PM) — A	3:00	3:00 KAY MAUPIN E2 / MARY MURRY E2 (To 4:00 PM)	3:00

pointments. (Exhibit 18–3 is a typical week from the dental hygienist's appointment book.) Appointments for the hygienist were made from 7:30 A.M. until 3:30 P.M. on Monday through Thursday and from 7:30 A.M. until 12:30 P.M. on Fridays. These appointments were an hour long for new patients, 40 minutes for regular patients, and 30 minutes for children.

Dr. Gambo's office was busiest on Mondays because of weekend emergencies. He preferred not to take walk-ins, however, and would attempt to reschedule them whenever possible. Dr. Gambo had few no-shows because the receptionist always confirmed appointments by phone the day before the appointment.

APPOINTMENT PROCEDURES FOR TYPICAL PATIENT

The receptionist typically answered the phone when someone called for an appointment. People requesting an appointment generally fit into one of the two categories previously described: a new or regular patient or a recalled patient who was coming in for restorative care. (Exhibits 18–4 and 18–5 illustrate the complete procedures for these two categories of patients.)

NEW OR REGULAR PATIENT

If the person wanting an appointment was a new patient, the receptionist would ask how they found

----- EXHIBIT 18–3 -----

■ *William T. Gambo, D.D.S.: Typical Weekly Appointment Schedule for Dental Hygienist*

	Monday, Oct. 24	Tuesday, Oct. 25	Wednesday, Oct. 25	Thursday, Oct. 27	Friday, Oct. 28
7:30	BEN PUMPHREY	TOM ATKINSON	IDLE	CLARA SUTTON	STAN HARDI
8:00	TOM HARLAN		JUDY OLDSON		
8:30	BRENDA BATTIN	JONNIE COPLAND	PHIL OWENS	DOT COLLIER	LARRY CORCA
9:00		BILL DAUGHERTY	FRED SADLER	DANNY WHALEN	
9:30	DENISE YANSROLL	DONNA DUVALL	RAY SHUMAN		PAT DEVIVI
9:50				JILL SMITHS	
10:00	JOHN BRADFORD	DANNY McKINNEY	PHIL SHOWALTER		KIM TISDALE
10:30				BREAK	
10:40	BREAK	JIM KENDALL		BREAK	DONNA SAGER
11:00	RONNIE HOMRA			BRUCE ASBURY	
11:20		WHIT CRISWELL	RAY TAYLOR		BUDDY HARDIN
11:30				LOUIS BISHOP	
11:50					KATHY WILLARD
12:00	PAM SPIES		IDLE / IDLE	IDLE	
12:40	IDLE / LUNCH	LUNCH	LUNCH	LUNCH	LUNCH
12:50	IDLE				
1:00	ALAN BECKENSTEIN				
1:20		MARY LaFRANA	PAUL BIDDLE	ELAINE BROWN	OFF
1:30	JULIE ADAIR				
1:50			BENTON DAY		
2:00		JOE B. LANTER		LARRY RITZMAN	
2:30			CHARLOTTE TERRY	LEE KRAJEWSKI	
2:40	TOM BENTON				
3:00		JAMES PENN	CAROLYN BABER		
3:20	IDLE			IDLE	
3:30	IDLE			IDLE	
3:40	OFF	OFF	OFF	OFF	

out about Dr. Gambo and then engage the caller in conversation about specific dental problems and general personal information. The point of this dialogue was to have the office staff interact with the prospective patient in a personal way. New patients were then scheduled for a one-hour appointment with the hygienist. Regular patients needing a routine six-month checkup were also scheduled for an appointment with the hygienist.

On the day of the appointment, the employee at the office reception window would cheerfully greet the patient. (See Exhibit 18–6 for a layout of the dental office.) All conversation in the dental office was required to be on a first-name basis. If the patient were visiting for the first time, he or she would complete any necessary paperwork, then sit in the reception room, supplied with current magazines, until the dental hygienist was ready for the patient or the second hygiene room was prepared. Dr. Gambo liked to have patients wait in the second hygiene room until the dental hygienist was finished with the previous patient. He felt that a wait in the treatment room did not seem as long to a patient as a wait in the reception area. On average, a patient spent about 10 minutes in the reception room; however, a few patients had waited as long as 20 minutes.

Once the second hygiene room was ready for

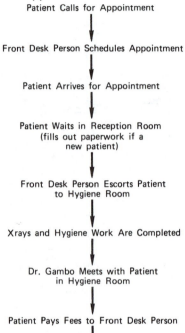

—— EXHIBIT 18–4 ——————————————————————————————————

■ *William T. Gambo, D.D.S.: Appointment Procedure for New or Regular Patient*

Patient Calls for Appointment

↓

Front Desk Person Schedules Appointment

↓

Patient Arrives for Appointment

↓

Patient Waits in Reception Room
(fills out paperwork if a
new patient)

↓

Front Desk Person Escorts Patient
to Hygiene Room

↓

Xrays and Hygiene Work Are Completed

↓

Dr. Gambo Meets with Patient
in Hygiene Room

↓

Patient Pays Fees to Front Desk Person

↓

Patient Leaves

—— EXHIBIT 18–5 ——————————————————————————————————

■ *William T. Gambo, D.D.S.: Appointment Procedure for Recall Patient*

Front Desk Person Calls Patient and
Schedules an Appointment

↓

Patient Arrives for Appointment

↓

Patient Waits in Reception Room

↓

Patient Is Escorted to Dental Room

↓

Dental Procedures Are Performed by
Dr. Gambo

↓

Patient Arranges for Fees Payment
at Front Desk

↓

Patient Leaves

—— EXHIBIT 18–6 ——————————————————————————

■ *William T. Gambo, D.D.S.: Dental Office Layout*

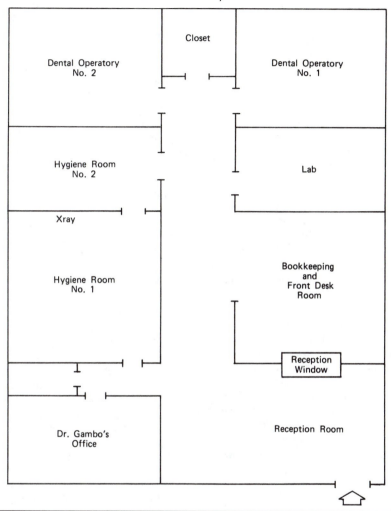

the patient, the receptionist escorted the patient there and, if this was a first visit, subsequently introduced him or her to the dental hygienist. The dental hygienist would inquire about specific problems and general medical history. During the one-hour appointment, the hygienist would take x-rays, fully examine and chart the mouth, clean the teeth, measure gum pockets, and check the mouth for oral cancer. While working, the hygienist would discuss the procedures and their purposes as well as review the x-rays with the patient. The purpose of these discussions was to "raise the patient's dental I.Q." and provide "premium service."

At some point during the appointment, Dr. Gambo would enter the dental hygiene room. If the patient was visiting the office for the first time, the hygienist would make the introductions. Dr. Gambo would then chat with the patient on a personal note before discussing the patient's x-rays with the dental hygienist and the patient. He would next perform a head and neck examination and an intraoral examination and review the hygienist's work. Dr. Gambo talked with the patient about any problems and recommended initial treatment. He recorded the results of his examination on the patient's chart as well as the length of time to schedule for any recall appointment. He often instructed the patient to call him at home or at his office if the patient had any questions. He then left the patient with the dental hygienist.

Dr. Gambo estimated that these unscheduled meetings with the hygienist's patients took from 5 to 10 minutes each. Virginia state law required that a dentist check every patient treated by a hygienist.

RECALLED PATIENTS

Recalled patients had previously visited the dental hygienist and were returning for an appointment with Dr. Gambo. The receptionist contacted these patients in order to schedule an appointment. Upon entering the office, the patient was cordially greeted by the receptionist and then remained in the front office until Dr. Gambo was ready or the second dental room was prepared. This wait was seldom more than 10 minutes. Either the receptionist or the dentist escorted the patient to one of the two dental rooms. Before numbing the patient's mouth, Dr. Gambo reviewed what he would do during the appointment. While the numbing was taking effect—5 to 15 minutes elapsed after the shot of novocaine—Dr. Gambo usually visited the dental hygienist's patients. He then returned to his patient and performed the appropriate procedure. Throughout the procedure, he carefully explained where he was in the treatment. After completing the appointment, Dr. Gambo walked the patient to the receptionist, who then arranged for payment and the next appointment. Dr. Gambo followed up some appointments with phone calls to ascertain how the patient was feeling.

CUSTOMER SERVICE AND QUALITY

Dr. Gambo was very conscious of quality and wanted to project an image of quality. He recognized three categories of quality: his rapport with patients, his equipment and the appearance of his office, and the professional care he provided his patients.

Dr. Gambo strove to have his office perceived by patients as a "fun and professional" operation. The staff were to make it clear that they were all friends and that they enjoyed working together. Dr. Gambo believed patients sensed that his personnel were having a good time and were relaxed and that this perception helped to relax the patients. His employees were thoroughly instructed on how to deal with a patient in a caring fashion. Dr. Gambo emphasized that "you have to put yourself in their shoes." He approached patients with a soft voice and touch and worked diligently at projecting a "caring attitude."

Dr. Gambo equated his office and equipment with an "investment in yourself." The office was designed to look like someone's house, with careful attention to color and surroundings. He tolerated nothing "stuffy" about the office. He had added one room during each year that he had practiced and felt that his patients liked the changes. Dr. Gambo used only the best equipment. Fancy drills with lights and multiple handpieces impressed patients and saved the dentist time. By using the best equipment, Dr. Gambo minimized his repair expenses.

Dr. Gambo divided his dental care for a patient into two phases. In the first phase, he emphasized good oral hygiene and attempted to rid the patient's mouth of decay and disease. He insisted that patients exercise good habits in oral hygiene. He might even go so far as to drop uncooperative patients because he did not want to risk tarnishing his professional image. The second phase of dental care was the long-term restorative work. Before beginning this work, Dr. Gambo met with the patient to discuss the long-term plan for his or her teeth. This meeting was relaxed and free of charge to the patient.

MEETING PROFESSIONAL REVENUE GOALS

Dr. Gambo felt that his hectic days and shortfalls in revenue resulted largely from his appointment system. He wondered if his weekly schedules were as efficient as possible. Also, he was curious about the feasibility of trying to change patient appointments that he may have set a week or two earlier. Should he reschedule patients to attain his revenue goals? How would he know when to reschedule?

Finally, he wanted to determine if his revenue goals were realistic. He knew that raising prices was not an option because he already charged on the high end of the scale in a small target market.

QUESTIONS FOR CASE 18.1

1. Using the information in Exhibits 18–1 and 18–2 of the case, calculate Dr. Gambo's revenue for the week. If Dr. Gambo works a maximum theoretical schedule, what is his revenue capacity? If he works a realistic schedule, what is his revenue capacity and can he attain his current revenue goals? (*You* must define maximum and realistic schedule.)

2. What actions can Dr. Gambo take to improve his revenues? How do these actions fit with the nature of his practice?

3. What would be the effect on Dr. Gambo's practice if he rescheduled previously confirmed ap-

pointments in order to eliminate idle blocks of time?

4. Can the appointment system be improved? If so, specify in detail what improvements you recommend.

5. Is Dr. Gambo's two-week planning horizon for scheduling appointments appropriate? If it is not, how might one determine the proper horizon?

6. How would Dr. Gambo define quality? How might Dr. Gambo measure quality? Can a cost be put on Dr. Gambo's level of quality?

7. What are your final recommendations to Dr. Gambo?

CASE 18.2

The New Orleans Hilton & Hilton Towers

"We are selling time. You can't put a hotel room on a shelf," Joseph F. Frederick, Jr., general manager of the New Orleans Hilton & Hilton Towers, said as he was addressing the issue of planning in the lodging industry. Joe stressed how important the issue of "capacity management" is to a hotel. A vacant hotel room for one night is revenue lost forever; thus it is important to monitor future bookings and no-shows as closely as possible to avoid a substantial block of unrented rooms. Profitability is directly related to booking rooms. To complicate the management task, no-shows, booking behavior, and arrival and departure patterns differ substantially by convention, conference, and association group.

Joe was in the process of reviewing the advance bookings for weeks no. 32 and no. 33 that had just been brought to him by his Front Office Manager Mark Wasiak and his Director of Sales Stan Skadal. They had pointed out a major gap in room bookings and were concerned that the time for action was growing short.

THE NATIONAL LODGING INDUSTRY

The lodging industry, as traditionally defined, is made up of four types of facilities:

— Hotel—a multistory building with its own dining rooms, meeting rooms, and other public rooms
— Motel—"a low-rise building" with limited dining facilities and, usually no meeting or other public rooms
— Motor Hotel—a fairly new hybrid of the motel and hotel
— Resort—lodging that could include any of the above but typically is located at a destination site with recreational facilities

The U.S. lodging industry in 1979 had estimated guest revenues of over $20 billion. The growth in revenues from 1963 to 1979 was approximately 350 percent. Generally speaking, the profit margin for a lodging establishment is a func-

Source: This case was written by Kenneth M. Scott and Professor David A. Collier, Faculty of Management Sciences, The Ohio State University. Copyright 1984 by the Colgate Darden Graduate School of Business Administration, Sponsors Case Research Program, University of Virginia.

tion of the occupancy rate. Higher occupancy rates mean higher profit margins, so great emphasis is placed on "selling out the house." The operating cost structure of a hotel or motel varies according to its age, size, location, and range of services. Once the hotel occupancy rate is above the breakeven occupancy rate, the contribution to profit and overhead per additional customer (room) is quite high.

The industry is susceptible to changes in the economy; in times of economic downturn, business people are not likely to travel as much as in good times and the overall number of conventions and seminars usually decline. The lodging industry generally lags by about six months on both ends of the economic downturn as some time is required for businesses to adjust to economic changes.

NEW ORLEANS LODGING MARKET

Forecasting and planning effectively for the New Orleans Hilton & Hilton Towers necessitated a thorough understanding of the overall New Orleans lodging market and how it functioned. In the late 1970s, the top three convention cities in the United States were Las Vegas, San Francisco, and New Orleans. By the 1980s, the top three had become Orlando, Philadelphia, and again, New Orleans. When asked why he thought New Orleans was still among the leaders, Joe Frederick noted a variety of reasons.

New Orleans was centrally located, which made it an ideal site for companies with employees nationwide as well as for many regional companies in the United States. New Orleans was also located in the Sun Belt, which in recent years had been experiencing rapid population growth. Perhaps one of the strongest reasons for New Orleans' popularity as a convention city was the "ambience" of the city itself. According to Joe, New Orleans was "the only true seven-day-a-week city in the U.S." This level of liveliness was currently valid for about 10 months of the year, but it was hoped that the coming of the Louisiana World Exposition in 1984, with the promotion activities and additional hotel capacity and convention center construction, would transform New Orleans into a seven-day-a-week, 12-month-a-year city.

There were some identifiable seasonal trends in the New Orleans convention lodging industry.

December was typically a slow month, as most businesses did not schedule conferences or conventions around the holidays. (The one big exception to this lull was the influx of out-of-town visitors every year for the Sugar Bowl football game played in the New Orleans Superdome.) Bookings started to build again by the second week of January and remained strong until June, when businesses again held off on meetings when schools let out. August was most often the lowest demand month for the New Orleans Hilton & Hilton Towers.

Exhibit 18–7 shows the current and planned capacities of the Hilton and its major competitors in the downtown and French Quarter lodging market. To Hilton's advantage was the fact that the actual World Expo site was directly next door. In fact, the World Expo would lease about 10 acres of Hilton's land. Exhibit 18–8 is a map of downtown New Orleans showing relevant points of interest. A large part of the Expo building complex was to be converted into a mammoth convention

_____ EXHIBIT 18–7 _____

■ *The New Orleans Hilton & Hilton Towers: Current and Planned Room Capacities of Hilton's Major Competitors in Downtown New Orleans*

Current downtown		
Marriott		1300
Hyatt		1200
Sheraton		1200
Fairmont		700
Royal Orleans		400
Sonesta		400
Subtotal		5200
Under construction downtown		
Intercontinental		500
Meridian		500
Trust House 40		500
Crown Regent		500
(as yet unnamed)		400
Windsor Court		360
Subtotal		2760
Hilton		
Current		1146
Under construction		454
Subtotal		1600
	Total	9560

───── EXHIBIT 18–8 ─────

- *The New Orleans Hilton & Hilton Towers: Map of Downtown New Orleans*

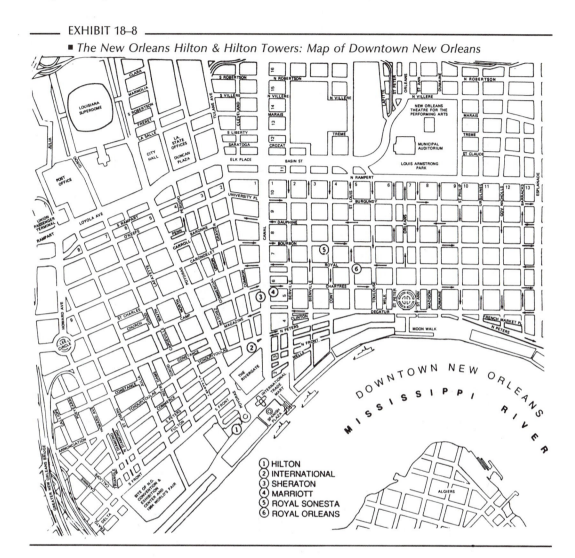

center for the Hilton at the end of the Fair. In addition, the row of buildings behind the Hilton along the Mississippi River was to be developed into a shopping center by the Rouse Co., famous for its development of such areas as Baltimore's Harbour Town and Boston's Faneuil Hall. Hilton managers believed that the attraction of the Rouse development would continue to benefit the downtown Hilton even after the Expo.

The New Orleans Hilton was, like many of the hotels in the downtown area, primarily a convention hotel. It drew about 60 to 70 percent of

its revenue from conventions. Room capacity was an important selling factor when trying to book convention groups, as were the capacities of the actual convention center meeting rooms and banquet rooms. In turn, the number and capacity of these meeting and banquet rooms imposed constraints on management's booking of guest rooms.

Hotels that were close to the New Orleans Superdome had the advantage of being the host hotel for conventions in the Superdome's huge meeting and banquet areas. The Hyatt Hotel actually adjoined the Superdome, making it one of

EXHIBIT 18-9

■ *The New Orleans Hilton & Hilton Towers: Organizational Chart*

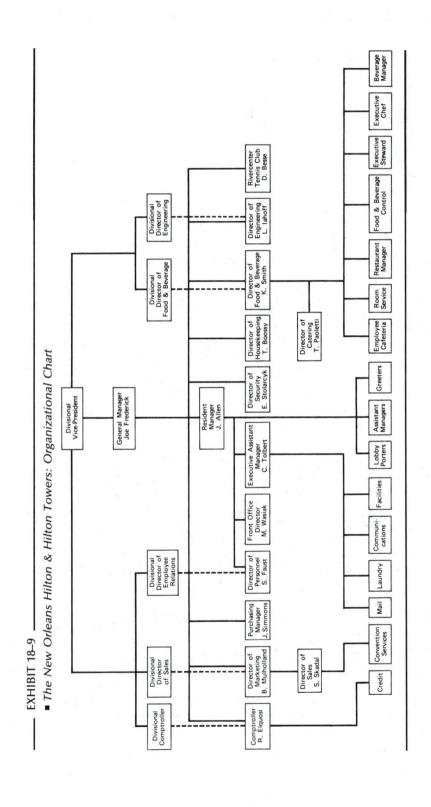

the Hilton's primary competitors. Given the size of many of the large conventions (as many as 10,000 people), there was, of course, an overflow of guests from the host hotel that went to the other hotels in the downtown area. The emphasis, however, was on being the host hotel since the banquets were profitable. How to feed 500 to 5000 people dinner within a two-hour period in your hotel or someone else's banquet room was a unique operational problem in itself. But getting the customers booked in the first place at close to a 100 percent occupancy rate was everyone's first and most important objective: as Joe stated, "No bookings, no banquet."

GENERAL HOTEL OPERATIONS

The New Orleans Hilton & Hilton Towers was a partially owned and managed property of the Hilton Hotels Corporation. As general manager, Joe Frederick had direct management control of all functions within the hotel, but there were indirect links between most of the hotel functional areas and the divisional functional areas of Hilton Corporation. Joe reported directly to the divisional vice-president. (See Exhibit 18–9 for an organizational chart.)

In August, the hotel employed 1081 people with the largest group of employees, 477, in the Food and Beverage Division. Exhibit 18–10 shows the actual employment figures by area.

Employees of the Hilton were drawn from the diverse local labor force. There were about 100 employees who spoke very little English (¾ Spanish-speaking, ¼ Haitian). Joe Frederick described the management problem of training employees with limited language skills and low socioeconomic background: "We have to teach some employees in a couple of days the skills it took the business guest a lifetime to acquire. Quality control starts with training all my employees." The two hotel operations in which this training problem was most evident were, not surprisingly, the ones with the largest number of employees: the Food and Beverage Division and the Housekeeping Division.

Major convention hotels in the large cities of the United States typically experienced employee turnover rates ranging from 30 to 65 percent per year. The New Orleans Hilton & Hilton Towers was no exception.

_____ EXHIBIT 18–10 _____

- *The New Orleans Hilton & Hilton Towers: Number of Employees by Functional Area*

Food and Beverage	
Service	119
Operation	228
Restaurants	130
Housekeeping	183
Accounting	101
Engineering	47
Facilities	42
Security	39
Service	36
Front Office	33
Conventions and Sales	28
Laundry	20
Administration	16
Telephone	16
Rivercenter (tennis club)	15
Personnel	9
Catering and Banquet Sales	8
Purchasing	7
Towers	4
Total	1,081

The Hilton met the difficult task of employee training and human resources management with a period of comprehensive and intensive training under simulated conditions and actual on-the-job training. There were also a number of employee recognition awards within the organization, such as newsletters; employee-of-the-month, -year, and -corporation awards; and years-of-service ceremonies. The company sponsored company picnics and softball and basketball teams. These activities and awards were received well by the employees. Employee morale at the New Orleans Hilton & Hilton Towers was good.

The Food and Beverage Division received a great deal of management attention because it accounted for about one-third of Hilton's revenue. The Hilton had three restaurants and one cocktail lounge. The Hilton had begun weekend special events in its lobby restaurants in an attempt to boost restaurant revenues and to attract weekend vacationers from the surrounding area. These specials included Friday night seafood buffets, a Saturday evening "Italian festival" with Italian food and strolling operatic musicians, and a Sunday jazz brunch with typical New Orleans jazz and Creole food. Reaction to these events had been extremely good, and preliminary results indicated that they would be profitable. Local advertising helped to fill up hotel restaurants with local guests who were "out-on-the-town" for one or two evenings.

The capacity-management issue was particularly vital to Ken Smith, director of the Food and Beverage Division, since the number of people who were to be in the hotel on a given shift day, whether they were "regular" guests or convention and conference groups, determined staffing and equipment levels for the restaurants and the banquet facilities.

Perhaps the most important division in terms of managing the capacity of the hotel on a continuing basis was the Front Office. Mark Wasiak, director of the Front Office, reported directly to the general manager. It was Mark's duty to track the long-range and the midrange (i.e., smaller conferences that were put together by the Sales Division) convention booking forecasts and to follow events all the way up to the day-by-day booking decisions.

DEVELOPING THE ROOM FORECAST: BOOKING CATEGORIES

The Hilton classified its bookings into four categories: Conventions, Conference Center, Tour and Travel, and Transient. These categories exhibited different characteristics such as number of rooms, length of planned stay and actual stay over, degree of use of hotel facilities, and lead time for bookings.

As stated previously, the Hilton was primarily a convention hotel. Conventions were booked as far as two to four years in advance with as many as 1000 rooms being committed. A convention for which the Hilton served as host hotel might also require meeting and banquet facilities for as many as 3500 people.

Conference Center bookings were typically smaller groups than conventions that make use of the Hilton's meeting areas. These groups usually had shorter stays (1 to 2 days versus 3 to 4 days). In addition, a Conference Center group was often a local or regional business or association, which meant that only a small core group of individuals might be staying in the hotel, with the rest of the participants just driving in to the meetings and dinners. Thus, predicting revenue and staffing levels

for Food and Beverage for a Conference Center group was different from predicting for a Convention group. Conference Center bookings were typically made six months to one year in advance but could be done more quickly if necessary.

Tour and Travel bookings were groups of anywhere from 10 to 100 individuals who were on tours arranged by travel agencies to visit New Orleans. There was seldom any related use of banquet facilities with these groups, and they typically stayed only briefly (i.e., 1 to 2 days). They might be booked anywhere from a few weeks to one year in advance.

The Transient bookings were people traveling alone or with a family who might call only a few days or weeks in advance for a reservation or come to the hotel without a reservation (walk-ins). The length of stay and impact on hotel food services with this group were unpredictable. Their impact on hotel revenues was significant, however, since transient bookings helped to fill up idle room capacity between major conventions.

OVERBOOKING

As the time to a particular time slot grew short, Hilton's reservation activity would become more complex. The hotel management knew that all the booked rooms for any given night would not actually be rented. Therefore, in its effort to maintain a "full house," the hotel would book to capacity subject to calculated casualty (i.e., no-shows).

Historical data were used to estimate what percentage of rooms would not be booked on any given night, based on the mix of customers. For example, the Tour and Travel groups historically had a 30 to 50 percent no-show or "casualty" rate. Conventions might have a 10 to 15 percent casualty rate, and Conference Center an 8 to 12 percent rate. If there was a 50-room booking for a Tour and Travel group on a particular night, the Front Office might plan on overbooking by 15 rooms. The hotelier and customer alike disliked the negative connotation associated with the idea of "overbooking," but it was simply a reality of managing a hotel.

Detailed management knowledge of the booking, no-show, arrival, and departure rates and behavior by *specific* group was critical in booking hotel rooms. For this reason, the entire Hilton organization kept detailed records, called "Report of Convention," on every group that stayed in a Hilton hotel. The report recorded the number of rooms booked and the number of rooms actually taken on each night of a convention or conference. Exhibit 18–11 is an example of this report. All this information allowed the front office director to make an educated decision as to how many rooms to try to book.

On any given day, the front office would actually be making decisions as to when to open reservations for transient business on an hourly basis, as it monitors the actual number of rooms available. The standard overbooking rate ranged from 5 to 15 percent for all booking categories, but as might be expected, it varied considerably by booking group and by the specific organization within a group.

Overbookings held some disadvantages. Sometimes the hotel would actually run out of rooms, and someone with a reservation had to be denied a room. If this happened, company policy was to pay the person's cab fare to another hotel and the first night's lodging bill. Management attempted to get the customer back in the hotel the next day. Records were kept on the people who were denied rooms, and a letter was sent by the general manager apologizing for the inconvenience. A list was kept of names of individuals who were denied a room once to ensure that the same person was not denied again.

FORECASTING METHODOLOGY—AN EXAMPLE

The primary responsibility for developing forecasts of room occupancy for the hotel rested with Front Office director, Mark Wasiak. The Front Office was always working on a daily forecast of rooms for the subsequent 18 months. Thus, the planning horizon has about 550 daily time periods. As the sales force booked groups, a Room Block Sheet for that particular group was prepared. (Exhibit 18–12 is an example.) The Room Block Sheet provided information as to the number of rooms that the group had requested for each day of its meeting. The information from those sheets, along with the Report of Convention sheets for the group, if available, was used to make an estimate of the number of rooms that would actually be taken up on each

night. That estimate of rooms was then entered on a Group Supplement Sheet. (See Exhibit 18–13.)

The actual mechanics of this estimating process can be seen by comparing Exhibits 18–11, 18–12, and 18–13. The number of rooms requested by the Paris Alumni Association in Exhibit 18–12 has been adjusted by the percentage no-show/cancellation rate in Exhibit 18–11 for each day of the convention before being entered in Exhibit 18–13. (The number might be further adjusted according to any additional information available on the group or on the judgment of the Front Office manager.) For example, the actual rooms booked in Exhibit 18–13 were computed as follows: $(1.0 - 0.036)110 = 106$ rooms, $(1.0 - 0.098)250 = 226$ rooms, $(1.0 - 0.229)400 = 308$ rooms, $(1.0 - 0.146)800 = 683$ rooms, $(1.0 - 0.274)1,000 = 726$ rooms, $(1.0 - 0.53)900 = 420$ rooms, and a 19 percent no-show rate used for all remaining days. When to use or not use the no-show rates on the arrival and departure patterns per group was based on managerial judgment. Moreover, stay-over behavior per group complicated the booking process.

The next step in aggregating the forecast was a large cumulative Spread Sheet (shown in Exhibit 18–14). Most of the information for this sheet was drawn directly from the Group Supplement Sheets. Convention blocks were put in first on a daily basis, then Conference Center, then Tour and Travel. The "regular base" row was then filled in for the transient business. The Front Office knew to a large extent how many rooms could be filled on a regular basis by the normal transient bookings, which were subject to the seasonal fluctuations explained earlier. The maximum number for this expected transient business was used unless it was obvious that there would be constraints on the 1146-room capacity because of group bookings.

The rooms committed to this point were then totaled to give the forecasted total occupied revenue-producing rooms for a given night. The number of expected vacant rooms was determined by subtracting this total from the total capacity of 1146 rooms. There were 30 rooms set aside at all times for complimentary purposes. A frequent incentive used to attract groups was to offer complimentary rooms to the leaders of the groups or the people responsible for making the convention arrangements. However, in emergencies, the complimen-

EXHIBIT 18–11

■ The New Orleans Hilton & Hilton Towers: Report of Convention and Group Meetings

Group *Paris Alumni Association*

REPORTING PROPERTY   Los Angeles Hilton

DATES (INCLUSIVE)   7/28-8/8   DAYS OF WEEK   Wednesday   THROUGH   Sunday

HEADQUARTERS: HILTON   Co-Headquarters   IF OTHER (name headquarters)   Bonaventure

LIST ALL PROPERTIES USED: ROOMS COMMITTED: ROOMS PICKED UP:

	ROOMS COMMITTED	ROOMS PICKED UP
HILTON Bonaventure	750	465
Biltmore	1,000	630
Hyatt Regency	800	215
TOTAL:	2,550	1,310

RESERVATION TALLY: Singles 333   Doubles 89   Twins 0   Triples 0   Quads 0

Parlor + 1   3   Parlor + 2   2   Parlor + 3   3   % Double Occupancy 25.81%

Date	Reservations	Arrivals	Departures	No-Shows	Cancellations	% of No-Show/Cancellations	Total Rooms for Day
Wed. 7/28	55	53	0	2	0	3.64	53
Thurs. 7/29	51	46	0	4	1	9.80	99
Fri. 7/30	144	111	0	21	12	22.92	210
Sat. 7/31	185	158	0	20	7	14.59	368
Sun. 8/1	124	90	0	30	4	27.42	458
Mon. 8/2	15	7	0	3	5	53.33	465
Tue. 8/3	0	0	23	—	—	—	442
Wed. 8/4	0	0	81	—	—	—	361
Thurs. 8/5	0	0	286	—	—	—	75
Fri. 8/6	0	0	50	—	—	—	25
Sat. 8/7	0	0	15	—	—	—	10
Sun. 8/8	0	0	10	—	—	—	0
TOTALS	574	465	465	80	29	18.99	2566

_____ EXHIBIT 18–12 _____

■ *The New Orleans Hilton & Hilton Towers: Room Block Sheet*

SUBJECT: Paris Alumni Association   DATE: _____

CONTACT: Charles Scroggin   FILE #: EBC 62149 _____

ADDRESS: 900 W. 62nd Street   TITLE: Executive Director ___

       New York, N.Y. 10021   PHONE: (212) 666-3000 _____

ESTIMATED DOUBLE OC.: 35%   SALESPERSON: Bonnie Ebelhar ___

ARRIVE: Week 31, Friday, July 1   DEPART: Week 32, Saturday, July 9

GUEST ROOM COMMITMENT   COMPLEMENTARY COMMITMENT:

1 room per 50 rooms

DAY	DATE	#ROOMS
Friday	7/1	110
Saturday	7/2	250
Sunday	7/3	400
Monday	7/4	800
Tuesday	7/5	1,000
Wednesday	7/6	900
Thursday	7/7	150
Friday	7/8	150

REMARKS:

TOTAL ROOM NIGHTS: 3760

RATES: REGULAR _____ SPECIAL XX

SINGLES: $58

DOUBLES: $75

_____

tary rooms could be used for regular hotel guests, but the impact on future sales could be damaging if a complimentary room was not available when needed.

     Management attention now focused on the vacant room numbers (or net vacant rooms) in Ex-

hibit 18–14. Wherever there were "gaps" in the capacity plan, the sales force had to fill them with some kind of "plug." These gaps are noticeable because of the large number of vacant rooms (i.e., 740, 620, 613, 213, 204, 451, 774 in Exhibit 18–14). The lead time to the date in question deter-

EXHIBIT 18–13

■ *The New Orleans Hilton & Hilton Towers: Group Supplement Sheet*

GROUP SUPPLEMENT

Month _____ Year _____

Groups		Day Date	1	2	3	4	5	6	7	8	9	10	11	12	13	14				30	31		Total
	Annual																						
Paris alumni	Monthly		106	226	308	683	726	420	122	122													
	Actual									122													
	Annual																						
	Monthly																						
	Actual																						
	Annual																						
	Monthly																						
	Annual																						
	Monthly																						
	Actual																						
	Annual																						
	Monthly																						
	Actual																						
	Annual																						
	Monthly																						

Actual	Annual	Monthly	Actual	Annual	Monthly	Actual	Annual	Monthly	Actual	Annual	Monthly	Actual	Annual	Monthly	Actual	Annual	Monthly	Actual

EXHIBIT 18–14

■ *The New Orleans Hilton & Hilton Towers: Sample Spread Sheet*

Date	1	2	3	4	5	6	7		30	31	Total
Total rooms revenue											
Actual											
Daily average rate											
Actual											
Daily house guest count											
Actual											
Convention rooms	106	226	308	683	726	420	122				
Actual											
Tour and travel											
Actual											
Conference center											
Actual											
Regular base (transients)	300	300	225	250	216	275	250				
Actual											
Total occupied revenue rooms	406	526	533	933	942	695	372				
Actual											
Vacant rooms	740	620	613	213	204	451	774				
Actual											
Complimentary	30	30	30	30	30	30	30				
Out of order	10	10	10	10	10	10	10				
House guest											
Daily room arrivals											
Net vacant rooms	700	580	573	173	164	411	734				
Convention plug rooms											
Paris Alumni Assoc.	106	226	308	683	726	420	122				

mined what type of plug was possible. For example, if a gap were only a month or two away, it was likely that it could only be filled by small seminars, transients, or tour and travel, rather than by large conferences or conventions. The total occupied revenue rooms in Exhibit 18–14 could be graphed. It would clearly show where "gaps" existed.

In many instances it was necessary to offer special deals to groups or travel agents to try to fill gaps. Or management would decide to run heavy local advertising via radio or newspapers or offer some form of coupon for a period of time to stimulate bookings. Special weekend rates might be offered to attract people from the regional market.

CAPACITY PLAN FOR WEEKS 32 AND 33

As Joe Frederick sat with his directors of Front Office and Sales, they looked over the bookings for weeks 32 and 33 (that is, 32 and 33 weeks into

---

_____ EXHIBIT 18–15 _____

- *The New Orleans Hilton & Hilton Towers: Room Block Sheet*

SUBJECT: Education Clubs of America   DATE: _____

CONTACT: Sandie Cummings   FILE #: DCGC 111924

ADDRESS: 2040 North Street   TITLE: National Education Director

Chicago, Ill.   PHONE: (303) 726-2010

ESTIMATED DOUBLE OCC.: 70%   SALESPERSON: Jane Joplin

ARRIVE: Week 31, Wednesday, day 28   DEPART: Week 32, Tuesday, day 3

GUEST ROOM COMMITMENT

COMPLEMENTARY COMMITMENT:

1 room per 50 rooms

REMARKS:

DAY	DATE	#ROOMS
Wednesday	28	75
Thursday	29	400
Friday	30	700
Saturday	31	700
Sunday	1	300
Monday	2	75

TOTAL ROOM NIGHTS: 2,250

RATES: REGULAR _____ SPECIAL XX

SINGLES: $50

DOUBLES: $65

the future). They knew that the Education Clubs of America was scheduled to depart from the Hilton on Sunday (day 1) and should be gone by Monday evening (day 2). Exhibit 18–15 shows the Room Block information on this group. No-show rates had very little to do with departure patterns.

Mark and Stan now had to evaluate the current status of bookings in the hotel for weeks 32 and 33 (days 1 to 14). In addition to the departure of the Education Clubs of America, the arrivals of the National Petrochemical Association and the Contract Bridge League were already booked. Exhibits 18–16 through 18–19 provide information on these groups.

EXHIBIT 18–16

■ *The New Orleans Hilton & Hilton Towers: Room Block Sheet*

SUBJECT: Contract Bridge League

DATE: _____

CONTACT: Susan Lambert

FILE #: BKC-11359

ADDRESS: 1706 West Broad

TITLE: President

Louisville, Ky.

PHONE: (929) 411-6036

ESTIMATED DOUBLE OCC.: 40%

SALESPERSONS: Robin Plummer/Susan Gould

ARRIVE: Week 32, Sunday, day 1

DEPART: Week 32, Friday, day 6

GUEST ROOM COMMITMENT

COMPLEMENTARY COMMITMENT:

1 room per 50 rooms

DAY	DATE	#ROOMS
Sunday	1	115
Monday	2	475
Tuesday	3	1,000
Wednesday	4	1,000
Thursday	5	600
Friday	6	175

REMARKS:

TOTAL ROOM NIGHTS: 3,365

RATES: REGULAR __ SPECIAL XX

SINGLES: $60

DOUBLES: $70

EXHIBIT 18–17

■ *The New Orleans Hilton & Hilton Towers: Report of Convention*

Name of Organization: Contract Bridge League
Reporting Property: St. Louis Hilton   Date: 5/11/82
Dates (inclusive): 3/7/82–3/13/82

Date	Reservations	Arrivals	Departures	No-Shows	No-Shows (%)	Total Rooms for Day
3/7	110	96	0	14	13	96
3/8	340	289	0	51	15	385
3/9	450	405	0	45	10	790
3/10	100	87	0	13	13	877
3/11	0	0	0	0	0	877
3/12	0	0	533	0	0	344
3/13	0	0	344	0	0	0
Total	1000	877	877	123	12	3369

Stan, when asked if he had any suggestions on how to increase the bookings for this period, indicated that the Sales Department had gone through its files and found several groups that had held conferences around this time of year in the past and had indicated some interest in holding meetings at the Hilton in the coming year.

He felt that if his sales force could approach them with a "special deal," some of them could be encouraged to schedule conferences during the idle time slots of weeks 32 and 33. Exhibits 18–20 and 18–21 provide all the available information on these groups.

Stan and Mark had already filled in the regular base (transient) row of the Spread Sheet shown in Exhibit 18–22. These numbers were based on 400 transient rooms on Friday and Saturday, 300 rooms on Sunday, and 250 rooms on Monday through Thursday. Also, as noted in Exhibit 18–22, 30 complimentary rooms and 20 out-of-order rooms must also be considered in all capacity planning decisions. Joe did not want to book anything beyond Saturday, day 14 because of the possibility of booking a huge all-week convention. In addition to Exhibit 18–22, management also used the graph worksheet shown in Exhibit 18–23 to evaluate full and idle hotel capacity.

The management team felt that these groups would probably be interested in such a deal, but they also knew that this particular time of year was historically a good time for transient business. This was reflected in the rather high number of rooms for the regular base demand indicated in Exhibit 18–22. They thought that the transient business during this period could be booked at the "normal" charge of $80.00 per night for a single occupancy and $100.00 per night for a double. (The normal double occupancy percentage rate for transient business was approximately 50 percent).

Joe hated to cut into this profitable base with group bookings that might be filled only by offering rates as low as $40–60 for singles and $60–80 for doubles. However, he did expect to get some extra revenue from the groups in the form of banquet and restaurant business. Transient bookings normally spent only about 25 percent as much as conference bookings on food and beverages.

The mangement team's decision involved not only how to fill idle hotel capacity, but how they might best maximize both the revenue of the bookings and customer service levels.

_____ EXHIBIT 18–18 _____

■ *The New Orleans Hilton & Hilton Towers: Room Block Sheet*

SUBJECT: National Petrochemical Ass'n   DATE: _____

CONTACT: Jerry Neptune/Ben Taylor   FILE #: CLEC 7357

ADDRESS: 421 Claiborne St.   TITLE: President/Vice-President

New Orleans, La.   PHONE: (217) 555-5300

ESTIMATED DOUBLE OCC.: 10%   SALESPERSONS: Betsy Wilson/Tarrol Collins

ARRIVE: Week 33, Monday, day 9   DEPART: Week 33, Thursday, day 12

GUEST ROOM COMMITMENT   COMPLEMENTARY COMMITMENT:

DAY	DATE	#ROOMS
Monday	9	75
Tuesday	10	400
Wednesday	11	400
Thursday	12	125

2 rooms per 50 rooms

REMARKS:

TOTAL ROOM NIGHTS: 1,000

RATES: REGULAR _____ SPECIAL XX

SINGLES: $65

DOUBLES: $80

_____ EXHIBIT 18–19 _____

- *The New Orleans Hilton & Hilton Towers: Report of Convention, New Orleans Hilton*

Name of Organization: National Petrochemical Association
Reporting Property: N.O. Hilton   Date: 7/30/83
Dates (inclusive): 7/12/83–7/16/83

Date	Reservations	Arrivals	Departures	No-Shows	No-Shows (%)	Total Rooms for Day
7/12	85	79	0	6	7	79
7/13	415	386	0	29	7	465
7/14	0	0	0	0	0	465
7/15	0	0	153	0	0	312
7/16	0	0	312	0	0	0
Total	500	465	465	35	7	1321

_____ EXHIBIT 18–20 _____

- *The New Orleans Hilton & Hilton Towers: Hotel Special Deal Booking Candidates**

The following is a list of possible groups for booking in weeks 32 and 33. Also, the planned number of rooms expected each day, the double-occupancy rate, and the historical Food and Beverage revenue per night per room is estimated.

	F&B Revenue (night/rm)	Expected Double Occupancy Rate	Expected Room Rate
La. Guild of Piano Technicians 4 days: Day 1, 75 rooms Day 2, 350 rooms Day 3, 425 rooms Day 4, 125 rooms	$17	60%	$40 (single) 55 (double)
So. La. Bankers Association† 3 days: Day 1, 180 rooms Day 2, 700 rooms Day 3, 450 rooms	42	50	$60 (single) 80 (double)
Southeastern Soccer Federation 5 days: Day 1, 50 rooms Day 2, 175 rooms Day 3, 325 rooms Day 4, 275 rooms Day 5, 90 rooms	27	70	$55 (single) 70 (double)
Institute of Food Technologists 3 days: Day 1, 410 rooms Day 2, 560 rooms Day 3, 175 rooms	24	65	$55 (single) 70 (double)

* These groups except where noted could probably be scheduled on any day of the week; therefore, the day number listed does not refer to a day of the week.
† This conference must start (i.e., day 1) on Monday or end (i.e., day 3) on Friday based on a preliminary phone conversation. They will not come otherwise.

───── EXHIBIT 18–21 ─────────────────────────────────────

▪ *The New Orleans Hilton & Hilton Towers: Report of Convention*

Name of Organization: La. Guild of Piano Technicians
Reporting Property: Atlanta Hilton   Date: 4/10/83
Dates (inclusive):   3/12/83–3/18/83

Date	Reservations	Arrivals	Departures	No-Shows	No-Shows (%)	Total Rooms for Day
3/12	60	40	0	20	33	40
3/13	240	190	0	50	21	230
3/14	350	298	0	52	15	528
3/15	50	44	0	6	12	572
3/16	0	0	7	0	0	565
3/17	0	0	241	0	0	324
3/18	0	0	324	0	0	0
Total	700	572	572	128	18	2259

EXHIBIT 18–22

■ *The New Orleans Hilton & Hilton Towers: Spread Worksheet*

Date	1	2	3	4	5	6	7	30	31	Total
Total rooms revenue										
Actual										
Daily average rate										
Actual										
Daily house guest count										
Actual										
Convention rooms										
Actual										
Tour and travel										
Actual										
Conference center										
Actual										
Regular base (transients)	300	250	250	250	250	400	400*			
Actual										
Total occupied revenue rooms										
Actual										
Vacant rooms										
Actual										
Complimentary	30	30	30	30	30	30	30*			
Out of order	20	20	20	20	20	20	20*			
House guest										
Daily room arrivals										
Net vacant rooms										
Convention plug rooms										
Paris Alumni Assoc.										

*Repeats for days 8 to 14.

EXHIBIT 18–23

■ *The New Orleans Hilton & Hilton Towers: Graph Worksheet*

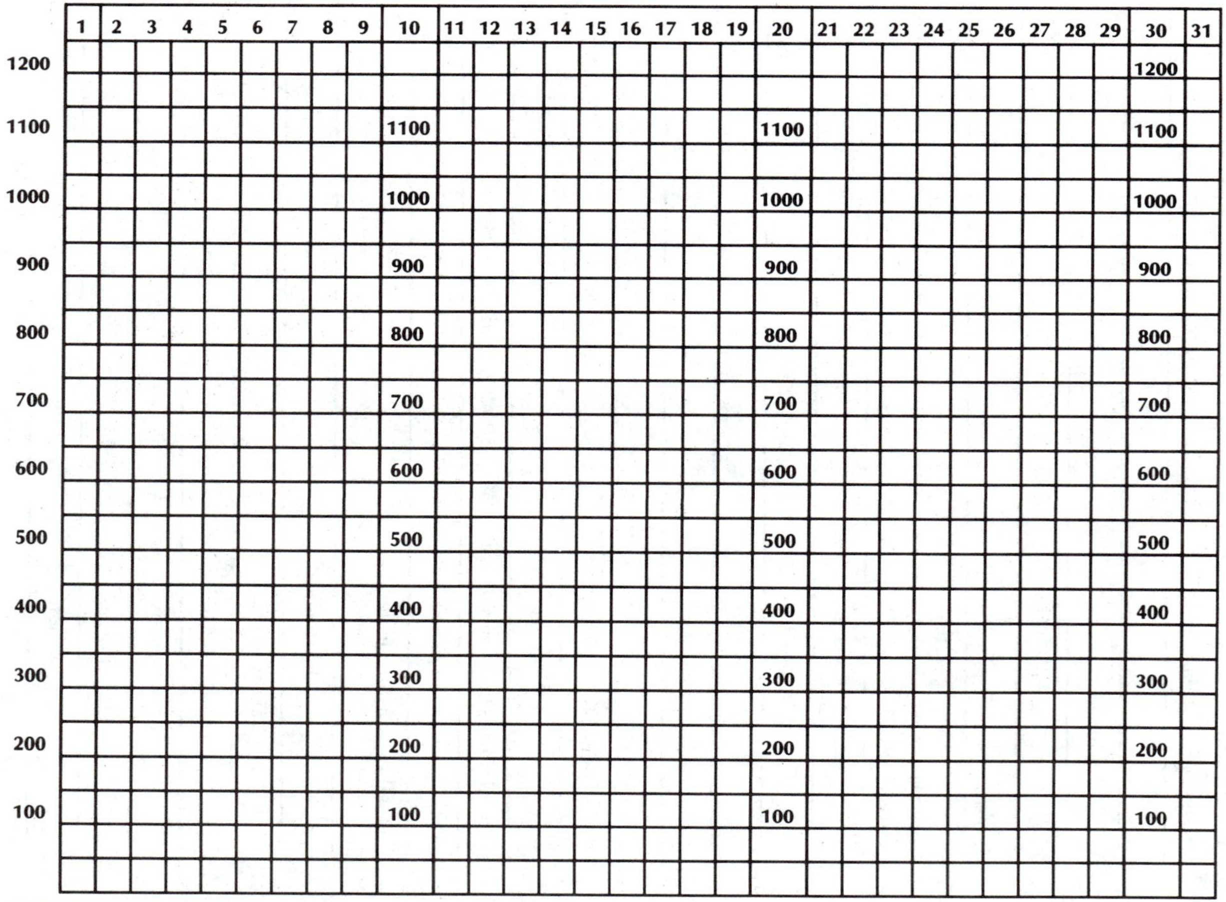

____ QUESTIONS FOR CASE 18.2

1. Develop a feasible bookings (capacity) plan for weeks 32 and 33. Use Case Exhibits 18–22 and 18–23 to work out your plan. What groups in Exhibit 18–20 will you offer a "special deal" to first, second, third, and last? Why? Is booking hotel capacity a marketing or operations function?

2. Define your strategy for booking hotel capacity (rooms), the economics of booking hotel groups, and the hotel service package.

Areas Under the Standard Normal Curve

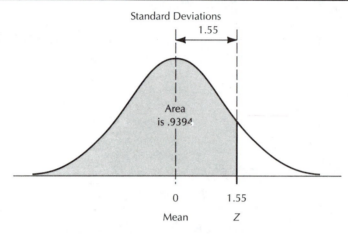

Standard Deviations

1.55

Area
is .9394

0
Mean

1.55
Z

Example of a One-Tail Test. To find the area under the normal curve, you must know how many standard deviations that point is to the right of the mean. Then the area under the normal curve can be read directly from the normal table. For example, the total area under the normal curve for a point that is 1.55 standard deviations to the right of the mean is 0.9394.

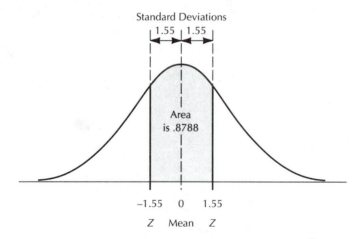

Standard Deviations

1.55   1.55

Area
is .8788

−1.55   0   1.55
Z   Mean   Z

Example of a Two-Tail Test. For some problems, you may want to find the area under the normal curve between two tails (e.g., when the problem states ± a certain number of standard deviations). Then, additional calculations are required. For example, the total area under the normal curve for a point that is 1.55 standard deviations to the right of the mean *and* −1.55 standard deviations to the left of the mean is

$$1.0 - [(1.0 - .9394) \times 2] = .8788$$

z	.00	.01	.02	.03	.04	.05	.06	.07	.08	.09
.0	.5000	.5040	.5080	.5120	.5160	.5199	.5239	.5279	.5319	.5359
.1	.5398	.5438	.5478	.5517	.5557	.5596	.5636	.5675	.5714	.5753
.2	.5793	.5832	.5871	.5910	.5948	.5987	.6026	.6064	.6103	.6141
.3	.6179	.6217	.6255	.6293	.6331	.6368	.6406	.6443	.6480	.6517
.4	.6554	.6591	.6628	.6664	.6700	.6736	.6772	.6808	.6844	.6879
.5	.6915	.6950	.6985	.7019	.7054	.7088	.7123	.7157	.7190	.7224
.6	.7257	.7291	.7324	.7357	.7389	.7422	.7454	.7486	.7517	.7549
.7	.7580	.7611	.7642	.7673	.7704	.7734	.7764	.7794	.7823	.7852
.8	.7881	.7910	.7939	.7967	.7995	.8023	.8051	.8078	.8106	.8133
.9	.8159	.8186	.8212	.8238	.8264	.8289	.8315	.8340	.8365	.8389
1.0	.8413	.8438	.8461	.8485	.8508	.8531	.8554	.8577	.8599	.8621
1.1	.8643	.8665	.8686	.8708	.8729	.8749	.8770	.8790	.8810	.8830
1.2	.8849	.8869	.8888	.8907	.8925	.8944	.8962	.8980	.8997	.9015
1.3	.9032	.9049	.9066	.9082	.9099	.9115	.9131	.9147	.9162	.9177
1.4	.9192	.9207	.9222	.9236	.9251	.9265	.9279	.9292	.9306	.9319
1.5	.9332	.9345	.9357	.9370	.9382	.9394	.9406	.9418	.9429	.9441
1.6	.9452	.9463	.9474	.9484	.9495	.9505	.9515	.9525	.9535	.9545
1.7	.9554	.9564	.9573	.9582	.9591	.9599	.9608	.9616	.9625	.9633
1.8	.9641	.9649	.9656	.9664	.9671	.9678	.9686	.9693	.9699	.9706
1.9	.9713	.9719	.9726	.9732	.9738	.9744	.9750	.9756	.9761	.9767
2.0	.9772	.9778	.9783	.9788	.9793	.9798	.9803	.9808	.9812	.9817
2.1	.9821	.9826	.9830	.9834	.9838	.9842	.9846	.9850	.9854	.9857
2.2	.9861	.9864	.9868	.9871	.9875	.9878	.9881	.9884	.9887	.9890
2.3	.9893	.9896	.9898	.9901	.9904	.9906	.9909	.9911	.9913	.9916
2.4	.9918	.9920	.9922	.9925	.9927	.9929	.9931	.9932	.9934	.9936
2.5	.9938	.9940	.9941	.9943	.9945	.9946	.9948	.9949	.9951	.9952
2.6	.9953	.9955	.9956	.9957	.9959	.9960	.9961	.9962	.9963	.9964
2.7	.9965	.9966	.9967	.9968	.9969	.9970	.9971	.9972	.9973	.9974
2.8	.9974	.9975	.9976	.9977	.9977	.9978	.9979	.9979	.9980	.9981
2.9	.9981	.9982	.9982	.9983	.9984	.9984	.9985	.9985	.9986	.9986
3.0	.9987	.9987	.9987	.9988	.9988	.9989	.9989	.9989	.9990	.9990
3.1	.9990	.9991	.9991	.9991	.9992	.9992	.9992	.9992	.9993	.9993
3.2	.9993	.9993	.9994	.9994	.9994	.9994	.9994	.9995	.9995	.9995
3.3	.9995	.9995	.9995	.9996	.9996	.9996	.9996	.9996	.9996	.9997
3.4	.9997	.9997	.9997	.9997	.9997	.9997	.9997	.9997	.9997	.9998

Source: Adapted from John Neter, William Wasserman, and G. A. Whitmore, *Applied Statistics,* 3rd Ed. Copyright © 1988 by Allyn and Bacon. Used with permission.

INDEX